Drama of a Na

# Drama of a Nation

*Public Theater in Renaissance England and Spain*

WALTER COHEN

CORNELL UNIVERSITY PRESS

ITHACA AND LONDON

THIS BOOK HAS BEEN PUBLISHED WITH THE AID OF A GRANT FROM THE HULL MEMORIAL PUBLICATION FUND OF CORNELL UNIVERSITY.

First published 1985 by Cornell University Press.
First published, Cornell Paperbacks, 1988.

Printed in the United States of America

LIBRARY OF CONGRESS CATALOGING IN PUBLICATION DATA

Cohen, Walter, 1949–
    Drama of a nation.

    Includes bibliographical references and index.
    1. English drama—Early modern and Elizabethan, 1500–1600—History and criticism. 2. English drama—17th century—History and criticism. 3. Spanish drama—Classical period, 1500–1700—History and criticism. 4. Literature, Comparative—English and Spanish. 5. Literature, Comparative—Spanish and English. 6. Theater—England—History. 7. Theater—Spain—History. I. Title.
PR651.C64   1985      822'.3       85-2633
ISBN 0-8014-1793-7 (alk. paper)
ISBN 0-8014-9494-x (paperback)

*For Laura Brown*

# CONTENTS

Preface   9

Introduction   15

1. Medieval Theater and the Structure of Feudalism   33

2. Renaissance Theater and the Transition from Feudalism to Capitalism   82

3. The Emergence of the Public Theater   136

4. Aristocratic Adaptation: Romantic Comedy and the National History Play   186

5. The Crisis of the Public Theater   255

6. Aristocratic Failure: Satiric Comedy and the Forms of Serious Drama   282

7. The Passing of the Public Theater: Intrigue Tragedy and Romance   357

Conclusion   405

Index   407

# PREFACE

When the idea of this project first crossed my mind many years ago, I had hopes of composing a book that would appeal not only to specialists in my field but also to those people who merely shared my political beliefs. I soon realized, however, what the following pages will amply demonstrate—that such an enterprise was completely beyond my capabilities. The irony of that failure forms one of the subjects of the Conclusion. Here I would simply note the autobiographical connection of this study to the protest movements beginning in the 1960s, a connection that does not seem to me fortuitous, unusual, or idiosyncratic.

My aim in *Drama of a Nation* is to account for the unique similarities between English and Spanish drama of the late sixteenth and early seventeenth centuries. This apparently straightforward comparative and historical enterprise requires a broad perspective, a perspective coherently available, in my opinion, only in the assumptions, theories, methods, and commitments of Marxism. I therefore seek to establish a series of correlations and causations among economic and social structures, political systems, cultural milieus, theatrical institutions, dramatic genres, and individual plays. Detailed analyses of works by Shakespeare, Lope de Vega, and others open out onto considerations of the fundamental movements of the age. In addition, the Spanish and English materials are situated in relation to medieval and Renaissance European drama, theater, and society as a whole. This comprehensiveness has contradictory consequences, however. On the one hand, the result is an advanced introduction both to a crucial period of drama in two countries and to the entire range and development of European theater from the fall of the Roman Empire to the end of the seventeenth century. On the other, that very comprehensiveness justifies a procedure uncharacteristic of introductory studies: the construction of an alternative model that combines a specific governing hypothesis with general encompassing claims or, more precisely, the advocacy of an explicitly political framework that in many respects proves antithetical to the interpretive norms of the previous scholarship on which it depends.

In the course of my research, I incurred many debts. I thank the staffs of the following institutions: the University of California at Berkeley Library, the Stanford University Library, the University of California at Riverside Library, the Henry E. Huntington Library, the Hispanic Society of America Library, and the Cornell University Libraries. The College of Arts and Sciences at Cornell helped support the later stages of the research with a Humanities Faculty Research Grant in 1981 and again in 1983. Coraleen L. Rooney produced an excellent typescript from what were genuinely foul papers. The staff at Cornell University Press—Carol Betsch, Cynthia Gration, Marilyn M. Sale, and especially Bernhard Kendler—were kind, encouraging, and helpful. Alice Bennett did a superior job of copy editing.

Part of Chapter 4 appeared in *ELH* 49 (1982): 765–89; I am grateful to that journal for permission to reprint the material here. Several other portions of this book draw on essays first published in *Shakespeare: Contemporary Critical Approaches*, ed. Harry R. Garvin (Lewisburg, Pa.: Bucknell University Press, 1980), *Genre, Bulletin of the Comediantes, Theatre Journal, Shakespeare Jahrbuch, Ideologies and Literature*, and *Renaissance Drama*. I thank the editors for their earlier assistance.

Many other people also helped me with this book at various times. I cannot adequately describe a number of these contributions, some of them personal and among the most important. Instead I will limit myself, no doubt unfairly, to recognizing those who read part or all of the typescript and commented on it. I wish to thank, then, Barry Adams, Ciriaco Morón Arroyo, Cynthia Chase, Jonathan Culler, Terry Eagleton, John Ganim, David Grossvogel, Judith Herrin, Thomas D. Hill, Peter Hohendahl, W. Wolfgang Holdheim, William J. Kennedy, Richard Klein, Philip Lewis, Jeffrey Librett, Scott McMillin, Peter Molan, Edward P. Morris, John Najemy, David Novarr, Stephen Orgel, Annabel Patterson, Edgar Rosenberg, Mark Seltzer, Harry Shaw, Richard Terdiman, and Alice Wexler. David Bevington, Anthony Caputi, Stephen Greenblatt, Luis A. Murillo, Mary Ann Radzinowicz, Raymond Williams, and Anthony N. Zahareas each heroically read a version of the entire work. So too did Louise Clubb, who directed my initial dissertation research on this topic with a rare combination of critical acumen, erudition, encouragement, and patience. I am deeply grateful to her.

It is customary at this point to absolve everyone whose suggestions have improved the book of any responsibility for its failings. Yet if we take seriously the notion of a community of scholars, no such generous absolution is possible. This book draws on some of the strengths and is hampered by some of the weaknesses of contemporary American literary study. It could not be otherwise. The possibilities of collaborative work have scarcely begun to be exploited, however. I take special pleasure, then, in acknowledging the cooperative effort that went into this book by dedicating it to Laura Brown.

WALTER COHEN

*Ithaca, New York*

# Drama of a Nation

# INTRODUCTION

During the sixteenth and seventeenth centuries, amid an international florescence of drama in Europe, the English and Spanish theaters took on a uniquely similar cast. The parallels between these two stage traditions soon elicited comment. A handwritten note from Leonard Digges to Will Baker, on the flyleaf of a copy of Lope de Vega's 1613 *Rimas*, reads as follows: "Knowinge that M^r Mab: was to sende you this Booke of sonets, w^ch with Spaniards here is accounted of their lope de Vega as in Englande wee sholde of o^r: Will Shakespeare. I colde not but insert thus much to you, that if you like him not, you muste neuer neuer reade Spanishe Poet."[1] This passage compares the two men as lyric poets. Subsequent discussion focused on the theater, however. In Dryden's *Essay of Dramatic Poesy* Lisideius, the advocate of French classicism, remarks: "Another thing in which the French differ from us [the English] and from the Spaniards is that they do not embarrass or cumber themselves with too much plot."[2] Not surprisingly, his comment was echoed in France during the following century. Although Voltaire admired Shakespeare, Lope, and Calderón, he generally surpassed even Lisideius in his hostility to the Renaissance theaters of Spain and England. "Calderón is as barbarous as Shakespeare," he once wrote—a representative comment.[3] But Voltaire also noticed what Dryden had missed.

[1]Quoted in Paul Morgan, "'Our Will Shakespeare' and Lope de Vega: An Unrecorded Contemporary Document," *Shakespeare Survey* 16 (1963): 118.
[2]John Dryden, "Of Dramatic Poesy: An Essay," in *"Of Dramatic Poesy" and Other Critical Essays*, ed. George Watson (London: Dent, 1962), 1:47–48.
[3]Voltaire, Letter to Marquis Francesco Albergati Capacelli, June 4, 1762, in *Voltaire on Shakespeare*, ed. Theodore Besterman, Studies on Voltaire and the Eighteenth Century, vol. 54 (Geneva: Institut et Musée Voltaire, Les Délices, 1967), p. 83. See also pp. 61, 84, 154–55, 158.

"Certainly Spain and England did not give each other the cue for close to a century to applaud plays that disgust other nations. Besides, nothing is more opposed than the English spirit and the Spanish spirit. Why then do these two different nations meet in such a strange taste?" Arguing in proper eighteenth-century fashion, he added: "There must be a reason, and that reason must be in nature." Logically enough, he found his explanation in the common presence of genius undirected by the social and cultural refinement that to his mind made possible French and Italian neoclassicism.[4]

Early in the nineteenth century August Wilhelm Schlegel, though operating from an opposed and far more sympathetic framework, had much the same perception. To him a stage that entirely lacked foreign models would as a matter of course differ sharply from the theaters of those nations that consciously imitated a single such model. "But," he continued, "when two theaters that originated simultaneously and yet remained unknown to each other bear, in addition to their external and internal differences, the most remarkable features of kinship to each other, while the two peoples are as far distant from one another in physical, moral, political, and religious respects as are the English and Spanish, then indeed the most thoughtless person must become attentive to this phenomenon, and the suspicion will naturally force itself upon him, that the same or at least a similar principle predominated in connection with the development of both."[5] Schlegel agreed with Voltaire that the absence of neoclassicism in Spain and England precluded a theatrical development along the lines of the sixteenth-century Italian or seventeenth-century French stage. He also realized, however, that unless one assumed the unchanging character of barbarism, as Voltaire apparently did in this instance, a common deficiency of antique dramatic ideals would not necessarily produce common results, especially in two countries so at odds in other respects. To the mutual negative feature Schlegel therefore added what was for him a far more crucial, common, positive possession: the romantic. "What they have in common with each other is the spirit of romantic poetry, dramatically expressed."[6]

Nonetheless, this advance could not really solve the problem. Unless one believes, as Schlegel perhaps did, that the romantic constitutes the only alternative to the classic, why should specifically romantic drama have triumphed in England and Spain? Even the classic/romantic dichotomy renders incomprehensible the differences between a medieval Eu-

---

[4]Voltaire, from comments appended to his translation of *Julius Caesar*, 1764, in *Voltaire on Shakespeare*, p. 155.

[5]August Wilhelm Schlegel, *Vorlesungen über dramatische Kunst und Literatur*, part 2, Sprache und Literatur 38 (Stuttgart: W. Kohlhammer, 1967), p. 110.

[6]Schlegel, p. 111.

ropean stage, largely free of classical influence, and a Renaissance Spanish or English stage, also largely free of classical influence. Schlegel's answer thus leads simply to the reformulation of the question, especially given the modern scholarly demonstration that playwrights in sixteenth-century Spain and England knew and sometimes used the classical and neoclassical dramatic traditions. What Voltaire found monstrous and Schlegel romantic was in this limited sense a matter of choice rather than of necessity.

Today, although the parallel between the two theaters is a commonplace, explanation has lagged behind research. One recent critic suggests that the English and Spanish stages, possessed of a common European cultural and dramatic heritage, alone reached maturity before the consolidation of neoclassicism.[7] Why this happened nowhere else, or why, for that matter, it happened in Spain and England, goes unexplained. While such an account introduces a historical dimension generally lacking in Schlegel's discussion, it too merely results in new phrasing for an old question. Another student of the subject plausibly relates the plays of both countries to the important social changes of the sixteenth century.[8] What this explanation gains in sophistication it loses in logic: it offers no basis for distinguishing the English and Spanish theaters from the stages of the rest of Europe.

This book seeks to remedy that long-standing deficiency, to discover why the drama of the two countries took the course it did. Spanish and English plays stand apart from all other European drama because they synthesize native popular and neoclassical learned traditions. Although the two theaters developed in relative isolation from each other, they form a group because both combined what elsewhere appeared only separately. This integration occurred primarily in the regular, though not necessarily neoclassical, plays (in Spain called *comedias*) composed for the permanent, public, commercial theaters that opened in both countries in the late 1570s and only closed, under government order, seventy years later. The present work correspondingly excludes court masques, mythological spectacles, civic pageants, *autos sacramentales, entremeses,* and closet drama. The plays of the early-seventeenth-century English private commercial stage and the late-seventeenth-century Spanish court stage occupy an ambiguous position, their pervasive links with the more popular traditions of the public theaters blurring easy distinctions. Accordingly, no absolute demarcation is attempted here; but those works de-

[7]John Loftis, *The Spanish Plays of Neoclassical England* (New Haven: Yale University Press, 1973), pp. 17–21.
[8]Jean Duvignaud, *Les ombres collectives: Sociologie du théâtre,* 2d ed. (Paris: Presses Universitaires de France, 1973), pp. 163–228.

signed equally for the public and private theaters receive more extended consideration than those aimed at an elite audience alone.

"Popular culture" is employed here in a sense compatible with Peter Burke's usage: "it is perhaps best defined initially in a negative way as unofficial culture, the culture of the non-elite, the 'subordinate classes' as Gramsci called them. In the case of early modern Europe, the non-elite were a whole host of more or less definite social groups of whom the most prominent were craftsmen and peasants. Hence I use the phrase 'craftsmen and peasants' (or 'ordinary people') as convenient pieces of shorthand for the whole non-elite, including women, children, shepherds, sailors, beggars and the rest."[9] What does popular culture have to do with the theater? Spanish and English plays typically eschew classical form. They lack Terentian intrigue structure; they ignore the unities of time, place, and, on occasion, action; and they violate classical decorum in character, style, and genre. Aristocrats may be the protagonists in comedy, commoners in tragedy. In both forms, noble and base-born figures mingle freely: monarchs often speak colloquially, while peasants and artisans demonstrate insight as well as eloquence. Even in subordinate roles, lower-class characters often possess a seriousness and autonomy that prevent them from serving merely as adjuncts of a princely hero. From a classical point of view, then, the impact of popular culture accounts for the generic irregularity of the plays. The cultivation of romantic comedy and the corresponding neglect of dramatic satire, though not without contemporary parallels in other parts of Europe, may reveal a closer allegiance to popular taste than to neoclassical precept. The same goes, though with far less qualification, for the national history play in both countries, for Spanish peasant drama, and for English bourgeois tragedy.

On the other hand, the plays also reveal the influence of classical literature and especially of the classical stage. Many English and Spanish dramatic genres have ancient Latin or Renaissance Italian precedents. A limited heritage of this kind can even be discovered for chronicle histories and, more easily, for romantic comedies. A few plays observe the unities and employ intrigue structure; some borrow plots from classical drama, more from the Italian theater. Others retell stories found in classical or Italian nondramatic literature, deploy the standard themes of the Renaissance, or at least allude to ancient culture, mythology, or history. Similarly, the playwrights often display a consciousness of classical or neoclassical dramatic theory. In addition, the legacy of humanism may help account for the self-conscious artistry and secular seriousness of the drama.

[9]Peter Burke, *Popular Culture in Early Modern Europe* (New York: Harper and Row, 1978), p. xi.

These constituent popular and learned features of the two theaters will provide a standard of reference for the subsequent discussion. Yet any such static, abstract formulation evidently falsifies a more complex reality. First, the plays changed over time, with different genres coming to the fore, often from decade to decade. Strikingly, however, the English and Spanish theaters took much the same path. Second, a drama both classical and popular can have little of the categorical rigor implicit in such generic labels as lower-class farce or neoclassical intrigue comedy. The process of innovation in both national theaters at once offered the basis of similarity and the potential for divergence. Within a larger unity, English and Spanish plays significantly differ in sources, materials, versification, style, act division, speech length, genre, relative emphasis on theme and character, and, not least, ideas.

A pervasive mixing of popular and elite elements also characterized the immediate institutional context of the drama. Most of the actors in the public theaters came from the lower classes. Though often of comparably humble origin, many of the playwrights managed to acquire a university education or its equivalent. The theaters themselves, remarkably similar in structure in the two countries, drew on both popular and aristocratic stage traditions; similarly, they operated under royal licensing, patronage, and censorship while appealing to a large clientele in the pursuit of profit. Although the plays attracted virtually all urban social strata, the lower classes probably dominated the audience numerically. The public theater accordingly provided fertile ground for the fusion of popular and classical materials that distinguishes English and Spanish drama.

Both the plays and their theaters in turn depended on the larger cultural, political, and social contours of the age. First, a relative cultural homogeneity of town and country, of upper class and lower, helped the drama exploit a variety of heritages and attract a broad spectrum of the populace. That homogeneity simultaneously reinforced and was perpetuated by an incomplete but stable absolutist state that had temporarily abandoned centralizing efforts after the unrest of the middle of the century and the still earlier era of initial national consolidation. The state in the end served the interests of the neofeudal aristocracy against those of all other classes, in the epoch of western Europe's transition from feudalism to capitalism. One can discern a series of increasingly general conditions of possibility for the constitution of Renaissance English and Spanish drama—the legacies of drama and literature, the institution of the theater, the organization of culture, the structure of the state, and the pattern of social and economic relations.

The entire study pursues a single and simple hypothesis: that the absolutist state, by its inherent dynamism and contradictions, first fostered and then undermined the public theater. More precisely, the similarities between Spanish and English absolutism help account for the parallels between the two dramatic traditions, while the divergent courses of economic and religious development in England and Spain begin to explain the differences. For this reason, the investigation moves from the general to the specific rather than in the opposite direction. The opening chapter treats the connection between feudalism and medieval European theater. Beyond whatever intrinsic interest such an investigation may possess, it prepares for the later emphasis on England and Spain by focusing on a series of basic relationships—between popular and learned culture, between ideology and dramatic form, and between medieval and Renaissance theater. Chapter 2 has roughly the same geographical range but covers only the sixteenth and seventeenth centuries. Claiming that behind the development of Renaissance drama lies the transition from feudalism to capitalism, it complements the first chapter's consideration of popular theater with a survey focusing on the neoclassical heritage. Together these chapters introduce the two main traditions that merge in the drama of England and Spain. The last part of chapter 2 in fact turns to that merger, canvassing the Spanish and English theaters during the first three-quarters of the sixteenth century to determine the conditions of their subsequent unique convergence. Given the amount of material to be covered, these two chapters necessarily operate at a high level of generality, seeking to provide little more than an aerial photograph of the terrain.

The second part of the book, consisting of five more chapters, presents a generally chronological analysis of the two public theaters, from the 1570s to the 1640s in England and from the late 1560s to 1700 in Spain. The emphasis rests on the ideological significance of the main genres, with detailed attention reserved for selected plays and playwrights from both countries. Two chapters treat the late sixteenth century, the first investigating the nonhomologous relationship between artisanal stage and absolutist state, and the second stressing the ambiguously aristocratic implications of romantic comedy and the national history play. The last three chapters turn to the theater's role in the absolutist crisis of the early seventeenth century, and in particular to the representation of oppositional currents on the stage. Chapter 5 discusses social and theatrical trends. Chapter 6 looks at satiric comedy and heroic drama, including Shakespearean tragedy. It seeks to account in addition for the salient, symmetrically divergent, distinctively popular forms of the period, English bourgeois tragedy and the Spanish peasant play. In the final chapter, which chronicles the supersession of public-theater drama, tragedy and romance receive primary consideration, but the religious play, central in Spain and peripheral in England, is also scrutinized.

As the preceding pages undoubtedly have suggested, the methods, theories, and commitments of Marxism shape the ensuing analysis of the public theater. Yet the evocation of historical or dialectical materialism today lacks the specificity that it perhaps possessed in the United States a generation ago. During the past twenty-five years, a variety of distinct, often competing strains in Marxist thought and action have emerged, while earlier traditions have been rescued from oblivion. The best Marxist work, moreover, has always entered into complex relations with other intellectual and political tendencies: these affiliations also widen the range of available approaches. For better or worse, the present discussion adopts an eclectic procedure, eschewing uniform allegiance to any single version of Marxism while drawing instead on a spectrum of positions developed primarily in western Europe and the United States. Since the most important model for this account of English and Spanish drama comes not from cultural theory or criticism, but from comparative history, and specifically from the work of Perry Anderson,[10] students of literature or theater may find themselves additionally befuddled.

At least one theoretical aim of the following chapters may repay further attention here, however. The emphasis on the mediations between drama and society or on the mutual articulation of numerous Marxist perspectives perhaps has already indicated a totalizing strategy.[11] Although especially associated with the writings of Georg Lukács, the quest for totality has in fact preoccupied Marxism since the 1840s. Traditional scholars, avant-garde theorists, and many Marxists all may well object to precisely this universal claim. First, an overall interpretation of medieval and Renaissance theater, or even of Renaissance Spanish and English drama, risks premature synthesis, given the meager empirical basis for many of the generalizations and the damaging absence of necessary mediating categories such as psychology. Second, the act of totalization may suppress detail, difference, heterogeneity, and conflict, finding, for example, a fusion of learned and popular culture where tension actually prevails, ignoring the irreducible specificity of sex or race, and even justifying not only the reactionary organicist ideology of interclass unity but also the totally administered societies of the capitalist West and the outright totalitarianism of Stalinist Communism.

These charges do not merit dismissal. They point, at the least, to the potential dangers of a totalizing project and, at the most, to the price any such project must pay. Although the remainder of this Introduction attempts in passing to address these problems, it mainly presents instead

---

[10]Perry Anderson, *Passages from Antiquity to Feudalism* (London: NLB, 1974); idem, *Lineages of the Absolutist State* (London: NLB, 1974).

[11]For a recent discussion, see Fredric Jameson, *The Political Unconscious: Narrative as a Socially Symbolic Act* (Ithaca, N.Y.: Cornell Univerity Press, 1981), pp. 50–58.

the possible advantages of totalization. These benefits include not only an advance in explanatory power, but also the delineation of and contribution to a genuinely shared intellectual enterprise, the potentially disquieting confrontation with the largest issues raised by Renaissance theater, the promotion of an alternative conceptual schema for the study of that theater, and the elucidation of the drama's subversive political efficacy during the seventeenth century and radical potential today. A consideration of the chasm separating theory from scholarship, and of the relationship between popular and elite culture, may help clarify the argument. The gamble is not, of course, that the difficulties of totality will magically disappear, but that the gains will outweigh the losses.

If the previous generation lamented the divorce between scholarship and criticism, the present one worries about the conflict between criticism and theory. Today scholarship and theory have gone their separate ways. The attempt to reunite them through a theoretically informed history of Spanish and English theater accordingly constitutes one kind of totalizing operation. Presumably, such an enterprise should meet particular obstacles in the apparently recalcitrant field of bibliography and textual criticism, with its extraordinary array of scientific procedures and substantive accomplishments, and its pretensions to value-free objectivity. A brief look at this hard case, then, may illustrate the importance of reconnecting scholarship and theory.

Anyone interested in Renaissance theater much prefers working with the relatively reliable editions of Shakespeare to struggling with the generally more dubious texts of Lope de Vega and Calderón. Yet bibliography is as ideologically purposeful as any of the myriad theories circulating today, and in ways that often unnecessarily limit its utility and occasionally even distort its results. Its scientificity, first of all, only superficially distinguishes it from New Criticism. Whereas New Criticism responded to the rise of science and the decline of the humanities by distinguishing literary from scientific language and preferring the former, bibliography made scientific methods its own. In a somewhat self-contradictory move, New Criticism in turn mimicked scientific procedure in its elaboration of systematic protocols for critical analysis. Textual criticism and New Criticism also shared an unprecedented concern with the verbal detail of literature. Finally, bibliographical analysis, like Chicago school Neo-Aristotelianism, fundamentally aimed to reconstruct authorial intention.

Yet a recognition of the multiple forces that help shape any literary or theatrical work renders problematic an exclusive focus on authorial intention. In the case of Shakespeare, whose texts inspired much of the pioneering work in bibliography, the entire project has a curious irrelevance. Scholars possess neither manuscripts of the plays nor printed versions whose publication the dramatist supervised. Shakespeare's theatrical career reveals no concern with authorial individuality or autonomy, no commitment to a stable text. Instead, the Shakespearean canon responds nicely to a Derridean critique of the centered subject, the guaranteed origin, and the self-identical text. From this perspective the search for the true Shakespeare amounts to a modern rewriting, either a useful appropriation of the past for present needs or an ideologically misguided imposition that effaces historical difference.

On the other hand, Shakespeare lived during a transitional era in which a bourgeois belief in literary property was beginning to emerge and in which dramatic composition already possessed a self-consciously verbal dimension. Thus the premises of bibliography and textual criticism, though hardly validated by these trends, partly echo the subjectivity of the earlier age. Whatever the appropriateness of those premises to New Criticism and Neo-Aristotelianism, bibliography can perhaps contribute to contemporary literary and theatrical study most effectively by pursuing not the text, but the texts of the Shakespearean or Renaissance play. Given adequate materials, one would want to distinguish at least among the foul papers, the promptbook of the opening performance, and the first printed edition, as well as among later emendations of each. Useful theoretical models for bibliography therefore derive not only from a deconstructive concern with textuality, but also from reception aesthetics and semiotics. Concerted empirical research on the relations between text and text, and between text and performance, could then modify and perhaps challenge the new paradigms that provide theoretical points of departure.

These suggestions may acquire a certain concreteness from a review of the textual problems raised by Marlowe's *Doctor Faustus*. Marlowe died in 1593, theatrical entrepreneur Philip Henslowe ordered additions to the play in 1602, the First Quarto appeared in 1604, and the much longer second one came out in 1616. Scholars agree that Marlowe collaborated on the original version, that Q1 represents a memorial reconstruction designed for provincial performance during the mid-1590s, and that Q2 derives at least partly from Marlowe's foul papers. Here a bizarre debate begins, however. W. W. Greg counterintuitively argues that Q2 does not incorporate the 1602 emendations and hence offers a fairly reliable report of the play on which Marlowe worked. In reply, Fredson Bowers takes the more probable position that the greater length of Q2 does result from the 1602 changes and that Q1 accordingly reproduces the structure of the Marlovian original. But Bowers, swayed by the connection of Q2 with the foul papers, then bases his text on Q2. Greg may have erred by placing excessive trust in the scientificity of bibliographical methods; Bowers certainly went wrong in sacrificing all for love of authorial verbal intention.[12]

Yet the latent potential of this scholarly endeavor emerges not so much from correction of mistakes in fact or judgment as from positive exploitation of the multiplicity of texts: Marlowe's collaborative composition of 1593 or earlier, the memorial reconstruction of the mid-1590s (and its 1604 printing), and the revised, expanded version of 1602 (and its 1616 printing). Q1 and Q2 present very different plays. In Q2 the many comic scenes reduce Faustus's overarching aspiration to trivial buffoonery. In Q1 the protagonist remains grand and tragic, especially if one concentrates on the passages written by Marlowe to the exclusion of those contributed by his coauthor. A study of the texts of *Doctor Faustus* might, then, help elucidate the distinctiveness of Marlovian dramaturgy, the practice of collaboration, the nature of provincial playing, the principles of emendation of old plays, and the significance of the printing of drama. Yet it will be able to do so only if specialists in bibliography modify their theoretical allegiances, and only if theorists take seriously the rich, potentially challenging scholarship newly at their disposal.

This prospective interplay between scholarship and theory also suggests some of the benefits and characteristics of totalization. One would expect a sheer intellectual gain for the study of literature. The supersession of false conflicts might have the additional advantage of freeing energy to confront real ones. A different understanding of the progress of scholarship could well emerge, in which a synthetic effort like the present work would play a new role. From this perspective, totalization functions not as the last word, not as the mechanism for closing off debate, but as the means of opening it up, as a recurrent moment in an ongoing dialectical process. The power of a comprehensive interpretation depends as much on its ability to generate new problems as on its success in overcoming old ones. The solution to these new problems may in turn call into question the earlier synthesis. If, for example, a Marxist account of Renaissance theater neglects issues of gender, a feminist response might involve an alternative totalizing act, which would in similar fashion then invite the scrutiny of its adequacy. Or a feminist project might reject all totalities in favor of local specificity, thus paving the way at some later time for still another provisional synthesis. This model implies the possibility of a common critical, cultural enterprise, of a working coalition that thrives on the interaction of different activities and different beliefs, that overcomes intellectual isolation, and that accordingly has some chance of mattering.

[12]W. W. Greg, ed., *Marlowe's "Doctor Faustus," 1604–1616: Parallel Texts* (Oxford: Clarendon Press, 1950); Fredson Bowers, ed., *Doctor Faustus,* in *The Complete Works of Christopher Marlowe,* 2d ed. (Cambridge: Cambridge University Press, 1981), 2:121–271.

The model does not, however, entail a commitment to pluralism, except in the limited sense of encouraging multiple approaches to a problem. At best, academic pluralism today corresponds to the political fragmentation of oppositional movements in the United States. At worst, it opposes totalization in order to protect a small piece of professional turf and to evade big issues, among them the politics of criticism. A totalizing view, by contrast, not only helps clarify the limits of individual positions and the areas of mutual incompatibility, but also may bring to light hidden strengths. The present study deploys a sharply defined, encompassing hypothesis partly to risk refutation by the vast amount of medieval and Renaissance drama that it claims to account for yet does not discuss. Similarly, its profound debt to prior scholarship partly conceals the subversive aim of undermining conventional assumptions about English and Spanish theater through the juxtaposition of a large quantity of disparate data. An allegiance to a common cultural project cannot thrive on an indifference to the orientation of that project. Like all critical enterprises, the attempt to effect a paradigm shift in Renaissance drama studies draws on strong impulses, interests, or convictions, in this instance primarily of a political nature.

The relation of popular to learned traditions in the public theater provides a useful framework within which to spell out those convictions. Of course an emphasis on synthesis, rather than on either the popular or the classical heritage in isolation, fundamentally stands or falls on its explanatory adequacy. Yet explanatory adequacy is hardly a neutral or independent concept, inextricably bound as it is to questions of what sort of knowledge one seeks and why. And that pursuit depends at least partly on the critic's sense of what matters most. Whatever a writer's intent, however, the choice of a learned or popular focus has political implications. These form a schematically logical, if not entirely obvious, pattern. Subversive as well as conformist tendencies have been found in both the popular and the learned traditions, and each of these tendencies has received applause as well as attack. Leftists have of course praised subversion and castigated conformity, whereas rightists have taken the opposite stance. One can therefore distinguish eight possible positions, depending on whether the emphasis is on popular culture or learned culture, subversion or conformity, and celebration or lament.

Among rightist critics, an antagonism to the subversiveness of neoclassical letters emerges in the denunciation of Marlowe by his contemporaries for Machiavellianism or atheism in particular and freethinking humanist radicalism in general. These charges, obviously now out of favor, have nonetheless been echoed by twentieth-century critics such as Douglas Bush, who attempt to reduce Marlovian iconoclasm to personal im-

[25

maturity. By contrast a sympathetic presentation of elitist aesthetics in connection with conformist values has probably characterized most of the best work done on England and Spain since the First World War. One thinks of Madeleine Doran and of the British Calderonistas, especially Edward M. Wilson and Alexander A. Parker. In a self-conscious and virulent variant, the critic rejoices in the persistence of hierarchy, the manipulation of the masses by the playwright, who thereby serves those in power. Although René Girard's application of his notion of scapegoating to Shakespeare comes close to this view, perhaps T. S. Eliot remains the greatest exponent of the approach.

An attack on the popular subversiveness of the public theater is a recurrent feature in late-sixteenth- and early-seventeenth-century opposition to the stage, whether by Puritan and Catholic clergy, English and Spanish city fathers, or courtly aestheticians in London and Madrid. This conservative ideology has its modern counterpart in the occasionally expressed conviction that Shakespeare's need to appeal to the groundlings damages his plays. A far more important approach to the popular heritage, however, stresses the creativity of the common people while locating their achievements within an interclass, organicist unity that performs the dual and related functions of effacing the conflicts of the past and pointing to the fragmentation of the present. Lope de Vega studies—including Leo Spitzer's work—have tended to follow this path, as has the research of Alfred Harbage and of L. C. Knights. Knights's affiliation with the *Scrutiny* group in turn indicates a leading theorist of this position, F. R. Leavis.

On the other hand, one may detect a recent trend—especially recent in the United States—toward a leftist perspective, influenced either singly or in various combinations by Marxism, feminism, and what is perhaps erroneously called poststructuralism. Concern with the learned, elite orientation of the drama has led both to critique of the resulting conservatism and to advocacy of the resulting radicalism. The discussions of gender by Coppélia Kahn and by Lisa Jardine seem to represent the former group; Jonathan Dollimore's account of "radical tragedy" clearly belongs in the latter category.

But arguably the most crucial current writing on the public theater skeptically interrogates the role of popular culture. Motivated by an awareness of the rationalizing effects of ideology in both the Renaissance and the present, this mode of inquiry seeks to unmask the often hidden reactionary implications of an organicist view of the theater, to demonstrate how apparently popular initiatives reinforce the status quo. Such a demystifying strategy can as a result both settle accounts with the past and lead to political defeatism in the present. José Antonio Maravall and José María Díez Borque in Spain and Stephen Greenblatt in the

United States have published investigations along these lines, which find a possible, though by no means inevitable, model in the oeuvre of Michel Foucault and an anticipation in the theories of Marxist thinkers as different as Theodor Adorno and Louis Althusser. Finally, a leftist enthusiasm for popular dramaturgy, centered in Marxist scholarship, takes the form of an insistence on the efficacy of lower-class initiatives and the importance of social antagonism. Its danger therefore lies in overestimating the autonomy of the oppressed, in succumbing to a populist voluntarism. Here one might include the research of Noël Salomon, a Frenchman writing about Spain, of Robert Weimann, a German writing about England, and, to take the leading theoretician of this position, of Mikhail Bakhtin, a Russian writing—in his book on Rabelais—about France.

The following chapters, in general sympathy with leftist approaches, prefer the subversive to the conformist, the popular to the learned, and, of course, the synthetic to any single alternative. They attempt, on one hand, to demonstrate the pervasiveness of the popular tradition in the theater. Barrington Moore, Jr., offers an elegant defense of this procedure: "In any society the dominant groups are the ones with the most to hide about the way society works. . . . sympathy with the victims of historical processes and skepticism about the victors' claims provide essential safeguards against being taken in by the dominant mythology. A scholar who tries to be objective needs these feelings as part of his ordinary working equipment."[13] More than three centuries earlier, the Leveller John Wildman anticipated this argument: "Our very laws were made by our conquerors; and whereas it's spoken much of chronicles, I conceive there is no credit to be given to any of them; and the reason is because those that were our lords, and made us their vassals, would suffer nothing else to be chronicled. We are now engaged for our freedom; that's the end of parliaments, not to constitute what is already according to the just rules of government."[14]

Wildman's words, spoken in 1647 at the radical high-water mark of the English Revolution, suggest not only victimization but also the partial success of oppositional movements. In England, then, the Civil War provides the main basis for assigning a progressive political impact to drama. Insofar as the plays anticipated the conflicts of the Revolution, the stage may have contributed as well as responded to the fundamental transformations of the age. From the vantage point of late-twentieth-century America, whose dominant institutions often seem utterly resis-

[13]Barrington Moore, Jr., *Social Origins of Dictatorship and Democracy: Lord and Peasant in the Making of the Modern World* (Boston: Beacon Press, 1966), pp. 522–23.
[14]John Wildman, in "The Putney Debates," in *The Levellers in the English Revolution*, ed. G. E. Aylmer (Ithaca, N.Y.: Cornell University Press, 1975), p. 109.

tant to change, the English Revolution may recall the possibilities of political activity, while the plays that preceded it may suggest the political potential of cultural practices. The connection between late medieval theater and the struggle against feudalism invites similar reflections. More specifically, the discussion of the English Renaissance stage combines a prospective view, stressing the drama's conditions of possibility, with a retrospective glance, emphasizing the drama's possible involvement in the making of a revolution. The multiple fissures that fractured English society after 1640 present a model for analyzing class relationships in Elizabethan and especially Jacobean theater; similarly, the unprecedented political and literary energy of the lower classes at midcentury can guide an account of the popular dramatic tradition.

As a result, the organizing problematic of reception theory acquires, if only for a moment, a unique configuration. In a discussion of the difficulties of historicism, Fredric Jameson presupposes a fundamental bifurcation: "We are thus confronted with a choice between study of the nature of the 'objective' structures of a given cultural text (the historicity of its forms and of its content, the historical moment of emergence of its linguistic possibilities, the situation-specific function of its aesthetic) and something rather different which would instead foreground the interpretive categories or codes through which we read and receive the text in question."[15] Yet with English Renaissance drama one can perhaps have it both ways, linking "the historical moment" to "the interpretive categories" through which that moment has been understood. The procedure of reading the drama through the revolution, whatever its perils, induces somewhat more confidence than usual in a correlation between genesis and function, between the ideological effectivity conferred by the context from which a play emerges and the ideological effect of that same play in a later context. That later context may in turn extend beyond 1660 to the present. Christopher Hill remarks, "My object is not to patronize the radicals by patting them on the head as 'in advance of their time'—that tired cliché of the lazy historian. In some ways they are in advance of ours."[16] To the extent that the radical agenda of the revolutionary decades remains the radical agenda of today, English Renaissance drama may retain both critical and utopian force.

Yet the symptomatic exclusion of Spanish theater from this argument betrays a one-sidedness. Apparently radical Golden Age plays lack even indirect radical effects in Spain. In England, the men of property succeeded in thwarting the revolutionary aspirations of the poor. Gramsci's notion of hegemony—broadly speaking, domination by consent—

[15]Jameson, p. 9.
[16]Christopher Hill, *The World Turned Upside Down: Radical Ideas during the English Revolution* (Harmondsworth, Middlesex: Penguin, 1975), p. 384.

nicely captures the structured complex of ruling-class power and popular opposition, specifying both the limits and the possibilities of insurgency from below.[17] Indeed, a purely popular theater cannot exist in a class society. In Renaissance England and Spain, a relatively unified national culture rendered unthinkable any absolute demarcation between popular and learned traditions, while obscuring basic inequities and genuine class conflict. Thus, to adapt various contemporary formulations, a demystification of ideology and ideological state apparatuses must balance enthusiasm for the creativity, the autonomy, and the utopian thrust of popular culture.[18]

A purely repressive interpretation of elite involvement distorts the significance of the interaction of popular and learned traditions in the public theater, however. The classical heritage constituted not only a crucial condition of possibility for English and Spanish drama, but also a vehicle for critical commentary and the positive presentation of alternatives. A leap forward in time may clarify this point. In an important debate within German Marxism during the 1930s, Brecht persuasively showed that Lukács's commitment to formal unities, to artistic totalities, effectually banished the disruptive voice from drama and literature while valorizing a conservative view of reality.[19] Indeed, whereas the expression of hegemonic ideologies went hand in hand with recourse to organic form in medieval and Renaissance theater, popular impulses consistently worked against aesthetic coherence. Yet these subversive gestures in themselves necessarily stopped short of the full articulation of an opposing point of view, just as lower-class rebellions failed in part from an inability to imagine a pervasive reorganization of society in the interests of the rebels. One might argue that, in theater and society alike, only a combination of learned and popular culture made it possible to dismantle ruling-class views and replace them with new perspectives of greater scope, power, and social justice. Some such hypothesis informs the present study, which distinguishes between organicism and totality and accordingly searches for admittedly elusive examples of contradictory totalities in the theater. Finally, the parallel quest for totalization in this book as a whole rests on the analogous, but perhaps self-serving, assumption that radical change today requires the participation, though

[17]Antonio Gramsci, *Selections from the Prison Notebooks*, ed. and trans. Quintin Hoare and Geoffrey Nowell Smith (New York: International, 1971).

[18]Ideological state apparatuses: Louis Althusser, "Ideology and Ideological State Apparatuses (Note towards an Investigation)," in *Lenin and Philosophy and Other Essays*, trans. Ben Brewster (New York: Monthly Review Press, 1971), pp. 127–86; creativity: Raymond Williams, *Marxism and Literature* (Oxford: Oxford University Press, 1977), pp. 206–12; utopia: Jameson, pp. 281–99; popular culture: Mikhail Bakhtin, *Rabelais and His World*, trans. Hélène Iswolsky (Cambridge: MIT Press, 1968), pp. 1–58.

[19]Ernst Bloch et al., *Aesthetics and Politics* (London: NLB, 1977), pp. 28–99.

not the leadership, of what Gramsci called traditional intellectuals and what two American socialists have recently termed the professional-managerial class.[20]

Yet an insistence on granting equal weight to the learned tradition may well introduce an unintended elitist bias. A focus on literary drama excludes from consideration an enormous range of theatrical activity, much of it involving those in no position to leave written records. Though the category of theatricality usefully helps locate literary drama within a broad cultural context, it also effaces geographical, historical, and social discriminations: all of medieval and Renaissance Europe was theatrical. Such discriminations matter for two reasons. First, Renaissance men and women had no trouble distinguishing between a play by Shakespeare or Lope de Vega, on one hand, and a royal entry or rural May Day festival, on the other. Second, and more important, today the plays can be politically mobilized far more easily than can the other forms of theatricality.

Nonetheless, the history and institutional setting of that mobilization may well work against any radical project. In Spain, Golden Age drama has long provided one of the bulwarks of a dominant reactionary ideology. The work by Maravall and Díez Borque alluded to above has accordingly and appropriately adopted a strategy of demystification. In the United States, on the other hand, where the names of Lope de Vega and Calderón mean little even to most literary and theatrical critics, perhaps the plays of Renaissance Spain can exercise a certain ideological leverage. From this perspective, studies of English Renaissance drama would presumably have the opposite effect. Shakespeare in particular, perhaps the language's only "living" dead author, stands at the center of the arts and the humanities in America, justifying both theatrical practice and the profession of literary study. A playwright of infinite variety, made to serve the needs at one time or another of widely disparate ideological projects, he remains the guarantor of high culture.[21]

On the other hand, the conservative effect of institutionalization may represent the unavoidable overhead charge on a radical rereading of Shakespeare. Although that rereading undoubtedly should not elicit the same sense of urgency as other, more pressing political enterprises, the continuing cultural force of Shakespeare means that neither can it be entirely avoided. An oppositional or insurgent criticism cannot always choose the terrain of contestation. Second, the present work makes a

[20]Gramsci, pp. 3–23; Barbara and John Ehrenreich, "The Professional-Managerial Class," in *Between Labor and Capital*, ed. Pat Walker (Boston: South End Press, 1979), pp. 5–45.

[21]For a comparable claim, with reference to England, see Derek Longhurst, "'Not for All Time, but for an Age': An Approach to Shakespeare Studies," in *Re-Reading English*, ed. Peter Widdowson (London: Methuen, 1982), pp. 150–63.

modest effort to decenter Shakespeare by locating him in the general context of Renaissance England, by comparing England with Spain, and, most important, by treating the explication of texts simply as one strategy among many. The analyses of individual plays by Shakespeare and others do not retrospectively justify the extensive presentation of "background" information; they are not the payoff. Test cases or necessary mediating steps, they instead help constitute and validate a totalizing view of Renaissance public theater. Similarly, the act of totalization aims to forestall any unproblematic acceptance of the ensuing argument simply as an account of the sociological aspects of drama.

The following pages nonetheless rely upon the canonical status of many English and Spanish plays in order to transform other conventional assumptions. In doing so, they make claims only for the relative, rather than for the objective and transhistorical, value of Lope de Vega, Shakespeare, and their contemporaries. The logic is as follows. A Marxist point of view can generate the best understanding of the conditions of production of that drama most esteemed by the arbiters of taste since the seventeenth century. Popular and at times radical forces figured prominently among those conditions. In like manner, the plays themselves have acquired their prestige to a considerable extent because of their radical elements, much as dominant classes have traditionally drawn upon popular culture to reinvigorate their own artistic life. An attempt to appropriate the drama of the public theater for new uses, to enlist it in a socialist program, will therefore gain fundamental support from the plays themselves, as well as from their immediate historical circumstances. This book is designed to further that project. Whether it does so or not depends in part, of course, on its own merits, but more on the theatrical and critical work of others, and on larger movements for change in American society.

# [1

# Medieval Theater and
# the Structure of Feudalism

Western European feudalism emerged between the late eighth and tenth centuries from the clash and ultimate fusion of two prior, decaying modes of production—Germanic tribal communalism and the Roman slave economy. In its classical form, which persisted into the fifteenth century, it coalesced around a double and connected set of relationships. The first, between exploited and exploiter, characterized all posttribal, nonslave, precapitalist societies. Through extraeconomic coercion, large landowners extracted an economic surplus from small peasant producers of legally limited mobility. The second bond, between individual members of the ruling class, was unique to feudalism and institutionalized in the fief. A lord typically enjoyed only conditional control of his property, in return for which he owed military service to his overlord. The overlord occupied a similarly subordinate position with respect to a still higher noble, in a system of vassalage that ideally ascended pyramidally from the lowest knight to the monarch or emperor. In practice, however, since a king, like any other aristocrat, relied largely on the income from his own lands and the direct loyalty of his armed followers for his political strength, a particular peer might well amass more effective power, though less often greater authority, than his nominal ruler. Indeed, the very structure of the system allowed for the duplication of this apparent anomaly at any point in the hierarchy. Thus constituted, feudalism precluded centralization, its "parcellization of sovereignty," as Perry Anderson calls it, instead dispersing normal state activity throughout the landowning class and in that way everywhere joining political with economic power.[1]

---

[1]Perry Anderson, *Passages from Antiquity to Feudalism* (London: NLB, 1974), pp. 147–48. The quoted passage appears on p. 148.

Medieval theater reenacted at its own institutional level the Roman-Germanic synthesis of the feudal mode of production. Further, many of its plays appropriated feudal terminology to dramatize character relationships, in some instances as part of a fundamental social critique. Yet feudalism helped establish the conditions of possibility and hence, indirectly, the distinctiveness of medieval theater primarily in a curiously negative sense. The parcellization of sovereignty limited the extension of aristocratic authority over communal agriculture, ecclesiastical organization, and urban communes.[2] The theater thrived during the Middle Ages in precisely those interstices of the feudal world—socioeconomic, geographical, temporal, and ideological—that the ruling class only incompletely penetrated. Ruralized, territorially dispersed, and culturally backward, the nobility directly contributed little to the stage. The drama of feudal Europe developed in the village, the church, and the town.

The structural neatness of this hypothesis should not obscure the dynamism of the process, however. Responding to the changes in feudal society, the theater flourished first among the peasantry, then among the clergy, and finally among the urban populace. This progression—from popular agrarian to learned religious drama, and from there to the simultaneously popular and learned religious plays of the late medieval towns—invites initial interpretation as a dialectical synthesis akin to the one that governs discussion of English and Spanish Renaissance theater in later chapters. Such an approach should help define the specificity both of the transition from medieval to Renaissance drama and of the fusion of learned and popular traditions on the English and Spanish stages. Within the context of the Middle Ages, it raises the possibility of a correlation between a Roman-Germanic and a learned-popular synthesis.

More important, this structural and historical model offers a preliminary means of ascertaining the social function of theater. Both the drama of the village and the drama of the church derived from rituals that almost certainly once had much in common. Yet the consequent problems in determining the historical and formal steps in the gradual transformation of ritual into theater also suggest a way of understanding the role of the stage. If ritual reasserts community, then cognate drama, sharing its broadly theatrical impulse, might often serve a similar purpose. But whereas popular theater may have provided moments of utopian liberation, the church stage tended toward a reaffirmation of an inequitable social order.[3] If the former possessed implicit oppositional

[2]Anderson, pp. 148–53.
[3]Mikhail Bakhtin, *Rabelais and His World*, trans. Hélène Iswolsky (Cambridge: MIT Press, 1968), p. 9, similarly contrasts marketplace festivities with official feasts.

potential, the latter fulfilled the ends of an ideological state apparatus, although the generally dubious emphasis on the state in this formulation retains particularly little relevance for medieval society. By the same logic, the late medieval plays that drew on both prior traditions necessarily faced in two apparently contradictory directions, an embarrassment that an analysis of the ideology of form should clarify.

Similar considerations apply to the difficulties of discriminating spectacle or procession from play[4] and, more generally, of understanding theatricality and theatrical space. Once again the problem conceals its own solution. Medieval drama was performed not in permanent theaters, but in institutions or locales that ordinarily served other purposes. There thus were several theatrical spaces. No physical distance or barrier separates peasant drama from agricultural labor, liturgical drama from clerical ceremony, or urban drama from the economic, social, and cultural relations of the marketplace. The medieval audience did not enter the world of the theater; the theater entered the world of the audience. Part of a milieu more than a privileged sanctuary from which to comment on that milieu, the stage usually fit unproblematically into its surroundings. Contradictions arose here too, however, primarily in urban religious drama. The attempt to superimpose metaphysical hierarchies and conceptions of space on the relatively secular geographical, architectural, and social structures of a late medieval town produced a variety of ambivalences that call into question any univocal interpretation of the effects generated on the urban stage.[5]

The parcellization of sovereignty probably accounts for this range of functions, a range unusually wide even in an institution such as the theater that at times has enjoyed relative autonomy.[6] Nonetheless, the nobility exercised hegemonic control over feudal society. A successive review of the three main kinds of medieval drama will therefore seek not merely to work out some of the general relationships between theater and society,[7] but also to determine the constraints imposed by a hegemonic aristocracy and the openings available for the construction of a counterhegemonic alternative.

[4]A number of valuable studies on this topic, mainly focusing on the city of York, appeared in *Leeds Studies in English*, n.s., during the 1970s.

[5]Elie Konigson, *L'espace théâtral médiéval* (Paris: Editions du Centre National de la Recherche Scientifique, 1975), esp. p. 79.

[6]Relative autonomy: Louis Althusser, "Contradiction and Overdetermination: Notes for an Investigation," in *For Marx*, trans. Ben Brewster (London: NLB, 1977), p. 111.

[7]The early volumes of *Records of Early English Drama—York*, ed. Alexandra F. Johnston and Margaret Rogerson, 2 vols. (Toronto: University of Toronto Press, 1979), and *Chester*, ed. Lawrence M. Clopper (Toronto: University of Toronto Press, 1979)—suggest that an adequately detailed account of these relationships will have to draw on an enormous amount of local archival material throughout Europe, much of it still unpublished.

## EARLY MEDIEVAL POPULAR THEATER

The earliest medieval theater preceded by centuries the birth of feudalism. Indeed, its two main strands—one deriving from the late antique mimic stage and the other probably from primitive agrarian folk ritual—date back to well before the beginning of the Middle Ages. These dual traditions very loosely correlate with the Roman and Germanic heritages, between which, however, no synthesis ensued for centuries at least. Although the extremely skimpy dramatic records surely give no indication of the pervasiveness of theatrical activity from the fifth to the tenth century, they may accurately represent the scarcity of genuine plays. Perhaps neither the mimic nor the folk tradition produced much prefeudal drama;[8] perhaps popular drama, as distinguished from ritual, revel, pastime, festival, or entertainment, emerged only during the age of feudalism.

Descriptions of medieval popular festivities often invoke the same complex of practices as do accounts of medieval popular theater: prominence of clowns and fools; subversive verbal inventiveness; festive, affirmative laughter; comically ambivalent treatment of death and rebirth, linked to a penchant for open-endedness, disguise, and metamorphosis; bodily, materialist, grotesque realism designed to parody or undermine official political and religious ideologies; and collective, antihierarchical behavior at once archaic and utopian.[9] If popular drama therefore could not exist without belonging to an encompassing popular theatricality, the converse does not hold: popular theatricality need not imply the presence of popular drama. A brief historical summary accordingly may suggest some significant trends in the development and eventual crystallization of popular drama.

Neither form of medieval popular theater developed in complete isolation from ruling elites. Late classical mime, whatever its ultimate sources, flourished during the gradual decline of imperial Rome's slave economy. Similarly, although rural dramatic activities may have had roots in some prior, classless society, peasantries historically have almost always had to devote part of their labor to the support of privileged strata.[10] Even among the Germanic tribes, hierarchical organization be-

[8]Heinz Kindermann, *Das Theater der Antike und des Mittelalters*, vol. 1 of *Theatergeschichte Europas* (Salzburg: Otto Müller, 1957), p. 399, refers to a seventh-century Tyrolean play, however.

[9]Festivities: Bakhtin, chap. 1; theater: Anthony Caputi, *Buffo: The Genius of Vulgar Comedy* (Detroit: Wayne State University Press, 1978), esp. chaps. 2 and 3; Robert Weimann, *Shakespeare and the Popular Tradition in the Theater: Studies in the Social Dimension of Dramatic Form and Function*, ed. Robert Schwartz (Baltimore: Johns Hopkins University Press, 1978), chaps. 1 and 2, who carefully distinguishes between mimic and folk theater.

[10]Rodney Howard Hilton, *Bond Men Made Free: Medieval Peasant Movements and the English Rising of 1381* (London: Temple Smith, 1973), pp. 11, 25–26.

gan to replace primitive communalism during the first century, in response to Roman military and economic pressure. Following the collapse of the Western empire, both popular theaters therefore again functioned in societies based on class distinctions. The new Germanic monarchies remained in every instance prefeudal, however.

The mimic drama of the barbarian kingdoms constituted a simple survival from the imperial period rather than a fresh departure coincident with the ascendancy of a new political order. The rulers of the postimperial states lacked a uniform attitude toward the stage. The closest approximation to Germanic theatrical patronage—under the Ostrogoth Theodoric the Great—formed part of a more general effort to preserve ancient culture. This initial instance of dramatic neoclassicism proved no more enduring than the fragile institutional structure on which it rested: the last certain references to theaters in the West date from the sixth century.[11] In straitened conditions the practitioners of the mime persisted, although their activities, often lumped together with juggling by hostile contemporaries, generally bore little resemblance to modern or indeed late imperial notions of drama. On the other hand, the mimes preserved a tradition of acting, particularly in farcical comedy, for the later Middle Ages.[12]

Although mimic theater did not begin with the rise of Rome, its urban strains probably responded to social change more directly than did the cultural life of Europe's remarkably stable and ancient villages.[13] At the dawn of the Middle Ages, especially in regions relatively untouched by imperial influence, rural religious ritual may well have resembled prehistorical practices. Exactly what kind of folk ritual gave rise to theater remains contested, however. Against the overwhelming majority of scholars, who continue to emphasize communal agrarian fertility rites, at least one recent dissenter focuses on shamanist trance.[14] By either interpretation, the problem lies in determining the date and cause of the

[11]Allardyce Nicoll, *Masks Mimes and Miracles: Studies in the Popular Theatre* (1931; rpt. New York: Cooper Square Publishers, 1963), pp. 141–42; Anderson, p. 119. But see Erich Auerbach, *Literary Language and Its Public in Late Latin Antiquity and in the Middle Ages*, trans. Ralph Manheim (New York: Pantheon, 1965), pp. 259–60; E. K. Chambers, *The Mediaeval Stage* (London: Oxford University Press, 1903), 1:20–21.

[12]Kindermann, 1:393–97; J. D. A. Ogilvy, "*Mimi, Scurrae, Histriones*: Entertainers of the Early Middle Ages," *Speculum* 38 (1963): 603–19; Richard Axton, *European Drama of the Early Middle Ages* (London: Hutchinson University Library, 1974), chap. 1; Weimann, chap. 1.

[13]Hilton, *Bond Men Made Free*, pp. 28–29.

[14]Theater and fertility rites: Chambers, *Mediaeval Stage*, 1:89–419; Paolo Toschi, *Le origini del teatro italiano* (Turin: Edizioni Scientifiche Einaudi, 1955); Benjamin Hunningher, *The Origin of the Theater* (Amsterdam: Em. Querido, 1955), pp. 14–47; Alan Brody, *The English Mummers and Their Plays: Traces of Ancient Mystery* (Philadelphia: University of Pennsylvania Press, 1969). Shamanist theory: E. T. Kirby, *Ur-Drama: The Origins of the Theatre* (New York: New York University Press, 1975).

transition to genuine drama from the dramatic rituals that once apparently flourished throughout Europe.[15] The initial stages of this movement probably resulted from the ideological hostility of Christianity, in most instances centuries before the emergence of feudalism. The transformation of cultic worship into secular pastime entailed the abandonment of ritual content, though not of ritual form. In England, a further, though still incomplete, development—from pastime to professional entertainment—also preceded the Norman Conquest and the full feudalization of English society.[16] Early theater's independence from the main medieval social system thus largely, if negatively, accords with the general relationship between drama and feudalism.

Clear evidence of popular plays remains only from after the consolidation of feudalism. Mimic acting led to urban secular drama by the thirteenth century, if not earlier.[17] In rural England, the final step from ritual to drama—the establishment of the folk play itself—may not have occurred before 1200, with complex versions dating from later still. More generally, feudal society left its distinctive mark on peasant theater of the later Middle Ages, arguably through the effect of economic expansion on the dramatic forms of the period, and without question in courtly and chivalric motifs and plots.[18] Even the figure of Robin Hood, perhaps deriving from pre-Christian May ceremonies, probably changed profoundly under the impact of the social struggles of thirteenth- or fourteenth-century England.[19]

Yet the persistence of ancient folk customs is at least as striking as their transformation. The parcellization of sovereignty may help explain the village's relative cultural autonomy from the ideology of the dominant class. Especially in northern Europe, communal holdings and individual peasant private property survived from earlier societies. Even fully enserfed agricultural producers devoted only part of their time to

[15]Chambers, *The English Folk-Play* (1933; rpt. New York: Russell and Russell, 1964), pp. 3–13, 197–235.

[16]Kindermann, 1:397; Kirby, p. 149; Charles Reed Baskervill, "Dramatic Aspects of Medieval Folk Festivals in England," *Studies in Philology* 17 (1920): 20, 22–26. Caputi, passim and esp. pp. 234–35, suggests gradations between ritual and drama. J. O. Prestwick, "Anglo-Norman Feudalism and the Problem of Continuity," *Past and Present*, no. 26 (November 1963): 39–57, attributes the triumph of feudalism in England to the Norman Conquest. But see Michael Moïssey Postan, *The Medieval Economy and Society: An Economic History of Britain 1100–1500* (Berkeley and Los Angeles: University of California Press, 1972), pp. 73–87.

[17]On England, see Weimann, pp. 49–55.

[18]Baskervill, pp. 32, 79, 89.

[19]May rites: Toschi, pp. 468–73. Social roots: Hilton, "The Origins of Robin Hood," in *Peasants, Knights and Heretics: Studies in Medieval English Social History*, ed. Hilton (Cambridge: Cambridge University Press, 1976), pp. 221–35; J. C. Holt, "The Origins and Audience of the Ballads of Robin Hood," in *Peasants, Knights and Heretics*, ed. Hilton, pp. 236–57.

the manorial demesne, reserving the rest for their customary tenancies. Although the lord received a portion of the surplus from these fields as well, the villeins retained organizational control of their labor. In addition, the multiple, overlapping, and competing aristocratic jurisdictions built into feudalism allowed for limited village independence and even at times for gaps in the application of the legal system. In all these respects, the feudal system differed from both the preceding slave economy and the succeeding capitalist mode of production.[20] Although perhaps no agricultural work force has ever fully accepted the values of its rulers or entirely relinquished its own traditions, the characteristic organization of rural society in the Middle Ages may have enabled the lower classes to preserve their cultural practices to an unusual extent. Early medieval peasant dramatic activities lived on for more than a millennium. Possibly they contributed to the social solidarity, to the incipient class consciousness of the rebellious peasants of the late medieval period. Certainly together with the mimic theater they exercised a formative influence on the late medieval secular stage and ultimately contributed to religious drama as well.[21] The decisive impulse behind the development of Christian theater, however, came from outside the popular traditions.

## LITURGICAL THEATER

Unlike the drama of the peasants and the mimes, liturgical plays seem independent of feudalism not because they had roots in a prior society, but because they arose from religious ceremony. The simplest extant version of the dialogue from which church theater probably developed reveals nothing of specifically feudal significance:

INTERROGATIO:
>    Quem queritis in sepulchro, Christicolę?

RESPONSIO:
>    Ihesum Nazarenum crucifixum, o caelicolae.

>    Non est hic, surrexit, sicut predixerat.
>    Ite nuntiate, quia surrexit de sepulchro.

>        Resurrexi ⟨. . .⟩ . (c. 975)

(*Question*: Whom do you seek in the sepulchre, O followers of Christ? / *Answer*: Jesus of Nazareth who was crucified, O heaven-dwellers. / He is not

---

[20]Anderson, pp. 148–50.
[21]Kindermann, 1:397–402; Axton, pp. 33–60; Robert A. Potter, *The English Morality Play: Origins, History and Influence of a Dramatic Tradition* (London: Routledge and Kegan Paul, 1975), pp. 10–16; Weimann, chap. 2.

here, he has risen as he had foretold; / go, announce that he has risen from the sepulchre. / I have risen.)[22]

A similar distance from social life apparently characterized liturgical drama over the next six hundred years. Yet far more than the popular stage, this tradition belonged to the feudal mode of production. Only the particular conditions of western European feudalism—its dual heritage, parcellization of sovereignty, international character, and expansionist tendencies—made possible the emergence, development, and distinctive features of early church theater.

Western European religious drama arose not in the first days of Christianity, but in the age of the Carolingian empire, the formative period of feudalism. Its initial characteristics, whether aesthetic (liturgical form and content), theatrical (ceremonial purpose), sociological (monastic auspices), or geographical (Carolingian locale), reveal the imprint of the immediate circumstances. Through roughly the first two centuries of the liturgical stage, the most fully dramatic pieces came from northern France and western Germany, the former centers of the Carolingian domain, while quasi-dramatic texts appeared on the feudal periphery. Equally important, the spread of liturgical theater generally coincided more closely in time and space with the outward thrust of the leading medieval social system than with the geographical widening of the Christian world.[23] Even in the more heterogeneous circumstances of the twelfth century, the heartland of feudalism retained its priority in theatrical innovation. The plays of this period, whether in Latin or the vernacular, draw explicitly on the language and structures of the feudal mode of production. In the late medieval period, although other theatrical forms, many of them profoundly indebted to the liturgical stage, eventually came to the fore, liturgical drama continued to thrive and to spread, protected by the special position open to the church in the structure of feudal society. The present discussion, however, focuses on the period before 1200, first surveying early developments and then considering the twelfth-century expansion.

## Quem quaeritis and Visitatio sepulchri

Early liturgical drama grew out of a complex set of relationships among the Carolingian empire and its foes, the dynamism and structure

<hr>

[22]Walther Lipphardt, ed., *Lateinische Osterfeiern und Osterspiele* (Berlin: Walter de Gruyter, 1975), 1:94. Subsequent discussion of the dates and locales of liturgical drama for Easter draws on this collection and on volumes 2 through 5 of Lipphardt's edition (Berlin: Walter de Gruyter, 1976). Translation: David M. Bevington, ed., *Medieval Drama* (Boston: Houghton Mifflin, 1975), p. 26.

[23]For an attempt to link the rise of liturgical theater to the emergence of private property, see Leonard Goldstein, "On the Origin of Medieval Drama," *Zeitschrift für Anglistik und Amerikanistik* 29 (1981): 101–15.

of feudalism, the institutional church, the reform of culture and religion, and the modification of the Christian service. The Carolingian ascendancy of the eighth and ninth centuries involved the construction of the empire, the turn to classical antiquity, and the reorganization of religion. The birth of feudalism was the ultimate, unintended consequence of the first of these policies, and the territorial nobility its main beneficiary. But the church gained almost as much. The feudal parcellization of sovereignty allowed it a position of power and autonomy unequaled in its prior or subsequent history. With the ruling class dispersed over the countryside, there remained no single military and cultural authority, either national or international. On the one hand, the church could protect its organizational and even territorial independence; on the other, it could in theory exercise ideological hegemony over much of Europe.[24] To anticipate: the church's near monopoly on western European literate drama at least until the twelfth century depended on this parcellization of sovereignty. In the relative absence of towns or courts, it simply lacked competition, while its own institutional organization facilitated the wide distribution of the plays in fairly homogeneous texts.

The church could not achieve this position unaided, however. Charlemagne's clerically inspired neoclassical cultural reforms, followed by the collapse of the political structure that engendered them, helped Western Christianity realize its potential. Designed to buttress an empire with aspirations to the universalist legacy of ancient Rome, these reforms under new conditions instead benefited a different kind of institution altogether. The church already possessed impressive claims to the heritage of classical antiquity, owing to its triumph in the late imperial period, its seat in Rome, its international organization, and its own even more encompassing universalism. The cultivation of a purified Latinity during the Carolingian Renaissance only strengthened this position, while contributing to the uniformity and centralization of religious practice. At the same time, the apparent return to the past concealed a radical innovation—the creation of an essentially artificial language and hence a break with the vernacular.[25] Only this extraordinary disjunction between written and spoken language explains the relative divorce of early liturgical drama from popular impulses or, for that matter, from secular influences of any kind.[26]

---

[24]Anderson, p. 152.

[25]Ernst Robert Curtius, *European Literature and the Latin Middle Ages*, trans. Willard R. Trask (1953; rpt. New York: Harper and Row, 1963), pp. 25, 28–29, 31; Auerbach, *Literary Language*, pp. 111–23. But see Auerbach, *Literary Language*, pp. 262, 282.

[26]C. Clifford Flanigan, "The Liturgical Drama and Its Tradition: A Review of Scholarship, 1965–1975," *Research Opportunities in Renaissance Drama* 18 (1975): 81–102, and 19 (1976): 109–36. For a recent opposing view, see Timothy J. McGee, "The Liturgical Placements of the *Quem quaeritis* Dialogue," *Journal of the American Musicological Society* 29 (1976):

Carolingian ecclesiastical changes also aimed at standardization and centralization under the authority of Rome, a process that probably gave rise to liturgical theater. Since the reform of the liturgy involved a move toward conformity based primarily on the simple Roman ceremonies, the seemingly anomalous invention of tropes, the unauthorized musical and textual embellishments of the liturgy from which church drama apparently arose, may represent, however unconsciously, a local Frankish rebellion against homogeneity. Between the ninth and eleventh centuries liturgical poetry became one of the focuses of Latin creativity, and the tropes themselves became the center of European musical advances.[27] More generally, just as feudalism emerged almost paradoxically from a synthesis of Roman and Germanic elements, a corresponding ethnic blend came to dominate the church only in the eighth century, as the institution increasingly assumed a hierarchical, indeed specifically feudal, structure. Finally, Carolingian liturgical reform resulted in the adoption of a Roman-Frankish rite, perhaps partly becuse of the incorporation of various Germanic ritual and musical motifs.[28] A product of the revised liturgy, troping emerged from the same contrast between intention and effect that characterized the transition from imperial internationalism to feudal particularism.[29] Liturgical change thus both depended on and paralleled larger political, social, and institutional trends.

The events immediately following the death of Charlemagne in 814 may have provided a specific inspiration for troping. Louis the Pious, Charlemagne's son and successor, aimed to perpetuate a unitary Frankish empire far more than did his father.[30] In 817, at his directive, Benedict of Aniane convoked an ecclesiastical council in the imperial capital of Aachen designed to centralize control over monastic custom. Since Benedict's reforms also involved considerable liturgical innovation

---

25; idem, "The Role of the *Quem Quaeritis* Dialogue in the History of Western Drama," *Renaissance Drama*, n.s., 7 (1976): 187.

[27]Liturgical poetry: Auerbach, *Literary Language*, p. 270. Trope music: Robert Weakland, "The Beginnings of Troping," *Musical Quarterly* 44 (1958): 477.

[28]Church personnel and structure: Anderson, p. 125; Roy Pascal, "On the Origins of the Liturgical Drama of the Middle Ages," *Modern Language Review* 36 (1941): 374–75. Emergence of the Roman-Frankish rite: Jacques Chailley, *L'école musicale de Saint Martial de Limoges jusqu'à la fin du xi^e siècle* (Paris: Livres Essentiels, 1960), p. 186; Pascal, pp. 375, 377, 380–81; and esp. Flanigan, "The Roman Rite and the Origins of the Liturgical Drama," *University of Toronto Quarterly* 43 (1974): 263–84. But see O. B. Hardison, Jr., *Christian Rite and Christian Drama in the Middle Ages: Essays in the Origin and Early History of Modern Drama* (Baltimore: Johns Hopkins Press, 1965), p. 82.

[29]The accidental, unconscious development of early liturgical drama: Rosemary Woolf, *The English Mystery Plays* (Berkeley and Los Angeles: University of California Press, 1972), p. 4. Axton, p. 65, though generally agreeing, discerns a more deliberate dramatic intention.

[30]Geoffrey Barraclough, *The Crucible of Europe: The Ninth and Tenth Centuries in European History* (Berkeley and Los Angeles: University of California Press, 1976), pp. 62–66.

and elaboration, they perhaps occasioned the first tropes. Similarly, the honor of inventing the trope perhaps belongs to Benedict's new monastery near Aachen, which served as a model for the entire empire. The presence of tropes in a northeastern French manuscript possibly dating from before 900 tends to support this hypothesis, as does the strong evidence pointing to a common origin for the two earliest (tenth century) and most important extant trope repertories, those of Saint Martial de Limoges in southern France and Saint Gall in Switzerland. At the very least, the existence of tropes composed in classical hexameters in the earliest Saint Martial and Saint Gall collections suggests a Carolingian origin.[31] Monks of northern France or the Rhineland, the center of the empire and, in the case of France, later of feudalism as well, probably composed the first tropes about the middle of the ninth century.[32]

The same hypothesis may best resolve the similar uncertainties surrounding the *Quem quaeritis* trope in particular. Although its distinctively Frankish poetic and melodic style indicates its general provenance,[33] no single explanation unproblematically interconnects the early texts of the dialogue. Nonetheless, it most likely developed initially not in Saint Martial, Saint Gall, northern Italy, or even some combination of these, as various scholars have suggested,[34] but, like troping in general, in northern France or the Rhineland, perhaps in the mid or late ninth century.[35] During this period the Carolingian empire, and with it much of western Europe's economy, collapsed under the combined pressure of Viking, Saracen, and Magyar invasions. By wrecking the imperial apparatus, the attacks sped the consolidation of feudal landownership, especially in northern France, the location of Europe's most balanced social synthesis of Roman and Germanic elements.[36] Thus the appearance of the *Quem quaeritis* trope, at least on this argument, coincided with and formed part of the transition from empire to feudalism.

The textual record of the next two centuries, primarily from Benedictine monasteries, the centers of European religious life and learned cul-

---

[31]Paul Evans, *The Early Trope Repertory of Saint Martial de Limoges* (Princeton: Princeton University Press, 1970), pp. 17–27.

[32]David A. Bjork, "On the Dissemination of *Quem quaeritis* and the *Visitatio sepulchri* and the Chronology of Their Early Sources," *Comparative Drama* 14 (1980): 58.

[33]Bjork, p. 56.

[34]Saint Martial: Grace Frank, *The Medieval French Drama* (Oxford: Clarendon Press, 1954), p. 66; Saint Gall: Karl Young, *The Drama of the Medieval Church* (Oxford: Clarendon Press, 1933), 1:205; northern Italy: Helmut de Boor, *Die Textgeschichte der lateinischen Osterfeiern* (Tübingen: Max Niemeyer, 1967), pp. 68–80; multiple origins: Sandro Sticca, *The Latin Passion Play: Its Origins and Development* (Albany: State University of New York Press, 1970), p. 27.

[35]McGee, "Liturgical Placements," p. 24; Bjork, p. 59.

[36]Marc Leopold Bloch, *Feudal Society*, trans. L. A. Manyon (Chicago: University of Chicago Press, 1961), pp. 3–56; Anderson, pp. 154–57.

ture at the time,[37] provides additional evidence of the close linkage between feudalism and church drama. The striking parallels between mode of production, the dialogue's liturgical placement, and its geographical distribution suggest that the development of theater went with the development of feudalism. In effect, quasi-dramatic theater characterized the quasi-feudal periphery, more fully dramatic theater the feudal center.

Like most tropes, *Quem quaeritis* probably began as an embellishment to the Introit of the Mass. Specifically designed for this position on Easter Sunday,[38] it survives there primarily in manuscripts from Saint Gall (tenth-twelfth centuries), from Saint Martial (tenth–eleventh centuries), from several other areas of southern France (tenth–eleventh centuries), from Italy, particularly the north (eleventh–twelfth centuries), and from Catalonia (twelfth–sixteenth centuries). In most of these regions, it inspired the dialogue *Quem quaeritis in praesepe* (eleventh–thirteenth centuries), a trope to the Introit of the Nativity Mass and the probable germ of liturgical theater during the Christmas season. These lands, though part of the former Carolingian empire, underwent only incomplete processes of feudalization. In Switzerland, the survival of a free Germanic peasantry and the relative absence of classical civilization combined to impede the development of feudalism. On the shores of the Mediterranean, opposing tendencies had a similar effect. Especially in Italy, the urban legacy of Roman antiquity remained strong, while the Germanic overlay counted for relatively little. Even in southern France and Catalonia, where feudalism made considerable inroads, there never occurred a balanced Roman-Germanic synthesis.[39]

As Introit tropes, however, the two *Quem quaeritis* dialogues underwent no further changes. *Quem quaeritis in sepulchro* never developed into a Resurrection play; *Quem quaeritis in praesepe* never gave rise to a Christmas play. Only at the end of Matins, where the dialogues seemingly pos-

---

[37]De Boor, pp. 25–26.

[38]Evans, pp. 4–6; Young, 1:201–5; William L. Smoldon, "The Origins of the *Quem Quaeritis* Trope and the Easter Sepulchre Music-Dramas as Demonstrated by Their Musical Settings," in *The Medieval Drama*, ed. Sticca (Albany: State University of New York Press, 1972), pp. 121–54; Bjork, pp. 63–64. But see McGee, "Liturgical Placements," pp. 1–14, 19–23.

[39]Evidence on the less pervasive development of serfdom in southern France than in northern France is found in Robert Henri Bautier, *The Economic Development of Medieval Europe*, trans. Heather Karoly (London: Thames and Hudson, 1971), pp. 80–81; Bloch, *French Rural History: An Essay on Its Basic Characteristics*, trans. Janet Sondheimer (Berkeley and Los Angeles: University of California Press, 1966), p. 86; François Louis Ganshof and Adriaan Verhulst, "Medieval Agrarian Society in Its Prime: France, the Low Countries, and Western Germany," in *The Agrarian Life of the Middle Ages*, ed. Postan, vol. 1 of *The Cambridge Economic History of Europe* (Cambridge: Cambridge University Press, 1966), p. 335. Hereafter cited as *CEHE*.

sessed greater room for expansion and where impersonation for the first time accompanied singing, did their dramatic potential emerge. As the *Visitatio sepulchri*, the *Quem quaeritis in sepulchro* trope first survives at the close of Easter Matins in a manuscript from 975, though it probably had appeared there by the beginning of the tenth century at the latest. Documentary evidence of *Quem quaeritis in praesepe* at the end of Christmas Matins, as the *Officium pastorum*, dates from the twelfth or thirteenth century.[40]

Yet the placement at Matins generally did not occur in the partially feudalized periphery. Although the *Visitatio sepulchri* at first remained virtually identical to the *Quem quaeritis* dialogue both in text and in music,[41] in part perhaps because of the conservatism of monastic custom the regions that fostered the *Quem quaeritis* had little to do with the *Visitatio sepulchri*. Only a few of the latter survive from Italy, virtually all of them of foreign rather than domestic inspiration. Much the same goes for southern France, the other leading producer of the *Quem quaeritis* dialogue. In addition, the earliest extant version of the *Officium pastorum* does not come from southern France. The entire subsequent history of liturgical theater largely passed these territories by.[42] Although Switzerland and Catalonia possessed the *Quem quaeritis* as well as the *Visitatio sepulchri*, the latter derived from foreign traditions and survives almost exclusively in late manuscripts. The passage from trope to play proved almost as difficult here as elsewhere.

The first surviving *Officium pastorum*, the basic, first stage *Visitatio sepulchri*, and other more complex and more dramatic forms developed in the older centers of European feudalism.[43] Although in a general sense liturgical theater radiated out from northern France and western Germany, the specific configurations of this pattern may have depended on the interaction of social trends with religious institutions. The greater survival of tenth- and eleventh-century texts of the *Visitatio sepulchri* from Germany than from France might well simply reflect the vagaries of manuscript preservation. On the other hand, the monastic reforms centered at Cluny and Gorze may have conditioned the spread of liturgical drama at least between 950 and 1050. Both movements were founded in the early tenth century to reverse the destruction and dislocation wrought by the "barbarian" invasions and by the subsequent

[40]Young, 1:231, and 2:3–5, 9, 12–13; Lipphardt, 2:539–40; de Boor, 91–94; Bjork, p. 54. But see McGee, "Liturgical Placements," p. 27; Wolfgang F. Michael, "Tradition and Originality in the Medieval Drama in Germany," in *The Medieval Drama*, ed. Sticca, p. 24.

[41]Text: de Boor, p. 7; music: Smoldon, "The Melodies of the Medieval Church Dramas and Their Significance," in *Medieval English Drama*, ed. Jeremy Taylor and Alan H. Nelson (Chicago: University of Chicago Press, 1972), pp. 78–79.

[42]Italy: de Boor, p. 19; southern France: Frank, *Medieval French Drama*, p. 66.

[43]Bjork, esp. pp. 49, 60.

chaos of early feudal life. The former constituted an organizational and spiritual response to this collapse, gradually subordinating subject monasteries to the rule of Cluny in a hierarchical pattern that reproduced and strengthened the structure of feudal society. Liturgical elaboration beyond that introduced by Benedict of Aniane spiritually complemented this organizational complexity. Either the religious rigor that inspired these innovations or the mere quantitative increment to the liturgy that resulted from them may have inhibited the development of drama. Perhaps becuse of the Cluniac reform, almost no liturgical theater survives from northern France until the late eleventh century.[44]

Nonetheless, France at one time or another possessed almost every kind of liturgical play, overwhelmingly in the northern part of the country. The international dissemination of French church drama fell primarily to the restless and aggressive Normans who, from the mid-eleventh century, left their only recently acquired Duchy of Normandy to implant feudalism, and with it liturgical theater, in England and Ireland, in Sicily and southern Italy, and even in Jerusalem.[45] Of these derivative traditions, only the one from the British Isles poses difficulties. Although perhaps all of England's liturgical drama derived from Normandy, the earliest English manuscripts of the *Visitatio sepulchri*—including the oldest extant version of the play, mentioned above—have no surviving Norman antecedents and date from well before the final triumph of feudalism in England. On the other hand, late Anglo-Saxon society had spontaneously evolved far in the direction of feudalism, while in the century before 1066 French influence in England had markedly increased. Very few texts of Anglo-Norman liturgical theater have survived, however, perhaps owing to the destructive work of the sixteenth-century Reformation.[46]

Spain, too, came under French, though not Norman, influence. As part of the former Carolingian empire, Catalonia developed a liturgical theater. In the rest of the country, which in the age of Charlemagne and long thereafter remained overwhelmingly under Moslem control, almost nothing remains except for a few French-inspired texts of the *Quem quaeritis* dialogue and the *Visitatio sepulchri*, all in the far north along the pilgrimage route to Santiago de Compostella in Galicia and all

---

[44]Cluny: Barraclough, *Crucible*, pp. 150–55, 163–64; Noreen Hunt, ed., *Cluniac Monasticism in the Central Middle Ages* (London: Macmillan, 1971). Cluny's opposition to drama: Richard E. Donovan, *The Liturgical Drama in Medieval Spain*, Studies and Texts, 4 (Toronto: Pontifical Institute of Mediaeval Studies, 1958), pp. 69–70; de Boor, pp. 76–80. Cluny's support of drama: Flanigan, "Review of Scholarship" (1976), p. 113; McGee, "Liturgical Placements," pp. 15–18; Bjork, pp. 53, 67 n. 30.

[45]Frank, pp. 66–73.

[46]Richard Middlewood Wilson, *The Lost Literature of Medieval England*, 2d ed. (London: Methuen, 1970), pp. 209–33; de Boor, p. 18.

testifying to the dynamism of French feudal society. Perhaps little more ever existed. Spanish Christians living under Islamic rule followed not the Roman but the Mozarabic or, more accurately, Visigothic liturgy. After the Christian triumph in the north, ecclesiastical reconstruction and liturgical reform occurred under the leadership of Cluny, in the 1070s. Perhaps this timing helps explain the scarcity of surviving dramatic texts from medieval Spain.[47]

In Germany, on the other hand, Gorze apparently fostered the liturgical stage: nearly all of the earliest versions of the *Visitatio sepulchri* (tenth–eleventh centuries) owe something to the textual tradition characteristic of its area of influence. In this respect as in others, Gorze's possible distance from Cluny may have paralleled Germany's historical divergence from France. Partly because of the differential intensity of the invasions and partly because of disparities in pre-Carolingian social evolution, political disintegration and the consequent rise of feudal particularism transformed Germany far less than France during the ninth and tenth centuries. The eastern portions of the old Carolingian empire accordingly remained more faithful to bygone political and religious traditions. The Ottonian revival of the mid-tenth century restored order under imperial authority; in church affairs as well the crown retained direct control. These conditions both fostered the religious, cultural, and artistic revival centered at Gorze and facilitated its spread, perhaps in this way promoting the spread of liturgical drama as well. In the century between Otto I's death in 973 and the outbreak of the Investiture Conflict, Germany experienced a sixfold increase in the number of its monasteries. Nearly all of the new houses were reformed institutions, founded by and dependent on the aristocracy rather than the monarchy, which as a result lost control of the church. The nobility strengthened its own political and economic power in this process, while moving away from the crown and toward the papacy. Thus the Gorze reform, and perhaps with it the *Visitatio sepulchri*, contributed to the early class formation of the German feudal aristocracy.[48]

These developments centred in the far west, the most feudalized region of the country before the twelfth century. From there liturgical

[47]Spanish history: Gabriel Jackson, *The Making of Medieval Spain* (London: Thames and Hudson, 1972), pp. 40, 51, 53–57; Jaime Vicens Vives, *Approaches to the History of Spain*, trans. and ed. Joan Connelly Ullman (Berkeley and Los Angeles: University of California Press, 1967), pp. 40–44. Cluniacs in Spain: Justo Pérez de Urbel, *Sancho el Mayor de Navarra* (Madrid: Institución Príncipe de Viana, 1950), pp. 297–321, esp. p. 299. Spanish theater: Donovan, pp. 21–23, 26, 29; Humberto López Morales, *Tradición y creación en los orígenes del teatro castellano* (Madrid: Ediciones Alcalá, 1968), pp. 39–87.

[48]Barraclough, *Crucible*, pp. 72, 80, 86, 92, 94, 106, 114, 117, 120–21, 124, 136, 150. But see Christopher Nugent Lawrence Brooke, *The Monastic World, 1000–1300* (New York: Random House, 1974), p. 57. Gorze and drama: de Boor, pp. 36–37.

drama spread in several directions, occasionally anticipating the emergence of feudalism, at least to the southeast. Perhaps because of the eastward movement of Germany's political center of gravity, the subsequent initiative in theatrical innovation belonged to southern Germany, and particularly to Bavaria, which was, after the Rhineland, the most feudalized section of the country.[49] On the other hand, no texts survive from the northernmost areas of Germany, owing partly to the Reformation and partly, in eastern regions, to the dominance of the Cistercians, who were hostile to liturgical theater.[50]

The territory covered by German traditions also included Austria, Switzerland, and Italy; eastern France and the Low Countries; and Scandinavia and eastern Europe. Developments in Austria simply represented an extension of German practice. In Switzerland and Italy, the more complex liturgical theater drew primarily on German rather than indigenous models. In Italy, for instance, the only areas affected were the Patriarchate of Aquileia, formerly a part of Bavaria, and the nearby towns of Venice and Padua, all in the far northeast.[51] To the west of Germany, few texts survive from anywhere in the Low Countries, once again apparently because of the Reformation.[52] In southern Sweden, the earliest dramatic texts date from the thirteenth century, following the country's conversion to Christianity and coincident with the period in which it belatedly, and incompletely, came under feudal domination.[53] Little liturgical drama remains from the lands east of the Elbe, where German colonization occurred only in the twelfth and thirteenth centuries. The settlements, though they retarded the development of serfdom, were products of feudal expansion, in which Cistercian monasteries played a significant role.[54]

In summary, then, neither the Catholic liturgy nor the institutional church adequately accounts for the phenomenon of liturgical theater. A belated product of the Carolingian period, it generally developed in

---

[49]Barraclough, *The Origins of Modern Germany* (Oxford: Basil Blackwell, 1952), pp. 135–47, 250; idem, *Crucible*, p. 106; Anderson, p. 194.

[50]The relation of various religious orders to the drama: de Boor, p. 26.

[51]Texts: Lipphardt, 2:583–607, 900–902; 3:721–37, 856–57; 4:1414–15; 5:1504–7, 1513–17; Young, 2:335–36, 447–48, 458–60, 484. Argument: de Boor, pp. 34, 110–11, 18; Baraclough, *Origins*, pp. 51–52; Alessandro d'Ancona, *Origini del teatro italiano* (Turin: Ermanno Leoscher, 1891), 1:114–15.

[52]Theodoor Weevers, *Poetry of the Netherlands in Its European Context, 1170–1930: Illustrated with Poems in Original and Translation* (London: University of London, Athlone Press, 1960), p. 46.

[53]History: Anderson, pp. 178–81. Texts: Lipphardt, 2:651–52, 654–55, 658.

[54]Colonization: Barraclough, *Origins*, pp. 251, 271–72, 275–77. The Cistercians in eastern Europe: Brooke, *Monastic World*, p. 233. Texts of the puzzlingly early (eleventh–twelfth century) Hungarian first stage *Visitatio sepulchri*: Lipphardt, 2:680, 688–89, 696–97.

ways that formally, institutionally, and geographically paralleled the halting movement of European society toward feudalism. At first it may have consisted of only a brief Easter dialogue, the *Quem quaeritis* trope, composed mainly in peripheral areas of the former Carolingian empire —the Mediterranean and Switzerland—relatively spared by the barbarian invasions and, partly for this reason, only moderately influenced by feudalism. The *Visitatio sepulchri*, by contrast, thrived in more fully feudalized regions. Church theater accordingly remained, above all, the creation and property of northern France and of western and southern Germany. It made far fewer inroads into those more backward regions outside the imperial boundaries in which feudalism emerged relatively late—Spain west of Catalonia, Scandinavia, and eastern Europe.

A view of liturgical theater as a feudal institution offers a new perspective on the possible dialectical relationship between popular and learned drama before the twelfth century, on the ways the church may have responded to peasants and mimes. The temporal coincidence of the *Visitatio sepulchri* with popular rituals of spring only underscores the obvious point that Christianity itself grew partly out of such rituals and sought to supplant them. Although in this sense a wide range of church practices reacted to popular custom, the major uncertainties surrounding the invention of troping, the *Quem quaeritis* dialogue, and the *Visitatio sepulchri* preclude confident assertions about clerical intent. An attempt, for example, to show that the church employed mimes in its early drama as part of its self-conscious conversion campaign and fight against paganism has won little support.[55]

On the other hand, the quite deliberately nonpopular, if not antipopular, Carolingian Latinity of liturgical theater helped produce a ritual linguistically incomprehensible to most Christians. Although that theater, like peasant drama, thrived in the interstices of medieval society, it coincided far more closely than did agrarian pastime with the constitution and expansion of feudalism and with the class formation of the aristocracy. These latter processes consistently resulted in the subjugation and exploitation of the peasantry. The combination of alien utterance and impressive ceremony in the *Visitatio sepulchri* might, then, have encouraged popular acquiescence in an unjust system. Partly thinking of the monastic auspices of early liturgical theater, various scholars have designated the *Visitatio sepulchri* a drama of the clergy, by the clergy, and for the clergy while denying it any relevance to the populace at large.[56] Yet the manuscript containing the earliest extant text of the play unambiguously argues that ceremony strengthens the faith of the masses.[57]

[55]Hunningher, chaps. 5–6.
[56]Pascal, pp. 378–79; Konigson, pp. 8, 26.
[57]Tydemann, p. 223.

Perhaps the *Visitatio sepulchri* reconfirmed the ideology of the ideologues while promoting that ideology among the peasantry as well. Drawing on the church's position as the dominant ideological apparatus of feudalism, liturgical theater may have produced affectively coercive transcendental legitimation of the status quo. Before 1100, religious drama worked against the comic, critical, egalitarian, and utopian strains of popular festivity.

## Twelfth-Century Plays

Twelfth-century theater continued the conservative practice of the early Christian stage, only with more sophisticated procedures. Venturing outside the liturgy, it drew on a variety of religious and secular traditions, invoking popular culture and, more often, the hierarchy of feudal social relations in an attempt to produce an effectively didactic vehicle. Yet the resulting heterogeneity of dramatic materials cut in two directions, introducing an incipient ideological ambivalence that increased in the later Middle Ages. To grasp initially the overall distinctiveness of drama after 1100, however, one need only cast a retrospective glance. In one crucial respect the nature of most liturgical drama, especially before the late eleventh century, remains contested. Both the *Quem quaeritis* and the *Visitatio sepulchri* undoubtedly constituted crucial innovations, necessary steps on the road to drama. Critics have often viewed the *Visitatio sepulchri*, at least, as a genuine play. Recent scholarship, however, has reversed this tendency, insisting that both the *Visitatio sepulchri*—even in its more complex manifestations—and the *Officium pastorum*, as integral parts of the liturgy, served essentially communal, cultic, and ritualistic functions. German researchers in particular rigorously distinguish between *Feier* (ceremony) and *Spiel* (play).[38]

By the late eleventh or twelfth century, however, Europe was producing unmistakable plays, whether composed in Latin or the vernacular, whether performed within the liturgy or independently of it. Although earlier church theater fundamentally influenced every one of these works, the creation of more complex, more truly dramatic forms probably did not proceed from any inner evolutionary logic, especially since the liturgical structure itself inhibited innovation. An important consequence follows from this observation: without outside impulses, liturgical ceremony would not have developed into Christian theater.[39]

[38]Young (see n. 40), representing the traditional position, is challenged by Flanigan, "The Roman Rite" and "Review of Scholarship"; de Boor, pp. 3–13; and esp. Theo Stemmler, *Liturgische Feiern und geistliche Spiele: Studien zu Erscheinungsformen des Dramatischen im Mittelalter* (Tübingen: Max Niemeyer, 1970), pp. 47–87.

[39]In this sense Hunningher's doubts (chap. 4) about the ability of the liturgy to produce theater are plausible.

These impulses arose from the material prosperity of Europe and specifically from the increased surplus available for cultural appropriation.[60] In the twelfth century, feudalism entered its prime in the West. The most elaborate plays of the period almost all come from especially dynamic feudal regions, whose social conditions they respond to far more directly than earlier church drama responded to its milieu.

One may note, first of all, a shift away from the countryside. The cathedrals of Germany and, even more, of northern France replaced the monasteries as the innovative centers of European high culture in general and of religious theater in particular. Since the more elaborate plays frequently lacked a fixed place in the liturgical service, their institutional settings remain obscure. But many works, including the Anglo-Norman *Adam* and the Benediktbeuern *Nativity* and *Passion* plays, have plausibly been attributed to cathedrals. Insofar as the ascendancy of the cathedral schools depended on the revival of town life,[61] so too did the new direction of the religious stage between the late eleventh and early thirteenth centuries. The plays of the period undoubtedly incorporated far more of the secular world than did their strictly liturgical predecessors. They primarily looked not to the towns, however, but to the emergent courts of the period—ducal, monarchical, and imperial. Finally, some dramatists shaped their material by direct recourse to specifically feudal relationships of dependence, thereby achieving an ideologically potent mix of theological and social hierarchies.

As a group, the most innovative plays of the twelfth century increased the scope of religious theater both outwardly—by depicting a wider range of activities, institutions, and locales—and inwardly—by exploring human psychology. These complementary forms of expansion, which also characterized European literature and life in general during the period,[62] depended on the assimilation of multiple dramatic and cultural traditions. The interaction of these traditions, with each other as well as with the previously dominant liturgical forms, produced a considerable diversity in material, subject, genre, purpose, attitude, and, not least, language. The episode involving Pilate's wife in the Montecassino *Passion* play reveals the importance of apocryphal and patristic sources, while the entire work relies heavily on Gospel narrative. Similarly, the *Auto de los reyes magos* derives its most atypical feature from French reli-

---

[60]Goldstein's emphasis (see n. 23) on the role of private property may have greater bearing here than it does on the earlier period of liturgical theater.

[61]Cathedrals in relation to monasteries and towns: Charles Homer Haskins, *The Renaissance of the Twelfth Century* (1927; rpt. New York: Meridian Books, 1957), pp. 32–54; Richard W. Southern, *The Making of the Middle Ages* (London: Hutchinson University Library, 1953), pp. 185–203; Brooke, *Monastic World*, p. 85. Cathedrals and drama: Axton, p. 113; Young, 2:195.

[62]Southern, chap. 4.

gious literature.[63] Folk festivities contributed structural patterns and individual episodes to twelfth-century drama; mime introduced a more representational acting style and a more sophisticated relationship with the audience.[64] From popular culture as well came the taste for romantic adventure satisfied by saints' plays, whether treating the biblical career of Saint Paul or the legendary miracles of Saint Nicholas.

Popular impulses may also have had some part in the growing use of the vernacular, especially when the playwright entertained didactic intentions. Often the vernacular segments of primarily Latin plays dramatized human emotion, as in the macaronic (Latin-Provençal) *Sponsus* or, to a lesser extent, in Hilarius's *Lazarus*.[65] This concern with inner feeling and the internal pursuit of salvation had ties to the development of Christocentrism and probably grew out of a union of popular spirituality and erudite monasticism. Such trends in religious thought unleashed, apparently for the first time in the medieval West, the dramatic potential implicit in the life of Christ, in the experiences of his followers, and in the psychic and moral struggles of any Christian.[66] In the Benediktbeuern *Passion* play, the lengthy vernacular passages devoted to Mary Magdalene and especially to the Virgin Mary fully exploit the affective and theatrical tensions arising from the intersection of the human and the divine. Analogously, entirely Latin compositions like the Beauvais *Peregrinus* and the Benediktbeuern *Nativity* play elaborate the interest in ocular proof already evident in the *Visitatio sepulchri* by juxtaposing human rational doubt and transcendental miracle.[67]

Though more detached from popular or religious thought, the classicist revival known as the twelfth-century Renaissance subtly but perhaps decisively reshaped Christian drama. The relatively trivial concrete reminders of its influence on the theater—borrowed verse forms and literary allusions—suggest the primarily medieval quality of the renewed interest in antiquity at this time. Indirectly spurred by the general economic expansion of feudalism, it had only limited impact in its more original and nonmedieval form. Certainly the religious plays owed far less to the most overt workings of the twelfth-century Renaissance than did an elegaic comedy such as *Babio*.[68]

---

[63]The Montescassino drama: Sticca, *Latin Passion Play*, pp. 97, 87. The *Auto*: Winifred Sturdevant, *El Misterio de los Reyes Magos: Its Position in the Development of the Mediaeval Legend of the Three Kings*, Johns Hopkins Studies in Romance Literatures and Languages, no. 10 (Baltimore: Johns Hopkins Press, 1927), p. 78.

[64]Axton, *European Drama*, passim.

[65]Woolf, pp. 43–44, is among the critics who make this point.

[66]Southern, pp. 231–40; and, specifically on Christocentrism, Sticca, *Latin Passion Play*, pp. 42–45.

[67]Bevington, pp. 33, 179, is among the critics who make this point.

[68]The incompleteness of the twelfth-century Renaissance: see Erwin Panofsky, *Renais-

Yet the geographical coincidence of the centers of classicism and church drama suggests the possibility of subterranean interconnections. First, the "protohumanist" and belletristic cultivation of classical Latin grammar and rhetoric may have sped the emergence of the vernacular in northern France.[69] The Anglo-Norman *Adam* and *La seinte resureccion* both fall well within the twelfth century. Second, and more important, increased knowledge of the ancient Roman stage may have provided the final impetus in converting liturgical ceremony into drama. At least to judge from surviving documents, authors and censorious ecclesiastical reformers alike first recognized church theatrical performances as plays during this period.[70]

Twelfth-century historical trends also directly influenced the drama. Political centralization, entailing an incipient, incomplete, and as a rule temporary reversal of the parcellization of sovereignty, jeopardized the independence of the church. The problematic relationship of Christianity to state power, rooted in the early history of the religion, became a favored subject for stage presentation. Almost every complex play dealing with the life of Jesus includes at least one scene at court. According to the Gospels, after all, Christ did go on trial before Pilate. On the other hand, much of the inherent potential of early Christianity remained latent for centuries, only to emerge under the pressure of changed conditions. In addition, episodes involving royalty appear widely in non-Gospel plays, among them the *Antichrist*, the Beauvais *Daniel*, the Laon *Joseph*, and one of the Fleury Saint Nicholas plays, *The Son of Getron*. Especially in the first two of these, the representation of the court takes on far more elaborate trappings than in even such extended productions as the Montecassino and Benediktbeuern *Passions*, where the Gospel narratives apparently exercised a conservative and restraining influence. In every instance, however, political tyranny poses a threat to religion, personal liberty, or both. Perhaps the recurrence of this theme was a legacy of the papal-imperial disputes that issued in the Investiture Conflict.

A number of plays make occasional but specific use of feudal language. In *Joseph* and *The Son of Getron*, the protagonists temporarily find themselves in "servitio" ("service") at monarchical courts.[71] In the Laon *Prophets*, the Fleury *Herod*, and the *Auto de los reyes magos*, similar termi-

---

*sance and Renascences in Western Art* (New York: Harper and Row, 1960), pp. 106–7; Eva Matthews Sanford, "The Twelfth Century—Renaissance or Proto-Renaissance?" *Speculum* 26 (1951): 635–41.

[69]"Protohumanism": Panofsky, pp. 68–81. Relations between Latin and the vernacular: Auerbach, *Literary Language,* p. 277; and esp. Curtius, pp. 383–88.

[70]Woolf, pp. 29, 348 n. 21.

[71]*Joseph*: Young, 2:269, lines 73, 80; *The Son of Getron*: Bevington, p. 172, line 16.

nology defines the relationship between humanity and Christ, with a diametrically opposed valence. King David, in the *Prophets*, joyfully announced the coming of "Dominum, / cui futurum / seruiturum / omne genus hominum" ("the Lord, whom in the future the whole human race will serve").[72] The Magi, in the *Herod* play, recall the prophecy, "Adorabunt eum omnes reges, omnes gentes servient ei" ("All kings will worship him, all nations will serve him").[73] And the three kings in the *Auto* express the same bond from the other side: the infant Christ is repeatedly called "en pace i en guera senior . . . de todo el mundo, . . . de todas gentes" ("in peace and in war lord . . . of all the world, . . . of all nations"), and so on.[74]

The pervasive appropriation of feudal language, ceremonies, and institutions, however, occurs only in those works that, unlike the *Auto*, come from fully feudalized societies.[75] The dramatist responsible for *La seinte resureccion* transfers the contemporary institution of vassalage to the relationship between Pilate and Joseph of Arimathea. A play might also fuse the normally antagonistic social and religious senses of subordination. For the church, religious servitude meant initiation into the freedom that humanity had lost through original sin. Although clerical writers attempted to justify serfdom on related grounds, they could not remove the stigma attached to it. The closest secular parallel to Christian service therefore involved the ruling class alone, specifically in the ties of vassalage. Yet no lay lord or sovereign could ever truly stand in for Christ. The secular and transcendental notions of subordination ideally merged only in visions of the last days, when Christ would return to rule the earth and physically to occupy the apex of the feudal pyramid. The problems of even this moment emerge in the *Antichrist*, where the titular character's parodic impersonation of the Savior highlights the dangerous consequences of theocratic rule. Although the play served as a piece of imperial propaganda, the German king, like the other monarchs, is duped by Antichrist, whose concluding defeat brings an apolitical return to the church rather than the restoration of imperial power.[76] The multiple traditions that help shape the play thus produce an unintentionally contradictory effect.

Although the *Adam* less problematically adapts the feudal hierarchy to the relationship between God and his creatures, the even greater range of materials on which it draws gives its representation of social life

[72]Young, 2:148.
[73]Text and translation: Bevington, p. 59, line 14.
[74]Ramón Menéndez Pidal, ed., "*Auto de los reyes magos*," *Revista de Archivos, Bibliotecas y Museos* 4 (1900): 456, lines 24–25, 40, 42.
[75]See Axton's discussion (pp. 88–94, 108–30) of feudal and other traditions in the *Antichrist*, *La seinte resureccion*, and the *Adam*.
[76]Southern, pp. 98–107.

an unusual, problematic density. Feudal language dominates all three parts—Adam and Eve, Cain and Abel, and the Prophets—but alternative social perspectives occasionally surface. In the Prophets sequence, Habakkuk marvels at the humble birth of the King of Kings, and Solomon evokes with pleasure the reversal of rich and poor:

> Char mult dor vengement serra
> En cels qui furent li plus halt:
> Il prendront toit un malvais salt.
> Del petit avra Dex pité.

(Extremely harsh vengeance will be visited / On those who were the most high: / They will take a fearful fall. / God will have pity on the lowly.)[77]

Abraham, however, makes clear the limits of this subversiveness. Of Christ, he remarks, "n'iert pas vilains" ("he will be no serf": p. 114, line 762). Similarly, some of Abel's first words to Cain implicitly distinguish glorious religious service from degrading social serfdom: "De Deu servir ne seom pas vilain" ("In serving God let us not be churlish": p. 106, line 594).

As in the *Antichrist*, then, service to Christ corresponds to secular vassalage. In the first section of the play, God, the ultimate "Seignor" ("Lord": e.g., p. 82, line 30), grants to Adam "De tote terre . . . la seignorie" ("dominion over all the earth": p. 83, line 61). It is against this condition that Adam and Eve, goaded by the devil, rebel. Adam "est mult serf" ("servile"), Satan cleverly tells Eve, thus implicitly equating the nobility of vassalage with the ignominy of serfdom (p. 91, line 224). He then proceeds to flatter her in courtly terms, appropriating the language of romance in order to disrupt the feudal hierarchy. If she eats the forbidden fruit, he asserts, she will become "dame del mond" ("mistress of the world"), her Lord's equal (p. 92, line 255; p. 93, lines 264–70). Emboldened by the devil's words, Eve addresses her husband with uncharacteristic aggressiveness. As a result, Adam loses sight of another crucial hierarchy at the moment of his fall, calling his wife "ma per" ("my partner": p. 95, line 313).

Courtly ideology thus encourages Eve to reject the dual subordination she had earlier accepted when speaking to her Lord:

> Toi conustrai a seignor,
> Lui [Adam] a paraille e a forzor.

(I will acknowledge you as sovereign, / Him [Adam] as my partner and stronger than I. [p. 82, lines 43–44])

[77]Text and translation: Bevington, p. 116, lines 800–803. Subsequent citations and translations of the *Adam* are from this edition and are noted in the text.

[55

It threatens both social and marital ties, as well as the religious relationships they specify. A product of twelfth-century feudalism, courtly values can nonetheless snap the most fundamental bonds of that society. In this sense the play reveals the subversiveness of the ideology, the contradiction built into aristocratic culture. Adam and Eve's marriage, on the other hand, fits smoothly into the hierarchical ordering of life, despite its striking domesticity and even burgherlike qualities.[78] Eve's final confession similarly serves orthodox doctrinal and didactic purposes, though its grandeur may point in the direction of the far more radical humanization of the identical story by a poet living five hundred years later in England, perhaps the homeland of the author of the *Adam* as well. Thus the work's heterogeneity of social materials primarily buttresses, but secondarily undermines, conventional hierarchies. The *Adam* begins to realize the possibilities and complications of a dialectical synthesis of learned and popular elements on the medieval stage.

Although both the *Antichrist* and the *Adam* reassert the hegemony of Christian-feudal values, they express ideological misgivings about the possibility of reconciling religious and social allegiances. The vernacular play also gives brief representation to the incipient consciousness of nonaristocratic social classes. Though strictly speaking nonliturgical in character, these and other plays of the time represent the culmination of two or three centuries of the liturgical dramatic tradition. But their distinctiveness largely derives from those innovations that gained increasing prominence in subsequent medieval theater. The years from 1050 to 1250 separate the early and late periods of European feudalism.[79] The dynamism of that intermediate era, including the emergence of town life, made possible the notable religious plays and left its mark on them. Inevitably, however, it produced new conditions, only adumbrated on the twelfth-century stage, that proved largely inimical to earlier dramatic traditions. A continuous process of social development first engendered and then bypassed medieval church theater.[80] In the thirteenth century, the towns became the permanent centers of western European drama.

## Urban Theater

Medieval towns have traditionally and accurately been seen as revolutionary innovations, hostile institutions in a predominantly agrarian and

[78]Auerbach, *Mimesis: The Representation of Reality in Western Literature*, trans. Trask (Princeton: Princeton University Press, 1953), pp. 151, 156, 158–59, emphasizes the everyday, middle-class realism of the exchanges between Adam and Eve. But see Axton, pp. 123–26, for discussion of courtly elements in the play.

[79]Bloch, *Feudal Society*, p. 69.

[80]Brooke, *The Twelfth Century Renaissance* (n.p.: Harcourt, Brace and World, 1970), pp. 184–92, presents some cultural explanations for the decline of the twelfth-century Renaissance.

feudal polity. Based in theory on the freedom and equality of all citizens, principles antagonistic to the hierarchical ordering of the rest of society, they struggled against feudal fiscal subordination and servile relations in pursuit of municipal autonomy. Furthermore, the early development of capitalism resulted from the commodity production and exchange characteristic of western European towns as early as the tenth century and especially after 1100. In the later Middle Ages, the cities contributed to the decisive transformation of the countryside as well, disrupting feudal ties commercially, ideologically, politically, and on occasion even militarily. Many distinguished historians have argued that the urban impact on rural society constituted an intrusion from outside, the corrosive intervention of nonfeudal or even antifeudal forces in a feudal world. Especially when considered retrospectively from the point of view of the modern, urbanized West, the originality and importance of medieval towns stand out unmistakably.[81]

But the cities of the Middle Ages were not wholly external to feudal society. Often founded by lay or ecclesiastical lords and at times possessing a distinct noble stratum, they initially developed economically in response to both the rebirth of commerce and the rise of agrarian productivity. Many of the cultural and material achievements of western European feudalism after the year 1000 in turn depended on the contributions of the towns.[82] The High Middle Ages thus saw complementary urban and rural growth. In most parts of the continent, the municipalities never succeeded in freeing themselves entirely from feudal restraints. Even in the fully autonomous commune, the ascendant patriciate increasingly took on the features of a traditional aristocracy. It appropriated both economic and political power in its control of the town and, at times, the nearby rural hinterland, while reinvesting capitalist profits in feudal landed estates.[83]

In addition, the economic activities of the towns normally retained a feudal cast. The largest profits accrued to merchant and finance capitalists, specifically from long-distance trade and usury, both of which damaged feudal social relations and boosted European productivity. But because merchants and moneylenders often lived parasitically upon feudal production rather than producing goods themselves, they could coexist with feudalism. Although manufacturing eventually presented a far more revolutionary challenge, its typical forms long paralleled those

---

[81]Henri Pirenne, *Economic and Social History of Medieval Europe*, trans. I. E. Clegg (London: Routledge and Kegan Paul, 1936), chap. 2, and many others since.

[82]A. B. Hibbert, "The Origins of the Medieval Town Patriciate," *Past and Present*, no. 3 (February 1953): 15–27; Georges Duby, *The Early Growth of the European Economy: Warriors and Peasants from the Seventh to the Twelfth Century*, trans. Howard B. Clarke (Ithaca, N.Y.: Cornell University Press, 1974), pp. 234–48.

[83]Rural policies of the Italian towns: Daniel Philip Waley, *The Italian City-Republics* (New York: McGraw-Hill, 1969), pp. 110–12.

of the feudal countryside. Even when merchant employers subordinated the artisans, industry depended on small-scale crafts in individual workplaces. Medieval commodity production thus qualitatively differed from the factory system that later dominated the capitalist world.[84]

Hence the towns of western Europe constituted at once external invaders and internal bulwarks of feudal society. As consideration of classical or modern cities immediately reveals, this ambivalent function does not inhere in urban life. The unique position of medieval towns instead depended on the parcellization of sovereignty, which allowed an unprecedented autonomy for urban enclaves and thus a dynamic tension between town and country. Though medieval cities ultimately opposed feudal society, they also belonged to its development.[85]

This structurally conditioned dual perspective characterizes urban drama as well. Given the relative weakness of the monarchies and their courts, the towns, once they had reached a certain size, offered the main demographic and material basis for large-scale theatrical productions, whether designed for Christian instruction, secular profit making, or some more complex combination. The urban playwrights had access to an array of social and intellectual traditions, which they mingled to produce a spectrum of forms. The stage of the late medieval town thus provided the arena for the possible synthesis of popular and learned dramaturgy, of secular and religious values, of lower- and upper-class experience, and even of the Germanic and Roman heritages. Although most of the surviving dramatic texts present a clear hierarchical organization, dominated by a Christian or an aristocratic outlook, the disproportionate loss of secular pieces renders any grand generalization suspect. Some plays, overwhelmingly popular or bourgeois in material, go so far as to dispense with a religious or feudal frame altogether, at times with radical implications. In such instances, actors and audiences could at least briefly experience alternative modes of organizing the life of their community. Even here, bourgeois values rarely predominated: the new class had not yet reached maturity.[86] Or to put the matter more positively, such works give expression to the traditions of popular culture. Pehaps ideology in this instance lagged behind material conditions;[87] more likely, the continued ascendancy of prebourgeois values in medieval urban theater corresponded primarily to the structural position of towns in feudal society.

[84]Maurice Dobb, *Studies in the Development of Capitalism*, 2d ed. (New York: International Publishers, 1963), chaps. 1–4.

[85]Anderson, pp. 150–51, 193–94; John Merrington, "Town and Country in the Transition to Capitalism," *New Left Review*, no. 93 (September–October 1975): 71–92.

[86]See Auerbach's similar comments on Boccaccio in *Mimesis*, p. 231.

[87]Wallace K. Ferguson, *The Renaissance* (1940; rpt. New York: Holt, Rinehart and Winston, 1967), pp. 66–67, explains the delayed arrival of the Italian Renaissance in this way.

## The Plays of Arras

The earliest extant tradition of secular drama in a medieval vernacular consists of four elaborate works from thirteenth-century Arras, in northern France. The plays raise a series of related questions: What conditions accounted for their production? What forms did the resulting theatrical pieces take? What attitudes found expression in them? And what purposes did the works serve? No single explanation does justice to all four texts. In general, however, despite the unusual development of the Arrageois bourgeoisie, the town's stage conformed to the general, dual articulation of medieval urban theater. In particular, the plays of Arras offer an initial opportunity to investigate the formal and ideological specificity of popular drama.

If these works actually point to the historical precocity of theater in Arras rather than to the accidents of survival, an interaction of economic, political, and cultural forces probably helped give the town a lead over other major European cities. Through most of the twelfth century, Arras formed part of the County of Flanders, owing its impressive success in textile manufacturing to the peacefulness and the geographical location of the region. But the accumulation of capital in itself does not sufficiently distinguish the town from urban centers in northern Italy and elsewhere in Flanders.[88] A political change supplemented economic prosperity in 1194, when Arras fell under the control of the French monarchy. Its closer integration into the cultural sphere of northern France came at a most opportune time. Though itself relatively free from feudal domination, Arras now drew more easily on the Latin and vernacular literary products of French feudal society in its most dynamic phase, especially because the town, like the rest of southern Flanders, traditionally spoke French.[89] It thus possessed from the start linguistic and geographical assets absent not only in Italy, but in the Flemish-speaking areas of northern Flanders as well. In this respect Arras only illustrated a general phenomenon: a strong development of feudalism resulted in a thriving medieval literature.[90]

Arras's debt to the feudal literature of northern France paralleled the social position of the town's patriciate. Often of landed or clerical origin, these bourgeois entrepreneurs retained connections with their previous

[88]Jean Lestocquoy, *Aux origines de la bourgeoisie: Les villes de Flandre et d'Italie sous le gouvernement des patriciens, xi^e–xv^e siècles* (Paris: Presses Universitaires de France, 1952).

[89]Unless otherwise noted, all information on Arras comes from Marie Ungureanu, *La bourgeoisie naissante: Société et littérature bourgeoises d'Arras aux 12^e et 13^e siècles* (Arras: Mémoires de la Commission des Monuments Historiques du Pas-de-Calais, 1955), chaps. 1–3, 6.

[90]For a related point—the weakness of medieval Italian literature as a consequence of the limited emergence of feudalism on the peninsula—see Ferguson, p. 72.

[59

sources of livelihood even after they had amassed manufacturing or mercantile fortunes; they continued to owe feudal obligations to various lay and clerical lords; and during the thirteenth century they apparently forged alliances with the local aristocracy, from which they derived their characteristic literary genres. Incapable of justifying the economic system it was helping to create, the patriciate inevitably borrowed precapitalist forms for its artistic production. The literary expression of a relatively independent ideology came from those classes beneath, and opposed to, the patriciate—especially the lesser bourgeoisie and the artisans. Their intellectuals, however, also failed to articulate a coherent and distinctive set of ethical and social beliefs. The implicitly egalitarian and antiauthoritarian values with which the commons challenged the oligarchic rule of the patriciate did not consistently extend to a general critique of the clerical and feudal hierarchies that remained overwhelmingly dominant in western Europe. The main oppressors of the artisanate were the leading capitalists of the town, not the rural exploiters of servile labor.

A characteristic feature of the nonpatrician literature of thirteenth-century Arras arose from this social and ideological situation. Almost completely free from modern bourgeois notions of aesthetic individuality and authorial personality, the poets of the popular classes often belonged either to the artisanate or to literary organizations analogous to the town's craft guilds. This rough equation of artist and artisan corresponded to economic conditions in which commodity production remained dispersed in small shops. Although by the twelfth century the Arrageois patriciate had largely succeeded in subordinating the guilds to its own interests and thus in establishing capitalist relations between the direct producers and the appropriators of the product, popular resistance, which grew intense by 1250 or earlier, operated from an essentially precapitalist commitment to craft independence that retarded the development of capitalism. Since the theater of Arras belonged mainly to the cultural milieu of these nonpatrician classes, it was not fundamentally bourgeois in character. Though strong guilds ultimately threatened the persistence of the established social order less than did the incipiently revolutionary economic activities of the patriciate, the commons did not draw on feudal and courtly literary models as directly as did the rulers of the town. The plays therefore seem to possess unusual originality, an appearance due in part, however, to the subsequent disappearance of the prior medieval popular stage traditions from which they derived. Indeed, the dramatization of popular culture primarily in an urban milieu gives a somewhat specious bourgeois coloring to the thirteenth-century theater of Arras.

Yet popular values rarely reign unchallenged in this drama. The latest of the four plays,[91] Adam de la Halle's *Le jeu de Robin et de Marion* (c. 1283), rests on aristocratic presuppositions, though it utilizes folk-dramatic motifs and modifies the pastoral idealization of the countryside with an infusion of urban realism. By contrast, the anonymous *Courtois d'Arras* (early thirteenth century) ridicules courtly affectation, converts the religious significance of the tale of the Prodigal Son into a species of secular, prudential moralizing, and instills a cynical and materialistic distrust of the world. It adds a faintly and incipiently bourgeois recommendation of hard work, the spiritual narrowness of which indicates the limits of that very bourgeois outlook independent of feudal society's dominant ideology.

The other two plays draw more pervasively on popular culture. Jehan Bodel's *Le jeu de Saint-Nicolas* (c. 1200) derives whatever intellectual structure it possesses from religious-feudal habits of mind. The intervention of Saint Nicholas saves the life of a Christian prisoner at a Moslem court and leads to the conversion of the Islamic monarch and his vassals. The affective force of the piece lies elsewhere, however, in the realistic low plot that takes up half the play. Although these tavern scenes make an attractive foil to the often ridiculous antics of the feudal infidels, they hardly offer a systematic alternative. Bodel thus juxtaposes an elaborate and explicit code of values with the vivid representation of a realm of experience utterly devoid of any ideological justification. Since no apparent hierarchy orders the relationship between the two plots,[92] the work escapes from total incoherence only through the pervasively playful tone of its author. Thus *Le jeu de Saint-Nicolas* acutely brings into focus the ideological contradictions already dimly apparent in the *Adam*; the copresence of popular and learned traditions leads to synthesis only in the loosest sense of the term.

Adam de la Halle's other play, *Le jeu de la feuillée* (c. 1276), helps clarify the significance of these contradictions. Bakhtin emphasizes the "typically carnivalesque" character of the work: temporary liberty from the official world, links to folk festival, grotesque and obscene treatment of bodily functions, license, revelry, feasting, gaming, fairies, folly, gaiety, religious parody, and archaic and utopian vistas.[93] The play's colloquial style, punning, improvisational quality, intimate and shifting relations between actor and audience, and evocation of both tavern and town square also indicate its profound indebtedness to popular culture. Per-

[91]Discussion of the four plays: Axton, chap. 7, and Ungureanu, chap. 6.

[92]Frank, *Medieval French Drama*, p. 212. But see Jean Duvignaud, *Les ombres collectives: Sociologie du théâtre*, 2d ed. (Paris: Presses Universitaires de France, 1973), p. 94.

[93]Bakhtin, pp. 257–63. Quoted phrase: p. 257.

haps influenced by the mimic tradition, it topically attacks individual patricians by name, in addition to satirizing the church. Though unquestionably a theatrical expression of class partisanship, the *Jeu* is far clearer about what it opposes than about what it advocates. Extraordinarily secular and realistic, bursting with scenes, characters, and opinions, it nonetheless lacks a consistent shape or plot. *Le jeu de la feuillée* is the low episodes of *Le jeu de Saint-Nicolas* writ large.

These two plays offer an initial opportunity to discuss the ideology of form, and in particular the problems of organicism and totality that have troubled aesthetic as well as political analysis for much of the twentieth century. In the Middle Ages, whereas the hegemonic ideologies stressed organic wholeness, formal closure, corporatist unity, philosophical homogeneity, intellectual coherence, and high seriousness, popular culture—the culture of peasants and artisans—favored fragmentation, openness, disunity, heterogeneity, incoherence, and high spirits. The major conflicts of the age, in theater and society alike, thus pitted two asymmetrical, qualitatively distinct forms of class consciousness against one another. The lower orders opposed the careful programs of the feudal and clerical hierarchies less with alternative, more equitable programs of their own than with a rejection of the programmatic. Thus, as *Le jeu de la feuillée* reveals, the incoherence of *Le jeu de Saint-Nicolas* derives not only from the formal and ideological incompatibility of the high and low plots, but also from the internal antistructural structure of popular culture.

A student of medieval theater ought to have no difficulty in preferring—to load the terms—the drama of popular culture to the drama of hegemonic ideology. Indeed, in other eras as well, a dismantling of ruling class belief systems necessarily includes a critique of organicism through a counteremphasis on dispersal, disunity, and dissemination. This position entered Marxist aesthetics in Brecht's telling attack on Lukács discussed in the Introduction and has been further developed in the Althusserian tradition.[94] Yet a further consideration of the plays from Arras may suggest the possible utility of a Lukácsian approach, the need to temper any unambiguous celebration of antiorganicist art. Although medieval popular culture by no means limited itself to negative subversion, the efficacy of its alternative positive vision remains suspect. "For a class to be ripe for hegemony," Lukács claimed, "means that its interests and consciousness enable it to organise the whole of society in accordance with those interests. The crucial question in every class strug-

[94]Althusser, "The 'Piccolo Teatro': Bertolazzi and Brecht," in *For Marx*, pp. 129–51; Pierre Macherey, *A Theory of Literary Production*, trans. Geoffrey Wall (London: Routledge and Kegan Paul, 1978); Terry Eagleton, *Criticism and Ideology: A Study in Marxist Literary Theory* (London: NLB, 1976).

gle is this: which class possesses this capacity and this consciousness at the decisive moment?"[95] For Lukács, since the peasantry never possessed such consciousness, its major, revolutionary struggles did not and could not succeed. Perhaps the antiorganicist plays of Jehan Bodel and Adam de la Halle reveal the lower-class need not for a hegemonic organicism of its own, but for a counterhegemonic construction of a contradictory totality or, better still, for a counterhegemonic process of demystification followed by totalization. Such a perspective hardly entails a political dismissal of Arrageois drama, however, particularly in its local impact. The feudal parcellization of sovereignty allowed independent or oppositional ideologies to have substantive force. *Le jeu de la feuillée* belonged to the popular struggle against the patriciate, may have furthered the formation of an insurgent artisan consciousness, and perhaps had the effect of contributing to the partial triumph of that struggle by the beginning of the fourteenth century.

Feudalism structurally accorded an ambivalent position to towns. Within these parameters, Arras experienced an advanced and early development of capitalism, on which the striking secularism and realism of its stage depended. Primarily in this indirect way, the bourgeoisie played a crucial role on the Arrageois stage. Composed neither by nor for the patriciate, the plays actually come closest to expressing the consciousness of a class threatened with extinction by the progress of capitalism. Their essentially prebourgeois values do not necessarily challenge the dominant ideology of the feudal and clerical hierarchy. When the plays instead ignore or reject the beliefs of the surrounding agrarian and ecclesiastical society, they present previously neglected aspects of life, but only an ambiguously efficacious alternative view of that life. The theater of the guilds could never have done more; the theater of the bourgeoisie could not yet do as much. The medieval stage, even in a town like Arras, could not entirely transcend the limits set by feudal society as a whole.


## Fourteenth- and Fifteenth-Century Theater

Problems of dialectical synthesis and class struggle also arise with the urban drama that thrived in most of Europe during the fourteenth and especially fifteenth centuries. By approximately 1280, if not earlier, western European towns had largely succeeded in freeing themselves from seigneurial control.[96] The definitive, international triumph of the

[95]Georg Lukács, *History and Class Consciousness: Studies in Marxist Dialectics*, trans. Rodney Livingstone (Cambridge: MIT Press, 1971), p. 52.

[96]Michael Mollat and Philippe Wolff, *The Popular Revolutions of the Late Middle Ages*, trans. A. L. Lytton-Sells (London: George Allen and Unwin, 1973), p. 11.

vernacular on the stage dates from this period as well. The plays composed between 1300 and 1500 did not merely repeat the procedures of Arras, however. Whereas Adam de la Halle and his predecessors wrote during the final epoch of feudal expansion in western Europe, the drama of the fourteenth and fifteenth centuries coincided with the general crisis of feudalism, to which it constituted a striking response.

The sequence of calamities that devastated Europe after 1300 probably resulted from the inability of the feudal mode of production to overcome its inherent limitations. On the land, the combination of rising population and falling yields led to poor harvests, famines, and a physically weakened people who, in 1348, fell easy prey to the Black Death. In the mines, technical problems in silver extraction eventually produced a wild rate of inflation. Faced with falling agricultural income, a shortage of labor, and rising costs, the aristocracy turned to international plunder and, when that failed, to civil war. At the same time, it sought throughout Europe to tie the peasantry more securely to the soil. Instead, such efforts fused the minor local protests of previous generations into resistance struggles as extraordinary as the immediately preceding catastrophes themselves: major peasant rebellions fundamentally threatened ruling classes from England to Czechoslovakia. Nearly all these movements failed. In eastern Europe, the nobility reduced the rural work force to a servile and degraded condition of dependence that persisted in many regions into the present century. In the more feudalized West, however, the towns, far stronger than their eastern counterparts, blocked this seigneurial solution. The evolution of social relations on the land proceeded in the opposite direction, toward the dissolution of serfdom.

In the towns, internal strife became endemic after 1300. Although rebellions in the most advanced regions—Flanders and northern and central Italy—at times took on a radical cast, craftsmen and shopkeepers typically and more modestly attempted, with partial success, to wrest some control over municipal affairs from the ruling oligarchies. The characteristic institutional expressions of these triumphs were the artisan guilds, which multiplied rapidly during the period, partly in response as well to economic contraction and to trends in manufacturing that threatened either to reduce their members to the status of wage workers or, worse still, to bypass them entirely.[97] Both product of the crisis and agent of subsequent history, the trade and craft guilds proved the crucial theatrical institution of the period, especially in England and Germany. In France, Italy, and, later, Spain, dramatic or religious guilds known as companies or confraternities and recruited from roughly the

[97]Anderson, pp. 197–209, 246–64; Mollat and Wolff, passim; Hilton, *Bond Men Made Free*, passim.

same social strata as the trade and craft guilds took responsibility for the stage. In France in particular, wealthier or better-educated groups—often organized in guilds of their own—also produced and performed plays.[98] The economic, social, and ideological turmoil of the age thus influenced the theater not only as general context but as specific institutional configuration as well. Because religious and secular authorities also exercised some control over the stage, within the plays oppositional ideas usually developed in overt or covert conflict with hegemonic views. Nonetheless, during the fourteenth and fifteenth centuries urban drama provided a forum for the representation of new, more radical political and social options.

*Religious Theater*

Medieval vernacular religious plays survive in English, Cornish, Welsh, Dutch, French, Provençal, Catalan, Spanish, Italian, Swedish, Polish, Czech, Croatian, Greek, and Russian.[99] The extent of dramatic development in most of these languages depended primarily on the growth of towns and secondarily, perhaps, on the strength of the prior theatrical tradition. More specifically, internal urban social and political relations often established the limits and possibilities of popular expression on the late medieval stage. In this relatively secular milieu, Christian doctrine could take on an ambivalence rarely evident in church theater. An insurgent perspective entered the drama both in struggle and in harmony with theological orthodoxy.

A brief survey of the social parameters of the theater will help locate more precisely the interaction of religion and radicalism. France and Germany, the leading centers of late medieval drama, combined established towns with large bodies of earlier, especially liturgical, plays. By contrast, Bohemia and Spain apparently proved inhospitable to drama. In Bohemia, the Hussite Wars of the early fifteenth century extinguished the preexistent Czech vernacular dramatic tradition.[100] In Catalonia, literary subordination to Provençal and economic ruin—in part the product of class war—perhaps had a similar result. Despite the region's liturgical drama and advanced urban economy, little survives beyond a simple and brief fourteenth-century Resurrection play.[101] The

[98]William Tydeman, *The Theatre in the Middle Ages: Western European Stage Conditions, c. 800–1576* (Cambridge: Cambridge University Press, 1978), pp. 132, 200–201.

[99]See Kindermann, 1:207–392.

[100]H. Jelinek, *Histoire de la littérature tchèque*, vol. 1, *Des origines à 1850*, 4th ed. (Paris: Editions du Sagittaire, 1930?), p. 153; Kindermann, 1:383.

[101]Catalan drama and the relations between Catalan and Provençal: Arthur Terry, *Catalan Literature*, vol. 8 of *A Literary History of Spain*, gen. ed. R. O. Jones (London: Ernest

rest of the Hispanic peninsula lacked not only an earlier theater but also towns comparable to those often found in western Europe. No true artisan guilds emerged until the end of the fifteenth century. Only Gómez Manrique's *Representación del nacimiento de Nuestro Señor*—performed in a nunnery rather than a town—remains from the period between 1300 and 1490.[102] Lower-class insurgency may have undermined theater in Bohemia and Catalonia; lower-class weakness may have had the same effect elsewhere in Spain.

Between these extremes, popular initiative could foster religious drama. The establishment of the Corpus Christi cycles and other elaborate plays in northern England followed upon the belated emergence of guilds in the country's provincial towns.[103] In thirteenth-century Italy, repeated lower-class religious movements, at times both revolutionary and heretical led to the formation, especially in Umbria, of popular religious organizations. These groups elaborated vernacular Christian lyrics (*laude*) and theatrical pieces (*laude drammatiche*) that, perhaps because of the relative scarcity of Italian liturgical drama, soon came to form a popular liturgy attached to the older Latin service at the appropriate places in the Christian year. Disseminated throughout the country, the *laude drammatiche* eventually provided the basis for the *sacra rappresentazione*, the characteristic form of fifteenth-century Italian religious drama.[104]

In Florence this drama took on a distinctive cast not only from the cultural traditions of a predominantly bourgeois city, but also from the tactical alliances with the artisanate through which the Medici family

---

Benn, 1972), pp. 53–55, 4. Late medieval Catalonia: Vicens Vives, *An Economic History of Spain*, in collaboration with Jorge Nadal Oller, trans. Frances M. López-Morillas (Princeton: Princeton University Press, 1969), pp. 176–80, 183–85, 215, 228–31; Jackson, pp. 125–26.

[102]Drama: J. P. Wickersham Crawford, *Spanish Drama before Lope de Vega*, 2d ed., bibliographical supplement by Warren T. McCready (Philadelphia: University of Pennsylvania Press, 1967), pp. 1–11; N. D. Shergold, *A History of the Spanish Stage from Medieval Times until the End of the Seventeenth Century* (Oxford: Clarendon Press, 1967), pp. 26–142; López Morales, pp. 68–87; A. D. Deyermond, *The Middle Ages*, vol. 1 of *A Literary History of Spain*, gen. ed. Jones (London: Ernest Benn, 1971), pp. 209–13. History: Pierre Vilar, *Spain: A Brief History*, trans. Brian Tate, 2d ed. (Oxford: Pergamon Press, 1977), p. 22; Vicens Vives, *Economic History*, pp. 260–62, 269, 284; Jackson, pp. 129, 132–33; Elena Lourie, "A Society Organized for War: Medieval Spain," *Past and Present*, no. 35 (December 1966): 54–76.

[103]A. R. Myers, *England in the Late Middle Ages*, 8th ed. (Harmondsworth, Middlesex: Penguin, 1971), p. 187; H. van Werveke, "The Rise of the Towns," in *Economic Organization and Policies in the Middle Ages*, ed. Postan, E. E. Rich, and Edward Miller, vol. 3 of *CEHE* (Cambridge: Cambridge University Press, 1963), p. 36; Sylvia L. Thrupp, "The Gilds," in *CEHE*, 3:244; Martin Stevens, "The York Cycle: From Procession to Play," *Leeds Studies in English*, n.s., 6 (1972): 45, 57.

[104]History: Waley, *Italian City-Republics*, pp. 164–220; Hilton, *Bond Men Made Free*, pp. 103–9; Mollat and Wolff, pp. 36–37. Drama: d'Ancona, *Origini*, 1:106–9; Mario Apollonio, *Storia del teatro italiano* (Florence: G. C. Sansoni, 1943), 1:146; Toschi, pp. 676, 680.

gained hereditary possession of the *signoria*.[105] The triumph of a dicta-torship that patronized both the arts and the lower classes helps explain the unusual combination of courtly and popular elements in the Floren-tine *sacra rappresentazione* during the age of Lorenzo il Magnifico. Floren-tine playwrights tended to ignore the life of Christ in favor of the lives of saints, which offered them greater freedom for elaboration and expan-sion. *La rappresentazione di Rosana*, a Christianized version of courtly ro-mance, contrasts notably with Rome's *La passione e resurrezione del Colosseo*, a conservative retelling of the Gospels. Lorenzo's own play, *La rappresen-tazione di San Giovanni e Paulo*, somewhat incongruously unites a series of exemplary acts of Christian renunciation of the world with a chronicle history of the Roman Empire and a sustained meditation on the prob-lems of royal power. The consequent structural bifurcation indicates a hesitation between sacramental and secular history that anticipates sev-enteenth-century Spanish religious theater while retaining biographical interest. A good ruler, Lorenzo argues, must conform to the highest standards of personal morality in serving the interests of the people. An obvious form of self-flattery, the play points to the social dimensions of both Medici power and the Florentine *sacra rappresentazione*.[106]

The impact of popular participation emerges more clearly from Ger-man records. During the fourteenth and fifteenth centuries, guild movements for civil involvement generally succeeded in the older towns of the Rhine and the south but failed in the newer trading settlements on the Baltic.[107] The hell scenes of the surviving plays suggest the con-sequences of this social distinction. *Das Wiener Passionsspiel* damns a usu-rer, a sorceress, and a robber; in *Das hessische Weihnachtsspiel* the subordi-nate devils cheer up a despondent Lucifer by promising to bring him Jews, heretics, heathens, and the standard usurers, among others. Both works are of Rhenish origin. On the other hand, *Das Redentin Osterspiel*, from Lübeck or its immediate Baltic environs, condemns a baker, a shoemaker, a tailor, a tapster, a weaver, a butcher, and a fishmonger. Critics have considered this procedure an advance. Instead of punishing representatives of inherently disreputable groups, as do *Das Wiener Pas-sionsspiel* and *Das hessische Weihnachtsspiel*, the northern play focuses on the specific economic crimes of individuals engaged in otherwise re-spectable trades. Yet this sophistication in sensibility also reveals a purely

---

[105]L. F. Marks, "Review Article: Fourteenth-Century Democracy in Florence," *Past and Present*, no. 25 (1963): 77–85; Waley, *Later Medieval Europe: From Saint Louis to Luther* (New York: Barnes and Noble, 1964), p. 109; C. M. Cipolla, "The Economic Policies of Governments: The Italian and Iberian Peninsulas," in *CEHE*, 3:428.

[106]D'Ancona, *Origini*, 1:217–22, 254–63, 301, 411, 422, 426–31, and 2:58–60, 163–66; Apollonio, 1:219–22, 237–42; Silvio d'Amico, *Storia del teatro drammatico*, 5th ed. (Mi-lan: Garzanti, 1968), 1:228, 231–32; Toschi, pp. 691–92.

[107]Thrupp, pp. 242–43; Mollat and Wolff, pp. 74–75.

patrician consciousness: the lost souls all come from the repressed urban lower classes.[108]

In Germany, then, the religious stage provided a terrain for social conflict. With the artisanate relegated to a peripheral role, the upper class could conflate secular and religious hierarchies, thereby arming itself with transcendental weapons of exploitation. As the plays of Arras have suggested, however, the assertion of popular consciousness opened up, at least theoretically, a range of options, including the organicist subordination of lower-class views to a hegemonic outlook, the unintegrated juxtaposition of asymmetrically structured opposing ideologies, and the dialectical synthesis of learned clerical and popular secular culture. The difficulty of differentiating either conceptually or empirically among these alternatives testifies to the potential ideological ambivalence of urban religious drama. In the present context, dialectical synthesis offers the most intriguing possibilities. At once diachronic and synchronic in implication, it simultaneously specifies the historical development of medieval theater and the defining formal characteristic of its final phase. Particularly in its assumption of a balance between learned and popular elements, the term looks ahead to the treatment of the same problem in the remaining chapters of this book, on Renaissance drama. There the late medieval synthesis takes on the perhaps dubious function of contributing popular culture to a new and distinctive fusion, this time with the learned heritage of classical antiquity. Most important, whether applied to the Middle Ages or to the Renaissance, the notion of dialectical synthesis suggests the possibility of the very process of contradictory totalization that lay beyond the boundaries of Arrageois theater.

Debate on this issue—the ideology of form—has traditionally centered, at least in the English-speaking world, on the relative weight of Christian and popular elements in the drama. Earlier generations of scholars, looking for evidence of secularizing tendencies, emphasized the relative autonomy within the religious plays of material drawn from the life of the folk. Realism, comedy, satire, adventure, even random, senseless violence—all revealed the move away from the church.[109] So too did the at least partly popular character of the audience, actors, staging, and dramatists.[110] Reacting against this position, more recent in-

---

[108]The original locations of the plays: Rolf Steinbach, *Die deutschen Oster- und Passionsspiele des Mittelalters* (Cologne: Böhlau Verlag, 1970), pp. 47–48, 116; Michael, *Das deutsche Drama des Mittelalters* (Berlin: Walter de Gruyter, 1971), p. 84. But see *Das Innsbrucker Osterspiel*, from the Schmalkalden area of Thuringia in central Germany (Michael, *Das deutsche Drama*, p. 69), which parallels the Lübeck play in its hell scene.

[109]Chambers, *Mediaeval Stage*, 2:68–176; Nicoll, pp. 175–213.

[110]Tydeman, pp. 165, 184–221, 232. But see Nelson, *The Medieval English Stage: Corpus Christi Pageants and Plays* (Chicago: University of Chicago Press, 1974), and the reply by Johnston, "The Medieval English Stage," *University of Toronto Quarterly* 44 (1975): 238–48.

vestigators have had little difficulty in showing that the lower-class dimensions of the religious theater contributed, both aesthetically and thematically, to a larger, controlling doctrinal purpose. For the church, the plays constituted effective propaganda, a social function that some distinguished critics, imagining that medieval society formed an organic whole, have celebrated.[111]

Like the views it supplanted, this recent approach has failed to grasp adequately the relationship between religious and popular forces in the later Middle Ages. First, an organicist vision of any class society fails simultaneously as ideology and interpretation. It is particularly inapplicable to the late Middle Ages, however. Peasant rebellions of the time frequently singled out ecclesiastical seigneuries for attack, primarily because abbots and bishops proved unusually zealous in exacting labor and rent from their tenants. Similarly, an interpretation stressing the doctrinal and organic unity of the plays, though more defensible than a comparable understanding of the society from which they arose, simply cannot account for all that took place on the medieval Christian stage. Even in harmoniously structured works, the combination of clerical and popular values in the urban religious theater cut ideologically in two directions. In one sense the church manipulated the townspeople. But from another perspective the mere fact of the plays attests to the seriousness with which the church treated the lower classes of the towns, a new group within the feudal social formation.

The value and dignity of ordinary human life emerge not only in *Mary of Nijmeghen*, a complex Dutch Faustian miracle play that provides an extended representation of everyday urban society, but also in early and relatively restrained pieces like *La passion Provençale* or *La passion du Palatinus*. In addition, the historical consciousness implicit in much of this drama, but especially in some of the English cycles, constituted an important advance on the timeless cultic mentality of liturgical theater or, for that matter, of primitive folk ritual.[112] For example, whereas in the Chester cycle's account of the Fall a recurrent use of typology[113] and a focus on God at the expense of Adam and Eve produce a relatively undramatic sense of divine foreknowledge, in the N-town version of the

[111]See Harold C. Gardiner, S.J., *Mysteries' End: An Investigation of the Last Days of the Medieval Religious Stage*, Yale Studies in English, no. 103 (New Haven: Yale University Press, 1946); Frederick Millet Salter, *Mediaeval Drama in Chester* (Toronto: University of Toronto Press, 1955); Glynne Wickham, *Early English Stages, 1300 to 1660*, vol. 1 (London: Routledge and Kegan Paul, 1959); V. A. Kolve, *The Play Called Corpus Christi* (Stanford: Stanford University Press, 1966).

[112]Kolve, pp. 1–7; Stanley J. Kahrl, *Traditions of Medieval English Drama* (London: Hutchinson University Library, 1974), pp. 121–29; Patrick J. Collins, "Typology, Criticism, and Medieval Drama: Some Observations on Method," *Comparative Drama* 10 (1976–77): 303–4.

[113]Woolf, p. 122.

same event the choice of a more human perspective evokes, at least for a time, a suspenseful and open-ended world of chance and uncertainty, in which even God appears to be momentarily overtaken by events. Thus, the assertion of transcendental control near the end of the N-town pageant somewhat arbitrarily imposes order on chaotic human history. Clerical ideological hegemony did not and indeed, in the conditions of the late medieval town, could not entail the negation on the religious stage of all alternative points of view.

An organicist approach has even greater difficulty with those plays that flaunt their heterogeneity. One surely would not want to conflate the stately, doctrinal, learned *Everyman* with a far more popular morality like *Mankind*, which dramatizes a conflict of world views that indirectly serve opposing class interests. Although orthodoxy wins out, the emotional force of the work perhaps lies with diabolism. Similar arguments apply to the plays of the Wakefield Master, and particularly to *Secunda pastorum*. The pervasive thematic connections between the two parts of the piece indicate a systematic effort to unify disparate material, an effort that cannot entirely conceal, however, the secular, popular, and comic premises of most of the action. The conventional conclusion only begins to subsume the world of the fifteenth-century English shepherds.[114]

If these plays stage ultimately irreconcilable ideological and social struggles, however, they hardly lead to dialectical synthesis. The drama that most nearly achieves such a synthesis exploits the potential ambivalence of Christian values even more fully than do the works of the Wakefield Master. Accordingly, one may fundamentally challenge the conservative reading of late medieval religious theater by rejecting the dichotomy between Christian and popular without, however, succumbing to an organicist vision of medieval society. Early Christianity was, of course, profoundly popular in appeal and support and revolutionary in some of its implications. Its defining feature, the dual nature of Christ, offered to the urban masses of the eastern Mediterranean a deity who, like them, was poor and suffering but who, unlike them, could and would change the world decisively to their advantage. Though in the third and fourth centuries Christianity triumphed among the properties classes, who henceforth dominated the religion, its original content, if often obscured, was nonetheless preserved and transmitted by the monastic orders to the later Middle Ages, at which time it once again inspired the revolutionary hopes of the oppressed.[115]

The crucial agents in the final stages of this process were the lesser

[114]See Axton, pp. 175–204, and esp. Weimann, pp. 49–97, on the popular elements in these and other plays.

[115]John Morris, "Early Christian Orthodoxy," *Past and Present*, no. 3 (1953): 1–14.

clergy, particularly the Mendicants. Generally recruited from the lower classes, they frequently found themselves at odds with wealthier prelates. Their sermons, moreover, had revolutionary moral, if not social, implications, while they themselves proved unusually prone to heresies based on a radical rereading of the Gospels. The thirteenth-century Umbrian movements mentioned above, led by Dominicans and Franciscans, incurred the wrath of the urban ruling classes as well as of the papacy. French peasant protests were often organized on parochial lines, centered in the church, and spearheaded by poorer priests. In England, perhaps because the unusual absence of heresy had closed off a religious vehicle for the expression of discontent, the poorer clergy, most notably John Ball, took an active role in the Peasants' Rebellion.

More generally, lower-class rebels throughout the Middle Ages, but especially after 1300, recovered the mystical millenarianism and primitive egalitarianism of the Gospels. The English peasants, for instance, demanded the leveling of the entire ecclesiastical hierarchy. Heresy often played a role in these struggles, though decisively only in Bohemia during the Hussite period. Given the ideological dominance of the church, popular insurgency virtually necessitated an attack on religious orthodoxy.[116] But early Christianity proved a consistent aid to late medieval revolutionary thought: it provided the only perspective available to the poor that enabled them to attack the rich while asserting their own value.[117] A radical contradictory totalization depended on the life of Christ.[118]

The influence of Mendicant preaching on the drama[119] surely accounts for much of the satire directed against the wealthy and powerful in plays of the period from France, Germany, Italy, and England. A suggestive variation on this consciousness occurs at the beginning of the *Lauda in decollatione Sancti Johannis Baptiste*, from Rome, where Herod refrains from killing John because "lo populo se levarà contra noi / e farrau re colui" ("the people will rise up against us / and make him king").[120] Most important, however, is the treatment of Christ. The

[116]Frederick Engels, *The Peasant War in Germany*, in *The German Revolutions: "The Peasant War in Germany" and "Germany: Revolution and Counter-Revolution,"* ed. and introd. Leonard Krieger (Chicago: University of Chicago Press, 1967), p. 35.

[117]Toschi, p. 678; d'Ancona, *Origini*, 1:110–11; d'Amico, 1:220; Hilton, *Bond Men Made Free*, pp. 207–13, 223, 227; Mollat and Wolff, pp. 289–92, 304–9; Bloch, *French Rural History*, pp. 169–71.

[118]Peter Burke, *Popular Culture in Early Moden Europe* (New York: Harper and Row, 1978), p. 193.

[119]Gerald Robert Owst, *Literature and Pulpit in Medieval England: A Neglected Chapter in the History of English Letters and of the English People*, 2d ed. (New York: Barnes and Noble, 1961), pp. 471–547; Wickham, 1:122, 313.

[120]Vincenzo de Bartholomaeis, ed., *Laude drammatiche e rappresentazioni sacre* (1943; rpt. Florence: Felice Le Monnier, 1967), 2:137, lines 62–63.

transference of feudal terminology to the relationship between humanity and God, first observable in twelfth-century drama, became widespread in the later Middle Ages. One finds it, for instance, in the Catalan Resurrection play, in Feo Belcari's *La rappresentazione de Abramo ed Isac*, in *La passion Provençale*, and in *La passion du Palatinus*. The major innovation, however, involved a reversal that resulted in the imaginative, class-conscious re-creation of the relationship between Jesus and his society. In *The Cornish Ordinalia*, a cycle that consistently evinces concern for the suffering of the poor and outcast, the following exchange occurs at the Last Supper:

*Jesus.* Hitherto, certainly, kings have always held dominion over their subjects, and those in power have invariably been accounted great by young and old alike.

May it never be thus with you, however. Let him who is the most important among you and has the greatest power be like the least of you, while he who heads the table ranks himself with him who serves it.

So give me a thoughtful answer to this question: which of these two is the greater in your opinion—he who serves the food or he who is served?
*Simon.* Isn't it the one who eats? It seems to me that's surely right. A lord is greater than a butler.
*Jesus.* I have taken my place in your midst as a servant serving.[121]

The Welsh *Passion* develops this pattern more explicitly. Pilate presides over a feudal court, peopled with "lords of high estate"; Jesus refers to his enemies as "men of high degree." Pilate's court also exercises an important judicial function, ultimately making Christ a victim of the law. In the Towneley cycle, Pilate's legal oppression from above of Jesus, the common man, complements the complaints of the Wakefield Master's shepherds from below, while echoing the vigorous attack on the legal system made by the lower classes in 1381. This view of the law accurately responded to the structure of feudal society: the parcellization of sovereignty precluded centralized political authority. The exercise of justice accordingly involved most executive and administrative functions as well, for this reason functioning as the central mechanism of political power.[122]

Thus the dual nature of Christ facilitated the critique of social hierar-

---

[121]Markham Harris, trans., *The Cornish Ordinalia: A Medieval Dramatic Trilogy* (Washington, D.C.: Catholic University of American Press, 1969), p. 103.
[122]Wales: text in Gwenan Jones, *A Study of Three Welsh Religious Plays* (n.p.: R. Evans and Son, Bala Press, 1939), p. 155, line 35; p. 161, line 87. See also p. 159, lines 54, 60; p. 167, line 159; p. 201, lines 558, 559, 567, 571, among others. Towneley: Arnold Williams, *The Characterization of Pilate in the Towneley Plays* (East Lansing: Michigan State College Press, 1950), p. 39. Medieval justice: Anderson, pp. 152–53.

chy.[123] The representation and formation in the theater of lower-class consciousness involved both a creative response to late medieval reality and a return to the latent content of the Gospels. The plays could be radical because they were Christian.

## Secular Theater

The secular stage raises complementary issues. Given the absence of popular dramatic texts from the early Middle Ages, one cannot confidently assess the relationship of late medieval urban comedy, for example, to the antecedent theatrical activities of peasants and mimes. Scholars widely assume, however, that the *Fastnachtsspiel* (Shrovetide play) derives from pre-Christian Germanic cult and at least indirectly from the ancient mimic tradition as well.[124] Urban comedy in this sense constitutes a popular and belated version of the Roman-Germanic synthesis that centuries before had helped shape feudalism in general and liturgical drama in particular. Certainly, the *Fastnachtsspiel* substantially differs from a presumably less mediated survival of agrarian ritual like the English Mummers' Play. Its peculiar synthesis also distinguishes it, of course, from the contemporary religious theater. Just as secular drama as a whole reveals the possibilities of a theater generally independent of a religious perspective, the comedy provides the most appropriate material for assessing the range of options available in late medieval popular theater.

Nonetheless, late medieval comedy closely resembled the contemporary religious drama. The processional staging of northern England's Corpus Christi cycles paralleled, both formally and temporally, the civic pageantry of London. Comparable structural analogues characterized the French theater as well. Furthermore, in Paris, the comic actors shared a stage with the Confrérie de la Passion. Scholars have discovered significant affinities between miracles and secular romantic plays, and between moralities and mummers' performances. Similarly, a work like *La guerra di Carnevale e Quaresima* is a Christianized revision of a pagan, popular comedy.[125]

But the difference between the two stage traditions is simple, obvious, and fundamental: the comedy is the religious drama without a metaphysical dimension; the comedy is popular culture without antagonistic ideological closure. Its characteristic features follow from these dis-

---

[123]Duvignaud, pp. 156, 158.

[124]Eckehard Catholy, *Fastnachtspiel* (Stuttgart: J. B. Metzlersche Verlagsbuchhandlung, 1966), pp. 3–4.

[125]English staging: Wickham, 1:122–25; France: Konigson, passim; Frank, *Medieval French Drama*, pp. 250, 203; the morality-mummers parallel: Potter, pp. 10–16; Carnival and Lent: Burke, pp. 185, 188.

tinctions. The reductiveness and cynicism of the French farce and *sottie* (fools' play) and of the German *Fastnachtsspiel* constitute critiques of daily life.[126] Although an early piece such as *Der Tanaweschel* (1414), in which a united society takes a personified epidemic to court and obtains a death sentence in retribution for the havoc the disease has wrought, evades such generalities, not all misfortunes can be blamed on nature. *Maistre Pierre Pathelin* and Hans Folz's *Ein Fasnachtspil von einem Pawrngericht* and *Ein Spil von konig Salomon und Markolfo* give ample evidence of good humor and high spirits, yet all present a jaundiced view of the judicial process.

Many fifteenth-century plays take social criticism as their central purpose, among them *Vom Babst, Cardinal und von Bischoffen* and *Des Turken Vasnachtspil*, both attributed to Hans Rosenplüt, and four anonymous French farces and *sotties* from the mid-fifteenth century—*Mestier et Marchandise, Mieulx que devant, Pou d'acquest*, and *Les gens nouveaux*.[127] Rosenplüt's works attack the aristocratic ruling class, both lay and clerical, for its mistreatment of burghers and peasants. *Des Turken Vasnachtspil*, a proto-Oriental tale, uses an ahistorically benign Ottoman emperor to highlight the hypocrisy involved in the oppression of the European masses by their supposedly Christian leaders. A similar theme informs the French pieces, which emphasize the sufferings of merchants, artisans, and peasants. The German plays do not reveal internal urban social conflict of the kind portrayed in *Le jeu de la feuillée*. Fifteenth-century conditions apparently provide an explanation for this substantial solidarity against the nobility. Although in Nuremberg the patriciate retained control of civic life, the unusual prosperity of the city seems to have benefited the lower classes as well. Equally important, at this time the landed princes were encroaching upon the sovereignty of the towns in an attempt to construct territorial states.[128] For this reason artisan consciousness in the *Fastnachtsspiele* is generally not directed against the rulers of Nuremberg. In France, the lower and middle classses shared a community of misery brought on by English invasion, French defense, aristocratic faction, royal taxation, and a newly powerful high bourgeoisie. Though probably performed by an organization of Parisian law clerks called the Basoche, and hence deriving from a highly educated social stratum, the French drama consistently takes this popular perspective.[129]

---

[126]Duvignaud, pp. 145–46; Kindermann, 1:399.

[127]On the *sotties*, see Heather Arden, *Fools' Plays: A Study of Satire in the "Sottie"* (Cambridge: Cambridge University Press, 1980).

[128]Fritz Rörig, *The Medieval Town*, trans. from the German (Berkeley and Los Angeles: University of California Press, 1967), p. 154; Barraclough, *Origins*, pp. 341, 343, 348.

[129]History: Anderson, pp. 86–87; the Basoche: Frank, *Medieval French Drama*, p. 249.

Thus, the plays reveal the ideology of urban dwellers besieged and threatened primarily by the traditional wielders of feudal power.[130] The resultant class perspective is entirely negative. No positive sense of morality shapes the thinking of the characters who, in the French works, mainly worry about earning a living. The complete absence of the concept of progress, only much later a defining characteristic of the bourgeoisie, indicates both the social basis and the political impasse of this outlook. Rosenplüt can offer nothing more than the fanciful intervention of the Turkish sultan, *Mestier et Marchandise* stakes all on the hoped-for assistance of God and king, and *Mieulx que devant* promises the imminent arrival of the imaginary Roger Bontemps. *Pou d'acquest* and *Les gens nouveaux* explicitly deny all meliorist expectations, however. To the "mieulx que devant" ("better than before") of the work of that title, *Les gens nouveaux* answers "de mal en pire" ("from bad to worse") and "pis que devant" ("worse than before"). At the conclusion of this *sottie*, the oppressed Le Monde finds herself "Sans nul espoir" ("without any hope"), a phrase that accurately sums up the implications of all these plays.[131]

Thus both the religious and the comic theaters responded to the material and cultural dislocations of the later Middle Ages. A time of crisis characteristically leads to spiritual bifurcation, to the reassertion in a new form of traditional morality, on one hand, and to the abandonment of all values, on the other. Perhaps the dichotomy between the two kinds of drama arises as well from the structurally determined dual perspective of medieval towns. Yet such a polarization underestimates the critical, popular outlook of the Christian and secular stages alike, an outlook that later contributed to the distinctive synthesis of Renaissance Spanish and English public theater. A division of the drama along these lines also leads one to expect that religious plays would incorporate any oppositional thrust within an encompassing ideology of acquiescence, whereas comic pieces might at least occasionally promote resistance. The reverse is as likely, however, precisely because only the religious stage dramatized the dialectical tension and perhaps effected a dialectical synthesis of learned Christian theology and popular revolutionary aspirations. Lacking in transcendental illusion and consequently free of an ethical or historical outlook as well, secular drama could only accept a bad situation. In a sense this resignation involved a kind of perceptiveness, since the lower classes did not dislodge, and probably could not have dislodged, the aristocracy. Yet as a result the comedy missed what some of the religious plays registered and, arguably, furthered: the defeat of

---

[130]For related arguments, see Duvignaud, p. 92; Konigson, pp. 67–68.

[131]In *La farce en France de 1450 à 1550*, ed. André Tissier (Paris: Editions CDU et SEDES réunis, 1976), pp. 242–55, lines 320, 341, 329.

serfdom and the accompanying dissolution of the feudal mode of production in its classical form. At least in England, one can perhaps trace an unbroken tradition of religious radicalism extending from the Peasants' Rebellion to the Civil War.

On the other hand, the connection of these two revolutionary moments inevitably tempers any assertions of the political efficacy of Christian drama. Although lower-class income increased in the late fourteenth and fifteenth centuries, the main long-term beneficiaries of both the decline of serfdom and the much later overthrow of the monarchy were not the peasants or shepherds in the countryside and the humble artisans or tradesmen in the towns, but the bourgeoisie. Thus, an overview of medieval urban drama may profitably conclude by temporarily turning away from popular culture, by anticipating a new hegemony, by considering one of the earliest surviving theatrical specimens of bourgeois ideology, the Dutch *Lancelot of Denmark*. Composed in Brabant during the mid or late fourteenth century, it has tentatively, and unconvincingly, been assigned to the repertory of a traveling company of actors. Although deeply indebted to romance, and hence one of the relatively few extant works from a now largely lost tradition of late medieval, secular, romantic drama,[132] it apparently attacks the conventions of courtly love.[133] The play in fact fuses bourgeois and aristocratic consciousness. Because the heroine, Sanderijn, prefers her chastity and, having lost that, her married love to a sexual liaison with the aristocratic Lancelot, she is seen as noble and courtly. By contrast, Lancelot's cowardly participation in the schemes of his mother, whose obsession with class distinctions governs her boorish and eventually vicious conduct, undermines his moral credibility. The knight who weds Sanderijn appropriately reveals his nobility by forgiving her single sexual error and by loving her not for her birth, but for herself. Finally, Sanderijn's ultimate happiness and Lancelot's death from grief provide a class-based, moralized conclusion: bourgeois virtue is rewarded and aristocratic vice punished.

But the good knight rejoices to learn that Sanderijn, though poor, is of noble birth, while his prospective bride thanks him for stooping, both socially and economically, to marry her. Earlier, Sanderijn unquestioningly accepts the insuperability of the class barrier that divides her from Lancelot. Operating entirely in a chivalric setting, the characters repeat-

---

[132]Leo G. Salingar, *Shakespeare and the Traditions of Comedy* (Cambridge: Cambridge University Press, 1974), pp. 39–59.

[133]A. W. Reed, "Early Dutch Secular Drama," *Review of English Studies* 1 (1925): 159–63; Weevers, pp. 48–54; Reinder P. Meijer, *Literature of the Low Countries: A Short History of Dutch Literature in the Netherlands and Belgium* (Assen, Netherlands: Van Gorcum, 1971), pp. 40–45.

edly evoke admiration for their courtly demeanor and above all for their courteous speech. The epilogue emphasizes this notoriously aristocratic trait: "If anyone loves truly, and gains his true love, let him use courteous language to her. . . . use courteous language about all women, and . . . love them truly; and so you will have joy of them."[134] In short, the play injects bourgeois values into an aristocratic context. The higher morality implicitly belongs to the new class, but the social preeminence to the old, which is refined and perfected by the incorporation of innovative ideas. Without including a single characteristically urban figure, *Lancelot of Denmark* presents a more sophisticated and advanced version of bourgeois ideology than characterizes most medieval town drama. But it does so by accepting the feudal order, which remains essentially intact. In various guises, some such class compromise prevailed in the age of western European absolutism as well.

## CONCLUSION

This overview of medieval theater began by recalling Germanic tribal communalism; it ended, at least as a historical survey, by anticipating the triumph of capitalism. An analysis of feudalism and its drama helps restore the connection between the preclassical past and the postmodern present. One should of course not overestimate the distinctiveness of the Middle Ages in this respect. All societies that have advanced beyond the state of primitive communalism have been composite formations. A dominant class in each has exercised hegemony, but never absolute control, over a socially heterogeneous populace. In medieval Europe, the anterior modes of production from which feudalism arose did not simply disappear with the consolidation of the new system. The expansion of that system, moreover, encouraged the emergence of still other groups, whose interests eventually pointed beyond the limitations of feudal society. The landed nobility thus ruled over a polity comprising several changing, unevenly subordinated classes, some of which, in the late Middle Ages, overtly challenged its privileged status.[135]

The distinctiveness of feudalism lies in the parcellization of sovereignty, in the unusual inherent structural constraints on the exercise of aristocratic power. Because the theater developed in the partially protected enclaves of the village, the church, and the town, it highlighted the heterogeneity of feudal society. One may easily perceive, for exam-

---

[134]*Lancelot of Denmark*, trans. E. Colledge, in *Reynard the Fox and Other Medieval Netherlands Secular Literature*, ed. E. Colledge, trans. Adriaan J. Barnouw and Colledge (Leyden: Sijthoff, 1967), p. 183.
[135]Anderson, p. 154.

ple, the qualitative difference between the plays of the peasantry and the plays of the clergy. Yet the relative autonomy of the three main dramatic locales did not entail absolute independence either from each other or from the hegemonic class. The urban stage in particular drew on the two earlier theatrical traditions. Medieval theater thus helps clarify the composite quality of feudalism not only through the variety of the plays, but also through the variety within the individual play. In drama as in society, that heterogeneity reveals a historical pattern. Peasant drama, the earliest structural evasion of upper-class control, probably expressed residual, prefeudal views. Church drama, at its most important during the High Middle Ages, conformed far more closely to the dominant, feudal perspective. Urban drama, coincident with the late medieval period, at times gave voice to emergent, postfeudal ideologies. An ambiguously hegemonic theater thus was historically flanked by two ambiguously counterhegemonic theaters.[136] Yet for even the most explicitly insurgent plays of the end of the Middle Ages, the structure and dynamism of the feudal mode of production remained the fundamental conditions of possibility.

The history of the other medieval European theater, that of Byzantium, notably confirms this conclusion. For half a millennium and more after the fall of Rome, the Eastern Empire retained enormous material and cultural advantages over the barbarian West. Stable, wealthy, and urban, it preserved unbroken ties to the classical Mediterranean, inheriting both the pagan and the Christian cultures of the Greco-Roman past. In particular, it imported the mimic art of the West, for which it constructed several permanent theaters, and, until the Islamic conquests of the seventh century, drew heavily on the secular and religious dramatic activities of the East, centered in Syria. The flamboyant rituals of the Greek liturgy, moreover, provided fertile soil for the growth of the stage. Unlike the comparatively backward societies of western Europe, then, Byzantium apparently possessed in abundance everything necessary for a thriving theater.[137]

Yet almost nothing remains of medieval Byzantine drama. The secular, mimic stage probably flourished almost continuously from before the fourth-century founding of the Eastern empire down to the final

---

[136]Terminology: Raymond Williams, *Marxism and Literature* (Oxford: Oxford University Press, 1977), pp. 108–14, 121–27.

[137]History: Anderson, pp. 265–70. Drama: Albert Vogt, "Le théâtre à Byzance et dans l'empire du iv<sup>e</sup> au xiii<sup>e</sup> siècle, I: Le théâtre profane," *Revue des Questions Historiques*, 3d ser., 18 (1931): 259, 262, 270, 280–81; Marjorie Carpenter, "Romanos and the Mystery Play of the East," *University of Missouri Studies* 11, no. 3 (1936): 21–51; Egon Wellesz, "The Nativity Drama of the Byzantine Church," *Journal of Roman Studies* 37 (1947): 145–51; Theodore Bogdanos, "Liturgical Drama in Byzantine Literature," *Comparative Drama* 10 (1976–77): 200–202, 209.

Ottoman conquest in 1453 and beyond. Although not a single play text has survived, one may cautiously infer certain structural affinities with popular theater in the West. The religious stage, about which there is considerable uncertainty, is another matter, however. The hymns and homilies of the early medieval Orthodox church possessed a highly dramatic character. At least before the Iconoclastic movement of the eighth century, the homilies may have contained autonomous liturgical plays. The *Christos paschon*, probably a closet drama of the eleventh or twelfth century, perhaps was actually composed and performed as early as the fourth. Finally, a late-fourteenth-century manuscript includes something resembling a hymnographic mystery play for the feast of the Annunciation. In each instance, however, proof of dramatic performance is entirely lacking. Taken together, these texts and hypothetical texts fail to demonstrate either the existence of a tradition of religious theater or even the staging of a single play.[138]

From over a thousand years of Byzantine history, only two unquestionably dramatic religious works survive. One, a *Passion* scenario composed during the 1260s in the ecclesiastically independent province of Cyprus, has little value in determining the nature and extent of Christian theater in Byzantium proper. Though monastic in origin, it was not part of the liturgy and was perhaps performed outdoors. The other piece, a liturgical play of the Christmas season known as *The Three Children in the Furnace*, probably originated in the twelfth or thirteenth century, though possibly in the eleventh. This isolated and rather late product of Byzantium could not have influenced Slavic vernacular drama to nearly the extent that the Latin liturgical stage shaped theatrical practice in the Romance, Germanic, and Celtic languages. But though it had no impact on the empire's long-time Balkan possessions, it seems to have been performed in Russia. More important, it inspired there a vernacular rendition, the *Play of the Furnace*, performed in Novgorod during the 1540s but perhaps first adapted centuries before. If one excludes puppet theater, which may have originated in the thirteenth century, as well as other folk drama, it is the earliest play in Russian.[139]

---

[138]Secular drama: Vogt, "Le théâtre profane"; hymns: Carpenter, passim, and Wellesz, "Nativity Drama"; homilies: George La Piana, "The Byzantine Theater," *Speculum* 11 (1936): 175–85; *Christos paschon*: Sticca, "The *Christos Paschon* and the Byzantine Theater," *Comparative Drama* 8 (1974): 26–41; fourteenth-century mystery play: G. M. Proxorov, "A Codicological Analysis of the Illuminated *Akathistos* to the Virgin (Moscow, State Historical Museum, *Synodal Gr.* 429)," *Dumbarton Oaks Papers* 26 (1972): 245–50, 252; and no performance: Bogdanos, pp. 208–9.

[139]The scenario: Vogt, "Etudes sur le théâtre byzantin, I: Un mystère de la passion," *Byzantion* 6 (1931): 39–40; and esp. August C. Mahr, *The Cyprus Passion Cycle* (University of Notre Dame Publications in Mediaeval Studies, no. 9 (Notre Dame, Ind.: University of Notre Dame Press, 1947), pp. 2, 3, 12, 13, 77. Furnace plays: Miloš M. Velimirović, "Litur-

The explanation for this meager collection of texts probably lies in the particular social dilemma of the medieval Byzantine state. Though it survived the collapse of the Western empire, it could not return to the full slave economy of antiquity without a program of conquest well beyond its power to sustain. At the same time, it could not progress to feudalism, owing to the persistence of the imperial bureaucracy and the continued exploitation of slave labor in manufacturing and agriculture. Though strong enough to withstand the loss of the Balkans in the sixth and seventh centuries, Byzantium was incapable of integrating the Slav settlers into the empire after its reconquest of the region two hundred years later. Therefore, no eastern parallel to the western European synthesis of primitive-communal and slave modes of production was ever possible.

This failure to evolve toward feudalism perhaps proved decisive for the theater. At the cultural level, the Greek-speaking world could not duplicate the fusion of Roman and Germanic elements that lay behind the formation of Latin liturgical drama. The closest approximation to this process occurred in Russia, the only Slavic region in the orbit of the Orthodox church to produce a liturgical play. Moreover, in the absence of parcellized sovereignty, the towns of the Byzantine Empire lacked the autonomy of their western counterparts. The path to communalism, of which the late medieval urban stage was such a striking phenomenon, accordingly lay closed to them.[140] The juxtaposition and possible synthesis of learned and popular dramatic traditions remained even more remote.

The Byzantine state finally experienced the emergence of something resembling feudalism in its period of decline, especially after the sacking of its capital by the Crusaders in 1204. The extant plays apparently date from this period and, in addition, often reveal the impact of Western drama. The Cyprus *Passion* was written while the island was under Latin domination. Its author may have obtained a sense of the possibilities of theater from his rulers, though in keeping with the cultural and social differences between East and West, his scenario is less historical and more truly cyclical than comparable Catholic plays. The Russian *Play of the Furnace* was even more dependent on western Europe: it borrowed both characters and staging.[141]

gical Drama in Byzantium and Russia," *Dumbarton Oaks Papers* 16 (1962): 351–85. Puppet theater: Russell Zguta, "The Origin of the Russian Puppet Theater," *Slavic Review* 33 (1974): 708–20. Russian folk drama: Boris Vasil'evich Varneke, *History of the Rusian Theatre: Seventeenth through Nineteenth Century*, trans. Boris Brasol and Belle Martin (New York: Macmillan, 1951), pp. 1–10.

[140]Anderson, pp. 270–75, 234–36, 284–86.

[141]History: Anderson, pp. 280–84; Cyprus: Mahr, pp. 17–18; Russia: Velimirović, pp. 365, 374–75.

Appropriately, Byzantium may have made its most long-lasting contribution to drama through its influence on Latin theater. The exact dimensions of this relationship are unclear. The secular mimes could have indirectly inspired Hrosvita. The liturgical stage probably owed an even greater debt to the East. It may have profited from Byzantine innovation in biblical characterization, from dramatic elements originating in Syriac hymnody, and from entire scenes of the Byzantine dramatic homilies. One such homily probably left its mark on the Latin prophets play. Finally, Carolingian liturgical reform may have involved a conscious imitation of Greek ritual, also the possible source of the tropes themselves.[142] Only the dynamic and feudal West could realize the dramatic potential of the relatively more stable East.

The distinctive characteristics of medieval western Europe that have formed the basis for the preceding comparison also suggest a means of reformulating the relationship between the theater of the Middle Ages and that of the Renaissance. Each major kind of medieval drama occupied a determinate structural and historical position within feudal society. One might therefore hypothesize that the replacement of feudalism by another social system would lead to a radical transformation of the theater. In the absence of cataclysmic innovation, the partial survival of feudal relations would result in the persistence of some peculiarly medieval elements on the stage. New features in the drama would accordingly suggest social change, though not necessarily the advent of a different mode of production. In particular, the supersession of parcellized sovereignty would make possible unprecedented conflicts and syntheses in the theater and rich but difficult opportunities for the expression of popular and oppositional perspectives. Such are indeed the general contours of Renaissance drama.

[142]Vogt, "Le théâtre profane," pp. 293–96; Bogdanos, p. 210; Carpenter, p. 39; Wellesz, "Nativity Drama," p. 151; idem, *Eastern Elements in Western Chant: Studies in the Early History of Ecclesiastical Music* (Copenhagen: Munksgaard, 1947), p. 154; La Piana, pp. 182–83; Flanigan, "Review of Scholarship" (1976), p. 114; McGee, "Liturgical Placements," p. 26.

# [2

# Renaissance Theater and the Transition from Feudalism to Capitalism

The Introduction to this book traced similarities between the English and Spanish theaters from the 1570s to the 1640s to the simultaneous but independent fusion of popular and learned dramatic traditions in each country, a fusion that in turn depended on the development of the absolutist state. If this claim is plausible, one would expect to find not merely significant parallels between Spain and England, but also substantive divergences everywhere else in Europe from the pattern in those two countries. Thus, an approach to the English and Spanish stages must first answer the broadest questions about the relationship between theater and society in the sixteenth and seventeenth centuries. This chapter mainly involves a process of elimination, designed to explain why the other theaters of the Renaissance failed to achieve a balanced synthesis of the learned and popular heritages. It concludes, however, by considering the positive forces at work before 1575 that led to English and Spanish uniqueness.

As early as the sixteenth century, capitalism began to succeed feudalism as the dominant mode of production in western Europe. Its original development probably dates from twelfth-century Italy and Flanders and from thirteenth-century Germany. But the decisive steps forward throughout western Europe occurred only after the feudal crisis and the subsequent decline of serfdom, processes in which the towns of the West seem to have played a crucial role. Yet the sixteenth and seventeenth centuries witnessed not the definitive triumph of capital on an international scale, even in western Europe, but the gradual transition from feudalism to capitalism. The variable interaction of these two ultimately irreconcilable modes of production shaped both the heterogeneous social formations of the age and the structures of the emergent form of the state, the absolute monarchy.

At least at the political level, however, the struggle between feudalism and capitalism was unequal. Western European absolutism represented the reaction of the feudal nobility primarily to the decline of serfdom in the country and secondarily to the rise of capitalism in the city. The concentration of political power in the monarchy ended the feudal parcellization of sovereignty. Complementarily, economic power was consolidated in the aristocracy as absolute private property. Both changes facilitated the oppression and exploitation of the peasantry for the benefit of the traditional ruling class. The ideology of this new kind of state conflicted with reality as a matter of course: the centralizing monarchy presented itself and was often quite widely viewed as a national and nationalist institution, governing impartially in the best interests of an entire, albeit hierarchically ordered, polity. But, as Perry Anderson observes, absolutism "was never an arbiter between the aristocracy and the bourgeoisie, still less an instrument of the nascent bourgeoisie against the aristocracy."[1] A transitional reorganization brought about by a class that could never entirely control the social and economic forces that threatened its hegemony, the absolutist state was the mechanism for the perpetuation of feudal power.

Its social character is confirmed by its geographical distribution in Europe. Centralizing monarchies came to power almost wherever the feudal nobility was the dominant class. In western Europe, France under Louis XIV saw the fullest establishment of absolutism, but Spain, England, Sweden, Portugal, Piedmont, and Naples underwent similar developments. On the other hand, where towns were strong and the landed aristocracy relatively weak—as in northern and central Italy, Flanders, and southern and western Germany—the result was urban autonomy, a series of petty local microabsolutisms, or foreign domination, rather than a national monarchy. In eastern Europe the aristocracy emerged from the feudal crisis as the unambiguous victor in the class struggle, reducing the peasantry to serfdom for the first time and breaking the autonomy of the towns. Yet absolutism eventually became the characteristic form of the state there too, above all in response to the military threat posed by Western, and especially Swedish, absolutism in the seventeenth century. But Eastern absolutism also possessed an internal rationale, the strengthening of serfdom. The economic upturn throughout Europe during the sixteenth century spurred the resurgence of urban life in the East. More important, the vast and underpopulated regions of eastern Europe consistently attracted enserfed peasants, offering them both freedom and free land. Only a centralized state could exercise sufficient might to enforce feudalism.

[1]Perry Anderson, *Lineages of the Absolutist State* (London: NLB, 1974), p. 18.

What was the relationship between the theater and these broad economic and political configurations of the period? Perhaps the decisive innovation in the drama, as in many other areas of culture, was the recovery and adaptation of the structures, styles, subjects, and themes of the classical world—a process termed the Renaissance by the age itself as well as by subsequent commentators.[2] The classical heritage replaced clerical ideology, which had exercised hegemony through the late Middle Ages, as the dominant learned tradition in the theater. One side of the distinctive synthesis in England and Spain, it was revived first and most fully in Italy but ultimately had at least a fragmentary impact almost everywhere on the continent. In a general sense, the social basis for the recovery of antiquity in the theater was the gradual transition from feudalism to capitalism. The drama was as a result both evolutionary and revolutionary. Partly medieval and feudal, partly modern and bourgeois, it was in essence neither. Yet the uneven development of the classicizing impulse suggests the need for more precise specification. As a geographical survey from east to west will reveal, the urban fusion of aristocracy and bourgeoisie usually produced the combination of population, culture, liquid wealth, leisure, and social refinement in a largely secular context that typically underlay a classicist or Renaissance drama.[3] In other words, the end of parcellized sovereignty accorded to the nobility a far more active role in the theater than it had had during the Middle Ages. The extent of the synthesis between the new neoclassical drama—itself primarily a phenomenon of western Europe—and the popular theatrical heritage depended, however, on a particular moment in the trajectory of the absolutist state.

## EASTERN EUROPE

The eastern half of the continent may be treated briefly, since the weakness of the towns precluded a significant classicizing movement. The citizen classes were not strong enough either to create a powerful culture of their own or to draw the nobility from the countryside. A burgeoning absolutism in the absence of capitalism produced meager results on the stage. Yet the significant, though partial, exceptions to this

[2]Wallace K. Ferguson, *The Renaissance in Historical Thought: Five Centuries of Interpretation* (Cambridge, Mass.: Houghton Mifflin, 1948).

[3]Ferguson, *The Renaissance* (1940; rpt. New York: Holt, Rinehart and Winston, 1967), esp. pp. 8, 51, 60, 109, 112, emphasizes this class relationship for the Renaissance in general; Jacob Burckhardt, *The Civilization of the Renaissance in Italy*, trans. S. G. C. Middlemore, introd. Benjamin Nelson and Charles Trinkaus (New York: Harper and Row, 1958), 1:151, 180–82, and 2:353–60, for Italy alone.

pattern merit attention, in part because they suggest that the bourgeoisie had more to do with neoclassical theater than did the monarchy.

Far to the east in Russia there was little, if any, drama based on ancient models. Despite Latin influences, including the pedagogical advocacy of neoclassical dramatic theory, both the school and the court stage remained resolutely medieval.[4] Scarcely modified by western European theater of the Middle Ages and virtually untouched by a Latin cultural and religious tradition that had penetrated almost every other corner of the continent, Russia was simply too alien to adapt at first to the new aesthetic, with all its attendant implications. Socially, Russia's environment was not necessarily more inimical to Renaissance drama than were those of several other eastern European regions. But its cultural distance was such that neoclassicism did not affect the theater before conscious westernization set in during the eighteenth century. The country is thus important in demonstrating the autonomous force of national cultural heritage.

By contrast, the various lands of the Austrian Habsburg empire generally conformed to what was the typical eastern European pattern: a modest but discernible humanist drama before 1600 and Jesuit school plays in the late sixteenth and seventeenth centuries. Within this unity, however, the imperial homeland differed from its possessions. Directly influenced by Counter-Reformation Italy, the Austrian monarchy fostered a flourishing court theater from the time of the Thirty Years' War. The opposite occurred in the outlying areas. Both Hungary and Bohemia adopted Protestantism in the sixteenth century. At least in the former country, the Reformation spurred the development of neoclassical vernacular drama. The military triumph of the Counter-Reformation in Austria's territories during the Thirty Years' War in turn crushed Magyar and Czech humanism.[5]

Elsewhere in eastern Europe, generally in regions both closer to the West and enjoying relative commercial prosperity, the neoclassical stage

[4]Boris Vasil'evich Varneke, *History of the Russian Theatre: Seventeenth through Nineteenth Century,* trans. Boris Brasol, rev. ed. Belle Martin (New York: Macmillan, 1951), pp. 15–32; D. S. Mirsky, *A History of Russian Literature from Its Beginnings to 1900,* ed. Frances J. Whitfield (New York: Vintage Books, 1958), pp. 31–32, 36–38.

[5]Margret Dietrich, "Le livret d'opéra et ses aspects sociaux à la cour de Léopold I<sup>er</sup>," in *Dramaturgie et société: Rapports entre l'oeuvre théâtrale, son interprétation et son public aux xvi<sup>e</sup> et xvii<sup>e</sup> siècles,* ed. Jean Jacquot, with Elie Konigson and Marcel Oddon (Paris: Editions du Centre National de la Recherche Scientifique, 1968), 1:203; Heinz Kindermann, "Rapports entre le baroque de cour et le baroque populaire dans la vie théâtrale du xvii<sup>e</sup> siècle en Autriche," in *Dramaturgie et société,* ed. Jacquot, 1:191; Tibor Klaniczay, "From the Eleventh to the Eighteenth Century," in *History of Hungarian Literature,* by Tibor Klaniczay, József Szauder, and Miklós Szabolcsi, ed. Szabolcsi, trans. József Hatvany and István Farkas (London: Collet's; Budapest: Corvina Press, 1964), pp. 23, 26, 39–40, 45–46, 48, 53–54, 56; H. Jelinek, *Histoire de la littérature tchèque,* vol. 1, *Des origines à 1850,* 4th ed. (Paris: Editions du Sagittaire, 1930?), pp. 153–54, 172.

proved more durable. On the Dalmatian coast, and particularly in the free city of Dubrovnik, a secular Croatian Renaissance theater reached its height in the late sixteenth and early seventeenth centuries. Here Italian models were paramount, with the Republic of Venice's Dalmatian dominions providing the obvious and fundamental, but by no means unique, conduit by which their influence was transmitted.[6] The adoption of classicism was probably also smoothed by the political parallels between Dubrovnik and the Italian and classical cities from which the Croats borrowed.

A slightly different structural similarity may lie behind the development of Renaissance theater in eastern Germany. Somewhat surprisingly, the leading center of the humanist stage anywhere in the nation during the sixteenth century was the Duchy of Saxony, situated in the East. The explanation of this apparent anomaly perhaps lies in the area's distinctive social configuration. Saxony resembled the absolutist West not only in its powerful monarchy and nobility, but also in its relatively free peasantry, entrenched bourgeoisie, and high level of commercial activity. Yet its drama reveals its Eastern provenance ideologically, in an advocacy of quietism.[7] The significance of this last trait can be gauged by turning to the seventeenth century, by which time German theatrical preeminence had migrated eastward to the directly contiguous province of Silesia. Technically part of the Austrian Habsburg empire, of which it was the most commercialized region, Silesia probably was culturally influenced primarily by Saxony and other points farther west. It was in Silesia, as the Thirty Years' War drew to a close, that the *Trauerspiel*, or mourning play, was composed, mainly for the Protestant school stage, but also for the court.[8]

Andreas Gryphius's *Papinianus*, illustrative of the form, concerns the political martyrdom of the chief advisor to the Roman emperor Bassianus. Once the latter murders his brother and coruler, the plot, such as it is, turns on Papinianus's response to his vulnerable situation. In fact there is no suspense: the protagonist is unswervingly principled, stoical, and otherworldly. Unable to support Bassianus for ethical reasons, Papinianus remains equally unmoved by friend or foe, by the murder of his

[6]Antun Barac, *A History of Yugoslav Literature*, trans. Petar Mijušković (1955; rpt. Ann Arbor: University of Michigan, Department of Slavic Languages and Literatures, 1971), pp. 29, 32–34, 43.

[7]Roy Pascal, *German Literature in the Sixteenth and Seventeenth Centuries: Renaissance-Reformation-Baroque*, vol. 2 of *Introduction to German Literature*, gen. ed. August Closs (New York: Barnes and Noble, 1968), pp. 61–64; Derek van Abbé, *Renaissance Drama in Germany and Switzerland* (Melbourne: Melbourne University Press, 1961), pp. 21, 65, 75, 79–80, 88, 101–2; Anderson, pp. 256–59.

[8]Pascal, pp. 115, 118; Theodoor Weevers, *Poetry of the Netherlands in Its European Context, 1170–1930* (London: University of London, Athlone Press, 1960), pp. 124–39; Anderson, pp. 266, 317.

son or the opportunity to lead a popular rebellion. The play despairs of effective secular activity, a despair inadequately compensated for by a Christian resignation that promises, but does not deliver, transcendence. Behind it lies the experience of the Thirty Years' War and, more specifically, the overwhelming weight of absolutism on the aristocracy. Papinianus's refusal to serve the emperor simultaneously precludes worldly action of any kind. Although the monarchy may be oppressive, particularly to a Protestant playwright alarmed by Habsburg pressure, it cannot be challenged. In the dramatic stasis, even paralysis, of *Papinianus,* one may discern the historical and ideological impasse of an aristocracy more ruthlessly integrated into the state bureaucracy than was the case anywhere in the West.[9]

The experience of the Polish nobility was just the opposite. The triumph of an aristocratic republic based on religious toleration was accompanied by the most consistently antiurban policy of any European ruling class. Despite these seemingly unpropitious circumstances, Poland was the only country in the East to experience a major turn to the classical past in the sixteenth century. Its strong medieval tradition of Latinity may have encouraged this development. Moreover, in the social configuration of republican Rome—aristocratic dominance resting on coerced agricultural labor—the nobility, unlike any other class on the continent, was able to discover a striking parallel to its own position. Finally, benefiting from the enormous expansion during the sixteenth century of the Baltic grain trade with the West, Poland became the wealthiest and most powerful nation of eastern Europe. Among the towns, Cracow led this advance, becoming the center of Polish humanism as well.

*The Dismissal of the Grecian Envoys,* by Jan Kochanowski, an aristocrat and former student at Cracow University with close ties to the West, was performed by gentry youth before the king in 1578 to celebrate the wedding of one of the nation's wealthiest and most powerful aristocrats. Rigorously classical in form, the tragedy concerns the outbreak of the Trojan War. Perhaps because Poland's unusual political structure eliminated conflict between nobility and crown, the action of the play is considerably slighter even than that of *Papinianus.* But the same historical conditions ultimately give *The Dismissal of the Grecian Envoys* a more dynamic cast than Gryphius's *Trauerspiel.* Despite the presence of the monarch in the audience, Kochanowski makes no effort to magnify the authority of Priam. Instead modeling his portrayal of the Trojan council of state,

---

[9]Anderson, pp. 224–29, 306–9; Walter Benjamin, *The Origin of German Tragic Drama,* trans. John Osborne, introd. George Steiner (London: NLB, 1977), who overemphasizes the similarities of the *Trauerspiel* to the far more popular English and Spanish drama of the seventeenth century.

something of a collective protagonist in the work, on the operations of the Polish Diet, he presents an aristocracy in political command but riven by faction. The force of the tragedy derives not only from the audience's foreknowledge that the pacifistic course advocated by Antenor, and apparently by Kochanowski as well, will be rejected, but also from an awareness that in 1578 Poland was preparing for war against Russia, with which the playwright explicitly associates the ancient Greeks. Thus, on the one hand, *The Dismissal of the Grecian Envoys* conveys a sense of doom and fatality; on the other, its latent nationalism in an age of Polish power results in an insistence on at least the potential ability of the ruling class to make the proper decisions and so to master its own destiny. Poland scored a decisive victory over Russia in the war of 1578. But though Kochanowski's historical analogy was inaccurate in the immediate context, it was prophetic in the long run. The very political divisiveness and irrationality diagnosed in his tragedy finally led to the total dismemberment of the nation.[10]

## THE WESTERN PERIPHERY

In much of western Europe as well, the lack of an urban synthesis between nobility and bourgeoisie limited the vitality of a classicizing drama. Scandinavia, though possessed of a rural nobility, was hampered by a social configuration atypical of the West—feeble towns, a weak bourgeoisie, and low commercialization—but akin to eastern Europe's. Unlike the nations of the East, however, its economy rested to a considerable extent on free peasant labor, a condition that sufficed to align subsequent Scandinavian history fundamentally with that of the remainder of the West.[11] In a comparative survey of western European theater of this period, then, Scandinavia serves an exemplary purpose. Its embryonic stage—far more rudimentary an institution than in most other parts of Europe—suggests that the bourgeoisie, rather than the aristocracy, was the senior partner in the formation of neoclassical drama.

[10]Anderson, pp. 282–98; O. Halecki, "The Renaissance in Poland: Cultural Life and Literature," in *The Cambridge History of Poland*, vol. 1, *From the Origins to Sobieski (to 1696)*, ed. W. F. Reddaway et al. (Cambridge: Cambridge University Press, 1950), pp. 272–86; A. Brückner, "Polish Cultural Life in the Seventeenth Century," in *The Cambridge History of Poland*, vol. 1, ed. Reddaway et al., pp. 557–69; Manfred Kridl, *A Survey of Polish Literature and Culture*, trans. Olga Scherer-Virski (New York: Columbia University Press, 1956), pp. 42, 48–52, 74–75, 93–99; Czesław Miłosz, *The History of Polish Literature* (London: Macmillan, 1969), pp. xiii–xiv, 27–37, 60–61, 68–74, 95–99, 106–8, 111–19; Janusz Pelc, "Polish Literature of the Renaissance Epoch," trans. Piotr Groff, in *Poland: The Land of Copernicus*, ed. Bogdan Suchodolski, trans. Bogusław Buczkowski et al. (Wrocław: Polish Academy of Sciences Press, 1973), pp. 163–92.

[11]Anderson, pp. 178–80.

For Iceland there are no records of any dramatic activity before 1750. Norway's position is much the same, but during the third quarter of the sixteenth century the Bergen Cathedral school, located in what was then the nation's largest city, produced classical Latin comedy as well as vernacular plays perhaps influenced by humanism. By contrast, Danish drama developed well within the sixteenth century, primarily owing to the economic, social, and cultural impact of nearby Germany. Latin neoclassical plays date from the 1520s, and school drama in Latin, German, and Danish became fairly frequent after 1550. Although theater in Denmark remained predominantly religious until the end of the seventeenth century, the few extant texts, most of them from the period between 1570 and 1610, reveal a partial approximation to classical form. In addition, an isolated neoclassical satirical farce survives from the 1670s.[12]

That Sweden's school theater, though more extensive than Norway's, lagged behind Denmark's would not at first appear to occasion any surprise. But Sweden underwent rapid absolutist consolidation in the sixteenth century and the international triumph of its monarchy in the seventeenth—an experience reasonably close to the one so crucial for the theater in France, Spain, and England. The Swedish crown does seem to have taken a more active interest in the theater than did its Danish counterpart.[13] Otherwise, however, the country could not escape Scandinavian social reality, and in particular the absence of widespread towns, trade, industry, or commercial agriculture.[14] Within a larger Scandinavian context, the example of Sweden reveals that even a Western-style absolute monarchy could not in itself lead to neoclassical drama.

Western Germany and the Netherlands faced the opposite, more characteristically Western problem. In their cities, few aristocrats complemented the dominant burgher class. On the one hand, the density of urban settlement precluded the formation of absolutism and thus a political structure similar to France's, Spain's, or England's. On the other, the towns of Germany and the Low Countries rarely acquired adequate

[12]Stefán Einarsson, *A History of Icelandic Literature* (New York: Johns Hopkins Press for the American-Scandinavian Foundation, 1957), pp. 209–12; Theodore Jorgenson, *History of Norwegian Literature* (1933; rpt. New York: Haskell House, 1970), pp. 123–25; Harald Beyer, *A History of Norwegian Literature,* trans. and ed. Einar Haugen (New York: NYU Press for the American-Scandinavian Foundation, 1956), pp. 78–80, 98; and Phillip Marshall Mitchell, *A History of Danish Literature,* 2d ed. (New York: Kraus-Thomson Organization Limited, 1971), pp. 53–60, 71–72, 76.

[13]Alrik Gustafson, *A History of Swedish Literature* (Minneapolis: University of Minnesota Press for the American-Scandinavian Foundation, 1961), pp. 69–71, 107–8; Weevers, pp. 140–41; Lennert Breitholtz, "Le théâtre français à Stockholm aux xvii$^c$ et xviii$^c$ siècles," in *Dramaturgie et société,* ed. Jacquot, 1:419–23.

[14]Anderson, pp. 182–83.

weight in feudal society to conquer the surrounding countryside. Unable to become territorial city-states, they failed to incorporate the local aristocracy and hence to provide a geographical ground on which the urban and rural ruling classes might meet.[15]

Why was the bourgeoisie, in the absence of the feudal landowners, incapable of fostering a major Renaissance theater? In western Germany this question can usefully be rephrased: What forces prevented the development of a drama that was at once vernacular, secular, and humanist? Throughout northern Europe urban lay culture retained a more religious character than in Italy, while in Germany the continued separation of burgher and noble may have perpetuated this situation.[16] More specifically, the courts, aristocratic halls, and learned private societies that sponsored plays in Italy and the absolutist West had few parallels in Germany. There, neoclassical theatrical production was largely limited to the schools, institutions whose dramatic language was often Latin and whose ideological orientation was didactic and religious, particularly after the Reformation and Counter-Reformation.[17] As long as the humanist stage remained an adjunct of pedagogy, it could become neither secular nor vernacular.

If, on the other hand, it emerged from the confines of the school in search of a broader public, the nonexistence of either a homogeneously educated audience drawn from the upper classes or of a national secular literary language resulted in the loss of its classical features.[18] Perhaps this attempt to fuse popular and learned traditions also ran into a social barrier. The advanced development of capitalism may have produced a split not only between country and city, but also between bourgeoisie and artisanate within the towns. The result was the consolidation of two fairly distinct urban cultures. In Strassburg, the thriving humanist theater unsuccessfully attempted to bridge this gap. Instead of combining disparate materials into something new and original, it oscillated between classicist Latinity and a popular vernacular—evidence of its inability to make a simultaneous dual appeal, much less a single encompassing one. In Nuremberg, an analogous effort came from below, from the theater of the artisans. Hans Sachs, the master of the *Fastnachtsspiel*, borrowed from learned drama and also tried his hand at neoclassical composition. After 1550 his theater shows the influence of staging based on antique models. Yet his longer plays have not won admiration from

[15]Anderson, pp. 150 n. 12, 159–60 n. 29, 247, 250–51; Ferguson, *The Renaissance*, pp. 104–5.

[16]Ferguson, *The Renaissance*, pp. 111–12.

[17]Pascal, pp. 16, 61; Boris Ravicovitch, "Le dramaturge face à la société et au public dans le théâtre humaniste strasbourgeois (1538–1621)," in *Dramaturgie et société*, ed. Jacquot, 1:185.

[18]Pascal, p. 60; Ravicovitch, pp. 181, 189–90.

modern scholars, while his *Fastnachtsspiele* regularly convert characters derived from classical sources into contemporary German commoners, regardless of their historical, national, and social origins. The very strength of the tradition in which he worked may have had a similar institutional effect, inhibiting the emergence of a commercial theater and thus of a drama along French, Spanish, or English lines.[19] These dilemmas probably were insuperable in themselves. Any chance of a significant western German Renaissance theater was eliminated, however, first by the gradual decline of the towns after 1550 and then by the disastrous wars of the seventeenth century.

Within a common unity, Dutch drama seems to have differed in important respects from its German counterpart.[20] Its crucial period occurred later, in an international context more favorable to neoclassical theater than the early sixteenth century had been. The drama that developed in the United Provinces mainly after 1600 was vernacular, secular, neoclassical, and independent of the schools. In western Germany, medieval burgher corporatism inhibited humanist drama; in the northern Netherlands, a revolution and an ensuing republic made it irrelevant. Whereas in Germany the problem was the failure of the neoclassical tradition, in the United Provinces the problem was its success. One area had not yet reached a point where it could foster Renaissance drama; the other had irrevocably gone beyond that point. Dutch theater of the seventeenth century reveals the incompatibility of neoclassical drama and the bourgeois state.

During the fifteenth and most of the sixteenth centuries, the Low Countries remained under centralized aristocratic rule, first of the Burgundian dukes and then of the more genuinely absolutist Habsburg monarchs. No synthesis of foreign nobility and native bourgeoisie occurred, however, because of the ethnic and linguistic split between the two classes. Throughout this period and even beyond, Dutch drama developed primarily in the Chambers of Rhetoric, which preserved a didactic, allegorical, and meditative medieval heritage and specialized in the morality play.[21] With the outbreak of the eighty years' rebellion

[19]Ravicovitch, pp. 184–90; Pascal, p. 60; Joel Lefebvre, "Le jeu du carnaval de Nuremberg au xv<sup>e</sup> siècle et au xvi<sup>e</sup>," in *Le lieu théâtral à la Renaissance*, ed. Jacquot, with Konigson and Oddon (Paris: Editions du Centre National de la Recherche Scientifique, 1964), pp. 188–89; Carl Niessen, "La scène du 'Laurentius' à Cologne et le nouveau document sur le Heilsbrunner Hof à Nuremberg," in *Le lieu théâtral*, ed. Jacquot, pp. 197–200.

[20]Given the absence of basic research, this must remain a tentative statement. See the three essays on the subject in the initial issue of *Dutch Studies* (1974): W. A. P. Smit, "The Dutch Theatre in the Renaissance—a Problem and a Task for the Literary Historian," pp. 44–69; Lieven Rens, "The Project on Renaissance Drama in Antwerp," pp. 70–88; C. A. Zaalberg, "Studies on Hooft, 1947–1972," pp. 89–102.

[21]Reinder P. Meijer, *Literature of the Low Countries: A Short History of Dutch Literature in the Netherlands and Belgium* (Assen, Netherlands: Van Gorcum, 1971), pp. 48–49, 79; Weev-

against Spain in 1568, the theater, like virtually all other aspects of life in the Low Countries, changed fundamentally and permanently. The war moved the center of culture and of drama from its traditional southern location in present-day Belgium, which remained under Habsburg control, to the revolutionaries' more northerly holdings, roughly coextensive with the contemporary Netherlands.[22] Despite the contributions of the Dutch nobility and the often conservative aspirations of the rebels, the war against Spanish rule should probably be seen as a bourgeois revolution.[23] Certainly the new Dutch nation was characterized by the concentration of population, wealth, and power in the towns; the development of insurance, a stock exchange, and low-interest banking; the expansion of manufacturing and overseas trade; and, beneath even the substantial artisan-shopkeeper stratum, the emergence of proportionally the largest proletariat in Europe, which provided the basis for this growth.[24] Given this victory of the bourgeoisie and comparative weakness of the aristocracy, a strongly neoclassical vernacular drama might not have come into being at all. But by 1550, and especially after 1575, even the conservative Chambers of Rhetoric began to register the impact of classicism.[25] The literary inspiration for this change seems to have come partly from foreign example, ancient and modern, Latin and vernacular, but even more from the Latin school drama and dramatic theory of the university of Leiden.[26]

The relation of the resultant plays to Dutch society was problematic. Serious drama in particular faced grave obstacles. Leaving aside the large issue of the possibility of bourgeois tragedy, one may still question the potential efficacy of a strictly classical bourgeois tragedy. To be

ers, pp. 102, 104; J. E. Uitman, "Les fêtes baroques d'Amsterdam de 1638 à 1660: L'intelligibilité de leurs motifs allégoriques et historiques pour le public contemporain," in *Dramaturgie et société*, ed. Jacquot, 1:226.

[22]Meijer, pp. 72, 89–91, 100, 104; Weevers, p. 192; J. L. Price, *Culture and Society in the Dutch Republic during the 17th Century* (London: B. T. Batsford, 1974), pp. 12–15.

[23]Conservative tendencies: Weevers, p. 103; Arnold Hauser, *Renaissance, Mannerism, Baroque*, vol. 2 of *The Social History of Art*, trans. Hauser and Stanley Godman (New York: Vintage, 1963), p. 210. Bourgeois revolution: J. W. Smit, "The Netherlands Revolution," in *Preconditions of Revolution in Early Modern Europe*, ed. Robert Forster and Jack P. Greene (Baltimore: Johns Hopkins Press, 1970), pp. 19–54, esp. pp. 51–53.

[24]K. H. D. Haley, *The Dutch in the Seventeenth Century* (London: Thames and Hudson, 1972), pp. 9–99 and passim; Charles Wilson, *The Transformation of Europe, 1558–1648* (Berkeley and Los Angeles: University of California Press, 1976), pp. 138–82; Geoffrey Parker, "Why Did the Dutch Revolt Last Eighty Years?" *Transactions of the Royal Historical Society*, 5th ser. 26 (1976): 53–72.

[25]W. A. P. Smit, "The Dutch Theatre," p. 61; Meijer, pp. 79, 93–101, 109, 111, 118, 127; Weevers, pp. 102–4, 116.

[26]W. A. P. Smit, "L'évolution des idées sur la tragédie dans le théâtre de Vondel," in *Le théâtre tragique*, ed. Jacquot (Paris: Editions du Centre National de la Recherche Scientifique, 1970), pp. 287–94; idem, "The Dutch Theatre," pp. 46–50, 54, 67–68; Meijer, pp. 77, 100, 129; Weevers, pp. 103, 107–8, 112, 114; Price, pp. 90, 98–99, 105, 183.

sure, the intense earnestness and sobriety of much of the drama seems in keeping with the tenor of middle-class Dutch culture. In western Europe of this period, moreover, a specifically tragic seriousness often depended on the perceived legitimacy of the state, a legitimacy that the nascent republic undoubtedly possessed in the eyes of its populace. The cultivation of the national history play is an even more striking sign of bourgeois consciousness. Its frequent debt to the writings of Tacitus[27] suggests an important area of compatibility between antiquity and capitalism. But neoclassical dramatic form—or at least neoclassical tragic form—was not designed to embody the social reality or cultural ideals of a bourgeois state. Its doctrine of decorum in subject, style, and characterization rested on a class ideology that left scant room for the serious portrayal of everyday life. In addition, this principle was regularly combined with a commitment to the unity of place, which effectively restricted the action to the court and its surroundings at a time when the princes of Orange were geographically, economically, socially, culturally, and on occasion even politically peripheral to Dutch urban existence.[28]

The dramatists were generally unable to resolve this contradiction. In *Baeto* (1617) P. C. Hooft attempts a solution by means of constitutional monarchy. The play concerns the legendary founding of Holland by the Batavians, a pagan Germanic tribe of classical antiquity. Grotius, who helped popularize the subject, emphasized the Batavians' collective, moral, and republican character. Hooft's version projects similar contemporary values into the past, opposing absolutism and Spanish power while advocating Protestantism and popular rebellion. But at the same time *Baeto* includes a protagonist apparently modeled on William the Silent, prince of Orange and aristocratic hero of the early years of the Dutch rebellion, and promotes elective monarchy—substantive changes from Grotius's rendition of the myth. Both modifications are consequences of Hooft's support for the House of Orange against the class of his birth, the urban oligarchy, a shift of allegiances that simultaneously moved him toward the predominantly aristocratic ideological center of Renaissance serious drama but away from the fundamental orientation of the United Provinces.[29]

A number of difficulties followed from these aesthetic and political principles. First, Hooft seems to have been betrayed by his classicism. His witches, led by Medea, have little of the emotional and psychological power that they exercise in Senecan tragedy or for that matter in *Macbeth*.

[27]Weevers, pp. 192–93.

[28]Erich Auerbach, *Mimesis: The Representation of Reality in Western Literature*, trans. Willard R. Trask (Princeton: Princeton University Press, 1953), esp. pp. 554–57; Price, pp. 90, 99–101; Meijer, pp. 113–14.

[29]Weevers, p. 118; Wilson, pp. 229–30; Price, pp. 37, 111–12.

In fact they clash incongruously with the main model for the play, book 2 of the *Aeneid*. Functioning largely as external decoration, they inadvertently remove the theme of the drama from the present. Even the far more integral Virgilian material is curiously unsatisfying both as neoclassicism and as political commentary, probably because Hooft infuses it with his own pacifistic longings. Prince Baeto, like Aeneas a paragon of filial piety, abandons one city in order to found another, not, however, because he has been driven out, but because he refuses to triumph over his father, the king, who has been misled by Baeto's evil stepmother. In this way the young prince snatches defeat from the jaws of victory. When William the Silent chose exile over submission to the Spanish, on the other hand, the immediate motive was not piety but peril, and his long-term aim not migration but rebellion. Hooft's rendering, while faithful to the fact, is antithetical to the spirit of the Dutch republic. Finally, classical form prevents Hooft from portraying the relationship between crown and populace that a commitment to limited monarchy entails. The characters in *Baeto* are as aristocratic as those in *Phèdre*. Although Hooft attempts with some success to introduce the common point of view into his choruses, the crucial creation of an elective monarchy is entirely a matter of noble initiative, with the chorus of soldiers reduced to two brief cries of support.

Unlike Hooft, J. van den Vondel was not hampered by an aristocratic outlook. A consistent opponent of the House of Orange and defender of the republic, he particularly extolled Amsterdam's bourgeois commercial preeminence, despite himself being born in Brabant and always belonging to religious minorities. *Gijsbreght van Aemstel* (1638), like *Baeto* a national history play, depicts the siege of Amsterdam in 1300.[30] Deeply colored by bourgeois ideology, it celebrates the heroic resistance of the town's citizens to the treacherous, and ultimately successful, onslaught of local feudal forces. In its comic gatekeeper, a distant relative of *Macbeth*'s porter, it introduces a popular element absent from *Baeto*. More important, much of the play constitutes a hymn to married love: the plot comes to life in the domestic dispute between the titular character and his wife that occupies much of act 5. Finally, the conclusion offers a vision of the future greatness of an imperial, Protestant, republican, and bourgeois Amsterdam.

Because these values are less ambiguously expressed than in *Baeto*, their conflict with classicism is correspondingly more evident: the con-

---

[30]Price, pp. 105–7; H. H. J. de Leeuwe, "Le théâtre d'Amsterdam durant les saisons 1659 et 1660: Sa réaction à l'actualité politique et aux attaques calvinistes," in *Dramaturgie et société*, ed. Jacquot, 1:220; W. Gs. Hellinga, "La représentation de 'Gijsbreght van Aemstel' de Vondel: Inauguration du Schouwburg d'Amsterdam (1638)," in *Le lieu théâtral*, ed. Jacquot, pp. 326–27.

tent and form of *Gijsbreght van Aemstel* are at odds. Once again, the plot is modeled on the second book of the *Aeneid*, but perhaps even more than in Hooft's play this source imparts an epic, undramatic quality to the action. Equally disturbing is the inappropriateness of Virgil's story to Dutch history. Where Aeneas leaves Troy for Rome, the lesser city for the greater, Gijsbreght forsakes Amsterdam to establish an obscure town in Prussia, thus moving from the greater city to the lesser. The true analogue of Virgilian Rome has nothing to do with Gijsbreght's efforts: it is Amsterdam itself, but in the time of Vondel. The action of the play is thus at best peripheral and perhaps irrelevant to its ideological import.

Despite the prevalence of defeat, destruction, and death in both *Baeto* and *Gijsbreght van Aemstel*, neither work is deeply tragic in tone. As national history plays, they inevitably point toward a heroic future, to the successful formation and international triumph of the United Provinces. Genuine tragedy seems to have required a different vehicle, in this instance sacred history. Vondel's *Lucifer* (1654) was perhaps indirectly and partially inspired by the continuing struggle between the Amsterdam oligarchy and the House of Orange, a struggle Vondel had dramatized at least once before.[31] It may draw in particular upon the crisis of 1650, in which the Amsterdam regents triumphed over the increasingly monarchical William II. William's premature and accidental death resulted in a twenty-two-year vacancy in the office of stadholder, the leading post in the republic and one normally filled by the prince of Orange.[32]

In Vondel's tragedy, the post of stadholder is occupied by Lucifer. The rebellion that he eventually directs is at least partly the conservative act of a disloyal vassal, afraid that his firstborn rights will be usurped by the parvenu human race. Followed by a faithful retinue, he demonstrates his nobility in heroic defeat. *Lucifer*'s most interesting moments occur earlier, however, in the titular character's hesitations between fidelity and betrayal in act 4. Here Vondel conjures up the inner life fundamental to bourgeois literature. Arguably, *Macbeth* is a tragedy of bourgeois consciousness, created by a playwright imaginatively capable of a sympathetic rendering of that consciousness despite his profound antipathy to its consequences as he understands them. *Lucifer* is the reverse, a tragedy of aristocratic consciousness, written by a bourgeois dramatist who extends his understanding to the plight of the nobility. Vondel does not in this way dispose of all the problems of bourgeois classical tragedy. His play continues to suffer from a static stateliness. Perhaps he would have been wiser to anticipate Milton's decision to eschew drama in favor of epic. For all that, *Lucifer* represents an ingenious and original solu-

[31]Meijer, pp. 130–31.
[32]Haley, pp. 112–14.

tion to the central dilemma of Golden Age Dutch drama. *Baeto* is too aristocratic for its country but too bourgeois for its form; *Gijsbreght van Aemstel* succumbs to the latter difficulty even more visibly. *Lucifer*, on the other hand, moves an aristocratic figure to the center of the action, but apparently without sacrificing the ideology of Vondel's earlier play.

The difficult relation of neoclassical serious drama to ordinary Dutch life contrasts strikingly with the synthetic abilities of the comedy. G. A. Bredero's *Spanish Brabanter* (1617), based on *Lazarillo de Tormes*, neatly combines classical and popular materials in a way that recalls the plays of Aretino, Bruno, and Jonson. Its satiric vision seems to capture the language and life of Amsterdam's streets.[33] This achievement, generally denied to the Dutch history play or tragedy, surely depended in part on the neoclassical concept of decorum, which oriented comedy toward the depiction of everyday reality. Here, but not in tragedy, the gap between the learned and popular traditions was relatively easy to bridge. Tragedy thus provides the most telling sign of whether the full integration of those traditions in fact occurred.

## Italy

The problem of synthesis is raised even more acutely by the sixteenth-century Italian stage. A pioneering neoclassical drama spread throughout the peninsula, often drew on popular culture, and profoundly influenced the professional acting companies of the country—a pattern repeated in England, Spain, and France. Yet the outcome of this influence in Italy differed greatly from what later happened in the other three countries. Italian theatrical exceptionalism rested on Italian political exceptionalism. The Italian city-state and the Western absolutist state made possible divergent forms of drama. In Italy the precocious development of capitalism and the consequent absence of absolutism, national unity, and a national capital limited the extent of the fusion between popular and learned traditions in the theater.

The early development of mercantile capitalism in Italy established the preconditions of the classical revival by fostering the growth of urban civilization. The medieval towns proved sufficiently strong first to overthrow episcopal rule and then to defeat imperial efforts to install a peninsulawide feudal monarchy. Following the removal of the papacy from Italy soon after, in the fourteenth century, the northern and cen-

[33]H. David Brumble III, introduction to *The Spanish Brabanter: A Seventeenth-Century Dutch Social Satire in Five Acts*, trans. Brumble, Medieval and Renaissance Texts and Studies 2 (Binghamton, N.Y.: Center for Medieval and Early Renaissance Studies, State University of New York at Binghamton, 1982), pp. 1–34.

tral towns found themselves in a vacuum. With the main buttresses of feudalism gone, urban culture and society could develop freely for the first time since antiquity.[34] In addition, though nearly all of the medieval Italian communes eventually evolved into hereditary tyrannies, or *signorie*, two of the leading centers of the Renaissance—Florence and Venice—were capitalist republics. Well before classicism had spread throughout the country, the threat of tyranny inspired a specifically Florentine civic humanism, conscious of republican parallels in the great city-states of antiquity.[35] Most of the humanists, in Florence and elsewhere, were not aristocrats but professionals—lawyers, public secretaries, and teachers. The gradual diffusion of the Renaissance beyond Tuscany depended primarily on the common urban character of much of Italy, regardless of variations in government.[36]

Yet even in Florence and Venice other forces were also at work. Although Tuscany and the Veneto had among the highest urban densities in Europe, roughly three-fourths of the population in both regions continued to live on the land. More important, the social composition of the dominant classes in the towns differed noticeably from the pattern in northern Europe, probably because of the unique dynamism of the Italian city-states. Far earlier than elsewhere in Europe, commercial vitality exercised an attractive force on the rural aristocracy, drawing it to urban centers. The Italian towns actually reversed the prevalent power relations of feudalism, conquering the surrounding countryside, or *contado*, and thus incorporating a substantial portion of the traditional ruling class within their boundaries.[37] Finally, the transformation of the Renaissance from a Florentine into an Italian phenomenon followed a relative decline of the political and economic power of the bourgeoisie on the peninsula, roughly coincident with the rise of the urban tyrannies. Often of seigneurial origin and always dependent on rural military power, the *signori* encouraged a self-consciously aristocratic and courtly culture. Even Florence eventually succumbed to this process of "refeu-

---

[34]Anderson, pp. 143–48; Denys Hay, *The Italian Renaissance in Its Historical Background* (Cambridge: Cambridge University Press, 1961), pp. 58–59; Burckhardt, 1:21–22, 182.

[35]Hans Baron, *The Crisis of the Early Italian Renaissance*, rev. ed. (Princeton: Princeton University Press, 1966).

[36]Hay, pp. 69, 112–21, 150, 177–78; Peter Burke, *Culture and Society in Renaissance Italy, 1420–1540* (London: B. T. Batsford, 1972), pp. 34–43, 229–30, 268–70, 293–302; Ferguson, *The Renaissance*, p. 76; Paul Oskar Kristeller, *Renaissance Thought: The Classic, Scholastic and Humanist Strains* (New York: Harper and Row, 1961), pp. 11–13, 102–3; idem, *Medieval Aspects of Renaissance Learning*, ed. and trans. Edward P. Mahoney, Duke Monographs in Medieval and Renaissance Studies, no. 1 (Durham, N.C.: Duke University Press, 1974), pp. 3–25; M. L. Bush, *Renaissance, Reformation and the Outer World* (London: Blandford Press, 1967), pp. 158–64.

[37]Burke, *Culture and Society*, p. 252; Anderson, pp. 150 n. 12, 159–60 n. 29; Philip Lee Ralph, *The Renaissance in Perspective* (New York: St. Martin's Press, 1973), pp. 34–38, 93–96.

dalization."[38] In all these senses, then, one can speak of the copresence of nobility and bourgeoisie in Italian towns.

Neoclassical vernacular drama emerged shortly after 1500, during this final political stage of the Italian city-state, dominated the peninsula during the sixteenth century, and went on to influence theatrical developments almost everywhere else on the continent.[39] For this reason Italy may seem a norm from which other nations in varying degrees diverged. But in crucial respects the Italian stage, like the society in which it developed, was itself the anomaly, especially in comparison with the theaters in the main Western absolutist states. The most prominent dramatists of these other countries—Marlowe, Shakespeare, and Jonson; Lope de Vega, Tirso de Molina, and Calderón de la Barca; Corneille, Molière, and Racine—were known in their own times, and are remembered today, above all for the plays they composed for the commercial stages of the national capitals—London, Madrid, and Paris. Matters stand differently with the Italian playwrights. Ariosto and Tasso wrote chivalric epic, Bruno was a philosopher, Della Porta won fame during his lifetime mainly as a scientist,[40] Machiavelli was a political theorist and historian. Their plays were usually designed for an upper-class, learned audience, often at court as an accompaniment to other festivities. Further, Ariosto and Tasso wrote in Ferrara, Della Porta and Bruno in the Kingdom of Naples, and Machiavelli in Florence. The Italian neoclassical theater of the sixteenth century was largely an amateur, elite, occasional, regional affair.

Not surprisingly, the primary social orientation of this drama blocked a full appropriation of popular materials. The regional dispersal of the stage may have had a similar effect. In the absence of a centralized state, dramatists understandably found it difficult to write about the nation as a whole and to take seriously all of its classes. Yet regional variation also meant that some areas were more likely than others to effect at least a partial union of popular and classical materials. Theater in Tuscany,

[38]Alfred von Martin, *Sociology of the Renaissance*, trans. W. L. Luetkens (London: Kegan Paul, 1944), pp. 47–76; Anderson, pp. 154–62; J. R. Hale, *Florence and the Medici: The Pattern of Control* (London: Thames and Hudson, 1977), pp. 79–83.

[39]The following discussion depends primarily on the data presented in Marvin T. Herrick, *Tragicomedy: Its Origins and Development in Italy, France, and England*, Illinois Studies in Language and Literature, no. 39 (Urbana: University of Illinois Press, 1955); idem, *Italian Comedy in the Renaissance* (Urbana: University of Illinois Press, 1960); idem, *Italian Tragedy in the Renaissance* (Urbana: University of Illinois Press, 1965). See also Douglas Radcliff-Umstead, *The Birth of Modern Comedy in Renaissance Italy* (Chicago: University of Chicago Press, 1969); Louise George Clubb, introduction to *Italian Plays (1500–1700) in the Folger Library* (Florence: Leo S. Olschki, 1958), pp. vii–xl; idem, "Italian Renaissance Comedy," *Genre* 9 (1976): 469–88.

[40]Clubb, *Giambattista Della Porta, Dramatist* (Princeton: Princeton University Press, 1965), introd. and chap. 1.

and especially in Florence, retained a popular and, even more, a bourgeois character; in the Veneto popular impulses had some influence;
and in Urbino, Mantua, and above all Ferrara a courtly atmosphere prevailed.[41]

As seventeenth-century Dutch stage history suggests, synthesis was
more readily available in comedy than tragedy. Not surprisingly, Florence and, to a lesser extent, Venice were the leaders in comedy,[42] a
pattern that has led at least one critic to associate the form with the
intellectual autonomy of the bourgeoisie.[43] The triumph of a nationally
comprehensible, universalized Tuscan as the literary language of
learned comedy,[44] by contrast, must have impeded the verbal fusion of
upper- and lower-class culture anywhere but Florence and its environs.
Yet popular motifs entered neoclassical comedy throughout Italy—for
example, in Ariosto's *La Lena* (Ferrara), Machiavelli's *La mandragola*
(Florence), Bruno's *Il candelaio* (Kingdom of Naples), and Aretino's *La
cortigiana* (Rome, but composed by a Tuscan author). *La cortigiana*,
in particular, though very loosely classical, in many ways subverts the
norms of Italian regular comedy in addition to drawing freely on popular material and possessing an improvisational character.[45] On the other
hand, Aretino's closest analogue in the English theater is Jonson, probably the most rigorously classical of the London playwrights.

A more genuinely, though still ambiguously, popular figure is to be
found, significantly enough, in the Veneto. No other sixteenth-century
Italian playwright was better equipped than the Paduan actor-dramatist
Ruzante to bring about the kind of synthesis that later characterized the
English and Spanish theaters, nor was any other more successful in this
respect. The bastard son of an urban nobleman, he managed his family's
farm property, wrote plays about the local peasantry, and performed
them before elite audiences in Venice. His unusual sympathy for the rural lower class is derived in large measure from his personal experience,
of course, but also from the beleaguered military position of the Venetian republic in the immediately preceding years. At that time the urban
population came to recognize the importance of the peasants as both soldiers in the armed forces and suppliers of food. The result was a drama
at times both popular and learned. Yet Ruzante's plays seem to suggest
what was in fact the truth: that it was ultimately impossible to unite the

[41]Clubb, introduction to *Italian Plays*, p. xi; Radcliff-Umstead, passim; Mario Apollonio,
*Storia del teatro italiano*, vol. 2 (Florence: G. C. Sansoni, 1951), pp. 1–39.

[42]Herrick, *Italian Comedy*, p. 112; Apollonio, 2:141.

[43]Nino Borsellino, "Rozzi et Intronati: Pour une histoire de la comédie à Sienne au xvi[e]
siècle," in *Dramaturgie et société*, ed. Jacquot, 1:149–59.

[44]Clubb, introduction to *Italian Plays*, p. xi.

[45]Mario Baratto, *Tre studi sul teatro (Ruzante-Aretino-Goldoni)* (Venice: Neri Pozza, 1964),
pp. 71–102; Radcliff-Umstead, pp. 157–64.

urban and rural worlds. Symptomatically, he is most admired today not for his synthetic efforts but for *Parlamento* and *Bilora,* peasant farces composed in the Paduan dialect. Set in the period after the return of peace, the two works focus on the misery of the peasants and their oppression by Venice. Comedy proves, on the one hand, generically inappropriate to the protagonist's painful life but, on the other, psychologically necessary as a defense against a grim and irremediable situation. In this way Ruzante's plays reveal the impermanence of the historical conjuncture that made their creation possible.[46] Perhaps, finally, *Parlamento* and *Bilora* indicate paradigmatically the cultural gulf separating the upper classes of the city from the lower classes of the country, a gulf produced by an extraordinary urban vitality that in turn prevented the establishment of a national absolutism.

Yet just as popular material often found its way into a learned comic tradition, national perspectives at times emerged from a regionally based theater. Alone among the centers of Italian Renaissance drama, Naples, as part of the Spanish empire, was ruled by an absolutist state. Madrid in fact exercised tighter control there than it could in Barcelona.[47] Just as the Calvinists proved consistent foes of absolutism, the centralizing monarchs supported and in turn derived support from the Counter-Reformation, with the king serving as the earthly executor of the providential plan. The uniqueness of Naples should not be overemphasized, however. A somewhat weaker instance of Counter-Reformation monarchism helps to account for the transcendental implications of such pastoral tragicomedies as Tasso's *Aminta* and Guarini's *Il pastor fido* at the ducal court in Ferrara. In general, the impact of absolutism and the Counter-Reformation led to a movement from satiric to providentially romantic comedy on much of the peninsula in the late sixteenth century.[48]

Giambattista Della Porta, in his romantic comedy *Gli duoi fratelli rivali,* integrates Counter-Reformation absolutist ideology with the history of the Kingdom of Naples and of his own family. To control their southern

[46]Baratto, pp. 11–68; Radcliff-Umstead, pp. 209–36; Franco Fido, "An Introduction to the Theater of Angelo Beolco," *Renaissance Drama,* n.s., 6 (1973): 203–18.

[47]Anderson, p. 69.

[48]The following discussion of late-sixteenth-century Italian drama is primarily indebted to Clubb, "The Moralist in Arcadia: England and Italy," *Romance Philology* 19 (1965): 340–52; idem, "Italian Comedy and *The Comedy of Errors,*" *Comparative Literature* 19 (1967): 240–51; idem, "The Tragicomic Bear," *Comparative Literature* 24 (1972): 17–30; idem, "The Making of the Pastoral Play: Some Italian Experiments between 1573 and 1590," in *Petrarch to Pirandello,* ed. J. A. Molinaro (Toronto: University of Toronto Press, 1973), pp. 45–72; idem, "La mimesi della realtà invisibile nel dramma pastorale italiano e inglese del tardo rinascimento," *Misure Critiche* 4 (1974): 65–92; idem, "The Arts of Genre: *Torrismondo* and *Hamlet,*" *ELH* 47 (1980): 657–69; idem, "Shakespeare's Comedy and Late Cinquecento Mixed Genres," in *Shakespearean Comedy,* ed. Maurice Charney (New York: New York Literary Forum, 1980), pp. 129–39.

Italian possession, the Spanish had to reach a compromise with the local, entrenched aristocracy.[49] The marvelous unraveling of Della Porta's plot, which draws, not coincidentally, on a mixture of Italian and Spanish dramatic materials,[50] effects just such a reconciliation between two ethnically distinct branches of the same class, previously at odds with one another. After a series of conflicts, tricks, misunderstandings, mistaken identities, and near disasters, the two rival brothers, nephews of the Spanish viceroy, marry the two daughters of old Eufranone Della Porta, a gentleman from Salerno impoverished by his support for an unsuccessful rebellion against Spanish power. The result is a new, unified Spanish-Italian ruling class that is spiritually noble, providentially justified, immensely wealthy, and socially exclusive.

A rarefied sense of honor governs the conduct of every aristocrat in the play but Don Flaminio, the unscrupulous brother whose misdeeds motivate the action. Yet he is the exception who proves the rule, consistently recognizing that his passionate plots violate an exalted code that gives meaning to his life and, after some moral backsliding and much good fortune, ultimately repenting his rash errors. When this final resolution comes into view, his uncle unhesitatingly interprets the earlier troubles as part of a divine plan whose sole purpose was to unite the two brothers with the two sisters. Having at last understood the providential pattern, the good viceroy proceeds in appropriate Counter-Reformation monarchical fashion to assist in its fulfillment. As a reward for their virtue, he gives the Della Porta daughters huge dowries and makes them his heirs. He then extends his beneficence to the lower classes, freeing and pardoning all imprisoned debtors and personally paying their debts from his apparently limitless resources. Finally he spares Leccardo, the gluttonous and scheming parasite, who had earlier been sentenced to death. If the gifts to the brides represent the triumph of justice, then the acts of forgiveness signify an overflow of mercy. The lower-class characters in the play are socially incapable of understanding, much less accepting, the standard of conduct that the aristocrats live by. Della Porta's comedy, then, presents a nobility at play, but in such a way as to reveal that class's confidence in the validity of its dominant political, social, and economic position. *Gli duoi fratelli rivali* ends with the ruling class happily united and firmly in control of both the immorality of its own members and the amorality of the under classes.[51]

One would expect a still more overt consideration of political and in-

[49]Anderson, p. 69.
[50]Clubb, *Della Porta*, pp. 203–4. The subsequent discussion of this play is indebted to the same work, esp. pp. 202–13.
[51]See Anderson, pp. 54, 81–82, however, for seventeenth-century revolts against Spanish rule in the region—by no means the first of their kind.

deed national issues from tragedy. Yet scholars regularly note, and deplore, the lack of precisely such concerns in sixteenth-century Italian tragedy, despite the genre's appeal primarily to a courtly audience.[52] Perhaps the absence of an indigenous absolutism, of a fit dramatic subject, stood in the way. Though Naples formed a partial exception, its monarchy was foreign. Ducal power in a town like Ferrara, by contrast, was domestic but, to quote Anderson, as in most of the *signorie*, "in a deep sense illegitimate: it rested on recent force and personal fraud, without any collective social sanction in aristocratic hierarchy or duty behind it. The new princedoms had extinguished the civic vitality of the republican towns; but they could not rely on the loyalty or discipline of a seigneurialized countryside."[53] Republican Venice had, if anything, an even weaker feudal base than the tyrannies, but it derived its political authority from an entirely different source.

Aretino's *La Orazia*, first performed in Venice, ties the well-being of the state to serious conflicts. Set in the early, monarchical days of Rome, the play nevertheless has a republican orientation that guides the action. Although Orazio's military exploits receive their due, in no sense do they acquire transcendent importance. The heroic ideal of Rome in general and the Orazii in particular is unquestionably affirmed, but its locus is transferred from Orazio to his aged father, from martial to spiritual greatness. In this *tragedia di fin lieto* (tragedy with a happy ending), the military savior of Rome is pardoned for the murder of his sister not because he is innocent, for he is not, nor because he has performed extraordinary deeds and remains necessary to the defense of the state, since such considerations fail to sway those entrusted with deciding his fate. Instead, his father's pathetic pleas and his own spiritual constancy in the face of death eventually move his judges to leniency.

These judges are the Roman people, fully developed in the play, treated with dignity and respect by dramatist and characters alike, and representative of the just will of Rome. Aretino in this way attempts to mediate between mercy and justice, between personal heroic patriotism and the law, between aristocratic voluntarism and the popular will. In general, the corporate rather than the individualist position gets the best of it: the people's decision is largely vindicated by divine vocal intervention, itself the culminating anticipation in the play of Counter-Reformation themes and techniques. But this resolution is also rooted in Venetian life. The republic's famed rigorous legal tradition, later evoked in *The Merchant of Venice*, lies behind the stern treatment of the errant national hero. Finally, the state's unusual structure of power may have

---

[52]Claude Margueron, "La tragédie italienne au xvi^e siècle: Théorie et pratique," in *Le théâtre tragique*, ed. Jacquot, pp. 135–36.

[53]Anderson, p. 162.

shaped the play even more crucially. In Venice ultimate authority rested not, as elsewhere in Italy, with a single ruler, but with a long-established, highly legitimate, paternalistic oligarchy. Perhaps this collectivity, despite its exclusiveness, inspired Aretino to project a democratic ideal at once utopian and mystifying, to make Rome, rather than Orazio alone, the protagonist of his work.

Yet this highly selective look at a primarily learned tradition may partly miss the point. Perhaps these Italian playwrights are best compared not with Jonson, Calderón, and Corneille, but with Gascoigne, Torres Naharro, and Garnier, amateur neoclassical dramatists whose works eventually influenced the commercial theater. Something similar happened in Italy. The *commedia dell'arte*—popular, professional, and successful for well over a century—drew freely on the learned theater, converting its borrowings into standardized techniques, types, and scenarios. It effected, in other words, a genuine synthesis of popular and neoclassical traditions. Why was the literary result a series of scenarios, rather than the plays of Shakespeare, Lope de Vega, or Molière? K. M. Lea, a leading scholar in the field, writes: "The intercourse and interaction between the two types [*commedia erudita* and *commedia dell'arte*] . . . modifies but does not change the essential distinction between them. It might be hazarded that it was for lack of a co-ordinating genius that all the literary and theatrical talent failed to produce a national Italian drama."[54]

This formulation, though it begs the question, hints at a more plausible hypothesis. The *commedia dell'arte*, despite its appeal to all social strata, was directed mainly toward wealthier circles and in time toward an international, rather than a merely local or even national, audience. One can detect a distant echo of this pursuit of an elite clientele by the actors in seventeenth-century England and Spain, a pursuit that contributed to the supersession of the public theater. In Italy, the primarily upper-class orientation of the *commedia dell'arte* perhaps explains the scarcity of permanent commercial theaters,[55] elsewhere a crucial complement to professional acting companies. The political fragmentation of the country, furthermore, precluded the establishment of a national capital like those of the Western absolutist states, in which a disproportionate percentage of the upper classes regularly congregated. Perhaps, then, a permanent commercial theater catering especially to the rich, such as emerged in seventeenth-century Paris and London, had no ade-

[54]K. M. Lea, *Italian Popular Comedy: A Study in the "Commedia dell'Arte," 1560-1620, with Special Reference to the English Stage* (1934; rpt. New York: Russell and Russell, 1962), 2:341.

[55]For the possible Venetian exception, see Apollonio, vol. 3 (Florence: G. C. Sansoni, 1956), pp. 142–43; Licisco Magagnato, *Teatri italiani del Cinquecento* (Venice: Neri Pozza, 1954), p. 55; David Brubaker, *Court and Commedia: The Italian Renaissance Stage* (New York: Richards Rosen Press, 1975), p. 111.

quate material basis on the peninsula. In Italy, the failure to produce a national drama resulted not from the lack of a genius but from the lack of a nation.

## FRANCE

Even more than Italy, France represents a crucial negative test for an argument attempting to explain the distinctiveness of England and Spain. Absolute monarchs, centered in Paris, London, and Madrid, ruled the three countries. During the seventeenth century, important stage traditions developed in these national capitals, and especially in the permanent commercial theaters. Yet the result in France was a generally neoclassical drama, in this respect reminiscent of the Italian stage, rather than a synthesis of popular and learned elements, as occurred in Spain and England. This unique outcome arose from the complex interaction of theater and society, especially in Paris. An unusually potent amateur medieval theatrical tradition combined with an unusually rapid transition from a very weak to a very strong absolutism. A fusion like the one in Spain or England could probably have occurred only in the brief interval between these two historical periods of the state, but the inhibiting effect of the dramatic heritage guaranteed that it did not.

France, Spain, and England experienced nothing comparable to the social evolution of northern and central Italy. The development of capitalism remained far more rudimentary for centuries, with the result that the social and economic conditions for a classical revival on the Italian scale were long absent. For these countries even to imitate Italian culture, two conditions had to be fulfilled. First, the gradual "refeudalization" of Italian society rendered its cultural products both accessible and attractive elsewhere in western Europe, where feudalism remained far more entrenched.[56] On the other hand, the rest of the continent had to meet Italy halfway. In most of medieval western Europe outside Italy, burghers dominated the towns while aristocrats resided in the country. Following the feudal crisis, the decline of serfdom led to the spread of absolute private property on the land and, more generally, to the freer growth of capitalism. The rise of absolutism involved the creation of urban courts that attracted both the previously rural nobility and the burghers. In the sixteenth century, though England, Spain, and France remained largely aristocratic, interaction between the bourgeoisie and the nobility greatly increased: the bourgeoisie became more aristocratic, the

---

[56]Hay, pp. 179–203, esp. 188–89; Kristeller, *Renaissance Thought II: Papers on Humanism and the Arts* (New York: Harper and Row, 1965), pp. 69–88.

aristocracy more bourgeois.[57] The turn to antiquity in these countries nonetheless represented a far less decisive rupture with the Middle Ages than had been the case in Italy.[58]

In France during the second half of the sixteenth century, one can distinguish between humanist and popular drama, between amateur and professional performance, and between the provinces and Paris. These dichotomies are not strictly parallel to one another. The works of such neoclassical playwrights as Robert Garnier often entered the repertories of the touring commercial acting companies that first appeared in the provinces during the 1580s. In Paris, on the other hand, the amateur Confrérie de la Passion enjoyed a theatrical monopoly. Performing at the Hôtel de Bourgogne, the city's one permanent theater, the fraternity presented a generically medieval repertory, centered on the farce, in which classicizing drama had no place. The political situation posed even greater obstacles. Four decades of civil war—dividing France along religious, geographical, and class lines—ruled out national unity of any kind, much less the consolidation of absolutism. At the very time when the public theaters of Spain and England were being established, the possibility of a French national stage became increasingly remote.[59]

The end of the century brought major changes, however. Under Henry IV the civil wars came to an end, a policy of national reconciliation within the aristocracy was adopted, court and capital were fixed in Paris, and tentative measures toward royal centralization were introduced. At the same time, the Confrérie began leasing out the Hôtel de Bourgogne to professional companies: Paris had its first permanent, public, commercial theater. In other words, conditions in the French capital between about 1600 and 1625 roughly duplicated those in Madrid and London a quarter of a century earlier. And indeed, the plays of Alexandre Hardy, composed and performed during this period, significantly resemble much Spanish and English drama of the late sixteenth century. *Mariamne* employs a generally classical form to frame the character of the blustering Herod, adapted from the medieval popular stage.

[57]Ferguson, *The Renaissance*, pp. 90–112; Immanuel Wallerstein, *The Modern World-System: Capitalist Agriculture and the Origins of the European World-Economy in the Sixteenth Century* (New York: Academic Press, 1974), p. 160.

[58]Douglas Bush, *The Renaissance and English Humanism* (1939; rpt. Toronto: Toronto University Press, 1962), pp. 69–99.

[59]Brian Jeffery, *French Renaissance Comedy, 1552–1630* (Oxford: Oxford University Press, 1969); Geoffrey Brereton, *French Tragic Drama in the Sixteenth and Seventeenth Centuries* (London: Metheun, 1973), pp. 7–47, 50–51; idem, *French Comic Drama from the Sixteenth to the Eighteenth Century* (London: Methuen, 1977), pp. 1–9; Herrick, *Tragicomedy*, p. 172; Robert Weimann, *Shakespeare and the Popular Tradition in the Theater: Studies in the Social Dimension of Dramatic Form and Function*, ed. Robert Schwartz (Baltimore: Johns Hopkins University Press, 1978), p. 178; Henry Carrington Lancaster, *A History of French Dramatic Literature in the Seventeenth Century*, Part 1, *The Pre-Classical Period, 1610–1634* (Baltimore: Johns Hopkins Press, 1929), 1:13; Anderson, pp. 90–93.

Its concentration on the tyrant/martyr conflict turns, finally, into an apotheosis of married love that has a homey, even bourgeois, feel. *Scédase*, based on one of Plutarch's narratives, dramatizes the tragic and murderous victimization of the Boeotian peasantry by the unscrupulous Spartan nobility. Indebted to Seneca, replete with mythological allusion, but ignoring the unities of time and place, the play represents a genuine fusion of popular and learned culture. Its lament for the decline of traditional Spartan values and complementary idealization of the countryside might be taken for a typical expression of conservative aristocratic ideology during the transition to capitalism were it not for Hardy's unambiguous class sympathies. Having failed to obtain legal redress for the rape and murder of his daughters, Scédase doubts the existence of either social or metaphysical justice, decides that life is absurd, and concludes the tragedy in appropriate neoclassical fashion with his own suicide.[60]

Yet Hardy seems to have achieved little popularity in Paris until the 1620s. A number of forces were working against the drama during the first twenty-five years of the seventeenth century. French national unity, first of all, rested more on a truce between opposing parties than on a real community of interest. Instead of the relative religious uniformity of Spain or even of England, France enjoyed religious toleration following the Edict of Nantes. Its theater, moreover, especially compared with the London stage, lacked the patronage of crown or aristocracy. Whereas in the English and Spanish capitals during the late sixteenth century there were always at least two public theaters in operation and hence a constant competitive stimulus, the Hôtel de Bourgogne retained its monopoly. Probably more important was the relative youth of French professional acting, in 1600 perhaps no more than twenty years old. The commercial companies that played in the first permanent theaters of Madrid and London were heirs of longer traditions. Finally, even after 1600, the strong heritage of farce at the Hôtel de Bourgogne continued to interfere with any efforts at a popular-neoclassical synthesis. In England and Spain, interaction between the learned and popular stage preceded by decades the opening of the first public theaters. But the taste of Parisian audiences had been formed by the amateur repertory. Companies that brought to the capital plays like *Scédase*—popular, but deadly serious—accordingly received a cool reception. The only successful professional actors before the 1620s were the farceurs.[61]

These, then, are some likely reasons why France, during the first

---

[60]Anderson, pp. 93–95; Brereton, *French Tragic Drama*, pp. 52, 58–99.
[61]W. L. Wiley, *The Early Public Theater in France (1580–1630)* (Cambridge: Harvard University Press, 1960), pp. 150, 207, 239, 250, 254–57; Maurice Descotes, *Le public de théâtre et son histoire* (Paris: Presses Universitaires de France, 1964), pp. 28–38; Brereton, *French Tragic Drama*, pp. 52–53; idem, *French Comic Drama*, pp. 9–10.

quarter of the seventeenth century, did not produce a drama like England's and Spain's, despite an analogous social and institutional milieu. Thereafter that milieu changed, and with it the possibility of a synthesis of popular and neoclassical theater receded as well. Although the reality of the transformation is beyond dispute, its explanation remains unclear: the relation between cause and effect is particularly vexed. Some central motifs may be discerned, however. Peacetime brought with it a gradual elevation in urban aristocratic taste. Detectable in some branches of literature as early as 1610, it began to affect the theater in the 1620s. Audience preference turned from farce first to the more classical plays of Hardy and then, even before 1630, to the still more classical and polished work of his immediate successors. After 1640, a relative decline in the mixed genre of tragicomedy coincided with the rise of more regular, classical tragedy. These trends were probably accompanied by a reduction in the lower-class component of the theatergoing public, perhaps because of rising admission prices, but perhaps simply in response to the modification of the repertory. In any case, an audience that may have been overwhelmingly popular in the early decades of the century was mainly drawn from the middle and upper classes after 1630. While the nobility favored tragedy, the plebeian remnant retained its allegiance to farce. The audience did not change in isolation. The quality of acting may have improved by the 1620s, at which time writers of more classicist inclination began to be attracted to the theater: Corneille's first play appeared in 1629. As of 1622, two professional companies were performing in Paris; in 1629 the theatrical monopoly of the Confrérie de la Passion finally came to an end.

Behind all these developments lay the rise of absolutism, particularly after Richelieu assumed power in 1624. Its initial impact on the stage was indirect. The centralizing policies of the crown may be seen first of all in the military suppression of Huguenot territorial independence and in the consequent political unification of the country. Royal consolidation also drew the aristocracy to the capital in ever greater numbers, integrated it into the state machinery, and fostered its cultural refinement and self-conscious exclusiveness. Richelieu's direct intervention in the theater, which followed most of the changes outlined above, consistently reinforced existing tendencies, linking the stage socially to the court and nobility and aesthetically to the neoclassical rules. The centripetal force of the cardinal's programs for society as a whole was thus reduplicated in the Parisian theater. The main victims of the refurbished French political apparatus were the lower classes; the same was true in the smaller world of the theater. Considerably more centralized than either the Spanish or the English monarchy, the French absolutist state, by the very rapidity of its success, closed off the possibility of a synthesis of popular and learned traditions and opened the way to a commercial, classical theater.[62]

The Parisian plays of the classical period did not, of course, necessarily differ from the drama of London and Madrid in all important respects. In England, Spain, and France, the unity of the stage was primarily a product and secondarily an agent of national unity. As previously noted, the perceived legitimacy of the state provided the underpinning for a specifically political tragedy in western Europe of this era. In these three absolutist states, tragedy, as well as much tragicomedy and historical drama, depended in particular on the presence of a nation governed by a traditional aristocracy, though in a new political form. The principal subject of these genres was precisely this class's conduct, and especially its ability to rule.[63] Because of the influence of popular traditions, the issue often fundamentally involved interclass relations in the Spanish and English theaters. On the French stage, by contrast, the neoclassical orientation produced a more exclusive focus on the aristocracy.

That class's experience during the sixteenth and seventeenth centuries was extremely troubled. The transition from feudal particularism to royal centralism everywhere proved difficult, for economic, social, and above all political reasons. In fact, the changing position of the landed ruling class with respect to the state may have determined the history of absolutism in the West. For instance, since monarchical consolidation entailed the suppression of traditional aristocratic prerogatives, the triumph of absolutism in the seventeenth century was attended by numerous revolts by the nobility, most of them ultimately suppressed.[64] It is this conflict that shaped French classical tragedy, as a review of the standard comparison between Corneille and Racine will reveal.

In the heroic plays of Corneille's first period, the social, political, and ideological legitimacy of the hereditary aristocracy is affirmed by both form and content.[65] This affirmation is won rather than assumed. The

[62]John Lough, *Paris Theatre Audiences in the Seventeenth and Eighteenth Centuries* (London: Oxford University Press, 1957), pp. 43, 71, 79, 81, 98–99, 148–49, 155–57; idem, *Seventeenth-Century French Drama: The Background* (Oxford: Clarendon Press, 1979), pp. 56–78; Wiley, pp. 150, 214, 222–23, 263, 273–79; Georges Mongrédien, *Daily Life in the French Theatre at the Time of Molière*, trans. Claire Elaine Engel (London: George Allen and Unwin, 1969), pp. 28, 54, 59–60; Antoine Adam, *Grandeur and Illusion: French Literature and Society, 1600–1715*, trans. Herbert Tint (London: Weidenfeld and Nicolson, 1972), pp. 201–6, 214–16; Descotes, pp. 59–73, 91–103; Brereton, *French Tragic Drama*, pp. 53–55, 100–25; Anderson, pp. 95–98.

[63]G. K. Hunter, "Italian Tragicomedy on the English Stage," *Renaissance Drama*, n.s., 6 (1973): 130–31.

[64]Anderson, pp. 40, 51–55.

[65]Jean Duvignaud, *Les ombres collectives: Sociologie du théâtre*, 2d ed. (Paris: Presses Universitaires de France, 1973), p. 334; Brereton, *French Tragic Drama*, pp. 127, 145; Herbert Lindenberger, *Historical Drama: The Relation of Literature and Reality* (Chicago: University of

repeated, but rapidly shifting clash between love and honor has fundamental political implications, especially for the struggle and ultimate accommodation of the nobility and the monarchy.[66] *Le Cid* reveals a refractory nobility in the difficult process of reconciliation with a nascent
absolutism. The excuse offered to the king, Fernand, for the defiant behavior of the count, Chimène's father, captures the essence of the feudal
ruling class's dilemma:

> une âme accoutumée aux grandes actions
> Ne se peut abaisser à des submissions.

(a soul accustomed to great deeds / Cannot abuse itself by such submis-
sions.)[67]

For the king, of course, true honor can never be at odds with obedience
to the throne. The count is the only figure in the play openly to challenge royal authority and also the only one to die. His defeat in a duel
with Rodrigue hardly establishes monarchical supremacy, however,
since private vengeance is a customary feudal right, explicitly opposed
by Fernand. The main antagonism in the play—between Rodrigue and
Chimène—thus has its origins in a feudal combat, but one unwittingly
instigated by a royal edict slighting the heroine's father in the act of
honoring the hero's. Within the context of aristocratic ideology, this
conflict is unresolvable. Yet the possibility of a happy outcome never
disappears, because the crown, though absolutist in aspiration, is also
high-minded and merciful, and Rodrigue, though committed to the preservation of family honor, remains unswervingly loyal to his king. A
compromise between feudal and monarchical values offers a way of
transcending a potentially tragic struggle.

Immediately following the news of the duel, Chimène approaches

---

Chicago Press, 1975), p. 103; Jean Rohou, "The Articulation of Social, Ideological and Literary Practices in France: The Historical Moment of 1641–1643," in *1642: Literature and
Power in the Seventeenth Century*, Proceedings of the Essex Conference on the Sociology of
Literature, July 1980, ed. Francis Barker et al. (Essex: University of Essex, 1981), pp.
139–65.
[66]Lough, *Paris Theatre Audiences*, pp. 158–59; Adam, p. 55; Lindenberger, pp. 123–
24, 145; Paul Bénichou, *Man and Ethics: Studies in French Classicism*, trans. Elizabeth Hughes
(Garden City, N.Y.: Doubleday, 1971), pp. 38, 64. But Bénichou, pp. 1–74, generally
stresses the purely feudal, antiabsolutist implications of Corneille's drama.
[67]Corneille, *Le Cid*, in *Théâtre choisi de Corneille*, ed. Maurice Rat (Paris: Editions Garnier
Frères, 1961), 2.6.583–84. Subsequent references to Corneille's plays are to this edition
and are noted in the text. The English version is from Jacques Guicharnaud, ed., *Seventeenth-Century French Drama* (New York: Random House, 1967), p. 22. Subsequent translations of French plays, except for *Horace*, are from this edition and are also noted in the
text.

Fernand, speaking in conventional terms of duty, honor, and blood, but basing her appeal on radically different grounds:

> j'en demande vengeance,
> Plus pour votre intérêt que pour mon allégeance.
>
> . . .
>
> Immolez, dis-je, sire, au bien de tout l'Etat
> Tout ce qu'enorgueillit un si haut attentat.
> (2.8.689–96)

(I ask for vengeance / More for your sake than to relieve my soul. / . . . / sacrifice, Sire, to the welfare / Of the whole state, the man that such an outrage / Has filled with pride. [Guicharnaud, p. 26])

The killing of her father, Castile's leading warrior, is for her an injury to the crown. In reply, Rodrigue's father, Don Diègue, attempts to defend his son by proposing a similar, but somewhat less convincing, conflation of aristocratic and absolutist ideology. A genuine synthesis can be achieved only by imperialist exploit, however, as Don Diègue astutely perceives in recommending to his despairing son the exercise of heroic valor in the service of the state:

> Ne borne pas ta gloire à venger un affront,
> Porte-la plus avant, force par ta vaillance
> Ce monarque au pardon, et Chimène au silence.
> (3.6.1092–94)

(Don't circumscribe your fame by this revenge / Of a private insult; carry it further now. / By your valor, compel the King to pardon, / Chimène to silence. [Guicharnaud, p. 39])

In other words, aristocratic voluntarism retains its traditional raison d'être, but within a new political apparatus: the nobility, despite the rise of absolutism, is not yet a class without a vocation. Thus, when Rodrigue succeeds in overcoming the Moorish menace, he not only wins royal pardon, but also in effect turns Chimène's earlier argument against her. Since his military exploits have won him a place of national importance comparable to that formerly occupied by her father, the demand for vengeance against him is transformed from a defense of the monarchy into an attack on it.

Having lost Fernand's aid, Chimène insists on satisfaction by combat, the recourse she had earlier deferred. The king delivers a diatribe against dueling but reluctantly agrees, subject to a number of restrictions designed to put an end to the vendetta. This compromise predictably results in both Rodrigue's victory and Chimène's public admission of her love, with the result that the king feels justified in enforcing their marriage. When Chimène questions the propriety of an overhasty wedding, the obliging ruler accordingly effects the final mediation in the play between aristocratic and monarchical interests. He postpones the marriage for a year, during which time Rodrigue will carry the war into Moorish territory, serving his king and by this means becoming even more worthy of Chimène. In conclusion, Fernand urges him to leave all remaining doubts and conflicts to "le temps, ta vaillance et ton roi" ("time, your valor and your king"), a suitable summary of the new social configuration at work (5.7.1840; Guicharnaud, p. 62). Thus, in *Le Cid*, even if Chimène remains resentful, the last word belongs to the king, and the last word is, quite literally, "king."

*Horace* begins essentially where the earlier play leaves off, with aristocratic family honor firmly associated with the absolutist state. This conjunction is then put to the test by a sequence of events that in the strongest possible way pits patriotism against the domestic concerns of the nobility, represented in this work by love. Between Horace's unquestioning allegiance to Rome and Camille's antithetical view of public affairs as a form of barbarism, Corneille presents a full spectrum of responses to the conflict, thereby providing a multiple perspective on the central heroic action. In fact, the dominant figures during the first four acts are two women, Camille and Sabine, the primary emotional victims of the quasi-civil war between Rome and Alba Longa. Moreover, none of the characters is a walking abstraction; even in the most extreme of them, the major dilemma is both internal and external.

As a result, when Horace is finally vindicated, it is impossible to avoid realizing that his exceptional virtues are inseparable from his considerable defects, that his triumph involves real human loss. Nonetheless, in the terms of the play, Horace clearly deserves his victory. Affairs of state must always take priority over affairs of family in any opposition between the two. The final act, in which this debate is definitively resolved, also witnesses the apotheosis of monarchy:

> le ciel entre les mains des rois
> Dépose sa justice et la force des lois.
> (5.2.1469−70)

(into the hands of kings heaven / Deposits its justice and the force of laws.)

Yet divine law does not seem to curb a king in relation to his subjects:

[111

le plus innocent devient soudain coupable,
Quand aux yeux de son prince il paraît condamnable.

(5.2.1539–40)

(the most innocent suddenly becomes guilty, / When in the eyes of his prince
he appears condemnable.)

A more merciful corollary of this position enables King Tulle to pardon Horace despite his guilt. Finally, the grounds for royal clemency—that Horace, because of his overriding service to the state, stands above the law—neatly equate the outstanding members of the promonarchical nobility with the monarchy itself. The contrast with the corresponding moment in *La Orazia* starkly reveals the ideological distance between legalistic republicanism and divine-right absolutism.

Far more than *Le Cid, Horace* suggests the implications of this reinvigorated mechanism of aristocratic political power. It does so by making explicit the social assumptions and boundaries of the absolutist state. Excluded, according to Horace's father, are "le peuple stupide" ("the stupid people"), the "vulgaire ignorant" ("ignorant commoners"), that great, silent majority of the population who, as King Tulle agrees, though they love their rulers, "ne peuvent pas / Par d'illustres effets assurer leurs Etats" ("cannot / By illustrious effects secure their states": 5.3.1711, 1724, 1749–50). Earlier, the masses of the contending armies were sympathetically linked to Camille and Sabine, the primary ideological foes of Horace. The soldiers express spontaneous revulsion at the prospect of mortal combat between two families intimately joined to each other by marriage, love, and friendship. This interclass association was possible because Sabine and Camille, for all their nobility, do not primarily act on the specifically feudal, or even generally aristocratic premises that motivate the characters in *Le Cid*. Rather, they are first and foremost women, a social fact that partly explains the necessity of Horace's triumph and Camille's death. As Peter Burke suggests: "Perhaps one should see noblewomen as mediators between the group to which they belonged socially, the elite, and the group to which they belonged culturally, the non-elite."[68] If the nobility is to retain its privileged position, it must honor its military vocation against foreign foes while distinguishing itself rigorously from the larger domestic population of women and members of the lower class that it mistreats or exploits. However great the costs and however inevitable the accompanying ambivalence, only thorough incorporation into the absolutist state can preserve the aristocracy from the double danger—external and internal—that it confronts. In the

---

[68]Burke, *Popular Culture in Early Modern Europe* (New York: Harper and Row, 1978), p. 28.

course of the seventeenth century, much of Europe's traditional landed ruling class learned precisely this lesson, often through painful experience. Though not necessarily Corneille's explicit meaning, such is also the significance of *Horace*.

The contrast between the early heroic plays of Corneille and the tragedies of Racine, or more generally between early and late seventeenth-century French serious drama, is marked and defined by the Fronde, the final and unsuccessful aristocratic rebellion against absolutist consolidation in France. The outcome of this struggle in effect put an end to the heroic politics of the nobility and helped turn tragedy toward a concern with love.[69] Within this historical and theatrical development, Racine's work may be viewed as an answer and a challenge to Corneille's. On the one hand, the forms of aristocratic preeminence are accepted, refined, concentrated, even apotheosized.[70] At the same time, however, the content points in the opposite direction, revealing through the powerful, irrational passions of the protagonists the inner weakness of the aristocracy. Racinian tragedy is thus an attack from the inside, an act of subversion. Stage conventions confirm this point. In the seventeenth-century French theater, the three unities and perspective scenery generally reinforced the ideological norms of the upper-class sector of the audience. A play set at court, for example, focused exclusive attention on the highest circles of the aristocracy, while the single plot reduced the diversity of represented experience. Similarly, perspective staging fixed the characters in a coherent framework, a framework that offered a perfect visual vantage point, however, to only a lone seat in the house, the one characteristically occupied by the king. For Racine, however, the resulting intensity and formalism seem also to imprison the protagonists, to distort their souls, to suggest, above all, that conservative social codes fail to do justice to the complexity of the human psyche.[71] This doubleness is nicely evoked by Roland Barthes: "the tragedy is simultaneously prison and protection against impurity, against all that is not itself."[72]

*Athalie,* Racine's final play, apparently lacks such ambivalence, however. Chronicling the overthrow of Athalie, a follower of Baal, and the consequent restoration to the throne of the line of David, and hence of Christ, the work seems to side clearly with Joad, high priest of the temple of Jerusalem and organizer of the rebellion. Certainly, *Athalie* is con-

---

[69]Adam, pp. 221–26; Descotes, pp. 103–9.

[70]Auerbach, pp. 370–94.

[71]Duvignaud, pp. 271–353; Stephen Orgel, *The Illusion of Power: Political Theater in the English Renaissance* (Berkeley and Los Angeles: University of California Press, 1975), pp. 1–36; Timothy Murray, "Theatrical Legitimation: Forms of French Patronage and Portraiture," *PMLA* 98 (1983): 170–82.

[72]Roland Barthes, *On Racine,* trans. Richard Howard (New York: Hill and Wang, 1964), p. 5.

sistent with absolutist ideology in its support of Joas, the rightful heir. Perhaps, too, the surprising sympathy developed for Athalie indicates a loyalty to power, whatever its legitimacy. Yet these two positions are evidently incompatible: one cannot simultaneously defend de facto rule and legal succession. Furthermore, emphasis on the corruption of the court, on Athalie's past crimes, and, most striking of all, on Joas's future crimes works against allegiance to the crown. The absolute monarch is at once to be loved and hated, sought and shunned, defended and attacked.

*Athalie* concentrates on external, overtly political, action. Racine's focus, in some of his other works, on the emotional vagaries of the court has at times led, with some justification, to the conclusion that the plays are apolitical.[73] On the other hand, they succeed in constructing a direct connection between inner and outer life. In *Phèdre*, the heroine's illicit passion is set in a tense political context, involving contenders for the succession and the future of the state. Hippolyte's feelings about Aricie combine the dynastic with the amorous, Phèdre hopes to placate Hippolyte with the bribe of power, and Thésee repeatedly labels his son a traitor for supposed incestuous designs on Phèdre.[74] The relationship between the affairs of the psyche and the affairs of state emerges most clearly, however, in one of Phèdre's characteristic acts of self-examination. Offered political power in Athens, she replies:

> Moi, régner! Moi, ranger un Etat sous ma loi,
> Quand ma faible raison ne règne plus sur moi!
> Lorsque j'ai de mes sens abandonné l'empire!
>
> (3.1, p. 566)

(I reign? To place the State / Under my law, when reason reigns no longer / Over myself; when I have abdicated / From the empire of my senses. [Guicharnaud, p. 254])

The metaphorical equation of self-control and political control is a common motif in ruling-class ideology of the period. In *Gli duoi fratelli rivali*, when the viceroy hesitates to punish his beloved but guilty nephew, he is promptly rebuked: "Signor Viceré, chi non sa reggere e comandare a' suoi affetti, lasci di reggere e comandar agli altri" ("My lord viceroy, he who cannot rule and command his affections should leave off ruling and commanding others").[75] On the other hand, the presence of a female

---

[73]Auerbach, pp. 377–79.

[74]*Phèdre*, in *Théâtre complet*, ed. Rat (Paris: Editions Garnier Frères, 1960), 2.2; 3.1, pp. 567–68; 4.1–2, passim. Subsequent references are noted in the text.

[75]*Gil duoi fratelli rivali: The Two Rival Brothers*, ed. and trans. Clubb (Berkeley and Los Angeles: University of California Press, 1980), 5.1.5–7.

protagonist in a tragedy of sixteenth- or seventeenth-century Europe characteristically indicates a retreat from the unsatisfying world of politics.

*Athalie* and *Phèdre* thus provide grounds for linking Racine's deep pessimism, pervasive sense of doom, and tragic perspective—all of them less evident in Corneille's heroic plays—to the crisis of the aristocracy. For this reason, although one can trace a decline of the heroic mode or, complementarily, discern a rise of fatalism in French drama, it is wrong to attribute any such changes to a tendency intrinsic to serious drama.[76] The shift from Corneille to Racine depended on the evolving relations between aristocracy and monarchy, relations that impinged directly on the theater. Racine's drama may also have been more specifically influenced by the Jansenism he apparently shared with that branch of the *noblesse de robe* injured by absolutist consolidation. For these *officiers*, Jansenism became an offensive class weapon, directed against that fusion of feudal and monarchical ideology ultimately affirmed in Corneille's heroic plays.[77] Since the *officiers*, like the dissident nobility, had participated in the Fronde, Racine's personal experience may have reinforced, intensified, even given intellectual coherence to the less articulate malaise of the defeated aristocracy.

Yet the subversiveness of Racinian tragedy is inherently limited. The challenge from within denies the larger reality of which the court forms only a part. However harsh the judgment of the absolutist state, the critique fails to break with the conceptual framework of that state and can therefore be expressed only as negation.[78] A neoclassical theater dominated by aristocratic assumptions and self-consciously distanced from popular culture necessarily lacked an independent ground from which to judge experience. Symptomatically, Phèdre blames her own misdeeds on her confidante, Œnone. Racine takes this ideological stance as his own, explaining in his preface to the play that he has socially tidied up his Euripidean source.

> J'ai même pris soin de la rendre [Phèdre] un peu moins odieuse qu'elle n'est dans les tragédies des anciens, où elle se résout d'elle-même à accuser Hippolyte. J'ai cru que la calomnie avait quelque chose de trop bas et de trop noir pour la mettre dans la bouche d'une princesse qui a d'ailleurs des sentiments si nobles et si vertueux. Cette bassesse m'a paru plus convenable à une nourrice, qui pouvait avoir des inclinations plus serviles, et qui néanmoins

---

[76]For this error, see Lindenberger, pp. 64–72.

[77]Lucien Goldmann, *The Hidden God: A Study of Tragic Vision in the "Pensées" of Pascal and the Tragedies of Racine*, trans. Philip Thody (London: Routledge and Kegan Paul, 1964), esp. pp. 103–41. But see Brereton, *French Tragic Drama*, pp. 252, 257, 272.

[78]Louis Althusser, *For Marx*, trans. Ben Brewster (London: NLB, 1977), pp. 143–44.

n'entreprend cette fausse accusation que pour sauver la vie et l'honneur de sa maîtresse. (pp. 540–41)

(I have even taken care to render her a little less odious than she is in the tragedies of the ancients, where she resolves of herself to accuse Hippolytus. I thought that the calumny was too base and evil to put into the mouth of a princess who elsewhere displays such noble and virtuous sentiments. This baseness appeared to me more suitable to a nurse, who could have more servile inclinations, and who nevertheless undertakes this false accusation only to save the life and honor of her mistress. [Guicharnaud, p. 227])

A similar class condescension appeared, of course, in *Gli duoi fratelli rivali* and, significantly, in *Horace*.

The distinction between Corneille and Racine may in the broadest sense be traced to a curious structural anomaly in the history of French absolutism. That state's greatest international success did not coincide with or follow upon its full domestic consolidation. The triumphs abroad of Richelieu, achieved in the absence of complete institutional integration, preceded by a generation the internal splendor, unaccompanied by successful imperial expansion, of the age of Louis XIV.[79] In this respect Corneille's plays bear witness to the opportunities newly opened to France, Racine's to the constraints upon its actions in foreign affairs and to the weight of centralized authority at home. The tension between nobility and monarchy, however, lies at the heart of both dramatists' work and accounts for their basic similarities.

If a relatively narrow focus on this intraclass relationship differentiates French from Spanish or English serious drama, the same cannot be said of comedy. In France, as elsewhere, neoclassical comedy proved less impervious to popular influences than did neoclassical tragedy. The plays of Molière, a professional actor who worked for years in the provinces and was deeply indebted to *commedia dell'arte* and French farce, obviously offer abundant evidence of the mixing of neoclassical and popular traditions. One might, for example, contrast a relatively restrained classical comedy like *Le misanthrope* not only with such shorter, more popular pieces as *La jalousie du Barbouillé, Le médecin volant,*[80] *Le mariage forcé,* and *Sganarelle, ou Le cocu imaginaire,* but also with *L'avare* and *Le Tartuffe.* Yet Molière's plays, like many Italian neoclassical comedies before them, effect less a balanced synthesis than the subordinate incorporation of popular materials into a predominantly learned form.

*Le Tartuffe* illustrates some of the consequences of this asymmetry. Criticism of the play has focused on the uncertainty about the object of

[79]Anderson, pp. 105–6.
[80]These two plays may not be by Molière.

the satire and on the inadequacy of the ending.[81] Such slippages suggest the utility of reconstructing the logic of the contradictions on which the comedy turns. Molière's perhaps disingenuous claim to be unmasking only the religious hypocrisy of Tartuffe—which, after all, scarcely needs unmasking—diverts attention from the more disturbing attack on the religious gullibility, credulity, enthusiasm, or simply faith of Orgon, and on the religious tyranny that Orgon exercises over his family as a result. Clerical foes of Le Tartuffe correctly perceived this fundamentally antireligious thrust. Philosophically set against Tartuffe and Orgon is Cléante, the leading representative of the relatively secular, enlightened values of reason, common sense, moderation, and decorum, values implicit in Molière's restrained, unexuberant style and, as befits the dominant positive ideology of the play, verbally affirmed throughout the plot. Yet Cléante, though his dignity is never compromised, is absolutely unsuccessful in opposing Tartuffe.

On the other hand, the play does provide more effective means of combating religion, in the farcical materials of popular dramaturgy. Broad stage business operates as a weapon in the efforts of the waiting maid, Dorine, who in this sense is Cléante's agent, first to turn Mariane against Orgon's marital plans for her and then to reconcile her with her true lover, Valère. Even more crucially, farce informs the scene in which Damis leaps from a closet to catch Tartuffe in the act of attempting to seduce Orgon's wife Elmire and the later episode in which Orgon makes the same discovery by concealing himself in the most humiliating, but symbolically appropriate, fashion under the table.[82] Since the ideological assumptions behind this physical activity never receive explicit formulation, popular culture remains subordinate, indeed precognitive, in Tartuffe. Yet its boisterousness, for example, evidently conflicts with the calmness of common sense, which its greater practical ability in exposing Tartuffe only further undermines.

The ultimate failure of even farce to defeat religion, however, produces the necessity of that secular deus ex machina, the absolute monarch. The royal intervention that saves the day, almost totally unprepared for as it is by the prior action, demonstrates not that hypocrisy doesn't pay but that the prudent hypocrite, unlike Tartuffe, should quit while ahead.[83] The bitterness of the satire arises from this unsatisfying ending. The language works against any such perception, however, by

[81]Auerbach, pp. 360-61; Brereton, French Comic Drama, pp. 117–23.

[82]Molière, Le Tartuffe, in Théâtre choisi, ed. Rat (Paris: Editions Garnier Frères, 1962), 2.1, pp. 196–99; 2.3, pp. 207–9; 3.4, p. 218; 4.4, p. 230 to 4.7, p. 236. Subsequent references are noted in the text.

[83]Brereton, French Comic Drama, p. 120.

linking common sense, absolutism, and God. Cléante argues that men like Orgon

> veulent que chacun soit aveugle comme eux.
> C'est être libertin que d'avoir de bons yeux,
>
> . . .
>
> Je sais comme je parle, et le ciel voit mon coeur.
>
> (1.5, pp. 187–88)

(They want to make the whole world blind like them. / It's irreligion just to have open eyes! / . . . / I know what I say, and heaven can see my heart. [Guicharnaud, p. 100])

For the officer who arrests Tartuffe, the king is

> Un prince dont les yeux se font jour dans les coeurs,
>
> . . .
>
> D'un fin discernement sa grande âme pourvue
> Sur les choses toujours jette une droite vue;
>
> . . .
>
> Il donne aux gens de bien une gloire immortelle;
> Mais sans aveuglement il fait briller ce zèle,
>
> . . .
>
> Celui-ci [Tartuffe] n'était pas pour le pouvoir surprendre,
> Et de pièges plus fins on le voit se défendre.
> D'abord, il a percé, par ses vives clartés,
> Des replis de son coeur toutes les lâchetés.
>
> (5.7, p. 250)

(His eyes can penetrate his subjects' hearts; / . . . / And his great spirit, wise in the ways of men, / Watches his kingdom with discerning eyes. / . . . / To worthy men he gives immortal glory, / And yet his zeal for virtue is not blind. / . . . / Tartuffe was not the sort to hoodwink him / Who has avoided many a subtler snare. / Immediately he saw in its true color / The base conniving of that evil mind. [Guicharnaud, p. 151])

This seeing to the heart of the matter, as it were, makes possible the discrimination between true and false devotion. For Cléante,

> Il est de faux dévots ainsi que de faux braves:
>
> . . .
>
> Les bons et vrais dévots qu'on doit suivre à la trace
> Ne sont pas ceux aussi qui font tant de grimace.
>
> (1.5, p. 188)

(There's false devotion like false bravery. / . . . / The truly pious, whom we should imitate, / Are not the ones who show off their devotion. [Guicharnaud, p. 100])

As for the king,

> l'amour pour les vrais ne ferme point son coeur
> A tout ce que les faux doivent donner d'horreur.
> (5.7, p. 250)

(His love for genuine faith does not eclipse / The horror one should feel for false devotion. [Guicharnaud, p. 151])

Finally, this ability to distinguish depends on the exercise of reason. Cléante complains that "La raison a pour eux [most men] des bornes trop petites" ("The boundaries of reason are too narrow [for most men]": 1.5, p. 188; Guicharnaud, p. 101), while the king's "ferme raison ne tombe en nul excès" ("firm reason yields to no excess": 5.7, p. 250; Guicharnaud, p. 151). Yet these pervasive echoes obscure a more troubling connection. The king, for all his benevolence, exercises an autocratic power over society comparable to the autocratic power exercised by Orgon over his family and by Tartuffe over Orgon. Far from being enemies, the crown and religion belong in the same camp.

Le Tartuffe, then, asserts the value of reason while failing to demonstrate its efficacy. Reason conflicts with forces of religion that prove too strong for it, is saved by a monarchy that seems its ally but is actually affiliated with its foe, and is supported by a popular culture that would oppose it, though not in the fashion of crown and Christianity, if only allowed to articulate a position. This formulation, in turn, opens up social and temporal vistas on a play that apparently has little to do with class struggle and historical change. Reason and common sense may be seen as early, proto-Enlightenment fragments of a bourgeois ideology at odds with reactionary religion but not yet fundamentally in contradiction with royal power. Ultimately, however, absolutism shared more profound interests with religion. According to Perry Anderson, "Its feudal character constantly ended by frustrating and falsifying its promises for capital."[84] On the other hand, the hierarchical, asymmetrical alliance between bourgeois values and popular culture, however weak in the present, points toward the future, toward 1789, toward the bourgeois revolutionary moment when that coalition would finally possess sufficient strength to overthrow the absolutist state. The distinction between the theoretically persuasive but practically inept language of common sense and the mute but rather more effective action of popular culture also anticipates the decisive role of the lower classes in saving the bourgeoisie from its own timidity, in doing the dirty work of the Revolution. Finally, the implicit tensions between reason and farce look for-

[84]Anderson, p. 41.

ward to the dissolution of the revolutionary alliance and to the social conflicts of the modern world. To quote Anderson again, "Concrete *social formations* . . . typically embody a number of coexistent and conflicting modes of production, of varying date."[85] In this sense *Tartuffe* is a structural model for the history of France and of the absolutist West.

## ENGLAND AND SPAIN

The urban drama of the late Middle Ages, surveyed toward the end of chapter 1, possessed a significant popular dimension. The urban drama of the Renaissance, analyzed in the present chapter, often drew primarily on learned, classical material. What circumstances led to a balanced synthesis of these two theatrical traditions? In England and Spain between 1490 and 1575, a concurrence of social and political forces—most notable among them the early growth of capitalism and absolutism— helped foster the development of professional acting troupes. These companies initiated the crucial fusion that later made possible, if not inevitable, the plays of Marlowe, Shakespeare, Lope de Vega, and their successors.

### Society

Owing to the Norman Conquest, medieval England combined feudal relations of production with national unity under the crown; owing to the Islamic Conquest, medieval Spain generally lacked both feudalism and royal centralization. These differences may help account for the divergent theatrical experiences of the two countries before 1500. But during the late Middle Ages both England and Spain felt the political impact of the feudal crisis in the form of aristocratic civil war. The reigns of Henry VII and of Ferdinand and Isabella simultaneously inaugurated a new era, putting an end to most internal strife. As the account of French classical tragedy has already suggested, the process of absolutist consolidation begun by these monarchs and continued by their successors lay behind the later triumph of the drama, and especially of its serious genres, in the commercial theaters of the two national capitals. Similarly, the main contours of English and Spanish society during this first stage of national unification generally conformed to an international pattern. Deprived of political autonomy by the new state, the nobility received in return from the same source a more secure defense of its traditional so-

---

[85]Anderson, p. 421.

120]

cial and economic preeminence. The class was far from unanimous in perceiving the benefits, or even the necessity, of this reorganization of its means of domination. In England, local and unsuccessful aristocratic uprisings against the Tudors broke out repeatedly—though mainly prior to 1570—before finally attaining a national character and bringing down the absolutist state in the 1640s. In Spain, landowner parochialism, though rarely involving recourse to arms, ultimately issued in the rebellions of the 1640s and thus in irreparable damage to the monarchy.

But if efforts at royal centralism entailed the partial suppression, or at least transformation, of the nobility, they benefited from the generally favorable configuration of forces in the nation as a whole. Both western European absolutism and its attendant theatrical institutions required a relative social and cultural homogeneity that transcended class barriers. The monarchy was as much the agent as the product of unity during the sixteenth century. Only after 1600 did its centripetal tendencies systematically accentuate social divisions. Its activist role in the earlier period particularly stands out in the field of religion. The complex economic, social, political, and of course doctrinal significance of the Reformation and Counter-Reformation fall well beyond the purview of the present work.[86] One may simply note that Tudor policy had much to do with the triumph of English Protestantism. In Spain, Ferdinand and Isabella and their first two Habsburg successors introduced the Inquisition and gradually fashioned it into the nation's most effective instrument for enforcing ideological conformity. Although theological tolerance at times spurred drama during the Renaissance, the ensuing persecution and judicial murder in Spain and England may, ironically enough, have had the same effect. Benjamin's famous remark—"There is no document of civilization which is not at the same time a document of barbarism"[87]—epigrammatically captures this tragic paradox. In the precapitalist era a national stage such as England's or Spain's probably could not have functioned without religious uniformity.

The redeployed and increased power of the state can also be registered in international affairs, above all in the vastly expanded scale of conflict. War was the vocation of the feudal aristocracy. True to their social roots, the early Tudor and Habsburg absolute monarchs threw themselves into continental imperialism. The task fell mainly to Henry VIII

---

[86]Recent discussions of the Weber-Tawney thesis include Christopher Hill, "Protestantism and the Rise of Capitalism," in *Change and Continuity in Seventeenth-Century England* (Cambridge: Harvard University Press, 1975), pp. 81–102; G. R. Elton, *Reformation Europe, 1517–1559* (New York: Harper and Row, 1963), pp. 305–18; A. G. Dickens, *Reformation and Society in Sixteenth-Century Europe* (London: Harcourt, Brace and World, 1966), pp. 178–80.

[87]Walter Benjamin, "Theses on the Philosophy of History," in *Illuminations*, ed. Hannah Arendt, trans. Harry Zohn (New York: Schocken, 1969), p. 256.

and his Spanish counterpart, Charles V. Both men managed to empty the royal treasury without achieving their territorial aims. Yet in other respects the foreign policies of the two countries were hardly comparable. The offspring of the most successful dynastic marriage of the Renaissance, Charles inherited the largest and most imposing empire in Europe and conducted his international forays on the same scale. Henry received from his father a far smaller material bequest, one fatally linked, moreover, to the medieval legacy of intervention in France. As recently as a century before, in the age of Henry V, the superior organization of the English state had made continental imperialism a profitable strategy. French victory in the Hundred Years' War signaled the end of an epoch, however. By the early sixteenth century, with Spain and France now as centralized as England, the comparatively modest size of the Tudor realm transformed a previously lucrative policy into irrational adventurism. Whereas the barriers to Habsburg expansion were set by the universalist grandeur of the enterprise, the limits of Tudor aggression were established by the resources of England itself.

Yet even international failure required a financial outlay far beyond anything the Middle Ages had known. The fiscal base of absolutism therefore assumed decisive importance. Here the Spanish crown possessed the enormous advantage provided by the precious metals of its New World empire. The treasure of the Indies combined with oppressive taxation of Castile's peasantry in the countryside and merchant and manufacturing classes in the towns to give the monarchy monetary access to a military machine unequaled elsewhere in Europe until well after 1600.

The closest approach to a windfall of this sort for the Tudor dynasty resulted from Henry VIII's expropriation of the monasteries in the early years of the Reformation. Unlike the continuous source of revenue that the mines of the New World became for the Habsburgs, however, church lands could be taken over only once. When Henry then proceeded to sell off most of what he had seized in order to pay for war with France, he squandered the Tudors' best chance of constructing a powerful absolutism. Instead, perennially short of cash, the monarchy never could establish either an adequate bureaucracy or a standing army. Lacking the income for a coercive apparatus, the crown remained reliant on Parliament and above all on the gentry in the House of Commons.

This class received the main economic benefit from the double alienation of the monastic domain. Its turn toward commercial agriculture, begun in the fourteenth century, was accelerated by the Reformation land boom. In addition, the futility of Tudor imperialism, in conjunction with the natural protection offered by the English Channel, deprived the aristocracy of its military function. Increasingly civilian, commercial, and common—all anomalies in sixteenth-century Europe—the ruling class was losing its stake in an absolutist state. Its interests were converging instead with those of the rapidly growing capitalist classes in the towns. In Spain, too, the first half of the sixteenth century, with its attendant price inflation, witnessed prosperity and expansion for agriculture, commerce, and industry. But capitalist economic development did not transform the nobility and hence undermine the monarchy. War in Europe and conquest in America continued to provide outlets for the traditional skills of the landowning class. A similar distinction applies to the domestic political operations of the state. Whereas the English monarchy crushed peasant uprisings on more than one occasion, the most serious challenge to Habsburg absolutism in Castile came from the revolt of the *comuneros* in 1520–21, an urban movement of artisans and burghers that was ultimately bourgeois in character.

But despite an appropriately feudal aristocracy, abundantly supplied royal coffers, and after 1521 a docile bourgeoisie, the Habsburgs came no closer to implanting a full absolutism in Spain than did the Tudors in England. The marriage of Ferdinand and Isabella unified Castile and Aragon in name alone. Aragon and its overseas possessions retained their feudal liberties, prerogatives, and exemptions: only the Inquisition crossed the border with its strength unabated. The same noncentralizing policy was extended to the new territories added to the empire at the accession of Charles V, perhaps because American metals seemed to render genuine political integration superfluous. Royal taxation remained largely confined within Castile. The crown eventually paid dearly for its entirely characteristic respect for medieval aristocratic rights. But the significance of its inaction was just the opposite for the theater. The example of seventeenth-century France suggests that the complete consolidation of royal power precluded the fusion of popular and learned traditions on the public stage. Only the partial absolutism of England and Spain made possible the drama of Shakespeare and Lope de Vega.[88]

[88]This historical summary draws primarily on S. T. Bindoff, *Tudor England,* vol. 5 of *The Pelican History of England* (Harmondsworth, Middlesex: Penguin, 1950), pp. 7–211; A. R. Myers, *England in the Late Middle Ages,* 8th ed., vol. 4 of *The Pelican History of England* (Harmondsworth, Middlesex: Penguin, 1971), pp. 199–262; Hill, *Reformation to Industrial Revolution: The Making of Modern English Society, 1530–1780* (New York: Random House, 1967), pp. 4–95; Lawrence Stone, *The Causes of the English Revolution, 1529–1642* (London: Routledge and Kegan Paul, 1972), pp. 58–117; J. H. Elliott, *Imperial Spain, 1469–1716* (New York: St. Martin's Press, 1964), pp. 1–241; Jaime Vicens Vives, *An Economic History of Spain,* in collaboration with Jorge Nadal Oller, trans. Frances M. López-Morillas (Princeton: Princeton University Press, 1969), pp. 291–384; Antonio Domínguez Ortiz, *The Golden Age of Spain, 1516–1659,* trans. James Casey (New York: Basic Books, 1971), pp. 1–72, 112–316; Anderson, pp. 60–72, 113–28.

## Theater

The differences between the two nations were perhaps even greater on the stage than in society as a whole. Whereas England enjoyed a thriving theater during the Middle Ages, medieval Spain, and Castile in particular, generally proved inimical to drama. In a sense, then, the sixteenth century witnessed the evolution of the theater in one country and its creation, or at least transformation, in the other. This view ignores discontinuities in England and continuities in Spain, however. More important, English drama from 1490 to 1575 turned on a constant and complex interaction between learned and popular traditions, whereas the Spanish stage underwent a gradual popularization of an initially learned pastime. The present discussion seeks to elucidate these two distinct processes and their common outcome: the establishment of professional acting companies equipped with a socially and theatrically heterogeneous and increasingly secular repertory, and poised for triumph in the last quarter of the century.

### England

One can somewhat arbitrarily isolate three main English theaters after 1490, two popular, one learned, and all indebted to the medieval stage.[89] Although the learned tradition goes back at least to fourteenth- and fifteenth-century indoor aristocratic entertainments and plays, the humanist impact discernible from the 1490s on meant a break with the past.[90] The change is evident not in the imitation of classical dramatic form, which did not occur nearly as quickly in England as in Italy or even Spain. Rather, it appears in a new secular seriousness, a commitment to intellectual speculation derived from the rhetorical theory and practice of antiquity.[91]

Whether performed in aristocratic households or at court, in schools and universities or at the Inns of Court, humanist drama was amateur and occasional. Despite this diversity of setting, moreover, a review of the plays reveals central formal, theatrical, and ideological characteristics or trends in the tradition. The first, already alluded to, involved the

[89]Background: F. P. Wilson, *The English Drama, 1485–1585*, ed. with a bibliography by G. K. Hunter, vol. 4, pt. 1 of *The Oxford History of English Literature* (Oxford: Clarendon Press, 1968); comedy: M. C. Bradbrook, *The Growth and Structure of Elizabethan Comedy* (Berkeley and Los Angeles: University of California Press, 1956), pp. 3–41.

[90]Continuity: Glynne Wickham, *Early English Stages, 1300 to 1660*, vol. 1, *1300 to 1576* (London: Routledge and Kegan Paul, 1959), 179–253; break: E. K. Chambers, *The Mediaeval Stage* (London: Oxford University Press, 1903), 2:179–226.

[91]Joel B. Altman, *The Tudor Play of Mind: Rhetorical Inquiry and the Development of Elizabethan Drama* (Berkeley and Los Angeles: University of California Press, 1978).

transition from the early debate structures of Medwall's *Fulgens and Lu-crece* (1497), Rastell's (?) *Gentleness and Nobility* (1527), and John Heywood's *Play of the Weather* (1528) to the classical generic consciousness of Udall's *Ralph Roister Doister* (1552) and Gascoigne's *Supposes* (1566) in comedy and Sackville and Norton's *Gorboduc* (1562) in tragedy.[92] Second, throughout the period humanist drama freely borrowed from the popular theater—adapting forms, techniques, characters, subjects, and attitudes.[93] Medwall's *Nature* (1495), Redford's *Wit and Science* (1539), and the anonymous *Respublica* (1553) are all moralities; *Fulgens and Lucrece* exploits the intimate contact between actor and audience typical of popular dramaturgy;[94] relatedly, *Ralph Roister Doister* and the anonymous *Gammer Gurton's Needle* (1553) introduce the Vice to the world of Roman comedy; the latter, in addition, confines its plot to the rural lower classes; and *Gentleness and Nobility* sees social relations from the point of view of the peasantry. Finally, in accord with the political orientation of English humanism, the learned drama of the sixteenth century persistently concerned itself with affairs of state.[95]

What is the relationship among these defining features of humanist theater? The incorporation of popular materials obviously testifies to the flexibility of the tradition. In *Fulgens and Lucrece* and *Gentleness and Nobility*, to take the obvious examples, standard humanist themes gain added social and intellectual breadth from the presence of a critical lower-class perspective. More often, however, the limits of learned drama emerge. The grand social and political themes of the early humanists proved incompatible with the triumph of neoclassical form. The differentiation between tragedy and comedy extended to the choice of subject matter, with the latter genre restricted to everyday life. *Gorboduc* treats the succession and the role of Parliament, but *Ralph Roister Doister*, *Gammer Gurton's Needle*, and *Supposes* do not really stray beyond private experience. Although Lyly and others later solved this problem through allegory, in so doing they were inevitably moving away from classical norms. The constraints on tragedy may be estimated by considering the interaction between classicism and the popular theater. The pattern is identical to the one that emerged earlier in this chapter. The responsiveness of Terentian comedy to the popular tradition starkly contrasts with

[92]Unless otherwise specified, the dates of all English plays are taken from Alfred Harbage, *Annals of English Drama, 975–1700*, rev. ed. S. Schoenbaum (London: Methuen, 1964). Periodization by dramatic genre is inferred from the same work.

[93]Weimann, pp. 100–112.

[94]Weimann, pp. 106–12; and, for a more speculative interpretation, Jackson I. Cope, *The Theater and the Dream: From Metaphor to Form in Renaissance Drama* (Baltimore: Johns Hopkins University Press, 1973), pp. 98–110.

[95]David M. Bevington, *Tudor Drama and Politics: A Critical Approach to Topical Meaning* (Cambridge: Harvard University Press, 1968).

the narrowness and rigidity of Senecan tragedy. *Gorboduc,* for example, suffers theatrically and ideologically as a result. More generally, although the humanist stage effected a workable synthesis of popular and learned materials, today its drama rarely interests anyone but scholars primarily concerned with a historical understanding of Marlowe and Shakespeare, and thus with plays composed for a very different institution. The most important fact about the humanist theater therefore is not that it borrowed from popular drama, but that popular drama borrowed from it.

At least one popular tradition remained impervious to classicism, however. The virtual disappearance of the great amateur mystery cycles in the late sixteenth century was not the natural fate of a moribund medieval institution. The central government suppressed the cycles, despite strong popular support for them, following the Catholic Rebellion of the North in 1569. Elizabeth thus completed what her father had begun forty years earlier, when the break with Rome first necessitated, from the Tudors' point of view, constant scrutiny and ever-increasing censorship of an obviously Catholic dramatic tradition. The persistence of the *auto sacramental* and the *comedia a lo divino* in Golden Age Spain reveals, on this argument, the normal and natural sequence of events, in the absence of the discontinuity introduced by the Reformation.[96]

On the other hand, and despite the composition of most of the Chester Cycle in the sixteenth century,[97] the main creative period of the mysteries had probably passed by 1500. Other more recently developed and more secular dramatic traditions could better represent the rapidly changing facets of sixteenth-century life.[98] The suppression of the cycles, moreover, formed part of the general process of absolutist centralization and hence belongs to political as much as to religious history. A dramatic performance, for example, sparked the Norfolk peasant revolt of 1549.[99] Hardly a lone enemy of the medieval stage, Tudor policy was one of a series of forces contributing to a break with the past. Spanish evidence in fact confirms this view. The Habsburgs exercised, if anything, more rigorous censorship than did the Tudors. In addition, the movement from medieval to Renaissance theater involved a deeper rupture

[96]Harold C. Gardiner, S.J., *Mysteries' End: An Investigation of the Last Days of the Medieval Religious Stage,* Yale Studies in English, no. 103 (New Haven: Yale University Press, 1946). For statistical corroboration, see Leo G. Salingar, Gerald Harrison, and Bruce Cochrane, "Les comédiens et leur public en Angleterre de 1520 à 1640," in *Dramaturgie et société,* ed. Jacquot, 2:531, table 2.

[97]Lawrence M. Clopper, introduction to *Records of Early English Drama: Chester,* ed. Clopper (Toronto: University of Toronto Press, 1979), p. liii.

[98]Weimann, p. 98.

[99]Wickham, vol. 2, *1576–1660,* pt. 1 (London: Routledge and Kegan Paul, 1963), pp. 54–83.

in Spain than in England. Most important, the prominence of religious drama during the *Siglo de Oro* perhaps signifies not continuity but backwardness, Spain's failure to make the transition from feudalism to capitalism. This historical stagnation is no more normal or natural than the comparative historical dynamism of Renaissance England. Finally, despite the Inquisition, the Counter-Reformation, and the persistence of medievalism under the Habsburgs, professional actors exercised a monopoly over religious theater of all types; the *auto sacramental* proved less important than the fundamentally secular *comedia*; and within the *comedia* itself religious plays constituted only a small proportion of the dramatic output.

In any case, the future of English drama belonged even less with the amateur cycles than with the humanist stage. Although the mystery plays directly influenced other theatrical forms almost to the time of their suppression[100] and perhaps had an indirect impact on the works of Shakespeare and his contemporaries, they had bequeathed their main legacy to the late Tudor and early Stuart stage long before, in their profound effect on the moralities in which the professional actors specialized at least from the late fifteenth century. It was partly from this genre that the main line of Renaissance drama later emerged. One should not identify the sixteenth-century commercial companies too exclusively with the morality, however, even though that form obviously predominates among the extant plays from their repertory. A substantial number of secular romances have been lost from the period after 1560, and presumably from the earlier Tudor era as well. The romantic comedies and romances of Shakespeare and his contemporaries probably derive from this tradition.[101] Because far more moralities than romances survive, and because the structural continuity between the morality and late Elizabethan drama is far less evident, the form nonetheless may repay some attention.[102] Equally important, a focus on the morality will reveal the salient characteristic of the professional stage in the sixteenth century —its extraordinary responsiveness both to other dramatic traditions and to social change.

Although commercial troupes performed from the early fifteenth century at the latest, their main period of growth probably began after 1500. In playing their moralities before essentially the same audience

[100]Rosemary Woolf, "The Influence of the Mystery Plays upon the Popular Tragedies of the 1560's," *Renaissance Drama*, n.s., 6 (1973): 89–105.

[101]Salingar, *Shakespeare and the Traditions of Comedy* (Cambridge: Cambridge University Press, 1974), pp. 28–39, 47–75.

[102]Bevington, *From "Mankind" to Marlowe: Growth of Structure in the Popular Drama of Tudor England* (Cambridge: Harvard University Press, 1962); Weimann, pp. 98–160.

that witnessed the mysteries, they sought to re-create the scope, action, spectacle, burlesque, popular life, music, and dance of the more venerable form. Short on both personnel and finances, they resorted to the technique of doubling parts to achieve these ends. The exigencies of doubling not only generated a useful paradigm for the construction of subsequent plays, but also facilitated the later incorporation of new material and attitudes beyond the imagination of the early actors and dramatists.

The changes in the morality resulted from a series of interlocking tendencies. In line with the basic direction of Tudor England, the form became increasingly secular in orientation, concerning itself with ethical, social, and political matters at the expense of metaphysical ones. Innovation accompanied even a continued focus on individual salvation. Traditionally comic in the Dantean sense, the morality extended its range to homiletic tragedy in W. Wager's *The Longer Thou Livest the More Fool Thou Art* (1559), a work that strikingly anticipates *Dr. Faustus*. Yet this generic shift did not bring with it the constraints that accompanied the adoption of neoclassical dramatic form on the humanist stage. Unlike Terentian comedy, the morality did not abandon its broad political perspective;[103] unlike Senecan tragedy, it did not eliminate its popular dimension.

Indeed, although the process of secularization not surprisingly coincided with the decline of most allegorical figures, the Vice proved an exception. A combination of negative ethical exemplum and comic, theatrical showman, he was never reducible to a purely homiletic function. As his various antics lost their moral and structural logic with the decline of an explicitly Christian framework, the Vice was freer to express those aspects of his character that perhaps go back to pagan ritual. His wordplay, vitality, intimacy with the audience, disruption of mimetic illusion, and commitment to inversion and negation all assured the continuing presence of a popular perspective within the play—one, moreover, that gradually acquired a new formal rationale in the lowlife subplot, which served as a critical commentary on the actions of the aristocratic protagonists.[104] But at the same time that the morality was strengthening its ties to the lower classes, it was also attracting the talents of learned writers and thus expanding its capacities in quite a different way. In *Magnyfycence* (1515), Skelton provided a political allegory of state. Heywood's *Four PP* (1520) and *Johan Johan* (1520) introduced French farce to the English stage, while the former work in addition drew on the hu-

---

[103]See Bevington, *Tudor Drama and Politics*, passim.
[104]Weimann, pp. 112–60. For the more orthodox view, stressing the homiletic function of the Vice, see Bevington, *From "Mankind" to Marlowe*; Robert C. Jones, "Dangerous Sport: The Audience's Engagement with Vice in the Moral Interludes," *Renaissance Drama*, n.s., 6 (1973): 45–64.

manist tradition of debate. Bale's *King John* (1538) offered Protestant doctrinal and political zeal. Finally, this last play, together with Wager's Calvinist tragedy, also demonstrates the adaptability of the morality to the Reformation.

Preston's *Cambyses* (1561) illustrates the possibilities of the form by the beginning of the Elizabethan era. The tragic main plot, derived from ancient history, traces the career of a historical king of Persia, set against the backdrop of both human and allegorical figures. Although the punishment of tyranny is explained as a consequence of divine agency, that agency is never seen. Largely deprived of a homiletic role as tempter of an allegorical protagonist, the Vice Ambidexter primarily engages instead in burlesque of the serious action and in inconsequential comic escapades with lower-class characters. These scenes, notable for a verbal realism far in advance of the rhetorical declamation characteristic of Cambyses' plot, constitute the play's principal appeal. The work as a whole suffers from fundamental weaknesses, however, its fusion of popular and learned traditions notwithstanding. The popular theater, like its humanist counterpart, awaited the appearance of a writer gifted enough to exploit the opportunities that remained largely unrealized in Preston's dramatic synthesis. On the other hand, a talented playwright would not encounter the same obstacles with the professional companies that he would face on the humanist stage. Yet those companies had no obvious means of regularly obtaining the services of the leading poets of the time. A new institutional configuration with new conditions of performance was necessary. The commercial boom of sixteenth-century England, with its accompanying demographic expansion, centered on the capital city of London. Elizabeth's accession in 1558 eventually resulted in the establishment of internal stability; perhaps relatedly, the 1560s witnessed a sharp rise in both amateur and professional dramatic activity.[105] The suppression of the amateurs in the following decade then left the field almost exclusively to the commercial companies. The public theater emerged from this conjunction of theatrical, social, economic, and political forces.

*Spain*

In a very different and perhaps even more discontinuous fashion, sixteenth-century Spanish drama, too, gradually moved toward a hybrid form.[106] The earliest extant works in the tradition, Juan del Encina's

[105]Salingar, Harrison, and Cochrane, 2:531, table 2.
[106]Background: J. P. Wickersham Crawford, *Spanish Drama before Lope de Vega*, 2d ed., bibliographical supplement by Warren T. McCready (Philadelphia: University of Pennsylvania Press, 1967).

*Eglogas* of the 1490s, probably draw less on prior lost religious plays than on aristocratic mumming, biblical story, and *cancionero* poetry. In turn, the combination of lyricism and narrative with quasi-ritualistic social pastime apparently accounts for the static, undramatic quality of Encina's early works.[107] Yet this initial situation changed with astonishing rapidity. Torres Naharro's *Ymenea* (1516?) and Gil Vicente's *Don Duardos* (1522?) more fully anticipate the drama of Lope de Vega than do any Spanish plays of the next half-century. In England, the works of Marlowe and Shakespeare have no comparable extant precursors from this period.[108] Perhaps the very primitivism of early Spanish drama, the absence of a strong conventional tradition, gave Vicente in particular an aesthetic freedom he would have lacked in contemporary England.[109]

The contrast between humble beginnings and early mastery is not the sole, or even the most important, contradiction in the first generation of the Spanish theater. The auspices of this drama were consistently and pervasively aristocratic, even courtly. Encina and Lucas Fernández belonged to the circle of the duke of Alba, Vicente wrote for the bilingual Portuguese court, and Torres Naharro enjoyed the patronage of the Spanish and Italian nobility, both lay and clerical. Hence, whatever the subject matter of an individual play, the theater itself was for the most part institutionally secular. Even overtly religious works reveal a process of thematic secularization.[110] As the designation *Eglogas* demonstrates, moreover, the drama possessed a classical side from its inception. Especially in Encina's early plays, the allusion to Virgil indicated a thematic, rather than a generic debt. But Torres Naharro, writing in Italy and influenced by the neoclassical movement there, modeled his drama on both the form and the content of Roman comedy.[111]

On the other hand, the vestigial ritual elements of the drama militated against the creation of a purely illusionistic theater. The most important survival was the contact between actor and audience.[112] On the

[107]N. D. Shergold, *A History of the Spanish Stage from Medieval Times until the End of the Seventeenth Century* (Oxford: Clarendon Press, 1967), pp. 113–42; Humberto López Morales, *Tradición y creación en los orígenes del teatro castellano* (Madrid: Ediciones Alcalá, 1968), pp. 94, 110, 120; Charlotte Stern, "The Early Spanish Drama: From Medieval Ritual to Renaissance Art," *Renaissance Drama*, n.s., 6 (1973): 177–201.

[108]Dates for Spanish plays, unless otherwise noted, come from Edward M. Wilson and Duncan Moir, *The Golden Age: Drama, 1492–1700*, vol. 3 of *A Literary History of Spain*, gen. ed. R. O. Jones (London: Ernest Benn, 1971).

[109]For a similar argument about religious drama, see Alexander A. Parker, "Notes on the Religious Drama in Mediaeval Spain and the Origins of the 'Auto Sacramental,'" *Modern Language Review* 30 (1935): 170–82.

[110]López Morales, p. 144.

[111]Raymond Leonard Grismer, *The Influence of Plautus in Spain before Lope de Vega, Together with Chapters on the Dramatic Technique of Platus and the Revival of Plautus in Italy* (New York: Hispanic Institute in the United States, 1944), pp. 120–65.

[112]Stern, p. 189.

amateur, aristocratic stage, this interaction often overlapped with the complex and problematic relationship between lowborn dramatist and upper-class patron—part servile flattery, part aggressive self-assertion. Because a lower-class character usually maintained intimacy with the audience, both the ritual heritage and the poet-patron relationship served a crucial function in shaping the general ideology of a play. For this reason, although early Spanish drama predominantly confirmed and reinforced the privileged position of the nobility, it at times produced critical and probing effects.[113]

Of the three main traditions in England between 1490 and 1575, the humanist theater most closely resembles the Spanish stage. Aristocratic and secular, it too moved from a classicism emphasizing dialogue and debate toward a formal imitation of ancient dramatic practice. Although the English humanist playwrights may have borrowed the idea from the popular tradition, like their Spanish counterparts they exploited the possibilities of contact between the performer and his public, not only to develop their own stance toward their aristocratic or royal protectors, but also to express complicated ideological attitudes toward contemporary social and political problems. Given these pervasive and fundamental parallels, it is not surprising to discover that early Spanish drama had trouble producing an adequate synthesis of learned and popular materials. For example, Torres Naharro, unable to integrate the shepherd into neoclassical comedy, relegates him to the prologue.[114] Clearly, this juxtaposition provides no lasting substitute for a genuine fusion. The limitations of the early Spanish stage may also be registered geographically. The spread of Castilian drama in less than two decades from Spain to Portugal and Italy depended in part on the nation's swift emergence as a major international power.[115] Yet from a a slightly different perspective, the theater remained territorially restricted. Encina and Fernández were from Salamanca; Vicente from Portugal, just to the west; and Torres Naharro, Sánchez de Badajoz, and others from Extremadura, just to the south.[116] The western edge of the peninsula created Spanish drama. Seville and Madrid, the eventual social, economic, political, and

---

[113]Noël Salomon, *Recherches sur le thème paysan dans la "comedia" au temps de Lope de Vega* (Bordeaux: Féret, 1965), pp. 3–164 passim, esp. 49–59; Yvonne Yarbro-Bejarano, "The Sixteenth-Century Drama in Spain: A Theater of Class Conflict," in *Essays in Honor of Jorge Guillén on the Occasion of His 85th Year* (Cambridge, Mass.: Abedul Press, 1977), pp. 141–55.

[114]John Brotherton, *The "Pastor-Bobo" in the Spanish Theater before the Time of Lope de Vega* (London: Tamesis, 1975), p. 197.

[115]Wilson and Moir, p. 13.

[116]Américo Castro, *The Spaniards: An Introduction to Their History*, trans. Willard F. King and Selma Margaretten (Berkeley and Los Angeles: University of California Press, 1971), p. 486.

cultural centers of the sixteenth and seventeenth centuries, had yet to emerge. Not quite a nation, Spain could not produce a national theater.

Early Castilian drama possessed one important potential advantage over the English humanist stage, however. Although the Spanish shepherd or peasant could not in himself overcome the barriers to a genuine fusion of popular and learned traditions erected by aristocratic theater, he possessed profound transformational potential that might be realized if other forces intervened to convert the conditions of dramatic production. The rural lower classes are prominent in such English humanist plays as *Gentleness and Nobility* and *Gammer Gurton's Needle*. But they did not gain nearly the same centrality as in Spain, perhaps because the early English learned stage seems to have had a more pronouncedly urban orientation than its Spanish counterpart. Performed on a rural estate, Encina's *Eglogas* present stylized rustics, to be sure, but ones who are recognizably akin to the real shepherds of the time. The traditional pastoral motifs associated with the Nativity and with Christianity in general reinforced the historical basis of the character. The conjunction could yield surprising dramaturgical effects. In Vicente's *Auto da sibila Casandra* (1513), the shepherds who attempt to persuade the protagonist that she will not be the mother of God all turn out to be Old Testament patriarchs and prophets. Here the author plays with religious as well as, perhaps, social expectations. In other works, however, the social implications are primary. Encina's farcical *Aucto del repelón* (pub. 1509) places its *pastores* in the alien world of the town, where they are frightened and humiliated by their physical mistreatment at the hands of some students before obtaining a measure of restitution by beating one of their tormentors. By and large, the play evokes a good-humored condescension from its aristocratic audience. But the shepherds never entirely lack human dignity, a point emphasized by their final victory, which also constitutes an authorial repudiation of the social superiority with which the *studiante* treats the protagonists.[117]

Fernández's *Farsa o cuasi comedia de una doncella, un pastor y un caballero* (pub. 1514) simply resolves a class conflict over a lady by having a *caballero* administer a salutary beating to a *pastor*. Yet once again the shepherd retains some dignity. His ability to feel love, moreover, indicates the universality of the emotion and hence carries at least faint connotations of social leveling. Finally, not only does the *pastor* mock the *caballero*—for which, admittedly, he is punished; his mere juxtaposition with the *doncella* has the effect of deflating her romantic pretensions.[118]

[117]Yarbro-Bejarano, pp. 143–44, 145–49.
[118]Yarbro-Bejarano, p. 144, stresses the dominance of aristocratic ideology; Brotherton, pp. 68, 147, the importance of lower-class assertion.

The play thus presents an early version of the complementary perspective that later characterized the public theater. *Don Duardos* also turns on the relationship between love and class. Although chivalric ideals inform the action, courtly love receives its share of ridicule. Similarly, despite some harsh treatment of lower-class life, the hero must assume the disguise of a humble gardener in order to win the hand of the emperor's daughter. Just as Don Duardos insists that love should depend on merit rather than status, his final reward testifies to his unique ability to combine the contradictory experiences of aristocrat and peasant.[119]

Although the *pastor* of *Ymenea* exhibits a characteristic mixture of aggressiveness and servility, in the play itself urban servants take the social place of shepherds. Torres Naharro, while using the servants' antics to burlesque the main romantic plot, only barely develops the critical ideological potential of his material. In *Auto da barca de Glória* (1519), Vicente systematically excludes the lower classes of both town and country. Although the work harshly attacks the secular and ecclesiastical aristocracy, primarily for favoring the rich at the expense of the poor, it typically blunts the force of the critique. Just as the devil is preparing to take the ruling class en masse to hell, Christ appears and the characters are saved quite literally by the grace of God. All of these plays, and especially the ones with prominent *pastores*, present suggestive, but only partly realized ideological and dramaturgical possibilities. Spanish drama needed to transform the lower-class character from object into subject,[120] a process that could not consistently occur in the aristocratic theater.

As in England, the accomplishment of this basic task fell to the popular commercial tradition. That tradition itself may have depended on the gradual urbanization of the theater by midcentury.[121] Sánchez de Badajoz's *Farsa militar* (rev. ed. c. 1547), like many of its author's works, was probably performed as part of the religious service in the cathedral of Badajoz.[122] In the tradition of Vicente, the play nicely exploits both the social and the theological dimensions of the shepherd, who introduces a comic tone while almost in the same breath underscoring the serious issues of the plot. But the *pastor* appears only at the beginning and end of the action. At least in the former position, where he delivers the *introito*, he clearly represents a development of Torres Naharro's dramatic practice. With the popularization of the audience about 1550, the prologue went into decline.[123] Yet its very presence testifies to a prob-

[119]See Robert L. Hathaway, *Love in the Early Spanish Theatre* (Madrid: Editorial Playor, 1975), pp. 125–35.
[120]Salomon, pp. 160–64.
[121]Salomon, pp. 59–61.
[122]Crawford, p. 49; Shergold, pp. 45, 89. Date: Brotherton, p. 185.
[123]Brotherton, pp. 80–82, 135, 143.

lem that Sánchez de Badajoz shared with Torres Naharro: how to incorporate a rustic into an urban context. Considering the virtually unrelated generic interests of the two writers, Naharro probably did not influence *Farsa militar*. His neoclassical comedy is just the most obvious form of city drama ill at ease with rustic characters.

Timoneda's *Aucto de la fee* (pub. 1575) provides one solution to this difficulty.[124] *El mundo* and *La fee* are bread sellers who compete in hawking their wares at market. Their prospective customer is *El hombre,* an everyman figure who appears "como simple," that is, as a foolish rustic. In the entirely conventional plot, *El hombre,* once tempted, quickly falls only to be saved in the end. Yet, as *Aucto de la fee* reveals, Timoneda wrote with an eye on the Valencian theater public. His adaptations of classical and neoclassical comedy for the Spanish stage suggest an effort to reach a socially more heterogeneous audience than had attended performances early in the century. Perhaps he acted and managed a theatrical company as well. In all these ways, he may have been an important forerunner of the crucial late-sixteenth-century Valencian dramatic tradition.[125] But the central figure of this generation was almost certainly Lope de Rueda. From about 1540 until his death in 1565, Rueda combined the roles of actor, manager, and dramatist for a traveling professional troupe that performed both secular and religious plays, at times for the aristocracy, but more often before the populace of the nation as a whole. He probably wanted to establish a permanent public theater in Valladolid in 1558.[126] Thus he was an only slightly premature synthesis of Burbage and Shakespeare. His plays, moreover, give evidence of a different kind of fusion. Influenced by Italian drama and most likely by the Italian actors who performed in Spain as well, Rueda came very close to integrating the *pastor* into an urban, indeed neoclassical, form.

It has been claimed that the evolution of the shepherd into a *simple,* or dolt, by this period diverted him into the *paso,* a short, comic fragment, while all but exhausting his significance in the main forms of Spanish drama.[127] Although such a position perhaps fits even a *paso* like Rueda's *Las aceitunas* (by 1565),[128] it cannot account for the same dramatist's *Comedia Armelina* (by 1565). Essentially a neoclassical comedy, the play nonetheless derives most of its life from Guadalupe, the *simple,*

[124]Date: John J. Reynolds, *Juan Timoneda* (Boston: Twayne, 1975), p. 88.

[125]Shergold, p. 154; and esp. Rinaldo Froldi, *Lope de Vega y la formación de la comedia: En torno a la tradición dramática valenciana y al primer teatro de Lope,* trans. Franco Gabriele and Mrs. de Gabriele (Salmanaca: Anaya, 1968), pp. 44–90. Text: Juan de Timoneda, *Aucto de la fee,* in *El teatro anterior a Lope de Vega,* ed. Everett W. Hesse and Juan O. Valencia (Madrid: Alcalá, 1971), p. 269.

[126]Shergold, p. 155.

[127]Brotherton, pp. 194–95.

[128]Like Rueda's other drama, it was published posthumously by Timoneda.

who combines farce and folly, on the one hand, with incisive critical commentary, on the other. He represents a preliminary, rudimentary amalgamation of the Roman comic servant with the Spanish *pastor,* an amalgamation central to Lope de Vega's later constitution of that complexly synthetic figure the *gracioso.*[129] Thus the play demonstrates one means by which the commercial theater brought to the surface the latent popular content of the earlier aristocratic stage at the same time that it, paradoxically enough, adopted some of the crucial features of neoclassical form. *Comedia Armelina* took Spanish drama almost as close to Lope de Vega as *Cambyses* brought the English stage to Kyd, Marlowe, and Shakespeare. The remaining steps required changes like those that occurred in England.

Yet the comparison may also suggest an important difference between the two countries. The Spanish theater before 1575 preferred comedy to serious secular drama far more than did the English stage. The early plays of the Spanish public theaters were primarily tragedies, however, partly because of the literary interest at the time in imitating Senecan drama. The cultivation of tragedy may also have represented an attempt to respond to the newly available national possibilities implicit in the public theater. To some extent this bold innovation met with only limited success precisely because it lacked a strong stage heritage of the kind that had developed in England. Beginning in the late 1580s, the works of Marlowe, Kyd, and early Shakespeare tended toward tragedy. Before the late 1590s, Lope's plays grew out of a largely comic tradition. In both countries, however, the very condition of possibility of this drama was a qualitative institutional transformation: the constitution of the public theater.

[129]Charles David Ley, *El gracioso en el teatro de la península (siglos xvi–xvii)* (Madrid: Revista de Occidente, 1954), p. 36; Salomon, p. 164; and esp. Barbara Kinter, *Die Figur des Gracioso in spanischen Theater des 17. Jahrhunderts* (Munich: Wilhelm Fink, 1978), pp. 11–12. On Lope, see José F. Montesinos, "Algunas observaciones sobre la figura del donaire en el teatro de Lope de Vega," in *Homenaje ofrecido a Menéndez Pidal: Miscelánea de estudios lingüísticos, literarios e históricos* (Madrid: Editorial Hernando, 1925), 1:469–504; Juan Cano-Ballesta, "Los graciosos de Lope y la cultura cómica popular de tradición medieval," in *Lope de Vega y los orígenes del teatro español,* Actas del I Congreso Internacional sobre Lope de Vega, ed. Manuel Criado de Val (Madrid: EDI, 1981), pp. 777–83.

# The Emergence of
# the Public Theater

Most of the plays of Marlowe, Shakespeare, Lope de Vega, and their contemporaries were composed for the permanent, public, commercial theater, an institution that came into being in England and Spain during the last quarter of the sixteenth century. Previous chapters have considered the national and international matrixes from which the best-known Renaissance drama in the two countries emerged and, more specifically, the necessary conditions for its production. But necessary conditions are not identical to sufficient ones. The remainder of the book is accordingly designed to present those sufficient conditions and, in so doing, to clarify the nature and significance of the public theater and its plays. This chapter considers society and theater in the late sixteenth century, focusing on both the interaction and the asymmetry between absolutist state and artisanal stage.

## SOCIETY

The common, defining feature of late sixteenth-century England and Spain was the complementarity between internal stability and external imperialism, under the sway of an incompletely absolutist monarch. The age itself was aware of the relation between domestic and foreign affairs. Philip the Bastard concludes Shakespeare's *King John* (1596) with a ringing and famous assertion:

> This England never did, nor never shall,
> Lie at the proud foot of a conqueror
> But when it first did help to wound itself.
> Now these her princes are come home again,

Come the three corners of the world in arms,
And we shall shock them. Nought shall make us rue
If England to itself do rest but true.[1]

Toward the end of *2 Henry IV* (1597), the dying king sums up the cynical
political wisdom of a reign repeatedly punctuated by civil war:

Therefore, my Harry,
Be it thy course to busy giddy minds
With foreign quarrels.[2]

And, of course, at the beginning of *Henry V* (1599), the new king heeds
his father's words and prepares to invade France. Contemporary Spanish historical drama reveals a similar, if somewhat less self-conscious,
perspective. Plays such as Lope's *Arauco domado* (1599?) and *El asalto de
Mastrique* (1600?–1606?)[3] celebrate the foreign conquests of Spain in
the New World and the Old.[4] Finally, most of the comedies performed
during this period in both countries take national unity for granted.

Yet stability must have seemed a remote ideal in the late 1560s. According to S. T. Bindoff, between 1568 and 1572 "Elizabethan England
weathered its greatest crisis," while the comparable period, especially
1569–70, constituted, in John Lynch's words, "years of crisis for Spain,
perhaps her greatest crisis in the sixteenth century."[5] In England the
1569 Rebellion of the North, a Catholic, separatist, and feudal uprising,
was followed the next year by the papal bull excommunicating
Elizabeth and the year after by the Catholic Ridolfi Plot. The Spanish,
meanwhile, faced real or potential foes on several fronts at once: the rebellious Protestants in the Netherlands, the Huguenots in the Pyrenees,
the Catalans, the forces of Islam in Turkey and North Africa, and the
Moriscos of Granada. In both countries, however, the crown ultimately
emerged strengthened from the troubles of this period. Elizabeth's victories marked the end of the internal Catholic threat, the defeat of feudal particularism in the North, and thus the unification of the nation.

[1]Shakespeare, *The Life and Death of King John*, ed. Irving Ribner, in *William Shakespeare: The Complete Works*, gen. ed. Alfred Harbage (Baltimore: Penguin, 1969), 5.7.112–18.
[2]Shakespeare, *The Second Part of King Henry the Fourth*, ed. Allan G. Chester, in *William Shakespeare*, gen. ed. Harbage, 4.5.212–14.
[3]Unless otherwise specified, all dates for Lope de Vega's *comedias* come from S. Griswold Morley and Courtney Bruerton, *Cronología de las comedias de Lope de Vega: Con un examen de las atribuciones dudosas, basado todo ello en un estudio de su versificación estrófica*, rev. ed., trans. María Rosa Cartes (Madrid: Editorial Gredos, 1968).
[4]But see Charles Vincent Aubrun, *La comedia española (1600–1680)*, trans. Julio Lago-Alonso (Salamanca: Taurus, 1968), p. 55.
[5]S.T. Bindoff, *Tudor England*, vol. 5 of *The Pelican History of England* (Harmondsworth, Middlesex: Penguin, 1950), p. 247; John Lynch, *Empire and Absolutism, 1516–1598*, vol. 1 of *Spain under the Habsburgs* (Oxford: Basil Blackwell, 1964), p. 224. See also Lynch, 1:294.

The memory of the rebellion, moreover, may have dampened subsequent enthusiasm for civil war.[6] To the south, Philip II was spared the impossible task of simultaneously confronting all his enemies. His Dutch subjects proved intractable, and the Granada rebellion of 1568 took two years of fighting to suppress. But otherwise Spain was generally able to choose its military encounters, a freedom that did not prevent it from overextending itself. Despite the victory of Lepanto (1571), the Mediterranean struggle with the Turks ended in permanent stalemate, while the strain of fighting at the same time in Flanders drove the state to its second declaration of bankruptcy, in 1575. Fortunately for Philip, at this point higher yields from his American silver mines solved the financial crisis, allowing Spain, like England, to enter an era of what Fernand Braudel calls unusual "domestic tranquillity."[7]

The longevity of both monarchs undoubtedly contributed to the internal peace of the late sixteenth century. More important, however, was the general failure to pursue standard absolutist centralizing policies, Elizabeth because she could not and Philip because he did not have to. The motor of state centralization did not stall entirely, however. In England, bureaucratic advances were concentrated in the Privy Council and the police and were reflected in a reduced dependence on Parliament. In Spain, the annexation of Portugal in 1580 unified the peninsula for the first time, although no comparable administrative integration ensued. Both states largely continued to base their operations on a juridical conception of government, characteristic of the Middle Ages; similarly, both at least partly inherited from the past a dynastic, rather than a national, understanding of power.[8]

Given such limited policies and so overwhelmingly conservative an orientation, the crucial relationship between aristocracy and monarchy remained far less troubled than was to be the case after the turn of the century. Elizabeth attempted to freeze the social structure of England by making the peerage more hereditary and by virtually refusing to create any new lords. The magnates in both countries continued to influence

---

[6]G. R. Elton, *England under the Tudors* (London: Methuen, 1955), p. 297; Christopher Hill, *Reformation to Industrial Revolution: The Making of Modern English Society, 1530–1780* (New York: Random House, 1967), p. 19; W. T. MacCaffrey, "England: The Crown and the New Aristocracy, 1540–1600," *Past and Present*, no. 30 (April 1965): 61.

[7]Lynch, 1:271–72, links the 1575 bankruptcy to a two-front war. But see Fernand Braudel, *The Mediterranean and the Mediterranean World in the Age of Philip II*, trans. Siân Reynolds (London: Collins, 1973), 2:897. The quoted passage, applied only to Spain, is from Braudel, 2:753.

[8]Perry Anderson, *Lineages of the Absolutist State* (London: NLB, 1974), pp. 128, 75–76; Lynch, 1:345, 170, 181–83; Penry Williams, "The Tudor State," *Past and Present*, no. 25 (July 1963): 51; J. H. Hexter, *Reappraisals in History* (Evanston, Ill.: Northwestern University Press, 1961), pp. 29–31, 35; Pierre Vilar, *Spain: A Brief History*, trans. Brian Tate, 2d ed. (Oxford: Pergamon Press, 1977), p. 23.

the state, colonizing sectors of the bureaucracy to secure political and economic gains, engaging in feuds with each other, directing rival systems of clientage, and forcing the crown to grant them official positions corresponding to their rank. To the extent that the high aristocracy lost political power, it was replaced in royal administration not by commoners but by members of the lesser nobility—gentry, squires, and knights in England and *hidalgos* and *caballeros* in Spain. In other words, unable to break completely the quasi-feudal power of their mightiest subjects, the two monarchs utilized a species of checks and balances within the aristocracy to control the class as a whole.[9]

Socially and economically, the preeminence of the nobility was still more pronounced. To the end of the century, the English peerage was treated with deference, even by the gentry. The privileges of the Spanish aristocracy included exemption from military service and taxation, as well as legal barriers that protected its virtual monopoly of the land. Its holdings, moreover, remained profitable throughout Philip's reign. Finally, the traditional, hierarchical social order was buttressed by religious institutions. Although Spanish Catholicism nominally owed ultimate obedience to the papacy, Philip was actually able to master the Spanish church and its considerable economic resources even more completely than Elizabeth could direct the English national Protestant church, which she officially headed under the terms of the Anglican Settlement. The Habsburg king's leading asset in this regard was the Inquisition, whose role as an agent of royal centralization he consciously expanded.[10]

At the same time, both societies continued to benefit from the long secular boom of the sixteenth century, manifested in economic and demographic growth.[11] These advances, Perry Anderson writes, suggest the "potential *field of compatibility* at this stage between the nature and programme of the Absolutist State and the operations of mercantile and manufacturing capital."[12] Yet the monarchy was not a progressive force

---

[9]Lawrence Stone, *The Crisis of the Aristocracy, 1558–1641* (Oxford: Clarendon Press, 1965), pp. 53, 97–100; idem, *The Causes of the English Revolution, 1529–1642* (New York: Harper and Row, 1972), p. 85; H. R. Trevor-Roper, "The Gentry 1540–1640," *Economic History Review Supplements* 1 (1953): 34; Anderson, pp. 48–49; Antonio Domínguez Ortiz, *The Golden Age of Spain, 1516–1659*, trans. James Casey (New York: Basic Books, 1971), pp. 114, 116–17.

[10]Stone, *Crisis*, pp. 746–47, 726; Hill, *Reformation to Industrial Revolution*, p. 22; Lynch, 1:103–5, 248; Domínguez Ortiz, pp. 117, 173–89, 217; J. H. Elliott, *Imperial Spain, 1469–1716* (New York: St. Martin's Press, 1964), p. 88; Jaime Vicens Vives, *An Economic History of Spain*, in collaboration with Jorge Nadal Oller, trans. Frances M. López-Morillas (Princeton: Princeton University Press, 1969), p. 340.

[11]In addition to the works cited in the previous notes, see Earl J. Hamilton, "The Decline of Spain," in *Essays in Economic History*, ed. E. M. Carus-Wilson (London: Edward Arnold, 1954), 1:215–16.

[12]Anderson, p. 41.

serving the interests of an urban bourgeoisie. Spain, of course, scarcely had a middle class of any kind. In England, where capitalism was considerably more important, 90 percent of the population remained on the land. The predatory monopolies the crown granted to leading London merchants were a sign of royal conservatism and in fact hindered the overall development of capitalism. The relative absence of popular uprisings in these years points to the same conclusion: the aristocracy was the dominant, and virtually unchallenged, class in late-sixteenth-century England and Spain.[13]

The neofeudal character of state and society is also apparent in the foreign policies of the two countries. By the 1580s, the relative caution of the first halves of Philip's and Elizabeth's reigns had given way to imperial offensives. The theater of war was the Atlantic, the obvious and inevitable choice for England but a new direction for Spain. Possessed of a global empire, Philip was able to turn his attention to the emergent Protestant, capitalist threat in northwestern Europe precisely because of the simultaneous peace in the Mediterranean and spurt in the supply of New World treasure. The half-century after 1580 saw the highest level ever of bullion shipments to Spain and, not coincidentally, the monarchy's most costly and persistent imperial efforts.

Although the concentration on the Atlantic required an increased emphasis on the navy, it did not signify a fundamentally commercial orientation. During the final two decades of the century, England and Spain both intervened in the Netherlands, France, and Ireland, in addition to fighting each other. The object of war, unchanged from the Middle Ages, was to acquire territory, the traditional source of wealth. The military thus remained the primary expenditure of the absolutist states. Characteristically, the major campaigns of England and Spain were attempts to quell uprisings by unruly subjects in Ireland and in the Netherlands, respectively. The structural parallel between these two ferocious attacks on indigenous populations extended even to matters of organization and command: both countries employed armies that utilized large mercenary components and that were personally led by powerful grandees, Essex in Ireland and Alba in the Low Countries.[14]

The dominant ideology, which sought at once to understand, to master, to disguise, and to justify the realities of late-sixteenth-century Spanish and English life, was a familiar, refurbished version of the medieval commitment to hierarchy and organic unity. It accorded the greatest es-

[13]Lynch, 1:106; Hill, *Reformation to Industrial Revolution*, pp. 45, 54; Elton, *England under the Tudors*, pp. 229 n. 1, 249; Hexter, pp. 71–116; Braudel, 2:738–39.

[14]Lynch, 1:304, 334; Elliott, pp. 235, 262–63; Vicens Vives, *Economic History*, pp. 323–24; Elton, *England under the Tudors*, p. 357; Anderson, pp. 29–33, 130–33, 48; Stone, *Causes*, p. 78.

teem to the monarchy, the aristocracy, and the church, groups that, combined with the educational system, were in turn the main propagators of the ideology. Both Elizabeth and Philip were apparently adept at arousing the adulation and affection of their subjects, regardless of class, though the latter's success declined noticeably beyond the borders of Castile. Part of their achievement rested on an ability to convince the people of England and Spain to equate royal policy with larger religious and nationalistic enthusiasms. Of course neither sovereign was insincere. Rather, the crown pursued interests that inevitably diverged from and, at least in the case of nationalism, ultimately conflicted with the deep convictions that it mobilized on its own behalf.

Yet the broad ideological consensus of the age must have depended on social and cultural patterns as well as on manipulation or false consciousness. Absolutism could emerge only where the preceding medieval urban florescence had not been excessively sustained or pervasive. Compared with the old Italian cities, the towns of England and Spain—an island and a peninsula situated on the western periphery of the continent—were relatively recent arrivals. Capitalist development in them was more primitive, internal class divisions were not so pronounced, and relations with the countryside were less antagonistic. One of the conditions of monarchical centralization, then, was the persistence of a social structure that may have ensured the survival of a comparative homogeneity in cultural predilection and practice among different, even opposing, classes. Certainly aristocrats continued to participate in a popular culture that, more generally, entered into a mutual exchange with learned culture.[15] Although such an interaction was hardly limited to Spain and England, perhaps this genuine basis for unity partly lay behind the crown's successful appeal.

The ideological position of the aristocracy was equally ambivalent, but for somewhat different reasons. The practices and values of the earlier, classical period of feudalism no longer sufficed in the sixteenth century. In Anderson's formulation: "The history of Western Absolutism is largely the story of the slow reconversion of the landed ruling class to the necessary form of its own political power, despite and against most of its previous experience and instincts."[16] This transformation ranged from economic, social, political, and military conduct to the cultural and educational attainments generally associated with humanism and the Renaissance. Nonetheless, the behavior of the nobility remained the model of emulation for all classes in both countries. Although the traditional aristocratic contempt for work did not penetrate English as deeply

---

[15]Peter Burke, *Popular Culture in Early Modern Europe* (New York: Harper and Row, 1978), pp. 23–29, 58–63.
[16]Anderson, p. 48.

as it did Spanish society, wealthy London merchants proved eager to purchase landed estates and to retire to the country for a life of genteel conspicuous consumption.

Finally, the national churches of England and Spain were institutions whose most deeply felt spiritual activities were often indistinguishable from propaganda campaigns in support of monarchy and aristocracy. Internally structured according to the same hierarchical principles that defined lay society, they also contributed to a conservative ideological hegemony through their judicial power. In Spain, religious law protected the aristocracy by barring interclass marriage. And in England, though the ecclesiastical courts lacked the muscle of the Inquisition, Archbishop Whitgift's High Commission successfully crushed the Puritan movement within the Anglican church.[17]

These major tendencies in late-sixteenth-century England and Spain together resulted in a stable but partial absolutism. But absolutism was never genuinely absolute, especially before 1600. For though the failure to centralize tended to diminish internal opposition, it also necessarily left intact and unreduced a range of social forces that threatened the ultimate goals of the crown. A convenient means of registering this potential danger is to look at the evolving rivalry between the two powers. Stretching from the early 1560s to beyond the turn of the century, the conflict grew into open warfare by the mid-eighties. In this respect the fate of the Armada, though scarcely a sign of English supremacy or Spanish impotence, marked a genuine break, particularly for the Elizabethans. More generally, however, the asymmetrical relationship of the two powers throughout the struggle reveals the larger differences between them, as well as what is not quite the same thing, the specific foes of absolutism in each country.

The basic distinction is that Spain had an empire, whereas England did not. Philip's holdings stretched from Italy and Flanders to America, Asia, and Africa; Elizabeth had trouble hanging on to nearby Ireland. Habsburg wealth and power depended profoundly on Indies silver; late Tudor imperial gains often rested on raiding the Spanish bullion convoys, that is, on looting the looters. Spain's empire, especially after the revolt of the Netherlands, was thus fiscal rather than commercial; its primary military orientation, despite the need to protect American metals shipments, was terrestrial rather than naval. Elizabethan England, by contrast, began to break with the typical absolutist pattern. Unable to compete on land, the ruling class turned to the sea to promote its inter-

[17]Anderson, pp. 38–39; Williams, pp. 41–42; Hill, *Society and Puritanism in Pre-Revolutionary England* (London: Secker and Warburg, 1964), pp. 501–4; Stone, *Crisis*, pp. 21–49; Elton, *England under the Tudors*, pp. 253, 421–29; Lynch, 1:171; Hexter, pp. 93–99; Domínguez Ortiz, pp. 201, 209, 230.

ests. The decision to rely on a fleet, though its commercial potential went largely unrealized at the time, oriented the dominant propertied class in the countryside in the same direction as the overseas merchants, the major propertied class of the towns.[18]

By 1600, in other words, though Spain retained the overwhelming preponderance of power, England was making the transition to capitalism. This exceptional development may be traced in economics, social relations, politics, and culture and ideology, all of which interacted with each other and in all of which those forces working to undermine absolutist unity gained momentum after 1588.[19]

Although originally an urban phenomenon, capitalism had penetrated the countryside well before the end of the century. The Elizabethan period witnessed a booming land market and, more important, a continuing transition to commercial agriculture by the rural propertied classes. The aristocracy also participated in the general advance of trade and industry, in the process developing close economic and social ties to the bourgeoisie. Spurred by the century-long price inflation, English capitalism increased social mobility while developing in general independence of and often opposition to the crown. One consequence was the relative and absolute rise of the gentry, merchants, and professionals (especially lawyers); another was the emergence of a landless rural proletariat. But the lower classes were not the only victims of economic change. The peerage seems to have suffered as well. Rising expenses on consumption, court, and borrowing combined with declining revenues from estates to produce a fall in real income that coincided with a general deterioration of the titled nobility's position within the ruling class and in society as a whole.

Equally crucial was the financial, bureaucratic, and military weakness of the monarchy, a legacy of early Tudor policy. Consequently, Elizabeth was forced throughout her reign to rely far more than she would have liked on the support of the gentry, both as national legislators in the House of Commons and as rulers of the countryside in the capacity of justices of the peace. In the context of the war-induced depression of the 1590s, Parliament attacked the growing corruption and inefficiency of the court system, itself a result of the desperate situation of a royal treasury exhausted by sustained military expenditure. The same decade

[18]Immanuel Wallerstein, *The Modern World-System: Capitalist Agriculture and the Origins of the European World-Economy in the Sixteenth Century* (New York: Academic Press, 1974), pp. 137–38, 149, 182, 309; Elton, *England under the Tudors*, p. 349; Anderson, pp. 134–35.

[19]In addition to the works cited in previous notes, the following valuable studies may be mentioned: Barrington Moore, Jr., *Social Origins of Dictatorship and Democracy: Lord and Peasant in the Making of the Modern World* (Boston: Beacon, 1966), pp. 3–14; R. H. Tawney, "The Rise of the Gentry, 1558–1640," in *Essays in Economic History*, ed. Carus-Wilson, 1:173–214.

witnessed an early idealization of the country, in oppostion to the city and especially the court. Yet at the same time this was only a secondary feature of a crucial ideological movement, the most important dimension of which was the rise of Puritanism. Elizabeth's open contempt for and economic exploitation of the Anglican church and her refusal to accept a moderate Puritan national religious settlement produced a spiritual and institutional vacuum that invited heterodoxy. Although the Puritans were driven from the orthodox church particularly after the Armada, when the decline of the external threat made the cause of internal unity and the need for compromise less overriding to the state, Puritanism struck roots among the laity, influencing Parliament, the universities, the gentry, the common lawyers, and the urban and rural lower middle classes. It also benefited from the failure of official censorship, in an atmosphere that simultaneously proved conducive to the spread of nationalism, ultimately a bourgeois phenomenon, as well as of individualism and skepticism. In short, increasingly lacking the material, social, and ideological requisites of absolutism, Elizabeth ruled by depending on the general prestige of the monarchy and the particular loyalty she was able to command.

Yet too narrow an emphasis on Puritanism makes it impossible to gauge the significance of the relation between Protestantism in general and the theater. "The tragedies of Shakespeare," Trotsky argued, "would be entirely unthinkable without the Reformation. . . . As a result of the Reformation, religion became individualistic."[20] If this commonsense claim is hard to dispute, it is even harder to corroborate. Protestantism won out on the Germanic fringes of Catholic Europe, in countries or regions too weak to have their way with the papacy.[21] Although the theater may have flourished in Switzerland, Germany, and the Netherlands during the sixteenth and seventeenth centuries, the most memorable plays of the age, at least from the perspective of the present, were composed and performed in Italy, England, Spain, and France. Of these four nations, of course, only England was Protestant: the common basis for this drama was not the Reformation but the Renaissance. Shakespeare did not write for a Reformation theater influenced by the Renaissance; he wrote for a Renaissance theater influenced by the Reformation. Accordingly, the Protestant contribution to the London theater will most likely appear in those dimensions of Elizabethan dramaturgy without analogues in Catholic Italy, France, and especially Spain and will almost certainly involve some sort of creative interaction between Renaissance and Reformation.

[20]Leon Trotsky, *Literature and Revolution*, trans. Rose Strunsky (Ann Arbor: University of Michigan Press, 1960), p. 242.
[21]Hill, *Reformation to Industrial Revolution*, p. 21.

Yet the Elizabethan suppression of the mystery plays and the apparent Puritan hostility to the stage have led some scholars to contrast Protestantism with drama and Reformation with Renaissance.[22] An implicit reply may be found in Gramsci's sense of the necessary, temporary trade-off between high culture and popular political effectiveness: "The classical example, previous to the modern period, is undoubtedly that of the Renaissance in Italy and the Reformation in the Protestant countries." Whereas the Renaissance never reached the people, "The Lutheran Reformation and Calvinism created a vast national-popular movement through which their influence spread: only in later periods did they create a higher culture. . . . the Reformation, in its higher phase, necessarily adopted the style of the Renaissance and as such spread even in non-protestant countries where the movement had not had a popular incubation."[23] Viewing both Renaissance and Reformation as modernizing movements of which Marxism is the culmination, Gramsci would have at least partly agreed with Althusser's interpretation of early Protestantism: "It is no accident that all ideological struggle, from the sixteenth to the eighteenth century, starting with the first shocks of the Reformation, was *concentrated* in an anti-clerical and anti-religious struggle."[24]

German and English history abundantly confirms the hypothesis of a contradictory unity between Renaissance and Reformation. The humanists paved the way for Luther with their critique of the church, their anti-Roman nationalism, and their appeal to the laity. The early spread of the Reformation was promoted by the pamphleteering of pro-Lutheran humanists, the preaching of humanist-educated clergy, the reserved support of Erasmus, and the growing involvement of Melanchthon, whose educational reforms eventually influenced England as well.[25] Similarly, after reviewing the vicious debate between More and Tyndale, Stephen Greenblatt concludes: "there are certain significant similarities between [them]. . . . The link here between the two enemies, Catholic and Reformer, is humanism."[26] Perhaps most important, however, was

[22]For example, Glynne Wickham, *Early English Stages, 1300 to 1660*, vol. 2, *1576–1660*, pt. 1 (London: Routledge and Kegan Paul, 1963), pp. 13–53.

[23]Antonio Gramsci, *Selections from the Prison Notebooks*, ed. and trans. Quintin Hoare and Geoffrey Nowell Smith (New York: International Publishers, 1971), pp. 393–94.

[24]Louis Althusser, "Ideology and Ideological State Apparatuses (Notes towards an Investigation)," in *Lenin and Philosophy and Other Essays*, trans. Ben Brewster (New York: Monthly Review Press, 1970), p. 151.

[25]A. G. Dickens, *The German Nation and Martin Luther* (London: Edward Arnold, 1974), pp. 21–71, 117; Roland H. Bainton, *The Reformation of the Sixteenth Century* (Boston: Beacon, 1952), p. 203; idem, *Studies on the Reformation* (Boston: Beacon, 1963), p. 106; Clyde Leonard Manschreck, *Melanchthon: The Quiet Reformer* (New York: Abingdon Press, 1958), pp. 13, 131–57.

[26]Stephen Greenblatt, *Renaissance Self-Fashioning: From More to Shakespeare* (Chicago: University of Chicago Press, 1980), p. 109.

the biblical philological humanism of Erasmus, Colet, and others that lay behind the theological revolution of Luther and the vernacular Bibles published by both Tyndale and Luther. Although the heart of Luther's system—justification by faith—required him to make a popular appeal, the overwhelming response he elicited seems to have depended less on fine points of doctrine than on the injunction to read the Gospels. As A. G. Dickens puts it, "For the mass of . . . [England's] people, this was the true Renaissance, the creative revival of Antiquity."[27] Bible reading was the center of a series of complex interrelationships characteristic of the Reformation—the decisive importance of the printing industry; the predominantly urban support for Protestantism, particularly among the middle and lower classes;[28] and perhaps the connection to the rise of capitalism.[29]

Such considerations point toward the Elizabethan theater, as later sections of this chapter seek to show. A still more crucial linkage between Bible and drama will emerge from a brief look at the Anglican religious settlement. Its compromise formulations, however variously interpreted, seem aimed at uniformity more in outer behavior than in inner belief.[30] And with good reason. The reading of the Bible was indeed designed to cultivate interiority, but it inevitably led to conflicting interpretations, personal religion, an anarchy of individual consciences, and conflict with society as well. These unintended consequences parallel not only various Renaissance motifs, but also the psychological complexity that distinguishes the treatment of character in Elizabethan drama and is particularly striking in the famous soliloquies. The conjunction of subjective interiority and a standardized, widely circulated text like the Bible may also anticipate the peculiarly quasi-public character of the soliloquy, a monologue at once heard and overheard.[31] To be sure, the disjunction between religious ceremony and religious conviction is not the only model for this dramatic resource. Nor was interiority confined to the English theater in sixteenth- and seventeenth-century Europe. Yet it informed no other national tradition to the same extent. If a parallel exists, it is perhaps to be found in the tragedies of Racine, whose

[27]Dickens, *German Nation*, pp. 132, 134, 225; idem, *The English Reformation* (London: Fontana, 1967), pp. 97–102. The passage quoted is from the latter work, p. 193.

[28]Dickens, *German Nation*, pp. 102–99; idem, *English Reformation*, pp. 105–12, 262–68, 362–79; Hill, *Reformation*, pp. 87–90; Conrad Russell, *The Crisis of Parliaments: English History, 1509–1660* (Oxford: Oxford University Press, 1971), pp. 112, 126–29, 136–39, 141–42; Elton, *Reform and Reformation: England, 1509–1558* (Cambridge: Harvard University Press, 1977), pp. 386–89.

[29]In addition to the classic statements by Marx, Weber, and Tawney, see Hill, "Protestantism and the Rise of Capitalism," in *Change and Continuity in Seventeenth Century England* (Cambridge: Harvard University Press, 1975), pp. 81–102.

[30]Bainton, *Reformation*, p. 201.

[31]Greenblatt, pp. 86–87.

Jansenist beliefs enabled him to draw on that very Augustinian position denied to the main line of Catholicism but emphasized in the thought of Luther.[32] In the particular historical circumstances of England, then, a humanist-inspired Protestantism developed internal contradictions that helped determine both the conflictual structure of Elizabethan drama and the struggles of the Civil War era.

Little of this experience—material, social, or ideological—is to be found in Spain, although here too military overextension led to economic crisis and mass impoverishment during the 1590s. Habsburg absolutism faced impediments of a different nature, derived, ironically, from the crown's greatest assets. "If the American Empire was the undoing of the Spanish economy," Anderson argues, "it was its *European* Empire which was the ruin of the Habsburg State, and the one rendered the extended struggle for the other financially possible."[33] First, New World silver undermined domestic production, not only by reinforcing the antiwork ethic, but also by introducing serious material obstacles. The price rise, which aided manufacturing and trade in England and in early-sixteenth-century Spain, had the opposite effect in Castile after 1550. Inflation drove up the costs of Spanish products, especially textiles, rendering them uncompetitive at home and abroad. Cheaper foreign goods flooded the domestic market and began to undersell Castilian exports to America. Industry's dilemma was reinforced by the technical narrowness imposed by the guilds, by the aristocracy's luxury spending on foreign goods, and by the effects of the government's own policies—taxation of exports and encouragement of imports, huge and burdensome military expenditures, disruption of trade owing to the anti-Protestant war, and devastating bankruptcies. In these circumstances, urban capital found it safer to invest in state annuities or in agriculture. As a result, the towns became increasingly parasitic off the peasantry, an exploitative relationship best exemplified by the capital city, Madrid. Thus the crown and its bullion mines probably bear primary responsibility for the demise of the Castilian bourgeoisie in the late sixteenth century.[34]

The dominant agricultural sector suffered a similar fate. To cash in on the Indies trade, spurred as it was by silver imports, much of Castile abandoned grain for wine and olive oil production. Since the migratory sheep of the *Mesta* were already eating away at the area under cereal cultivation, here too America worsened a precarious situation. By the 1570s

[32]Dickens, *German Nation*, p. 97.
[33]Anderson, p. 74. See also Vicens Vives, *Approaches to the History of Spain*, trans. and ed. Joan Connelly Ullman (Berkeley and Los Angeles: University of California Press, 1970), chap. 16.
[34]See Vilar, "Problems of the Formation of Capitalism," *Past and Present*, no. 10 (November 1956): 15–38.

Spain was a major grain-importing nation, and by the next decade it faced an agricultural crisis. In the latter part of the sixteenth century the Castilian peasantry, the majority landless laborers rather than dependent tenants or smallholders, may have been on the edge of starvation.[35] The rural population fled the countryside at an astonishing rate: only one-third of Spanish males worked in agriculture, while a greater number were entirely outside direct economic production. Finally, a succession of disasters during the late 1590s brought the century to a gloomy end, as failed harvests led to famine, plague, soaring prices, falling wages, and a population loss that wiped out the steady growth of a hundred years.

Politically, the corrosive effect of American metals was still more subtle. On the one hand, the bullion encouraged imperialism on a scale far beyond the capabilities of any other European power. On the other, Philip's forays ultimately proved beyond the capabilities of Spain as well. Habsburg defeats in the Protestant North, significant though they were, did not decisively weaken Spain. More important was the financial strain that imperial enterprises imposed on the state and the economy. However fast the crown's revenues from the New World grew, expenditures in the Old World rose more quickly. The bankruptcy of 1596 put an end to Philip's plans for northwestern Europe as well as to the economic vitality of much of northern Spain.

Even earlier, however, taxes on the Castilian population, which actually provided twice as much to the war effort as did royal income from America, had begun to take their economic and human toll. Castile, the largest and wealthiest region of the peninsula, was bound to pay heavily as long as the monarchy pursued grandiose imperial strategies. But its share of the costs was disproportionately onerous because of still another indirect effect of the crown's American patrimony. The substantial funds the state obtained from across the Atlantic disinclined it to undertake the absolutist integration of the entire peninsula—admittedly an arduous task. Thus Portugal retained its separatist liberties after it was annexed in 1580, Aragon was able to do the same after the suppression of its rebellion in 1592, and Castile, or rather the 90 percent of its people below the rank of *hidalgo*, footed the bill. Indeed, this crucial limitation on absolutism may be observed in a striking anomaly: the capital of the nation was neither the largest nor, economically, the most important city of the realm.

[35]Noël Salomon, *Recherches sur le thème paysan dans la "comedia" au temps de Lope de Vega* (Bordeaux: Féret, 1965), pp. 14–15. But see Carmelo Viñas y Mey, prólogo to *Tráfico marítimo y comercio de importación en Valencia a comienzos del siglo xvii*, by Alvaro Castillo Pintado (Madrid: Seminario de Historia Social y Económica de la Facultad de Filosofía y Letras de la Universidad de Madrid, 1967), pp. xiv–xv.

Correspondingly, despite the evident intellectual narrowing and tight censorship of late-sixteenth-century Spain, there were still ideological positions available that remained relatively independent of the crown. These may be summarized as the agrarian, the antiimperialist, and the regionalist alternatives. The first arose from the crisis on the land, the second from Castile's painful financial contribution to the European wars, and the third from the periphery's resentment of the overwhelmingly Castilian, even Madrilenian, orientation of the monarchy. All these dissenting voices were audible toward the end of the century. In addition, Catholicism offered an implicit distance from the state in two respects. First, Philip's reign was a period of intense spiritual activity within the church, but activity that usually originated outside the upper reaches of the hierarchy. And second, the Jesuits, as direct servants of the pope, constituted a potential threat to a ruler who was continually at odds with the Holy See and who expected the Spanish clergy to owe its primary obedience to the Habsburg, rather than the papal, state.

In both England and Spain, then, the incompleteness of absolutist consolidation proved intellectually and emotionally liberating by leaving open economic, social, or political spaces that could provide the basis for the expression of distinct perspectives. During the closing years of the century, every one of the positions outlined above, as well as others, appeared in society and drama alike. England clearly had a comparative advantage, however. It was in the process of transition from one mode of production to another, a historical movement that in this era as in others gave rise to basic and irreconcilable conflicts. Here is one of the most important sources of the differences, within a common unity, between the English and Spanish theaters, and particularly of the London dramatists' interest in psychological depth and tragic dilemmas. Elizabethan playwrights were able to mingle communal and individualist attitudes, to draw upon a pervasive and unique mixture of feudal, monarchical, humanist, bourgeois, and popular elements.[36]

Like their Spanish counterparts, they could often transform this multiplicity of materials into a comprehensive and synthetic vision that was not simply reducible to any one narrow class orientation. But it would be misleading to overemphasize the resulting unity, for two reasons. First, different perspectives were genuinely opposed to one another, in life and on the stage. Second, not all ideologies carried equal weight. Although the monarchies of England and Spain had achieved only a limited degree of centralization, they were still absolutist and their ideology

[36]For a synoptic view of English culture and society in the Renaissance, see Robert Weimann, *Shakespeare and the Popular Tradition in the Theater: Studies in the Social Dimension of Dramatic Form and Function*, ed. Robert Schwartz (Baltimore: Johns Hopkins University Press, 1978), pp. 161–69.

was still hegemonic. As in France, the conduct of the aristocracy was the main subject of the drama. In a telling contrast with the popular theater of Italy, Thomas Nashe insisted that English plays were "full of gallant resolution, not consisting, like theirs, of a Pantaloun, a Whore, and a Zanie, but of Emperours, Kings, and Princes."[37] What may loosely be called the serious genres—history plays, tragicomedy, and tragedy—often narrowed the subject even further, to focus on the fitness of the noblity to rule and especially on the tense unity between class and state, between lord and monarch, between the traditional rulers of society and the new mechanism of their political power. It is almost always in this context that other positions developed—whether supportive, modifying, or critical—and that departures from the aristocratic norm occurred.

Yet these alternative perspectives, constituent features of the contradictory unity of the age, ultimately distinguish English and Spanish from French drama. The latter is the drama of a class, the ruling class; the former is the drama of a class, but it is also the drama of a nation. This is so in part despite the nonnationalist direction of absolutism. In the age of the Renaissance, the new and still subordinate ideology of nationalism marked a clear advance over a feudal particularist or an absolutist dynastic conception of politics, while enlarging the range and significance of the drama. Any adequate understanding of that significance, however, requires a direct look at the theater.

## THEATER

Since the public theater was a part of late-sixteenth-century society, one might assume that it mirrored the society's larger relations—that the aristocracy, led by the monarchy, occupied the dominant position in its operation while the remaining, partly opposed classes played subordinate roles. Yet no significant area of social life can be reduced to a simple projection of other, more basic areas. On the one hand, the theater was influenced by a multiplicity of forces, upon which it in turn reacted; on the other, it had a history of its own, with its own logic and temporality.[38] Though the public theater was primarily shaped by the structure of society, one cannot deduce its nature, or even its existence, simply from the salient historical movements of the age. Still less is it possible to

[37]The quotation is from an excerpt printed in E. K. Chambers, *The Elizabethan Stage* (Oxford: Clarendon Press, 1923), 4:239.

[38]See Frederick Engels's letter to Joseph Bloch (London, September 21–22, 1890) in *The Marx-Engels Reader*, ed. Robert C. Tucker (New York: Norton, 1972), p. 640; and, more recently, Althusser's "Marxism Is Not a Historicism," in *Reading Capital*, by Althusser and Etienne Balibar, trans. Brewster (London: NLB, 1977), pp. 119–44.

deduce the plays of Lope de Vega or of Shakespeare directly from such trends, in part because these works were conditioned in important ways by the theaters for which they were written. In Spain as in England, the public theater was a crucial mediation between drama and society.

A disparity like the one between theater and society also characterizes the internal relations of the theater itself. The origins, nature, and impact of its constituent parts are homologous neither with one another nor with the institution as a whole. Indeed, the theater's economic, social, political, and ideological heterogeneity precludes any simple categorization. An emphasis on effective control of the stage—on patronage, licensing, censorship, and the like—points to the nobility and monarchy, as do the thematic preoccupations of most of the plays. One might reasonably speak in this sense of a neofeudal theater. Yet the large sums of money, the evident quest for profit, and the array of financial instruments integral to the operation of the public stage seem to indicate the dominance of the capitalist mode of production—a position argued by Christopher Hill.[39] Finally, a concern with physical structures, audiences, dramatists, and especially actors reveals the popular dimensions of the theater. The institution, then, was a socially composite organization. An interpretation that seeks to avoid one-sidedness must come to terms with this reality; an interpretation that seeks to avoid mere accumulation of data must attempt a theoretically coherent synthesis. The remainder of this chapter accordingly moves from the upper classes to the lower, and thus from the outside in, ending with a view of the public theater as a contradictory, but fundamentally artisanal institution.

## The Crown and the Aristocracy

The English monarchy's handling of the theater in the late sixteenth century reveals the absolutist drive of the state. Beginning in the 1570s, the Privy Council attempted to increase its authority over the actors, audiences, plays, writers, and time and place of performance, a task it largely completed in the last years of Elizabeth's reign and the first of James's. Although the crown's quest for power suffered certain vicissitudes and reverses in the course of these thirty years, the general trend was toward the creation of still another royally controlled economic monopoly. To take a significant example: a 1572 law all but banned acting companies that lacked the patronage of a member of the peerage, in this way simultaneously limiting the number of professional troupes and drawing those that remained closer to the monarchy.[40]

[39]Hill, *Reformation to Industrial Revolution*, p. 69.
[40]Chambers, 1:236–347, and, for the relevant documents, 4:259–345; Wickham, 2 (pt. 1): 13–149; J. Leeds Barroll, "The Social and Literary Context," in *The "Revels" History of*

In Spain, too, state control of the stage entered a distinct phase in the last third of the century, to a considerable extent because of the increase in commercial acting. Although no comprehensive study of this phenomenon seems to exist, a brief summary of some of the relevant data may suggest the scope of the government's activity. In 1565, the monarchy authorized the foundation in Madrid of a religious charity known as the Cofradía de la Pasión. Three years later, the same confraternity obtained the exclusive right to sponsor plays in Madrid, in order to finance its hospital. The licensing agency in this instance, as in most others that were later to concern the theaters, was the Council of Castile, a somewhat weaker version of Elizabeth's Privy Council. During subsequent decades, the council intervened in and adjudicated disputes between *cofradías* or hospitals over the division of stage earnings. It assigned duties—mainly involving money, public order, and the sexual segregation of the audience—to the commissioners appointed to regulate the theater, and it established the prices of certain seats. The council also licensed acting companies, determined the frequency with which they could perform, and decided and redecided on the legitimacy of professional actresses. As in England, it could close the theater—for a day, for an extended period, or permanently.[41] It took this last step in 1598, a year after the Privy Council applied a similar ban to the London stage.

In these respects, state control of late-sixteenth-century professional drama was pervasively and remarkably alike in the two countries. The greatest contribution of the two monarchs was therefore identical as well. Beyond the general sense in which absolutism helped create the conditions of possibility of the public theater, the crowns of England and Spain both allowed that theater to exist. This assistance ranged from the passive absence, most of the time, of any compelling political motive for suppressing the drama to a more active protection of the actors against their enemies. In England this second function was crucial by the 1570s; in Spain, characteristically, it did not assume significant proportions until about the turn of the century.

---

*Drama in English*, vol. 3, *1576–1613*, by Barroll et al. (London: Methuen, 1975), pp. 1–46; Leo G. Salingar, Gerald Harrison, and Bruce Cochrane, "Les comédiens et leur public en Angleterre de 1520 à 1640," in *Dramaturgie et société: Rapports entre l'oeuvre théâtrale, son interprétation et son public aux xvi<sup>e</sup> et xvii<sup>e</sup> siècles*, ed. Jean Jacquot, with Elie Konigson and Marcel Oddon (Paris: Editions du Centre National de la Recherche Scientifique, 1968), 2:536.

[41]N. D. Shergold, *A History of the Spanish Stage from Medieval Times until the End of the Seventeenth Century* (Oxford: Clarendon Press, 1967), pp. 177–79, 184 n. 2, 185, 187, 188, 195, 198, 386, 516–17; Othón Arróniz, *La influencia italiana en el nacimiento de la comedia española* (Madrid: Editorial Gredos, 1969), pp. 212, 217, 218–19; J. E. Varey and Shergold, "Datos históricos sobre los primeros teatros de Madrid: *Contratos de arriendo, 1587–1615*," *Bulletin Hispanique* 60 (1958): 73–74; the documents printed in Emilio Cotarelo y Mori, ed., *Bibliografía de las controversias sobre la licitud del teatro en España* (Madrid: Real Academia Española, 1904), pp. 619–20.

In like manner, patronage during this period benefited the English companies far more than the Spanish. It operated at the Tudor court in two interlocking ways. First, Elizabeth liked having plays performed before her in the winter season, in part, no doubt, as a cultural ornament of power. When the permanent playhouses closed because of plague or religious holiday, moreover, the court often provided the main economic alternative for the actors. Thus the public theaters were saved not just by absolutism in general, but by court drama in particular.[42] Second, the protection of the great lords raised the status of the actors, proving especially helpful in London. Those companies nominally attached to the leading peers of the realm played at court frequently and, as Burbage's decision to build the Theatre in 1576 suggests, had the best chance of bucking the city authorities. Along with a London foothold, patronage by a titled member of the nobility offered the surest guarantee of a troupe's survival. For this reason, although the number of companies declined slightly after 1570, those that remained enjoyed an unusually good chance of success. In part because of the higher aristocracy, the Elizabethan era was the age of consolidation of professional acting in England. This was not a one-way proposition, however. Powerful patronage and court appearances were both cause and effect of a viable troupe. Similarly, some companies reaped the economic rewards of highly placed connections, but the Queen's Men, despite their name, went into decline after 1585.[43]

Although some scholarly effort has been expended to demonstrate a similar pattern of theatrical interest at the Spanish court, it seems likely that Philip virtually ignored the drama during this period. He witnessed scarcely any *particulares*, or private performances, except perhaps on occasion as part of a royal triumph or entry. On the other hand, the Italian actor Ganassa did perform an *auto sacramental*, Spain's distinctive short religious play, before the king. In addition, professional companies participated in Spain's closest analogue to Elizabethan court drama— Christmas *particulares* before the Council of Castile. Finally, Ganassa and his troupe graced aristocratic weddings and other festivities.[44] But in Spain the patronage of the nobility could also often extend to the dramatist. During the late sixteenth century, the most important instance was Lope de Vega's prolonged residence and service at the court of the

---

[42]Chambers, 1:267; Wickham, 2 (pt. 1): 98, and 2 (pt. 2) (London: Routledge and Kegan Paul, 1972), p. 25; Barroll, p. 36.

[43]Salingar, Harrison, and Cochrane, 2:535–38; Alexander Leggatt, "The Companies and Actors," in *The "Revels" History*, by Barroll et al., p. 101.

[44]Arróniz, pp. 211, 213; Shergold, pp. 240–44; Hugo Albert Rennert, *The Spanish Stage in the Time of Lope de Vega* (New York: Hispanic Society of America, 1909), pp. 346, 349, 351.

duke of Alba in the early 1590s. Nonetheless, the more potent role of the English ruling class is undeniable.

The search for a still more direct impact of crown or nobility on the plays, however, is apt to be disappointed. The absolutist state and the high aristocracy, through their domination of society, became a frequent focus of the drama and their ideology its fundamental orientation. The general support of the stage provided by this hegemonic class only reinforced such theatrical tendencies. Some of the most impressive discussions of the relationship between the drama and its leading patrons do not really demonstrate much more than that.[45] In England the prospect of free costumes and elaborate scenery could have affected plays composed specifically for court performance, as a few of Shakespeare's perhaps were. Elizabeth herself may have requested the work that eventually became *The Merry Wives of Windsor* (1600). Without question, a royal setting encouraged an interest in the aristocratic tradition of festivity, an exploitation of pageantry, myth, masque, debate, and pastoral—the qualities, in other words, that characterize such efforts as Peele's *Arraignment of Paris* (1581), the anonymous *Rare Triumphs of Love and Fortune* (1582), and, above all in this period, the plays of Lyly (mainly 1584–90). The latter's achievement was eventually adapted and transformed by Shakespeare, especially in *Love's Labour's Lost* and *A Midsummer-Night's Dream* (both 1595), two works that seem especially suitable for an aristocratic audience. But well before that, Lyly's court successes may have prompted the professional actors to seek the services of classically trained, university-educated playwrights for the public stage. More generally, the crown's longtime interest in both learned and spectacular drama left its mark on the commercial theater.[46]

The significance of Lope's stay with the duke of Alba is harder to assess, since the dramatist seems to have pioneered most of the characteristic features of his Alban plays earlier, in the late 1580s. At the least, however, this period reinforced Lope's interest in pastoral and his resort to rustic autobiographical disguise. Both are rooted in an aristocratic milieu and specifically in the unequal relationship between poet and patron. Most important, Lope's pastorals during these years constituted the point of departure from which he ultimately arrived at his well-

---

[45]E.g., Jean Duvignaud, *Les ombres collectives: Sociologie du théâtre*, 2d ed. (Paris: Presses Universitaires de France, 1973), pp. 201–11; Marion Jones, "The Court and the Dramatists," in *Elizabethan Theatre*, ed. John Russell Brown and Bernard Harris, Stratford-upon-Avon Studies, no. 9 (London: Edward Arnold, 1966), pp. 169–95.

[46]Barroll, p. 20; Chambers, 1:6; Jones, p. 185; G. K. Hunter, *John Lyly: The Humanist as Courtier* (Cambridge: Harvard University Press, 1962), pp. 89–158, 298–348; Salingar, Harrison, and Cochrane, 2:539; Wickham, 2 (pt. 1): 44–45.

known peasant plays.[47] The generative force behind this movement, however, was in large part the public theater.

Such a perspective inevitably calls into question the belief, particularly widespread in English scholarship, that, as E. K. Chambers put it, "On the literary side the *milieu* of the Court had its profound effect in helping to determine the character of the Elizabethan play as a psychological hybrid, in which the romance and the erudition, dear to the bower and the library, interact at every turn with the robust popular elements of farce and melodrama."[48] Yet the court was hardly alone in bringing popular and learned traditions together: the pervasiveness of social and cultural mixing to a considerable extent defined the age. But "the *milieu* of the Court" in particular, as opposed to the impact of the state in general, contributed little to the lower-class side of the drama, nor was it the primary source of the crucial neoclassical dimension. Marion Jones has aptly noted that "the masterpieces of Elizabethan drama were not what the patron ordered."[49] But of course, when it came to the plays themselves, the court was rarely the main patron. According to an anonymous writer of the early seventeenth century, "Howsoever he [the actor] pretends to have a royal master or mistress, his wages and dependance prove him to be the servant of the people."[50] To return to a basic theme of this study: the dramatic synthesis of popular and learned traditions was achieved only in the public theaters of Renaissance England and Spain.

Royal involvement with the stage also had a less attractive side, attributable to the state's absolutist tendencies. In the long run, patronage in England opened a breach between theater and populace. As early as the 1580s, the government's formation of the Queen's Men, centralist in intent, may have temporarily hindered the development of drama. The crown also cashed in on its monopoly by selling various stage licenses through the Office of the Revels, whose occupant seems to have followed standard late Elizabethan practice by supplementing his income through a regular system of bribery.[51] Most deleterious, however, was

---

[47]Salomon, pp. 448−51; Rinaldo Froldi, *Lope de Vega y la formación de la comedia*: *En torno a la tradición dramática valenciana y al primer teatro de Lope*, trans. Franco Gabriele and Mrs. de Gabriele (Salamanca: Anaya, 1968), pp. 134−59.

[48]Chambers, 1:3.

[49]Jones, p. 189. See also Louis Adrian Montrose, "'Shaping Fantasies': Figurations of Gender and Power in Elizabethan Culture," *Representations*, no. 2 (Spring 1983): 81−86.

[50]Excerpted from a 1615 document printed in Chambers, 4:256.

[51]Wickham, 2 (pt. 1): 19; Barroll, pp. 25, 37-38; Andrew Gurr, *The Shakespearean Stage, 1574−1642* (Cambridge: Cambridge University Press, 1970), pp. 92−94; M. C. Bradbrook, *The Rise of the Common Player: A Study of Actor and Society in Shakespeare's England* (Cambridge: Harvard University Press, 1962), p. 63.

the practice of political, religious, and ethical censorship that operated in both countries.[52]

Yet monarchical direction of the stage had its limits. Even the French government in the age of Louis XIV possessed nothing like the coercive power of a modern totalitarian state. The royal prerogative was more limited still in the late sixteenth century. It is often hard to know whether the gap between royal dictate and theatrical practice in Spain indicates such limits or merely arises from the absence of the relevant documentation. Clearly, however, the monarchy's legal restrictions on the number of dramatic companies never came close to realization.[53] In England the record is unambiguous. The centralizing 1572 law mentioned above neither entirely eliminated gentry patronage of professional troupes nor stemmed the growth of commercial theatrical performance. The prohibition against public playing during Lent was often evaded, and the government's attempt to use the stage during the Marprelate controversy backfired because the actors quickly escaped the control of their nominal masters. The weakness of central power, even as regarded the drama, is suggested by the opening passage of a 1601 letter from the Privy Council to the justices of Middlesex and Surrey, sites of the public theaters:

> It is in vaine for us to take knowledg of great abuses and disorders complayned of and to give order for redresse, if our directions finde no better execution and observation then it seemeth they do, and wee must needes impute the fault and blame thereof to you or some of you, the Justices of the Peace, that are put in trust to see them executed and perfourmed, whereof wee may give you a plaine instance in the great abuse contynued or rather encreased in the multitude of plaie howses and stage plaies in and about the cittie of London.

This plea, representing the unsuccessful culmination of a four-year effort, reveals the reliance of the Privy Council on the gentry for the enforcement of its administrative decisions, even on the outskirts of London. Eventually, of course, the crown paid dearly for precisely this dependence.[54]

[52]Defense of Spanish censorship: Edward M. Wilson and Duncan Moir, *The Golden Age: Drama, 1492–1700*, vol. 3 of *A Literary History of Spain*, gen. ed. R. O. Jones (London: Ernest Benn, 1971), pp. 28–29. English censorship: Gerald Eades Bentley, *The Profession of Dramatist in Shakespeare's Time, 1590–1642* (Princeton: Princeton University Press, 1971), pp. 145–96.

[53]Rennert, p. 146.

[54]Salingar, Harrison, and Cochrane, 2:535–36; Gurr, p. 56; Chambers, 1:294–95; Bradbrook, pp. 48, 61. The letter from which the quotation comes is printed in Chambers, 4:332–33.

## The Clergy and the Bourgeoisie

In addition, both governments faced open opposition to their policies toward the theater. Religious objections developed along parallel lines in the two countries,[55] most generally as part of an international learned movement to reform popular culture that began in the sixteenth century.[56] Nonetheless, Spanish clerical opinion, unlike its English counterpart, was mixed. Ony beginning in the late 1590s was the issue of the theater widely debated. The closest similarity was actually between the sixteenth-century Puritans in England and the seventeenth-century Jesuits in Spain. The explanation for this apparently anomalous consensus is not to be found simply in the standard biblical and patristic sources utilized by theater foes in both nations. It is also related to the common structural position of the two movements: neither one was adequately incorporated into the political-clerical hierarchy of the state. This relative autonomy was the institutional basis of ideological challenge. Indeed, most of the Spanish opposition came not from the secular clergy, which was mainly concerned with local affairs, but from the regular clergy, which, according to J. C. J. Metford, .evaluated the theater "in general terms as it affected the whole of Spain in particular and Christendom in the broader aspect."[57]

But what were the English and Spanish clerics challenging? The dates of the attack tell the story. In England, the Puritan assault began in 1577; in Spain, little Catholic invective survives from before 1581. Thus the object of controversy was not dramatic performance, which, after all, the Jesuits favored. Nor was it professional acting, which especially in England had a long history behind it by the late sixteenth century. It was rather the extraordinary popularity of an entirely new phenomenon, the permanent, public, commercial theater, that evoked religious hostility in this era. The opposition did not achieve much success. Certain minor changes owed something to clerical pressure, but except for the temporary suppression of the Spanish stage in 1598, little came of religious protest. Even this atypical victory depended more on the will and sensibility of a pious, dying monarch than on the independent power of the church. Precisely this lack of political clout accounts for the relative failure of the religiously based antitheatrical campaigns in both countries.

[55]See J. C. J. Metford, "The Enemies of the Theatre in the Golden Age," *Bulletin of Hispanic Studies* 28 (1951): 76–92, esp. 85. The documentary evidence on which the arguments in this and the following two paragraphs are based may be found in Chambers, 4:184–259, and Cotarelo y Mori, passim.

[56]Burke, pp. 207–22.

[57]Metford, p. 81.

But in England the Puritans found immediate allies in the city fathers of London.

During the late sixteenth century, the most important difference between the battle for control of the stage in England and the comparable struggle in Spain was the antipathy to the theater of the city officials of London, as opposed to the general enthusiasm of the urban government in Madrid. Not all Spanish cities emulated the capital, however, as some apparently unnoticed but significant parallels reveal. In a 1592 appeal to Archbishop Whitgift, the lord mayor of London claimed that as a result of the theater, "the prentizes & seruants [were] withdrawen from their woorks, . . . to the great hinderance of the trades & traders of this Citie," an argument that the mayor and aldermen repeated almost verbatim to Burghley two years later and to the Privy Council three years after that. Sevillian city officials complained of the theater in 1580 that "eran muchos los perjuicios que se seguían de que los *trabajadores con afán de ir tras* aquella novedad abandonaron sus oficios" ("many were the damages that followed from the fact that the *workers, with an eagerness to pursue* that novelty, abandoned their trades"), to the consequent detriment of the economy. The same year, local authorities in Valladolid sought to prevent performances by Ganassa's company because it "a sacado y saca gran cantidad de dinero desta villa y an rresultado otros muchos ynconbinientes" ("has taken and takes a great quantity of money from this city and many other difficulties have resulted"), an echo of the charge made in 1574 by the Common Council of London, which labeled the theater an "vnthriftye waste of the moneye of the poore and fond persons."[58]

The city of Madrid's 1598 *Memorial* to Philip requesting that the theaters be reopened offers an entirely different set of parallels. By arguing that in the drama "juntamente se mezcla el gusto y recreación del espíritu con la buena doctrina del entendimiento" ("pleasure and recreation of the spirit are mixed together with the good doctrine of the understanding"), it evoked the traditional Horatian mixture of delight and instruction found also in Sidney, among others. In claiming that plays showed the reward of virtue and the punishment of vice, the *Memorial* adopted another favorite humanist trope, used in England during this period by Whetstone, Harrington, and Nashe. Its insistence that religious theater accomplished "lo que la predicación santa del santo Evangelio de Jesucristo puede hacer" ("what holy preaching of the holy gospel of Jesus Christ can do") was sufficiently common in England to be

---

[58]The English quotations are taken from documents printed by Chambers, 4:307, 317, 322, 274; the Spanish ones are cited by Arróniz, pp. 215, 214. See also Jean Sentaurens, "Sobre el público de los 'corrales' sevillanos en el Siglo de Oro," in *Creación y público en la literatura española*, ed. J. F. Botrel and S. Salaün (Madrid: Editorial Castalia, 1974), p. 62.

quoted in outrage by foes of the stage like Stubbes. When the city defended the *comedia*, and therefore the basic Spanish play of the period, as a "memoria de las historias antiguas y hechos heroicos loables" ("memoir of old history and heroic, praiseworthy deeds") that preserved "la fama de los pasados" ("the fame of those from the past"), it was asserting no more than Nashe did of the Shakespearean history play. Madrid's suggestion that idlers were better off at the theater than anyplace else was also made by Nashe, as well as by Chettle. Finally, in reminding Philip that well-trained actors were essential on Corpus Christi Day, the city government was proceeding much as the English companies had in emphasizing to the Privy Council their need for practice so as better to serve the queen.[59]

These admittedly selective analogues do not convey the full range of arguments deployed for and against the stage in the late sixteenth century. But they do suggest the basic social issues in question. Seville was the commercial center of Spain. Its theaters, unlike most of those in the rest of the nation, were not run by religious confraternities. Instead, they operated according to a system of private enterprise fairly close to the one prevailing in London. Valladolid, too, had a privately owned and operated playhouse, or *corral*, though this was not the one at which Ganassa's performance elicited the irritated comments quoted above. In other words, while a neofeudal social class—the crown and the aristocracy—defended the stage, a capitalist ruling class attacked an at least partly capitalist industry as a threat to capitalism. Yet this is not really so strange a situation. Bourgeois class consciousness does not necessarily imply a defense of the conduct of every individual capitalist; conversely, the individual capitalist, or even capitalist sector, may often develop vital interests that conflict with those of the class as a whole. Thus, the Merchant Taylors, though opposing the stage, declined the mayor's request that they bribe the master of the Revels to suppress it: "albeit the Companie think yt a very good service to be performed yet wayinge the damage of the president and enovacion of raysinge of Anuyties upon the Companies of London what further occasions yt may be drawne unto, . . . they thinke this no fitt course to remedie this myscheife."[60]

Is it really fair, however, to reduce the city's grounds of opposition to the theater to a species of class consciousness? Given the sheer number of arguments employed by the mayor and aldermen, genuine motives

[59]The *Memorial* is printed in Cotarelo y Mori, pp. 421–25. Sidney's comments are from "An Apologie for Poetrie," in *English Literary Criticism: The Renaissance*, ed. O. B. Hardison, Jr. (New York: Appleton-Century-Crofts, 1963), pp. 106–7. The other English writers are excerpted in Chambers, 4:202, 211, 223, 237–38, 238–39, 242–44, 299, 312.

[60]Sentaurens, p. 57; Shergold, pp. 193–94. The document quoted appears in Chambers, 4:309.

are hard to disentangle.[61] But London's leaders showed a consistent concern, shared by the Puritans, with preserving the hierarchical social order. Their conservative brand of capitalism bore little resemblance to the individualistic, laissez-faire version that emerged in the nineteenth century. Nonetheless, their attitude went beyond a mere traditionalist's sense of political responsibility. The public theater's plebeian appeal involved the very class on which their wealth and social position largely depended. It is the stage's generally unverbalized threat to stable ties of domination and exploitation—a threat extending to sexual as well as to class relations—that they seem to have felt most deeply.[62]

In Madrid, the urban ruling class probably had a far larger rentier component than in London and in this sense was not really a bourgeoisie at all. The populace of the town seems to have lacked even the incipient class consciousness discernible among London's lower orders. In addition, the local government, or Ayuntamiento, did not have to face the dilemma of a theater industry organized for private profit. This was no accident: since the economics of the stage often mimicked the productive relations of the surrounding society, the contradictions that arose in London and Seville were intrinsic to capitalist development in those cities. Accordingly, the attitude of officials in the Spanish capital reveals less of the London aldermen's obsession with the social linkages of the under classes, though in 1602 they did prohibit artisans from attending the theater on workdays.[63] In general, however, the Ayuntamiento assumed an aristocratic stance of tolerant condescension toward its inferiors, explaining that the *comedia* teaches "los indoctos" ("the unlearned"). Its defense of the theater was couched in precapitalist terms: it speciously stressed the long, illustrious tradition of the stage abroad and in Spain and consequently counseled against any sudden change in so venerable an institution. Similarly, most of the late-sixteenth-century clerical attacks on Spanish drama ignored the social and economic issues so prominent in English religious criticism of the time. In fact, the one truly class-conscious thrust at the Spanish public theater in this period was launched by a layman, the former dramatist Argensola, whose perspective was openly and arrogantly aristocratic, most notably in its fear of the social consequences of sexual liaisons between the nobility and the actresses.[64]

The distinction between London and Madrid also clarifies the position of the Puritans. Although the city's open antagonism toward the stage

[61]Barroll, p. 30.

[62]Jonas Barish's emphasis in *The Antitheatrical Prejudice* (Berkeley and Los Angeles: University of California Press, 1981), pp. 80–117, esp. 114–17, on a transhistorical antitheatrical authoritarianism is compatible with this conclusion.

[63]Rennert, p. 215 n. 1.

[64]Argensola's *Memorial* is printed by Cotarelo y Mori, pp. 66–68.

preceded the religious campaign, it is not certain whether the Puritans took over this political opposition or, as is more likely, were themselves commissioned by the London bourgeoisie to join the fray.[65] Either way, their main function was to reinforce an existing attitude—one, moreover, that reflected a particular social bias. For, in fact, there is nothing more striking than the failure of this side of Puritanism to cut across class lines. Since the writing of history has usually belonged to the victors, the lower classes have not left behind many records of their opinions and motives. But this period offers no evidence for believing that Puritan values, though they struck deep roots in London, turned a substantial portion of the populace against the theater. The contrary, if anything, is suggested by the mayor's futile order of 1582 that the freemen of the companies not "suffer any of ther sarvants, apprentices, journeymen, or children, to repare or goe to annye playes, peices, or enterludes, either within the cittie or suburbs thereof."[66]

At the other end of the social scale, the evidence is unambiguous. Very few Catholic or pro-Catholic peers patronized professional actors; among militant Protestant, Puritan-leaning, or overtly Puritan aristocrats, the opposite was the case. Burghley at least acquiesced in the Privy Council's support of the stage; Walsingham had much of the responsibility for the formation of the Queen's Men, the most important troupe of the 1580s. Essex, Sussex, Lincoln, Warwick, and Leicester all had dramatic companies, of which the latter's was the crucial one during the 1570s. At least in the earlier part of Elizabeth's reign, Lord Hunsdon was sympathetic to Puritanism; in the 1590s he patronized Shakespeare's company, the Lord Chamberlain's Men. Hence, especially during the 1570s and 1580s, when the Puritan movement within the church was at its height, the leading peers of the realm simultaneously shielded it from state repression and protected the theater from its attacks.[67]

Yet as the discussion of the mystery cycles in the previous chapter has already suggested, the Reformation clearly complicated the problem of royal control of the theater. The stage posed genuine problems for the English monarchy. Even when its plays did not contain ideological challenges, an important, if subordinate, class attempted to suppress them. The state's centralizing policy toward the theater was a response to this dilemma. The stage thus became from the start an institutional battleground for some of the struggles that were fought out rather more de-

[65]For the former position, see Wickham, 2 (pt. 1):81; for the latter, see Bradbrook, pp. 67, 70,75, 294 n. 1.
[66]The Lord Mayor's "Precept" may be found in Chambers, 4:287.
[67]Stone, *Crisis*, pp. 727–39; Chambers, 1:266–67; Margot Heinemann, *Puritanism and Theatre: Thomas Middleton and Opposition Drama under the Early Stuarts* (Cambridge: Cambridge University Press, 1980), pp. 18–36.

finitively in the Civil War. Partly as a result, the same issues made their way into a number of the plays. By contrast, the Spanish crown faced no social threats. Since its power was uncontested in Castile, it confronted no organized impediments to its direction of the theater. For the same reason, the government could delegate responsibility, secure in the knowledge that local administrators would at least attempt to implement its programs. In these circumstances, neither magnate patronage nor monarchical consolidation of power was necessary.

The differences between London and Madrid thus helped generate the divergent conduct of the English and Spanish ruling classes. But in one important respect, the two city governments shared a common fate: neither was very successful. Madrid's *Memorial* fell on deaf ears. London's mayor and aldermen did a little better, gaining a prohibition on Sunday performances and, more significantly, preventing the construction of any commerical theaters within their jurisdiction. But although, unlike the Ayuntamiento of Madrid, they were not impotent before royal authority, the limits of their power were soon reached. London was in no position to take on the national government directly: the monarchy triumphed for precisely this reason. As long as the crown secured the support of the landed aristocracy, it was safe. But when the gentry defected, neither the absolutist state nor the stage it protected long survived.

In the late sixteenth century, members of the bourgeoisie influenced the theater less as politicians or ideologues than as capitalists. The capitalist system is adequately defined neither as a spirit of enterprise and economic rationality[68] nor as the organization of production for distant markets, motivated by a desire for profit.[69] It is characterized not only by generalized commodity production and circulation based on absolute private property, but also and more importantly by the contradiction within its forces of production—that is, by the separation of the immediate producer from the means of production. Since the forces of production circulate freely on the market, they too are commodities. This holds true not only for the means of production, including, at least as far as changes in property title go, the land itself, but also for the living human component of the forces of production. In other words, labor appears as a commodity that must be sold by a propertyless class, the proletariat, as its only means of livelihood.

Technically speaking, the capitalist, owner of the means of produc-

---

[68]For this position see Max Weber, *The Protestant Ethic and the Spirit of Capitalism*, trans. Talcott Parsons (New York: Scribner's, 1958).

[69]The trade-centered theory of capitalism, though foreign to Marx's conception, has appeared from time to time in Marxian scholarship. A recent and important instance is Wallerstein, passim.

tion, pays for the human capacity for labor, or labor-power. In return, however, he receives not labor-power but labor, not that part of the day's work needed for the maintenance of the laborer, but the entire day's work. The difference between the two constitutes surplus labor, the source of surplus-value. In feudalism surplus is extracted by extraeconomic coercion; in capitalism it is extracted by a voluntary wage contract. The classical locus of the capitalist mode of production is accordingly industry, rather than agriculture or even trade and finance.[70]

Some preliminary observations may clarify the significance of this theory, derived from Marx, for a study of the theater. First, the indisputably commercial character of the London playhouse must not in itself be taken as a sign of a capitalist enterprise. Commercialism is a necessary but by no means a sufficient condition of capitalism. Second, if the theater can be located in any one branch of economic activity, it inevitably appears as a kind of industry rather than as a form of trade or finance. Yet here a problem arises. The theory of surplus-value applies only to productive labor. Although Marx did not distinguish between productive and unproductive labor in an entirely consistent fashion, he may have considered the labor that goes into the formation of immaterial goods, such as a theatrical performance, to be unproductive.[71] Hence any discussion of the theater industry as a capitalist industry may have to rely at least in part on analogy.

It will therefore be useful to begin with those dimensions of the playhouse most influenced by capital. First of all, the public theaters were a consequence of the rise of capitalism, a fundamental change primarily responsible for the spread of commercialization and the development of centers of population and commodity exchange. During this period the presence of the crown had much the same effect, to some extent in London and especially in Madrid. But the principal cause of Renaissance urbanization is beyond question. Although the city in itself by no means sufficed to bring forth a public theater, no other locale provided the economic and demographic conditions necessary for the successful interaction of investor, actor, dramatist, and audience. On the other hand, in England at least, capitalist dynamism eventually helped undermine some of the other bases of the public stage.[72]

But in the late sixteenth century, the geographical distribution of permanent, commercial, outdoor theaters correlated closely with large con-

[70]Much of the technical terminology in the summary above is explained by Marx in *Capital: A Critique of Political Economy*, vol. 1, introd. Ernest Mandel, trans. Ben Fowkes (New York: Vintage, 1977), pp. 270–306, 873–940.

[71]Marx, *Capital*, vol. 2, introd. Mandel, trans. David Fernbach (New York: Vintage, 1981), pp. 207–77. See also Mandel's introduction, pp. 41–45.

[72]Weimann, p. 177.

centrations of population. With the opening of the Theatre in 1576 and of several other similar structures in succeeding years, London, essentially the sole city of the realm, also became the first and almost the only English town to possess any permanent playhouses. At that time the situation was very different in Spain, where urban development was far more evenly spread than in England. Madrid was smaller than Valencia and Seville and may also have been surpassed by Granada, Barcelona, Zaragoza, Toledo, and Valladolid.[73] *Corrales* were built in all these cities, as well as in many others, often before 1580. Madrid's Corral de la Cruz, for instance, opened in 1579.[74] The particular incompleteness of Spanish absolutism encouraged this national dispersal of theaters. But from a longer view, the position of state and stage alike resulted from historical trends that originated early in the Reconquest, just as the preeminence of London and its drama was generated by forces that in part antedated by centuries the rise of the Tudors. Most of the *corrales*, however, had little influence on the course of the *comedia*, since the administrative consolidation inherent in the establishment of a fixed capital inevitably resulted in Madrid's dominance. The winning formula for Renaissance absolutist drama was the copresence of court and commerce in the urban center of the nation. But at first Seville and Valencia were probably as important as Madrid, and Valencia may well have been the theatrical center of the country to the end of the century.

Capital also played a more direct role in the history of the public stage, in matters of ownership and management. Here, too, broad distinctions between the two societies, rooted in their very different heritages, produced contrasting organizational procedures that in turn helped lead to divergent paths of dramatic evolution. As already noted, in London the public theaters were run for private profit. The main beneficiaries were the owners of the property on which the playhouses were erected and especially the merchants who lent or invested the large sums necessary for their construction. Thus, James Burbage leased the land for the Theatre and then, in need of funds to cover building costs, entered into a partnership with a wealthy grocer. But even his limited entrepreneurial activity was extremely atypical among actors. Henslowe, a "citizen and dyer of London," constructed the Rose with a "citizen and grocer of London," and Francis Langley, "a citizen and goldsmith of London," built the Swan. Although with the exception of Henslowe all outside

---

[73]Domínguez Ortiz, pp. 134–35; Vicens Vives, *Economic History*, pp. 330, 428. See also n. 89 below.

[74]Shergold, pp. 177–86, 191–97; Thomas Middleton, "El urbanismo madrileño y la fundación del Corral de la Cruz," in *Cinco jornadas de teatro clásico español: El trabajo con los clásicos en el teatro contemporáneo*, Almagro, 1982, ed. Juan Antonio Hormigón (Madrid: Ministerio de Cultura, 1983), 1:135–69.

speculators were hurt by plague, fire, and licensing restraints, these men in general were able to exercise considerable power and make handsome returns on their investments.[75]

But how should these economic arrangements be understood? It is necessary to distinguish among the ownership and leasing out of land, the construction of a theater on that land, and the subsequent operation of the playhouse for profit. In his discussion of ground-rent, Marx repeatedly and explicitly links agriculture and the building industry: "this farmer-capitalist pays the landowner . . . a contractually fixed sum of money . . . , for the permission to employ his capital in this particular field of production. This sum of money is known as ground-rent, irrespective of whether it is paid for agricultural land, building land, mines, fisheries, forests, etc. . . . Ground-rent is thus the form in which landed property is economically realized, valorized. We have together here, moreover, and confronting one another, all three classes that make up the framework of modern society—wage-labourer, industrial capitalist, landowner."[76] The ground-rent received by the landowner, one step removed as it is from the actual production process, may in fact inhibit the accumulation of capital.[77] On the other hand, building a theater, insofar as it entails the employment of wage labor, is an unambiguously capitalist activity. Yet it also represents only a relatively brief moment in the economic history of the playhouse. The dominant mode of production of the theater therefore depends on the social relations that prevail when the structure is used for the performance of plays.

Such considerations at least raise the question of the extent of capitalist involvement in the theater. Another kind of modifying perspective is offered by contemporary events in Spain. Peninsular analogues to English institutional arrangements in Valladolid and especially in Seville have already been noted. Some lesser instances may also be mentioned. Ground-landlords were part of the Valencian theater and leased out some of Madrid's early *corrales*. But the normal pattern was quite different. The reign of Philip II witnessed the founding of numerous religious houses and charitable organizations. These latter groups regularly owned both the theaters and the land beneath, devoting their profits to the administration of their hospitals. The Cofradía de la Pasión and the Cofradía de la Soledad together managed the Madrid public theaters as a monopoly. Beyond the immediate eleemosynary intent, one purpose of this system was to prevent the theater from becoming a capitalist busi-

[75]Chambers, 1:395, 387, 406, 411, and 2:358; Wickham, 2 (pt. 1): 115, 134, 149, and 2 (pt. 2): 25–26; Gurr, pp. 48–49.
[76]Marx, *Capital*, vol. 3, introd. Mandel, trans. Fernbach (Harmondsworth, Middlesex: Penguin, 1981), pp. 755–56.
[77]Marx, *Capital*, 3:898–99. See also Mandel's introduction, p. 65.

ness. In Madrid, for instance, leases between private individuals and the *cofradías* placed limits on the former's profits. Similar concerns were expressed in Zaragoza.[78] Such practices went against the economic trends, however, and eventually had to be modified.

But in the late sixteenth century, the public theater operated along capitalist lines to a greater extent in England than in Spain. What consequences did this difference have? First, since it reflected in exaggerated form larger economic, social, and ideological distinctions between the two countries, it reinforced the corresponding divergences within the drama. The secularization of the English stage, an indication of the bourgeois future, and the roughly contemporaneous florescence of the Spanish religious play, a sign of the feudal past, provide obvious and important examples. Perhaps of still greater significance were the effects on the security of the theater. Even more than the need for accomplished actors to perform in the *autos sacramentales* given on Corpus Christi Day, the charitable destination of the admission receipts prevented the clerical attack on the *corrales* from leading to their suppression. Various critics, however, considered collecting alms from an immoral source to be a perversion of religion. Indeed, a 1598 recommendation to close the theaters, heeded by Philip, plausibly suggested that alternative sources be found. Apparently the work of Spanish hospitals was a less formidable defense than the recreational pleasures of an English queen. The financial requirements of the *cofradías* nonetheless carried considerable weight. A single example must suffice. In 1589, responding to a request from Madrid's Hospital General for a definitive judgment, the theologians at the University of Alcalá de Henares concluded that although the theater might well be immoral, the profits of immorality most certainly were not.[79] Lacking this double buttress of *auto* and hospital, the English stage was at once more vulnerable to religious hostility and more immediately dependent on royal favor. The long-range effects of its position suggest that, for the character and survival of the public theater, in the end charity was a more effective ally than monarchy.

## Playhouses and Playgoers

An interesting parallelism characterizes recent discussion of the physical structures of the London playhouses and the social composition of their audiences. In both instances, traditional scholarly emphasis on the

---

[78]Shergold, pp. 181–85, 194–98.
[79]Metford, p. 90; Shergold, p. 522; the documents printed by Cotarelo y Mori, pp. 64–65, 563, 396, 324–25.

predominance of the popular has been challenged by a revisionist insistence on the centrality of the elite. According to Richard Hosley, the Eizabethan platform stage seems to derive from "the booth stage of the marketplace," and the Fortune, opened in 1600, may owe its rectangular shape to the yards of the great inns, which housed semipermanent theaters in the late sixteenth century. These in turn probably resembled closely the *corrales* of Madrid, named for the urban streetyards in which they, like the semipermanent theaters that immediately preceded them, were built. The similarities extend to the platform stages of the English and Spanish public theaters as well as to their tiring-houses or *vestuarios*.[80] The explanation for these parallels is to be found in an international medieval inheritance, perhaps in the common influence of touring *commedia dell'arte* troupes, and certainly in the purpose of the buildings: professional performance before a large paying audience.[81] On the other hand, the long-held assumption that the larger structures of most of the English theaters originated in the animal-baiting house now seems to suffer from serious weaknesses. First, the only playhouse that was also a baiting ring was the Hope. Second, James Burbage had the option of leasing a beargarden at the time he constructed the Theatre, but did not, perhaps because he considered such a building unsuitable for dramatic performance.[82] Finally, a fairly close analogue to the structure of several of the public playhouses may be found in Henry VIII's temporary banqueting house in Calais in 1520.[83]

Despite the important structural similarities between English and Spanish playhouses, estimates of theater capacity and average audience size differ greatly for the two countries. For London, the best guesses are 3,000 for the former and 1,250 for the latter during the 1590s.[84] In Seville between 1611 and 1614, the comparable figures are 2,200 and 550.[85] The *corrales* of Madrid, however, probably held only about 1,050 people in the late sixteenth century,[86] though the average attendance may have run as high as 700.[87] These differences, at least between Lon-

---

[80]Richard Hosley, "The Playhouses and the Stage," in *A New Companion to Shakespeare Studies*, ed. Kenneth Muir and S. Schoenbaum (Cambridge: Cambridge University Press, 1971), p. 22; Shergold, pp. 164, 166, 175.

[81]John J. Allen, *The Reconstruction of a Golden Age Playhouse: El Corral del Príncipe, 1583–1744* (Gainesville: University Presses of Florida, 1983), pp. 111–17.

[82]Oscar Brownstein, "Why Didn't Burbage Lease the Beargarden? A Conjecture in Comparative Architecture," in *The First Public Playhouse: The Theatre in Shoreditch, 1576–1598*, ed. Herbert Berry (Montreal: McGill-Queens University Press, 1979), pp. 81–96.

[83]Hosley, "The Theatre and the Tradition of Playhouse Design," in *The First Public Playhouse*, ed. Berry, pp. 47–79.

[84]Harbage, *Shakespeare's Audience* (New York: Columbia University Press, 1941), pp. 30–33; Hosley, "The Playhouse and the Stage," p. 26.

[85]Computed from Sentaurens, pp. 57–58, 86, 92.

[86]Allen, p. 100.

[87]Computed from Shergold, pp. 183–86, 194, 198-99, 387, 526.

don and Madrid, may reflect larger demographic distinctions. In 1595, when London's population was 150,000 or more, total theater attendance was in the neighborhood of 600,000.[88] Madrid at the same time had about 75,000 inhabitants and an annual audience at the *corrales* of almost a quarter of a million.[89]

Who attended the theaters? The traditional study of England speaks of a popular majority,[90] a claim that receives circumstantial support from the more recent emphasis on the location of the theaters in rapidly growing lower-class suburbs.[91] The innovative and impressive counterargument, however, refers to "privileged playgoers."[92] Although this controversy will most likely not be soon resolved, the hypothesis of primarily elite spectators represents no more than an abstract possibility, and one fraught with logical and empirical problems. On the other hand, an insistence on a heterogeneous audience, with a plurality of artisans and shopkeepers, and a majority consisting of these groups and the ones beneath them—servants, prostitutes, transients, soldiers, and criminals—is compatible with the existing evidence and hence considerably more plausible.[93] This popular clientele, concentrated in the pit, was probably the heart of the English public theater audience and the section of it that seems to have determined the financial success or failure of a play.[94]

The Spanish groundlings, or *mosqueteros*, probably exercised a similar sway, a role they shared, however, with the equally vociferous *cazuela*, or women's gallery.[95] Both groups were part of an audience that, because of the presence of the clergy as well as the higher aristocracy, may have

---

[88]Population: Harbage, *Shakespeare's Audience*, p. 41—160,000 in 1605; Hill, *Reformation to Industrial Revolution*, p. 31—200,000 in 1600; Salingar, Harrison, and Cochrane, 2: 540, 547—250,000 in 1600. The estimate of theater attendance is based on two companies giving six performances a week, forty weeks a year. See Chambers, 2:142; Harbage, *Shakespeare's Audience*, pp. 37–38.

[89]Population: Jonathan Brown and Elliott, *A Palace for a King: The Buen Retiro and the Court of Philip IV* (New Haven: Yale University Press, 1980), p. 3. This estimate of the theatergoing public assumes 333 showings per year, a figure derived from Rennert's Appendix A, pp. 345–56.

[90]Harbage, *Shakespeare's Audience*.

[91]Salingar, Harrison, and Cochrane, 2:547, 549, 574–75; Weimann, pp. 170–71.

[92]Ann Jennalie Cook, *The Privileged Playgoers of Shakespeare's London, 1576–1642* (Princeton: Princeton University Press, 1981). Michael Hattaway, *Elizabethan Popular Theatre: Plays in Performance* (London: Routledge and Kegan Paul, 1982), pp. 46–50, and Peter Thomson, *Shakespeare's Theatre* (London: Routledge and Kegan Paul, 1983), pp. 24–25, agree with Cook.

[93]A single brief example must suffice here. Cook argues that only the privileged minority possessed the time, money, education, personal associations, geographical access, and inclination to attend the theater regularly. Yet she cannot quite deny a popular majority at the Fortune and Red Bull in Jacobean times (p. 137), an implicit concession that fundamentally undermines her basic claim.

[94]Leggatt, p. 113.

[95]Rennert, pp. 117–22.

surpassed in social range even the assembly at the English theaters.[96]
Nonetheless, just as in England, the popular element was probably predominant. The *mosqueteros* may have consisted of a relatively idle floating
population that ranged from manual workers, day laborers, and servants to inactive soldiers, false gentlemen, middlemen, picaros, and ruf-
fians. The *cazuelas* attracted the female analogues of these groups, while
the *gradas*, or stands, situated physically, socially, and financially only
slightly above the *patio*, or pit, included petty bureaucrats, industrial
workers, artisans, and traders, many of them associated with one or another of Madrid's five great guilds.[97] In neither country would the stratification of admission charges have seriously reduced the influence of
the groundlings, however. In Spain as in England, the owners of the theaters reaped the main benefits of the most expensive seats in the house,
while the actors depended for their income primarily on a uniform payment at the door by all members of the audience.[98]

These considerations suggest the importance of the attitudes of those
who attended the theater. But an attempt to reconstruct the ideologies
of the audiences and particularly of the presumably crucial popular sectors, especially when derived from the evidence of the dramatic texts
themselves, runs the risk of circularity. It seems possible to reduce this
danger, however, by postulating the values of the audience on the basis
of its social background. From this point of view, the London groundlings probably possessed a more developed, more coherent class consciousness than did the *mosqueteros* of Madrid. For both countries, however, the assumption that the plays made a consistent, self-conscious
double appeal—one to the vulgar and unlettered, the other to the refined and erudite—must be rejected. This notion, which has recently
enjoyed a revival,[99] is deeply misleading in at least two respects. First, it
reduces the audience to ideological passivity and victimization, despite
abundant contemporary evidence to the contrary and despite the only
partial success of the far more effectively manipulative electronic media
of the twentieth century in achieving this end. Second, it falsifies the experience of the plays, many of which create complex effects that derive
in significant part from popular culture. If the result is not necessarily a

---

[96]Shergold, pp. 534–36.
[97]José María Díez Borque, *Sociedad y teatro en la España de Lope de Vega* (Barcelona:
Bosch, 1978), pp. 140–59.
[98]Chambers, 1: 353–54; Shergold, p. 198.
[99]Díez Borque, pp. 150–52, with qualifications; José Antonio Maravall, *Teatro y literatura en la sociedad barroca* (Madrid: Seminario y Ediciones, 1972); René Girard, "'To Entrap
the Wisest': A Reading of *The Merchant of Venice*," in *Literature and Society*, ed. Edward W.
Said, Selected Papers from the English Institute, 1978, n.s., 3 (Baltimore: Johns Hopkins
University Press, 1980), pp. 100–119.

conservative organic unity, still less is it an equally, if not even more, conservative opportunistic bifurcation.

## Playwrights

Like the audiences, the dramatists had important connections with popular culture. In general, the social origins of the playwrights were more modest in England than in Spain. The men who wrote for the London public theaters before 1600 were characteristically from the artisanate: Chettle's father was a dyer, Greene's a saddler, Kyd's a scrivener, Marlowe's a shoemaker, Munday's a draper, Peele's a clerk, and Shakespeare's a glover. Although the Spanish poets generally came from a higher class, the exceptions are nonetheless noteworthy: Aguilar, Cervantes, and, most important, Lope de Vega.[100] Here it is worth mentioning the lifelong popular and rural ties of the most important dramatist in each country. On the other hand, the example of Shakespeare should not obscure the extraordinary impact of the university-educated playwrights—Marlowe, Greene, and Lodge, for instance—in the transformation of English drama.[101] Among the Spanish writers, comparable schooling seems to have been a common acquisition.

Regardless of the extent of their formal education, however, the dramatists unquestionably provided the primary conduit by which neoclassical theory and practice reached the public stage. In neither England nor Spain was neoclassicism an entirely new phenomenon. As already noted, the influence of court and aristocratic taste after 1575 may also have fostered an interest in the literary ideals of the Renaissance, while in London the predilections of the students at the Inns of Court most certainly did so. The playwrights, moreover, were not simply autonomous agents who chose to write for the theater. Their roots were in the revamped educational systems of the sixteenth century, behind which lay the growth of capitalism, the rise of the state, and the impact of humanism. Finally, the condition of their employment was the ability and desire of the actors to pay them a decent sum in return for the swift and prolific composition of plays. Such reservations and qualifications, however, merely serve to specify the nature, rather than belittle the significance, of the dramatists' decisive role in introducing a classicist strain. For within the plays it is this strain that qualitatively distinguishes the integration of popular and learned culture in the public theater from the

---

[100]Information on the playwrights: Chambers 3:201–518; Cayetano Alberto de La Barrera y Leirado, *Catálogo bibliográfico y biográfico del teatro antiguo español desde sus orígenes hasta mediados del siglo xviii* (1860; rpt. London: Tamesis, 1968).

[101]Bradbrook, pp. 96–138.

more Christian, but otherwise comparable, synthesis on the late medieval urban religious stage.

In social origin and education, then, the very real differences between the dramatists of the two countries were partly subsumed by more encompassing similarities. Yet a disparity resembling the national gap in background and education can also be found in some of the economic and social relations into which the dramatists entered. No English playwright achieved the prestige of Lope de Vega. Though Castro and especially Cervantes were poor at one time or another, they represent isolated cases in comparison with the long list of needy, imprisoned, short-lived, or otherwise marginal contemporary English dramatists: Chettle, Dekker, Greene, Jonson, Kyd, Lodge, Lyly, Marlowe, Nashe, Peele, and Porter. These authors were hardly social outsiders, but when considerable fortunes were amassed in the theater industry they were not made primarily from the composition of plays—a generalization that probably applies to Spain as well.[102] The relatively more modest position of the London dramatists also appears in the relationship between author and theater. Wilson, Munday, Heywood, Shakespeare, and for a brief time Jonson were all actors. Spanish actor-dramatists, by contrast, were rare by the late sixteenth century; perhaps the best-known examples are Ganassa and Claramonte. Even so, the playwrights often maintained close ties to the acting companies. Once again, Lope de Vega's career provides striking evidence, partly in his friendships with various *autores* (managers of acting companies), but even more in his prolonged and often stormy relations with two actresses, Elena Osorio and Micaela de Luján.[103]

How may these data be theorized? Aristocratic patronage such as the English companies enjoyed often extended to individual writers as well, including many of the public theater playwrights. But it had no part in these authors' involvement, as authors, with the public stage, a relationship that was instead purely commercial in character and that centered on the actors' purchase of dramatic manuscripts. Today, in the industrialized West, although large-scale printing has evolved into a capitalist industry, according to Terry Eagleton it "incorporates as a crucial constituent a *subordinate* mode of production: the artisanal mode of the literary producer himself, who typically sells his product (manuscript) rather than his labour-power to the publisher in exchange for a fee."[104] A comparable interlocking of capitalist and artisanal production defined

---

[102]Aubrun, pp. 105–6.
[103]Rennert, p. 164; Aubrun, pp. 86–87.
[104]Terry Eagleton, *Criticism and Ideology: A Study in Marxist Literary Theory* (London: NLB, 1976), p. 51.

the professional relations of the dramatists in late-sixteenth-century England and Spain.

One sign of the impact of capital on the theater was the establishment of the category of playwright. Like the modern writer, the dramatist of the Renaissance public theater was, on the one hand, an artisan rather than a wage-earner, but, on the other, an artisan who did not sell directly to a clientele that could consume his commodity as a use-value. Of course, since the dramatic performance itself, as opposed to the acting script, was the product bought by an audience, the distance between playwright and public was not a result of capitalist penetration but merely a specific manifestation of a more general and far older social division of labor. The emergence of capitalism did not simply accelerate the process of division, however. The position of the dramatist also parallels an important contemporary economic phenomenon. Under the putting-out system, traditional, often rural, domestic industry was falling partially under the control of urban merchants. Although this early stage of capitalism did not fully reduce producers to wage-workers, at times it did remove them from direct contact with the market, convert the output of their labor into piecework, and increase their dependence on an antagonistic and unequal class relationship with an employer.[105]

The analogous, though less extreme, trend in the theater was the gradual separation of playwright and actor. This distinction does not always seem to have been the norm. In Spain, the generation that followed Lope de Rueda dissolved the unity of actor, manager, and playwright that had characterized his career, while anachronistically continuing to designate the actor-manager of a troupe as the *autor de comedias*. Although English actor-playwrights flourished longer, their decline apparently dates from the early seventeenth century. The separation did not, at least initially, benefit the playwrights. If Lope de Vega could often dictate terms to the troupes that performed his plays, less prestigious dramatists in Spain and nonacting dramatists in England were relatively at the mercy of their main customers, the acting companies. Thanks to the rise of the public theaters, professional playwrights probably did better commercially than both contemporary nondramatic writers who lived by their pens and earlier professional actor-dramatists. Moreover, unlike the victims of the putting-out system, who were simply former artisans, the playwrights were not actor-dramatists who had lost part of their vocation but often men of letters looking for a remunerative outlet for their specifically literary talents. Nonetheless, in their segregation of mental from physical labor and in their consequent lack of control over a

---

[105]The putting-out system: Maurice Dobb, *Studies in the Development of Capitalism*, 2d ed. (New York: International Publishers, 1963), pp. 123–76 passim.

crucial step in the process of dramatic production and distribution, they partly paralleled the artisans in the putting-out system and more fully anticipated the writers of the capitalist era.

Two other indications of the playwrights' subordination to capital can be illustrated in this period only from English records. The first is indebtedness. Theater owner and entrepreneur Philip Henslowe lent money to at least ten dramatists, twice obtaining in return exclusive rights to his debtor's services.[106] In such cases the playwright, having lost the option of selling his product to the highest bidder on the open market, approached the status of a wage-worker. Second, collaboration in dramatic composition, which may have occurred on half the plays of the late-sixteenth-century English public theater, and especially on those composed for the Admiral's Men,[107] fragmented the coherence of creative labor. Its effects are in many respects comparable to those that Marx noted in the early development of preindustrial manufacture.[108] Beyond the common purpose of speeding up production and the common breakdown of an integrated work-process into component parts, presumably with deadening psychological consequences, one parallel stands out in particular. The division of labor in society results in itself only in a series of independent producers of commodities, but the "division of labour in manufacture" gives rise to a sequence of specialized workers, each of whom individually "produces no commodities. It is only the common product of all the specialized workers that becomes a commodity."[109] The same is true in the theater. The playwright working alone produces a commodity, but the dramatist commissioned by the company to write one act of a play does not. Only when the individual products of the collaborating writers are combined does a commodity come into being. This occurs not in the hands of any or all of the authors, but in the possession of the actors.

These arguments, however, do not entirely remove the professional playwrights from the artisanate. Further, a substantial body of evidence suggests that this class affiliation was their primary one. First, the practice of collaboration is ambiguous in its significance, in part because cooperation is essential in the theater and does not inherently connote personal degradation of any kind. During the Renaissance, plays written by more than one author do not appear to have been deemed inferior to the work of a single man. Actor-playwrights, the dramatists closest to the artisanal tradition, were particularly involved in their composition.[110]

---

[106]Chambers, 1:363, 374.
[107]Bentley, *Profession of Dramatist*, p. 199; Salingar, Harrison, and Cochrane, 2:545.
[108]Marx, *Capital*, vol. 1, chap. 14.
[109]Marx, *Capital*, 1:475.
[110]Bentley, *Profession of Dramatist*, pp. 197–98, 210–11.

The chronology of collaboration suggests, albeit inconclusively, the same judgment. In Spain a dramatist, rather than an *autor*, introduced multiple authorship after the turn of the century, apparently in response to an increased demand for plays that, surprisingly enough, did not result in a simultaneous rise in the income of playwrights.[111] In England, on the other hand, collaboration declined in the Caroline period, coincident with an improvement in the status of dramatists.[112] Perhaps this decline may be interpreted as a victorious return to an artisanal conception of creativity; far more likely, it represents the demise of such a conception. In general, modern suspicion of collaborative art reflects a bias in favor of bourgeois values like originality, individuality, projection of personality, and aesthetic unity, a set of ideals, in short, that was rarely paramount in the public theaters.

The typical treatment of authorship, publication, ownership, and revision all actually point toward a very different orientation. For perhaps the majority of the plays performed in the English public theaters during the late sixteenth century, either the dramatist or the text or both dramatist and text are unknown. In Spain the situation is almost certainly similar, if not more extreme. Clearly, the playwrights were not much concerned with claiming or even preserving their writings, an attitude reinforced by laws that, unlike capitalist copyright regulations, granted them no proprietary rights. Jonson's careful publication of his works, classical in inspiration and bourgeois in implication, was unusual even for the early seventeenth century.[113] Although Lope de Vega and his successors saw their plays into print more frequently than did their English contemporaries,[114] particularly after 1600, in Spain as well dramatic publication was an entirely subordinate matter. The same conclusion applies to revision. If the rifling of previous literature conformed to the Renaissance notion of imitation, the pervasive tampering with the plays that went on in the public theater testifies to another heritage entirely—to the anonymous and multiple authorship, oral performance, and fluid texts of the popular tradition. It is this precapitalist legacy that the predominantly artisanal dramatists of the public theaters accepted, reworked, and transfigured.[115]

---

[111]Rennert, pp. 177, 180.

[112]Bentley, *Profession of Dramatist*, pp. 220–21.

[113]Bentley, *Profession of Dramatist*, pp. 14–17, 264–92, and passim; on Jonson in particular, Timorthy Murray, "From Foul Sheets to Legitimate Model: Antitheater, Text, Ben Jonson," *New Literary History* 14 (1983): 641–64.

[114]Froldi, p. 18.

[115]Bentley, *Profession of Dramatist*, pp. 235–63; Salomon, pp. 739–40; Arróniz, pp. 277–81, 302–3.

## Players

The immediate beneficiaries of their efforts were the secular, professional players, most of whom, at least during the late sixteenth century, came from relatively modest social backgrounds, made little money during their lifetimes, and died poor.[116] The few wellborn Spanish actors or the considerable fortunes amassed by Burbage, Shakespeare, and above all Alleyn are the exceptions. Despite a genuine rise, particularly in England, in the status, security, and income of the profession between 1570 and 1600,[117] the social relations of the theater industry precluded any widespread or equitable distribution of the gains. The position of English actors was defined by both the external connections and the internal organization of the dramatic companies. As the servants or retainers of the powerful lords who patronized them, the players enjoyed a form of feudal protection still vital in an aristocratic age. But they earned their living, of course, in a business that largely depended on the vicissitudes of the market in a nascent capitalist economy. By the 1590s the leading London actors held shares in their companies, an organizational format with some affinities to the structure of the guilds. In principle, the roughly ten or twelve sharers horizontally divided the costs, responsibilities, and profits among themselves, in the manner of petty commodity production. The use of boy apprentices to play female parts conforms to this pattern. In practice, the sharers also entered into vertical, hierarchical ties in two directions, in this respect approximating the social relations of capitalism. On the one hand, since they often fell into debt to the capitalists from whom they leased their theaters, they could effectively decline to the status of wage-workers. On the other, they employed perhaps twenty hired men—journeymen actors as well as miscellaneous workers—at fairly low wages. Yet this practice did not turn the sharers into capitalists. As Marx's comments make clear, a two-to-one ratio between employees and employers is far too low to bring about this conversion. "The guild system of the Middle Ages therefore tried forcibly to prevent the transformation of the master of a craft into a capitalist, by limiting the number of workers a single master could employ to a very low maximum."[118] Inscribed in the lives of the actors, then, were

[116]Rennert, pp. 110, 159–61; Chambers, 1:351. For illustrative material, see Rennert, pp. 531, 571–73; Chambers, 2:305, 341, 345, and 3:352–53. The discussion of the English actors, though mainly composed before the publication of Bentley's *The Profession of Player in Shakespeare's Time, 1590–1642* (Princeton: Princeton University Press, 1984), is compatible with the evidence in that book.

[117]Rennert, pp. 181–82, 189; Bradbrook, pp. 282–83.

[118]Chambers, 1:363–68; Bentley, *Profession of Player*, pp. 6, 42, 65; Marx, *Capital*, 1:423.

the multiple and shifting class relationships that characterize English Renaissance society, theater, and drama. But in this instance, too, the artisanal dimension was unmistakably dominant.[119]

In Spain, actor-shareholders are unattested before 1614. Peninsular troupes of the late sixteenth century depended on a single leading actor, the *autor*, who served as manager, financier, and employer of the other members of the repertory group. Although this difference may partly be attributed to Spanish belatedness, it had structural causes as well. Unlike their London counterparts such as the Admiral's Men or the Chamberlain's Men, even the leading Spanish companies were never allowed to establish a permanent base in any theater, in Madrid or elsewhere. Constantly forced to travel, their organization paralleled that of the English provincial companies, who suffered a similar plight. Though in England the itinerant professionals earned considerably less than did the relatively sedentary London players, in Spain successful touring actors may have commanded salaries that approached the incomes of London sharers.[120]

In both countries, however, the continued linkage between playing the provinces and performing in the capital helped constitute the latter work as a genuinely national theater. The Spanish troupes may have carried the drama from the cities to rural regions. On the other hand, the triumph of the London companies, especially after 1580, depended on the prior and continuing success of the professional actors in outlying areas. The Queen's Men in particular brought the new and strengthened drama of the city back to the towns and villages of England, where the commerical theater consequently reached its apogee between 1585 and 1594. These, of course, were also the years in which the London stage came into its own, with the appearance of Marlowe and Shakespeare. Such synchronicity is a bit misleading, however: the rise and fall of provincial professional playing generally anticipated the comparable trajectory of acting in the capital's permanent, public theaters by about a decade. In addition, the earlier decline of the one seems partly to have been caused by the centralization, consolidation, and urban concentration of the other, which, though it actually began in the 1570s, assumed serious proportions only from the late nineties.[121] Nonetheless, the extent, as well as the geographical extension, of professional playing made the London public theater less an oasis than an entrepôt of drama in the age of Elizabeth.

These social origins and relations also help clarify the way the compa-

[119]Bradbrook, pp. 39, 283; Gurr, pp. 31–32, 50.

[120]Rennert, pp. 146–47, 188–89; Shergold, p. 181 n. 3; Díez Borque, p. 33; Gurr, pp. 46, 63; Chambers, 1:370.

[121]Salingar, Harrison, and Cochrane, 2:525–76, esp. 531–32, 538–41, 560.

nies performed the plays. The available evidence points to the continuity of the popular, professional acting tradition. As previously noted, in earlier sixteenth-century English drama it is possible to observe a dialectical relation between the form of the play and the doubling of parts. The need to incorporate an increasing range of material inspired the development of doubling, but doubling in turn influenced dramatic structure and hence the manner in which new themes and subjects were thereafter assimilated. Thus, even beyond the likelihood that some dramatists, probably including Shakespeare, wrote with the talents and resources of a particular troupe in mind,[122] the plays of the late-sixteenth-century public theater bear the marks of the companies for which they were composed. Doubling patterns affected a prospective author not only extrinsically, as a production technique to which he had to adapt, but also intrinsically, as the driving force behind a series of now well-established generic conventions.[123]

The tradition of professional playing also shaped the way an individual character was interpreted. The reconstruction of acting styles depends on a partly hypothetical, often speculative, and inevitably circular analysis of the at times contradictory relationships among performer, role, playwright, stage, and audience. One difficulty lies in assessing the extent to which acting changed in the closing decades of the sixteenth century. Though recent students of the English theater have modified the realist bias of the early 1950s, itself a reaction to the extreme formalist consensus of the interwar years, they tend to believe that the eclipse of the clown by the tragic protagonist, of Tarlton by Alleyn, and the more general transition from conventional to naturalistic acting, from Alleyn to Burbage, were well under way, if far from complete, by 1600.[124] In this sense too, then, Renaissance public theater was a unique, precarious product of a brief historical moment.

But in one respect such a view is profoundly misleading. The popular tradition included both formalism and realism, a duality rooted in primitive ritual as well as, more proximately, in the relation between actor

---

[122]Gurr, pp. 57–59.

[123]David M. Bevington, *From "Mankind" to Marlowe: Growth of Structure in the Popular Drama of Tudor England* (Cambridge: Harvard University Press, 1962), pp. 199–262; William A. Ringler, Jr., "The Numbers of Actors in Shakespeare's Early Plays," in *The Seventeenth-Century Stage*, ed. Bentley (Chicago: University of Chicago Press, 1968), pp. 110–34; Bentley, *Profession of Player*, pp. 228–33. Spanish evidence: Rennert, pp. 145–46, 360–79; Shergold, p. 505.

[124]For the realist argument, see the two essays collected by Bentley on this subject in *The Seventeenth-Century Stage*: Brown, "On the Acting of Shakespeare's Plays," pp. 41–54; Marvin Rosenberg, "Elizabethan Actors: Men or Marionettes?" pp. 94–109. For the more recent position, consult Bradbrook, pp. 96–138; Gurr, pp. 60–81; Daniel Seltzer, "The Actors and Staging," in *A New Companion to Shakespeare Studies*, ed. Muir and Schoenbaum, pp. 35–54; Leggatt, pp. 95–117. But Hattaway, pp. 50–98, argues against a realistic or naturalistic view of Elizabethan acting and performance.

and role. The physical basis of this conjunction in the public theater was the platform stage. In sequences of dialogue, this stage was capable of fostering an illusionistic representation of reality. But in passages of monologue—whether soliloquy, aside, or direct address—it became an unlocalized acting space, particularly when the speaker was downstage near the audience. The characteristic occupant of this position was a lower-class figure, the clown. Descended from the Vice, he was both subject and object of mirth, laughing with the audience, speaking to and for it, and thus existing in both unity and contradiction with the witnesses to his performance. His language, replete with couplet, proverb, and wordplay, violated the mimetic quality of the drama both by its nonsensical turns and by its anachronistic approximation to the speech of his audience. In this respect the clown may be said to have called attention to the reality of the theater.

At the same time, he enriched the fiction of the play by offering an alternative perspective that pierced the illusion (in the bad sense) of the stage action. It would be misleading, however, to contrast the realism of dialogue with the formalism of monologue. For not only did the downstage speaker penetrate appearances to discover truth and reality, the actor's self-expression in this role was also dramatically integrated into a coherent action. The character's physical position signified a genuine difference from the other dramatis personae, most often a rejection of pretense and of acting. Thus, in late Elizabethan drama antiillusionistic playing merged with psychological realism. Moreover, as the distance between the downstage acting area and the localized space of the central plot continued to diminish in the course of this period, dramatic structure underwent a corresponding modification. Through a low-comedy subplot, a choric interlude, the reception of comic figures into the ranks of the aristocratic main plot, or the assimilation of popular elements in the protagonist, the possibility was created of a fully integral, simultaneous elevation and mockery of the central action, of a perspective alert to the tensions as well as the harmonies of life. On the other hand, these latent features of the popular theatrical tradition could only have developed under the impact of the general movement toward naturalism that was spurred by the larger social and cultural trends of the age.[125]

Although the comparable necessary research on the Spanish theater does not exist, the late-sixteenth-century drama of the *corrales* reveals a number of characteristic elements of popular theater—audience address, asides, proverbs, wordplay, disguise, dance, and the mingling of comic and serious moments.[126] Many of these practices go back to the

[125]The paragraphs above are derived from Weimann, pp. 208–60.
[126]Weimann, p. 10; Jean Canavaggio, "Lope de Vega entre refranero y comedia," in *Lope de Vega y los orígenes del teatro español*, Actas del I Congreso Internacional sobre Lope de Vega, ed. Manuel Criado de Val (Madrid: EDI, 1981), pp. 83–94.

*pastor* of the earlier sixteenth-century dramatic prologue and entered the *comedia* with the *gracioso*, the figure who most fully embodies these traits and habits, and who most closely resembles the English clown. Yet the *gracioso* did not come into his own until the late 1590s. One reason for the precocity of English drama, at least in comparison with Spanish, was the greater length and richness of its tradition of acting in general and of professional playing in particular.[127] As the evidence on French and German drama developed in chapter 2 suggests, however, too much should not be attributed to the autonomous workings of the popular legacy in the absence of a commercial stage.

Nonetheless, the relatively impoverished heritage of the early Spanish public theaters appears in at least two striking phenomena. The first is the success and influence of Ganassa and, to a lesser extent, the other Italian actors, as well as the evident emulation of their procedures by the fledgling Spanish troupes.[128] The second and more important is the prominence in the drama of the *romances*, the anonymous, primarily popular ballards of medieval origin that narrate the heroic and legendary history of Spain. The transference of their lyric qualities was facilitated by the platform stage, which, as in England, proved extremely suitable for poetic recitation. In addition, the full use of the *romances* helped confer a narrative character on Spanish drama, at least in comparison with most English plays. But the result of this adaptation was by no means the structural clumsiness that might have been expected. Given the relative absence of the popular stage tradition, the Spanish theater found a partial substitute source of the crucial unity between audience and actor by recreating, through the *romance*, the conditions of medieval, juglaresque performance. Especially in its more popular genres, the *comedia* may have utilized this roundabout route to develop a mode of acting that generated a sense of community and that thus bears comparison with the more theatrically based English heritage.[129]

## Conclusion

It is now time to attempt a synthesis, to determine which mode of production the public theater belonged to. A theatrical mode of production

---

[127]The importance of this legacy is emphasized by Harbage, *Shakespeare and the Rival Traditions* (New York: Macmillan, 1952), pp. 3–28.

[128]Arróniz, pp. 208–309; Nancy L. D'Antuono, "Lope de Vega y la *commedia dell'arte*: Temas y figuras," in *Lope de Vega*, ed. Criado de Val, pp. 217–28.

[129]Ramón Menéndez Pidal, *La epopeya castellana a través de la literatura española*, 2d ed. (1910; rpt. Madrid: Espasa-Calpe, 1959), pp. 175–207; Shergold, p. 551; Salomon, pp. 554–56; Jorge A. Silveira y Montes de Oca, "El *Romancero* y el teatro nacional español: De Juan de la Cueva a Lope de Vega," in *Lope de Vega*, ed. Criado de Val, pp. 73–81. For Lope's popular dramatic heritage, however, see two other essays from Criado de Val's collection: Frida Weber de Kurlat, "Elementos tradicionales pre-lopescos en la comedia de Lope de Vega," pp. 37–60; Fernando de Toro-Garland, "El 'entremés' como origen de la 'comedia nueva' según Lope," pp. 103–9.

may be understood to comprise the range of social relations and practices discussed above rather than the narrower spectrum of activities normally associated with stage production. Such a redefinition, however, only emphasizes the difficulty of ascertaining the specific nature of that productive mode. For like sixteenth-century society in general, the theater was a composite formation in which disparate modes coexisted and intertwined. A process of elimination may help determine the institution's primary, if by no means single, orientation.

First, feudalism can be excluded. The absolutist state dominated politics and ideology; its influence on theater and society was thus largely superstructural. This is not to denigrate the importance of the monarchy, however. In Perry Anderson's words, "The 'superstructures' of kinship, religion, law or the state necessarily enter into the constitutive structure of the mode of production in pre-capitalist social formations."[130] On the other hand, one can discover well before the late sixteenth century a rift between base and superstructure unlike feudalism's amalgam of economics and politics in surplus extraction. This ultimately explosive contradiction typifies the theater of the period as well. For all its continued potency, feudalism scarcely penetrated the economic organization of the stage. Totally commercialized, the theater lacked dependent or servile labor, as well as any form of extraeconomic coercion. The complexity not only of its structure, but also of its products thus derives in part from a fundamental, internal asymmetry of base and superstructure.

The same peculiar configuration also raises doubts about a capitalist interpretation of the stage. The extensive political restriction, control, and licensing under which the theater operated characterized precapitalist rather than capitalist industry. In addition, the Spanish theater lacked a bourgeoisie. Arguably, the hospitals, unlike medieval churches that staged plays, were forced to function as capitalists by the overall economic development of society. But this contention cannot be pushed too far. First of all, the hospitals did not reinvest their profits. Equally important, in England as well as in Spain, there was only a fairly small and proportionally indecisive working class in the theater. Partly feudal, partly capitalist, the public theater of the late sixteenth century was predominantly neither.

The combination of widespread commercialization, relative absence of a proletariat, and extensive regulation of the conditions of production suggests the operation of a qualitatively different system. Marx began the first volume of *Capital* with an analysis of the commodity. According to some scholars, the logical development from simple commodity pro-

[130]Anderson, p. 403.

duction to capitalist production in his exposition may also be seen as a historical progression from the era of petty commodity production to the age of capitalism.[131] At least in the towns and cities of England and Spain, petty commodity production seems to have been the characteristic mode of economic organization in the late sixteenth century. It is this fundamentally artisanal historical form that the theater most closely approximated.

Such a perspective, however tentative, points to additional conclusions. Once again, an analogy to an argument about economic history may prove helpful. The same mode of production can emerge in different places from different anterior modes of production. Yet once the new system is constituted, it operates according to an inner logic that generates its own reproduction. The internal contradictions of the society inevitably modify but do not, at least for some time, destroy this reproductive mechanism. On the other hand, the consolidation of a new mode of production does not obliterate all traces of the anterior ones that went into its making. These continue to exercise a subordinate influence that at some later date may well prove decisive.[132] For a study of the theater, this latter point is obvious enough. What most clearly separated England from Spain in the period before the 1570s was the comparative weakness of the latter's popular, professional theatrical tradition. This debility survived into the era of the public theaters, as evidenced, for example, by the prominence of aristocratic motifs, the narrative character of the plays, the borrowing from the *commedia dell'arte* not only of types but also of the *comedia*'s three-act structure, and the tendency for the dramatists to be men of letters rather than actors.

Similarly, both the public theater synthesis and the concomitant parallels between the two countries were fragile, precarious, and transitional. Most of the differences between the Spanish and English stages, within a common unity, had roots in the decades and often centuries before 1575. It is as if the two countries briefly converged, only to separate once again for a considerably longer time. The causes of that separation were already present in the late sixteenth century, if not earlier. In both countries, some of the forces that made the emergence of the public theater possible were, by a kind of internal logic, undermining their own product from the very start. The most important period of the institution fell between the moment when the evolution of the propertied classes, aristocratic and to a lesser extent bourgeois, brought into being the necessary conditions of its formation, and the later point on that trajectory

[131]Mandel, introduction to *Capital*, 1:13–16.
[132]Anderson, pp. 420–22.

[181

when the same classes were responsible for the sufficient causes of its destruction.[133]

It is nonetheless the similarities between the two theaters that remain most striking. Once established, the public theater became a self-replicating mode of dramatic production that obeyed the same internal logic in both countries. From this point of view, some of the evidence of Spain's weak tradition takes on a new meaning: the structural exigencies of the public theater impelled the appropriation of popular elements from foreign or nondramatic sources. Even more, the social conditions of performance led to the exhumation and even the invention of popular motifs, to the gradual realization of inherent, but latent, possibilities. In what may have been Shakespeare's earliest comedy, the lower-class dimensions of Plautine theater come to life as they generally do not in Italian Renaissance drama. Lope de Vega reconverted the medieval Spanish prose chronicles back into the popular poetry from which they derived. The emergence in his plays of a serious, sympathethic view of the peasantry involved a transformation, at times a negation, of preexistent, more aristocratic treatments of the same class.[134] The puzzlingly belated appearance of the *gracioso* may be understood in much the same way. Institutional configurations made his invention possible; all that was required was an appropriately situated and talented dramatist to seize the opportunity. Thus the reproductive mechanism of the public theater helped bring about not only the initial convergence between England and Spain but also, as later chapters will argue, the subsequent deepening of the significance of the popular tradition at the very time it was being superseded, and hence the perpetuation of the parallels between the two national dramas well into the seventeenth century, when the societies to which they belonged were sliding ever further apart.

Equally important, a view of the stage as an artisanally dominated, composite mode of production also focuses attention on the profound interaction between the theater and its drama. Although one obviously cannot deduce the nature of Renaissance plays even from the immediate context, the dramatic performance is quite literally what the theater produced. This once controversial position is now almost universally accepted, at least in principle. The current chapter has offered in passing various instances of the relation between the stage and its plays that, for cumulative effect, might be recapitulated and supplemented. But since the issue will arise repeatedly in the discussion of the drama in the remaining chapters, the present inquiry into the social dimensions of the theater may conclude by concentrating on a single crucial problem—the

[133]On England, see Weimann, pp. 171,176, 178, 191.
[134]Weimann, p. 10; Menéndez Pidal, p. 185; Salomon, pp. 39, 637–44.

question of the inherent subversiveness of the institution. The concern, then, is less with whether *Fuente Ovejuna* or *King Lear* or any other play undertakes a radical critique than with whether the theater itself necessarily does so.

From the perspective adopted here, the public theaters constituted part of both the base and the superstructure, their function in one conflicting with their role in the other. However aristocratic the explicit message of a play, the conditions of its production introduced alternative effects. The total theatrical process meant more than, and something different from, what the dramatic text itself meant. The medium and the message were in contradiction, a contradiction that resulted above all from the popular contribution. Yet as chapter 1 argued, a similar disjunction characterized much late medieval drama of the towns, and especially the religious plays. The public theater differed from this earlier stage tradition, however, in the greater range of its social and cultural material, in the more secular cast of its ideologies, and in its replacement of an urban perspective by a national one.

The practical consequences of its particular structural contradiction are observable first of all in Nashe's proud assertion, quoted earlier, that the subject of English drama was kings and princes. But as early as 1559 a royal proclamation on the drama had ordered local authorities to "permyt none to be played wherin either matters of religion or of the gouernaunce of the estate of the common weale shalbe handled or treated, beyng no meete matters to be wrytten or treated vpon, but by menne of aucthoritie, learning and wisedome, nor to be handled before any audience, but of graue and discreete persons."[135] Yet any drama of state performed in the public theater automatically converted a heterogeneous and, it seems, largely popular audience into judges of national issues, a position from which most of its members were excluded in the world of political affairs. "Shortly they will play me in what forms they list upon the stage," Essex complained to Elizabeth in 1600. A year later she responded to his attempt to use the theater as an adjunct of a putsch by remarking, "I am Richard II, know ye not that?"[136] The accuracy of these comments is perhaps atypical. Most of the time, the higher aristocracy and especially the queen herself, remembering the polemics of mid-century and accustomed to the allegorizing tendencies of the court play, discovered veiled personal references where nothing of the sort may have been intended. The public theater in particular was unlikely to present dramatized romans à clef.[137] Nonetheless, Nashe's great royal

[135]Excerpted from a document printed in Chambers, 4:263.
[136]Quoted in Chambers, 1:324–25, 3:206 n. 4.
[137]Bevington, *Tudor Drama and Politics: A Critical Approach to Topical Meaning* (Cambridge: Harvard University Press, 1968), pp. 1–26.

themes, subjected to implicitly egalitarian scrutiny when dramatized in the artisan playhouse, could, ironically, become a social threat to the upper ranks of the nobility.

The subversion of aristocratic and clerical superstructure by artisanal substructure may also be inferred from the attacks on the theater and especially on acting. The frequent references in both countries to the pagan, idolatrous, or outright diabolical origins and significance of the theater were presumably inspired by the patristic view of the late classical stage. Yet this charge unwittingly may have contained an element of validity. The popular acting tradition of the late sixteenth century retained structural parallels to and perhaps inherited vestiges of non-Christian mimetic ritual. In particular, the social unity of "the clowning actor and the laughing spectator—a connection that has its ultimate origins," according to Robert Weimann, "in the rituals of a less divided society," points as well to an egalitarian, utopian future.[138] Appropriately, the antitheatrical bishop of Barcelona found the stage's greatest threat to religion in the words of the *gracioso*.[139]

Finally, the hostility to dramatic impersonation suggests a deep confusion and unease about the relation between actor and role. For Gosson and Argensola, a player's portrayal of a character different from himself or herself was tantamount to a lie. Both writers especially objected to extreme disjunctions, Gosson to a boy playing a woman or "a meane person" taking "vpon him the title of a Prince," and Argensola to sinful performers mimicking the lives of saints or even of Christ, "pintadas las llagas de nuestra Redención en aquellas manos que poco antes estaban ocupadas en los naipes ó en la guitarra" ("with the wounds of our redemption painted on those hands that shortly before were busy with cards or the guitar").[140] Yet precisely this sort of impersonation was a regular feature of medieval drama. At that time, however, there was little possibility of the actor's disappearing into the role: the moral being who performed the part never entirely escaped from view.

By the late sixteenth century, such was no longer the case. Under the impact of classical drama and the general secularizing trends of society, the popular theatrical tradition had developed new and more radical mimetic techniques by which to create a temporary belief in the illusion of reality produced by the play. But the logical and historical conclusion of this development in the absolute separation of the private life of the actor from the public performance of the role had not yet been reached. For this reason, both foes of the theater insisted on a homol-

[138]Weimann, pp. 171, 259–60. The passage quoted is from p. 259.
[139]Cotarelo y Mori, p. 417.
[140]Gosson is excerpted in Chambers, 4:217. Argensola's comment: Cotarelo y Mori, p. 67.

ogy—whether sexual, social, or ethical—between player and character. Otherwise insincerity, deception, or fraud might ensue. Only because of the contradiction between base and superstructure in the theater, however, did the actors' mastery of more powerful methods of impersonation and representation present a danger to moralists of the time. An important purpose of the remaining chapters will be to investigate this conflict as it shaped the plays themselves.

# [4

# Aristocratic Adaptation: Romantic
# Comedy and the National History Play

The remaining chapters of this book entail a shift of emphasis. The main issue is now the drama itself, and especially the ideology of form —of the individual genre and the individual work. The following pages are accordingly not meant to be autonomous: they form part of the elucidation of larger significance outlined in the Introduction. Instead of converting everything into concerns congenial to Marxism, the argument seeks to discover why so broad a spectrum of themes and forms occurs and to gauge the effects these have on society. In this respect the analysis partly deviates from the tendency toward explication that dominates criticism of Renaissance drama, often approaching, on the contrary, what Althusser has called symptomatic reading[1] and what Fredric Jameson has termed metacommentary.[2] Symptomatic reading seeks to show the systematic relation between presences and absences, between the visible and the invisible, between what is said and what cannot be said, within any problematic, any genre, or any play. Metacommentary's purpose is not merely to arrive at an interpretation, but also to interrogate interpretation itself, to ask why it is needed at all and to determine what its response to the text or performance of a play reveals or, more important, obscures. These methods are in turn designed not only to help elucidate the more general workings of ideology specified, for example, in Lukács's theories of reification and class consciousness[3] or Gramsci's notion of hegemony, but also to connect ultimately with the central, classical categories of political power, class struggle, and mode of production.

[1]Louis Althusser, "From *Capital* to Marx's Philosophy," in *Reading Capital*, by Althusser and Etienne Balibar, trans. Ben Brewster (London: NLB, 1970), pp. 19–30, esp. p. 28.
[2]Fredric Jameson, "Metacommentary," *PMLA* 86 (1971):9–18.
[3]Georg Lukács, *History and Class Consciousness: Studies in Marxist Dialectics*, trans. Rodney Livingstone (Cambridge: MIT Press, 1971).

The present chapter is devoted to romantic comedy (in Spain often known as the *comedia de capa y espada*: cloak-and-sword comedy) and the national history play, the major dramatic forms of the late sixteenth century. But the remarks of Schlegel quoted in the Introduction suggest that almost all the plays of Renaissance England and Spain may be regarded as essentially romantic. And though national history ceases to be a prominent subject on the English stage after 1600, this is not so in Spain. One purpose here, then, will be to define these central forms in a way that is faithful to the elements of continuity after the turn of the century at the same time that it clarifies the generic specificity of the preceding area. The basic argument is that romantic comedy and the national history play are complementary forms for expressing, enacting, and securing the successful adaptation of the aristocracy to social and political change.

## ROMANTIC COMEDY

### Forms of Romantic Comedy

Dramatic form frequently provides an ideological resolution to deep social problems. When a plot ends in reconciliation and joy, as in comedy, this process is most apparent. It is less clear why Renaissance comedy should have taken a specifically romantic turn or in what ways it differs from romantic comedy of other times and places. Plautus and Terence, for all their relevance to the sixteenth-century stage, scarcely anticipate the Renaissance's concern with love and marriage, much less with married love.[4] Just as an initial social distinction between classical and Renaissance literature depends on the presence or absence of slavery, so in comedy the first principle of differentiation is the relative liberation of women, a movement that in some ways has its roots in primitive Christianity and that has continued, with inevitable false starts and regressions, to the present.

The rather dismal position accorded to women, both theoretically and institutionally, in the early Middle Ages nonetheless marked an advance on female status in antiquity. Subsequent gains also coincided with basic changes in European civilization. The triumph of romantic love in the medieval romance involved a profound interlocking of sexual relations with marvelous, often quasi-religious adventure. Renaissance Neopla-

---

[4]For the Renaissance's romantic interpretation of Roman comedy, see Madeleine Doran, *Endeavors of Art: A Study of Form in Elizabethan Drama* (Madison: University of Wisconsin Press, 1954), pp. 171–82. The generic categories employed in the remainder of this study, particularly with regard to English drama, draw on chaps. 5–8 of her work.

tonists, especially in the era of the Counter-Reformation, discovered a providential hand in the wonderful untangling of romantic imbroglios and thus gave them a new valence. Humanism and, in England, the Reformation led to the revaluation of women, and in particular to the conflation of romantic and married love.[5] In Spain, Christóbal Acosta's *Tratado en loor de las mugeres* argued "que fue la muger como madre de todas las sçiençias pues lo es del hombre" ("that woman was like the mother of all the sciences since she is it [the mother] of man") —admittedly a backhanded compliment.[6] In England, the Puritan battle against property marriage led to the rise of the love marriage.[7] The Renaissance's penchant for festivity and celebration, moreover, found an outlet in the wedding ceremony. In this way married love came to be viewed as a crucial buttress of the social order. Improvement in the actual condition of women did not necessarily accompany these ideological shifts. Nonetheless, the love marriage remained a contested ideal in the sixteenth and seventeenth centuries and accordingly a primary source of conflict in romantic comedy. On the one hand, married love could be a progressive step for women and men alike. On the other, the concluding matrimony of many a comedy reintegrates women into a family and a society dominated by men, thereby alleviating male sexual, procreative, and emotional anxieties. In addition it constitutes a transference, defusing, or suppression of conflict, designed to produce reconciliation.[8] *The Merchant of Venice* (1596) and Gaspar de Aguilar's *El mercader amante* (before 1605; probably the early 1590s),[9] two extreme and somewhat atypical works, transform intractable economic problems partly through their love matches. Consequently they integrate the bourgeoisie into aristocratic society without undermining traditional hierarchies. To this extent the extremism of both plays is revelatory. Romantic comedy, firmly founded on marital love, its climactic weddings presided over by great lords, dramatizes the adaptation of the nobility to a new social configuration, an acceptance of change inextricable from a reassertion of dominance.[10]

[5]Juliet Dusinberre, *Shakespeare and the Nature of Women* (London: Macmillan, 1975).

[6]Christóbal Acosta, *Tratado en loor de las mugeres* (1585?), sig. Cc4$^r$.

[7]Christopher Hill, *The World Turned Upside Down: Radical Ideas during the English Revolution* (Harmondsworth, Middlesex: Penguin, 1975), p. 308.

[8]Carolyn Ruth Swift Lenz, Gayle Greene, and Carol Thomas Neely, eds., *The Woman's Part: Feminist Criticism of Shakespeare* (Urbana: University of Illinois Press, 1980), pp. 7–8; Coppélia Kahn, *Man's Estate: Masculine Identity in Shakespeare* (Berkeley and Los Angeles: University of California Press, 1981), pp. 14–16; Lisa Jardine, *Still Harping on Daughters: Women and Drama in the Age of Shakespeare* (Brighton: Harvester, 1983), pp. 43–58; Louis Adrian Montrose, "'Shaping Fantasies': Figurations of Gender and Power in Elizabethan Culture," *Representations*, no. 2 (Spring 1983): 81–86.

[9]Date: Courtney Bruerton, "La versificación dramática española en el período 1587–1610," *Nueva Revista de Filología Hispánica* 10 (1956): 352–53.

[10]Paul N. Siegel, *Shakespeare in His Time and Ours* (Notre Dame, Ind.: University of Notre Dame Press, 1968), pp. 163–212.

The form carries out this function in a doubly theatrical process.[11] First, an unusual, even extraordinary event may impel one or more of the characters to don a disguise and engage in various kinds of acting that lead to mistaken identities, still wilder plot complications, and deeply ironic but relatively unbitter comic situations. A manifestation of dramatic self-consciousness, this complex phenomenon also responds to the simultaneous instability and rigidity of the ruling class's position. The aristocracy's effort to define strictly the acceptable limits of its own behavior implicitly admits the precariousness of its customary exclusivity and privileged status. The improbable situations that the protagonists of romantic comedy must confront signal uncertainty, insecurity: the social code has socially failed. But they also designate preferred alternatives to the imposed constraints of daily life: the social code has humanly failed. Pastoral, intrigue, lower-class disguise, acting, the atmosphere of holiday or of release—all testify to a utopian impulse toward freedom and an extended range of self-expression. Appropriately enough, women— still, of course, subordinate and mistreated in the Renaissance—are often dramatized in flight from social convention. As chapter 2 suggested, noblewomen of the period may have served as conduits between the upper class, to which they belonged socially, and the mass of the population, to which—given their exclusion from formal schooling—they belonged culturally. The plays can accordingly involve an investigation of psychology and the production of a deepened, more efficacious sense of identity. In this way playing and pretense often help resolve the problems of the action. Whether exiles or rebels, the main characters ultimately forgo masquerade and return to the common conduct of a class whose collective sense of purpose their experience has renewed and reformed.

The act of playing operates in much the same fashion on an institutional plane. More than most other dramatic genres, romantic comedy tends to reinforce the audience's experience of a trip to the theater as a festive occasion. Played in the artisanal public theater, the form evokes recollections of popular pagan ritual and thus can inspire fears of religious heterodoxy. The same interaction of dramatic genre and theatrical mode of production generates socially subversive effects from the recurrent use of lower-class disguise as a means of aristocratic validation. In *As You Like It* (1599) a male actor impersonates a woman (Rosalind) impersonating a man (Ganymede) impersonating a woman (Rosalind). Carnival, the leading popular festival of the year, especially in southern Europe, encouraged a similar sexual reversal of costumes and roles.[12]

[11]Leo Salingar, *Shakespeare and the Traditions of Comedy* (Cambridge: Cambridge University Press, 1974), pp. 1–27.
[12]Peter Burke, *Popular Culture in Early Modern Europe* (New York: Harper and Row, 1978), pp. 183, 190.

In class terms, an artisan plays an aristocrat playing a farmer playing an aristocrat. But stage performance also rationalizes and contains such implications, not only by the specific resolution of the plot, but also by channeling anarchic instincts that may result from attendance at a play. The public theater in this respect offers communal affirmation and social ratification, a means of confronting instability in a manner that promotes reassurance about the existence and legitimacy of a new order. The theater within a nation, like theatricality within a play, helps restore a stratified social unity.

Yet the conservative, integrative effect of romantic comedy does not entirely negate the liberating dimensions of the form. From this perspective one can understand a distinctive feature of the plays: their appeal does not reside primarily in social mimesis. Although the form can criticize contemporary life, its main power lies in the representation of comic, anarchic freedom issuing in an ideal solution. From here, moreover, its most enduring social criticism usually derives. The late-sixteenth-century aristocracy had to face a rising bourgeoisie, urban—as opposed to rural—residence, a centralizing monarchy, and an emancipated peasantry. A look at the dramatic expression of each of these interdependent changes will reveal that, as a rule, the festive side of a play is inversely proportional to both the social seriousness of the subject and the prominence of other, potentially antagonistic classes.[13]

This relationship clearly emerges in works that concern a potent threat to the nobility—the capitalist economic practices associated with the bourgeoisie. Here the thematic intention requires the integration, rationalization, or even repression of the celebratory moment. In *El mercader amante* and *The Merchant of Venice* role playing and the assumption of disguise are almost grimly purposeful. Relatedly, the critical thrust of both comedies leads to various structural disjunctions and incongruities, as if the capacities of the form were being strained. Aguilar's and Shakespeare's plays thus reveal the limits of aristocratic theatricalism as a social device. In so doing they point beyond romantic comedy, not only forward to satire and tragedy, but also backward to the predominantly anticapitalist and popular English morality tradition, represented in this period by such works as Robert Wilson's *Three Ladies of London* (1581), Thomas Lodge and Robert Greene's *A Looking Glass for London and England* (1590), Thomas Dekker's anachronistic *Old Fortunatus* (1599), and ambiguously, Greene's romancelike *Scottish History of James IV* (1590).

Many other plays, though also concerned with the marital integration of aristocracy and bourgeoisie, consistently maintain a lighter tone. Typ-

---

[13]Elliot Krieger, *A Marxist Study of Shakespeare's Comedies* (New York: Barnes and Noble, 1979), pp. 6–8.

ically they involve at least an implicit test, in which the characters over-come aristocratic social condescension, bourgeois economic grasping, and mutual class antagonism through various playfully assumed humble disguises. England, of course, provides more examples than Spain, espe-cially if, in accordance with the fluid class distinctions of the time, one somewhat improperly extends the notion of a bourgeoisie to include ur-ban artisans and rural independent farmers as well: Greene's *Friar Bacon and Friar Bungay* (1589), Dekker's *Shoemakers' Holiday* (1599), and Shake-speare's *Merry Wives of Windsor* (1600) fall into this category. So too does *The Taming of the Shrew* (1594), where the titular action transforms the man's commitment to property marriage and the woman's to class pride into a mutual love firmly located within a neofeudal hierarchy. More strikingly, Thomas Heywood's *1 Fair Maid of the West* (c. 1600)[14] weds a gentleman to a barmaid whose simultaneous allegiance to prudent economics and exemplary morality, on the one hand, and to romantic adventure and good fun, on the other, suggests the continued compati-bility at the end of the century of traditional popular culture and a nas-cent Puritan bourgeois ideology.[15]

In Spanish drama, Lope de Vega's *Belardo el furioso* (1587)[16] pits the autobiographically inspired protagonist against a baseborn but far wealthier rival for the common object of their affections. The play in this respect demonstrates its author's uncanny ability to find in his own life the material by which to represent the concerns of his society.[17] In Aguilar's *La fuerza del interés*, partly a satiric rewriting of Lope's play, the comfortable but subordinate position within an aristocratic hierarchy accorded to the bourgeoisie by the concluding marriages, analogous to the status of a mercantile city such as Aguilar's Valencia in an absolutist state, depends overtly on the superior morality of the nobility, but co-vertly on its superior financial resources.

Finally, in some English plays with an unusually pronounced bour-geois focus, interclass tension is virtually nonexistent and, complemen-tarily, festive release almost uninterrupted. Henry Porter's *1 The Two Angry Women of Abingdon* (1588) achieves this effect by concentrating on the middle classes while taking for granted the traditional social order.

[14]Date: Robert K. Turner, Jr., chronological appendix to his edition of both parts of the play (London: Edward Arnold, 1968), p. 206. The favorable references to Essex might ac-tually suggest a period of composition between mid-1598 and late 1599.

[15]David M. Bevington, *Tudor Drama and Politics: A Critical Approach to Topical Meaning* (Cambridge: Harvard University Press, 1968), pp. 294–98, perhaps overemphasizes the fragility of this consensus.

[16]Date: Rinaldo Froldi, *Lope de Vega y la formación de la comedia: En torno a la tradición dramática valenciana y al primer teatro de Lope*, 2d ed., trans. Franco Gabriele and Mrs. de Gabriele (Salamanca: Anaya, 1968), pp. 147–49.

[17]Noël Salomon, *Recherches sur le thème paysan dans la "comedia" au temps de Lope de Vega* (Bordeaux: Féret, 1965), pp. xviii, 740.

Heywood's *Four Prentices of London* (1600) offers heroic exploit as artisanal wish-fulfillment. Upward mobility is imagined in feudal terms long anachronistic for the nobility but apparently well suited to the assertion of bourgeois merit. The play thus reveals both the continuation of aristocratic ideological hegemony and the means by which a rising class disguises even from itself the revolutionary significance of its struggle for self-consciousness and self-realization. Heywood's work also suggests that freedom from social restraint might mean freedom from lower-class status and that in this way popular aspiration could fuse with aristocratic longing in the theater.

Appropriately enough, a spirit of play similar to that in the predominantly bourgeois comedies also emerges when the emphasis shifts to the nobility alone. Given the prominence of the London bourgeoisie, an urban setting for the aristocracy's internal intrigues is more common in Spain than in England. In both countries, however, the plays implicitly concern the way the aristocracy has adjusted to its new environment. *Much Ado about Nothing* (1598), *Twelfth Night* (1600), Tárrega's *El prado de Valencia* (1588–91),[18] Guillén de Castro's *Los mal casados de Valencia* (1595?–1604?),[19] and Lope's (?) *El sufrimiento premiado* (probably 1603)[20] offer a range of responses to this problem. A number of the relevant issues arise in *Las ferias de Madrid* (probably 1587–88),[21] another of Lope's autobiographically resonant early works. The play has recently escaped from a legacy of misunderstanding through the simple recognition that it is not a seventeeth-century wife-honor drama but a sixteenth-century romantic comedy. Yet in continuing to attempt to moralize the play, revisionist critics have failed to grasp the full logic of their own arguments.[22] The main plot involves an adulterous couple who evade death at the hands of the jealous husband only when the woman's father preemptively murders his wronged son-in-law. The remainder of the comedy, hardly a subplot, concerns the hijinks of some idle young *caballeros* who wander about town amusing themselves, often at others' expense. *Las ferias de Madrid* thus presents a fantasy of freedom from social codes and constraints. But it also partially censors that fantasy, in the

[18]Bruerton, "Versificación," p. 339, opts for a date of 1590–91; Froldi, p. 119 and n. 80, prefers a slightly earlier date.

[19]Date: Bruerton, "The Chronology of the *Comedias* of Guillén de Castro," *Hispanic Review* 12 (1944): 125–26, 150.

[20]Victor Dixon, prólogo to his edition of the play, *El sufrimiento premiado: Comedia famosa* (London: Tamesis, 1967), p. xxvi, argues for this date and, pp. vii–xxvii, for the attribution to Lope, now widely accepted.

[21]Date: Froldi, pp. 140–46.

[22]Donald McGrady, "The Comic Treatment of Conjugal Honor in Lope's *Las ferias de Madrid*," *Hispanic Review* 41 (1973): 33–42; Donald R. Larson, *The Honor Plays of Lope de Vega* (Cambridge: Harvard University Press, 1977), pp. 28–37. For the moralistic readings, see McGrady, p. 42, and Larson, pp. 33–34.

lovers' agreement to marry eventually and in the ejection of the *caballeros* from a wedding feast for their carnivalesque recitation of satiric verses directed against the bride.[23] The play in this respect implicitly questions the social possibility of the very wish-fulfillment it offers.

More generally, the urban setting itself is the source of repression in *Las ferias de Madrid*. Even this restraint disappears, however, when the action occurs in the country. Broadly speaking, pastoral involves a literary and theatrical reaction by the nobility to the twin pressures of capitalism and absolutism. The construction of the pastoral world resolves the intractable dilemmas of aristocratic life in the city or at court. The form also responds to the increased independence of the peasantry. Pastoral does not really involve a flight from town and court to a traditional world. It leaves behind present social life not to return to the past, but to construct an alternative and imaginary rural reality, from which the indigenous population has been exiled precisely because of its insufficient servility. The idealization of pastoral life reveals as well the aristocratic assumption that shepherds did not engage in manual labor.[24] The form rarely occurs in all its purity, even in an authentic pastoral like *Belardo el furioso*. A verisimilar landscape and its inhabitants enter in varying degrees such works as Miguel Sánchez's *La guarda cuidadosa* (1580s),[25] the anonymous *Mucedorus* (1590), George Peele's *The Old Wives Tale* (1590), *The Two Gentlemen of Verona* (1593), *Love's Labour's Lost* (1595), *A Mid-Summer-Night's Dream* (1595), and Anthony Munday's *The Downfall of Robert, Earl of Huntingdon* (1598),[26] among many others. All, however, share a common method: the solution of aristocratic problems by a process of ruralization.

A closer look at two comedies by Lope and Shakespeare suggests the possibilities and limits of pastoral. Until well into the final act, *Los donaires de Matico* (1589–90?)[27] seems a conventionally romantic comedy, in which the titular royal heroine dons a lower-class, masculine disguise in order to win her mate. But the play is actually an intrigue, a dramatic genre that at times confirms the Russian Formalist insistence on the primacy of form. When the intrigue serves as an end in itself, rather than merely as a means, issues arise not because of their cognitive importance, but for their contribution to the plot, whose elegance points only

[23]Carnival and verbal aggression: Burke, p. 187.

[24]Salomon, esp. pp. 167–96, 222–23, 451–73; Raymond Williams, *The Country and the City* (New York: Oxford University Press, 1973), pp. 18–21; Krieger, 85–88; Hill, p. 327.

[25]Date: S. Griswold Morley, "Strophes in the Spanish Drama before Lope de Vega," in *Homenaje ofrecido a Menéndez Pidal: Miscelánea de estudios lingüísticos, literarios e históricos* (Madrid: Editorial Hernando, 1925), 1:524.

[26]Attribution: John C. Meagher's introductory comments to *The Downfall of Robert Earl of Huntingdon*, 1601 (n.p.: Malone Society Reprints, 1964), pp. vi–vii.

[27]Date: Froldi, p. 154 n. 157, believes that the play was written during Lope's Valencian exile.

to the playwright's ingenuity.[28] Ideologically, the intrigue, unlike Shakespearean comedy, proclaims that people bear no responsibility for their conduct, that social rules have no consequences, that things will work out, that the status quo remains secure. In *Los donaires de Matico*, the resolution of the complicated plot, rather than fulfilling the prior thematic premises, instead requires that the lovers marry two other people, with scarcely a regret. The symbolic resonance of humble attire, evident throughout the action, accordingly proves meaningless. Much of the attraction of *Los donaires de Matico* lies precisely in the fantasy and irresponsibility that have troubled even the play's defenders.[29] Yet the other side of these virtues is triviality. The intrigue form ultimately removes all difficulty from the aristocracy's adaptation to the new role prescribed for it by the rise of absolutism.

In *As You Like It*, by contrast, the ruling class earns its position, rather than having it handed over. The comic business of the plot requires the creative exercise of free will: Rosalind makes and therefore deserves her destiny. As opposed to intrigues or even most romantic comedies, here how the woman gets her man is more important than that she gets him. But the encompassing and critical vision attained by Rosalind may obscure the ideological underpinnings of that perspective.[30] The forces of usurpation, injustice, and exile, which motivate the action and give it special significance, prove in the end hardly less illusory than the problems of *Los donaires de Matico*. In this sense Shakespeare's work simply deploys a more sophisticated mechanism of repression.

The comparison of these plays can provide a basis for a general contrast between the two dramas before 1600. In England romantic comedy triumphed; in Spain the intrigue persisted as well. In addition to *Los donaires de Matico*, *Los mal casados de Valencia*, Lope's *El rufián Castrucho* (c. 1598), and other early works by Lope [31] exhibit strong tendencies toward intrigue. Romantic comedy remains only a genre in formation. The English plays evince a correspondingly greater interest in depth of characterization. If aristocratic theatricality responds to the combined social instability and rigidity of the class's position, the rigidity is felt more fully in Spain, the instability in England. The greater weight of the

[28]Laura Brown, "The Divided Plot: Tragicomic Form in the Restoration," *ELH* 47 (1980): 67–79; Viktor Shklovsky, "Art as Technique," in *Russian Formalist Criticism: Four Essays*, trans. Lee T. Lemon and Marion J. Reis (Lincoln: University of Nebraska Press, 1965), p. 12.

[29]E.g., Emilio Cotarelo y Mori, prólogo to *Los donaires de Matico*, in *Obras de Lope de Vega*, n.s., 4 (Madrid: Real Academia Española, 1917), xxvii–xxviii; Edward M. Wilson and Duncan Moir, *The Golden Age: Drama, 1492–1700*, vol. 3 of *A Literary History of Spain*, gen. ed. R. O. Jones (London: Ernest Benn, 1971), pp. 50–51, 53.

[30]Bevington, *Tudor Drama and Politics*, pp. 297–98, provides an example of this failing.

[31]See Richard F. Glenn, "The Loss of Identity: Towards a Definition of the Dialectic in Lope's Early Drama," *Hispanic Review* 41 (1973): 609–26.

English bourgeoisie helps account not only for this distinction but also for the unusual psychological complexity of the protagonists in Shakespearean romantic comedy.

The differences between English and Spanish drama also grow out of the respective theatrical traditions. In England, romantic comedy draws on various strains of neoclassicism, as well as on the morality play, romantic drama, and, more generally, the entire popular legacy.[32] The artisanal dimension of theatrical practice cuts across the tension between mimesis and festive release in the form, reinforcing one or both tendencies, introducing an alternative and independent perspective on the action, and increasing the social breadth and significance of the representation. The analogous Spanish plays are more exclusively neoclassical. Recent efforts to locate the origin of the *comedia* in the Valencian theater[33]—more persuasive for comedy than for serious drama—merely highlight the indebtedness to Italy, despite the willingness of the Valencian playwrights to dispense with neoclassical dramatic rules in order to appeal more effectively to their public. Valencian origins also imply a link between the relatively weak popular dimension and the defining feature of Spanish comedy, theatrical regionalism. England's romantic comedies often have national implications; Spain's comedies—romantic or intrigue—are narrower socially as well as geographically. Only after the turn of the century, with the triumph of Madrid as the theatrical center of the country, could a genuine parallel to English practice occur. By then, however, other forces had also intervened to modify further the course of Spanish comedy.

## Shakespeare, *The Merchant of Venice*

*The Merchant of Venice* offers an embarrassment of socioeconomic riches. It treats merchants and usurers, the nature of the law, and the interaction between country and city. But since it is also about the relation between love and friendship, the meaning of Christianity, and a good deal more, a thematically minded critic, regardless of his or her persuasion, may be in for a bit of difficulty. In the most comprehensive study of the play yet produced, Lawrence Danson attempts to solve this problem by arguing that *The Merchant of Venice* dramatizes not the triumph of one set of values over another, but the transformation of conflicts into harmonies that incorporate what they at the same time transcend.[34] Shake-

---

[32]M. C. Bradbrook, *The Growth and Structure of Elizabethan Comedy* (Berkeley and Los Angeles: University of California Press, 1956).

[33]Froldi, passim.

[34]Lawrence Danson, *The Harmonies of "The Merchant of Venice"* (New Haven: Yale University Press, 1978).

speare's procedure thus resembles both medieval figura and Hegelian dialectics.[35] Because the intellectual and structural design posited by Danson elegantly accommodates not only thematic diversity but also the audience's ambivalent responses to both Shylock and the Christian characters, it is the appropriate object of a skeptical scrutiny of interpretation in *The Merchant of Venice*.

Perhaps Shakespeare needs to be interpreted simply because of the antiquity and complexity of his art. Yet far from being ideologically neutral, such an enterprise, by juxtaposing an alternative and richer reality with contemporary life, involves an implicit critique of the present. Even more, Shakespeare's plays, despite their elaborateness, appealed to a broadly heterogeneous primary audience whose constitution depended on a comparative social and cultural unity, long since lost, in the nation as well as the theater. This underlying coherence emerges in the logical and, one would expect, inherently meaningful unfolding of the dramatic plot,[36] a strong example of which is provided by the rigorously interlocking, causal development of *The Merchant of Venice*. Presumably, then, the best criticism would deepen, rather than overturn, a sense of the play's meaning widely shared in space and in time.[37]

This is precisely not the case in discussions of *The Merchant of Venice*, however. The play has been seen as the unambiguous triumph of good Christians over a bad Jew;[38] as the deliberately ambiguous triumph of the Christians;[39] as the unintentionally ambiguous, and hence artistically flawed, triumph of the Christians;[40] as the tragedy of Shylock, the bourgeois hero;[41] and as a sweeping attack on Christians and Jews

[35]Figural interpretation: Erich Auerbach, "Figura," in *Scenes from the Drama of European Literature*, trans. Ralph Manheim (New York: Meridian Books, 1959), pp. 11–76; dialectics of the trial scene: Danson, p. 70; general "dialectical element in Shakespeare's comic structure": Northrop Frye, *A Natural Perspective: The Development of Shakespearean Comedy and Romance* (New York: Harcourt, Brace and World, 1965), p. 133.

[36]For the social and ideological implications of the well-made plot in the novel, see Jameson, "Metacommentary," pp. 12–13. Sigurd Burckhardt, *Shakespearean Meanings* (Princeton: Princeton University Press, 1968), pp. 206–36, offers a symbolic, modernist, self-referential analysis of the rigors of the plot in *The Merchant of Venice*.

[37]Richard Levin, "Refuting Shakespeare's Endings—Part II," *Modern Philology* 75 (1977): 132–58.

[38]C. L. Barber, *Shakespeare's Festive Comedy: A Study of Dramatic Form and Its Relation to Social Custom* (Princeton: Princeton University Press, 1959), pp. 163–91; Frank Kermode, "The Mature Comedies," in *Early Shakespeare*, ed. John Russell Brown and Bernard Harris, Stratford-upon-Avon Studies, no. 3 (New York: St. Martin's Press, 1961), pp. 220–24; Siegel, "Shylock, the Elizabethan Puritan and Our Own World," in *Shakespeare in His Time and Ours*, pp. 337–38.

[39]Danson, passim.

[40]Doran, pp. 318–19, 347, 362–64.

[41]Erich Auerbach, *Mimesis: The Representation of Reality in Western Literature*, trans. Willard S. Trask (Princeton: Princeton University Press, 1953), pp. 314–15, 316, 320, 325, 328, offers elements of this reading, though also acknowledging that the resolution of the play precludes a tragic interpretation. The stage tradition described by John Russell

alike.[42] No other Shakespearean comedy before *All's Well That Ends Well* (1602) and *Measure for Measure* (1604), perhaps no other Shakespearean comedy at all, has excited comparable controversy. Probably the most promising way out of this dilemma is to see the play as a new departure for Shakespeare, as his earliest comedy drawn from the Italian *novelle*, as the first of several not entirely successful attempts to introduce more powerful characters, more complex problems of conduct, more realistic representation, and a more serious vision of life into a traditionally light genre.[43] Such a perspective has its drawbacks. Nonetheless, it has the virtue of suggesting that the play is by and large a romantic comedy; that it is partially flawed; that it calls for an unusual set of critical questions;[44] and, most important, that it requires not so much interpretation as the discovery of the sources of difficulty in interpreting, the view of the play as a symptom of a problem in the life of late-sixteenth-century England.

Critics who have studied *The Merchant of Venice* against the background of English history have justifiably seen Shylock, and especially his lending habits, as the embodiment of capitalism.[45] The last third of the sixteenth century witnessed a sequence of denunciations of the spread of usury. In *The Specvlation of Vsurie*, published during the year in which Shakespeare's play may first have been performed, Thomas Bell expresses a typical sense of outrage. "Now, now is nothing more frequent with the rich men of this world, than to writhe about the neckes of their poore neighbours, and to impouerish them with the filthie lucre of Usurie."[46] Behind this fear lay the transition to capitalism: the rise of banking, the increasing need for credit in industrial enterprises, and the growing threat of indebtedness facing both aristocratic landlords and,

---

Brown, "The Realization of Shylock: A Theatrical Criticism," in *Early Shakespeare*, ed. John Russell Brown and Harris, pp. 187–209, seems to fall primarily into this category.

[42]Anselm Schlösser, "Dialectic in *The Merchant of Venice*," *Zeitschrift für Anglistik und Amerikanistik* 23 (1975): 5–11; Burton Hatlen, "Feudal and Bourgeois Concepts of Value in *The Merchant of Venice*," in *Shakespeare: Contemporary Critical Approaches*, ed. Harry R. Garvin (Lewisburg, Pa.: Bucknell University Press, 1980), pp. 91–105; René Girard, "'To Entrap the Wisest': A Reading of *The Merchant of Venice*," in *Literature and Society*, ed. Edward W. Said, Selected Papers from the English Institute, 1978, n.s., 3 (Baltimore: Johns Hopkins University Press, 1980), pp. 100–119; Marc Shell, *Money, Language, and Thought: Literary and Philosophical Economics from the Medieval to the Modern Era* (Berkeley and Los Angeles: University of California Press, 1982), pp. 47–83.

[43]Salingar, pp. 298–325.

[44]For this argument see Ralph W. Rader, "Fact, Theory, and Literary Explanation," *Critical Inquiry* 1 (1974): 249–50, 258–61.

[45]John W. Draper, "Usury in *The Merchant of Venice*," *Modern Philology* 33 (1935): 37–47; E. C. Pettet, "*The Merchant of Venice* and the Problem of Usury," *Essays and Studies* 31 (1945): 19–33; Siegel, "Shylock."

[46]Thomas Bell, *The Specvlation of Vsurie* (London, 1596), sig. A2ʳ. For similar statements, see Thomas Lodge, *An Alarum Against Vsurers* (London, 1584), sig. E1ʳ, and Roger Fenton, *A Treatise of Vsvrie* (London, 1611), sig. B1ʳ.

above all, small independent producers, who could easily decline to working-class status.[47] Although the lower classes were the main victims, it is as misleading to emphasize the popular character of opposition to usury in Shakespeare or elsewhere as to argue, with L. C. Knights, that "Elizabethan drama, even in its higher ranges, was not the expression of a 'class' culture at all."[48] Rather, the ideology ultimately served the interests of the hegemonic nobility. Artisans and peasant smallholders might fall into the proletariat, but once the majority of the traditional ruling class had adapted to capitalism, the issue of usury faded away.

This had not occurred by 1600, however. *The Merchant of Venice* offers a number of specific parallels to the antiusury campaign,[49] most notably the contradiction between usury and assistance to the poor, as well as the related contrast between usurers and merchants. Miles Mosse, for example, laments that "lending upon *vsurie* is growne so common and usuall among men, as that free lending to the needie is utterly overthrowne."[50] The distinction between merchants and usurers, also of medieval origin, could be drawn on the grounds that only the former operated for mutual benefit, as opposed to self-interest. Or it might be argued, in language recalling Shakespeare's high valuation of "venturing," that the usurer does not, like "the merchant that crosse the seas, adventure," receiving instead a guaranteed return on his money.[51]

A number of dubious consequences follow from concentrating too narrowly on the English background of *The Merchant of Venice*, however. From such a perspective, the play as a whole seems unproblematic, noneconomic issues unimportant, and related matters like Shylock's religion or the Italian setting irrelevant.[52] Even explicitly economic concerns do

---

[47]R. H. Tawney, introduction to *A Discourse upon Usury by Way of Dialogue and Orations, for the Better Variety and More Delight of All Those That Shall Read this Treatise* [1572], by Thomas Wilson (New York: Harcourt Brace, [1925]), pp. 1–172. See also Lawrence Stone, *The Crisis of the Aristocracy, 1558–1641* (Oxford: Clarendon Press, 1965), pp. 158, 183, 541–43.

[48]L. C. Knights, *Drama and Society in the Age of Jonson* (London: Chatto and Windus, 1937), p. 11.

[49]See Draper, pp. 45–46; Pettet, pp. 26–27.

[50]Miles Mosse, *The Arraignment and Conviction of Vsvrie* (London, 1595), sig. C3$^v$. See also H. A. [Henry Arthington?], *Provision for the Poore, Now in Penurie* (London, 1597), sig. C2$^v$; Philip Caesar, *A General Discovrse Against the Damnable Sect of Vsurers* (London, 1578), the title page of which refers to "these / later daies, in which, Charitie being ba- / nished, Couetousnes hath got- / ten the vpper hande."

[51]*The Death of Vsvry, or the Disgrace of Vsvrers* (London, 1594), sig. E1$^r$. See also Nicolas Sanders, *A Briefe Treatise of Vsvrie* (Lovanii, 1568), sig. D1$^r$; and Lodge and Thomas Greene's *A Looking Glasse for London and England* (1590), ed. Tetsumaro Hayashi (Metuchen, N.J.: Scarecrow Press, 1970), 1:iii and 3:i. A sympathetic view of merchants is taken for granted—a position impossible at the time with regard to usurers—in John Browne, *The Marchants Avizo* (London, 1591), and in *A True Report of Sir Anthony Shierlies Iourney* (London, 1600).

[52]Draper, pp. 46–47; Pettet, pp. 19, 29, 32; Siegel, "Shylock," pp. 249, 252.

not make adequate sense. An emphasis on the difference between trade and usury might imply that Antonio and his creator are resolutely medieval anticapitalists.[53] But not only do Shakespeare's other plays of the 1590s show few signs of a hostility to capitalism, *The Merchant of Venice* itself is quite obviously procapitalist, at least as far as commerce is concerned. Perhaps Shakespeare is merely criticizing the worst aspects of an emergent economic system rather than the system itself. In this respect, moreover, he deviates from the antiusury tracts and English reality alike. Writers of the period register both the medieval ambivalence about merchants and the indisputable contemporary fact that merchants were the leading usurers: suspicion of Italian traders ran particularly high.[54] Shakespeare may intend a covert parallel between Shylock and Antonio. Yet no manipulation will convert a comedy in which there are no merchant-usurers and in which the only usurer is a Jew into a faithful representation of English economic life.

Similar trouble arises with Shylock, whom critics have at times allegorically Anglicized as a grasping Puritan.[55] The identification is unconvincing, however, partly because one can just as easily transform him into a Catholic, partly because he is too complex and contradictory to fit neatly the stereotype of Puritan thrift, and partly because the stereotype was by no means universal. In *The Massacre of Money*, for instance, Auarus contemptuously addresses the virtuous Liberalis as "thou base Puritan, who hast much wealth / And on the poore bestow'st it frivolously."[56] It is also unclear exactly what kind of capitalist Shylock is. The crisis of the play arises not from his insistence on usury, but from his refusal of it. The contrast is between usury, which is immoral because it computes a charge above the principal from the moment of the loan, and interest, which is perfectly acceptable because, as Mosse makes clear, it "is never due but from the appointed day of payment forward."[57] Immediately recognizing that Shylock's proposal falls primarily into the latter category, Antonio responds appropriately, if naively:

> Content in faith, I'll seal to such a bond,
> And say there is much kindness in the Jew.[58]

[53]Draper, p. 39; Pettet, pp. 19, 22, 23, 27, 29.

[54]Bell, sigs. B4$^v$ and C3$^v$; Tawney, *Religion and the Rise of Capitalism: A Historical Study*, Holland Memorial Lectures, 1922 (New York: New American Library, 1954), pp. 20–39; *A Discovery of the Great Svbtiltie and Wonderful Wisedome of the Italians* (London, 1591), sig. B1$^r$.

[55]Siegel, "Shylock"; A. A. Smirnov, *Shakespeare: A Marxist Interpretation* (New York: Critics Group, 1936), p. 35.

[56]Danson, pp. 78–80; T. A., *The Massacre of Money* (London, 1602), sig. C2$^v$.

[57]Mosse, sig. F2$^r$; Tawney, *Religion*, pp. 43–44; W. H. Auden, *The Dyer's Hand and other Essays* (New York: Vintage, 1968), pp. 227–28.

[58]The Arden edition of Shakespeare, *The Merchant of Venice*, ed. John Russell Brown (London: Methuen, 1955), 1.3.148–49. Subsequent references are noted in the text.

In addition, the penalty for default on the bond is closer to folklore than to capitalism: stipulation of a pound of flesh, after all, is hardly what one would expect from *homo economicus*. To be sure, Shakespeare is literalizing the traditional metaphorical view of usurers.[59] Moreover, Shylock's desire for revenge is both motivated by economics and possessed of a large degree of economic logic (e.g., 1.3.39–40 and 3.149, 117–18). But when the grasping moneylender refuses to relent in return for any repayment—"No not for Venice"—he goes beyond the bounds of rationality and against the practices of a ruthless modern businessman (4.1.226).[60] In short, although it is proper to view *The Merchant of Venice* as a critique of early English capitalism, that approach fails to account even for all of the purely economic issues in the work. Can tolerable sense be made of the play's economics? An answer to this question requires scrutiny of the Venetian setting of the action.

To the English, and particularly to Londoners, Venice represented a more advanced stage of the commercial development they themselves were experiencing. G. K. Hunter's telling remark about the predilections of the Jacobean theater—"Italy became important to the English dramatists only when 'Italy' was revealed as an aspect of England"— already applies in part to *The Merchant of Venice*.[61] Yet Venetian reality during Shakespeare's lifetime contradicted almost point for point its portrayal in the play. Not only did the government bar Jewish usurers from the city, it also forced the Jewish community to staff and finance low-interest, nonprofit lending institutions that served the Christian poor. Funding derived primarily from the involuntary donations of Jewish merchants active in the Levantine trade. The Jews of Venice thus contributed to the early development of capitalism not as usurers, but as merchants involved in an international, trans-European economic network. Ironically, elsewhere in the Veneto, by the late sixteenth century the public Christian banks on which the Jewish loan houses of Venice were modeled drew most of their assets from interest-bearing deposits.[62]

---

[59]Barber, p. 169; *Whartons Dreame* (London, 1578), sig. A3$^r$; Robert Wilson, *The Three Ladies of London* (1581), ed. John S. Farmer (Tudor Facsimile Texts, 1911), sig. D4$^v$. The subsequent reference to Wilson's play is to this edition.

[60]Stephen J. Greenblatt, "Marlowe, Marx, and Anti-Semitism," *Critical Inquiry* 5 (1978): 295.

[61]G. K. Hunter, "English Folly and Italian Vice: The Moral Landscape of John Marston," in *Jacobean Theatre*, ed. John Russell Brown and Harris, Stratford-upon-Avon Studies, no. 1 (London: Edward Arnold, 1960), p. 95. On Venetian trade, see Robert Johnson's translation of Giovanni Botero, *Relations of the Most Famovs Kingdoms and Common-weales thorovgh the World* (London, 1611), sigs. Gg2$^v$–Gg3$^v$; George Sandys, *A Relation of a Iourney* (London, 1615), sig. B1$^r$.

[62]Brian Pullan, *Rich and Poor in Renaissance Venice: The Social Institutions of a Catholic State, to 1620* (Oxford: Basil Blackwell, 1971), pp. 538–621; Fernand Braudel, *The Mediter-*

From a longer historical view of Italy and Venice, however, *The Merchant of Venice* assumes a recognizable relationship to reality. Between the twelfth and the early fourteenth centuries in Italy, international merchant-usurers were often required by the church to make testamentary restitution of their profits from moneylending. Thereafter this occupation decomposed into its constituent parts. Without changing the character of their financial transactions, the merchants experienced a sharp rise in status, eventually evolving into the great philanthropical merchant princes of the Renaissance. The other descendants of the earlier merchant-usurers, the small local usurer-pawnbrokers, suffered a corresponding decline in social position. This latter group, the main victim of ecclesiastical action against usury in the fifteenth and sixteenth centuries, increasingly consisted of immigrant Jews.[63]

Jewish moneylenders benefited the Venetian republic in two principal ways. They provided a reliable, lucrative source of tax revenues and forced loans to finance the state's military preparations. They also drove down interest rates for private citizens, rich and poor, by underselling the Christian usurers, whom, consequently, they gradually replaced. The Christian banks, founded beginning in the late fifteenth century, were designed not only to assist the poor, but also to eliminate Jewish moneylenders by providing cheaper credit. Although never established in Venice itself, the *monti di pietà*, as they were called, were soon widespread in the cities and towns of the republican mainland. They rarely succeeded in completely replacing Jewish pawnbrokers, however.[64]

This, then, is the other, Italian historical background to *The Merchant of Venice*. None of Shakespeare's probable sources refers to any prior enmity between merchant and usurer, much less to a comparable motive for the antagonism. English discussions of Italy, on the other hand, regularly mention both Jewish usury and Venetian charity,[65] while Bell, among others, speaks of the *mons pietatis*, a bank where the poor can "borrow money in their neede, and not bee oppressed with usury."[66]

---

*ranean and the Mediterranean World in the Age of Philip II*, trans. Siân Reynolds (London: Collins, 1973), 2:817, 823. Fynes Moryson, *Shakespeare's Europe: A Survey of the Condition of Europe at the End of the Sixteenth Century; Being Unpublished Chapters of Fynes Moryson's "Itinerary"* (*1617*), ed. Charles Hughes, 2d ed. (1903; rpt. New York: Benjamin Blom, 1967), p. 488, gives a reasonably accurate picture of the position of Italian Jews.

[63]Benjamin N. Nelson, "The Usurer and the Merchant Prince: Italian Businessmen and the Ecclesiastical Law of Restitution, 1100–1550," *Journal of Economic History*, Suppl. 7 (1947): 104–22.

[64]Pullan, pp. 431–537.

[65]Wylliam Thomas, *The Historye of Italye* (London, 1549), sigs. U4ᵛ–X1ʳ, Y2ᵛ, Y3ᵛ; Lewes Lewkenor's translation of Gasparo Contarini, *The Commonwealth and Gouernment of Venice* (London, 1599), sig. T2ʳ; Moryson, *An Itinerary* (London, 1617), sig. H1ᵛ–H2ʳ.

[66]Bell, sig. D4ᵛ. See also Fenton, sig. P4ᵛ; Tawney, introduction, pp. 125–27; idem, *Religion*, p. 53; Draper, pp. 45–46; Nelson, *The Idea of Usury: From Tribal Brotherhood to Univer-*

From this point of view, the hostility between Antonio, the openhanded Christian merchant, and Shylock, the tightfisted Jewish usurer, represents not the conflict between declining feudalism and rising capitalism, but its opposite. It is a special instance of the struggle, widespread in Europe, between Jewish quasi-feudal fiscalism and native bourgeois mercantilism, in which the indigenous forces usually prevailed.[67] Both the characterization and the outcome of *The Merchant of Venice* mark Antonio as the harbinger of modern capitalism. By guaranteeing an honorable reputation as well as a secure and absolute title to private property, the exemption of the Italian merchant-financier from the stigma of usury provided a necessary spur to the expansion of the new system.[68] Shylock, by contrast, is a figure from the past, marginal, diabolical, irrational, archaic, medieval. Shakespeare's Jacobean tragic villains—Iago, Edmund, Macbeth, and Augustus—are all younger men bent on destroying their elders. Shylock is almost the reverse, an old man with obsolete values trying to arrest the course of history.[69]

Obviously, however, the use of Italian materials in *The Merchant of Venice*, for all its historicity, remains deeply ideological in the bad sense, primarily because of the anti-Semitic distinction between vindictive Jewish usurer and charitable Christian merchant. Shylock's defense of usury is not as strong as it could have been,[70] nor was Shakespeare's preference for an Italian merchant over a Jewish usurer universally shared at the time.[71] Indeed, the very contrast between the two occupations is a false dichotomy, faithful to the Renaissance Italian merchant's understanding of himself but not to the reality that self-conception sought to justify.

The apparently contradictory implications of English and Italian economic history for *The Merchant of Venice* are responses to the intractability of contemporary life. The form of the play results from an ideological reworking of reality designed to produce precisely the intellectual and structural pattern described at the beginning of this discussion. The prominence of duality, especially in Shylock, is necessary to this end. In *The Merchant of Venice* English history evokes fears of capitalism, and Italian history allays those fears. One is the problem; the other

*sal Otherhood*, 2d ed. (Chicago: University of Chicago Press, 1969), p. 73 n. 2. Greenblatt, "Marlowe, Marx, and Anti-Semitism," p. 294, seems to be the only critic to suggest a parallel between Antonio and the *monti di Pietà*.

[67]Fiscalism versus mercantilism: Immanuel Wallerstein, *The Modern World-System: Capitalist Agriculture and the Origins of the European World-Economy in the Sixteenth Century* (New York: Academic Press, 1974), pp. 137–38, 149. But see Pullan, p. 451.

[68]Nelson, "The Usurer and the Merchant Prince," pp. 120–22.

[69]For similar perceptions, see Barber, p. 191; Frye, p. 98.

[70]Draper, pp. 43–44; but see Danson, pp. 148–50.

[71]See, for example, Wilson, *Three Ladies*, sig. D3ᵛ.

the solution, the act of incorporation, of transcendence, toward which the play strives.

A similar, if less striking, process of reconciliation is at work with Antonio, whose social significance varies inversely to Shylock's. As a traditional and conservative figure, he nearly becomes a tragic victim of economic change; as the embodiment of progressive forces, he points toward the comic resolution. But Antonio cannot be too progressive, cannot represent a fundamental rupture with the past. Giovanni Botero attributed his country's urban preeminence partly to the fact that "the gentlemen in *Italy* does dwell in Cities."[72] Chapter 2 argued that the fusion in the towns of nobility and bourgeoisie helped make the Renaissance possible. The concluding tripartite unity of Antonio, Bassanio, and Portia[73] enacts precisely this interclass harmony between aristocratic landed wealth and mercantile capital, with the former dominant. A belief that some such relationship provided much of the social foundation of the English monarchy partly accounts for Shakespeare's essentially corporatist defense of absolutism in the 1590s.

A brief consideration of Marx's views on Jews, on usurers, on merchants, and on *The Merchant of Venice* will make it possible to restate these conclusions with greater theoretical rigor and to point toward additional, related issues. In the "Contribution to the Critique of Hegel's *Philosophy of Right*: Introduction," Shylock is an exploiter of the lower classes. Characterizing the German historical school of law, Marx comments: "A Shylock, but a servile Shylock, it swears upon its bond, its historical, Christian-Germanic bond, for every pound of flesh cut from the heart of the people." The second part of "On the Jewish Question" basically equates Judaism with capitalism, a position that volume 1 of *Capital* reasserts in a discussion of the efforts of nineteenth-century English manufacturers to force children to work long hours. "Workers and factory inspectors protested on hygienic and moral grounds, but Capital answered:

> My deeds upon my head! I crave the law,
> The penalty and forfeit of my bond. . . .

This Shylock-like clinging to the letter of the law," Marx adds, "was, however, only a way of introducing an open revolt against the same law." But the extended discussion of usury in volume 3 of *Capital* implicitly reaches a very different conclusion. Usurer's capital, Marx claims, arises long before the capitalist system itself, its parasitic action weakening the

---

[72]Robert Peterson's translation of Giovanni Botero, *A Treatise, Concerning the Causes of the Magnificencie and Greatnes of Cities* (London, 1606), sig. I3$^v$.
[73]Danson, p. 55.

precapitalist mode of production off which it lives. But unassisted it cannot generate a transition to capitalism. When that transition does occur, however, usury inevitably declines, partly as a result of the determined opposition of mercantile capital. Finally, commercial capital itself is, like usury, an early and primitive form of capital and, as such, ultimately compatible with precapitalist modes of production. Thus Marx's comments in effect recapitulate the argument on the economics of *The Merchant of Venice* presented in the previous pages.[74]

In one instance, however, they lead beyond that argument. Up to now the discussion has primarily attempted to show how dramatic form, as the product of an ideological reworking of history, resolves those contradictions that prove irreconcilable in life. But of course many critics do not feel a final coherence to *The Merchant of Venice*. In volume 1 of *Capital*, after showing how industrial capital endangers the worker, "how it constantly threatens, by taking away the instruments of labour, to snatch from his hands the means of subsistence," Marx quotes Shylock's reply to the duke's pardon:

> You take my life
> When you do take the means whereby I live.[75]

The passage implies exactly the opposite of what is suggested by the lines previously cited from the same volume. There Marx identifies Shylock with capital, the Christians with labor; here the Christians represent capital, Shylock labor. Such a reversal does not conform to the other dualisms of the play: instead, Marx's use of selective quotation succeeds in capturing Shylock as both victimizer and victim, a double role incompatible with the ostensible design of the play.

That Shylock is grand as well as pitiable does not in itself imply any structural flaw in *The Merchant of Venice*. Shakespeare needed an antagonist possessed of sufficient stature to pose a credible threat. The sympathy elicited by the Jewish usurer, often a consequence of his mistreatment by Christian characters who resemble him more than they would admit, also serves a plausible formal purpose in the overall movement toward mercy and harmony. By the end of the trial scene most of the Christian characters have fairly settled accounts with Shylock.[76] The

---

[74]Marx's remarks may be found in "Contribution to the Critique of Hegel's *Philosophy of Right*: Introduction," in *The Marx-Engels Reader*, ed. Robert C. Tucker, 2d ed. (New York: Norton, 1978), p. 55; "On the Jewish Question," in *The Marx-Engels Reader*, pp. 47–52; *Capital: A Critique of Political Economy*, vol. 1, introd. Ernest Mandel, trans. Ben Fowkes (New York: Vintage, 1977), pp. 399–400; *Capital*, vol. 3, introd. Mandel, trans. David Fernbach (Harmondsworth, Middlesex: Penguin, 1981), pp. 728–45, 440–55.

[75]*Capital*, 1:618.

[76]Danson, pp. 123–25.

trouble is that Christianity has not. Although the Christian characters in the play are better than Shylock, the Christian characters not in the play are not. In his famous "Jew" speech and in his declamation on slavery to the court, Shylock adopts the strategy of equating Christian with Jew to justify his own murderous intentions (3.2.47–66, 4.1.89–103). But by the end of act 4 his analogies are strictly irrelevant to most of the Christian characters in the play. The Christians either have given up the practices that Shylock attributes to them or have never been guilty of them at all: certainly no Christian slaveholders appear in *The Merchant of Venice*. On the other hand, Shylock's universalizing accusations are never challenged in word by his Christian auditors and cannot be sufficiently answered in deed by the individual charitable acts with which the trial concludes. The devastating judgments particularly of the second speech, allowed to stand, reveal that although Shylock is defeated and then incorporated in the world of the play, in the world beyond the play his values are pervasive.

This bifurcation is a consequence of the fundamental contradiction in Shakespeare's social material. English history requires that the threat embodied in Shylock be generalized, Italian history that it remain localized. Yet if Shakespeare had fully responded to both imperatives, *The Merchant of Venice* would have lapsed into incoherence. If the play showed that merchants were as exploitative as usurers, that they were in fact usurers, then its entire thrust toward harmonious reconciliation could only be a fiendish oblique instance of ironic demystification. But if instead Shakespeare took the movement toward transcendent unity at least as seriously as the dangers of nascent capitalism, he needed to present the latter in a way that would not undermine the former. He needed to transform materialist problems into idealist ones—Antonio cannot very well give up commerce, but he can learn to be more merciful—or to project them harmlessly away from the Christian characters in the play—some Christians who do not take the stage own and mistreat slaves. To achieve a convincing resolution, Shakespeare had to begin with a partly imaginary dilemma. But only partly. For had his premise been wholly imaginary, his treatment could easily have been free of contradiction. That it is not is a testimony to both his strengths and his limitations.

Such a perspective enables one to understand and in a sense to justify the opposed responses to *The Merchant of Venice*, to see in its flaws not signs of artistic incompetence but manifestations of preformal problems. It also suggests answers to the questions with which the discussion began. This play requires interpretation particularly because its formal movement—dialectical transcendence—is not fully adequate to the social conflict that is one of its main sources of inspiration and principal subjects. Some of the merit of *The Merchant of Venice*, ironically enough, lies in the failure of its central design to provide a completely satisfying resolution to the dilemmas raised in the course of the action. If one purpose of the form is to reconcile the irreconcilable, one effect of interpretative methods that view explication as their primary end is a complicity of silence with the play, in which the ideology of the form is uncritically reproduced and the whole—*The Merchant of Venice*—is replaced by the part—Shakespeare's possible intention.

On the other hand, a critical consideration of the ideology of form in *The Merchant of Venice* from the vantage point of economic history mainly constitutes an antiorganicist act of demystification. An exclusive preoccupation of this sort fails to do justice to the play, however. To locate the merit of the work in Shakespeare's inability to accomplish precisely what he intended hardly corrects the deficiency, instead merely betraying the critic's wish that *The Merchant of Venice* were *The Jew of Malta* (1589). The positive value of Shakespeare's comedy naturally includes the significant concerns that it voices, a prominent example of which is the problem of usury. But at least as important is the utopian dimension of the play: what may seem escapist from one perspective from another becomes liberating. Although art does not necessarily transcend the constraints of its time, in *The Merchant of Venice* much of this aspiration is right on the surface. The play persistently attempts to establish a congruence between economic and moral conduct, between outer and inner wealth, to imagine a society based on nonexploitative human relationships. Such a vision, quite literally a fantasy, simultaneously distracts members of the audience from the deficiencies of their lives and reveals to them the possibility of something better. Utopian mystification and liberation are always inseparable and often, as here, strictly identical.

Similar lines of analysis would help elucidate the other major issues in the play. Here, however, only the outlines of such an inquiry are necessary. The supersession of justice by mercy, of the letter by the spirit, and of the Old Law by the New in the trial that occupies act 4 at once reveals the fairness of the legal system and the ethical premises of the entire plot.[77] Shakespeare's demonstration that the principle of equity inheres in the rigor of the law is rooted, according to W. Gordon Zeeveld, "in the adjustment of the common law to the practice of Equity in the Court of Chancery" during the sixteenth century.[78] Beginning in the 1590s,

---

[77]On act 4, see Alice N. Benston, "Portia, the Law, and the Tripartite Structure of *The Merchant of Venice*," *Shakespeare Quarterly* 30 (1979): 367–85. The relation between trial and drama: Herbert Lindenberger, *Historical Drama: The Relation of Literature to Reality* (Chicago: University of Chicago Press, 1975), pp. 21–23.

[78]W. Gordon Zeeveld, *The Temper of Shakespeare's Thought* (New Haven: Yale University Press, 1974), pp. 141–42. See also Maxine MacKay, "*The Merchant of Venice*: A Reflection

however, the officials of the old, comparatively popular common law courts and their counterparts on the newer, royally dominated courts like chancery entered into a struggle that ultimately resulted in the common lawyers joining the militant opposition to the crown.[79] In this respect Shakespeare's ideological project represents an anticipatory and, in the event, futile attempt to reconcile absolutist values with popular, traditional, but, ironically, revolutionary institutions, so as to prevent civil war. Another version of this compromise is implicit in Shylock's demand of his bond from the duke: "If you deny it, let the danger light / Upon your charter and your city's freedom!" (4.1.38–39). The case acquires such political reverberations because Shakespeare assumes a feudal conception of law, in which justice is the central peacetime conduit of aristocratic power. Yet Shylock's threat proves so grave because the trial is based on a bourgeois commitment to binding contracts. Portia's integrative solution reveals the compatibility of rigor and freedom, of bourgeois self-interest and aristocratic social responsibility. But the profound allegiance to contractual law can make this ideological yoking seem either unjust or precarious, responses that indicate the tension between the limits of reality and the promises of utopia in *The Merchant of Venice*.

The relation between country and city, perhaps the other major, overtly social issue raised by the action, situates the play in the tradition of Renaissance pastoral. Rather than representing a species of evasion, however, the recourse to the country bears a weighty thematic burden in *The Merchant of Venice*. The strictly causal logic of the action is identical to the interplay between Belmont and Venice. Because the multiple plot extends the social range of the representation, the traditional ruling class, ensconced in the second or "green" world, is tested and validated by its ability to master the deepest conflicts of the first world. Shakespeare's goal is thus, once again, to bind what had been torn asunder into a new unity, under aristocratic leadership. The symbolic repository of value is the great country house, home not of reactionary seigneurial barons but of a rising class, increasingly dependent for its revenues on capitalist agriculture and soon to align itself against the monarchy. The play, of course, remains oblivious to these developments: no one does any work at Belmont, Portia's apparently endless wealth has no source,

---

of the Early Conflict between Courts of Law and Courts of Equity," *Shakespeare Quarterly* 15 (1964): 371–75; George Williams Keeton, *Shakespeare's Legal and Political Background* (New York: Barnes and Noble, 1967), pp. 132–52; E. F. J. Tucker, "The Letter of the Law in *The Merchant of Venice*," *Shakespeare Survey* 29 (1976): 93–101; O. Hood Phillips, *Shakespeare and the Lawyers* (London: Methuen, 1972), pp. 91–118.

[79]Stone, *The Causes of the English Revolution* (London: Routledge and Kegan Paul, 1972), pp. 62, 75, 97–98, 103–5, 114.

and all comers are welcome to a communism of consumption, but not of production.[80] The aristocratic fantasy of act 5, unusually sustained and unironic even for Shakespearean romantic comedy, is partly a formal effort to obliterate the memory of what has preceded.

The treatment of love is also socially hybrid. The fairy-tale-like affair between Bassanio and Portia is constrained by the harsh will of a dead father, motivated by a concern for property, and premised upon the traditional sexual hierarchy. But largely for these very reasons, it produces a love match in which virtue counts for more than wealth or beauty and the wife is in practice at least the equal of her husband. Shakespeare's typical synthesis here represents a response to the unsettled position of the late-sixteenth-century aristocracy, whose practices and ideology were in the process of transition from a feudal to a bourgeois conception of marriage.[81] The striking characteristic of love in *The Merchant of Venice*, however, is that it is not unambiguously primary. For Leo Salingar, Shakespeare's comedies regularly enact an unresolved conflict in their author's mind "over the claims of love and the claims of law in Elizabethan society."[82] But in this play the controlling intellectual pattern requires what is partly a romantic and personal solution to a social problem. From this perspective, however, act 5 may also be viewed as a playful and graceful effort by the aristocratic heroine to carry out the serious business of reestablishing the bourgeois assumptions of her marriage, assumptions endangered by the very romantic solution to a social problem that she has just provided.[83]

Since the present discussion seeks to complicate and at times to challenge ideologically a Christian interpretation, it may appropriately conclude by examining directly the religious dimension of the action. The problem is not particularly the tendency of some critics to overemphasize the allegorical meaning of the plot's unfolding,[84] although attempts to incorporate such moments as Shylock's anguished response to Jessica's sale of his ring or his forced conversion, as opposed to his daughter's voluntary one, may seem a bit strained.[85] It is rather the difficulty of transforming the play into a paraphrasable meaning of any kind. Founding his argument upon the critical controversy over *The Merchant of Venice*, Norman Rabkin has questioned "the study of meaning" and the "bias towards rationality" in general, pronouncing "all intellection . . .

---

[80]Stone, *Causes*, pp. 105–8; Williams, pp. 22–34; Krieger, pp. 8–36.

[81]Stone, *Crisis*, pp. 589–671.

[82]Salingar, p. 312.

[83]On love, see R. F. Hill, "*The Merchant of Venice* and the Pattern of Romantic Comedy," *Shakespeare Survey* 28 (1975): 75–87. On marriage in act 5, see Shell, pp. 74–78.

[84]E.g., Barbara K. Lewalski, "Biblical Allusion and Allegory in *The Merchant of Venice*," *Shakespeare Quarterly* 13 (1962): 327–43.

[85]See Danson's efforts, pp. 136–39, 164–69.

reductive" because of "its consistent suppression of the nature of aesthetic experience."[86] Although Rabkin opportunistically relies on a notoriously hard case, it is quite true that "aesthetic experience," especially when induced by more than words alone, does not neatly convert into argumentative meaning. Religious interpretation has proved symptomatically incapable of understanding the play as a comedy, except to the limited extent that romantic comedy and Christian myth share a common ritual movement. On the other hand, as part of an effort to elucidate the overall significance of the work,[87] a demystification of allegorical reading can specify the comic side of *The Merchant of Venice*, in its integral relationship to the popular tradition in the theater.

Allegory may involve a utopian drive to assimilate alien experience, to create or restore unity where only incoherence and fragmentation are felt, to confer meaning upon a secular existence that seems intrinsically meaningless.[88] Shakespeare's intermittently quasi-allegorical mode in *The Merchant of Venice*, in its moving revelation of the correspondence between human agency and divine plan, represents the most profound version of the Christian Neoplatonism that flourished especially in the pastoral tragicomedy of the Counter-Reformation court.[89] The providential pattern of Neoplatonism in turn moralizes the intrigue, which in turn domesticates a still more anarchic impulse toward misrule and liberation at the root of comedy. Today, literature often censors some fantasy about work;[90] in the Renaissance, however, when hierarchy was more open and alienated labor not yet the norm, dramatic form often submerged an aspiration toward freedom from social convention and constraint. Shakespeare's own religious interpretative strategy in *The Merchant of Venice* thus simultaneously constitutes an act of humane sophistication and a process of repressive concealment.

But the repression is incomplete. The internal distancing produced by the subversive side of the play justifies the transformation of the learned surface, a comedy mainly in the Dantean sense, into a deep comic structure with affinities to popular festivity, folklore, and ritual. In general, Shakespeare's synthetic enterprise in an age of transition ran a considerable risk: the ultimately antiabsolutist implications, invisible to the playwright, of even a qualified allegiance to the country and to the common

[86]Norman Rabkin, *Shakespeare and the Problem of Meaning* (Chicago: University of Chicago Press, 1981), pp. 20–21.

[87]See E. D. Hirsch, Jr., "Introduction: Meaning and Significance," in *The Aims of Interpretation* (Chicago: University of Chicago Press, 1976), pp. 1–13.

[88]Jameson, "Metacommentary," p. 10, drawing upon Walter Benjamin, *The Origin of German Tragic Drama*, trans. John Osborne (London: NLB, 1977), e.g., pp. 220–24.

[89]Louise George Clubb, "La mimesi della realtà invisibile nel dramma pastorale italiano e inglese del tardo rinascimento," *Misure Critiche* 4 (1974): 65–92.

[90]Jameson, "Metacommentary," p. 17.

law are obvious examples. But these conflicts mainly concern the upper classes, just as much of the material considered in the previous pages and still more that could be cited place the work within the neoclassical literary and dramatic traditions. An understanding of the tensions generated within the synthesis by the popular theatrical heritage, an exploration of the consequences of the contradiction between artisanal base and absolutist superstructure, requires attention to matters of stage position and of dramatic speech, to deviations from the norms of blank verse and Ciceronian prose.[91]

One can easily demonstrate that the clown, Launcelot Gobbo, has an integral role in *The Merchant of Venice*, that, for example, his abandonment of Shylock for Bassanio foreshadows and legitimates Jessica's similar flight from Jew to Christian.[92] Nonetheless, his physical, social, ideological, and linguistic proximity to the audience comically challenges the primary mimetic action and intellectual design. Launcelot's penchant for malapropism illustrates his function. In seeking service with the understandably bewildered Bassanio, the socially mobile clown explains that "the suit is impertinent to myself" (2.2.130). Having somehow obtained the job, he revisits his old employer to invite him to dinner with his new one: "I beseech you sir go, my young master doth expect your reproach," to which Shylock replies, "So do I his" (2.5.19–21). Shylock's recognition that the apparent misuse of "reproach" for "approach" is at some level intentional points to the linguistically and socially subversive connotations of young Gobbo's double meanings, to the "impertinent" quality, again in two senses, of his speech and conduct.

In his final major appearance, Launcelot begins by expressing his theological concern for Jessica: "I speak my agitation of the matter: therefore be o' good cheer, for truly I think you are damn'd,—there is but one hope in it that can do you any good, and that is but a kind of bastard hope neither" (3.5.4–7). The confusion of "agitation" and "cogitation," the proposed response of "good cheer" to the prospect of damnation, the ironic play on bastardy—all hopelessly jumble and thus undercut the serious religious issues of the plot. Later in the same scene the clown systematically and wittily misconstrues Lorenzo's apparently straightforward order that the kitchen staff "prepare for dinner!" (3.5.43). His quibbling replies range from an aggressive assertion that the servants, too, are hungry—"they have all stomachs!"—to a pre-

---

[91]Shakespeare and Ciceronian prose: Jonas A. Barish, *Ben Jonson and the Language of Prose Comedy* (Cambridge: Harvard University Press, 1960), pp. 1–40. The remainder of the present discussion is primarily indebted to Robert Weimann, *Shakespeare and the Popular Tradition in the Theater: Studies in the Social Dimension of Dramatic Form and Function*, ed. Robert Schwartz (Baltimore: Johns Hopkins University Press, 1978).

[92]Geoffrey Bullough, *Narrative and Dramatic Sources of Shakespeare*, vol. 1 (London: Routledge and Kegan Paul, 1957), p. 457; Frye, p. 97.

tended retreat into deferential humility—"I know my duty" (3.5.44, 49). In general, then, from his very first appearance, significantly in soliloquy, when "the devil himself" prompts him to run from his master "the Jew . . . the very devil incarnation" (2.2.25–26), Launcelot provides an alternative perspective on the related matters of Christian orthodoxy and social hierarchy. On the one hand, his nonsense paradoxically demystifies; on the other, it uniquely combines archaic memories and utopian vistas.

As Marx's comments suggest, this complex vision is compatible with the disturbingly ambiguous implications of Shylock, himself a figure with important ancestors in the popular tradition.[93] Like the Vice, he is associated with the devil; is the leading manipulator of the action; elicits from the audience fascination as well as revulsion, laughter as well as terror; functions as both homiletic foe of Christianity and incisive critic of Christian society; and accordingly ranges linguistically from rhetorically polished, mimetic dialogue to popular, self-expressive monologue. Thus, insofar as *The Merchant of Venice* combines a formally dominant Christian, aristocratic ideology with that ideology's inherent structural qualification in large part by the process of artisanal theatrical production, the play escapes standard categories of interpretation while strikingly embodying the central creative tension of Shakespearean drama.

## Aguilar, *El mercader amante*

Although Aguilar's *El mercader amante* bears striking resemblance to Shakespeare's play, it raises very different critical problems. Where *The Merchant of Venice* has been extensively studied, *El mercader amante* has been benignly neglected. Aguilar's comedy nonetheless merits attention, in part because of its important differences from subsequent developments in the *comedia*. This distinctiveness is less formal than ideological. As the title suggests, Aguilar gives even greater prominence than does Shakespeare to a character who is almost totally absent from the seventeenth-century Spanish stage.

A brief plot summary will reveal the extent of the divergence from the later, antibourgeois norms of the peninsular theater. Belisario, "aquel mercader / que fué de España el más rico" ("that merchant / who was the richest in Spain"),[94] must decide which of two apparently interchange-

---

[93]Frye, p. 93, sees the affinity between the two characters, though in somewhat different terms. Bernard Spivack, *Shakespeare and the Allegory of Evil: The History of a Metaphor in Relation to His Major Villains* (New York: Columbia University Press, 1958), generally tends to exclude Shylock from the Vice tradition, but he neglects most of the relevant evidence.

[94]*El mercader amante*, in *Poetas dramáticos valencianos*, ed. Eduardo Juliá Martínez (Madrid: Real Academia Española, 1929), vol. 2: act 2, p. 136. Subsequent references are noted in the text.

able women he should marry. In order to make the proper choice, he feigns poverty while entrusting his fortune to his faithful servant Astolfo. The stratagem succeeds: Lidora quickly displays her mercenary motives and Labinia her true love. Though his dilemma is seemingly resolved, Belisario must then suffer through a series of unfortunate misunderstandings that twice lead him to conclude he has been betrayed by both Astolfo and Labinia. The second such round of errors almost produces the deaths of the three main virtuous characters before all confusions are dispelled and the concluding match is made.

What is a merchant doing in the role normally reserved for the *caballero* in Spanish drama? A look at the history of Valencia, not only Aguilar's home but also the city where his play was presumably first performed, may help answer the question. The course of economic evolution on the Levantine coast differed considerably from trends in the Castilian interior. Both regions experienced the long boom of the sixteenth century, itself partly a consequence of the sharp decline in the real income of the overwhelming majority of the population. In Castile, the growth rate tailed off after 1550, with capitalist development suffering in particular. But in Valencia, the period of greatest prosperity and most rapid expansion occurred late in the century, was centered on maritime trade, and especially enriched the merchant class. Thus, when *El mercader amante* was composed, Valencia's traditional Mediterranean commercial orientation was at its most pronounced.[95] Elsewhere in Spain, Thomas de Mercado could say of trade that "su ocasion fue el peccado" ("its occasion was sin") and criticize the merchant for being "muy amante de su dinero y codicioso del ageno" ("a great lover of his own money and covetous of others'").[96] Even in Barcelona, in a work by no means hostile to international commerce, Fray Marco Antonio de Camos subjects merchants to extensive, entirely traditional abuse. His discussion of the body politic, moreover, takes the biological metaphor quite seriously, only belatedly turning to "los mercaderes y gente de trato, que comparamos a las piernas" ("merchants and men of dealings, whom we compare to the legs").[97] In Valencia, on the other hand, the paragon protagonist of a comedy might follow that very occupation. Similarly, a manuscript manual on navigation composed in Castile refers to the different people its sailor-author met through his voyages,

---

[95]Emilia Salvador and Juan Reglá, "Contribución al estudio de la coyuntura económica en Valencia en el siglo xvi," *Estudios Geográficos* 29 (1968): 359–67; Alvaro Castillo, "La coyuntura de la economía valenciana en los siglos xvi y xvii," *Anuario de Historia Económica y Social* 2 (1969): 239–88.

[96]Thomas de Mercado, *Tratos y contratos de mercaderes* (Salamanca, 1569), sigs. A6$^r$ and A7$^r$—representative passages.

[97]Fray Marco Antonio de Camos, *Microcosmia, y govierno vniversal del hombre christiano, para todos los estados y qvalquiera de ellos* (Barcelona, 1592), sig. Mm7$^r$.

whereas a comparable volume published in Valencia by Pedro de Syria, a native of the city, emphasizes "quan necessaria sea la nauegacion al comercio humano" ("how necessary navigation is to human commerce").[98] Regionalism thus proved a source of ideological opposition.

This distinction should not be overstated, however. An aristocracy resided in the city of Valencia as well as in the surrounding countryside, an absolutist state exercised ultimate dominion, and capitalist economics threatened to disrupt traditional social relations. Aguilar's play represents an attempt to reconcile the potential conflicts of a transitional age. In a sense the central dilemma is intrinsic to capitalism: marriage for love is largely a bourgeois creation, but its antithesis, marriage for money, also has obvious attractions for a certain kind of bourgeois consciousness. The two must be radically separated, not only by Belisario, but also by Aguilar, who is at pains to validate his lovers by stressing their intrinsic moral worth and freedom from any taint of self-interest. First, the play rejects an excessive aristocratic preoccupation with class and rank at the expense of character. The opening scene offers a comic, antifeudal perspective on a duel between two Old Christian *escuderos* (squires), in which the motivating point of honor and the duel itself are equally illusory.[99] Similarly, Don García, Belisario's rival for Labinia, repeatedly stresses the social superiority of his birth and appropriately ends the play unmarried and embittered.

More important, however, is the problematic nature of money. Just as Lidora wants Belisario only because of his fortune, García justifiably fears that Labinia's padre is guided by the same principles in desiring the merchant for a son-in-law. Later, when Astolfo seems to have acquired all of Belisario's wealth, Lidora and Labinia's father both shift their marital aspirations to him. Belisario, meanwhile, falsely concludes that financial considerations have come to dominate first Astolfo's and then Labinia's conduct. His apparent sudden impoverishment causes alarm, yet because his wealth is not in land but in mercantile, and hence movable, capital, it can be lost: other merchants can make off with his goods or, like Antonio, he can lose all his ships at sea. Astolfo's complementary rapid economic ascent undermines traditional notions of hierarchical stability even more radically:

> la persona rica
> es hidalga, es noble y grave,

[98]Luis de la Cruz, *YnstRucion y auisos . . . Para la buena nauegacion Delas yndias*, Huntington Library MS 30957, c. 1600, p. 1; Pedro de Syria, *Arte de la verdadera navegacion* (Valencia, 1602), p. 4ʳ.

[99]John G. Weiger, *The Valencian Dramatists of Spain's Golden Age* (Boston: Twayne, 1976), p. 94.

> porque la hacienda es jarabe
> que la sangre purifica.

(the rich person / is genteel, is noble and grave, / because property is a syrup / that purifies the blood. [3, p. 151])

In act 1, García accuses Belisario of being "tan pobre de linaje / que de sí mismo deciende" ("of such poor lineage / that he descends from himself": p. 129). Near the climax of the action, Astolfo wittily retorts that "si es bueno el hijodalgo, / el padre de algo es mejor" ("if the son of something [i.e., gentleman] is good, / the father of something is better": 3, p. 158). As father of his line, he takes precedence over the scion of a noble family.

The virtuous characters operate in the space between these two extremes of social fixity and social anarchy. Astolfo remains so unswervingly loyal to Belisario, so unmoved by pecuniary enticements, that at the end, when his master offers to reward his service liberally, he replies: "cuando no me des nada, / te quedaré yo a deber" ("if you should give me nothing, / I will remain indebted to you": 3, p. 161). Labinia is similarly uncompromising in her preference for love over money and her affection for poverty because of Belisario's plight. Given the choice of marrying García or being killed, she unhesitatingly opts for death. Faced with the same alternative, this time, however, with the apparently treacherous and newly enriched Astolfo as the prospective mate, she escalates her response: pretending to yield, she secretly plans to murder the groom and then commit suicide. Finally, Belisario is not merely a merchant who desires a love match, who "en tesoro / excede al próspero Fúcar" ("in treasure / exceeds the prosperous Fugger": 1, p. 126), on the one hand, and, like Antonio, lends money interest-free, on the other. The action also rigorously tests his response to what he believes to be the loss of both his fortune and his love. The nobility with which he bears the horrible fate of poverty evokes admiring comments from even such a mercenary figure as Labinia's father. Belisario himself, moreover, cares far more about Labinia than about the state of his finances. Hence, when he learns to his dismay that she has agreed to marry Astolfo, he goes off to attempt suicide.

By these means, Aguilar domesticates the threat of capitalism. Boldly associating idealism and nobility of soul not with the aristocracy but with the one unambiguously bourgeois figure in the play, he shows that money, though potentially destructive, need not determine human relations. Subordinated to the traditional ties between man and woman or between master and servant, the new economics reinforces, rather than overturns, the social order. Like *The Merchant of Venice, El mercader amante* fully expresses and then allays the anxiety about the movement from one mode of production to another. Its concluding utopian vision presents a world in which wealth or especially birth counts for less than individual merit and deep feeling, and in which the latter are tried and found efficacious.

This, at any rate, seems to be what Aguilar had in mind. But the process of the action involves an array of qualifications, retreats, evasions, and deflections—some clearly conscious, others less so—that seriously compromise the ostensible ideological intention. First of all, Belisario, though a bourgeois, is also an aristocrat. Unlike other wealthy merchants, he is untouched by Jewish blood or by base ancestry of any kind. As Labinia's father tells García,

> yo sé que de tan buenos
> parientes como yo viene,
> y si alguna falta tiene
> es haber venido a menos.

(I know that he comes from as / good relatives as I, / and if he has any fault / it is to have come to less. [1, p. 134])

The play simply demonstrates that even this hedging is unwarranted: it is acceptable for the nobility to go into business. By no means a trivial point in the late sixteenth century, an insistence on this principle is, however, something less than an assertion of bourgeois equality or individualism. Again, although the characters express astonishment over economic and social upheaval, their fears prove unfounded. No transfers of wealth, power, or status actually occur, nor does the possession of any or all of these advantages in itself guarantee marital success. On the other hand, although the plot values love above money, the concluding marriage remains absolutely dependent on Belisario's enormous income. Since this state of affairs is never challenged in *El mercader amante*, the implicit moral critique of the social status quo derives from an ideological contradiction of which the author too seems unaware.

A comparable failure to confront unresolved dilemmas extends to the treatment of the minor characters. Labinia's father, forever eager to auction his daughter off to the highest bidder, ultimately gets precisely what he wishes: "Para mí no hay bien mayor" ("For me there is no greater good": 3, p. 160). The relationship between Lidora and Astolfo is more troubling still. Though the pay is slightly ambiguous, it seems that they will be married. In a sense, the beautiful and aristocratic Lidora is deservedly punished: contrary to her expectations, she is stuck with a socially servile and financially insolvent mate. But she is also rewarded, since Astolfo is an admirable human being and has access to large sums of money if he so desires. The same polarity recurs, only in reverse, if one considers the match from Astolfo's point of view. The problem stems from the difficulty in finding some correspondence between the values that are asserted to be triumphant and the social structures that actually persist. The play reveals, almost against itself, that its resolution of conflict is illusory.

This symptomatic problem in a way makes sense: the conflict itself is also imaginary. Belisario does not set his initial intrigue in motion to surmount opposition to his marriage with Labinia, for in fact no serious opposition exists. He requires subterfuge because of the impenetrability of social surfaces, the impossibility of distinguishing true from false love by normal means. By early in act 2, even this potentially disquieting problem has disappeared. In a sense the play might well end at this point. Aguilar needs to sustain the plot, however, not only to fill out three acts, but also to test and thereby to validate his protagonists, in this fashion deepening the resonance of his thematic material. The difficulty arises from his recourse to such conventional devices as eavesdropping and comic misunderstanding to generate the remainder of the action. First, one may well wonder if Belisario's subsequent suffering merely constitutes the bad luck resulting from his repeated and purely fortuitous presence in the wrong place at the wrong time. Or rather does his own conventional, manipulative intrigue logically entail just such a consequence, his subjection to an ordeal that is morally and symmetrically necessary to balance his ethically questionable testing of others?

It is hard to decide this question. Astolfo raises objections to the scheme when Belisario first broaches it. Labinia's final words express her resentment at having been tested. Belisario's attempt to mollify her seems to acknowledge a certain justice in what he has endured. She should not be angry, he argues, because "casi he venido / a perderte por probarte" ("I have almost come / to lose you by testing you": 3, p. 161). He has apparently been punished by manipulative devices comparable to the one he had originally employed. Yet though two eavesdropping scenes lead him falsely to despair, a third such episode enables him to discover part of the truth. Comic convention is thus morally neutral. There nonetheless may be a sense in which Belisario's amoral tactic, necessitated by the problematic nature of reality, is itself problematic. The plot reveals that things do not always work out according to human, as opposed to authorial, design.

In other words, because of the potential incompatibility of generic convention and thematic intent, *El mercader amante* resists interpretation. This problem may be further illustrated. First, what purpose is served by the belabored symmetries of Belisario's experience in acts 2 and 3—a

loss of faith in Astolfo and then Labinia, followed by a recovery of faith
in Labinia and then Astolfo, followed by a repetition of the entire chias-
mic process? No purpose at all, it seems, except to emphasize inadvertently the hero's dimwittedness. Still more unfortunate is the trivializa-
tion of the issues that results. Although Aguilar evidently takes quite
seriously the troublesome impact of money on human relations, he can
only dramatize his concern irrelevantly, not through genuine clashes of
will but through eavesdropping and misunderstanding. This tendency
toward displacement governs the entire form of the play. As its very title
suggests, *El mercader amante*, like other romantic comedies, systematically
converts economic problems into marital ones. Although it presents a social world debased by the triumph of the values of mercantile capitalism,
it rigorously and ideologically excludes the mercantile capitalist from
the general condemnation. For this reason, the play cannot examine
the sources of commercial wealth. Aguilar's predicament in one sense
emerges from his admirable and ambitious, if not quite successful, effort
to extend the range of a traditional form, to deepen its presentation of
character and idea. But it also and unmistakably derives from the transference of conflicts from the arena of production and exchange, where
they are irreconcilable, to the sphere of private relations, where they
may be resolved. Romantic comedy constitutes the generic solution to
the problems created by the rise of capitalism.

Much the same might be said of *The Merchant of Venice*, with allowance
made, of course, for its presentation of more genuine conflict, its superior adaptation of technical means to ideological ends, and its more actively achieved, more fully integrative, and more moving conclusion.
But Shakespeare's comedy also contains an internal popular qualification of the main plot for which *El mercader amante* offers no real parallel.
The characters and language of the Spanish play are overwhelmingly
neoclassical in orientation. Although *El mercader amante* conforms to the
standard *comedia* division into three rather than five acts and, more important, eschews Italian for Spanish verse forms in its polymetric system,
Aguilar does little with these possibilities.

His closest approach to popular theatrical practice comes in his use of
soliloquy and aside. These are almost entirely reserved for the sympathetic characters, and especially for the intriguers, Belisario and Astolfo,
who appropriately stand closest to the audience, where they can explain
what is happening, reveal the purity of their motives, generalize on the
meaning of events, and, in Astolfo's case, promise a happy outcome. But
these passages of self-revelation also serve an essential nonsemantic
function by dissolving the illusion of place created by mimetic dialogue,
restoring the sense of an unlocalized acting space, and thus facilitating
the transition from scene to scene. Of the twelve scenes in the play, three

[217

of course end the individual acts and consequently pose no problems of change of locale. Of the remaining nine, seven end with soliloquies, one is followed by a scene that begins with a soliloquy, and the other falls directly before the final scene, when the accelerating pace of events precludes leisurely reflection. Aguilar's multiple uses of monologue in *El mercader amante* are perfectly compatible with one another. But it took years, even decades, of experimentation by a dramatist more attuned to popular culture to discover and develop the full latent social potential of the intimacy between actor and audience in the Spanish public theater.

## THE NATIONAL HISTORY PLAY

### Forms of the National History Play

The preeminence of national historical drama in late-sixteenth-century England and Spain, but in few other regions of Renaissance Europe, provides one of the more striking indications of the unique similarities between the two theaters. Yet the genre eludes conventional categorization. Indebted to morality, romance, tragicomedy, chronicle, and intrigue and *de casibus* tragedy, among others, the form cannot be conceptualized as a characteristic movement in the way that romantic comedy, for instance, can.[100] This untidiness extends to the serious drama of the period as a whole: tragedy in particular constitutes an alternative generic focus to the national history play in the 1580s and 1590s. Accordingly, the latter form is usefully defined in terms of intention and materials: "If a play appears to fulfill what we know the Elizabethans considered to be the legitimate purpose of history," argues Irving Ribner, "and if it is drawn from a chronicle source which we know that at least a large part of the contemporary audience accepted as factual, we may call it a history play."[101] With minor modifications, the same is true of Spain.[102] Although one can specify numerous "legitimate purposes of history," these conveniently fall into three large groups.

[100]For emphasis on the formal diversity of the national history play, and especially on its relationship to tragedy, see Doran, pp. 112–47; Irving Ribner, *The English History Play in the Age of Shakespeare*, 2d ed. (New York: Barnes and Noble, 1965), pp. 26–29; Lindenberger, passim. But see David Scott Kastan, *Shakespeare and the Shapes of Time* (Hanover, N.H.: University Press of New England, 1982), pp. 37–57, who emphasizes the open-ended, contingent sense produced at least by Shakespeare's national history plays.

[101]Ribner, *English History Play*, p. 25.

[102]Elaine Ann Bunn, "The Early History Plays of Lope de Vega: Classification and Analysis," Ph.D. diss., University of Pennsylvania, 1976, chaps. 1–2; Stephen Gilman, "Lope, dramaturgo de la historia," in *Lope de Vega y los orígenes del teatro español*, Actas del I Congreso Internacional sobre Lope de Vega, ed. Manuel Criado de Val (Madrid: EDI, 1981), pp. 19–26.

First, a dramatist may use a real historical setting to intensify emotionally a relatively timeless plot. Since the past serves primarily as a source of dramatic energy while history itself becomes marginal, some scholars would exclude plays of this sort from the canon of historical drama.[103] The other two types depend more directly on the relation between past and present. If the focus is on contemporary life, history offers a species of analogy, a means of projecting current concerns back in time or of investigating and establishing parallels between past and present, whether celebratory, exemplary, hortatory, or admonitory. Derived from the humanist tradition,[104] this use of history as pastoral runs the obvious risk of distorting the past to make it conform to the present. A concern with history as subject, with the past as past, on the other hand, faces the danger of antiquarianism. But it can also lead to a sense of process, to a vision of the development of the playwright's own times out of the very different conditions of a prior age.[105] This concern with process, adapted from medieval Christian providential historiography,[106] suggests once again the dynamic temporal perspective of the Latin church. When grafted onto a secular political narrative, it proved, despite its universalist premises, one of the distinctive features of the national history play. To be sure, the genre draws as frequently on analogical linkages of past and present as on the idea of process. But humanist analogical methods, though capable of promoting nationalist ends, are not unique to the national history play: they are largely applicable to foreign history and tragedy as well. The notion of historical development proved less adaptable, however. In the first age of the nation-state and of national consciousness, belief in the continuity between past and present inherent in the providential view found its amplest and most appropriate embodiment in the national history play.

Pure examples of any of these categories rarely occur, however. The issue, rather, is the ways multiple uses of history interact in a single work, at times under the dominant sign of one of them. The most important potential conflict is between history as pastoral and history as subject. For, if a play is organized around a strict identity between past and present, how can there be any change? Renaissance playwrights found a partial solution to this problem by imagining past and present as different stages in the same process. If, therefore, romantic comedy depicts the social adaptation of the aristocracy, serious drama occupies a complementary position, focusing on the political adaptation of the aristocracy.

[103]E.g., Bunn, p. 53.
[104]Ribner, p. 24.
[105]These distinctions are adapted from Harry E. Shaw, *The Forms of Historical Fiction: Sir Walter Scott and His Successors* (Ithaca, N.Y.: Cornell University Press, 1983), chaps. 1–3.
[106]Ribner, p. 24.

Probably the central political event in western Europe during the sixteenth and seventeenth centuries was the emergence of nationhood. As long as that historical tendency carried ideological conviction, the main vehicle for evaluating it in the public theater was the national history play. Since nationbuilding was usually synonymous with absolutist consolidation, the genre repeatedly treats the changing relations between nobility and monarchy. In England at least, no other dramatic form of the time evinces so consistent an interest in the topic.[107] Although Marlowe's *Edward II* (1592) and most of Shakespeare's history plays turn on the antagonism between class and state, in Marlowe's other works and in *Titus Andronicus* (1594) and *Romeo and Juliet* (1595) the same issue is peripheral.

An important deduction follows from the complementarity of romantic comedy and national historical drama: each form presents a partial and hence distorted view of reality. The problem is less incompleteness, which is, after all, inevitable and perhaps desirable as well, than the systematic suppression of material that would make it possible to see a restricted range of experience as part of a larger whole. Although Shakespeare at times represents something of an exception, the portrayal of social life in romantic comedy largely omits the substantial role of the state in perpetuating aristocratic social and economic power. The basic fallacy of the history play is to assume that politics is everything and consequently to minimize the impact on national affairs of social relations between the aristocracy and other classes.

But this formulation too closely aligns the history play with other forms of serious drama. It fails to distinguish, for example, between seventeenth-century French classical tragedy and the sixteenth-century English and Spanish national history play, between the drama of a class and the drama of a nation. In national drama, peasants, artisans, and common soldiers often take an active part in the destiny of the state or, at the least, register the impact of the deeds of their rulers. The advantages of this more encompassing dramaturgy of the public theater should not be underestimated. But such plays, precisely because of their focus on the nation, cannot depict the fundamental social mediations of their political concerns. One never really learns why aristocrats foment civil war, why England is fighting in France, or why Spain faces rebellion in Europe as well as America. An investigation of these questions would eventually lead to an awareness of the exploitation of one class by another. If the central category is not nation but class, however, then the national history play loses its raison d'être. Thus, the most profound explorations of these class issues occur in those later works where the na-

---

[107]Bevington, *Tudor Drama and Politics*, p. 301.

tional perspective, though still apparent, is sufficiently muted to allow alternative emphases to emerge.

The contradictory significance of the popular dimension in the national history play may also be understood theatrically. The complicated and beguiling social inversions associated with Henry V in *The Famous Victories of Henry V* (1586) as well as in Shakespeare's three plays on his life are evidence at once of popular assertion and of reactionary integration. These works generate lower-class disorder only to recontain it as the very condition of royal power.[108] Similarly, as a result of the more general tendency for the popular acting tradition to be adapted to the characterization of serious, as opposed to comic, figures, aristocratic protagonists acquired a three-dimensionality and accompanying emotional persuasiveness that they previously lacked.[109] These double-edged meanings are also discernible in the functioning of the theater. The audience witnessing a national history play at the public theater comes to feel that its own history is being performed. In a sense, such a belief is a corporatist illusion, especially since the crown's interests were not ultimately national. But it is also a progressive insistence on the right of the populace to judge the ruling class's exercise of state power. In this respect the national history play in the public theater inherently subverts aristocratic ideology.

This larger significance of the popular contours of the national history play goes beyond the narrower, but still important question of the social material treated by the genre. Although the presence of lower-class characters is a common distinguishing feature of the form, it is by no means ubiquitous. The social range of the genre varies from work to work, in a manner that roughly correlates with the use of the three main versions of history already outlined. Not surprisingly, plays in which history is a source of dramatic energy pay scant attention to class relations, tending to take some version of aristocratic ideology for granted while ignoring the experience of other classes. Other categories are a bit fuzzier. History as pastoral tends to allow an investigation of only one set of relations at a time. Either the homogeneity of crown and nobility is assumed and the issue is the interaction between upper and lower classes, or the dramatist confines himself to the aristocracy as in the first type of history play but concentrates on the antagonism between class and state. Finally, in works that render history as past, both sets of conflicts are elaborated simultaneously.

---

[108]Greenblatt, "Invisible Bullets: Renaissance Authority and Its Subversion," *Glyph* 8 (1981): 53–57.

[109]Weimann, *Shakespeare and the Popular Tradition*, pp. 176, 189–91, 224–25, and passim, documents these phenomena but apparently does not believe they have a repressive side.

Each of these groupings bears further scrutiny. The use of the past as a source of dramatic energy is best exemplified in England not by historical drama proper, but by the pseudohistorical romantic comedies and romances of Greene, Dekker, and Heywood already considered. Lope's *El testimonio vengado* (1596–1603) closely resembles these plays. Despite displaying a superficial interest in historical process and national destiny, which emerges in a concern with monarchical succession and in the protagonist's prophetic, allegorical dream, Lope's play is primarily a pastoral romance preoccupied with the private life of the royal family. Otherwise, Spanish historical drama of this sort clusters in the late 1570s and early 1580s. Argensola's *Isabela* (1581) offers general analogies to the present in the Catholicism and nationalism of the play, but the plot really turns on a series of tragic love intrigues at the Moorish court that have virtually no historical reverberations.[110] *Los siete infantes de Lara* (1579), like Juan de la Cueva's other plays, might seem an exception: it has recently been understood as a covert attack on Philip II's ultimately successful effort to annex Portugal.[111] More likely, the play points to the present only in a general sense, by means of the heroic model it provides, while offering a vision of historical process in its transformation of immediate defeat into eventual victory. But in the end *Los siete infantes* uses history primarily for emotional intensification. Relations between Moor and Christian produce not national resonance so much as local color, while the action itself, symptomatically, involves a private squabble confined to the Christian aristocracy.

These tendencies are still more pronounced in another play on the same subject, *La gran comedia de los famosos hechos de Mudarra* (1583 or 1585).[112] The intrigue structure of the work succeeds in suppressing even the secondary sense of historical process created by Cueva's more sprawling plot. Instead, the play presents a moment in the distant past when emotions were simpler, more powerful, and more romantic; when life was more exotic and colorful; when neither character nor ethics revealed, or required, any sign of complexity. It is a fantasy of an uncomplicated world in which retributive justice is efficacious and final. The work assumes the ideology of an almost tribal military aristocracy, though without the customary tragic outcome, and accordingly consti-

[110]Date: Otis Howard Green, *The Life and Works of Lupercio Leonardo de Argensola*, Publications of the University of Pennsylvania Department of Romanic Languages and Literatures no. 21 (Philadelphia: University of Pennsylvania Press?, 1927), pp. 23–24, 105. See also J. P. Wickersham Crawford, *Spanish Drama before Lope de Vega*, 2d ed., with a bibliographical supplement by Warren T. McCready (Philadelphia: University of Pennsylvania Press, 1967), p. 177.

[111]A. I. Watson, *Juan de la Cueva and the Portuguese Succession* (London: Tamesis, 1971), chap. 5. The date is given in the argumento of the play.

[112]Date: Ramón Menéndez Pidal, *La leyenda de los infantes de Lara* (Madrid: Imprenta de los Hijos de José M. Ducazcal, 1896), p. 126.

tutes a celebration of class conduct in the absence of high civilization that is nostalgic in its appeal. Thus Renaissance pastoral has affinities not only with history-as-pastoral drama, but also with those works that use history as a source of dramatic energy.

The two categories should not be conflated, however. Plays like *The Famous Victories*, *The Life and Death of Jack Straw* (1591), Munday, Dekker, Chettle, and Shakespeare's *The Book of Sir Thomas More* (1595), and Cervantes's *El cerco de Numancia* (early 1580s),[113] as well as *Edward II* and Lope de Vega's *La vida y muerte del rey Bamba* (1597–98), are far more explicitly concerned with social and political issues than are any of the works just considered. The presence of such issues suggests that here the past functions as pastoral. Once again, subordinate intentions intervene: *Bamba* and *Numancia* both make claims for historical process, the latter especially employing the characteristic Spanish defeat-into-victory mode. More important are the internal divisions within the group. *Numancia* and all the English plays with the exception of Marlowe's concentrate on the interaction between the upper and lower classes. But *Edward II* opposes aristocracy to monarchy, and *Bamba* dramatizes both intraclass and, rather less successfully, interclass antagonism.

The inherent constraint on the representation of interclass issues in the Renaissance national history play helps explain why Marlowe's and Lope's works might have greater power and appeal, especially from a twentieth-century perspective. Serious treatment of the relationship between the nobility and the classes dominated by it cannot avoid a portrayal of conflict that undermines the premises of the national history play. Dramatists interested in interclass relations but committed to a patriotic appeal must accordingly choose between two alternatives, neither of them entirely satisfactory. They must either deny the reality of class struggle and posit social unity instead, as in *The Famous Victories* or *Numancia*, or view popular rebellion in a relatively unsympathetic light, as in *Jack Straw*, *Thomas More*, or *2 Henry VI* (1591). These problems do not automatically disappear even if the playwright stresses hostilities within the ruling class. *Edward II* achieves much of its force by essentially repudiating a nationalist perspective, and the almost equally tragic conclusion of *Bamba* calls into question the reality, if not the ideal, of such a perspective. Furthermore, these plays, too, cannot trace the causes of aristocratic conflict to the crisis of surplus extraction that began in the fourteenth century.

Yet because class antagonism is less central in *Edward II* and *Bamba* than in the interclass plays, the inadequacy of the treatment is also less debilitating. The strength of these two plays, then, lies in the acceptance

---

[113]The date is from Crawford, pp. 179–80.

of certain structural limits. This difficult matter was considered at length by Lukács. Writing of a later era, he argued: "The class consciousness of the bourgeoisie may well be able to reflect all the problems of organisation entailed by its hegemony and by the capitalist transformation and penetration of total production. But it becomes obscured as soon as it is called upon to face problems that remain within its jurisdiction but which point beyond the limits of capitalism."[114] The same goes, perhaps even more strongly, for the hegemonic aristocratic consciousness of the late sixteenth century. *Edward II* and *Bamba* turn on the problem of intraclass conflict, which was solvable from within that consciousness, while downplaying the problem of interclass conflict, which was not.

Lukács was therefore quite right to focus his later discussion of Renaissance historical drama on "the decline of feudalism," on the artistic creation of "forceful, interesting historical types among the older, declining human stock of feudalism and the new type of hero, the humanist noble or ruler," on the "class [*sic*] struggle between monarchy and feudalism."[115] Two related deductions follow from this emphasis. The first is that, although the age generally witnessed the transition from feudalism to capitalism, the conflict between these two modes of production is not directly represented, even ideologically, in the national history play. Its subject is one crucial dimension of that transition, a struggle within the hegemonic class between aristocracy and monarchy, between feudalism and absolutism. Second, the treatment, mistreatment, or simple lack of treatment of the lower classes in the genre, and hence the very viability of the genre itself, are partly consequences of the inability of any one of these underclasses to produce a hegemonic class consciousness of its own.

This is not to say, however, that the lower classes are wholly devoid of class consciousness. Such a recognition directs attention to those plays in which the past is past, in which both intraclass and interclass relations are dramatized. Although *Bamba* generally sees the past as pastoral, some of its social material at least ambiguously places it in the past-as-past group. Roughly the reverse is true in two other works by Lope de Vega, *Arauco domado* (probably 1599) and *El asalto de Mastrique* (probably 1600–1606). Both seem to acquire their sense of historical process from the fact that they are set in the recent past and hence have an immediate connection to the present. But *El asalto de Mastrique* simply assumes ruling-class unity while investigating the relationship between military commanders and common soldiers, and *Arauco domado* takes all forms of social harmony for granted.

[114]Lukács, *History and Class Consciousness*, p. 54.
[115]Lukács, *The Historical Novel*, trans. Hannah and Stanley Mitchell (Boston: Beacon, 1963), pp. 153, 137.

The only body of work that consistently treats the past as past is Shakespeare's historical drama of the 1590s. Its unparalleled sense of process derives in part from the linkages between individual plays provided by the tetralogy form. But of course this form in turn depends on a coherent theory of English history. All of the plays consider both interclass and intraclass relations, although one or the other may be more prominent at any given time. *Richard II* (1595) is concerned mainly with aristocratic infighting, whereas *Henry V* (1599) concentrates on the relationship between king and commoner. The most equal balance of these two emphases, in *1 and 2 Henry IV* (1597–98), is achieved largely through a strategy of symmetrical plotting. In the standard reading of these plays, Hal is the mean between Hotspur and Falstaff, killing the first at the end of part 1 and rejecting the second at the close of part 2. The inherent limitations of absolutism emerge from the critical judgments offered on the future of Henry V from both aristocratic and popular perspectives, but so too does the superiority of royal centralism to either alternative. Like the selfless noblemen of Shakespeare's earlier historical plays, Hal demonstrates his moral responsibility by his willingness to subordinate his own freedom to the interests of the nation.[116]

This view requires qualification in at least three respects, however. First, in assuming, plausibly enough, that Falstaff has affinities with popular culture, it tends to obscure his connections with a variety of other sources, traditions, and groups, especially, in the present context, with the declining feudal aristocracy.[117] Indeed, the paradoxical status of the character may partly correspond to the ideologically contradictory position of that sector of the gentry which lost ground because of its inability to adapt to commercial agriculture. In the Civil War, certain members of this apparently reactionary subclass formed part of the militant Independent officer corps of the New Model Army. As some of the strongest advocates of the execution of Charles, these men performed the typical chore of victims of historical change: they did the dirty work

[116]See, for example, Bevington, *Tudor Drama and Politics*, pp. 246–48; Philip Edwards, *Threshold of a Nation: A Study in English and Irish Drama* (Cambridge: Cambridge University Press, 1979), pp. 110–30. For a more negative view of the same pattern see Greenblatt, "Invisible Bullets," pp. 53–57; Steven Mullaney, "Strange Things, Gross Terms, Curious Customs: The Rehearsal of Cultures in the Late Renaissance," *Representations*, no. 3 (Summer 1983): 57–62. Unlike Greenblatt and Mullaney, who seek to demystify the plays' legitimation of royal power, H. R. Coursen, *The Leasing Out of England: Shakespeare's Second Henriad* (Washington, D.C.: University Press of America, 1982), pp. 99–150, attributes this negativity to Shakespeare's critical intention.

[117]The association of Falstaff with the lower classes: William B. Stone, "Literature and Class Ideology: *Henry IV, Part One*," *College English* 33 (1972): 891–900. Falstaff's social ambivalence: T. A. Jackson, "Marx and Shakespeare," *International Literature*, no. 2 (1936): 75–97; Siegel, "Falstaff and His Social Milieu," *Shakespeare Jahrbuch* (Weimar) 110 (1974): 139–45.

for the newly dominant classes.[118] Second, the symmetry on which Hal's mediating position depends ultimately breaks down. While the refractory feudal nobility is systematically excluded from the polity, the lower classes, because they are thought to pose no threat to state power, live on with their independent consciousness intact as part of a national synthesis in *Henry V*. In *1 and 2 Henry IV*, Shakespeare thus realized the possibilities of national historical drama in the age of absolutism. Intraclass conflict, represented in its full severity, issues in the triumph of absolutism; interclass conflict, depicted in far more oblique form, conduces to the same end. Third, however, though these plays first helped strengthen a sense of nationhood, they nonetheless seem to have acquired subversive force during the revolutionary upheavals a half-century later. Yet the full revolutionary significance of taverns and inns, emergent only in the years of civil war,[119] was unrepresentable in the national history play. These are the structural limits of the form. Any further advances required a different set of generic premises.

The foregoing typology reveals a far more consistent stress in England than in Spain on social conflict, a divergence that stems from the different national histories of the two countries. In England the Norman Conquest was decisive, bringing with it the establishment of feudalism and of the most centralized medieval monarchy. National unity was disrupted by the feudal crisis, only to be more solidly restored by the Tudors. Most English history plays accordingly treat events from the fourteenth or fifteenth century. In Spain, although the feudal crisis occupied a similar structural position, by an act of only partial ideological distortion it could be assimilated to the larger historical pattern of the Reconquest, to an unbroken national experience focused for centuries on the single definitive struggle against Islam. The temporal options available to the Spanish historical dramatist were consequently far greater than those open to his English counterpart.[120]

This distinction is symptomatic. In England, the enemy is within and the subject is conflict. Spain is the opposite: the English define themselves by what they are, the Spanish by what they are not. All appearances to the contrary, the Hispanic nation is internally harmonious; it

[118]H. R. Trevor-Roper, "The Gentry, 1540–1640," *Economic History Review Supplements*, no. 1 (1953): 22, 32, and passim; for a more moderate view, Barrington Moore, Jr., *Social Origins of Dictatorship and Democracy: Lord and Peasant in the Making of the Modern World* (Boston: Beacon, 1966), pp. 15–16. For more on the declining gentry, see the discussion of satiric comedy in the next chapter.

[119]Edwards, p. 68; Walter Cohen, "*Heinrich IV. und die Revolution*," *Shakespeare Jahrbuch* (Weimar) 121 (1985), 57–63; Christopher Hill, pp. 198–99.

[120]Wilson and Moir, p. 59; Bunn, p. 115; Carol Bingham Kirby, "Observaciones preliminares sobre el teatro histórico de Lope de Vega," in *Lope de Vega*, ed. Criado de Val, pp. 329–37, who rightly argues that Spanish plays set during the feudal crisis at times emphasize conflict.

has exported its problems. The late-sixteenth-century Golden Age national history play, regardless of its temporal or geographical setting, tends to emphasize the struggle between Catholic Spain and its infidel, external foes. When the dramatized events postdate the Reconquest, the structure of the Christian/Moor struggle is simply shipped abroad, for instance to the New World in *Arauco domado* or to Flanders in *El asalto de Mastrique*. At the other temporal extreme, classical or Visigothic Spain, though relatively inconsequential for later peninsular development, can also be incorporated into the paradigm of the Reconquest. The Spanish history play's relative lack of tragedy, self-criticism, or complex characters, though primarily rooted in late-sixteenth-century conditions, was thus reinforced by earlier historical trends and the ideologies they engendered. But in both countries reactionary social corporatism discovers its crucial buttress in imperial mythology.

What, then, is one to make of the substantial number of plays that, far from straining the conventional assumptions of the form, either take the dominant values for granted or explicitly seek to reinforce them? Such works, precisely because of their relatively uncritical allegiances, inadvertently tend to place aristocratic ideology in an unflattering light. In *Mudarra* and in *Los siete infantes*, the refined conduct of most of the characters, typical of the playwright's own age, conflicts with the hero's prefeudal commitment to bloody vengeance to such an extent that, in Cueva's play at least, sympathy is unintentionally elicited for the villainous victims.[121] In *Arauco domado* and *El asalto de Mastrique*, Lope's unquestioning acceptance of orthodox justifications of imperialism allows alternative interpretations to be voiced precisely because they are not taken seriously. The Indians of *Arauco domado* plausibly explain their resistance to Spanish rule as a defense of their freedom. In *El asalto de Mastrique*, Lope reworks his sources so as to aggrandize the aristocratic protagonist at the expense of the soldiers, while generally whitewashing Spanish military behavior. Nonetheless, he portrays the siege as an attack on an indigenous population, defends Spanish aggression in the broadest sense on absolutist rather than nationalist grounds, and motivates the attack more narrowly as the only means of pacifying restive soldiers whose services will be needed again. The purpose of war, in other words, is to make possible not peace, but more war—a classic instance of feudal logic.

A similar pattern of unconscious revelation can be discerned in English plays about popular rebellion. The allegiances of the author of *Jack Straw* are so unambiguously monarchical that he can present the rebels' position in the serene confidence that it will be contemptuously dis-

[121]Alfredo Hermenegildo, *La tragedia en el Renacimiento español* (Barcelona: Editorial Planeta, 1973), pp. 288–89.

missed. Shakespeare's methods are more subtle in *2 Henry VI*, but the result is not qualitatively different. Although similar remarks might be made about the treatment of the rebellious citizens in *Thomas More*, the most interesting connection between ideology and form in that work is generated by a very different political problem, the protagonist's relationship to Henry VIII. The play must be pro-More, but since it was dangerous to scrutinize Tudor policy too closely, it must also be pro-monarchy. This dual imperative is easy enough to fulfill during the first half of the action, when the two men agree. It is in this section that interclass issues are discussed. Once More falls from royal favor, however, the dramatists must sytematically suppress the basis of the conflict, thus draining the hero's downfall and death of its historical meaning. Finally, in *Richard III* (1593), Shakespeare violates the ideal of loyalty to *de facto* rule that runs through his national history plays, in order to justify the Tudor line's claim to the throne. Although his technique of evasion is characteristically far more sophisticated than the one adopted in *Thomas More*,[122] *Richard III* clearly belongs with those works that, through their very blindness, communicate significant insight.[123]

An independent perspective on the national history play may be obtained by returning to the point of departure of this discussion and, as it were, viewing the form from the outside. The impossibility of strictly distinguishing historical drama from tragedy is evident in such plays as *Richard II*, *Edward II*, and *Bamba*, works that consequently possess a certain representative status in the serious drama of the period. But several of the best-known late-sixteenth-century plays—most of Marlowe's corpus, Thomas Kyd's *Spanish Tragedy* (1587), *Romeo and Juliet*, and Lope's *El marqués de Mantua* (1596) and *La imperial de Otón* (1597)—are tragedies with little or no explicit reference to national experience. The overall significance of the national history play may emerge more clearly from a general comparison with these plays. If the tragedies are divided by subject matter according to whether they portray private citizens, the domestic life of the court, or affairs of state, the resulting categories very roughly correspond to the three kinds of historical drama described above. A successive consideration of these three main types of tragedy, however, uncovers less parallelism than complementarity: tragedy's greater critical freedom is inseparable from its relative social and political impoverishment.

An overt political referent is secondary at best in such works as Micer Andrés Rey de Artieda's *Los amantes* (written 1577–78, published

[122]Ribner, pp. 116–18.

[123]For this formulation, though put to a very different end, see Paul de Man, *Blindness and Insight: Essays in the Rhetoric of Contemporary Criticism*, 2d ed. (Minneapolis: University of Minnesota Press, 1983), esp. pp. 102–6.

1581),[124] *The Jew of Malta, Doctor Faustus* (1592), and *Romeo and Juliet.*
Cueva's *El infamador* (1581),[125] a tragicomedy, might be included in this
group as well. Since these plays, like other tragedies, reveal that something has gone fundamentally wrong, they are at odds with the dominant, corporatist ideology of national historical drama. But their crucial
innovation lies in their serious treatment of everyday life, their break
with generic, ideological, and social convention. On the other hand, such
works eliminate almost by definition that concern with public affairs
which characterizes the history play. This tendency is less pronounced in
England than in Spain, however. Yet even *Los amantes* has a national feel
that extends to a victory-from-defeat admiration for the star-crossed lovers. The evocation of such a feeling, finally, has affinities with the use of
history as a source of dramatic energy.

Court tragedy shares many of the features of the private plays, though
its intrigues rely more consistently on sex and violence, and its plots cannot avoid political implications. *El marqués de Mantua* and Castro's *El
amor constante* (1596?–99?)[126] end with reassertions of a social harmony and political order temporarily disrupted by the misbehavior of
royalty. The solutions are not entirely bland, however. Castro's play, like
Argensola's before it, makes use of the freedom offered by a foreign setting to justify regicide, while Lope's, in which Charlemagne must all but
order the execution of his son and heir, closes with a profound sense if
not of doubt, then certainly of loss. But revealingly, both works, as well
as *Los amantes, El infamador,* and *Romeo and Juliet,* resemble the contemporary romantic comedy. One may almost feel as if the conventional material of that genre had been reinterpreted to produce an unexpectedly
dissonant conclusion.

Probably a more important, though scarcely more political, subgroup
of court tragedy comprises those plays within the Italian Senecan tradition.[127] Cristóbal de Virués's *La cruel Casandra* (perhaps 1579),[128] *The
Spanish Tragedy,* and *Titus Andronicus* are hardly unique in their indebtedness to the Roman tragedian, but the mixture of rhetoric, horror,

[124]The first date is from Froldi, p. 101; the second is from Juliá Martínez, 1:xxxii.
[125]The date is given in the argumento.
[126]The date is from Bruerton, "Chronology of Castro," p. 150.
[127]For the Italian influence on both English and Spanish Senecanism, see John W.
Cunliffe, *The Influence of Seneca on Elizabethan Tragedy* (1893; rpt. Hamden, Conn.: Archon
Books, 1965), pp. 7–9; F. L. Lucas, *Seneca and Elizabethan Tragedy* (1922; rpt. New York:
Haskell House, 1966), pp. 99–104; H. B. Charlton, *The Senecan Tradition in Renaissance
Tragedy* (1921; rpt. Manchester University Press, 1946), pp. 147–53; T. S. Eliot, *Selected
Essays* (New York: Harcourt, Brace and World, 1950), pp. 67–68; Cecilia Vennard Sar-
gent, *A Study of the Dramatic Works of Cristóbal de Virués* (New York: Instituto de las Españas
en los Estados Unidos, 1930), pp. 137–38; Karl Alfred Blüher, *Seneca in Spanien: Untersuch-
ungen zur Geschichte der Seneca-Rezeption in Spanien vom 13. bis 17. Jahrhundert* (Munich:
Francke Verlag, 1969), pp. 244–49.
[128]Date: Froldi, p. 111.

blood, vengeance, and the supernatural produces far deeper pessimism in these works than in the most closely comparable history plays. How firmly is this pessimism rooted in the life of the time? Although a recent argument plausibly attempts to connect Spanish Senecan drama to late-sixteenth-century crisis,[129] it is extremely difficult to discover any conscious attempt by the playwrights to establish the linkage. Such works are more popular than earlier Renaissance Spanish tragedy, but they still seem to have been aimed at a socially, culturally, and numerically restricted audience.[130] This is one of the reasons the peninsular Senecan tradition largely precedes the main age of the *comedia*, exercising only minor influence after 1590.[131]

In England, on the other hand, Senecan influences fused with the popular heritage.[132] A recognition of this development contributes, from one point of view, to the current depreciation of the Latin tragedian's importance for Elizabethan dramaturgy.[133] But it is also the clue to his significance. In England, but not in Spain, Seneca was naturalized, domesticated, and incorporated into a larger theatrical movement.[134] Kyd differs from the early Spanish Senecans in his position at the beginning of an important tradition rather than at the end of a minor one that to some extent had to be superseded before the *comedia* could come into its own. English interest in the divided consciousness and particularly in the complex psychology of the revenger may also have prompted the assimilation of Seneca. In Spain, on the other hand, revenge was not inherently problematic, as the "siete infantes" legend suggests.[135] The more multidimensional appropriation of this particular classical source in England ultimately leads back to the basic social distinctions between the two countries and substantiates the recent critical claim that Seneca has historically exercised his greatest appeal in ages of strain.[136] Yet

[129]Herbert E. Isar, "La question du prétendu 'sénéquisme' espagnol," in *Les tragédies de Sénèque et le théâtre de la Renaissance*, ed. Jean Jacquot (Paris: Editions du Centre National de la Recherche Scientifique, 1964), pp. 47–60.

[130]Green, pp. 104–5; Sargent, p. 16 n. 1; Hermenegildo, pp. 11–20, 68, 109.

[131]Raymond R. MacCurdy, "La tragédie neo-sénéquienne en Espagne au xviiᵉ siècle, et particulièrement le thème du tyran," in *Les tragédies de Sénèque*, ed. Jacquot, pp. 73–85, assembles the evidence on this later period.

[132]Catherine Belsey, "Senecan Vacillation and Elizabethan Deliberation: Influence or Confluence?" *Renaissance Drama*, n.s., 6 (1973): 67–68, 88; Weimann, *Shakespeare and the Popular Tradition*, pp. 128–29.

[133]Anna Lydia Motto and John R. Clark, "Senecan Tragedy: A Critique of Scholarly Trends—Review Article," *Renaissance Drama*, n.s., 6 (1973): 219–35.

[134]Fredson Thayer Bowers, *Elizabethan Revenge Tragedy, 1587–1642*, rev. ed. (Gloucester, Mass.: Peter Smith, 1959).

[135]But see Jean-Louis Flecniakoska, "L'horreur morale et l'horreur matérielle dans quelques tragédies espagnoles du xviᵉ siècle," in *Les tragédies de Sénèque*, ed. Jacquot, pp. 61–72.

[136]C. J. Herington, "Senecan Tragedy," *Arion* 5 (1966): 460–62.

much late-sixteenth-century revenge tragedy remains curiously detached from its own time and place, at least in comparison with the plays in the tradition after 1600 or with the contemporary national historical drama. In England Senecanism seems associated with an ideological revulsion against the court, but one that evinces only intermittent understanding of the source of the malaise. It is an analogy without substance,[137] a problem as well in many of the history plays that treat the past as pastoral.

A small number of tragedies undertake a direct depiction of national or international political events, however, and thus more closely approximate those national history plays that take history as their subject, with the concomitant combination of process, relevance, and social range. Although one finds this tendency in Diego López de Castro's *Marco Antonio y Cleopatra* (1582)[138] and in *Tamburlaine* (1587–88), even the English play keeps its distance from contemporary reality. However narrow *Edward II* may seem in comparison with the full possibilities of the English history play, it still has a noticeably broader and more immediate social perspective than its two-part predecessor in Marlowe's canon.[139] A work that comes closer to combining social range with a sense of process in the manner of past-as-past national historical drama is *La imperial de Otón*. Although the play dramatizes thirteenth-century German politics, it systematically celebrates Spanish national glory. To this end, Lope must introduce into the story considerable extraneous material in praise of Spain and things Spanish. But since the tragedy concerns the struggles surrounding the election as Holy Roman emperor of Rudolph, founder of the Habsburg line, the inclusion of a prophecy of Spain's sixteenth-century imperial greatness possesses a certain logic.

The same cannot be said, however, of the relation between this overt ideological intention and the main plot, which recounts Otto of Bohemia's disappointment at not winning the imperial election, his consequent rebellion against Rudolph, and his defeat and death. Translated into Renaissance terms, the play pits feudalism against absolutism. Though orthodox in insisting on the injustice of Otto's cause, Lope treats his protagonist's ethically correct, but temporary decision not to rebel as an act of cowardice. When Otto does fight, the playwright emphasizes the heroic nobility of his effort. The play thus attempts to have it both ways, honoring both destined imperial triumph and quixotic personal defeat. Like Rey de Artieda, Cueva, and Cervantes, Lope snatches

[137]Weimann, *Shakespeare and the Popular Tradition*, p. 89 n. 5.

[138]The date refers to the moment when composition was completed and is found in the sole extant manuscript of the play.

[139]Paul H. Kocher, *Christopher Marlowe: A Study of His Thought, Learning, and Character* (1946; rpt. New York: Russell and Russell, 1962), pp. 205–8.

victory from the jaws of defeat: "venció Otón, aunque vencido" ("Otto conquered, although [he was] conquered").[140] In Otto's case, however, this "victory" does not result from historical process. Since future Spanish ascendancy requires his defeat, he can expect no posthumous revenge and vindication. Lope's sympathy for his doomed hero in this way contradicts the explicit ideology of the tragedy. This glaring flaw is symptomatic of the obstacles facing tragedy, even when it seeks to conform to the norms of the national history play. Although tragedy implicitly challenges the social and political order by its negativity, it has great difficulty in taking on that order. In this sense, orthodoxy and relevance are inextricable: during the late sixteenth century, national historical drama is central and tragedy, with a few crucial exceptions, peripheral.

### Marlowe, *Edward II*

Just as it is difficult to parody a parodist, so a demystifying dramatist proves unusually resistant to demystification. The national history play deals with the fates of kings and princes, and of the nations they attempt to govern. Although the sense of reality created by any individual work may of course be ideologically suspect, the form itself, unlike the contemporary romantic comedy, would seem to be the opposite of escapist. When, moreover, a particular play in effect undermines the illusions fostered by most other specimens of the genre, the critic can apparently do little more than reduplicate the dramatist's performance. Such, at any rate, are some of the problems raised by Christopher Marlowe's *Edward II*.

These are hardly the problems with which Marlowe begins, however. His point of departure is the question of absolutism, of the relations between aristocracy and monarchy, between class and state.[141] Yet the opening scenes of the play might seem remote even from these considerations. The barons, after all, initially oppose Edward because he slights them in favor of the lowborn Gaveston. The conflict accordingly turns on the class opposition between nobility and commoner, only gradually developing into an open rebellion of the peerage against the crown. But although the aristocrats long hide their true motives even from themselves, the ultimate transformation of the struggle is inherent in the initial situation. Throughout western Europe, royal centralization required the partial exclusion of the titular nobility from political power and its replacement by men of humbler station, whose influence depended en-

---

[140]*La imperial de Otón*, in *Obras escogidas*, vol. 3: *Teatro*, ed. Federico Carlos Sainz de Robles, 2d ed. (Madrid: Aguilar, 1962), 3:596.

[141]Michael Poirier, *Christopher Marlowe* (London: Chatto and Windus, 1951), p. 173.

tirely on monarchical goodwill. The following exchange neatly captures
this process:

> *Edward.* Tell me, where wast thou borne? What
>      is thine arms?
> *Baldock.* My name is *Baldock*, and my gentrie
> I fetcht from Oxford, not from Heraldrie.
> *Edward.* The fitter art thou *Baldock* for my
>      turne.[142]

Hostility to the king's minions thus constitutes not only a form of aristocratic class condescension common to the reigns of Edward II and Elizabeth I alike,[143] but also and more important a fundamental feudal attack on the formation of the absolutist state. Symptomatically, Marlowe
changes the class status of Gaveston, Spencer, and Baldock downward
from his source in Holinshed, which is silent about both absolutism and
class conflict.[144]

Forced to make an abstract choice between nobility and monarchy, the
public theater audience would have had no difficulty opting for the latter. But the course of the action complicates the decision. It is not that
the barons are particularly attractive. Although they occasionally com-
plain of the nation's sufferings, their primary concern is always their
class position.[145] Marlowe even refuses his aristocracy the glamorous
feudal allure with which Shakespeare endows Hotspur, instead granting
Gaveston an opportunistic, but telling, taunt:

> Base leaden Earles that glorie in your birth,
> Goe sit at home and eate your tenants beefe.
>                    (2.2.74–75)

In fact, the unruly lords seem attractive only in comparison with their
monarchical antagonist. Edward's personal and, even more, political
failings are commonplaces of criticism: his ineffectual defense of royal
prerogative rests on private pleasure rather than national interest. In
the first two acts, both Kent and "the murmuring commons" (2.2.158)
come to prefer the barons to Edward—evidence of the proper disposi-
tion of audience sympathies.[146] The early part of the play, then, pits a

---

[142]Christopher Marlowe, *Edward II*, in *The Complete Works of Christopher Marlowe*, ed.
Bowers, 2d ed. (Cambridge: Cambridge University Press, 1981), vol. 2: 2.2.242–45. Subsequent references are noted in the text.

[143]On the hardening of social divisons and class consciousness after 1550, see Stone,
*Crisis*, pp. 30–34.

[144]Roma Gill, ed., *Edward II* (London: Oxford University Press, 1967), p. 20.

[145]Clifford Leech, "Marlowe's *Edward II*: Power and Suffering," *Critical Quarterly* 1
(1959): 187.

[146]But see Kocher, p. 205.

feudal aristocracy, viewed coolly and without nostalgia, against a monarch whose absolutist aims are still more profoundly undercut.

How does Marlowe obtain a dramatic resolution to a conflict in which the triumph of either party would be unsatisfactory? He does so in largely conventional moral terms.[147] Every character who violates social and political norms is severly punished. Gaveston, the parasitic social climber, is killed by the barons, a fate that his successors, Spencer and Baldock, later meet at the hands of Mortimer. The homosexual and irresponsible king is deposed and then killed on Mortimer and Isabella's orders. In the period of captivity before his murder, moreover, Edward agonizes over the ethical culpability of voluntary abdication. This scene, added by Marlowe to his source,[148] is one of the reasons some critics have discovered in the beleaguered royal consciousness a belated, but redemptive realization of the value of kingship.[149] Finally, in retribution for their crimes, Isabella is imprisoned and Mortimer executed. The profound deterioration of their characters and conduct under the pressure of historical crisis[150] reveals that rebellion against the crown, however much provoked by royal highhandedness, inevitably leads to a dictatorship far worse than the one it replaces. For these reasons the assumption of power by the young Edward III provides an adequate conclusion to the dilemmas of the plot. The implicit defense of a strong monarchy may be seen as an ideological solution to a political problem —as the censorship of a new individualism by traditional values.[151]

Few viewers or readers of the play would find this summary satisfactory, however. A consideration of *Edward II* in the context of its author's dramatic practice as a whole may help explain why. In general Marlowe's works constitute acts of double and reciprocal demystification, carried out both formally and ideologically. The plays characteristically begin in a secular and realistic vein but increasingly draw upon morality structures as they move toward conclusion; complementarily, they open with assertions of individualist aspiration but close if not with the reimposition of conventional religious and political values, then at least with a cri-

[147]See, for example, Douglas Cole, *Suffering and Evil in the Plays of Christopher Marlowe* (Princeton: Princeton University Press, 1962), pp. 186–87; Bevington, *Tudor Drama and Politics*, pp. 216–17.

[148]Cole, p. 174.

[149]Charles G. Masington, *Christopher Marlowe's Tragic Vision: A Study in Damnation* (Athens: Ohio University Press, 1972), p. 86; Judith Weil, *Christopher Marlowe: Merlin's Prophet* (Cambridge: Cambridge University Press, 1977), pp. 165–69.

[150]Ribner, *English History Play*, p. 125.

[151]Jean Duvignaud, *Les ombres collectives: Sociologie du théâtre*, 2d ed. (Paris: Presses Universitaires de France, 1973), pp. 193–210, esp. 193–98, considers this pattern typical of English and Spanish Renaissance drama.

tique of aspiration.[152] Such a pattern is of course never found in a pure form. But the sources of Marlowe's unusually modern techniques and attitudes and, even more, their juxtaposition with traditional dramaturgical and intellectual modes nonetheless require explanation.

In the broadest sense, of course, Marlowe felt the conflicting pulls of a transitional age in theater and society alike. Although Marlovian iconoclasm did not simply emanate from the bourgeoisie, it can no more be separated from that class than can the Renaissance in general.[153] Marlowe may further be understood as one of the growing number of frustrated intellectuals created by the inability of the society to provide suitable employment for all of the graduates of its universities.[154] This difficulty was exacerbated in his case by the class structure of Elizabethan England. Marlowe's talent and education led him to treat his artisanal origins with condescension and contempt, yet those very origins imposed powerful constraints on his upward mobility.[155] His probable career as a government spy, the rash behavior that got him in trouble with the same government, and to a lesser extent his decision to write for the professional acting companies—all are indications of his social marginality.

This perspective suggests the significance of the recurrent formal and ideological fissures of the plays. The result is neither compromise nor supersession nor, for that matter, anything much like Shakepeare's attempted solution in *The Merchant of Venice*. It is, rather, simple contradiction. The initial secularism and individualism effectively undermine neofeudal values, while the plot resolutions demonstrate the impossibility, the inaccuracy, and in some instances the undesirability as well, of the earlier positions. Although Marlowe apparently anticipated many of the convictions of the revolutionary sects of the mid-seventeenth century,[156] he remained cut off not only from aristocratic ideology but from popular culture as well. Since he also lived before the bourgeoisie had more than begun to articulate a hegemonic ideology of its own, he necessarily lacked a sufficiently secure yet independent vantage point

---

[152]For the formal point, see Bevington, *From "Mankind" to Marlowe: Growth of Structure in the Popular Drama of Tudor England* (Cambridge: Harvard University Press, 1962), pp. 199–262. For the ideological argument, see Greenblatt, "Marlowe and Renaissance Self-Fashioning," in *Two Renaissance Mythmakers: Christopher Marlowe and Ben Jonson*, ed. Alvin B. Kernan, Selected Papers from the English Institute, 1975–76, n.s., no. 1 (Baltimore: Johns Hopkins University Press, 1977), pp. 51–55.

[153]Linkages between Marlowe and the bourgeoisie are made by Bevington, *Tudor Drama and Politics*, pp. 212–15, and by Greenblatt, "Marlowe and Renaissance Self-Fashioning," p. 42.

[154]Stone, *Causes*, pp. 95–96, 113–14.

[155]Poirier, pp. 39–43.

[156]Compare Kocher, pp. 21–68, with Christopher Hill, passim, e.g., p. 227.

from which to survey and judge experience. The price of his radical inquiries was thus a form that risked incoherence and an ideology that bordered on nihilism.[157]

What are the consequences of the confrontation between Marlowe's dramatic strategy and the national history play? *Edward II* by and large conforms to the pattern of its author's other works. In some ways like *The Merchant of Venice*, it criticizes the assumptions of its form. It offers no providential or nationalist justification for absolutism: the significance of events does not transcend the lives of the people involved.[158] On the other hand, Mortimer's feudal rebellion in the second half of the play proves even less satisfying. Not only does power corrupt Mortimer, converting him into a bizarre Machiavellian; in addition to misusing power, he is incapable of retaining it, as the ending reveals. This ideological transformation is accompanied and largely accomplished by Marlowe's regular formal shift toward morality structure, a move that correspondingly complicates the aesthetic and theatrical assumptions of the play. Thus the changes in Mortimer and Isabella are not so much evidence of complex characterization as signs of relative flaws in the design,[159] flaws, however, that arise not from unaccountable errors in an otherwise elegantly constructed plot, but from the unsettled state of English dramaturgy and especially of Marlowe's own social and ideological situation. The effect of the reciprocal critique of the two halves of the play is conflict without resolution; the use of conventional morality in unconventional fashion; a *de casibus* pattern without affirmation, exhortation, theory, moral, or justice; and a consequent pessimism from the dual tragedies.[160]

Yet *Edward II* modifies Marlowe's typical pattern in several important respects, all of them related to the exigencies of the national history play. Although one may speak of formal and ideological bifurcation elsewhere in the playwright's canon, the split is usually between one form and another and between one ideology and another rather than between form and ideology. Indeed, it is possible to discern at least a crude homology between realist form and bourgeois ideology or between morality form and aristocratic-absolutist ideology. In *Edward II* this parallel is

[157]Bevington, *From "Mankind" to Marlowe*, pp. 199–262; Greenblatt, "Marlowe and Renaissance Self-Fashioning," pp. 59–63.

[158]Leech, pp. 192–93; Cole, p. 186; Ribner, pp. 126–30; Bevington, *Tudor Drama and Politics*, p. 217.

[159]Robert Fricker, "The Dramatic Structure of *Edward II*," *English Studies* 34 (1953): 210–12; Bevington, *From "Mankind" to Marlowe*, pp. 234–44.

[160]Leech, pp. 194–96; Cole, p. 184; Ribner, pp. 127–28; Bevington, *Tudor Drama and Politics*, pp. 217–18; Joel B. Altman, *The Tudor Play of Mind: Rhetorical Inquiry and the Development of Elizabethan Drama* (Berkeley and Los Angeles: University of California Press, 1978), p. 362.

disturbed by a qualitative change in subject matter from the other plays. When they first appear, Tamburlaine, Barabas, and Faustus are a shepherd, a merchant, and a humanist scholar, respectively. All stand outside the traditional ruling class, with which their aspirations bring them into conflict. There is thus a rough compatibility in the first parts of their plays among form, ideology, and social material. Although Gaveston and, to a lesser extent, Spencer and Baldock occupy analogous positions in *Edward II*, they are treated with far less sympathy and are in fact peripheral to the central conflict, which occurs within the ruling class and pits aristocracy against monarchy.

If Marlowe viewed the two sides with equal contempt, no major problems would occur. But given the greater sympathy for the aristocracy than for the monarchy in the first half of the play, while the form moves, loosely, from bourgeois to aristocratic, the ideology simply moves from one species of aristocratic to another. Beyond Marlowe's standard contradictions within form and ideology, in other words, there is in the first half of *Edward II* a conflict between form and ideology. It is not surprising to discover an absence of homology among a play's constituent parts when the public theater reveals similar asymmetries. One could find comparable instances in many other dramas of the time as well. Nor is the conflict absolute: the earliest scenes demonstrate that a secular and realistic dramaturgy can produce an impressively detached perspective on traditional feudal conduct.

Yet even if the disjunction between form and ideology is minimized, the problem of a focus on the nobility remains. What place, for instance, can the concern with individualist aspiration, widespread among English Renaissance dramatists, occupy in the portrayal of a ruling class? An obvious answer is that an aristocrat may try to become a king. This striving might be understood in a number of ways, all of them related to the breakdown of feudalism and the rise of capitalism. In *Macbeth* (1606), Shakespeare takes the extreme position of essentially equating his protagonist's quest for power with bourgeois consciousness, an insight that was not generally available during Queen Elizabeth's lifetime. As early as *Richard II*, however, he seems to have perceived that process, with rather mixed emotions, as a drive toward absolutism. But even this solution was not really open to Marlowe, in part because of his emphasis in the first half of the play on baronial class solidarity rather than aristocratic individualist ambition. For these reasons he had no credible means of motivating Mortimer's usurpation. Ironically, aristocratic aspiration is dramatized in homiletic terms and accordingly understood as a form of corruption within the feudal class inspired by some unspecified modern developments. In these respects, *Edward II* calls to mind *Richard*

*III*,[161] and certainly both Mortimer and Richard defend their class's traditional prerogatives against upstart aristocrats.

Schematically stated, then, the turn to national history and to the political affairs of the aristocracy and crown reflexively converts Marlowe's characteristically subjective concerns into an independent and objective point of view. There is correspondingly less scope for individualist aspiration. Because the nobility is always seen from the outside, a tolerable unity is maintained between the two halves of the play, despite the greater prominence of morality elements here than in *Tamburlaine* or *The Jew of Malta*. Likewise, for all the obvious antipathy to absolutism, the allegiance to hereditary monarchy is, paradoxically, greater in *Edward II* than in Marlowe's other works.

These consequences are inextricable from the other main distinctive feature of the play within its author's canon. Instead of portraying the heroic pursuits of a lowborn protagonist, Marlowe focuses on the defeat and death of a weak ruler. The utopian vistas opened up by the movement of romantic comedy or by the grandeur of tragic struggles are scarcely evoked by Edward's pathetic desires. As many critics have noted, the emphasis is on the personal at the expense of the political.[162] Edward's tragedy consists of his private misery: though his agonies are intensified by the fact that he is king, they have no apparent bearing on affairs of state.[163] This orientation depends on Marlowe's modern and more bourgeois side. The secular and realistic dramaturgy that so effectively dismantles Edward's absolutist pretensions also makes possible the complexity of characterization that engenders sympathy for the helpless monarch. Similarly, the ideology of individualism provides imaginative access to the experience of the aristocracy from a perspective originating outside that class, precisely when that experience is overwhelmingly one of isolation. For Marlowe, then, English history, insofar as it possesses any significance at all, consists of the tragedy of individual suffering. *Edward II* offers its most telling critique of the corporatist, absolutist, and nationalist norms of its own genre in its pervasive privatization of public issues.

Although an interpretation of the play along these lines may succeed in specifying the critical thrust of the action, in so doing it largely duplicates Marlowe's own achievement. A discussion of the ideology of form that stops at this point has stopped too soon. The difficulty is less the almost inadvertent acceptance of absolutism at the end of the play than a

[161]Lukács, *The Historical Novel*, p. 153, refers to "the types representing the social-moral, human-moral decay of feudalism" in Shakespeare's history plays.

[162]See, for example, Harry Levin, *Christopher Marlowe: The Overreacher* (London: Faber and Faber, 1953?), pp. 110, 125–126; Lindenberger, pp. 120, 136, 182 n. 38.

[163]Leech, pp. 183–87, 195–96; Cole, pp. 184–85.

systematic narrowness of outlook. Although Marlowe is profoundly right to consider the various justifications of political behavior only so many masks of self-interest, he is wrong to conclude that the struggles over the state in the later Middle Ages and in the Renaissance, and particularly the rise of absolutism, were of no importance either to the aristocracy or to the English people as a whole. This crucial absence of social vision accompanies an analogous distance from the popular tradition in the theater, a distance that is evident in the restricted range of characters and the neoclassical language and style of *Edward II*. Symptomatically, Marlowe excises his source's emphasis on the economic crisis and on the hardships of the common people that resulted from Edward's misrule.[164] The compensatory depiction of the king as a kind of tragic emblem of suffering humanity is thus a gesture at once of generous generalization and of elitist obscurantism. Although Marlowe is not trapped by the ideology that he rejects to the extent that Racine is in *Phèdre*, his independent perspective is not the strongest one that was available at the time. *Edward II* constitutes a typical act of demystification, powerful in its destructiveness but incapable of producing a constructive alternative. This is to say, however, that Marlowe does what Shakespeare does not and vice versa, that the ideological weaknesses of the play are inseparable from its strengths, that its socially constituted blindness is the enabling force behind its unusual insight.


## Lope de Vega, *La vida y muerte del rey Bamba*

Like *Edward II*, Lope de Vega's *La vida y muerte del rey Bamba* recounts the history of a monarch besieged by a fractious nobility. Each king has little affection for his office; each increases the hostility of his courtiers by the unwise choice of a foreign favorite to whom he is deeply, almost mystically attracted. In both plays the royal protagonist faces a foreign invasion, defeats a domestic aristocratic rebellion, and has the traitors executed but in turn is murdered and succeeded by one of the surviving dissident magnates. This largely tragic movement means that neither work constitutes an unambiguous celebration of national destiny. Otherwise, however, the two plots have little in common. *Bamba* may almost be seen as a photographic negative of *Edward II*. As such it helps to complete the picture of the limits and possibilities of the national history play in the late-sixteenth-century public theater.

Lope's drama focuses on one of the last Visigothic rulers of Spain (672–80). It begins, in an atmosphere of religious heresy, with a narra-

---

[164]Gill, p. 19.

tive of the miraculous visit of the Virgin Mary to Saint Ildefonso, late in the reign of Bamba's predecessor Recisundo. After the king's death, aristocratic strife leads to an impasse over the succession, finally broken only by a series of divine interventions and injunctions pointing unmistakably to Bamba, a recently married young peasant whose humility, piety, and overall ability have already caused his fellows to make him the local mayor. In the second act, he and his wife Sancha adapt to life at court. Bamba repels an Arab invasion but befriends Paulo, a Greek Christian advisor to the Islamic chieftain and the inspirer of his attack on Spain. The final *jornada* (act) finds the peasant monarch hard at work running his country when he is brought the news of a rebellion in the North. Sent to suppress the uprising, Paulo instead joins it and is crowned king. Bamba defeats his foe but soon after is fatally poisoned and succeeded by Ervigio, whose misdeeds depend on the services of a Moorish magician.

As this brief summary indicates, *Bamba* neither represents a historically accurate staging of its subject matter nor possesses even a rudimentary structural unity. Disunity and inaccuracy do not automatically go together, however. The untidiness of a chronicle play is often a sign of the dramatist's inability to transmute the recalcitrant material of history, or rather of historical sources, into a form suitable for theatrical performance. But here Lope may have compounded the inherent difficulties, partly, it seems, out of simple carelessness or ineptitude. A review of the source tradition and of what Lope did with it, however, may begin to reveal the contours of his possible intentions in the play, the considerable coherence that results, and, finally, the relation between the flaws in the structure and certain ideological contradictions that he could not successfully overcome.[165]

The earliest documents are virtually contemporaneous with the events they discuss. Saint Ildefonso composed a tract entitled *De virginitate perpetua Sanctae Mariae adversus tres infideles liber unicus*, referred to by Saint Julian in his *Beati Hildefonsi elogium*, and extant today.[166] Another bishop of Toledo, Cixila, provides an almost firsthand account of Mary's visit to Ildefonso.[167] The most important record, however, is Julian's *Historia rebellionis Pauli adversus Wambam Gothorum regem*, composed dur-

---

[165]For the sources and a critique of Lope's use of them, see Marcelino Menéndez y Pelayo, observaciones preliminares to his edition of the *Obras de Lope de Vega*, vol. 16, *Crónicas y leyendas dramáticas de España*, Biblioteca de Autores Españoles, vol. 195 (Madrid: Ediciones Atlas, 1966), pp. 10–18. References to *Bamba* are to the edition printed in this volume, pp. 295–342, and are cited in the text.

[166]Several Latin background texts to *Bamba* are printed in J. P. Migne, ed., *Patrologia Latina* (hereafter *PL*), vol. 96 (Paris, 1851). Ildefonso's *De virginitate* appears in cols. 53–110, the reference to it in Julian's *Elogium* in col. 44.

[167]*Vita S. Hildefonsi*, in *PL*, 96, col. 46, par. 5.

ing the king's lifetime.[168] Though free, with one small exception, of supernatural intervention and largely accurate in detail, the *Historia* was sufficiently striking to foster the legendary accretions and emendations of later centuries.[169] Finally, at the Twelfth Council of Toledo, which convened in early January 681, the assembled bishops asserted that three months previously Wamba, believing he was near death, had named Erwig to succeed him. At this point, however, uncertainties arise. It is likely that the old king, who in fact recovered from his illness, subsequently struggled unsuccessfully to regain the crown. But no suspicions of the official version of the episode appear in writing before the *Crónica de Alfonso III*, traditionally dated at the end of the ninth century, which accuses Erwig, perhaps correctly, of poisoning Wamba, who seems to have been none too popular with the higher clergy.[170]

Recent scholarship increases the likelihood that this counterinterpretation of the succession is accurate. On the one hand, the *Crónica* was almost certainly compiled in the early tenth, rather than the late ninth, century. On the other, the section dealing with Wamba may have originally been composed by a contemporary of King Pelayo (718–37), who recorded his narrative in the age of Alfonso I (739–56).[171] The increased credibility that this text acquires from an earlier dating is important in other respects. After summarizing Paul's rebellion, the narrative goes on to mention that Wamba's reign also witnessed an unsuccessful attack on Spain by "ducentae septuaginta naues Sarracenorum" ("270 Saracen boats").[172] In addition, two minor points may be noted. Erwig is here given Greek ancestry—perhaps a source of the subsequent ethnic identification of Paul. And in the slightly later of the two surviving manuscripts of the *Crónica* (significantly, the one that does not refer to Julian's *Historia*), Wamba is known as Bamba.[173]

The texts that unquestionably date from the eighth century do not add anything crucial to the tale.[174] Unambiguous fictionalization begins four hundred years later with the false attribution to Bamba of a division

---

[168]In *PL*, 96, cols. 763–800.

[169]Menéndez y Pelayo, observaciones preliminares, p. 11. The veracity of the *Historia* may be gauged by comparison with two other contemporary documents: the *Espistola Pauli perfidi qui rebellionem fecit in Gallia Wambano principi Magno Toletano*, in *PL*, 96, cols. 761–62, and the *Judicium in tyrannorum perfidia promulgatum*, in *PL*, 96, col. 801–8.

[170]E. A. Thompson, *The Goths in Spain* (Oxford: Clarendon Press, 1969), pp. 229–32, gives a slightly more complex account.

[171]Antonio Ubieto Arteta, prólogo to his edition of the *Crónica de Alfonso III*, Textos Medievales 3 (Valencia: Editorial Anubar, 1971), pp. 12, 14–15.

[172]*Crónica de Alfonso III*, p. 22.

[173]*Crónica de Alfonso III*, pp. 22–25.

[174]These are the *Continuatio Byzantia Arabica* (741) and the *Continuatio Hispanica* (754), both in Theodore Mommsen, ed., *Monumenta Germaniae historica: Auctores antiquissimae* (Berlin: Weidmann, 1894), 11:323–68.

of the bishoprics.[175] In 1236 the *Chronicon mundi* by Lucas, bishop of Túy, revises the *Historia* by adding that Paul, whom Julian had treated as a Gothic leader, *"erat de Græcorum nobili natione"* (*"was from the noble nation of the Greeks"*).[176] The same position is taken in Rodrigo Ximénez de Rada's *De rebus Hispaniae* (1243), which, in addition, incorporates other material not found in Lucas.[177] The *Estoria de España*, compiled under the direction of Alfonso X in the second half of the same century, draws on these as well as other sources for its discussion of Bamba.[178] Used by Lope in the 1541 edition of Florián de Ocampo entitled *Cronica de España*, it includes not one but two Islamic attacks on Spain.[179]

Most important, Diego Rodríguez de Almela's *Valerio* (1487) offers an entirely different version of Bamba's election. Unable to agree on the succession, the Goths ask the pope to decide. His prayer for guidance is answered by a divine command to choose Bamba, now a young peasant rather than the elderly aristocrat he was in prior sources. Additional miracles confirm his identity; he is graced with a wife, a religious temperament, and, even after his coronation, a love of poverty; and his murder is seen as a consequence of the sins of the Goths.[180] Lope took all this and more from Rodríguez de Almela, borrowing some felicitous phrases from a late-sixteenth-century *romance* based on the *Valerio*,[181] which during the same period also influenced Iulian del Castillo's *Historia de los reyes Godos*,[182] another possible source. Although the play may get some details that go back to the early Latin documents from still a third work composed in the reign of Philip II, Ambrosio de Morales's continuation of the *Corónica general de España*, it eschews Morales's critical use of the sources.[183]

---

[175]Menéndez y Pelayo, observaciones preliminares, p. 12.

[176]Lucas of Túy, *Eadem Historia*, in *PL*, 96 col. 768, par. 7. It is conceivable, though doubtful, that Paul was a Roman rather than a Goth. (See Thompson, p. 226.) He could not have been a Greek.

[177]Rodericus Ximenius de Rada, *Historia de rebus Hispaniae*, in *Opera*, ed. Mª. Desamparados Cabanes Pecourt, facsimile of the 1793 ed. (Valencia: Editorial Anubar, 1968), book 2, chap. 22, pp. 45–46; book 3, chap. 2, p. 48; book 3, chap. 9, pp. 56–57; book 3, chap. 12, pp. 58–59.

[178]A. D. Deyermond, *The Middle Ages*, vol. 1 of *A Literary History of Spain*, gen. ed. Jones (London: Ernest Benn, 1971), pp. 82–90.

[179]Florián de Ocampo, *Las quatro partes enteras dela Cronica de España* (Zamora, 1541), sigs. cxciii[r], cxcv[v].

[180]Diego Rodríguez de Almela, *Valerio de las historias de la Sagrada Escritura y de los hechos de España*, ed. Don Juan Antonio Moreno (Madrid: For Don Blas Román, 1793), pp. 101–4, 144–45, 301–2. This is the eighth edition of the work (Menéndez y Pelayo, observaciones preliminares, p. 13).

[181]Menéndez y Pelayo, observaciones preliminares, pp. 15–16.

[182]Iulian del Castillo, *Historia de los reyes Godos* (Burgos, 1582), sigs. G1[v]–G3[v].

[183]Ambrosio de Morales, *Corónica general de España* (Madrid: Don Benito Cano, 1791), 6:211–304.

Whatever unified meaning some of the original narratives of Bamba's reign may possess, the elaborated versions that reached Lope are incoherent. What relation, for instance, is there between the king's class background and either the Goths' inability to agree upon a successor to Recisundo or the peasant's subsequent experiences in power? What is the link between Paul's rebellion and the Islamic invasion? What connects the supernatural circumstances of Bamba's election to his piety and to his division of the bishoprics? Why was he poisoned? Does his life have any bearing on the significance of the Spanish past or present? These are some of the questions that, as a practicing dramatist, Lope had to answer. He attempted to solve his problems by conceiving of Bamba's reign as a tragic class conflict set against the larger providential pattern of Spanish history.

Most of the plot turns, causally as well as thematically, on the antithesis and interaction between peasant and lord. In Camos's *Microcosmia*, an attack on "labradores" ("husbandmen") by one speaker is effectively answered by the next.[184] Lope's procedure may be seen as a more extreme and socially committed version of this dialectical strategy. Contempt for Bamba is not merely one-sided; it is voiced exclusively by noblemen who have already revealed their flaws and whose class condescension only blackens them even further. Alternating, contrasting scenes repeatedly demonstrate Bamba's moral, political, and military superiority to an array of aristocrats, whose continuing opposition, however, ultimately proves decisive. Consistently in the opening act and intermittently thereafter, Bamba and, more generally, Lope compare the court unfavorably with the country.[185] In *The Merchant of Venice* the basis of opposition to the dominant ideology is popular and bourgeois, in *Edward II* it is individualist, and in *El mercader amante* it is regionalist. *Bamba* offers an early example of the agrarian perspective, later to become the most potent vehicle of independent expression in the *comedia*. Camos praises peasants for living "apartados de ambicion y de pretensiones del cortesano" ("secluded from ambition and the pretensions of the courtier"), while adding, "A Saul con ser Rey, dizen las letras sagradas, que andaua tras los bueyes" ("Holy Scripture says that Saul, on becoming king, was walking behind oxen")[186]—the very activity by which the Gothic leaders recognize Bamba. But ironically, precisely because of his own specifically peasant virtues and the complementary deficiencies of an egotistical aristocracy in crisis, Bamba is the only suitable replacement for Recisundo and must accordingly forsake his farm and village. The central social distinction is then naturally extended by pre-

[184]Camos, sigs. 001$^r$–005$^v$.
[185]Salomon, pp. 224, 310–11, 322–35, 345, 368.
[186]Camos, sigs. 005$^r$, 003$^r$.

[243

senting the naive, often humorous reactions of Bamba and his wife to the unfamiliar world of the urban nobility.

The distinction becomes a genuine conflict only with the Arab attack, an incident about which the historical sources are extremely terse. Lope utilizes a number of strategies to develop and integrate this material. First, Alicán, the Islamic king, is foolishly emboldened by Paulo to undertake his campaign against the Goths by the knowledge that Spain is ruled by a *villano*. Bamba has little difficulty in defeating Alicán and dispelling his enemy's class illusions—"¡Aguarda, villano!" ("Wait, peasant [or villain]!") are his first, resonant words to the invading king (2, p. 323)—but he betrays his own political inexperience by his excessively generous treatment of Paulo. The Grecian captive in this way connects the two major military episodes of the play, unrelated in all the sources, with the result that the causal logic of the plot is greatly strengthened. The easily disgruntled Gothic aristocracy resents being passed over for a foreign favorite and at the same time recalls the ignominy of owing feudal allegiance to a peasant. This latter sentiment proves contagious: it is the animating principle of the northern rebellion. Because Paulo is nobly born, he proves an acceptable alternative to Bamba from the point of view both of the rebels and of the very courtiers who had previously resented his privileged position with the king. As far as the aristocrats go, this change of loyalty, an obvious violation of character consistency, makes no political sense. For that very reason, however, it is a sign of the controlling ideological intention of the play.

Meanwhile, Bamba is bogged down in the daily business of monarchy, effectively managing affairs of state, mercifully administering justice, and always keeping in mind his roots. Though he of course reveals no traits in common with the aristocrats by whom he is surrounded, neither does he anticipate the heroic ideal of the nobility as it develops on the seventeenth-century stage. He instead displays a rounded humanity inextricable, in this play at least, from the class of his origin. News of Paulo's treachery allows Lope to demonstrate the military superiority of his peasant hero to a dissolute, decadent aristocracy. By now, however, Bamba has learned that he must temper his instinctive mercifulness with a commitment to justice necessitated by the political exigencies of monarchical rule.[187] Against his own feelings, the king orders the execution of Paulo and his coconspirators, a sentence found nowhere in the sources and in fact explicitly repudiated by them. This is not Lope's only reworking of the history of this incident. As all the chronicles report, the rebellion actually occurred soon after Bamba's coronation and well before the Arab attack, real or imaginary. By instead placing it at the end

[187]Bunn, p. 235, argues that *Bamba* fundamentally explores the idea of kingship.

of the reign, Lope makes it the climax of his drama and as such a clear indication that the crucial problem of Gothic Spain was not the external threat of Islamic invasion, but the internal failure of the aristocracy.

The conclusion of the play emphasizes this point by an equally pervasive transformation of the sources. When leaving to fight Paulo, Bamba must entrust political control to the aristocracy, specifically designating Ervigio to govern in his absence. Ervigio's poisoning of the monarch on his triumphant return thus constitutes a culminating act of betrayal by the ruling class. Lope underscores the tragic implications of the deed in two other ways. Ervigio's reliance on Moorish aid indicates the victory of personal, aristocratic ambition over national concern, in a manner that precisely foreshadows the legendary account of the fall of Spain to Islam soon after. Vulnerability to foreign invasion depends on prior internal collapse. And collapse seems all the more imminent because Bamba dies from the poision, rather than merely falling temporarily ill as he does in the sources. Here, even more than in the fate of Paulo, Lope's insistence on death contributes to the somber mood of the ending. The accession of Ervigio at the close of *Bamba* appropriately places in power a man who has amply demonstrated that he is the social, moral, and political antithesis of his murdered predecessor. The class conflict that informs the play and leads to so potent a critique of the nobility represents, on the one hand, an impossibly anachronistic imposition on history. On the other, it is an imaginatively plausible explanation of the decline of Gothic Spain, a society militarily dependent on a slave population that was increasingly escaping the control of the dominant class.[188] This dual significance, past and present, suggests the seriousness of the play.

What technical means were available to Lope for the dramatization of a social conflict in which the moral advantage lies entirely with the peasant? He was able to draw on the multiple resources of the public theatrical tradition and thus to achieve a range of reference that characterizes *The Merchant of Venice* but not *El mercader amante* or *Edward II*. The synthesis of learned and popular embodied in the peasant-king finds its most important linguistic and theatrical analogue in the functioning of the play's polymetric system.[189] This system does not always have a directly sociological import. A new verse form often merely denotes a change of scene and thus works in much the same fashion as do the soliloquies in Aguilar's comedy. For most of the play, nearly every time the stage is cleared a different strophe is employed; thereafter, this principle is adhered to about half the time. Metrical variation occurs rather

---

[188]Thompson, pp. 262–73, 317–19.
[189]For descriptions of late-sixteenth-century metrical practice in Lope, his predecessors, and his contemporaries, see Morley, "Strophes," pp. 519–31; Bruerton, "Versificación," pp. 337–64.

frequently within the individual scene as well, where it has much the same effect. The shift, in *Bamba* commonly from *redondilla* to *romance*, introduces a new character or alters the mood or both.

But the versification of the play also has a crucial social significance, one that is latent, moreover, in the very structure of the polymetric system of the *comedia*. An initial distinction may be made between those verse forms based on hendecasyllables (*canción*, *tercetos*, *soneto*, *sueltos*, and *octavas reales*), and those employing octosyllables (*quintillas*, *romance*, and especially *redondillas*). The former, borrowed from Italian Renaissance poetry, are learned; the latter, of domestic vintage, are medieval and popular. The situation is thus roughly parallel to the contrast between pentameters and prose on the Elizabethan stage. *Sueltos* can be viewed as a kind of blank verse, and the epic quality of the English meter is duplicated in the *octava real*. Analogies also exist between the indigenous Spanish strophes and popular British prose, but there is no direct correlation in *Bamba* between downstage monologue and the language of the speaker. The several short soliloquies in the play, all delivered by Bamba or Ervigio, are indifferently in native or Italianate meters. It is also true, of course, that poetry is not prose and that most of the verse in *Bamba*, whether popular or learned, is both stanzaic and lyrical. On the other hand, Lope does not exploit lyrical possibilities here as successfully as he does in many other plays, while in Shakespeare's work blank verse can become an effective vehicle of lyricism.

Such qualifications and complications notwithstanding, the alternation between Spanish and Italianate meters in *Bamba* is generally class based. When the hero and his wife first appear, they converse in *quintillas*. The immediately following scene, composed in *sueltos*, depicts the triumphal return from war of Teófilo, a general and aristocrat. The effect of the juxtaposition is particularly striking if the intervening stage directions are suppressed:

> *Sancha.* Yo voy: mil bienes publica
> de vos la ribera y prado.
> *Teófilo.* Cesen las cajas y la dulce pompa
> que vienen celebrando mis victorias.

(*Sancha.* I go: the riverbank and field / proclaim a thousand good things about you. / *Teófilo.* Let cease the drums and the sweet pomp / that come celebrating my victories. [1, p. 301])[190]

Soon after, the movement is reversed. The courtiers' decision to have the pope determine the succession, dramatized in *tercetos*, precedes Bam-

[190]The stage directions also contribute to the contrast. Bamba and Sancha appear "*vestidos de villanos*" ("*dressed as peasants*"); Teófilo enters equipped "*con un bastón de general*" ("*with a general's staff*": 1, pp. 300, 301).

ba's apostrophe to the crown in *quintillas* (1, p. 305). And at the end of
the act, *redondillas* give way to *sueltos* as the scene shifts from a peasant
baptism to the Gothic nobility's visit to the pope (1, pp. 309–10).

Much of the second *jornada* alternates between Bamba's first experiences as king, in *redondilla* passages, and the invasion of Alicán and
Paulo, rendered in *octavas reales* (2, pp. 314–22). But by then the metrical characterization of Bamba has already begun to change. In his opening appearance of the act, just before the aristocrats inform him of his
new job, his soliloquy takes the form of a *canción*. Moments later, he
reaches the decision to accept the throne in a *soneto*. The versification of
the soliloquy is particularly appropriate. The *canción* was traditionally
used in the pastoral eclogue, and Bamba here echoes the *menosprecio de
corte* theme in general and Horace's *Beatus ille* in particular. More important, throughout this scene the nobility speaks entirely in native strophes, primarily *redondillas*: the social and metrical relations are simultaneously reversed (2, pp. 311–16). In the later part of the play, with the
issue of class slightly muted by the rustic's royal right, no consistent distinction between Bamba and the nobility is maintained.

Before this, however, the social uses of the polymetric system are accompanied and reinforced by other comparable stylistic contrasts. As
Bamba's *canción* suggests, classical allusion is mainly confined to learned
poetic forms. The lines of Sancha and Teófilo quoted above reveal that
peasant syntax in native meters is far more paratactic than aristocratic
speech in Italianate verse. Significantly, Bamba, who from the start is
marked out for better things, usually occupies a linguistic position intermediate between his wife and his courtiers, in this respect verbalizing the
social phenomenon he represents. Within an individual scene, moreover, where characters of all classes tend to employ the same strophes,
syntax often must carry the weight of the social distinction. The following exchange between a genteel *caminante* and his self-conscious peasant
interlocutor, which turns on that favorite popular clerical hero, Saint
Martin,[191] illustrates the point:

> *Caminante.* Un Martín de vos no escapa,
> con que el pobre se remedia,
> aunque él dió sola la media,
> y vos dais toda la capa.
> *Cardencho.* Muy retórico sois vos.

(*Traveler.* A Martin does not escape from you, / by whom the poor person
remedies himself, / although he gave only half, / you give the whole cloak. /
*Cardencho.* You're very rhetorical. [1, p. 308])

[191]Burke, p. 155.

As both Cardencho's unceremonious reply and the entire action of the play suggest, linguistically and metrically based social differentiation is not necessarily tantamount to the conservatism of Renaissance aesthetic decorum. More generally, the range and flexibility of the language and versification of *Bamba* contribute to a new verisimilitude in the adaptation of word to character and action.

In his major theoretical discussion and defense of his dramatic practice, the *Arte nuevo de hacer comedias en este tiempo* (pub. 1609), Lope briefly explains the proper uses of most of the verse forms found in *Bamba*. Although his recommedations are largely irrelevant to this play, his insistence that "Las relaciones piden los romances" ("Stories demand *romances*") is strictly applicable in almost every instance.[192] The *romance* passages are usually third-person narratives of events in the recent past or in the future, delivered by characters who come on stage for no other reason than to present their information. What relation can this procedure have to popular dramaturgy? At first sight, none at all. It seems the antithesis of the English downstage monologue, since it so obviously depends upon the presence not of the public theater spectators, but of an internal, fictional audience. Yet it has genuine affinities with Shakespeare's technique in one important respect. Although the report in *romances* appears to be called forth naturally and logically by the dramatic situation, this show of verisimilitude is something of an illusion.

Since the switch to *romances* is Lope's only regular means of metrical variation within a scene, the verse form conveys a sense of change, of interruption. In act 2, when Bamba asks how he came to be chosen king, Atanagildo replies:

> En el tiempo de los godos,
> que no había Rey en Castilla,
> cada cual quiere ser Rey
> aunque le cueste la vida.

(In the time of the Goths, / there was no king in Castile, / each one wants to be king/ although it might cost him his life. [2, p. 313])

This passage, based on the late-sixteenth-century *romance* mentioned earlier, has more than one peculiarity. Atanagildo is among the nobles who contended for the throne, yet he refers to himself here in the third person and continues to do so throughout the first twenty lines of his tale. The events he recounts have all taken place in the previous year or

---

[192]Lope, *Arte nuevo de hacer comedias en este tiempo*, ed. Juana de José Prades (Madrid: Consejo Superior de Investigaciones Científicas, 1971), p. 297, line 309. This text is based on the edition of 1613.

so, yet the first two lines locate them in the distant past, in the age of the Goths, as if the present moment were no longer a part of that age. The *romance* is thus adapted neither to the speaker nor to the occasion. In act 3, Bamba tells Atanarico that he would like to know how the bishoprics are to be divided. Atanarico accordingly recites a first-person proclamation to that effect, ostensibly composed by "yo, Bamba, Rey de la España" ("I, Bamba, king of Spain": 3, p. 331). Hence, either Bamba was aware of the contents of Atanarico's speech beforehand, or he had little to do with what for Lope was one of the glorious moments of his reign. Neither possibility makes good dramatic sense.

In general, then, the *romances* in *Bamba* have the effect of set pieces. They are not comparable to the English play within the play, since the fictional audience has no consciousness of itself as an audience or of the speaker as a performer. But the *romance* narratives evoke the poet-audience relationship of the medieval popular ballad tradition. The apparent awkwardness in the *romances* of *Bamba* largely disappears if it is understood that the primary auditors for these speeches are not, as is usually the case, the dramatis personae but the real people in attendance at the public theatre, who for once hear, rather than overhear, what is going on onstage. Or one might say that the fictional characters temporarily adopt the perspective of the late-sixteenth-century audience.[193] For better or worse, the subject matter of the *romances*—the miracle of Ildefonso, the manner of Bamba's election, the division of the bishoprics, and the prediction of the fall of the peninsula to Islam and of the subsequent Christian Reconquest—reproduces and reinforces the popular national culture of Renaissance Spain, fostering a certain kind of historical consciousness even where the events are ostensibly set in the future.

These, then, are some of the ways the polymetric system enables Lope to introduce a crucial popular dimension into material derived from a predominantly Latin, and hence learned, tradition.[194] The content of the *romances* suggests, however, that an explanation based exclusively on class cannot adequately account for the play. Christian themes, and especially the connection between the workings of providence and the course of national history, have much to do with the meaning of *Bamba*. It is true that the age consistently connected religion and rusticity,[195]

[193]Morley and Bruerton, *Cronología de las comedias de Lope de Vega: Con un examen de las atribuciones dudosas, basado todo ello en un estudio de su versificación estrófica*, rev. ed., trans. María Rosa Cartes (Madrid: Gredos, 1968), pp. 117–39, discuss the evolution of Lope's use of the *romance*. In his later plays, Lope adapted the *romance* to a wider range of purposes than those discussed here. *Bamba*, 3, pp. 334, 340–42, provides early instances of this extension of use.

[194]Menéndez y Pelayo, observaciones preliminares, p. 11, says that the legend of Bamba was "nada popular en su formación" ("not at all popular in its formation").

[195]Salomon, pp. 404–18, discusses this link. His remarks on *Bamba* appear on pp. 409, 411–13.

that Bamba is a Christlike martyr, an unheeded model for a fallen aristocracy,[196] and that in this respect the influence of the church on the Spanish theater fostered a critical distance from the dominant ideology. Yet the numerous Christian motifs in the play cannot all be reduced to this paradigm.

Instead, they function as a kind of glue, binding together thematically, if not causally or logically, the otherwise disparate and unrelated incidents of the plot. They provide, first of all, a religious sanction for the anomaly of a peasant king. Bamba is justified not only by his piety and his Christian works, but also by the supernatural circumstances of his election. He assumes an honored place in the providential history of the nation by his defeat of an Arab attack, and the final events of his life are inextricable from the subsequent lengthy Reconquest of Spain. It is of course symbolically appropriate that a Moor provides Ervigio with the poison he uses to kill Bamba. Soon after, the dying king, though aware of the identity of his murderer, nonetheless submits to divine will and names Ervigio to succeed him. These concluding moments also announce both the coming Islamic domination of Spain and the string of Christian victories against the intruders, partly anticipated by Bamba and stretching from Pelayo to Philip II. Ultimately, the life and death of Bamba take their place in a larger historical and transcendental pattern that incorporates the fall of the Goths and culminates in the triumph of the Habsburgs. In this context the first scene of the play, structurally superfluous to the succeeding action, acquires its purpose. In it, Recisundo prepares to crush a heresy that parallels sixteenth-century Protestant beliefs and that the miracle of Ildefonso tends to disprove.[197] More generally, the insistently Christian opening offers, if not a motive for the plot, then at least a means of comprehending and accepting it.

What is the relation between these more-or-less overt intentions and the less conscious ideologies that shape the play and are produced by it? *Edward II* calls the bluff of the inherently aristocratic political focus of the national history play. *Bamba* is the opposite, its pivotal class conflict notwithstanding. The king's involvement in the petty day-to-day affairs of his country, for instance, is a flattering allusion to the bureaucratic obsessions of Philip II. More important, the basic social issues of the play are fraudulently presented. The felt need both to flee and to attend the court was a genuine contradiction, but one confined to the historical experience of a single class, the aristocracy. Transferring the dilemma to the peasantry simply obscures this fact. At the same time and despite the obvious sympathies of the dramatist, it mystifies the condition of the

---

[196]Bunn, pp. 228–29, 232.
[197]Bunn, pp. 236, 225, 221, 207–8.

lower class. Most of the peasants of the play are at one time or another treated by Lope with genteel condescension. More important, the conflict between lord and peasant is relegated to the realm of politics, where, furthermore, the peasant is metamorphosed into a king. The real roots of antagonism in the struggle over production are consequently ignored. In this respect Lope's propeasant bias expresses and serves the interests of the nobility.[198]

Yet to a considerable extent this is not the case. The peasant perspective does function as a critique of the aristocracy. If, further, the peasantry's real struggles are badly distorted, the battle between class and state is not. Unlike interclass oppositions, intraclass conflict can be plausibly rendered without going beyond the bounds of the dominant ideology and thus of the national history play. Nonetheless, here the play symptomatically betrays its ideological impasse, most notably in the structural flaws mentioned at the outset. For, in fact, the relationship between conflict and Christianity, or between history and providence, is uneasy at best. Lope wants his tragedy and his redemptive pattern too. The first is comfortably carried by the plot, whether Bamba is viewed as a peasant victim of a social conflict or as a royal victim of a political one. Either way, the play ends in a disaster for which the ruling class as a whole is to blame: from this point of view Lope's hortatory purpose seems clear. The transcendent significance of the events, on the other hand, is harder to discern. If Bamba's reign bears some analogy to Lope's own time, then the meanings for the present are grim indeed. If it is seen as part of some larger process leading to the felicities of the late sixteenth century, its specific function in that process remains mysterious. Bamba's efforts are futile, his accomplishments wasted. His life and death plausibly point nowhere but to the coming defeat. The only tragic setbacks that could reasonably be seen in relation to an overarching historical movement are those temporary ones that occurred in the context of the Reconquest, following the almost total eradication of Visigothic Spain by the Islamic invaders.

The structurally awkward or intrusive religious episodes are an attempt to overcome the problem, or at least to disguise the difficulty, of unusually inappropriate historical material. The first scene is an obvious and extreme instance of this effort. Yet Lope did not have to compose a play on the subject. That he did so suggests his deeply ambivalent attitude toward the issues raised in *Bamba*. This is especially evident at the end of the play, where he in a sense presents two competing, prophetic conclusions. The first, delivered by the Moorish magician to Ervigio, is

---

[198]Salomon, passim, is particularly effective at stressing the aristocratic ends served by idealizations of the peasantry.

conventionally providential. It predicts the Islamic conquest of Spain but continues the narrative forward to the contemporary exploits of Philip II. The second is almost the opposite. The angel tells the sleeping Bamba no more than that he will die and that Spain will fall. The king then dreams that he is defeating the Moors, only to awake, first, to the illusion of his victory and, second, to the reality of his death. One version is triumphant; the other, at best, resigned. This double vision is ultimately a product of the central position of the Reconquest in Spanish history and of its even more dominant role in Spanish ideology. An attempt to view the Visigothic era in these terms might well produce problems, however. Since the events in *Bamba* precede the Islamic victory, the enemy must fundamentally be within. This is the source of the play's ambivalent conclusion and the reason the work is an anomaly, its relationship to providential history tenuous, and its plot essentially tragic. Such a vision may have become available to Lope in the late 1590s because of the temporary political and economic collapse of Spain following two decades of overextension. The moment of uncertainty was at any rate brief. In the peasant dramas of the early seventeenth century, the popular materials of *Bamba* are given a more pervasive, profound, and radical treatment, but at the expense of jettisoning the conflicted conclusion of the atypical, earlier, and in a sense prophetic play: less than half a century later, aristocratic rebellion against the crown began the final decomposition of the Habsburg state.

## CONCLUSION

A synoptic view of the period discloses certain discontinuities. The first is temporal: in both countries the years between 1575 and 1600 can be divided almost right down the middle. The two main genres discussed in this chapter characterize only the second half of the era. Judging from the scanty dramatic remains, the first half may have been dominated by tragedy in Spain and the morality and romance in England. Although these early forms and others that were cultivated at the time influenced later developments, such a split demands explanation. It probably bears witness to a chronological lag of drama behind theater, to the gradual adaptation of aesthetics to changed material conditions, and to the belated recognition by actors and playwrights of the possibilities of a new theatrical mode of production. The transition seems to have been particularly difficult in serious drama. The national history play had small precedent, marked more of a break with the past than did romantic comedy, was uniquely rooted in the public theater as romantic comedy was not, and hence was harder to invent. Works by Marlowe and

Kyd precede by a few years Shakespeare's first experiments with English historical drama. In Spain, Lope's centrality is far less ambiguous in the creation of the national history play than in the formation of romantic comedy. With one early exception, moreover, it is only in the late 1590s that he begins to discover his material in Spain's past.[199]

These temporal and generic distinctions of the period also suggest the differences between the countries. The English first of all possessed a richer popular theatrical tradition than did the Spanish. The new departures in the second half of this period entailed a fresh infusion of classicism in England but, significantly enough, a retreat from learned models in Spain. The commanding position of London, unequaled by any peninsular city, also favored the English theater most clearly in the development of the national history play. Even one of the staunchest defenders of Valencia's influence in shaping the *comedia* admits that the theater in that city lacked a national stamp.[200] Finally, England's social and ideological matrix seems to have been more conducive to complex theater than Spain's. Although causality of this kind is particularly difficult to prove, it may have been unusually important. The most extraordinary moments of the English stage generally came in the early seventeenth century, after its initial lead had in all other respects disappeared.

It would nonetheless be a mistake to ignore the overall coherence of the drama composed for the late-sixteenth-century public theater. Its primary genres are vehicles for portraying and examining the adaptation of the aristocracy to the new conditions of its supremacy. Although the movement toward reconciliation in most of the plays, often accompanied by providential sanctions, ratifies this process of adaptation, the approval is critically qualified by the workings of the popular tradition. This formal-ideological complex did not long remain unmodified. Since the changes brought by the new century are the subject of the next chapter, here it is necessary to note only that the transition was not always smooth. Shakespeare's closest sixteenth-century approximation to his late romances is probably *The Comedy of Errors* (1592); his strongest anticipation of his problem comedies is *The Merchant of Venice*. Yet his final romantic comedies are probably *Much Ado about Nothing*, *As You Like It*, and *Twelfth Night*. Similarly, the culmination of Shakespeare's serious drama of the period occurs in *1 and 2 Henry IV* and in *Henry V*, whereas his more tragic plays date from 1595 or before. Only as the century approached its end did Shakespeare fulfill the potential of the forms he had been practicing, a fulfillment that did not point directly toward his later achievement.

[199]Bunn, pp. xi–xii.
[200]Weiger, p. 132.

In Spain, the unusual prominence of tragedy in Lope's work of the late 1590s—*El marqués de Mantua* and *La imperial de Otón*, as well as *Bamba*—does not indicate the future direction of the *comedia*. In general, late-sixteenth-century Spanish drama retains a flexibility, even looseness, uncharacteristic of the works performed in the *corrales* after 1600. The prevalent definitions of the *comedia* accordingly do justice to these early plays less often than to their more famous successors.[201] In different ways, then, both English and Spanish drama of the seventeenth century represented new departures. The earlier plays in each country depended on a similar fragile synthesis that they in turn scrutinized and, with some misgivings, reinforced. New conditions not only produced a different drama, but also changed relationships among drama, theater, and society. Although the basic problems of class remained, they were approached in a fashion that the sixteenth century had scarcely known. Finally, since the course of events was not the same in Spain as in England, the coming decades saw the emergence both of new parallels and of even more pronounced divergences between the plays of the two public theaters.

[201]See A. A. Parker, "The Approach to the Spanish Drama of the Golden Age," *Tulane Drama Review* 4 (1959): 42–59; Arnold Reichenberger, "The Uniqueness of the 'Comedia,'" *Hispanic Review* 27 (1959): 303–16. For the openness of this drama, see Lavonne C. Poteet-Bussard, "Algunas perspectivas sobre la primera época del teatro de Lope de Vega," in *Lope de Vega*, ed. Criado de Val, pp. 341–54.

# 5

# The Crisis of
# the Public Theater

The discussion of the late sixteenth century in the two preceding chapters provided the occasion for developing a number of themes that remain as relevant after 1600 as before. Rather than attempting to demonstrate these unquestioned elements of continuity, the remainder of the book attends instead to matters of change. The present chapter surveys national and theatrical history, primarily in the first half of the seventeenth century, arguing that the absolutist drive toward centralization was largely responsible for gradually undermining the public theater. Here, as in chapters 6 and 7, which treat in roughly chronological fashion the consequences of this development for the drama, the revolts of the middle of the century provide a recurrent point of reference and a fundamental interpretive orientation.

## SOCIETY

In the early seventeenth century both England and Spain entered periods of crisis that culminated, during the 1640s, in aristocratic rebellion against the crown, civil war, and consequently the virtual destruction of absolutism. The age, in other words, reversed the dominant trends of the generation after 1575. This development may also be viewed, however, less as a radical break with the past than as an elevation to preeminence of those subversive tendencies that were present all along, beneath the superficial calm of the absolutist state. The early-seventeenth-century monarchs were forced to live out the secretly troubled legacies of their more illustrious predecessors. Nonetheless, the passage from the old era to the new was marked at least initially by discontinuity. The sixteenth century ended in disaster for Spain. In England the seventeenth century opened with a series of unsuccessful aristocratic plots and conspiracies against the crown. The people at the top changed as well. Philip III became king on the death of his father in 1598; James I succeeded Elizabeth in 1603. The following year the two countries reached a peace settlement that inaugurated for each a much-needed period of quieter foreign policy. At home, both monarchs fostered an inflation of honors and an extravagance at court unknown in the reigns of their predecessors. Such policies do not really give any indication why the two crowns soon faced determined opposition, however. In England as in Spain, profound economic problems lay behind the political eruptions of midcentury. The complex chain of causality differed in the two nations, but in both it led to aristocratic revolt against the state—the defining feature of the general crisis of the seventeenth century.[1]

The early Stuart monarchs inherited from the Tudor line both irreducible feudal premises and intractable conflict with an increasingly capitalist nation. Earlier economic trends—the commercialization of agriculture, the growth of manufacturing, and the increase of domestic and foreign trade—all accelerated after 1600, as England embarked on its great colonialist adventure. So too did the corresponding social changes —the rise of the gentry, the merchants, and the common lawyers and the simultaneous decline of the crown, the peerage, and the clergy.[2] "No Bishop, no King, no nobility," King James supposedly remarked,[3] a position not only borne out by the events of the Civil War, but also indicative of the difficulties confronting any English monarch who pursued the centralizing policies inherent in absolutism. More specifically, without an adequate fiscal base the crown possessed no remedy for its traditional lack of an integrated nationwide administrative apparatus or sizable armed forces, and no simple means of establishing religious unity. Yet it could not raise taxes unless it obtained the consent of the gentry-dominated House of Commons. And that body, though the class it represented was grossly underassessed, was not eager to finance out of its own pocket programs that were designed to curb its power.[4]

[1]Perry Anderson, *Lineages of the Absolutist State* (London: NLB, 1974), pp. 53–55, revising the earlier proposals by E. J. Hobsbawm, "The Crisis of the Seventeenth Century," and H. R. Trevor-Roper, "The General Crisis of the Seventeenth Century," both in *Crisis in Europe, 1560–1660: Essays from "Past and Present"*, ed. Trevor Aston (London: Routledge and Kegan Paul, 1965), pp. 5–58 and 59–95, respectively. For graphic evidence, see the map in Geoffrey Parker, *Europe in Crisis, 1598–1648* (Ithaca, N.Y.: Cornell University Press, 1979), p. 18.
[2]R. H. Tawney, "The Rise of the Gentry, 1558–1640," in *Essays in Economic History*, ed. E. M. Carus-Wilson, vol. 1 (London: Edward Arnold, 1954), pp. 192, 199; Christopher Hill, *The Century of Revolution, 1603–1714* (New York: Norton, 1966), pp. 15–42; Lawrence Stone, *The Crisis of the Aristocracy, 1558–1641* (Oxford: Clarendon Press, 1965), pp. 139, 162–64, 269; idem, *The Causes of the English Revolution, 1529–1642* (New York: Harper and Row, 1972), pp. 68, 71–72.
[3]Quoted in Hill, *Century of Revolution*, p. 78.
[4]Stone, *Causes*, p. 62.

The Stuarts had a limited number of other options open to them, however, all of which they pursued energetically. Perhaps the most important of these was pacifism. Although James made peace after coming to the throne, he had to sell off over three-quarters of a million pounds worth of crown lands to liquidate the war debt run up by Elizabeth. The international conflicts of the late 1620s cost Charles almost as much in royal capital. When Parliament put the remainder of the monarchical estate on the market in 1649, it brought in under two million pounds. In peacetime, on the other hand, the state could make ends meet even without having to rely on taxes voted by Commons. The nonexpansionist foreign policy of the early Stuarts was thus motivated not by an aversion to imperialism, but by the need to balance the budget and to dispense with Parliament. That body met regularly in the first decade of James's reign, just as it had in the last years of Elizabeth's. But after 1614 the crown called it into session only irregularly and after 1629 not at all, until the onset of the crisis of 1640.[5]

The monarchy could also pursue absolutist consolidation by increasing extraparliamentary revenues. The Stuarts found it far easier to raise money in Ireland, where English arms had finally prevailed in 1603, and in Scotland, which became part of the kingdom with James's accession, than they did in England proper. Charles was particularly successful in that endeavor during his personal rule of the 1630s, during which time he also seems to have attempted to create an army in Ireland that would lie beyond the control of Commons.[6] At home, although the government occasionally resorted to forced loans and taxes, its main expedient was the sale of monopolies, offices, and titles. In the 1620s, with patronage in the hands of the duke of Buckingham, the royal favorite, virtually anything could be bought. But the policy was a general one, and especially in the case of the inflation of honors, it represented a reversal of Elizabethan practice. Finally, during the 1630s Charles intensified these procedures by reviving a series of obsolete feudal dues—among them the rights of wardship, purveyance, knighthood fines, and ship money—in order to supplement his income.[7]

It would be a mistake, however, to concentrate exclusively on the narrowly financial motives of the Stuarts, as important as these were. Most of the fund-raising methods also served the more general conservative purpose of strengthening absolutism by stabilizing the social structure, building up the higher aristocracy, aligning the crown with the peerage and urban patriciates while excluding the gentry and newer mercantile interests, centralizing the economy, and restricting the growth of capital-

---

[5]Hill, *Century of Revolution*, pp. 47, 72, 315 (Appendix A). See also Stone, *Causes*, p. 92.
[6]Anderson, *Lineages*, pp. 138, 140–41; Hill, *Century of Revolution*, p. 73.
[7]Hill, *Century of Revolution*, pp. 29, 52–53, 69–70; Stone, *Causes*, p. 86; idem, *Crisis*, pp. 65–128; Anderson, *Lineages*, p. 141.

ism. The same goes for the state's promotion of guilds and opposition to enclosures. Again the 1630s, a period of economic, social, political, and religious reaction, marked the systematization of earlier efforts. Charles and his ministers largely succeeded in ruling without Parliament, in refurbishing the hierarchy of the church, and to some extent in controlling the judiciary. But by 1640 their overall administrative and military apparatuses remained inadequate, they had failed to achieve religious conformity, and they had at best retarded, rather than reversed, the country's economic development.[8]

Equally fateful, absolutist dynamism generated an increasingly vocal, organized, and united opposition. Conflict arose from the first year of James's reign and soon ranged over such issues as economic policy, international trade, finance, court extravagance and corruption, diplomacy, religious ritual, and the legal system. The period from 1610 to 1614 represents something of a turning point. The first of these years saw the failure of the Great Contract, a compromise that would have abolished the monarchy's feudal economic prerogatives in return for an annual grant from Parliament of a fixed sum. By then any chance of a national church had also disappeared. In both 1610 and 1614 the king dissolved Parliament without receiving the supplies he wanted. And in the latter year the monarchy's disastrous intervention in the economy via the Cokayne Project helped end a decade of prosperity and inaugurate a prolonged depression that lasted until midcentury. When Commons, by then the central institution in the struggle against the crown, met again in the 1620s, it tended to view specific local issues in broader, constitutional terms. Well before 1640, a crown that combined High Church Anglicanism or even Catholicism with prerogative courts, restrictive economic regulation, and arbitrary exercise of power found itself dangerously isolated against a coalition of Puritan ministers, common lawyers, free traders, and, most important of all, the gentry both in Commons and in the country.[9]

For in the decades of the midcentury, primarily this section of the ruling class provided the leadership of the revolution. Despite the complex political alliances and conflicts of the period, the top 2 percent of the population never lost control of the nation.[10] And despite the multiple and at times contradictory motives that led the gentry to rebel, one of its most conscious and significant accomplishments was to remove the remaining feudal barriers to capitalist development in the country and the

[8]Stone, *Causes*, pp. 117–35; Anderson, *Lineages*, p. 140; Hill, *Century of Revolution*, pp. 72–73.
[9]Stone, *Causes*, pp. 83, 92–95; Hill, *Century of Revolution*, pp. 10, 35–37, 49–51, 80, 321 (Appendix D); Anderson, *Lineages*, p. 138.
[10]Stone, *Crisis*, p. 51.

city and to prevent any new ones from being erected. Lawrence Stone, a historian with only limited sympathy for this interpretation, nonetheless concedes: "Many things were restored at the Restoration, but it is surely significant that among those which were not were feudal tenures, restraints upon enclosure of land, such monopolies and economic controls as did not suit the convenience of influential interest groups, and a foreign policy which gave little weight to commerical objectives."[11] The significance of a revolution lies less in its intentions than in its effects. The English Civil War was a bourgeois revolution not because of the class of the revolutionists, but because of the class of its beneficiaries.[12]

The capitalist landlords, together with their urban analogues and allies, were not the only forces of change in the period, however. The Scottish invasion of England in 1640 and the Irish rebellion of the following year set off the sequence of events that resulted in the victory of Commons over the crown. These uprisings on the periphery revealed the crucial vulnerability of English absolutism. Lacking an army, Charles could no longer rule without Parliament: civil war broke out over the question of who should control the military.[13]

The final social variable was the vast mass of the population. Real wages had fallen precipitously at the turn of the century and remained low. In response to particularly hard times, riots broke out during 1596 and 1607 and again between 1628 and 1631. More generally, it is possible to catch fleeting glimpses of popular restiveness or radicalism, whether social, political, economic, or religious, throughout the early seventeenth century.[14] But various historians have argued that, for a number of reasons, among them the growing internal stratification of the class, peasant militance was on the wane in these years. As a result, the aristocracy may have gained confidence in the social stability of the countryside, leaving it with no interest in a standing army and reducing the risk that it ran in breaking with the crown.[15] On the other hand, a recent study has argued for an increase in both peasant and craftsman rebelliousness during the reign of Charles I. This popular radicalism may have proved the driving force behind the revolutionary events that followed upon the convening of the Long Parliament in November

[11]Stone, *Causes*, p. 72.

[12]Barrington Moore, Jr., *Social Origins of Dictatorship and Democracy: Lord and Peasant in the Making of the Modern World* (Boston: Beacon, 1966), pp. 17–20, 427.

[13]Stone, *Causes*, pp. 135–38; Anderson, *Lineages*, pp. 141–42.

[14]Hill, *Century of Revolution*, pp. 317–19 (Appendix C); idem, *The World Turned Upside Down: Radical Ideas during the English Revolution* (Harmondsworth, Middlesex: Penguin, 1975), pp. 19–56; idem, "The Many-Headed Monster," in *Change and Continuity in Seventeenth Century England* (Cambridge: Harvard University Press, 1975), pp. 182–92.

[15]Immanuel Wallerstein, *The Modern World-System: Capitalist Agriculture and the Origins of the European World-Economy in the Sixteenth Century* (New York: Academic Press, 1974), pp. 254–56; Anderson, *Lineages*, p. 139; Stone, *Causes*, pp. 76–77.

1640.[16] At the very least, the gentry discovered that it needed the help of the people against the monarchy. Its appeal for support was answered by small freeholders and yeomen in the countryside and by the largely Puritan, often radical tradesmen, petty merchants, shopkeepers, artisans, and apprentices of the towns. In particular, the political intervention of these groups in London proved decisive for the parliamentary cause. But once the lower and middling strata were unleashed, it was not easy to keep them in their place. In the late 1640s, power almost slipped from the hands of the landlords. The Levellers came fairly close to gaining control of the New Model Army before Cromwell subdued them and opened the way for the reunification of the ruling class.[17]

In Spain, too, the seventeenth-century monarchs inherited the basic problems from their predecessors only to exacerbate them. Before 1600 New World imperialism precluded both capitalism and absolutism while helping to finance an imperial strategy in the Old World that was beginning to wreck the Habsburg state. After the turn of the century, deepening agricultural difficulties engendered significant social conflict in the countryside. More important, imperial overextension in Europe forced the crown to attempt a belated centralist solution to its problems, with the not surprising result that the aristocracies of the periphery threw off the Castilian yoke. Many of the same components went into the absolutist crisis in Spain as in England, but their structural and historical significance differed because of the absence of capitalism and radical Protestantism.

Although the pace of events is open to debate, the seventeenth century was unquestionably an age of serious decline for the Spanish economy.[18] In agriculture, contemporary awareness of the problem dates from about 1600. The expulsion of the largely peasant *morisco* (nominally Christian Moor) population between 1609 and 1614 hurt rural production in Aragon and especially in Valencia. Castile, meanwhile, suffered from a loss of overseas markets as its New World empire grew increasingly self-sufficient in the traditional exports of the region, wine and oil.[19] The agricultural depression culminated in the plague of

[16]Brian Manning, *The English People and the English Revolution, 1640–1649* (London: Heinemann, 1976).

[17]Hill, "The Many-Headed Monster," pp. 193–204; idem, *Century of Revolution*, pp. 129–33; Stone, *Causes*, pp. 55, 145.

[18]For the historiographical problems, see Ralph Davis, *The Rise of the Atlantic Economies* (Ithaca, N.Y.: Cornell University Press, 1973), pp. 143–56.

[19]On the timing of the slump, particularly in agriculture, see Fernand Braudel, *The Mediterranean and the Mediterranean World in the Age of Philip II*, trans. Siân Reynolds (London: Collins, 1973), 2:894; Antonio Domínguez Ortiz, *The Golden Age of Spain, 1516–1659*, trans. James Casey (London: Weidenfeld and Nicolson, 1971), pp. 194–95; Noël Salomon, *Recherches sur le thème paysan dans la "comedia" au temps de Lope de Vega* (Bordeaux: Féret, 1965), pp. 197–206, 251. For regional trends, see J. H. Elliott, *Imperial Spain, 1469–1716*

1648–54, but bad harvests also led to a visitation from 1629 to 1631. The peasantry, which constituted the overwhelming majority of the 80 percent of Spain's population living in the country, naturally bore the brunt of this collapse. But perhaps owing to the strength of the state in Castile, the widespread discontent of the class rarely took the form of organized resistance.[20]

The notable exceptions to this rule were the middling-to-wealthy peasant proprietors of Castile, who were able to take advantage of the agricultural crisis to consolidate their holdings at the expense of the majority of the rural population. But they also opposed the aristocracy, attempting, for instance, to wrest village political control from the local *hidalgos*. Similarly, the *villanos ricos*, as these peasants were called, sought village juridical autonomy from the small, unusually exploitative landlords common in the region. Such a movement usually meant in practice the transfer of allegiance to a more powerful but less demanding *señor* or, ideally, to the crown itself. Underlying these struggles was a desire to escape from the peasantry altogether. But in the social conditions of Castile, as opposed to those of England, this aspiration represented less a sign of revolutionary consciousness than a simple wish for upward mobility within the class hierarchy. Owing to the conditions of the Reconquest, the Castilian peasantry had partially avoided some of the more brutal versions of feudalism prevalent elsewhere on the peninsula. The attitudes of its wealthier members in the early seventeenth century accordingly drew on a medieval egalitarian heritage. More generally, the social and ideological impasse of Spain is suggested by the idealization of the *villanos ricos* in the contemporary campaign to persuade not only the peasantry but also the absentee aristocracy, which had taken up residence in Madrid, to return to the land.[21]

The agricultural problems of Castile, along with the simultaneous industrial decline, limited the tax revenues available to the crown, especially since the government, somewhat like its Jacobean counterpart, could not obtain any contribution from the rich. After 1600, moreover, the flow of American bullion into the royal treasury slowed down: the volume during the 1620s was less than half what it had been as recently

(New York: St. Martin's Press, 1964), pp. 287–88, 299–303; Alvaro Castillo, "La coyuntura de la economía valenciana en los siglos xvi y xvii," *Anuario de Historia Económica y Social* 2 (1969): 239–88; Anderson, *Lineages*, p. 77. "Aragon" refers to the kingdom of Aragon; the "Crown of Aragon" designates a larger entity: Valencia, Catalonia, and the kingdom of Aragon.

[20]Jaime Vicens Vives, *An Economic History of Spain*, in collaboration with Jorge Nadal Oller, trans. Frances M. López-Morillas (Princeton: Princeton University Press, 1969), pp. 413–15; Braudel, 2:704, 738–39; Elliott, pp. 289–90.

[21]Domínguez Ortiz, p. 149; Salomon, pp. 72–74, 97–100, 158–59, 168–69, 270–73, 668–78, 744–45, 748–50, 780–88, 808–10, 860–63, 868–69, 893–97.

as the 1590s. The chronic fiscal crisis of the state, unsolved by the wide-spread sale of offices, led to bankruptcies in 1607 and 1627, as well as to the alternating inflation and deflation of the currency—a recurrent pattern throughout the century. Perhaps the best opportunity for Spain lay in Philip III's relative pacifism, which again has an analogue in English diplomacy of the time. But the opportunity for desperately needed domestic reform was squandered by the king and his corrupt *privado*, or favorite, the duke of Lerma. Unlike Charles I's closing of ranks with the peerage, which was part of a conscious absolutist strategy, the rearistocratization of the highest levels of the state machinery under Lerma was symptomatic of the weakness, even immobility, of the crown. Given the relative absence of a bourgeoisie, it merely accentuated the division of Spain into a two-class society. Similarly, the Twelve Years Truce with the United Provinces, signed in 1609, primarily enabled Holland to take over a growing portion of traditional peninsular trade with America.[22]

The turning point for Habsburg absolutism probably came in the two decades following 1618 or 1621, with the revival of imperialism. As late as 1628 Spain could have extricated itself from its European involvements, serious military reverses began only after 1635, and genuine collapse was a phenomenon of the second half of the century. But the logic of the Spanish state was always to sacrifice domestic economics and politics—capitalism and absolutism—to imperial needs. The onset of the Thirty Years' War in 1618 therefore evoked a predictable response in Madrid. The opening of Philip IV's reign in 1621, coincident with the expiration of the Dutch peace treaty, then determined the course of the monarchy. Under the new *privado*, the count-duke of Olivares, Philip IV's government, like Charles I's, pursued a more aggressive program than had its predecessor.

On the one hand, Olivares's grandiose European strategy led inexorably to conflict with France's refurbished military apparatus and hence to the defeat of Spain.[23] On the other, Olivares realized that the success of his foreign policy depended on the absolutist integration of the Habsburg empire, and especially of the two main peripheral regions of the peninsula, Portugal and the Crown of Aragon. The expulsion of the *moriscos* under Philip III, over the objection of the aristocracies of Valencia and Aragon, merely continued the centralist direction of religious affairs established in the late fifteenth century. In other areas no comparable royal progress had been made. Olivares, however, hoped to equalize the fiscal and military burdens, as well as the benefits, of empire across the breadth of the peninsula. His proposals, detailed in a secret memo-

[22]Elliott, pp. 175, 297–99, 320–21; Domínguez Ortiz, pp. 144–45; Vicens Vives, pp. 446–50, 463; Braudel, pp. 755–56; Anderson, *Lineages*, pp. 76–77.
[23]Elliott, pp. 330, 375; Domínguez Ortiz, pp. 90–97; Anderson, *Lineages*, pp. 78–79.

randum of 1624 and a more moderate public statement of 1626 called the Union of Arms, met overwhelming opposition, especially in the Crown of Aragon. But when a French army invaded Catalonia in 1639, he decided to use a Spanish counterattack there as a means of implementing his plans.[24]

This desperate gamble failed disastrously the following year when the Catalans rebelled. A few months later, the Portuguese took advantage of Castile's preoccupation with its eastern flank to stage a successful revolt of their own. With signs of unrest in Valencia and Aragon, coupled with the Andalusian aristocracy's attempted secession in 1641, Spain faced the dismemberment not only of its European empire, but also of its territorial homeland. Six years later, moreover, Naples and Sicily rose against Habsburg power, and in 1648 the Aragonese plotted to establish an independent kingdom. But with the exception of Portugal, which was permanently lost, Spain recovered all of its possessions by 1652. The reasons for this reversal are perhaps best illustrated by the revolutions of Catalonia and Italy. Both depended on French support, which in the former instance proved oppressive and in the latter insufficient. The outbreak in turn of the Fronde enabled Spain to win back these wayward territories. Aristocractic separatism in France minimized the efficacy of aristocractic separatism within the Habsburg empire. Equally important, in both Catalonia and Italy the rebellion soon spread well beyond the confines and control of the ruling class and thus began to transform aristocractic particularism into its antithesis: social revolution. In the end, the nobility preferred loose control by Madrid to the more authoritarian domination of French absolutism and especially to losing class supremacy altogether.[25]

But the events of the 1640s nonetheless revealed the fatal weakness of Spanish absolutism. Olivares's attempted remedy, coming much too late as it did, proved more catastrophic than inaction. For most of the remainder of the century, the economy continued to plummet, with Castile hit the hardest. Foreign reverses also mounted. By the conclusion of the War of the Spanish Succession, which coincided with the end of the Habsburg line on the peninsula, Spain had lost its entire European empire.[26]

Yet the implications of national evolution were evident over a century earlier. But in the absence of a strong Castilian bourgeoisie, the often sensible programs of the *arbitristas*—the social theorists of the time— never stood a chance. Increasingly as the century progressed, all open

[24]Elliott, pp. 324−29, 335−37, 339.
[25]Elliott, pp. 339−51; Domínguez Ortiz, pp. 98−108; Anderson, *Lineages*, pp. 80−82.
[26]Elliott, pp. 351−73; Domínguez Oritz, pp. 108−11; Vicens Vives, pp. 465−66; Anderson, *Lineages*, p. 82.

ideological roads instead led backward. As in politics, 1620 represents a point of demarcation, after which reformism gave way to escapism. Feudal separatism on the periphery triggered off in the center not a capitalist revolution, as in England, but just more feudal separatism. For those unwilling to abandon monarchical consolidation for aristocratic particularism, the options were even narrower. There was Spain's famous *desengaño*, or disillusion; an increasingly narrow and otherworldly religion in striking contrast not only to contemporary revolutionary English Puritanism, but also to sixteenth-century Spanish Catholicism; or the somewhat earlier and more plausible idealization of the peasantry, combined with an injunction to go back to the land. In the words of Pierre Vilar, "around 1600, on its own soil in Castile, *feudalism entered upon its death struggle without there being anything to replace it.*"[27] Within the common context of the crisis of absolutism in the public theater, the contrasts between English and Spanish drama during the early seventeenth century primarily resulted from the different range of ideological perspectives available in each country.

## THEATER

During the first half of the seventeenth century, absolutist centralization, combined with deepening social conflict, gradually led to the decline of the public theater. A comparative study of this process may help clarify its significance in both England and Spain. Permanent public theaters first opened in London and Madrid during the 1570s. Toward the end of the 1590s, both monarchies closed down the stages—permanently, it seemed at the time. Finally, amid the international crisis of the 1640s, the two governments really did ban the theater for several years. Yet parallels of this sort, as striking and revealing as they are, obscure more fundamental relationships.

A periodization that accounts for the different pace of events in the two countries might instead stress the following analogies: England 1597–1608 and Spain 1598–1621, England 1609–14 and Spain 1622–43, England 1615–19 and Spain 1644–50, and England 1620–42 and Spain 1651–1700. These divisions should be treated tentatively. Not only do the moments of demarcation rarely, if ever, constitute absolute barriers; a rather different chronology could easily be constructed

[27]*Arbitristas*: Vicens Vives, pp. 450–53; Earl J. Hamilton, "The Decline of Spain," in *Essays in Economic History*, ed. Carus-Wilson, 1:215–26; ideological periodization: Pierre Vilar, "The Age of Don Quixote," *New Left Review*, no. 68 (July–August 1971): 59–71, esp. pp. 60, 67–68; *desengaño*: Elliott, pp. 293–95; religion: Domínguez Ortiz, p. 200. The quotation from Vilar appears on p. 66 of his essay.

for each nation and for the comparisons between the stage traditions.[28] For example, the opening years of the seventeenth century are a period of ambiguity in Spain, perhaps because of Philip III's temporary shift of the court from Madrid to Valladolid. The purpose of the dates is simply to suggest the trajectory of the theater, to establish the parallels between England and Spain, to insist in particular that what occupied a century in one country took its course in less than half that time in the other, and to propose some rough temporal correlations between history, theater, and drama. Toward those ends, it is necessary to reverse the priorities of the previous discussion of the public theater, to look less at the artisanal mode of production as it persisted in the seventeenth century than at the forces that undermined it—to focus, in other words, on the propertied classes.

Following the suppression of playing near the end of the 1590s, the public theaters of England and Spain reopened under tighter royal control. In England, between 1598 and 1604 the state narrowed the right to patronize acting companies until, in the latter year, this privilege was restricted to the royal family. The number of professional troupes was correspondingly reduced,[29] although especially outside London the absolutist intention of the policy was partially thwarted.[30] The crown's actions in effect guaranteed the social and financial stability of the actors. A second generation of public theaters ensued—the Globe in 1599, the Fortune in 1600, and the Red Bull in about 1605. The exact movements of the Chamberlain's Men in 1599 are impossible to trace, but it is very possible that *Henry V* (1599) was composed for one of the older playhouses, perhaps the Curtain, whereas *Julius Caesar* (1599), representing a theatrical as well as a generic shift, was designed to help inaugurate the Globe.[31] The improved position of the companies is also indicated by their partial ownership of these new theaters, a procedure initiated at the Globe in 1599 and imitated, apparently with less success, by the

[28]For the perils of periodization, especially in Spanish drama, see Charles V. Aubrun, "Nouveau public, nouvelle comédie à Madrid au xviiᵉ siècle," together with the intervention by Salomon and the réponse by Aubrun, in *Dramaturgie et société: Rapports entre l'oeuvre théâtrale, son interprétration et son public aux xviᵉ et xviiᵉ siècles*, ed. Jean Jacquot, with Elie Konigson and Marcel Oddon (Paris: Editions du Centre National de la Recherche Scientifique, 1968), 1:1–12.

[29]E. K. Chambers, *The Elizabethan Stage* (Oxford: Clarendon Press, 1923), 1:299–302, 308–9; Glynne Wickham, *Early English Stages, 1300 to 1660*, vol. 2, *1576–1660*, pt. 1 (London: Routledge and Kegan Paul, 1963), pp. 90–96, and vol. 2, pt. 2 (London: Routledge and Kegan Paul, 1972), pp. 9–29.

[30]Leo G. Salingar, Gerald Harrison, and Bruce Cochrane, "Les comédiens et leur public en Angleterre de 1520 à 1640," in *Dramaturgie et société*, ed. Jacquot, 2:560–62.

[31]M. C. Bradbrook, *The Rise of the Common Player: A Study of Actor and Society in Shakespeare's England* (Cambridge: Harvard University Press, 1962), pp. 41–42; Chambers, 1:308–9, and 2:196–97, 203, 364–66, 402–3, 415.

Queen's Men at the Red Bull and the Prince's Men at the Fortune.[32] Finally, the accession of James brought with it a sharp rise in the frequency of court dramatic performances as compared with the late Elizabethan period, an economic windfall from which Shakespeare's company, now renamed the King's Men, benefited disproportionately.[33]

The other main theatrical event between 1597 and 1608 was the reopening at the turn of the century of the indoor private playhouses. As the exploitation of amateur child actors rather than the employment of professional adult companies suggests, the performances at Paul's and Blackfriars, resumed after a hiatus of about a decade, depended on very different social relations from those that governed production at the public theaters.[34] In general, and despite a tendency in the comedies, and perhaps the tragedies as well, to attack the court of King James, the private playhouses had far stronger royal, aristocratic, and ecclesiastical ties. They attracted dramatists interested in genteel status and aristocratic patronage, drew their high-paying audiences from the upper-class neighborhoods in which they were situated, and seem to have enjoyed special protection from members of the peerage as well as, perhaps, from the crown itself.[35] In later years, of course, the private theaters gradually replaced the public playhouses as the centers of London dramatic activity. During this period, however, the boy companies did no lasting economic damage to their adult rivals, while their repertories actually broadened the range of accomplishment in the public theater.

In Shakespeare's decreased use of the clown after 1600 it may be possible to detect an early symptom of the decline of popular dramaturgy.[36] Although additional evidence pointing in the same direction is

[32]Chambers, 1:356, 358, 364.

[33]Salinger, Harrison, and Cochrane, 2:531. The relevant information is presented in Chambers, *Elizabethan Stage*, 4:108–23.

[34]For the distinctions between the public and private theaters, see Alfred Harbage's valuable, though overstated, *Shakespeare and the Rival Traditions* (New York: Macmillan, 1952). But compare Alexander Leggatt, "The Companies and Actors," in The *"Revels" History of Drama in English*, vol. 3, *1576–1613*, by J. Leeds Barroll et al. (London: Methuen, 1975), p. 99; Juliet Dusinberre, *Shakespeare and the Nature of Women* (London: Macmillan, 1975), p. 14.

[35]Robert Weimann, "Le déclin de la scène 'indivisible' élisabéthaine: Beaumont, Fletcher et Heywood," in *Dramaturgie et société*, ed. Jacquot, 2:826; Harbage, *Rival Traditions*, pp. 56–57, 78–80, 90–102; William A. Armstrong, "The Audience of the Elizabethan Private Theatres," *Review of English Studies*, n.s., 10 (1959): 235; Salingar, Harrison, and Cochrane, 2:549–51, 554; W. R. Gair, "La Compagnie des Enfants de St. Paul: Londres (1599–1606)," in *Dramaturgie et société*, ed. Jacquot, 2:655–74; Louis Lecocq, "Le Théâtre de Blackfriars de 1596 à 1606," in *Dramaturgie et société*, ed. Jacquot, 2:682–83; Chambers, 1:325–28; Gerald Eades Bentley, *The Profession of Dramatist in Shakespeare's Time, 1590–1642* (Princeton: Princeton University Press, 1971), pp. 165–67.

[36]Weimann, *Shakespeare and the Popular Tradition in the Theater: Studies in the Social Dimension of Dramatic Form and Function*, ed. Robert Schwartz (Baltimore: John Hopkins University Press, 1978), pp. 178, 191.

available,[37] in retrospect the innovations before 1608 were merely ominous rather than immediately harmful. The absolutist drive toward monopoly, manifest in the reduction of the number of companies, was no threat to the public stage only so long as the professional troupes did not seek to appeal to a different audience. But increasing visits to court encouraged the actors to aim at a more aristocratic clientele than previously. At the same time, the mere presence of the court in London continued to spur the migration of the nobility to the capital and hence the formation of precisely such an audience, while the private theaters offered an institutional framework capable of undermining the public stage. In all these respects, monarchical centralization, without changing its essential character or purpose, gradually reversed its effect upon the public theater.[38]

The crown was aided at every point, however, by the bourgeoisie. City opposition sped royal intervention in the affairs of the stage; later, market forces helped limit the number of acting companies. The players' turn toward the court and the aristocracy was also partly a response to the hostility of London's mayor and aldermen, particularly after 1596, when the city succeeded in suppressing the stage within its boundaries. The private theaters, their aristocratic and royal connections notwithstanding, were commercial enterprises, while the residence of the gentry and peerage in London testified to the city's preeminent position in the development of British capitalism. This unintentional intertwining of monarchy and bourgeoisie is characteristic of English stage history from the 1570s to the 1640s.

In Spain, where the crown was not comparably hemmed in by capitalist forces, the danger to the public theater came more exclusively from the state and as a result emerged more slowly. A number of the defining features of the Spanish stage already discussed—among them the *gracioso*, dramatists' collaboration, actor-sharers, and clerical attacks on the theater—date either from the very end of the sixteenth century or from the seventeenth century itself. But royal centralization also increased between 1598 and 1621. The permanent establishment of the court in Madrid in 1606 assured the triumph of the public theaters in the capital and the eclipse of their regional rivals. The reopening of the stage at the turn of the century answered not only to the financial needs of the

---

[37]See John Russell Brown, "On the Acting of Shakespeare's Plays," in *The Seventeenth-Century Stage*, ed. Bentley (Chicago: University of Chicago Press, 1968), p. 44; Daniel Seltzer, "The Actors and Staging," in *A New Companion to Shakespeare Studies*, ed. Kenneth Muir and S. Schoenbaum (Cambridge: Cambridge University Press, 1971), p. 50.

[38]Gair, 2:664–65, notes the aristocracy's attraction to the court; Wickham, 2 (pt. 1): 90–96, blames the decline of the public theater on the crown. Weimann, "Le déclin," 2:827, although partly accepting this conclusion, believes that court control did not increase so much as change in character.

hospitals, but also to the predilections of the new monarch and his *privado*.[39] As in England, all playing without a royal license was prohibited. Although this provision was never absolutely enforced, the number of companies seems to have fallen as a result. Relatedly, the mechanisms of censorship were explicitly codified.[40]

Court patronage of the theater, all but nonexistent in the late sixteenth century, increased sharply in the reign of Philip III, just as it did in Jacobean London. In both instances the drama apparently received especially strong support from the queen. Performances before royalty took the form either of *particulares*, private palace showings of *corral comedias*, or of spectacle plays designed specifically for a courtly audience.[41] The first twenty years of the seventeenth century saw a marked increase in the use of stage machinery in the public theater, perhaps a sign of the influence of the crown upon the *corrales* and in any case a sufficiently prominent phenomenon to elicit a protest from Lope in 1621 over the excessively visual, as opposed to aural, emphasis of the theater.[42] Though the weakness of Spanish capitalism precluded any changes as portentous as those occurring in England, even the theaters of Madrid could not wholly evade the economic tendencies of the age. Subcontracting of various money-making activities related to the *corrales* became the norm after 1600. In 1615 a financial crisis that bears some affinities to exactly contemporary problems in the English public theaters led the Council of Castile to implement a pervasive system of leases, whereby a single *arrendador* paid a large lump sum to the hospitals in return for the right to administer the *corrales* and retain the profits that the *cofradías* had formerly earned.[43] Thus, paradoxically, a precapitalist conception of charity found its most efficient means in the bourgeois entrepreneur.

The subsequent periods, 1609–14 in England and 1622–43 in Spain, were the last ages during which the public theater dominated dramatic activity in each country. Although it is customary to date the decline of the London public stage from this era, by 1609 it was the children's companies that were in trouble. Three of their leading dramatists—Chapman, Marston, and Day—seem to have left the theater at this time. Of

---

[39]See N. D. Shergold, *A History of the Spanish Stage from Medieval Times until the End of the Seventeenth Century* (Oxford: Clarendon Press, 1967), p. 517; and the relevant passages in Emilio Cotarelo y Mori, ed., *Bibliografía de las controversias sobre la licitud del teatro en España* (Madrid: Real Academia Española, 1904).

[40]Shergold, pp. 516, 518; Hugo Albert Rennert, *The Spanish Stage in the Time of Lope de Vega* (New York: Hispanic Society of America, 1909), pp. 214–16, 220–23.

[41]Shergold, pp. 230–31, 236, 245, 248, 250, 252, 261, 263. For the role of Queen Anne in England, see Chambers, 1:326.

[42]The evidence is assembled by Shergold, pp. 213–15, 217, 235, but he draws no conclusions about the possible relation between court spectacle and *corral* stage machinery.

[43]Rennert, p. 224; Shergold, pp. 383–85.

the three troupes performing in the city the previous year, only one survived. The problem was primarily financial. Under the pressure of the plague closing of 1608–9, the Children of the King's Revels fell apart, the Children of Paul's were successfully bribed twenty pounds a year not to play, and the Children of the Queen's Revels relinquished their lease to Blackfriars and moved to Whitefriars. There, four years later, they were amalgamated with Lady Elizabeth's Men. By 1617 at the latest they had ceased to exist.[44]

The real threat to the public theaters came from within, specifically in the form of the King's Men's decision in 1608 to spend their winter season at Blackfriars. The events surrounding this crucial innovation[45] have been variously interpreted, and a number of obscurities remain.[46] Perhaps the simplest explanation is as follows. James Burbage purchased Blackfriars in 1596 as a winter replacement for the Cross Keys Inn, from which the Chamberlain's Men had been driven by the recent prohibition against playing in the city. There is no reason to believe that he was seeking by this maneuver to attract a wealthier and more aristocratic audience than the one that patronized the open-air theaters. When local opposition thwarted the plan in 1600, Burbage's sons, having no other use for Blackfriars, leased it for twenty-one years as a private theater to the Children of the Chapel (later known as the Children of the Queen's Revels, among other names). Although negotiations to surrender the lease took place in 1603, these were both instigated and broken off by the boy company. The transfer of Blackfriars back to the Burbages occurred in 1608, again it seems at the initiative of the lessee. Only from this point on did the King's Men significantly turn their attention to the private theater audience.[47] The long-run theatrical significance of the children's companies, in other words, was to reveal to the professional actors a means of raising their profits by concentrating primarily on an upper-class clientele.

After Shakespeare's death, Blackfriars was the main theater of the King's Men. By the 1630s the company seems to have spent almost two-thirds of the year at it, performing in the summer at the Globe. Average daily receipts ran more than twice as high at the indoor as at the outdoor playhouse, with a comparably great discrepancy in prestige.[48] This

[44]Salingar, Harrison, and Cochrane, 2:556; Chambers, 2:7, 22–23, 54–55, 60–61, 67.
[45]Bentley, *Shakespeare and His Theatre* (Lincoln: University of Nebraska Press, 1964), pp. 125–28.
[46]Lecocq, 2:679–83.
[47]The evidence for this reconstruction comes from Chambers, 1:297–98, 319–20, and 2:49, 54, 214, 359–60, 383, 479, 503, 508–9.
[48]Bentley, *The Jacobean and Caroline Stage*, vol. 1 (Oxford: Clarendon Press, 1941), pp. 3, 23–24, and vol. 6 (Oxford: Clarendon Press, 1968), pp. 12–17, 192–94. If the Globe was so little used, however, it is surprising that half or more of the extant new plays of the

may not have been the case between 1609 and 1614, however. During 1610–11, the first full season at the new theater, the King's Men did not spend more than half the year there. Although right from the start Blackfriars profits probably surpassed former winter earnings at the Globe, it is less likely that they also exceeded contemporary summer income from the Bankside playhouse. Certainly the Globe was still considered London's leading theater. The status of Shakespeare's last plays is similarly ambiguous. *Cymbeline* (1609), *The Winter's Tale* (1610), and *Henry VIII* (1613) all were performed at the Globe by 1613, but their original destination remains unknown.[49] Like *The Tempest* (1611), these works at once reveal an adherence to the conventions of popular dramaturgy and a consciousness of the most avant-garde English and international theatrical trends.[50] For these reasons such plays, and others like them, may be seen as instances of transitional drama.

Even if the King's Men and their theaters are excluded as atypical, the position of the public theaters during this period appears quite strong. Prince Henry's (later Palsgrave's) Men prospered, as did Queen Anne's Men until at least 1612. Perhaps in the hope of filling the theatrical void left by the decline of the boy troupes, two recently formed provincial companies, the Duke of York's (later Prince Charles's) Men and Lady Elizabeth's Men, established themselves in London by 1610 and 1611, respectively. The number of active public theaters accordingly increased as well. In addition to the three main outdoor playhouses—the Globe, the Fortune, and the Red Bull—the Curtain and the Boar's Head may have reopened after periods of disuse to serve the Duke of York's Men. The Swan unquestionably came out of retirement to accommodate Lady Elizabeth's Men. Finally, in 1614 the latter company moved into the Hope, a newly constructed theater on the Bankside.[51]

It is often asserted that the public theater audience was stagnant or declining between 1609 and 1614, or that the fall in attendance had already begun by 1605 or even as early as the turn of the century.[52] The

King's Men between 1622 and 1641 were first performed there. See Bentley, *Jacobean and Caroline Stage*, 6:195–96.

[49]Chambers, 1:369, and 2:215, 217, 369, 419; Bentley, *Jacobean and Caroline Stage*, 6:13 n. 1, 16 n. 1.

[50]Popular dramaturgy: Weimann, *Shakespeare and the Popular Tradition*, pp. 213, 294 n. 80; English avant-garde: Bentley, *Shakespeare and His Theatre*, pp. 65–99; international avant-garde: Louise George Clubb, "La mimesi della realtà invisibile nel dramma pastorale italiano e inglese del tardo rinascimento," *Misure Critiche* 4 (1974): 67.

[51]Chambers, 2:236–40, 242–43, 246–47, 404, 413–14, 464–69; Bentley, *Jacobean and Caroline Stage*, 1:158–60, and 6:124, 130–31, 134, 200–201, 206–7.

[52]Harbage, *Shakespeare's Audience* (New York: Columbia University Press, 1941), p. 38 n. 35; idem, *Rival Traditions*, pp. 27–28; Weimann, "Le déclin," 2:827; idem, *Shakespeare and the Popular Tradition*, pp. 172, 178; David M. Bevington, *Tudor Drama and Politics: A Critical Approach to Topical Meaning* (Cambridge: Harvard University Press, 1968), pp. 294–95.

obvious expansion of companies and theaters casts this argument, unsupported as it is by any data, into serious doubt. But there are additional documentary reasons for rejecting such a position. The daily take at the Red Bull from 1612 to 1617 still averaged eight to nine pounds, exactly the sum Alfred Harbage determined for the Rose in the halcyon days of the 1590s and on the basis of which he estimated attendance for each performance at 1250. A petition of early 1614, moreover, claimed that every day "three or four thousand people" patronized the Middlesex theaters—primarily the Fortune and the Red Bull, no doubt, but perhaps the Curtain or the Boar's Head as well. These mutually compatible figures have the added attraction of approximating Harbage's estimate for the combined daily attendance at all the public playhouses in their supposed heyday, about 1605 or a little earlier.[53] But the 1614 petition excludes the Swan, the Hope, and above all the Globe. Assuming that these theaters were closed at the time, that their operation, when open, cut into attendance in Middlesex, and even that the figures for Middlesex are somewhat exaggerated, there seems little doubt that the total audience at the public playhouses continued to grow throughout the first fifteen years of the seventeenth century. The population of London also rose rapidly during these years, but theater attendance probably kept pace.

Finally, the public theater plays themselves do not reveal signs of decline. Dekker was active until 1611 or 1612 at the Fortune and the Red Bull, while Heywood continued writing through 1612 for the latter theater. In the same year, the Red Bull was also the site for the initial performance of Webster's *White Devil*. Middleton's *Chaste Maid in Cheapside* opened at the Swan in 1613;[54] Jonson's *Bartholomew Fair* inaugurated the Hope in 1614. In a manner partly reminiscent of Shakespeare's final plays, these last three works do not entirely belong to the popular dramatic tradition. But they demonstrate the centrality of the public theaters through 1614.

Although the overall pattern was much the same in Madrid from 1622 to 1643, the Spanish material calls for the opposite approach. It has been necessary to counter the tendency in English scholarship to pronounce a premature death for the public theater. Owing to the recent, and justified, revaluation of Calderón and his school, it is equally essential to stress the early symptoms of decline in Spain not of the stage in general, but of the public stage in particular. The first two decades in the reign of

[53]Bentley, *Jacobean and Caroline Stage*, 6:219; Chambers, 2:371; Harbage, *Shakespeare's Audience*, p. 33 and n. 31; idem, *Rival Traditions*, pp. 24, 45, 124 n. 56. The quoted passage is from Chambers, 2:371.

[54]R. B. Parker, introduction to his edition of *A Chaste Maid in Cheapside*, by Thomas Middleton (London: Methuen, 1969), pp. xxviii–xl.

Philip IV saw an extension and intensification of the centralizing trends of the early seventeenth century. In the winter of 1622–23, over forty *particulares* were performed before the new queen, a figure that compares with the more avid seasons of the early Stuarts. The king, too, remained a steady patron of the drama.[55] The machine play, meanwhile, began to pose a still more serious challenge to the traditional *comedia*. The arrival at the court in 1626 of Cosme Lotti, Spain's answer to Inigo Jones, led to an increase and a sophistication of court spectacle. In 1629 Lotti introduced perspective scenery. The opening in 1633 of Buen Retiro, the new royal palace, provided another impetus to stage pageantry, and between 1635 and 1640 a number of elaborate machine plays were performed at its theaters. In the latter year, the Coliseo, a new and more distinguished theater designed by Lotti, made its debut at Buen Retiro. Modeled on the Madrid *corrales*, it could handle not only unusually complex spectacular effects but also the simpler visual demands of the ordinary *comedia*. In fact, at times it played to a paying audience much like the one that frequented the public theaters.[56]

But the continuing ties of court and *corral*, and the imitation of the latter by the former, should not obscure the threat that monarchical enthusiasm for drama posed to the public theater. The physical reproduction of the *corral* at court inevitably entailed a loss of spontaneity and authenticity. For the benefit of the queen, who in this respect anticipated Marie Antoinette, an attempt was made to recreate the atmosphere of the public theater: derisive whistles from the audience, jeers from the pit, and physical battles amid scurrying rodents in the *cazuela* all were faked at the Coliseo. Significantly, the Coliseo was an indoor rather than an outdoor theater, whose stage differed from those at the *corrales* in not projecting into the auditorium. The traditional interplay between actor and spectator was in this way undercut, though perhaps not entirely eliminated. This change in turn suggests the contingent status of the public theater audience at the Coliseo, where it usually did not play the same integral commerical and cultural role as it did in the *corrales*. In addition, what is often claimed of the *comedia* in the public theater was undoubedly true of the court play, whether open to a popular audience or not: it was a conscious instrument of royal propaganda.[57]

[55]Rennert, pp. 233–37.

[56]Ruth Lee Kennedy, *Studies in Tirso*, vol. 1, *The Dramatist and His Competitors, 1620–26*, North Carolina Studies in the Romance Languages and Literatures, Essays no. 3 (Chapel Hill: University of North Carolina Department of Romance Languages, 1974), pp. 65, 194–95; Shergold, pp. 275, 278, 284, 293, 295–96, 298–300; Jonathan Brown and John H. Elliott, *A Palace for a King: The Buen Retiro and the Court of Philip IV* (New Haven: Yale University Press, 1980), pp. 42–47.

[57]The facts, though not all the conclusions, of this paragraph may be found in Shergold, pp. 297, 299, 329, 549; Auburn, *La comedia española (1600–1680)*, trans. Julio Lago Alonso (Madrid: Taurus, 1968), p. 81.

Crown patronage of the drama also had the effect of turning players and playwrights from the *corrales* to the court. Beginning in the 1630s, spectacle plays in particular earned them far more than they could hope to receive in the public theater. Despite coming into conflict with Lotti over the place of stage machinery, in a fashion that recalls both Lope's earlier grumblings and Jonson's battles with Inigo Jones, Calderón began writing as much for the palace theaters as for the *corrales* from about 1635 on. In this period as well, Rojas Zorrilla, Solís y Ribadeneyra, and Coello y Ochoa composed most of their work for the court. The tastes of a more aristocratic audience than attended the public theaters partly account for the elevation of style and tone in the *comedia* after 1620, even though most plays, wherever their premiere, ultimately found their way to the *corrales*. There were also tentative efforts at court to produce a more refined drama than the *comedia*. By the early 1630s the *arrendadores* of the *corrales* were having trouble making their required payments to the hospitals, with the result that, though the leasing system continued, the public theaters fell even more firmly under the control of the city of Madrid.[58] It is not clear, however, whether the economic problems of the *corrales* were already at this relatively early date a consequence of court competition.

After this ambiguous era, in which the open-air, commerical stages of London and Madrid continued to thrive despite the encroachments of more aristocratic drama, there came a period of collapse that quickened earlier tendencies and from which the public theaters never fully recovered. Between 1615 and 1619 England suffered a crisis of overexpansion. The growth of the audience resulted in a bigger economic pie, but the increase in the number of companies and theaters meant that the pie had to be divided into more pieces. Individual shares probably thus remained unchanged, particularly if, as is possible but by no means certain, the cost of admission also did not go up. But prices in general did rise, at least 15 percent in the preceding twenty years.[59] Accordingly, companies with fixed gross revenues were likely to face a financial squeeze that may have substantially reduced personal income. The overall slump of the economy that began in 1615 could only have worsened the situation.

[58]Shergold, pp. 280, 288–89, 292, 360–61, 384, 527; Edward M. Wilson and Duncan Moir, *The Golden Age: Drama, 1492–1700*, vol. 3 of *A Literary History of Spain*, gen. ed. R. O. Jones (London: Ernest Benn, 1971), pp. 107–12, 130, 133; Cayetano Alberto de La Barrera y Leirado, *Catálogo bibliográfico y biográfico del teatro antiguo español desde sus orígenes hasta mediados del siglo xviii* (1860; rpt. London: Tamesis, 1968), p. 95; Aubrun, *La comedia española*, p. 78; Kennedy, pp. 24–25, 77–150, 334.

[59]Andrew Gurr, *The Shakespearean Stage, 1574–1642* (Cambridge: Cambridge University Press, 1970), p. 142; Bentley, *Jacobean and Caroline Stage*, 1:30–31 n. 6, and 6:111, 171; Hill, *Century of Revolution*, pp. 317–18 (Appendix C). The best account of the crisis is by Salingar, Harrison, and Cochrane, 2:550, 555–58.

The consequences were predictable. Queen Anne's Men had financial problems from 1612 to 1619. Lady Elizabeth's Men, it will be recalled, amalgamated with the Children of the Queen's Revels in 1613, only to be joined two years later by Prince Charles's Men. All but the last of these companies had left London by early 1616. The number of professional companies thus fell from five to four. In 1617 Queen Anne's Men moved into a newly opened private theater, the Phoenix. Their place at the Red Bull was probably taken by Prince Charles's Men, who had been playing at the Hope. The number of active public theaters thus fell from five to three—the Globe, the Fortune, and the Red Bull. As for the dramatists, Dekker and Heywood were silent from 1613 to 1619, Massinger and to a lesser extent Middleton switched from comparatively unsuccessful companies to the King's Men, and Jonson, probably owing to the patronage of King James, abandoned the commerical stage for almost a decade. In this period, then, one can first detect what proved a permanent defection by the leading dramatists from the public theater.[60]

In Spain during the 1640s, the difficulties were less economic than political. The revolutions of these years, combined with royal deaths in 1644 and 1646, sharply curtailed dramatic activities. Court performances were rare throughout the decade, with the public theaters remaining closed almost continuously from 1644 on. To a government in search of scapegoats for its own misdeeds, the supposed moral laxity of the theater seemed an appropriate target.[61] Convenient rhetoric lay ready to hand. Fructuoso Bisbe y Vidal, to cite but one foe of the theater, concluded that plays cause "la corrupcion de costumbres, y daños de la Republica" ("the corruption of customs, and harm of the Republic").[62] Hence a 1644 government decree ordered that "se prohibiesen casi todas las [comedias] que hasta entonces se habían representado, especialmente los libros de Lope de Vega, que tanto daño habían hecho en las costumbres" ("almost all the [comedias] were to be prohibited that up to then had been performed, especially the books of Lope de Vega, which had done such great harm to customs").[63] Under these conditions professional troupes disbanded and the actors sought other employment.

This dismal period for the drama did not last in either country. But by the beginning of the recovery of 1620 in England and of midcentury in Spain, the public theater was in clear, irrevocable decline and had relin-

[60]Chambers, 2:8; Bentley, *Jacobean and Caroline Stage*, 1:158–64, 177, 201; ibid., vol. 3 (Oxford: Clarendon Press, 1956), p. 243; ibid., vol. 4 (Oxford: Clarendon Press, 1956), pp. 556, 609–10, 754, 857; ibid, 6:208–9.

[61]Shergold, pp. 301–5, 520–21, 527.

[62]Fructuoso Bisbe y Vidal, *Tratado de las comedias* (Barcelona, 1618), sig. o8^r.

[63]*Consulta del Consejo de Castilla*, in Cotarelo y Mori, p. 164.

quished the lead to the private playhouses and the court. This was particularly true in London after 1629, with the opening of still another private theater, Salisbury Court, and the much increased involvement of
Charles and Henrietta Maria's court with the stage. The public theater
was not entirely moribund, however. During the late teens and early
twenties, the Fortune continued to receive praise for its physical appearance and its distinguished audience. If Harbage's methods are applied
to receipts from the Globe during the Caroline era, the result is an average daily attendance of roughly a thousand, far more than regularly patronized Blackfriars. Indeed, even though the King's Men performed in
their Bankside theater for only about one-third of the year, the total annual audience there probably surpassed that at the company's far more
lucrative private playhouse. Although the Globe could not financially
match Blackfriars, its average daily earnings may have been greater than
those at the Phoenix and almost certainly exceeded those at Salisbury
Court. Finally, to take an extraordinary instance, the daily profits from
Middleton's *Game at Chess*, performed at the Globe in 1624, cannot be
paralleled in the history of Renaissance English commerical theater.[64]

On the other hand, while the population of London continued to
swell, the attendance at the Globe shrank. The Fortune and especially
the Red Bull became renowned for their violent audiences and their vulgar and old-fashioned plays, a reputation that dates back to the early
years of James I but that grew especially prominent in Caroline times.
Very few plays remembered today were composed for these three playhouses after 1620, nearly all of them appearing at the Globe. The center
of dramatic innovation shifted to the private stages, which catered to an
increasingly aristocratic, even courtly, coterie.[65]

These changes occurred not, as most critics have argued, because the
audience abandoned the actors, but because the actors abandoned their
audience. The move of the King's Men to Blackfriars is in retrospect
paradigmatic. As the success of *A Game at Chess* reveals, the public theater audience survived, at least potentially. But the companies were either unwilling or unable to appeal to it as effectively as they once had
done. Those successful dramatists of the private theater who occasionally wrote for the outdoor stage increasingly lacked the appropriate cultural and social sympathies as well as the necessary training in the conventions of popular dramaturgy. Despite the deep indebtedness of the
private to the public theater, Marlowe, Shakespeare, and even Jonson in
this respect had no successors. *The Antipodes* (1638), a Salisbury Court

[64]Bentley, *Jacobean and Caroline Stage*, 1:23–24, 136, 140–41; ibid., 4:746, 873, 876;
ibid., vol. 5 (Oxford: Clarendon Press, 1956), p. 1024; ibid., 6:93, 152–53.
[65]Salingar, Harrison, and Cochrane, 2:560; Bentley, *Jacobean and Caroline Stage*, 1:47,
and 6:32–36, 146–49, 166, 194, 238–47; idem, *Shakespeare and His Theatre*, pp. 111–25.

comedy written by Richard Brome, one of the sons of Ben, offers a well-known and telling example. In the following exchange, a lord instructs one of his servants in the art of acting.

> *Letoy.* But you, sir, are incorrigible, and
> Take license to yourself to add unto
> Your parts your own free fancy, and sometimes
> To alter or diminish what the writer
> With care and skill compos'd; and when you are
> To speak to your coactors in the scene,
> You hold interlocutions with the audients—
> *Byplay.* That is a way, my lord, has bin allow'd
> On elder stages to move mirth and laughter.
> *Letoy.* Yes, in the days of Tarlton and Kemp,
> Before the stage was purg'd from barbarism,
> And brought to the perfection it now shines with.
> Then fools and jesters spent their wits, because
> The poets were wise enough to save their own
> For profitabler uses.[66]

Hence to Brome, his admiration for Shakespeare notwithstanding (1.5.69), one of the fundamental resources of the public theater was literally incomprehensible.

Parliament's order of September 2, 1642, thus dealt a final blow to an already troubled institution while simultaneously closing down the private playhouses. Why did this happen? As in the earlier and less systematic defeat of provincial playing, the authorities may not have acted primarily on the basis of a supposed Puritan aversion to the stage or out of hostility to the court.[67] The evidence presented in chapter 3, it will be recalled, in fact suggests considerable Puritan support for the commercial theaters during the late sixteenth century. Under the first two Stuarts, parliamentary Puritan foes of the crown promoted oppositional drama, a strategy that continued at least until 1640 and perhaps as late as June 1642.[68] The majority of the members of the Long Parliament, which convened in November 1640, failed to attend afternoon sittings of that body, instead frequenting the bowling green, the park, or the the-

[66]Richard Brome, *The Antipodes*, ed. Ann Haaker (Lincoln: University of Nebraska Press, 1966), 2.2.39–53. The subsequent reference is noted in the text. See also Armstrong, *The Elizabethan Private Theatres: Facts and Problems* (1958; rpt. Folcroft, Pa.: Folcroft Press, 1969), pp. 16–17.

[67]Salingar, Harrison, and Cochrane, 2:566–72.

[68]Margot Heinemann, *Puritanism and Theatre: Thomas Middleton and Opposition Drama under the Early Stuarts* (Cambridge: Cambridge University Press, 1980), esp. pp. 200–236; Bentley, *Jacobean and Caroline Stage*, 4:714–15, and 5:1355–56.

ater.[69] Antipathy to Caroline absolutism also does not adequately account for the suppression of the stage. The promulgation of the closing order, for example, did not follow immediately upon the defeat of Charles in London and the concomitant consolidation of parliamentary control over the city: that had already occurred in January 1642.[70] The following month, however, "there was a great complaint made against the Play-houses, and a motion made for the suppressing of them."[71] Yet Parliament took no action at this time.

Opposition of Puritans to the theater and of the gentry to the court, then, only partially explains the September decision. The same goes for other forces pointing in that direction, most notably a traditional bourgeois commitment to public order and a corollary fear of popular rioting. Mass demonstrations and protests in London, many of them dominated by the lower classes, began not in mid-1642 but in 1639 or earlier. More important, these unprecedented assemblies overwhelmingly favored the parliamentary cause.[72] Finally, in the course of 1642, the theater lost much of its clientele. That spring, James Shirley attributed the decline in attendance—at least by the aristocracy—to the king's flight to the north: "*London* is gone to *York* . . . / . . . and a Play / Though ne'r so new, will starve the second day."[73] As the two sides gathered their military forces during the summer, thousands of London tradesmen and apprentices joined the parliamentary armies. On the very day of the suppression order, 2,400 foot soldiers and four regiments of horse were being raised in the city.[74] In the absence of its traditional supporters, the theater probably proved unusually vulnerable.

Yet these contributing causes could not spontaneously and decisively coalesce. It was the outbreak of the Civil War that sealed the fate of the English public theater. In this context, parliamentary fears of popular disorder or of propaganda by Royalist dramatic companies may well have acquired a special urgency.[75] Certainly the suppression order, though obviously indebted to Puritan rhetoric, stops well short of an absolute condemnation of the theater, specifying instead a temporary closure only for the duration of the conflict: "Whereas . . . the distracted Estate of England [is] threatned with a Cloud of Blood, by a Civill Warre

[69]Conrad Russell, *The Crisis of Parliaments: English History, 1509–1660* (Oxford: Oxford University Press, 1971), p. 167.

[70]Manning, pp. 95–98.

[71]Quoted in Leslie Hotson, *The Commonwealth and Restoration Stage* (Cambridge: Harvard University Press, 1928), p. 5.

[72]Manning, pp. 1–111; Valerie Pearl, *London and the Outbreak of the Puritan Revolution: City Government and National Politics, 1625–43* (London: Oxford University Press, 1961), pp. 107–8.

[73]James Shirley, quoted in Bentley, *Jacobean and Caroline Stage*, 1:67–68.

[74]Manning, pp. 163, 196–97, 241–42; Pearl, p. 251.

[75]Heinemann, *Puritanism*, pp. 235–39.

. . . ; and whereas . . . publike Stage-playes [disagree] with the Seasons of Humiliation, this being an Exercise of sad and pious solemnity, and the other being Spectacles of pleasure, too commonly expressing laciuious Mirth and Levitie: It is therefore thought fit . . . that while these sad Causes and set times of Humiliation doe continue, publike Stage-Playes shall cease, and bee forborne."[76] Although clandestine performances continued for well over a decade, at the Phoenix and Salisbury Court but especially at the Fortune and the Red Bull, the revolutionary parliaments never lifted the ban. In time, indeed, its purpose may have changed: the vehement suppression decree of early 1648 perhaps reflected the government's fear of a Leveller uprising in London.[77]

The decline of the Spanish public theater after 1650 was less dramatic but equally unambiguous and strikingly parallel. The *corrales* remained open to 1700 and beyond, but by midcentury the focus of theatrical activity had shifted to the court. Things did not go as far as in England, of course. Even Calderón's court plays continued to rely on audience address, and a socially heterogeneous public witnessed *comedias* at the royal palace as well as in the *corrales*. But a bifurcation of the audience along class lines had clearly begun to develop. The populace could attend court festival plays, for example, only after prior performances before the king, the councils of state, and the municipal authorities of Madrid. Although Bautista Diamante wrote for both the court and the *corrales*, Juan Vélez de Guevara, Moreto, and Calderón concentrated exclusively on the former. By royal command, actors were often whisked away from the public theaters at a moment's notice to begin long runs at Buen Retiro, during which time the *corrales* might stand empty. As the number of dramatists and companies fell, the public theaters came to specialize in reruns of early-seventeenth-century plays, a phenomenon paralleled at the Fortune and the Red Bull.[78]

This running comparison of the English and Spanish stages in the seventeenth century suggests, more clearly than a consideration of either in isolation could, that the primary responsibility for the demise of the public theater belongs to the absolutist state, at one time the leading benefactor of that theater. The centralizing tendencies of the monarchy in the end revealed their feudal, antipopular basis. In England the bourgeoisie played a secondary role in undermining the public theater, speeding the process and giving it an air of finality that it lacked in Spain, but not

[76]Bentley, *Jacobean and Caroline Stage*, vol. 2 (Oxford: Clarendon Press, 1941), p. 690.
[77]Hotson, pp. 3–59; Bentley, *Jacobean and Caroline Stage*, 6:76–77, 112–14, 173–77, 230–37, 247; Salingar, Harrison, and Cochrane, 2:572–73.
[78]Wilson and Moir, pp. 69, 74, 112, 122, 126, 136–42; Aubrun, *La comedia española*, pp. 68, 81–82, 93–94; Shergold, pp. 310–12, 314–15, 359, 527, 540; Rennert, pp. 226 n. 1, 341.

initiating it. In both countries, however, the underlying conflict over the stage pitted the upper classes against the lower, with predictable results. If the fundamental logic of absolutism was to destroy the public stage, it cannot be maintained that the institution in its heyday unambiguously served the interests of the state. This is only a historical reformulation of a relationship hitherto posed formally as the contradiction between artisanal base and absolutist superstructure. The social function of the public theater, or of its plays, cannot be adequately understood in the absence of some such perception.

A preliminary way of pursuing this difficult issue is to investigate more systematically the chronological parallels between national and theatrical history that have guided the previous discussion. A thriving public theater required an early species of nationalism that combined genuine commitment to nationhood by the bourgeoisie with traditional lower-class xenophobia and a more-or-less illegitimate royalist appropriation of the ideology. The loss of this homogeneity, partly produced by centralizing policies as well as by the inability of the monarch any longer to represent the country,[79] spelled the end of the stage. From this point of view, the decline of the public theater removed illusion, revealing the reality of the state and particularly its failure to deliver the goods. But well before, the structure of the institution had made this crucial insight available. The claims of absolutism could be tested against its actual operations. The extent to which the crown served the population as a whole could be judged not merely by its abstract identification with some larger national interest, but also in terms of its concrete impact on the lives of ordinary people. This form of scrutiny, pursued to relatively optimistic conclusions in the national history play of the 1590s, continued after the turn of the century, at which time the monarchy was found wanting.

In Spain, since the centralization of the drama under Philip III constituted less a component of a larger strategy than a reflection of royal taste, it had only a modest effect on the public stage. After 1621, however, the coordination of political and theatrical consolidation began to take its toll, especially as the government suffered reverses abroad and met opposition at home. By 1640 or soon after, generations of Habsburg policy finally acquired sufficient cumulative force to tear the nation apart. This act of decomposition was of course the ironic consequence of the opposite intention. The influence of the state upon the drama during the 1640s was accordingly straightforward in its destructiveness. Thereafter, the widening cultural gap between court and populace, co-

[79]The nationalist role of the monarchy in the public theater: Jean Duvignaud, *Les ombres collectives: Sociologie du théâtre*, 2d ed. (Paris: Presses Universitaires de France, 1973), pp. 200–210.

incident with repeated demonstrations of the monarchy's powerlessness to prevent steady national deterioration, precluded a continuation and extension of the previous practices of the public theater.

Whether one judges by impact during the Renaissance or by critical esteem today, that theater reached its height in England between the late 1580s and 1614, the era of the most frequent parliamentary activity. Whatever the conflicts between crown and Commons, their joint, if unequal, rule during these years testified to the aristocracy's continued community of interest and hence to the possibility of national unity. Partly as a result, increased royal control of the theater during this period only belatedly revealed its main negative consequences. The struggles between Parliament and the monarchy became more intractable between 1610 and 1614, the last, and challenged, moment of the supremacy of the public stage. From that point on, English society was incapable of providing the necessary cultural, political, and economic milieu. There immediately followed a brief hiatus in theater and politics alike. When James called the two legislative houses back into session in 1621, the constitutional crisis of the state and the bifurcation of the stage simultaneously emerged, both of them detrimental to the public theater. These tendencies reached an extreme after 1629, when the full weight of Caroline absolutism was felt in drama and society.

What, then, was the relationship between the conflict within the theater and the divisions of the Civil War? The political conflicts of the 1640s fell roughly into three stages, each more radical than the last. Initially, an extremely unpopular court found itself isolated from a restive country, belatedly represented in the Long Parliament. The Civil War proper, beginning in 1642, pitted one section of the aristocracy, aligned with the crown, against another, allied with the artisanate. The victory of the latter forces in the late 1640s then led to the dissolution of the triumphant coalition, to the outbreak of a social conflict in which the Levellers offered a comprehensive, but in the event unsuccessful, radical challenge to traditional upper-class rule.

Each of these moments has its analogue in the theater. First, all of London's commercial playhouses, both private and public, were situated in the liberties or suburbs, areas that, because of their relative freedom from city jurisdiction, became centers of Puritanism as well as of drama. Early Stuart theater may have picked up much of its oppositional thrust, noticed briefly above, from its immediate surroundings, a thrust that monarchical patronage of the drama and the subsequent royalism of the actors have largely obscured. In this limited sense, the stage sided with the country against the court. Second, the distinction between the private theater, which mainly appealed to the upper classes and the court, and the public theater, whose much broader audience ranged from the

upper classes to shopkeepers and below, loosely parallels the conflict between Royalists and Parliamentarians in the Civil War. To this extent the
public theater in the age of Shakespeare was antiabsolutist, or at least opposed to the logic of absolutism. Finally, as the upper classes of late Jacobean and Caroline England withdrew from the public theater, which as a
result became an increasingly popular institution, the division between
private and public playhouse came to anticipate the later split between
upper class and lower. During the 1640s the suburbs, in which all the
public theaters were situated, were the centers of popular radicalism.
This was especially true of Southwark, site of the Globe, of several large
demonstrations in 1641, and of crucial left-wing support for the New
Model Army in 1647.[80] The situation partly recalls the dilemma of late
medieval, urban, popular drama, described in chapter 1. Just as the Levellers failed to push through a lower-class revolution, so too the Caroline
public theater, relatively cut off from the resources of high culture,
could not sustain the amplitude and depth of the late Elizabethan and
early Jacobean stage.

[80]Heinemann, *Puritanism*, p. 9; Manning, pp. 67–68; Pearl, pp. 28, 40–41; Hill, *World*,
pp. 41 n. 7, 112, 354.

# 6

# Aristocratic Failure: Satiric Comedy
# and the Forms of Serious Drama

Although basic similarities between English and Spanish plays persisted in the early seventeenth century, the generic parallels were no longer always so close. In the major dramatic forms that came to prominence about 1600 or shortly thereafter, the differences resulted primarily from the intensification of prior social, religious, literary, and theatrical divergences between the two countries, but also—and especially in the case of satiric comedy—from the reopening of the London private theaters. In comedy satire dominated the field, but in serious drama at least four emergent forms—political tragedy, heroic drama, bourgeois tragedy, and the peasant play—demand attention. All these genres, however, reversed the ideological norms of the late sixteenth century, testifying instead to the failure of the aristocracy to adapt to social and political change.

## SATIRIC COMEDY

### Forms of Satiric Comedy

Satiric comedy provides a useful point of departure, its long life on the stage rendering it an appropriate vehicle for viewing the historical contours of the entire period considered in this chapter and the next. As a form, it structurally excludes a positive moral perspective from the action. Its vigor derives from the disjunction between the social assumptions and resolution of the plot, on the one hand, and the implicit moral judgment by the author, on the other. An audience may, for instance, admire a character's mastery of society while simultaneously faulting her or his deviation from ethical norms. The more pronounced the disjunc-

tion, the more satiric the work. In England, at least, such comedies generically transform the formally didactic, allegorical, popular morality
play. To be sure, the change is not absolute. Just as satires offer intermittent moralizing, moralities often seek the effects of local satire. But although satiric comedy, like the morality, may demonstrate the self-
destructiveness of vice, unlike the morality it rarely shows the social
efficacy of virtue, much less the ordering presence of a just and benevo-
lent deity. Similarly, the implicit moral judgement of this drama may
possess unusual breadth, extending even to the attractive but hypocritical intriguers in a general exposé of a society whose gullibility reveals a
shallowness and defectiveness of values that know no class limitations.
Nonetheless, the social resolution always accepts the status quo, although
the implicit moral judgment may not. The satiric playwright has much
to criticize but wishes to offer no positive alternative to contemporary
reality, either because he has none or because he considers reform
unattainable. Indeed, the negativity of the form at least theoretically allows dramatists of widely varying beliefs to produce relatively similar effects. Since the objects of the satire are not permanently vanquished, the
conclusions may be resigned, bleak, or even bitter. Satiric form thus
proves an ideal vehicle for a playwright convinced of both the necessity
of attack and the improbability of reform.[1]

If satiric comedy is compared with romantic comedy, it is immediately
evident that the contrast between the two forms can easily be overstated.
Jonson's claims to the contrary, the first major classicist in English comedy was Shakespeare, in the series of romantic comedies he composed
during the 1590s.[2] Those plays, moreover, regularly include local satiric
objects, characters, or moments, as well as a more general ironic deflation of the protagonists, carried out by means of the techniques of popular dramaturgy. A comparable procedure may be found in Lope's *Las
bizarrías de Belisa* (1634), as well as in numerous other seventeenth-century works. And to reverse the analogy, satiric comedies often conclude
with love matches that pair off at least some of the main characters. But
of course important differences remain. Although romantic comedy
hardly accords women equal status with men, its treatment of sexual relations has little in common with the antifeminist vision of much satiric
comedy. Similarly, although the lovers in romantic comedies often make
financial calculations, their societies, unlike those of the satires, rarely

---

[1]The distinction between satiric and didactic employed here is adapted, with changes,
from Sheldon Sacks, *Fiction and the Shape of Belief: A Study of Henry Fielding with Glances at
Swift, Johnson and Richardson* (Berkeley and Los Angeles: University of California Press,
1967), chap. 1.

[2]Leo G. Salingar, *Shakespeare and the Traditions of Comedy* (Cambridge: Cambridge University Press, 1974), p. 27.

face serious social and economic threats. And when such threats arise, as in *The Merchant of Venice*, the limits of the form come into focus as well.

Underlying the distinction is the difference between two modes of production. If romantic comedy renders the successful adaptation of the nobility to social change, satiric comedy dramatizes the class's failure to adapt, regardless of whether a given aristocrat emerges victorious in any individual play. In romantic comedy, the timelessness of the pastoral world may offer an opportunity for growth, a means of mastering the whole of society. That other world and its options are systematically excluded from satiric comedy. A play like Lope's *La Arcadia* (probably 1615) remains something of an anomaly in the early seventeenth century. Pastoral atemporality is transformed into its opposite, an urban sense of the brevity, the pressure, the contraction of time that is constraining, even claustrophobic, in effect. Cut off from its rural roots, the aristocracy, traditional ruler of the land, confronts the alien existence of the city.

The public theater did not prove particularly hospitable to satiric comedy, however. A satirist may well take a position opposed to the dominant values of the society and rooted in an unrecoverable and imaginary past. Although the *corrales* of Madrid and the open-air playhouses of London did not presuppose any thoroughgoing social equality, they did depend on a certain community of belief and acceptance of the present. The seventeenth-century plays of the two public theaters accordingly belong more often to a looser, less generically specific category: city comedy.[3] But satiric comedy flourished far more in England than in Spain, a discrepancy that has no parallel in the nondramatic satire of the two countries, as Quevedo's works will immediately suggest.

Perhaps the relatively advanced stage of English capitalism recommended a satiric perspective to the London playwrights, while the Spanish nobility's all-but-uncontested domination of Madrid and other towns, and its consequent freedom from urban disorientation, had the opposite effect. The related tendency of *comedias de capa y espada* to focus on the aristocracy may also have blunted a satiric impulse. But the main

[3]See Salingar, Gerald Harrison, and Bruce Cochrane, "Les comédiens et leur public en Angleterre de 1520 à 1640," in *Dramaturgie et société: Rapports entre l'oeuvre théâtrale, son interprétation et son public aux xviᵉ et xviiᵉ siècles*, ed. Jean Jacquot, with Elie Konigson and Marcel Oddon (Paris: Editions du Centre National de la Recherche Scientifique, 1968), 2:551; Edward M. Wilson and Duncan Moir, *The Golden Age: Drama, 1492–1700*, vol. 3 of *A Literary History of Spain*, gen. ed. R. O. Jones (London: Ernest Benn, 1971), p. 51; Alexander Leggatt, *Citizen Comedy in the Age of Shakespeare* (Toronto: University of Toronto Press, 1973); Gail Kern Paster, "The City in Plautus and Middleton," *Renaissance Drama*, n.s., 6 (1973):29–44. For a general theory of Spanish comedy, see C. A. Jones, "Some Ways of Looking at Spanish Golden Age Comedy," in *Homenaje a William L. Fichter: Estudios sobre el teatro antiguo hispánico y otros ensayos*, ed. A. David Kossoff and José Amor y Vázquez (Madrid: Editorial Castalia, 1971), pp. 329–39.

cause of the difference was probably the English private theater. Toward the turn of the century, the public stages of both countries witnessed at least tentative moves toward satire, by Chapman and Jonson in London, and on the peninsula in two plays briefly considered as intrigues in a previous chapter, *Los mal casados de Valencia* and *El rufián Castrucho*. Little came of Castro's and Lope's efforts, however. In other words, though not the cradle of dramatic satire, the private theater was certainly the home where the form grew up. As a social institution, it was well suited to express satire's characteristic combination of exclusivity and insecurity in a way that the Spanish court theater, to take the relevant analogue, was not. This institutional proclivity was probably reinforced by the bishops' order of 1599, which banned the publication of verse satire and, as an inadvertent result, impelled literary satirists to turn their attention to drama.[4] Satiric comedy was thus the private theater's fundamental contribution to the public stage, a crucial impetus behind the expanded range of representation available to audiences at the Globe and elsewhere in the early seventeenth century. Its influence may be discerned in tragicomedies such as *All's Well That Ends Well* (1602) and *Measure for Measure* (1604),[5] in some of Shakespeare's tragedies, and in a number of satires written expressly for the public theater by dramatists who often catered to the private stage.

The disjunction between the social premises of the action and the author's implicit moral judgment elaborated above may be of further use in establishing subclassifications within the general category of satiric comedy. The extent of this disjunction, the strength of the satire, roughly corresponds to the social breadth of the critique. As in romantic comedy, the representation of interclass relations usually downplays festivity in favor of negativity. Plays in which social resolution and moral evaluation coincide tend to define their satiric objects rather narrowly; by contrast, those with an extreme disjunction may attack all humanity.[6] A work of the former, narrower kind, often called a *comedia de figurón* in Spanish scholarship, centers on a single ridiculous or otherwise defective character, whose defeat immediately entails a happy resolution of the plot. As a satiric butt, the *figurón* offers a handy vehicle for the reassertion of community through a collective rejection of social misbehavior.

---

[4]Edward Arber, *A Transcript of the Registers of the Company of Stationers of London, 1554–1640*, vol. 3 (1876; rpt. New York: Peter Smith, 1950), p. 677.

[5]The designation of these two plays as tragicomedies is made by Arthur C. Kirsch, *Jacobean Dramatic Perspectives* (Charlottesville: University Press of Virginia, 1972), pp. 52–74. See also G. K. Hunter, "Italian Tragicomedy on the English Stage," *Renaissance Drama*, n.s., 6 (1973): 123–48. Paul N. Siegel, *Shakespeare in His Time and Ours* (Notre Dame, Ind.: University of Notre Dame Press, 1968), pp. 190–93, discusses Shakespeare's debt here to satiric comedy.

[6]Most of the plays discussed below fall into Northrop Frye's first, or ironic, phase of comedy. See *Anatomy of Criticism: Four Essays* (Princeton: Princeton University Press, 1957), pp. 177–79. A few conform to his third, or "normal," phase, pp. 180–81.

Not surprisingly, the form remained popular on the Spanish stage through much of the seventeenth century.

But the notion of the *comedia de figurón*, if extended only slightly beyond its standard usage, can comprise a spectrum of possible effects, ranging from conventional affirmation to bitter, pessimistic irony. When aristocratic characters are purged of their affectations by the process of the action, they may actively participate in the romantic conclusion. Such is the case in Moreto's *El desdén, con el desdén* (1653–54?) and *No puede ser el guardar una mujer* (1659).[7] A similar result can be achieved if the *figurón* is from a lower class and hence poses no ultimate threat to the nobility's conception of itself or control of society. In Solís y Ribadeneyra's *El doctor Carlino* (before 1667),[8] the titular figure, an attractively mercenary charlatan, is responsible for the complications and near catastrophes of the plot and remains cheerfully unreformed to the very end. As a result and in studied contrast, the two pairs of aristocratic lovers generally conform to their class's norms of conduct. Moreover, because the doctor finally untangles the imbroglio rather than allowing it to issue in tragedy, his frankly self-interested, witty machinations produce no retrospective moral qualms. Even when the unregenerate figure is an aristocrat near the center of the plot, a predominantly romantic tone remains possible. In Calderón's *Mañanas de Abril y Mayo* (1633)[9] and Moreto's *El lindo don Diego* (1654–62),[10] the unmasking of the *figurón* leads directly to the marriages of the true lovers.

But a much grimmer outcome is also available. Alarcón's *La verdad sospechosa* (by early 1621)[11] concludes with two marriages, one matching two admirable lovers and the other uniting a virtuous woman to the aristocratic young man of her choice. The man, however, is the constitutionally dishonest protagonist, whose misconduct steadily increases in the course of the play despite the sympathetic attention of the other characters and the repeated moral lessons administered by the *gracioso*, in this instance a mouthpiece for the author. Solely because of his own failings, the protagonist is forced at the end of the work to forgo a

[7]The first date is from Francisco de Rico, introducción to his edition of *El desdén, con el desdén; Las galeras de la honra; Los oficios*, by Agustín Moreto (Madrid: Editorial Castalia, 1971), pp. 38–43; the second from Eduardo Juliá Martínez, "Obras de Moreto," in his edition of *El lindo don Diego*, by Moreto, 4th ed. (Zaragoza: Editorial Ebro, 1966), p. 10.

[8]Date: Ramón de Mesonero Romanos, "Apuntes biográficos y críticos," Biblioteca de Autores Españoles, vol. 47 (Madrid: Atlas, 1951), p. xix.

[9] For this date and all other dates of plays by Calderón, see Kurt and Roswitha Reichenberger, *Bibliographisches Handbuch der Calderón-Forschung*, vol. 3 (Kassel: Thiele und Schwarz, 1981), pp. 731–42.

[10]For the date see Juliá Martínez, "Análisis de *El lindo don Diego*," in his edition of the play, p. 15.

[11]For the date see Alfonso Reyes, apéndice 4 to his edition of *La verdad sospechosa; Las paredes oyen*, by Ruiz de Alarcón (1923; rpt. Madrid: Clásicos Castellanos, 1967), p. 259.

woman he loves in order to marry one he does not. The conventions of romantic comedy are thus turned back upon themselves, as marriage becomes the punishment of youth. Although the criticism is restricted to a single figure, the serious treatment of his faults produces a social resonance unusual in *comedias de figurón*. It is as if the protagonist functioned as a lightning rod for a moral defect that the dramatist believed to be widespread. Yet even here there is no real divergence between social action and moral judgment. For an example of a genuinely satiric effect produced by having an immoral character serve as a scapegoat for general social ills, one would have to turn to Tirso de Molina's *El burlador de Sevilla* (perhaps 1616–20, more likely c. 1625).[12] Although Tirso's play transcends the limits of satire, the breadth of its critique points toward a second grouping of satiric comedy.

Most dramatic satires occupy an intermediate position. The disjunction between social plotting and moral understanding is partial rather than minimal or absolute, and several, though rarely all, of the characters are objects of attack. Such plays regularly result in the witty and at least morally acceptable intriguers achieving their desired ends. Among English public theater plays, Jonson's *Every Man in His Humour* (1598) is exemplary. The protagonists are drawn from the gentry and its aides, but the series of fools and knaves who populate the comedy include gentlemen as well as citizens. In this way Jonson's satire acquires a significant social range. But the overall satiric force of the action is weak, not only because the main characters get what they want, but also because what they want focuses on wedded love, all extramarital sex is avoided, and, perhaps most important, the witty means of the intrigue are themselves given a moral valence of sorts.[13] The workings of society thus approximate the ethical norms of the playwright.

A similar pattern is discernible in such later public theater satires as Brome's *Northern Lass* (1629) and Davenant's *News from Plymouth* (1635).[14] The latter work appeals to its audience in its salute to the English navy, its commitment to interclass marriage, and its satire on both foreigners and the gentry. But it is interesting today for the unintended conflict between these values and the author's ill-concealed hostility to-

---

[12]Date: Paul M. Lloyd, "Contribución al estudio del tema de Don Juan en las comedias de Tirso de Molina," in *Homenaje a William L. Fichter*, ed. Kossoff and Amor y Vázquez, pp. 447, 451.

[13]For this last argument, see Joel B. Altman, *The Tudor Play of Mind: Rhetorical Inquiry and the Development of Elizabethan Drama* (Berkeley and Los Angeles: University of California Press, 1978), pp. 179–95. Martin Seymour-Smith, introduction to his edition of *Every Man in His Humour*, by Ben Jonson (New York: Hill and Wang, 1968), pp. xxvi–xxvii, is somewhat more skeptical.

[14]For the assignment of these plays to the Globe, see Gerald Eades Bentley, *The Jacobean and Caroline Stage*, vol. 6 (Oxford: Clarendon Press, 1968), p. 197.

ward the very citizen classes for whom the play was meant. In Brome's piece, a reworking of *Bartholomew Fair*, a witty gentleman-intriguer, Tridewell-Quarlous, marries a wealthy city widow, Fitchow-Purecraft. His gentleman friend, Luckless-Winwife, forsakes his interest in the widow to win a virtuous gentlewoman, Constance-Grace, from an idiotic country gentleman, Widgine-Cokes, and from the clutches of the woman's uncle and guardian, Squelch-Overdo, a justice of the peace who ultimately finds himself on the wrong side of the law. Although additional parallels of plot, character, and local satire might be cited, the two plays are utterly dissimilar: *The Northern Lass* is a vision of *Bartholomew Fair* as romantic comedy. Both marriages are love matches—indeed, love at first sight—and the *miles gloriosus* labors faithfully to forward them. So does the prostitute, who, in addition, resolves to change her profession. But the conversion of satire into romantic comedy is not accompanied by any real sense of regeneration. The work is thus a perfect satiric comedy for the public theater.

Two analogous *corral* plays, Tirso's *Marta la piadosa* (1614–15)[15] and especially Lope's *El perro del hortelano* (probably 1613) offer more encompassing social critiques. Although the centrality of the romantic plot in each softens some of the harshness of the judgment, it also allows for a complexity of characterization extremely rare in satiric comedy and thus for a reversal of the usual relations between the two national dramas on this important matter. Because of the depth of the portrayal, the protagonists are inevitably attractive, even beyond the normal identification with young lovers. This sympathetic identification in turn largely enables the audience to deflect the main brunt of the satire from itself. But the central characters are also seriously compromised by their intrigues. Better than the society they manipulate, they nonetheless are objects of the general satire. In Tirso's play, the monetarization of human relations, linked to a characteristically slighting treatment of American wealth, combines with the general folly of society to outbalance the religious, even sacrilegious, hypocrisy of the resourceful heroine. In Lope's, the dubious conduct of the lovers results from the strength and potential destructiveness of rigid social stratification. In both, the reasonably happy endings must systematically exclude any general rectification of basic economic and social injustice. The way of the world is not the way of morality.[16] The integration of this profoundly satiric vision with an

[15]For the date, see Melveena McKendrick, *Woman and Society in the Spanish Drama of the Golden Age: A Study of the "Mujer Varonil"* (London: Cambridge University Press, 1974), p. 136 n. 1.

[16]For some similar comments on Lope's play, see Kossoff, introducción biográfica y crítica to his edition of *El perro del hortelano; El castigo sin venganza*, by Lope (Madrid: Editorial Castalia, 1970), pp. 26, 38–42.

equally well-realized romantic plot, the simultaneous affirmation and negation, is the special achievement of these plays, and one that was not duplicated in the later Spanish theater or, for that matter, on the Renaissance English stage.

A final kind of intermediate satiric comedy was performed in London's private theaters. The plays composed for the children's companies in the first decade of the century bear an ambiguous relation to the Spanish works just discussed. Although the satire in the English comedies is more bitter and insistent, it is also more narrowly focused, primarily on London's citizen classes—merchants, tradesmen, and apprentices—and secondarily on the court. The court, however, is more frequently an object of attack in tragicomedies like Marston's *Antonio and Mellida* (1599) and *The Malcontent* (1604), the earlier of these plays actually attempting to establish some connection between the corruption of the court and the rise of capital. With either social focus, the potential conflict between the dramatist and his audience disappears. Although members of the aristocracy are often satirized, the main target remains safely outside the enclosed private theater. Paradoxically, then, vituperative satire may reinforce a sense of community.

A possible analogue to this ideological and social matrix may be found in the signs of ruling-class unrest right after the turn of the century—the Essex Rebellion (1601), the Main and Bye Plot (1603), and the Gunpowder Plot (1605). The conspirators, motivated by a combination of thwarted ambition at court and financial distress, often accompanied their desperate political activity with various forms of religious heterodoxy. Although the tendency of these men was toward reaction, they were sufficiently unstable to dabble in radicalism of the left as well. Thus—to recall an argument of a previous chapter—in the mid-1640s, while most of the small or declining gentry understandably lined up behind the king, a minority formed the backbone of the Independents.[17] Economically threatened, on the one hand, equally attracted and repelled by the court, on the other—such was the position of the rebels at the beginning of the seventeenth century, and such, too, may have been the motive force behind the often backward-looking, unpredictable subversiveness of private theater drama.

In Middleton's *A Trick to Catch the Old One* (1605) and, in a sense, in Marston's *Dutch Courtesan* (1604), members of the gentry triumph at the expense of the city's commercial classes, who frequently are further tarred by their association with prostitution, Puritanism, and perhaps popular rebellion. Even where the plot itself does not signal this victory,

---

[17]Lawrence Stone, *The Crisis of the Aristocracy, 1558–1641* (Oxford: Clarendon Press, 1965), pp. 12, 482–88; idem, *The Causes of the English Revolution, 1529–1642* (New York: Harper and Row, 1972), pp. 27–29, 55–56.

the underlying ideology is usually evident enough, as in Chapman's *Widow's Tears* (1605) or, most obviously, Beaumont (and Fletcher's?) *Knight of the Burning Pestle* (1607). The vigor of these plays is accordingly inseparable from their principal bias. Their satiric disjunction, rooted in a simultaneous aristocratic desire to exclude the citizen classes from the national polity and fear that the opposite might actually be occurring, may also be the source of their often noticed moral waverings and imbalances. For in such a case the resulting perspective lacks the sanction of a traditional corporatist ideology that, though rationalizing class privilege, also finds a place for all classes within a single social order.

Later satiric dramatists found a solution of sorts to this problem. If one could not read the citizen classes out of the nation, one could at least write them out of the plays. Something of this strategy may be detected as early as Jonson's *Epicene* (1609), a work that Dryden, symptomatically, singles out for analysis and praise in his *Essay of Dramatic Poesy*. But the excision becomes regular only after 1620, with the adult troupes in the private theaters. In Massinger's *A New Way to Pay Old Debts* (1625) and *The City Madam* (1632), the narrowing of scope simplifies the central problem of interclass harmony. The moralistic aim of both comedies is realized in social terms, as the determined reconstruction of a class hierarchy: crown, peerage, gentry, and wealthy merchants, in descending order. This achievement requires either that the merchants have some sense pounded into them or, if they refuse to learn their place, that they be dispensed with entirely. More broadly, it also requires a manipulation of social fact. Sir Giles Overreach in the earlier play is loosely based on Sir Giles Mompesson, a monopolist impeached by Commons in 1621. His patent for licensing inns and alehouses threatened the autonomy and power of local justices of the peace. When Overreach boasts of his conflict with the gentry, he is being accurate enough. It may also be true that to this extent Overreach is a typical big city merchant. But Massinger carefully ignores the general unity of country landlords and urban capitalists, in this instance against the patents and monopolies granted by the crown. For to admit as much would be to recognize the true contours and seriousness of the crisis.[18]

A still more extreme constriction characterizes Shirley's *Lady of Pleasure* (1635), an overtly moralistic and hence only intermittently satiric comedy. Here the London commercial classes have been excluded en-

[18]For a warning against too close an identification of Overreach and Mompesson, see Philip Edwards and Colin Gibson, introduction to *A New Way to Pay Old Debts*, in their edition of *The Plays and Poems of Philip Massinger* (Oxford: Clarendon Press, 1976), 2:276–78. See 2:273–76 for the assignment of the play to 1625. Martin Butler, "Massinger's *City Madam* and the Caroline Audience," *Renaissance Drama*, n.s., 13 (1982): 157–87, argues for a pro-Puritan, procitizen orientation in *The City Madam* but concedes the absence of small shopkeepers from the play.

tirely: the social world consists only of the peerage and the gentry, to which class a steward, a bawd, a pimp, and a barber somewhat incongruously belong. The play proposes an absolutist ideal that combines praise of the court with a commitment to return to the country, there to reestablish human relations with the peasantry on neofeudal lines. This diminution of social range is typical of the Caroline private theater. It suggests, moreover, that the Renaissance English stage was best situated to dramatize the conflicts of its day before those contradictions became irreconcilable in society and theater alike.[19]

It is appropriate, then, to conclude a discussion of satiric comedy by returning once again to that earlier period. In a small number of plays performed in the London public theaters before 1615, the divergence between the social development of the action and the moral judgment on that action is almost absolute, and the object of satire all humanity. The theatrical function of such plays is inherently problematic, since by definition the critiques they offer are also directed at the very audience whose approbation the playwrights and actors seek. At the end of *A Chaste Maid in Cheapside*, Tim accepts his unwitting marriage to a whore: "I'll love her for her wit, I'll pick out my runts there; / And for my mountains, I'll mount upon—." At this point the sexually obscene rhyme is forestalled either by Tim's father or by the censor, thus producing a final moment poised between reconciliation and bitterness. The superficially good-humored epilogue to Chapman's *All Fools* (1599) also concludes with the suppression of the subversive rhyme: "We can but bring you meat, and set you stools, / And to our best cheer say, you all are— welcome."[20] There were other ways of softening the blow, of course. *All Fools* and Jonson's *Every Man out of His Humour* (1599) and *Volpone* (1606) are set in Italy. Chapman's play combines an utterly cynical view of humanity, and especially of sexuality, with a series of witty intrigues that, far from aiming to promote premarital or extramarital affairs, actually have as their object wedded love. It thus offers an extreme version of a pattern observable as well in such other public theater satires as *Every Man in His Humour* and *The Northern Lass*. Finally, faced with a more intractable obstacle to evasion, the London comedies opt for a delicate interplay between universal satire and universal forgiveness.

The encompassing satire of such plays suggests that in this instance the public stage reaped what the private one had sown. Only in the open-air theaters could satire transcend social and ideological narrow-

[19]Robert Weimann, "Le déclin de la scène 'indivisible' élisabéthaine: Beaumont, Fletcher et Heywood," in *Dramaturgie et société*, ed. Jacquot, 2:824, 827.

[20]Middleton, *A Chaste Maid in Cheapside*, ed. R. B. Parker (London: Methuen, 1969), 5.4.111–12; Chapman, *All Fools*, ed. Frank Manley (Lincoln: University of Nebraska Press, 1968), p. 93, line 11.

ness to attain a genuine comprehensiveness, even in negativity. Yet this is perhaps to overstate the argument. *The Alchemist* (1610), *Bartholomew Fair, A Chaste Maid in Cheapside,* and perhaps *All Fools* have—to change the metaphor—one foot in the private theater as well. Except for Chapman's comedy, these plays were composed between 1609 and 1614, in the crucial period of transition for stage and society alike. It would seem, then, that satiric comedy depended on the fusion of two closely related, but diverging traditions, and that it reached its height at the brief moment when that fusion was possible.

This conclusion has the advantage of accounting for the relative eclipse in the form of the leading figure from popular dramaturgy, the English clown and his Spanish equivalent, the *gracioso.* The classical heritage of satire involved a reorientation toward the leading intriguer in Latin comedy, the *servus,* a popular character as well, but primarily in *his* theater. In England, the function of the *servus* was often taken over by the witty gentleman. In Spain, for reasons of decorum, the *gracioso* frequently fulfilled the role. Tarugo, the *gracioso* of *No puede ser el guardar una mujer,* all but usurps the plot from the young lovers. But his extraordinary prominence requires a qualitative shift in purpose. Tarugo offers not a detached and critical perspective on the main action, but loyal aid to his master. This integration may reflect the greater prominence of servants in Madrid and its *corrales* than in London, where the lower-class sector of the public theater audience occupied a more independent and less subordinate position with respect to the aristocracy. It certainly contrasts with the more peripheral role of the clown in Shakespearean comedy or, for that matter, of the *gracioso* in *Las bizarrías de Belisa.* Not simply a result of the distinction between romantic and satiric comedy or between Spain and England, this difference also accords with the decline of popular theater in general in the course of the seventeenth century.

## Jonson

Recent scholarship has effectively demonstrated the indebtedness of Jonsonian comedy to the popular dramatic tradition and particularly to the late morality play. This legacy extends from forms, themes, ethics, and satiric temper to matters of theatrical self-consciousness and techniques of staging.[21] Native nondramatic literature similarly contributed

[21]L. C. Knights, *Drama and Society in the Age of Johnson* (London: Chatto and Windus, 1937), esp. pp. 179–227; Eugene M. Waith, "Appendix II: The Staging," in his edition of *Bartholomew Fair,* by Ben Jonson (New Haven: Yale University Press, 1963), pp. 205–17;

to Jonson's linguistic and satiric practice.[22] Even many critics disposed to emphasize the classical and neoclassical dimensions of the plays have conceded significant divergences from antiquity.[23] Although Jonson repeatedly attempted to distinguish his dramatic methods from those of his contemporaries, today he is merely going the way of all English Renaissance playwrights. While classical influence is respectfully admitted and its interaction with native material at times indicated, it has been increasingly relegated to a walk-on part: the popular heritage now occupies center stage.[24] Given this persuasive yet undogmatic critical trend, it may well seem unreasonable to return to a major theme of this study, to insist that the plays of Marlowe, Shakespeare, Jonson, and their contemporaries would simply not have been written in the absence of the classical inheritance. Neither the generic nor the ideological significance of the classical impact on Renaissance drama, and especially on the works of Jonson, has been adequately understood.[25] The following discussion of *Volpone, The Alchemist*, and especially *Bartholomew Fair* accordingly attempts to outline some of these relationships.

The classicist movement in Renaissance comedy was dialectically related to Europe's approximation to the material conditions of antiquity. It appropriated a dramatic form—Roman comedy—specifically designed to represent the new and distinctive reality of urban commodity exchange and, for all its mastery of verisimilitude and illusionism, produced a self-conscious theatricalism as an inherent reflex of bourgeois culture. Jonson's plays combine this generic heritage with another, the ancient world's tradition of nondramatic satire in verse and prose. Roman satire from Horace to Juvenal responded to a later phase of classical civilization than did the works of Plautus and Terence. It appeared at the time of the violent transition from republic to empire and of the economic apex of the slave mode of production. These momentous changes

---

Brian Gibbons, *Jacobean City Comedy: A Study of Satiric Plays by Jonson, Marston and Middleton* (Cambridge: Harvard University Press, 1968), pp. 19–21, 24–25; Alan C. Dessen, *Jonson's Moral Comedy* (Evanston, Ill.: Northwestern University Press, 1971); Irena Janicka, *The Popular Theatrical Tradition and Ben Jonson* (Łódź, Poland: Uniwersytet Łódzki, 1972); Kirsch, pp. 20–24.

[22]Gibbons, pp. 24–25.

[23]Madeleine Doran, *Endeavors of Art: A Study of Form in Elizabethan Drama* (Madison: University of Wisconsin Press, 1954), p. 169; Jonas Barish, *Ben Jonson and the Language of Prose Comedy* (Cambridge: Harvard University Press, 1960), pp. 79–80.

[24]Kirsch, p. 23, attempts to reconcile the satiric and didactic veins in Jonson.

[25]Recent studies dealing with Jonson's classicism include Salingar, "Comic Form in Ben Jonson: Volpone and the Philosopher's Stone," in *English Drama: Forms and Development—Essays in Honour of Muriel Clara Bradbrook*, ed. Marie Axton and Raymond Williams (Cambridge: Cambridge University Press, 1977), pp. 52–56; L. A. Beaurline, *Jonson and Elizabethan Comedy: Essays in Dramatic Rhetoric* (San Marino, Calif.: Huntington Library, 1978); Altman, pp. 179–95.

undermined the political and social bases of early Roman ascetic ideals, a loss that the satires of the period lament.[26]

Jonson's comedies bear witness to the decline of medieval agrarian civilization and its attendant values, that is, to a historical transition in some ways reminiscent of the conjuncture from which antique satire emerged. More specifically, the dichotomy between social action and moral evaluation renders the prerevolutionary crisis of the absolutist state. The plays share the hostility to the citizen classes of London and the reactionary opposition to capitalism typical of the formerly hegemonic ideology of those sectors in the traditional aristocracy threatened by economic change. Perhaps their central theme is the devastating social and moral effect of early capitalism. By employing the critical cutting edge of satire, Jonson in effect turns a rational, secular tool against its own material origins. The hierarchical class perspective prescribed by neoclassical concepts of decorum, combined with the exigencies of satiric form, reduces human life to fixed social categories, generally precluding complexity or development of character. The detailed settings provide not the means of analyzing the interaction between character and environment, as happens for instance in modern prose fiction, but an instrument of antipathy serving to typify a social milieu and to depict concretely the psychology of the classes inhabiting and responsible for it. The very density of social reference emphasizes the moral and social perversion of the citizen classes. The plays do not confine their critique to these classes. Nonetheless, since Jonson senses that the direction of history runs counter to his hopes, that any dynamism would only be degenerative, he can hope for no more than a static future. His characteristically weak plots are therefore symptomatic, his recourse to the unities of time and place particularly functional.

More than *The Alchemist* or *Bartholomew Fair*, *Volpone* is indebted to classical literature and remote from English life. What is the relation between these two aspects of the play? As one of the oldest and most advanced centers of mercantile capitalism, Venice constituted an appropriate setting in which to investigate the contemporary manifestations of human greed. The city's economic precocity was at the same time partly a cause and partly a consequence of the Renaissance and the recovery of the classical world. Allusions to antiquity by author or characters in this respect serve a verisimilar function. Although Volpone's and Mosca's commitment to wit, play, and the imagination can be overstated—Mosca, after all, proves in the end to be simply a young man on the make—the tricksters' economic practices acquire at least a specious philosophical depth by recourse to a perverted classicism. One thinks es-

[26]Perry Anderson, *Passages from Antiquity to Feudalism* (London: NLB, 1974), pp. 67–76; Noël Salomon, *Recherches sur le thème paysan dans la "comedia" au temps de Lope de Vega* (Bordeaux: Féret, 1965), pp. 171–96.

pecially of Volpone's opening invocation of the Golden Age, of Mosca's Pythagorean show in the following scene, and again of the Catullan and Ovidian echoes in Volpone's attempted seduction of Celia in act 3. All these references are ironic in intention: they point to the positive moral norm absent from the action of the play. In other words, the object of neoclassisal satire is a certain kind of neoclassicism itself, especially insofar as the latter is properly viewed in close relation to the economic practices in conjunction with which it emerged. The same contradiction recurs in *The Alchemist* and, even more sharply, in *Bartholomew Fair*.

These classicist concerns extend to *Volpone*'s subplot as well. Lady Wouldbe's imitative recital of the names of the major Italian vernacular poets testifies to the international influence of the Italian Renaissance. The distinction between the good lady's foolish Italianism and the protagonists' vicious classicism corresponds to a larger contrast between English folly and Italian vice, between London and Venice.[27] Volpone's city, both more classical and more capitalist than Jonson's, thus represents in one sense a mirror of London, but in another a cautionary example of what London was rapidly becoming. But *Volpone* is a cautionary example of a specific kind. The satiric form through which its morality is delivered allows for the rather accidental meting out to the wicked of a justice of sorts. But it leaves no room for a comparable distribution of rewards to the virtuous or, least of all, for any generalized social regeneration. Though freed from the schemes of a few unpleasant individuals, Venetian society remains much the same at the end of the play as it was at the beginning.

*The Alchemist*'s difference from *Volpone* may be measured in terms of geographical distance. A Venetian location evoked the entire history of European civilization on the Mediterranean, a unique inland sea that for over two thousand years had been the continent's primary means of commerce and communication. The switch to London in *The Alchemist* meant a corresponding reorientation toward Europe's future, toward the modern Atlantic economy whose origin went back only to the late fifteenth century. The play, though clearly designed to expose alchemy and perhaps opposed to the aspiring science's radical associations,[28] in part responds as well to growing English interest in overseas trade and perhaps even to the founding of the country's first permanent colony in North America at Jamestown in 1607. For Sir Epicure Mammon, alchemy offers an equivalent to Spanish treasure in Peru and the Indies,

[27]Barish, "The Double Plot in Volpone," in *Ben Jonson: A Collection of Critical Essays*, ed. Barish (Englewood Cliffs, N.J.: Prentice-Hall, 1963), pp. 104–5. For the equation of English folly and Italian vice, see Hunter, "English Folly and Italian Vice: The Moral Landscape of John Marston," in *Jacobean Theatre*, ed. John Russell Brown and Bernard Harris, Stratford-upon-Avon Studies 1 (London: Edward Arnold, 1960), p. 111.

[28]Christopher Hill, *The World Turned Upside Down: Radical Ideas during the English Revolution* (Harmondsworth, Middlesex: Penguin, 1975), p. 290.

and hence to the leading mechanism of the primitive accumulation necessary for the triumph of European capitalism. Marx saw a similar relationship, ironically praising those European exploiters of America, Africa, and Asia who, "cleverer than the alchemists, made gold out of nothing."[29] The aspirations of the émigré Anabaptists in Amsterdam are tied to Dutch maritime expansion, and Surly's crucial Spanish disguise provokes references to the overlapping rivalries among three of the new Atlantic economies—England, Spain, and the Netherlands—on commercial, political, and ideological issues.

The imagined benefits of alchemy may be compared, however, not only to the flow of American gold or to the enormous profits available from speculative investment in long-distance trade, but also to lending at interest and the resulting apparent, mysterious ability of money to create more money.[30] Again Marx addressed this problem at length in *Capital*, noting that "in interest-bearing capital, on the other hand, the self-reproducing character of capital, self-valorizing value, the production of surplus-value, appears as a purely occult quality."[31] He argued, however, that in reality capital accumulated by incorporating unpaid labor in the form of surplus-value. Jonson captures the "occult quality" of alchemy in its full psychological effectiveness, denying gold any self-expansive capacity and locating the source of value in human beings. As many critics have noticed, the base metals transformed into gold are the gulls themselves. The restless activity of the play results, however, not in the creation, but in the transfer of value. On the other hand, Marx might have approved of the satiric disjunction of the plot: the ultimate beneficiary of the alchemical schemes is not the best character, but the trickiest of an amoral lot. The classicism of *The Alchemist* may also be seen in its verbal texture. Amid the play's multitude of mutually incomprehensible languages and pseudolanguages, Mammon's stands out for its specific configuration of referents. When the prospect of alchemical wealth does not lead the knight to evoke the metallic bounties of America, it reminds him of the opulence of antiquity. In this respect as in others, *The Alchemist* embodies the specific combination of forces that determined Europe's future: the Old World almost simultaneously discovered the New World and rediscovered the Ancient World, and by these means it made the transition to capitalism.[32]

[29]Marx, *Capital: A Critique of Political Economy*, vol. 1, introd. Ernest Mandel, trans. Ben Fowkes (New York: Vintage, 1977), p. 917.

[30]Knights, *Drama and Society*, pp. 54–55, 124, 128.

[31]Marx, *Capital*, vol. 3, introd. Mandel, trans. David Fernbach (Harmondsworth, Middlesex: Penguin, 1981), p. 744.

[32]Anderson, *Lineages of the Absolutist State* (London: NLB, 1974), p. 422; D. B. Quinn, "Renaisance Influences in English Colonization," *Transactions of the Royal Historical Society*, 5th ser., 26 (1976): 53–72.

Unlike Volpone, the tricksters in *The Alchemist* act on purely pecuniary motives, attaching no transcendent significance to their deceptions. The association between money and imagination is accordingly relegated to Mammon, only one of many gulls. *Bartholomew Fair* represents an extreme development of this tendency, a narrowing in on England and London, a division of the world into buyers and sellers, and a reduction of human relationships to commodity exchanges. The women at the fair, including even Grace Wellborn, are themselves commodities, and in the spirit of the feeble wordplay with which John Littlewit opens the first act, one might say that Knockem deals in horseflesh by day and whores' flesh by night. As the framing induction and puppet show make clear, the theater itself is an almost exclusively economic institution, its grand classical themes debased beyond recognition by their removal to contemporary London. Similarly, the moralized classicism of Justice Overdo, though self-deluding, is not so much perverse as irrelevant. The ethical system toward which *Volpone* gestures is hard to discern behind the well-intentioned justice's words precisely because of the pervasive, random reality of the fair.

The same point may be made in another way. In *Volpone*, and even more in *The Alchemist*, perhaps because of the thematic emphasis on playing, on acting, one is apt to feel a powerful link between the dramatic construction of a convincing sense of reality, on the one hand, and the provisional status of that reality, on the other. Alchemy in the later work, for instance, appears to be a phenomenon of language, created quite literally ex nihilo. The explosion of the unseen alchemical laboratory near the end of the comedy not only sends a variety of dubious schemes up in smoke; it also seems to put an end to the characters themselves, who, deprived of a raison d'être, reasonably enough cease to exist. The conclusion of *The Alchemist* may accordingly leave an audience with an impression of the fragility both of theatrical reality and of its own world.

At a comparable moment in *Bartholomew Fair*, Rabbi Busy heatedly debates and eventually succumbs to a puppet. The overwhelming impression of reality that the puppet theater produces in the zealous but credulous Puritan once again highlights the artifice of Jonson's plays. This is not the dominant response elicited by the comedy, however. The play within the play continues, as do the larger drama and the fair it renders. One of Jonson's striking achievements in *Bartholomew Fair* is the creation of the palpable, insistent, even oppressive reality of a fair that is also a popular festival. The events of Smithfield fill the play and come to seem an adequate representation of the rich and varied existence lived outside the theater. The ability to reproduce on stage a facsimile of the secular world is a fundamental classicist legacy. But ironically, in *Bartholomew*

*Fair*, as in such other urban satiric comedies as Aretino's *La cortigiana*, Bruno's *Il candelaio*, and Bredero's *The Spanish Brabanter*, the extreme success of this enterprise leaves scant room within the action for those very classical impulses that inspire and shape the play.

This exclusion is one aspect of the satiric thrust of the play: Jonsonian realism is no more ideologically neutral than any other mimetic method. Appropriately, the satiric intention is subject to the very contradiction that operates in relation to the realist impulse. Just as the fair stands for the world, so the scope of the satire is universal: no one is entirely spared. Jonson's repeated and unconvincing attempts to deny the generalizing force of his satire testify to the resulting difficulty. In this context the pervasiveness of commodity relations in *Bartholomew Fair* acquires its full effect. When Winwife, a snobbish gentleman, wonders how Trash and Leatherhead could have considered him a potential customer, his gamester friend Quarlous explains: "Why, they know no better ware than they have, nor better customers then come. And our very being here makes vs fit to be demanded, as well as others."[33] The prologue to the court performance begins, "Your majesty is welcome to a Fair" (p. 11, line 1). Similarly, echoing James's position, Justice Adam Overdo delivers a foolish lecture against smoking, a habit particularly favored by the religious sects during the revolutionary decades.[34] Partly as symbolic punishment for his snooping, Overdo spends act 4 in the stocks, a typical carnivalesque inversion of authority[35] that may also recall the playwright's hostility to informers in *Sejanus His Fall* (1603). It can have been no part of Jonson's intention to insult the king, much less to recommend radical practices, but the logic of his play nonetheless produces a satiric, and perhaps subversive, effect.

In these circumstances, two conclusions are possible. One is that all people are animals—Swift's position in *Gulliver's Travels*. The other is that all people are, nonetheless, also humans—Jonson's solution in *Bartholomew Fair*. Partly from this perspective, the concluding scenes constitute a defense of both popular culture and the public theater, an institution to which their author was deeply, if ambivalently, indebted. As satire approaches its limits, it begins to reverse directions, to transform itself into its own antithesis, universal forgiveness. For these reasons *Bartholomew Fair* marks the culmination of Jonsonian satirical comedy, its

---

[33]Ben Jonson, *Bartholomew Fair*, in *Ben Jonson*, ed. C. H. Herford and Percy and Evelyn Simpson, vol. 6 (Oxford: Clarendon, 1938), 2.5.16–18. The subsequent reference is noted in the text.

[34]Hill, *World*, pp. 198–201.

[35]Peter Burke, *Popular Culture in Early Modern Europe* (New York: Harper and Row, 1978), p. 190.

noticeable geniality deriving from a drastically constricted vision of human possibilities.[36]

That constriction may be understood by reference to what Marx termed the fetishism of commodities, the "metaphysical subtleties and theological niceties . . . , the mystical character of the commodity." In commodity exchange "the relationships between the producers, within which the social characteristics of their labours are manifested, take on the form of a social relation between the products of labour. . . . the commodity . . . reflects the social relation of the producers to the sum total of labour as a social relation between objects, a relation which exists apart from and outside the producers. . . . It is nothing but the definite social relation between men themselves which assumes here, for them, the fantastic form of a relation between things." But "the whole mystery of commodities, all the magic and necromancy that surrounds [sic] the products of labour on the basis of commodity production, vanishes therefore as soon as we come to other forms of production. . . . Whatever we may think, then, of the different roles in which men confront each other in such a society [feudalism], the social relations between individuals in the performance of their labour appear at all events as their own personal relations, and are not disguised as social relations between things, between the products of labour."[37] The fetishism of commodities, then, increasingly becomes the central analytical category of Jonsonian satire. In retrospect, it appears as the destination toward which Jonson was always heading, the common theme that would unify both the individual play and the *oeuvre* as a whole.

Some such principle of unity was a considerable achievement, especially for a playwright who could not or would not rely on his plots to attain this end. *Every Man out of His Humour* has a satiric scope comparable to that of the later comedies, but its coherence is largely confined to a pervasive satiric temper that ultimately derives from Asper-Jonson. By contrast, *Volpone*, *The Alchemist*, and *Bartholomew Fair* give the satiric impulse an object, a content that distinguishes these works within the long literary and theatrical tradition denouncing greed and avarice. "As the commodity-form is the most general and the most undeveloped form of bourgeois production," Marx writes, "it makes its appearance at an early date, though not in the same predominant and therefore characteristic manner as nowadays. Hence its fetish character is still relatively easy to penetrate." For Georg Lukács, who substitutes reification for fetishism, "it is not to be wondered at that the personal nature of economic rela-

---

[36]For geniality, see Barish, *Ben Jonson and the Language of Prose Comedy*, e.g., p. 225. For the opposing view, consult Dessen, pp. 148–220.

[37]Marx, *Capital*, 1:163–65, 169–70.

tions was still understood clearly on occasion at the start of capitalist development, but that as the process advanced and forms became more complex and less direct, it became increasingly difficult and rare to find anyone penetrating the veil of reification."[38] Writing near the start of capitalist development, Jonson could penetrate the veil of reification. The great ideological advantage of his satiric comedies is precisely a point of reference in a prior mode of production, a historically determined possibility of insight. Marx's language—"appears," "occult," "metaphysical," "theological," "mystical," "mystery," "magic," "necromancy," "manifested," "reflects," "fantastic form," "disguised"—suggests that Jonson understood the fetishism of commodities as representation, rather than reality. But he could also see that the commodity-form was on its way to social predominance. In this sense, although his insight is a phenomenon of a relatively brief historical moment, its significance extends into the fetishized world of the present.

Jonson was a man of paradoxes. Manifest in the style and structure of his plays, his ambivalence extends to his attitude toward the Renaissance celebration of individualism, his career as a playwright, and his social position.[39] His classicism was equally riddled by contradictions, ones that no writer of the age could entirely escape. For though the revival of antiquity was vitally related to the rise of capital, it was neither in origin nor in effect a purely bourgeois event. Unquestionably a force for change in relation to a mainly feudal-clerical society, classicism was nonetheless easily adopted by the courts of Renaissance Italy and of the absolute monarchies in western Europe. By contrast, bourgeois societies that sought to preserve neoclassical dramatic practice—such as seventeenth-century Holland and eighteenth-century England—inevitably foundered in the attempt. Jonson could affirm classicism at one level and attack it at another for similar reasons. Although it offered him the basic means by which he could criticize the direction of social change, it was itself inseparable from that change. Without the development of capital, Jonson would have lacked both a technique and a theme: in this respect his critique of capitalism occurs from within. Moreover, as he seems to have realized, the progress of the bourgeoisie was gradually rendering classicism obsolete. *Volpone*, *The Alchemist*, and *Bartholomew Fair*, in their very contradictions, accordingly suggest both the possibilities and the limitations of vigorous social criticism from a primarily reactionary ideo-

[38]Marx, *Capital*, 1:176; Georg Lukács, *History and Class Consciousness: Studies in Marxist Dialectics*, trans. Rodney Livingstone (Cambridge: MIT Press, 1971), p. 86.

[39]Barish, *Ben Jonson and the Language of Prose Comedy*, pp. 85–89; Alfred Harbage, *Shakespeare and the Rival Traditions* (New York: Macmillan, 1952), pp. 92–102; esp. Don E. Wayne, "Drama and Society in the Age of Jonson: An Alternative View," *Renaissance Drama*, n.s., 13 (1982): 103–29.

logical perspective that nonetheless is inevitably complicit with the forces of its own negation.

## SERIOUS DRAMA

If satiric comedy depends on a turn to antiquity, serious drama— exclusive preserve of the nobility in neoclassical theory and prac- tice—broadens and deepens the popular tradition. Two basic types of this characteristically aristocratic form dominate each theater, one he- roic and national, the other private, rural, and scarcely, if at all, aristo- cratic. Although the latter represents more of an innovation, at least when compared with the main lines of Renaissance drama in Italy and France, both rely fundamentally on the resources of popular drama- turgy. This common pattern nevertheless conceals distinctions between the two countries at least as significant as those in satiric comedy. The main cause of the difference here is surely the Protestant nation's histor- ically more advanced social and ideological structures. Spain's nonaristo- cratic plays deal with the peasantry, whereas England's have a relatively bourgeois cast. Moreover, the London stage favors tragedy in both he- roic and rural plays far more than do the *corrales*. In both nations, how- ever, serious drama tends to depict either the failure of the aristocracy to adapt to political change or, indeed, the supersession of the traditional ruling class altogether. Much as satiric comedy reverses the norms of ro- mantic comedy, serious drama undermines the assumptions of the na- tional history play.

### Forms of Serious Drama

In the first decade of the seventeenth century, London playwrights broke with the past by abandoning English history for tragedy—an un- common genre in the 1590s—and particularly for tragedy on classical themes.[40] This shift proved a turning point in English Renaissance drama: in subsequent years tragedy maintained its prominence, while the national history play all but disappeared. The causes of change were undoubtedly multiple—the possible exhaustion of the earlier form, the tightening of censorship, the construction of new theaters, the rise of satire together with the reopening of the private stage, and the increase in social and ideological conflict. Each of these will repay at least brief attention.

[40]Jonathan Goldberg, *James I and the Politics of Literature: Jonson, Shakespeare, Donne, and Their Contemporaries* (Baltimore: Johns Hopkins University Press, 1983), pp. 164–209, em- phasizes the connection between absolutism and classicizing, specifically Roman, tragedy.

With the completion of a second historical tetralogy, perhaps Shakespeare felt he had used up the dramatic potential of England's past. But it will be recalled from chapter 4 that Shakespeare's last national history plays of the 1590s—*1 and 2 Henry IV* and *Henry V*—if anything lead away from tragedy rather than toward it. There was no inherent generic logic in the switch. If it had never taken place, if after 1599 Shakespeare had instead followed the path taken by early-seventeenth-century Spanish heroic drama, scholars would plausibly have found anticipations of that new direction in the immediately preceding works. More likely, he was responding to the same censorship law that spurred the development of satiric comedy. The 1599 bishops' order, although it did not enact a strict ban on English history and did not refer to the national history play at all, did require prior licensing of English histories by the Privy Council. In these circumstances, a foreign setting might have seemed safer, especially after the tightening of ideological control at the accession of James in 1603.[41] Whatever the intentions of the censorship, however, the recourse to tragedy also allowed playwrights and actors alike a critical freedom impossible within the bounds of the national history play.

In Shakespeare's career, tragedy absolutely and unambiguously replaced English history. The two tragedies and nine history plays of the 1590s gave way to a sequence of nine tragedies between 1599 and 1608. In that period Shakespeare set *Julius Caesar, Antony and Cleopatra* (1607), and *Coriolanus* (1608) in the Roman world and both *Troilus and Cressida* (1602) and *Timon of Athens* (1607) in the Greek. Even *King Lear* (1605) is nominally classical, a pattern that continues into the late romances as well. Yet closer scrutiny inevitably modifies this perspective. First, Shakespeare's main concern with antiquity apparently occurred only after 1605. More important, at the other public theaters the national history play remained at least as prominent as tragedy up to that time. Perhaps, then, the 1599 order had only relative impact until reinforced by Jacobean theatrical centralization a few years later. Perhaps, too, the earlier switch by Shakespeare reflected the caution of his company in avoiding the wrath of the authorities, although such a hypothesis is not easily reconciled with the Chamberlain's Men's reckless agreement to perform *Richard II* on the eve of Essex's Rebellion.

Shakespeare's decision may also have owed something to the opening of the Globe. Its Bankside location, combined with its greater physical attractiveness, enabled the Chamberlain's Men to draw a section of their audience from the fashionable areas of London more easily than had

[41]Margot Heinemann, *Puritanism and Theatre: Thomas Middleton and Opposition Drama under the Early Stuarts* (Cambridge: Cambridge University Press, 1980), pp. 36–47.

been possible at the older Middlesex theaters. Perhaps partly with this consideration in mind, Shakespeare offered, in *Julius Caesar*, a more overtly neoclassical play than had been his custom. The success of that tragedy, as well as the problems it raised, might then have led to *Hamlet* (1601).

Whatever the merit of these speculations, *Julius Caesar* did function as a generic shifter, inaugurating Shakespeare's tragic period and with it new possibilities of representation. At the other end of that period, *Coriolanus* realizes some of these possibilities. The opening of the play pits the oppressed plebeians against the Roman senators, who "make edicts for usury, to support usurers; repeal daily any wholesome act established against the rich, and provide more piercing statutes daily to chain up and restrain the poor."[42] The plebeians may here be echoing the popular protests of 1607, in which Levellers and Diggers first appeared.[43] Although Shakespeare hardly advocates the overthrow of patrician rule, he at least shows the legitimacy of lower-class grievances. Coriolanus, both the noblest and the most arrogant member of the aristocracy, lives and dies in relation to this struggle. That the resolution of the crises of early republican Rome depends on his exclusion[44] reveals the radical difference between *Coriolanus* and a play such as Corneille's *Horace*. For the French dramatist, the recourse to classical Rome provided a means of approaching his own nation; for Shakespeare, it offered a way of establishing critical distance. In England the closest generic analogue to Corneille's play, the proper vehicle for depicting the potential harmony between class and state or between upper class and lower, was the national history play.

Jonson's *Sejanus*, a failure at the public theater, produces a somewhat different subversive effect from *Coriolanus*'s. The true tragic complement to dramatic satire in general and, of course, to Jonson's comedies in particular, it replaces Juvenal by Tacitus as part of its abandonment of the exclusively social for the exclusively political. As in the comedies, Jonson pursues loosely didactic ends, attacking dictatorship and informers while insisting that principled action will prove victorious. Yet the plot shows this belief in the ability of human freedom to shape society to be illusory. The ineffectual good characters prove easy prey for the villainous protagonist, who in turn can be defeated only by another consummate villain. Thus Jonson represents politics as a sordid power struggle. Since the lower classes are objects of contempt, Jonson's aristocratic

[12]Shakespeare, *Coriolanus*, ed. Harry Levin, in *William Shakespeare: The Complete Works*, gen. ed Harbage (Baltimore: Penguin, 1969), 1.1.77–80.

[13]Hill, "The Many-Headed Monster," in *Change and Continuity in Seventeenth Century England* (Cambridge: Harvard University Press, 1975), p. 182.

[14]See Anselm Schlösser, "Reflections upon Shakespeare's *Coriolanus*," *Philologica Pragensia* 6 (1963): 11–21; Siegel, pp. 149-55.

spokesman has no potential allies, human or divine, at the end of the play. For the survivors of the tyranny, the final note is not hope but paranoia.[45]

Chapman's *Caesar and Pompey* (1605), perhaps never performed, is also troubled by unconscious ideological contradictions. Though nominally a tragedy, it ends somewhat incongruously with a sense of Cato's triumph. Yet the Senecan Stoicism that motivates the hero is a philosophy of defeat. As the climax approaches, Cato's passionate concern for the destiny of Rome and the welfare of its populace, whom Chapman, in defiance of historical fact, aligns with the Republicans, fades into insignificance before the stirring scene of one man's pursuit of personal freedom in life and in death. So as not to detract from the rather narrowly aristocratic moral, the simultaneous political dimension of suicide so prominent in *Julius Caesar* must here be suppressed. Thus the important national issues raised by both Jonson and Chapman prove insoluble at the political level. The virtuous characters, essentially helpless victims of circumstance, can retain their moral stature only as private, aristocratic individuals incapable of influencing the course of events. The ideological distortions in both works arise from the playwrights' unwillingness to face the obvious, but admittedly depressing, implications of the historical material they dramatize. The plays, in other words, reveal more, and more of significance, about the authors and their society than Jonson and Chapman apparently intended.

Related difficulties beset *Timon of Athens*. Both literally and figuratively, money rules Athens, shaping government policy, social class, and human relations. Timon, disillusioned by the city's previous exploitation of his neofeudal extravagant hospitality, curses all humanity, attributing to gold the absolute power to invert traditional values, to make "Black white, foul fair, wrong right, / Base noble, old young, coward valiant"—a rhetorical formulation of moral outrage typical of the time.[46] Also a feudal figure of sorts, Alcibiades responds to his banishment by the Senate with a vow to destroy Athens. This parallel between main plot and subplot gives rise to the central interpretive problem of the play, however. Although the selective vengeance for which Alcibiades ultimately settles seems juster than Timon's universal misanthropy, Timon is surely right in insisting on the irredeemable depravity of Athens. Since the practices of Alcibiades' and Timon's enemies quite clearly conform to the norms of the entire society, Alcibiades' final victory carries

---

[45]Barish, introduction to Jonson, *Sejanus His Fall*, ed. Barish (New Haven: Yale University Press, 1965), pp. 1–24.

[46]Shakespeare, *Timon of Athens*, ed. Charlton Hinman, in *William Shakespeare*, gen. ed. Harbage, 4.3.29–30. For expressions like Timon's, see Thomas Lodge, *An Alarum against Vsurers* (London, 1584), sig. B1ᵛ and C1ᵛ; Thomas Bell, *The Specvlation of Vsurie* (London, 1596), sig. A2ʳ.

with it no likelihood of the profound changes necessary for a return to a precapitalist economy. This ideological impasse is manifested in the fractured form of the play.[17] *Antony and Cleopatra*, however, does not try to have it both ways. The dichotomies of the play issue in no reconciliation; the verbal paradoxes that in *Macbeth* (1606) reflect the hero's, rather than the world's, disorder are never resolved. The suicide with which Cleopatra caps her career removes her from a new world in which she, like Antony, has no real place. In this respect the lovers' deaths constitute a judgment on the processes of history.[48] The play faces directly what remains oblique in *Sejanus, Caesar and Pompey*, or even *Timon of Athens*.

Both *Sejanus* in particular and the classicizing tendencies of all these plays in general suggest the similarity of tragedy to satiric comedy. The setting for tragedy, as for satire, is a new mode of production. Again like satire, tragedy derives its critical perspective on capitalism from a rootedness in a prior mode of production. Finally, it too reveals a disjunction between social action and moral judgment, the most extreme divergences coinciding with the widest range of social representation. In Shakespeare's career, the turn to tragedy responds in part to the interconnected rise of satire and of the private theaters. The imprint of satiric comedy may be discerned at least in *Hamlet, Troilus and Cressida, Othello* (1604), *King Lear*, and *Timon of Athens*.

Yet it would be misleading to overstress the similarities between tragedy and satiric comedy. Shakespearean tragedy does not consistently, and certainly does not structurally, offer approbation for social mastery. Audience response to the vitality of a belated Vice figure like Iago or Edmund, whose ancestry derives significantly from the popular theatrical tradition, is qualitatively different from the admiration elicited by the adroitness of more neoclassical characters such as Volpone, Subtle, and Face. Nor does Shakespearean tragedy merely complement dramatic satire. It also attempts to incorporate the latter form, in ideological sympathy as well as in social breadth. It is not concerned only with political adaptation. These asymmetries are partly consequences of distinct institutional affiliations. The widest-ranging satiric comedy was generally a product of a transitional balance between public and private theater, in the years from 1609 to 1614. Shakespearean tragedy dates from the pre-

[17]See E. C. Pettet, "*Timon of Athens*: The Disruption of Feudal Morality," *Review of English Studies* 23 (1947): 321–36; Kenneth Muir, "*Timon of Athens* and the Cash-Nexus," *Modern Quarterly Miscellany* 1 (1947): 57–76; Leonard Goldstein, "Alcibiades' Revolt in *Timon of Athens*," *Zeitschrift für Anglistik und Amerikanistik* 15 (1967): 257–78; Siegel, pp. 155–62.

[18]See John F. Danby, *Poets on Fortune's Hill: Studies in Sidney, Shakespeare, Beaumont and Fletcher* (Port Washington, N.Y.: Kennikat Press, 1952), pp. 128–51; Dipak Nandy, "The Realism of *Antony and Cleopatra*," in *Shakespeare in a Changing World*, ed. Arnold Kettle (New York: International Publishers, 1964), pp. 172–94.

vious decade and was composed exclusively for a public theater that was in the process of absorbing the secondary influences of the private stage. Partly as a result, it was more indebted to the tradition of popular dramaturgy.

The strength of that tradition, combined with Shakespeare's critical commitment throughout his career to aristocratic rule in general and monarchical power in particular,[49] helps account for the relative continuity between the national history play and tragedy. Well before 1600, the institutional configuration of the theater, reinforced for Shakespeare by his own modest social origins, opened the way to a judgment of the absolutist state according to its ability to live up to the full popular, humanist, and bourgeois dimensions of its claims. Since, however, that state's actual social basis lay elsewhere, even the history plays offer a critical perspective on the triumph of the monarchy over the separatist feudal nobility. In his entire career Shakespeare presents many admirable aristocrats but few good rulers.

In this sense his tragic period is the climactic dramatic representation of the failings of absolutism. From his history plays, Shakespeare retains a sense of the dynamism of history, the overriding importance of national unity, and the grandeur of human aspiration.[50] *King Lear* and *Macbeth* are even set in the British Isles. On the other hand, the change of subject—from the triumph of a people to the death of a single, often isolated noble figure—suggests a declining belief in the correlation between individual action and the larger movements of social and political transformation. At the beginning of this period, for instance, *Julius Caesar* and *Hamlet* portray the heroic defeat of the finest representatives of the aristocracy by those other members of their class who embody the more typical and despicable features of power. Yet neither these plays nor *Troilus and Cressida*, the last of the Elizabethan tragedies, offers a

---

[49]Marxist critics who take the opposite position, emphasizing the progressive, bourgeois, or radical and democratic humanist essence of Shakespeare, of the state he supported, or of both, or who at least place primacy on his ideological independence of any class position, include, but are not limited to: A. L. Morton, "Shakespeare's Historical Outlook," *Shakespeare Jahrbuch* (Weimar) 100/101 (1964/65): 216; Miklós Szenczi, "The Nature of Shakespeare's Realism," *Shakespeare Jahrbuch* (Weimar) 102 (1966): 50; Heinemann, "Shakespearean Contradictions and Social Change," *Science and Society* 41 (1977): 7–16; Annette T. Rubinstein, "Bourgeois Equality in Shakespeare," *Science and Society* 41 (1977): 25–35; Weimann, "The Soul of the Age: Towards a Historical Approach to Shakespeare," in *Shakespeare in a Changing World*, ed. Kettle, pp. 17–42; idem, *Drama und Wirklichkeit in der Shakespearezeit: Ein Beitrag zur Entwicklungsgeschichte des elisabethanischen Theaters* (Halle [Saale]: Veb Max Niemeyer Verlag, 1958), e.g., p. 310. Some of these positions are challenged by Michael B. Folsom, "Shakespeare the Marxist," *Studies on the Left* 5, no. 4 (1965): 106–19.

[50]For a similar point, see A. A. Smirnov, "Shakespeare, the Renaissance and the Age of Barroco," in *Shakespeare in the Soviet Union*, ed. Roman Samarin and Alexander Nikolyukin, trans. Avril Pyman (Moscow: Progress Publishers, 1966), pp. 58–83.

consistent perspective on the social or ideological significance of such struggles.[51]

In *Hamlet*, for example, even before the truth about Claudius becomes known, Hamlet's inwardness is a matter of conscience, a rejection of the external and hollow rites of the Danish court. As the prince contemptuously retorts to Guildenstern later on, "You would play upon me, you would seem to know my stops, you would pluck out the heart of my mystery, you would sound me from my lowest note to the top of my compass; . . . Call me what instrument you will, though you fret me, you cannot play upon me."[52] At the end of the play, Horatio accepts the responsibility of faithfully reporting Hamlet's story to the world:

> So shall you hear
> Of carnal, bloody, and unnatural acts,
> Of accidental judgments, casual slaughters,
> Of deaths put on by cunning and forc'd
>     cause,
> And, in this upshot, purposes mistook
> Fall'n on th' inventors' heads. All this can I
> Truly deliver.
>
> (5.2.385–91)

Accurate though this account may be, it utterly fails to capture the depth of Hamlet's experience, a depth available only to the audience. Yet even to the audience, and even to those members of it who could see in Hamlet's identification with Wittenberg a synthesis of Renaissance and Reformation[53] of the kind described in chapter 3, the precise ideological significance of *Hamlet* remains somewhat obscure.

After 1603, in the Jacobean tragedies, Shakespeare shifts his focus subtly but crucially. Most of his protagonists in the plays of the next five years are victims, if not always of the rise of capitalism, then at least of some dimensions of bourgeois ideology. The private theaters, in addition to fostering satire, may have impressed upon Shakespeare, by their very existence and by the kind of appeal they made, the growing divisions in English society. These divisions provide the basis of Shakespearean tragedy. They constitute the necessary, though by no means the sufficient, conditions of its formation. Even this qualification is by itself

---

[51]For a view of *Troilus and Cressida* as a critique of capitalism, see Raymond Southall, *Literature and the Rise of Capitalism: Critical Essays Mainly on the 16th and 17th Centuries* (London: Lawrence and Wishart, 1973), pp. 70–85.

[52]Shakespeare, *Hamlet*, ed. Harold Jenkins (London: Methuen, 1982), 3.2.355–63. The subsequent reference is cited in the text.

[53]Thomas Metscher, "Shakespeare in the Context of Renaissance Europe," *Science and Society* 41 (1977): 20–22.

inadequate, however, It is not possible to demonstrate a break in English history during 1599 sufficiently sharp to motivate so major a generic reorientation. The conflicts in society began earlier. On the other hand, the struggles between Parliament and the crown increased toward the end of the 1590s and continued thereafter, conspiracies and rebellions against the state punctuated the first years of the new century, and the accession of James immediately intensified preexistent antagonisms while engendering new ones. Shakespeare's histories coincide with a period of war and depression, his tragedies with an era of peace and prosperity. The conflicts that underlie Shakespearean tragedy, like the oppositions on which satiric comedy turns, are not military or economic, but social.

At this point the implications of the rejection of national history in favor of tragedy emerge. In mediated fashion, the earlier form pits feudalism against absolutism; the later, absolutism against capitalism. Shakespeare's general failure to treat the two stages of the transition at once does not constitute a defect, a distorting incompleteness of vision, however. Virtually nowhere in western Europe did capitalism directly succeed feudalism: the absolutist state regularly intervened. But again, and as the dramatic forms themselves imply, that state was not a neutral entity. Because the struggle between the feudal nobility and the centralizing monarchy occurred within a single class, its outcome, from the point of view of that class, was not necessarily tragic. It could therefore be treated in the national history play. But the antagonism between absolutism and capitalism involved two classes and hence more fundamental issues. As Marx suggested in a celebrated passage, "The *ancien régime* had a *tragic* history, so long as it was the established power in the world while liberty was a personal fancy; in short, so long as it believed and had to believe in its own validity. So long as the *ancien régime*, as an existing world order, struggled against a new world which was just coming into existence, there was on its side a historical error but no personal error. Its decline was, therefore, tragic."[54]

Awareness of the shattering force of the new economic and social relations could easily have caused Shakespeare to retreat to a relatively uncritical defense of absolutism, to commit, in other words, the "historical error." But the confrontation with bourgeois ideology instead led him to recognize that the standard justifications of absolutism were equally ideological.[55] Shakespearean tragedy thus is a synthetic achievement that at times almost transcends the dual and complementary impasses of the

[54]Marx, "Contribution to the Critique of Hegel's *Philosophy of Right*: Introduction," in *The Marx-Engels Reader*, ed. Robert C. Tucker (New York: Norton, 1972), pp. 14–15.

[55]Terry Eagleton, *Criticism and Ideology: A Study in Marxist Literary Theory* (London: NLB, 1976), p. 96.

two main kinds of late-sixteenth-century serious drama. It retains the critical freedom of earlier tragedy but without a corresponding political or social impoverishment. This political and social richness, a legacy of the history play, is in turn sufficiently freed from its nationalist constraints. The inherent limits discernible even in *1 and 2 Henry IV* no longer strictly apply. Subjecting the moral claims of the traditional order to a more searching analysis than at any other time in his career, Shakespeare is particularly sensitive to the nobility's treatment of the lower classes. The hard-won reaffirmation of aristocratic values in these plays, insofar as it occurs at all, is accompanied not only by the death of the main character, but also by the painful acknowledgment of his unfitness to rule. Between 1604 and 1608, then, Shakespeare exploits the ideological opportunities presented by his new form. Every one of the tragedies draws at least partially on the tripartite interrelationships of aristocracy, bourgeoisie, and urban and rural poor, emphasizing both irreconcilable, destructive social conflict and the creative nobility of the hero's unsuccessful struggles.[56]

As the earlier discussion of the shift to classical tragedy may have suggested, *Timon of Athens* offers the clearest account of the antagonism between aristocratic and bourgeois ideology, *Coriolanus* the most direct representation of the opposition between upper class and lower. Similar claims about the other Jacobean tragedies may well seem excessively allegorical, however. The social conflicts of early-seventeenth-century England are not so much the subject of the plays as the crucial force behind them. But of course other forces also intervene, and often in the formation of a single character. For instance, in *Othello*, significantly the earliest of these works, Iago somewhat inconsistently combines the Vice's perverse pleasure in amoral destruction with a cynical self-interest and reductive materialism that, from a certain point of view, are the harbingers of a new economic system.[57] *Macbeth* turns on a related internal tension, but this time one that is at the center of the character's consciousness as well as of the play as a whole. In murdering Duncan, a man who is at once his kinsman, his guest, and his lord, Macbeth violates specifically feudal social relations, not, of course, in the name of economic calculation, but in allegiance to an amoral ambition whose superficial rationality leads inexorably away from personal fulfillment and toward a

---

[56]Lukács, *The Historical Novel*, trans. Hannah and Stanley Mitchell (Boston: Beacon, 1963), pp. 99, 122, discusses the nobility of struggle in tragedy. Kenneth Muir, "Shakespeare and Politics," in *Shakespeare in a Changing World*, ed. Kettle, pp. 65–83, reviews changes in Shakespeare's attitudes. On this subject, see also Morton, pp. 219–20, 224–26.

[57]On *Othello* see G. M. Matthews, "*Othello* and the Dignity of Man," in *Shakespeare in a Changing World*, ed. Kettle, pp. 123–45; Georg Muri, "*Othello*," *Shakespeare Jahrbuch* (Weimar) 104 (1968): 85–108.

meaningless nihilism.[58] And in *Antony and Cleopatra* the irresolvable dichotomies point to the same underlying problematic. Furthermore, the absence of the cataclysmic feel of the two earlier tragedies, combined with the supersession of the protagonists by the pragmatic and business-like Caesar, perhaps indicates a resigned acceptance of change previously resisted, but ultimately unavoidable.

Lower-class expression is also polyvocal in these tragedies. It falls loosely into two overlapping categories, an indebtedness to the practices of popular dramaturgy and an explicit portrayal of popular concerns and grievances. The first is perhaps most important when it involves the assimilation of popular elements into a major character, such as Hamlet or Iago. But of course the popular heritage also plays a significant structural role in the persons of comic, lower-class figures who directly or indirectly comment on the main plot. From the tragedies alone the list would include the gravediggers in *Hamlet*, Thersites in *Troilus and Cressida*, the Porter in *Macbeth*, Apemantus in *Timon of Athens*, and the simple countryman who brings the heroine the asp in *Antony and Cleopatra*.[59] This first popular dimension, however, is evidently less prominent in the classical tragedies and especially in the works from after 1605. In a sense, then, the unusually overt and extended presentation of lower-class ideology in *Coriolanus* compensates for the decline of a traditional mode of popular dramaturgy. Finally, as will later become clear, *King Lear* achieves the fullest synthesis among the tragedies not only of these two appropriations of popular culture, but also of the dual social oppositions, between upper class and lower and between aristocratic and bourgeois ideology.

A comparable national perspective often informs Spanish heroic drama of this period. In another respect, however, a focus on Shakespearean tragedy leads to an overemphasis on the differences between the English and Spanish stages. From 1599 to 1608, the vast majority of pieces performed in the private theaters were comedies. As noted above, however, tragedy did indeed supersede the national history play not only in Shakespeare's career, but in the public theater as a whole. Thus the generic differences between the two national dramas after 1600 remain undeniable. The social and theatrical changes in Spain during the first two decades of the seventeenth century were less pronounced than those that had occurred in England by 1608. In particular, the relative absence of a conflict between modes of production reduced the ideolog-

---

[58]On *Macbeth* see J. K. Walton, "*Macbeth*," in *Shakespeare in a Changing World*, ed. Kettle, pp. 102–22.

[59]Weimann, *Shakespeare and the Popular Tradition in the Theater: Studies in the Social Dimension of Dramatic Form and Function*, ed. Robert Schwartz (Baltimore: Johns Hopkins University Press, 1978), pp. 215–46, esp. 238–39.

ical space for tragedy.[60] Peninsular heroic drama does not consistently reveal the failure of the aristocracy to adapt to a new political situation, much less jettison the Spanish people as an object of representation. The national history play, like romantic comedy, continued to flourish long after the turn of the century.

Indeed, Tirso de Molina's celebrated *La prudencia en la mujer* (probably 1622)[61] represents something like the apotheosis of the genre. At least ambiguously feminist in perspective,[62] it may be seen as a nontragic reworking of some of the major issues of *Bamba*, with a woman replacing a peasant as guardian of the state. The potential interchangeability of sexual oppression and class oppression, or at least the association between the two, generally characterizes early-seventeenth-century serious drama in both countries. More particularly, *La prudencia en la mujer*, drawing its subject from the political conflicts of the late Middle Ages—its historical setting is virtually contemporaneous with that of *Edward II*—ties its feminist concerns to a national and dynastic focus. It turns on the struggle between aristocracy and monarchy, between class and state. Tirso's allegiances are unambiguously with the latter. In all these respects the work is perhaps the closest Spanish analogue not to Shakespearean tragedy, but to the Shakespearean national history play. A national and dynastic perspective also shapes the second part of Castro's *Las mocedades del Cid* (1610?–15?).[63] Both plays, however, present unusually sordid views of the high aristocracy. The struggle between the nobility and the crown recurs at the end of the century in Bances Candamo's *El esclavo en grillos de oro* (1692),[64] although the plot is set in imperial Rome rather than Spain and its composition for a court audience further narrows the frame of reference.

Yet these elements of continuity and the corresponding absence of tragedy should not obscure the real break with earlier serious drama that occurred after 1600 in response to the growing national crisis. The Spanish equivalent to Shakespearean tragedy took the form of a symptomatic moral belt tightening, an aggressive effort to cope with the unfa-

[60]For alternative explanations, see Raymond R. MacCurdy, "Lope de Vega y la pretendida inhabilidad española para la tragedia: Resumen crítico," in *Homenaje a William L. Fichter*, ed. Kossoff and Amor y Vázquez, pp. 525–35; idem, *The Tragic Fall: Don Alvaro de Luna and Other Favorites in Spanish Golden Age Drama*, North Carolina Studies in the Romance Languages and Literatures, no. 197 (Chapel Hill: University of North Carolina Department of Romance Languages, 1978), pp. 17–37.

[61]Date: MacCurdy, introduction to his edition of *"El burlador de Sevilla y convidado de piedra" and "La prudencia en la mujer"*, by Tirso de Molina (New York: Dell, 1965), p. 26.

[62]But see McKendrick, pp. 199, 201–3, 204, 207.

[63]Date: Courtney Bruerton, "The Chronology of the *Comedias* of Guillén de Castro," *Hispanic Review* 12 (1944): 150. See Sturgis E. Leavitt, "Una comedia sin paralelo: *Las Hazañas del Cid*, de Guillén de Castro," in *Homenaje a William L. Fichter*, ed. Kossoff and Amor y Vázquez, pp. 429–38.

[64]Date: Wilson and Moir, p. 141.

miliar experience of defeat, an extreme reconsolidation of aristocratic ideology, a reassertion of the values that had accompanied earlier success, and hence a return to the past for a stylized and exaggerated code of honor.[65] A fundamental issue throughout seventeenth-century Spanish drama,[66] the honor code, though traceable to primitive Germanic society, is rooted in the material and ideological conditions of the feudal aristocracy, the operative component of which was the complementary combination of military vocation and freedom from manual labor. Its hierarchical assumptions were an international inheritance of the European ruling class in the Renaissance. During this period, it served to perpetuate sexual inequality far less in the Protestant North than in Catholic, and especially Mediterranean Catholic, nations. The unusual importance of honor in Spain was also a consequence of the atypically strong survival of feudal relations, at least by western European standards, as well as of the legacy of Moorish influences. The Reconquest and the subsequent subjugation of the New World, both agents of that survival, also contributed to the diffusion of the concept of honor to classes beneath the nobility.[67]

Most recent discussion of this phenomenon, though properly attuned to the formative role of the Middle Ages, has nonetheless tended to ignore these particular influences and to concentrate instead on the problem of the *conversos* (Jews forced to accept Catholicism) and the resulting societal obsession with *limpieza de sangre* (purity of blood).[68] It is easy enough to see how attention to the racial and religious purity of blood might reinforce pride in the social purity of blood. But *limpieza de sangre* could also work against hierarchical principles, becoming a vehicle for an egalitarian notion of honor of sorts and as such a mystified ideological weapon of the poor against the rich.[69] Given the general context of

[65] For the change in Lope's treatment of honor in this direction after 1600 see Donald R. Larson, *The Honor Plays of Lope de Vega* (Cambridge: Harvard University Press, 1977), p. 161.

[66] General discussions of honor on the *Siglo de Oro* stage include Ramón Menéndez Pidal, "Del honor en el teatro español," in *De Cervantes y Lope de Vega* (Buenos Aires: Espasa-Calpe, 1940), pp. 153–84; Arnold Reichenberger, "The Uniqueness of the 'Comedia,'" *Hispanic Review* 27 (1959): 307–9; C. A. Jones, "Spanish Honour as Historical Phenomenon, Convention, and Artistic Motive," *Hispanic Review* 3 (1965): 32–39.

[67] J. H. Elliott, *Imperial Spain, 1469–1716* (New York: St. Martin's Press, 1964), pp. 215, 229, 303–4.

[68] See, for example, Américo Castro, "El drama de la honra en la literatura dramática," in *De la edad conflictiva*, vol. 1, *El drama de la honra en España y en su literatura*, 2d ed. (Madrid: Taurus, 1963), pp. 59–107; Antonie A. van Beysterveldt, *Répercussions du souci de la pureté de sang sur la conception de l'honneur dans la "comedia nueva" espagnole* (Leiden: Brill, 1966); Joseph H. Silverman, "Some Aspects of Literature and Life in the Golden Age of Spain," in *Estudios de literatura española ofrecidos a Marcos A. Morínigo* (Madrid: Insula, 1971), pp. 133–70.

[69] For the two dimensions of honor outlined here, see Gustavo Correa, "El doble aspecto de la honra en el teatro del siglo xvii," *Hispanic Review* 26 (1958): 99–107. The egalitarian

the Inquisition and the Counter-Reformation, this was possible because the nobility in the towns intermarried with men and women of Jewish descent more frequently than did the rural masses, because it was easier to trace the lineage of an aristocrat than of a peasant, and because wealthy Jews had traditionally served as fiscal agents of the state and thus as direct oppressors of the lower classes. Yet the effectiveness of *limpieza de sangre* was fairly limited when directed against the higher and more powerful circles of the aristocracy. It is nonetheless far preferable to see the concern with purity of blood as an issue in its own right that sometimes became an adjunct of class struggle than to reverse the relationship, as some contemporary scholars do, and to transform depictions of social conflict into covert allusions to racial antagonism.[70]

As a defining feature of early-seventeenth-century Spanish heroic drama, the code of honor did not entail an abandonment of affairs of the nation. But it did deflect attention from the destiny of the state in general and the conflict between feudalism and absolutism in particular toward a demonstration of the efficacy of an ideal norm of aristocratic conduct in protecting the nation and its ruling class. Perhaps the central form of political drama was the *comedia de privanza* (play about royal favor), cultivated assiduously during the first third of the century and intermittently thereafter. *La prudencia en la mujer* and *El esclavo en grillos de oro* both belong ambiguously to this subgenre, which often has a tragic outcome. In general, however, *comedias de privanza* concentrate on the emotional and personal side of the relationship between king and favorite rather than on its larger political significance.[71]

An extreme example of the attenuation of national concerns is provided by Alarcón's *Ganar amigos* (1619–21),[72] in which the *privado*'s extraordinary spiritual nobility leads him to increasing peril in a society incapable of understanding the selfless motives underlying his behavior. As the title suggests, however, his conduct simultaneously wins him friends, who are furthermore impelled by his example and by the complications of the plot to adopt for themselves the protagonist's exalted standard of honor, in order to restore him to his former felicity. The

---

and democratic aspects of Spanish society are emphasized, indeed overemphasized, by Carmen Olga Brenes, *El sentimiento democrático en el teatro de Juan Ruiz de Alarcón* (Valencia: Editorial Castalia, 1960), pp. 13–32, 45–58.

[70]The argument here follows Elliott, pp. 213–17, and Salomon, pp. 114–25, against the position represented by the scholars cited in n. 68 above.

[71]Leicester Bradner, "The Theme of *Privanza* in Spanish and English Drama, 1590–1625," in *Homenaje a William L. Fichter*, ed. Kossoff and Amor y Vázquez, p. 106; MacCurdy, *The Tragic Fall*, passim.

[72]Date: Sister Mary Austin Cauvin, O.P., "The *Comedia de Privanza* in the Seventeenth Century," Ph.D. diss., University of Pennsylvania, 1957, p. 432 n. 7. For the relative lack of political interest in *Ganar amigos*, see p. 431.

play concludes with the aristocracy and the crown at a higher moral plane than before. Yet the most desirable female marries a rapist, the hero ends up with a woman of questionable character, and the second most honorable figure in the play is left unwed. Since this resolution is entirely a consequence of the code of honor,[73] *Ganar amigos* unwittingly reveals, against Alarcón's obvious intention, that the exercise of honor even by the entire aristocracy does not completely answer to that class's needs. In this respect the play has affinities with the tragedies of Jonson and Chapman.

Although national and dynastic issues are more prominent in the famous first part of Castro's *Las mocedades del Cid* (1612?–15?),[74] even here there is no absolute equation of aristocratic honor and the triumph of Spain. Honor dominates the central love plot and is intermeshed with affairs of state through the acts of military prowess by which the Cid wins over first the king and then Ximena. But it has almost nothing to do with matters of royal succession or with the conduct of the heir, Prince Sancho, and his sister Urraca. The continuation of the play moves this background activity to center stage. In *Le Cid*, Corneille excises it entirely as part of a general process of narrowing and intensification: his adaptation, after all, is by definition no longer a national history play.[75] But at the same time, he fully integrates honor and politics. *Le Cid* works toward the accommodation of private feudal values to the needs of the absolutist state. The absence of a comparably complete fusion in *Las mocedades del Cid* is an indication both of the comparative weakness of Habsburg absolutist pressure on the nobility and of the limited potency of aristocratic honor as a solution to the crisis of Spain.

It would be wrong, however, to stress such unresolved contradictions while ignoring the at least superficially successful achievement of reconciliation and related preservation of a conservative social order. The early-seventeenth-century Spanish nobility, as depicted in the public theater, retains much of its traditional vocation as a class. Its ideals and behavior, however exclusive, continued to possess a corporatist dimension. The heroine of *La prudencia en la mujer* is identified with humble shepherds, who come to her aid at the climactic moment of the play. In *Ganar amigos* a servant shows himself the moral equal of most of the aristocracy and accompanies this demonstration with a diatribe against class-based definitions of honor that is ideologically of a piece with the critical treatment of the protagonist in *La verdad sospechosa*. *Las mocedades del Cid*

---

[73]Cauvin, p. 439.

[74]Date: Bruerton, p. 150.

[75]For a recent comparison of the two plays, see William E. Wilson, *Guillén de Castro* (New York: Twayne, 1973), pp. 77–82.

is profoundly indebted to the *romances* and hence to a popular conception of national history.[76] This interclass perspective aligns Spanish heroic drama with Shakespearean tragedy.

Yet the fullest utilization of popular culture on the Spanish stage occurs in peasant honor drama, a form that finds an important analogue in English bourgeois tragedy. The fundamental role of *romances* in such plays as Lope's *Peribáñez y el comendador de Ocaña* (1604–14)[77] and Luis Vélez de Guevara's *La serrana de la Vera* (1613)[78] is paralleled in Heywood's *A Woman Killed with Kindness* (1603).[79] The relics of pagan festival preserved in many of the peasant plays[80] may be compared to the Morris dance in Dekker, John Ford, and William Rowley's *The Witch of Edmonton* (1621). Popular parody or qualification of the serious plot occurs briefly in *A Yorkshire Tragedy* (1606) and in *Arden of Feversham* (1591), and more profoundly, especially in the character of Nicholas, in *A Woman Killed with Kindness*.[81] There is something of this sort in Lope's *El mejor alcalde el rey* (1620–23) and more, in Nuño, in Calderón's *El alcalde de Zalamea* (1636?, early 1640s?). But the true peasant *gracioso* is almost a contradiction in terms.[82] At any rate, the popular dimension of the Spanish plays is carried above all by the protagonists themselves. Relatedly, the vast majority of bourgeois tragedies and peasant dramas have national settings. In addition, most of the English works and a number of the Spanish plays—Lope's *Fuente Ovejuna* (probably 1612–14) and *El mejor alcalde el rey* among them—are based on actual events.

The resemblances between the two forms extend to ideology as well. A pervasively religious context, common in the Spanish plays and perhaps most evident in *Peribáñez*, regularly emerges at the conclusion of the English works. In the latter it is associated with a rapid sequence of repentance, pardon, and promise of salvation that blunts the tragic force of the action,[83] just as happens in *La serrana de la Vera* through the uni-

[76]See Menéndez Pidal, *La epopeya castellana a través de la literatura española*, 2d ed. (1910; rpt. Madrid: Espasa-Calpe, 1959), pp. 191–201.

[77]For the continuing debate on the date, see Alonso Zamora Vicente, ed., *"Peribáñez y el comendador de Ocaña" y "La dama boba"*, by Lope de Vega (Madrid: Clásicos Castellanos, 1963), pp. vii–xiv. Subsequent references to *Peribáñez* are to this edition and are cited in the text. For the function of the *romance*, see Salomon, pp. 384, 555–58.

[78]Date: Salomon, p. 22; *Romance*: Menéndez Pidal, *La epopeya castellana*, p. 201.

[79]Michel Grivelet, *Thomas Heywood et le drame domestique élizabéthain* (Paris: Didier, 1957), pp. 203–4.

[80]Salomon, p. 663.

[81]Arthur Brown, "Thomas Heywood's Dramatic Art," in *Essays on Shakespeare and Elizabethan Drama in Honor of Hardin Craig*, ed. Richard Hosley (Columbia: University of Missouri Press, 1962), p. 336.

[82]Salomon, pp. 160–63, who perhaps overstates the case.

[83]Cf. T. S. Eliot, *Selected Essays* (New York: Harcourt, Brace and World, 1950), p. 158.

versally acknowledged justness of the heroine's punishment.[84] The apparent generic contrast between all these tragedies and most of the peasant drama is thus somewhat blurred. Again, the comfortable rural domesticity that provides the backdrop for the plays involves an implicit association of wealth, concentrated in landed private property, with moral virtue.[85] One thinks especially of Frankford in Heywood's tragedy, Old Carter in *The Witch of Edmonton*, Peribáñez, Pedro Crespo in *El alcalde de Zalamea*, Juan Labrador in Lope's *El villano en su rincón* (1611), and the titular figure in Francisco de Rojas Zorrilla's (?) *Del rey abajo, ninguno o El labrador más honrado, García del Castañar* (1631?–44?).[86] But for a number of these characters, the highest satisfaction of their middling, private existence derives from married love, the threat to which causes them extreme misery. Several of the plays accordingly reveal a transformation of extreme aristocratic and masculine notions of honor into what for the time represented a far more humane system of morality, implicitly based on a conviction of at least relative sexual and social equality.

Strictly speaking, however, most of the protagonists in Spanish peasant drama or English bourgeois tragedy do not belong to the bourgeoisie. This is evident enough with the peasant heroes, whose birth is either humble or, in *El mejor alcalde el rey* and *Del rey abajo, ninguno*, aristocratic—an incongruity that owes something to the geographical vagaries of peninsular history. Similarly, the main characters of the English plays are consistently members of the gentry: *A Yorkshire Tragedy* scarcely extends beyond that class. Yet not only were the gentry integrally linked to the rise of capitalism; the themes and attitudes that shape the plays of both countries possess in retrospect a distinctively bourgeois quality. Although one would of course not want to push this argument too far with the Spanish plays, it is surely symptomatic that Lukács, after twice referring to Pedro Crespo as a peasant, goes on to describe *El alcalde de Zalamea* as one "of the important bourgeois dramas."[87] Even Noël Salomon, who labors under no such misconception, remarks: "in the opening in a still feudal horizon, this aspiration of the peasant to issue forth on the free sea of dignity already causes us to catch a glimpse of the distant brightness of equality of the bourgeois type."[88] Yet the plays also reveal

---

[84]See McKendrick, pp. 115–18.

[85]For the Spanish plays, see Salomon, pp. 236–307, 755–78.

[86]The range of dates, relevant only if the play is by Rojas, indicates his first known association with court literary circles, on the one hand, and the closing of the theaters, on the other. Rojas died in 1648. See Jean Testas, introducción to his edition of *Del rey abajo, ninguno o El labrador más honrado, García del Castañar*, by Francisco de Rojas Zorrilla (Madrid: Editorial Castalia, 1971), pp. 17–27.

[87]Lukács, *Historical Novel*, pp. 104, 119, and, for the quoted phrase, 129.

[88]Salomon, p. 832.

the problematic quality of this consciousness. The placidity of everyday life in all of them is interrupted by sudden bursts of violence that are often engendered by sexual conflict and that produce significant formal and ideological contradictions.

The subject may be best approached, however, by reversing direction and considering the major contrasts between peasant drama and bourgeois tragedy. The latter category comprises only a miniscule percentage of the plays performed on the English Renaissance stage. Peasant dramas, on the other hand, are not only far more numerous, but also far more influential: *Peribáñez*, *Fuente Ovejuana*, and *El alcalde de Zalamea*—admittedly, ideologically heterodox specimens—have won a place in European culture as a whole. This distinction ultimately depends on the difference between two modes of production. Bourgeois tragedy is rooted in early English capitalism. There is some interesting juxtaposition of classes in *A Woman Killed with Kindness* and *The Witch of Edmonton*. *Arden of Feversham* briefly but suggestively dramatizes the social conflict over the land that helped lead to the initial formation of the British working class. But all the plays reveal a social narrowness inseparable from the historical immaturity of the English bourgeoisie and of English capitalism as late as the early seventeenth century. They take on neither national politics nor class struggle. The deepening conflict between absolutism and capitalism, like the incipient one between capitalist and proletarian, is beyond their range. Bourgeois tragedy is static: it conceives of the bourgeoisie neither as a rising force in conflict with the traditional order nor as an established class challenged from below. Almost despite itself, it points beyond the present to what could not yet be thought, at a time when aristocratic ideology remained hegemonic.

The limits of bourgeois self-consciousness, pervasively evident in these plays, especially take the form of an uncertain relationship between the represented action and the conventional values by which it is judged. In *Arden of Feversham*, the homiletic conclusion seems strangely inadequate to the passions and inner conflicts that motivate the characters. The multiple plots of *A Woman Killed with Kindness* and *The Witch of Edmonton* raise similar difficulties. Although the two plots of Heywood's play result in a generalization and fertile ambiguity of meaning,[89] they also reveal the dramatist's reluctance to choose between the behavior of different social classes, a desire to subsume real oppositions into a specious unity, and, most important, a sense that the central bourgeois values lack sufficient generalizing force in themselves, that they require an aristocratic buttress. Similarly, in *The Witch of Edmonton*, although the crimes in both

[89]Grivelet, *Thomas Heywood*, p. 206; idem, "The Simplicity of Thomas Heywood," *Shakespeare Survey* 14 (1961): 65.

plots seem to have social causes, the audience is actually presented with two different worlds. One, relatively realistic, involves the gentry and yeomanry; the other, pervaded by superstition, folklore, and witchcraft, concerns the peasantry. Human freedom is insisted upon, but, unlike the drama and literature of later centuries, the play can demonstrate the seriousness of everyday life only by diabolical intervention.[90] In *Othello*, on the other hand, Shakespeare superimposes these two perspectives by introducing Iago's apparently demonic powers into a domestic tragedy. The play's famous double time—a sign of ideological ambivalence—socializes this metaphysical dimension. Whereas the compressed temporality lends intensity to the action, allusions to a more leisurely chronology anchor the tragedy in a more realistic social world. Finally, and perhaps most telling, the main plot of *A Woman Killed with Kindness* simultaneously asserts the equality and inequality of man and woman, of husband and wife.

The continued domination of the nobility that lies behind these evasions is in the Spanish peasant drama, by contrast, a crucial source of strength. The wealthy protagonists, like the aristocracy, exploit lower-class labor and in this sense are miniature analogues, rather than antagonists, of the traditional rulers of the countryside. Yet their real historical models, by their very success and the further expectations it aroused, did come repeatedly into conflict with the nobility. Their struggle, then, turned on the basic coercive relationship of feudal society—between lord and peasant. This irreconcilable contradiction distinguishes peasant drama from bourgeois tragedy, and indeed from nearly all other Renaissance drama and popular culture as well.[91] An unexpansionist, politically quiescent bourgeoisie did not automatically find itself opposed to a feudal nobility: neither class depended on the exploitation of the other. But much of the peasantry, as a normal and inevitable part of its daily life, had a portion of its surplus product appropriated by the aristocracy. The centrality of this experience made it possible for peasant drama to retain a national dimension, evoking not only the monarchy and its wars, but also the intraclass conflict between the aristocracy and the absolutist state. A few of the plays, moreover, did so indirectly enough to avoid the inherent ideological constraints of the national history play. For these reasons, though peasant drama is rooted in less modern relations of production than is domestic tragedy, its resonance for the social conflicts of the contemporary industrialized West remains far greater.

The triumph of the peasant play about 1610 probably depended not only on the general social conditions already outlined, but also on more

[90]Cf. the title of an older work in the field: Otelia Cromwell, *Thomas Heywood: A Study in the Elizabethan Drama of Everyday Life* (1928; rpt. n.p.: Archon Books, 1969).
[91]Burke, p. 159.

immediate events and relationships, in all of which Lope, the founder of the form, may have had a personal stake. These included the expulsion of the *moriscos* between 1609 and 1614, which gave added ideological weight to the assertion of *limpieza de sangre*; temporary intraaristocratic conflicts; and declining respect for the military orders. A less specific impulse was the long-term struggle between the peasantry and the troops that, against its will, were quartered in its villages.[92] But the plays also grew out of a long prior generic evolution, a gradual process of popularization, a movement from pastoral to peasantry, a transfer of attention from aristocratic desires to peasant needs. The increasing intrusion of reasonably authentic aspects of peasant life into pastoral drama produced an important modification in the ideological function of the form. To be sure, the theatrical image of rural retreat, especially in a play like *El villano en su rincón*, remained for the nobility a fantasy of freedom from the combined pressures of court and city. The apparent intensification of the honor code may even have reinforced this meaning. But like that code, the idealization of the peasantry seems to have been a means of returning to the sources of the Spanish people, to a lost vitality that could be recovered, surprisingly enough, only in agricultural labor. For the aristocracy, then, peasant drama may have come to constitute a fantasy of precapitalist work.

But in *Peribáñez* the ideological impetus has changed even more radically. Motifs formerly used to ridicule the peasantry are refashioned to add to the dignity of the class, the devices of pastoral, for instance, now applying to Peribáñez and his wife Casilda. More important, in a manner adumbrated by *Bamba*, the very literary resources of aristocratic culture are called into question. Peribáñez can say of Casilda:

> El olivar más cargado
> de aceitunas me parece
> menos hermoso, y el prado
> que por el mayo florece,
> sólo del alba pisado.

(The olive-grove most laden / with olives and the meadow / that flowers in May, / trampled only by the dawn, / seem to me less beautiful. [1.1.46–50])

But the comendador, his belated, upper-class rival for her affections, must fall back on:

> Hermosa labradora,
> más bella, más lucida

[92]Salomon, pp. 819–28, 863, 890–97. The subsequent discussion is indebted to this work.

> que ya del sol vestida
> la colorada aurora;
> sierra de blanca nieve,
> que los rayos de amor vencer se atreve.

(Beautiful peasant, / more beautiful, more shining / than the colored dawn / already dressed in sunlight; mountain of white snow, / which the rays of love dare to conquer. [1.11.522–27])

Peribáñez knows and loves Casilda and compares her to the earth; the comendador knows the language of love and compares her to the sky. Again, when describing an encounter with Casilda, the comendador says:

> yo, con los humildes ojos,
> mostraba que sus enojos
> me daban golpes mortales.

(I, with humble eyes, / showed that her anger / gave me mortal blows. [2.3.1253–55])

The appropriation here of a Petrarchan love conceit bears a complex relationship to reality. In portraying himself as the servant or victim of Casilda, the aristocratic lover inverts the actual social situation. Yet this reversal neatly establishes the proper ethical order, since the comendador's language expresses his moral inferiority.[93]

Nonetheless, modern critics tend to minimize the significance of class conflict both in this work and in the peasant drama in general.[94] Of course most of the plays find means of softening or evading the issue. In *Del rey abajo, ninguno*, for instance, not only does the peasant hero turn out to be of noble birth, his enemy, whom he had assumed and feared was the king, also proves to be simply another aristocrat. *El mejor*

---

[93]On these issues, as well as on the play in general, see Aubrun and José F. Montesinos, prólogo to their edition of *Peribáñez* (Paris: Hachette, 1943), pp. xv–xlviii; José Manuel Blecua, "Análisis de la comedia," in his edition of *Peribáñez* (Zaragoza: Editorial Ebro, 1944), pp. 9–22; Wilson, *Spanish and English Literature of the 16th and 17th Centuries: Studies in Discretion, Illusion, and Mutability* (Cambridge: Cambridge University Press, 1980), pp. 130–54; R. G. Sánchez, "El contenido irónico-teatral en el *Peribáñez* de Lope de Vega," *Clavileño* 5 (1954): 17–25; Correa, "El doble aspecto de honor en *Peribáñez y el comendador de Ocaña*," *Hispanic Review* 26 (1958): 188–99; Alison Turner, "The Dramatic Function of Imagery and Symbolism in *Peribáñez* and *El caballero de Olmedo*," *Symposium* 20 (1966): 174–86.

[94]The most extreme example of this position is José Antonio Maravall, *Teatro y literatura en la sociedad barroca* (Madrid: Seminarios y Ediciones, 1973), pp. 57–145. But see also Eva R. Price, "The Peasant Plays of Lope de Vega," *Modern Language Forum* 20 (1937): 214–19; R. D. F. Pring-Mill, introduction to his edition of *Lope de Vega (Five Plays)*, trans. Jill Booty (New York: Hill and Wang, 1961), pp. xx–xxvi; R. O. Jones, "Poets and Peasants," in *Homenaje a William L. Fichter*, ed. Kossoff and Amor y Vázquez, pp. 341–55.

*alcalde el rey* removes political autonomy from the peasantry, reserving all power for the wise, just, and disguised monarch—a familiar popular motif.[95] The profound sexual and social rebellion of *La serrana de la Vera* is ideologically censored, at least in part, from the point of view of traditional morality.[96] A concluding peasant acquiescence that violates the emotional force of *El villano en su rincón* resolves the relatively plotless but genuine ideological conflict between rural retirement and courtly concerns. More generally, the transfer of social and economic struggles to the arena of sexual relations, despite having certain historical analogues and despite expressing authentic feminist concerns, helps avoid the full tragic implications of irreconcilable antagonism.

But in at least three plays—*Fuente Ovejuna, Peribáñez,* and *El alcalde de Zalamea*—even most of these limited qualifications do not apply. Not only can royal intervention at the ends of these works be interpreted equally well as reactionary corporatism and progressive affirmation; the role of the monarchy is essentially limited to the acceptance of a fait accompli. *Fuente Ovejuna* may be left for separate, more extended treatment. In *Peribáñez* the king abandons his plan to punish the hero when he hears Peribáñez's defense of private vengeance. But he retains an aristocratic sense of surprise that a peasant could act on such noble values. And in *El alcalde de Zalamea,* though the monarch agrees with Pedro Crespo about the guilt of the offending captain, he denies Zalamea's jurisdictional rights until presented with the captain's corpse. It is hard to imagine how a fully sympathetic portrayal of the peasantry literally getting away with murder at the expense of the aristocracy, with the crown confined to ambivalent acquiescence, could have served to reinforce the social status quo.

Yet the monarchist resolutions of the plots cannot be lightly dismissed. Salomon's solution to the problem does justice to their prominence. These peasant plays, he argues,

> are an attempt to "comprehend" (embrace) some of the internal conflicts of monarcho-seigneurial society and to master the tangling up of its contradictons by a sort of ideological miracle. Thanks to monarchist sentiment and thanks to the appearance of the royal figure in the dénouement, the accumulated problems disappear in an absence of problems or, more exactly, these pass away through having received their solution and remain not open but closed as if by decree. Finally, the unanimity about the king, which emerged from these "comedias," made it possible to blur the existing disagreements in the interior of monarcho-seigneurial society and gave the spectators the illusion that it was perfected, coherent, definitive.[97]

[95]Burke, p. 152.
[96]See Duvignaud, p. 197, for a general application of this paradigm to English and Spanish Renaissance drama.
[97]Salomon, pp. 910–11.

Thus, as in much Renaissance drama, the form is designed to reconcile the irreconcilable. But peasant plays, unlike most domestic tragedy, for instance, present a conflict between what is said at the end and what is shown throughout. What is said points to integration; what is shown, to revolution. Similarly, Shakespeare's tragedies portray violent upheaval, only to end either without reconciliation, or with a plot resolution that violates the logic of prior events, or at least with a concluding statement inadequate to the experience of the play. Despite the generic differences, Spanish peasant drama should ultimately be compared with Shakespearean, rather than bourgeois, tragedy. Each group of plays represents the most profound legacy of the popular tradition in its nation to the public theater. In the absence of that institution no combination of social conditions with literary and dramaturgical heritage could have produced such works. The formal resolution of social conflict in Shakespearean tragedy and in the Spanish peasant play may be understood as the full dramatic realization of the inherent contradiction between artisanal base and absolutist superstructure in the public theater.

## Lope de Vega, *Fuente Ovejuna*, and Shakespeare, *King Lear*

These claims may acquire a certain concreteness through a more extended, comparative analysis of *Fuente Ovejuna* and *King Lear*. That analysis primarily adopts the characteristic strategy of the present work: it interprets the plays by situating them with respect to their conditions of possibility. Yet its final sections reverse direction, running history backward as it were and thus reading the works in relation not to their past but to their future.

*Fuente Ovejuna*, perhaps one of the many plays dashed off hurriedly by its author,[98] focuses on the murder of a sexually predatory feudal overlord, or comendador, by the peasants of the village of Fuente Ovejuna. Forced to undergo a royally instituted judicial investigative torture, these peasants nonetheless insist on taking collective responsibility for the killing: "¡Fuente Ovejuna lo hizo!" ("Fuente Ovejuna did it!": 3.10.2106). The play concludes with the arrival of King Ferdinand and Queen Isabella, who, confronted with the choice between exterminating the entire population of the village and issuing a general pardon, reluctantly opt for the latter and even take Fuente Ovejuna directly under their benign protection, to the joy of the inhabitants. In other words,

---

[98]Francisco López Estrada, ed., *Fuente Ovejuna: Dos comedias*, by Lope de Vega and Cristóbal de Monroy (Madrid: Editorial Castalia, 1969), p. 24. References to both versions of *Fuente Ovejuna* are noted in the text.

*Fuente Ovejuna* combines the sympathetic portrayal of lower-class revolutionary insurgency with the concluding incorporation of that insurgency into a harmonious conservative resolution.

This ideological sleight of hand is prepared for in various ways. The subplot describes the evil overlord's illegal and, in the event, unsuccessful rebellion against the monarchy, with the result that peasant violence can be interpreted as a form of local vigilante patriotism in support of the crown. To achieve this national closure, Lope deviates from his source, which does not connect the comendador of Fuente Ovejuna with the military struggle against Ferdinand and Isabella. The subplot may also constitute a compliment to a powerful aristocratic family that had patronized Lope's works.[99] More important, the peasants of Fuente Ovejuna consistently express royalist sympathies. For instance, to the embattled comendador's desperate claim, "¡Yo soy vuestro señor!" ("I am your lord!"), the villagers retort, "¡Nuestros señores / son los Reyes Católicos!" ("Our lords / are the Catholic Monarchs!": 3.6.1885–86). Their desire at the end of the play to be placed directly under monarchical control— "tuyos ser queremos" ("we want to be yours": 3.21.2434)—conflicts with the source narrative, in which they shift their allegiance to the city of Córdoba.[100] Frondoso's eagerness to deny the insurrectionary implications of his armed confrontation with the comendador at the end of act 1—"Yo me conformo / con mi estado" ("I conform / to my station": 1.13.851–52)—testifies to the same general pattern: the peasantry of Fuente Ovejuna is, at least initially, a class in itself, but not a class for itself. Similarly, the contemporary disrepute of the comendador's military order and the more general tension between monarchy and aristocracy in early modern Europe allow Lope not to recognize the ultimate class solidarity of nobility and crown. An attack on the local oppressor need not imply hostility toward the national oppressor; a representation of the fundamental antagonism in the feudal mode of production from the point of view of a successfully rebellious peasantry need not challenge the ultimate guarantor of that productive mode, the absolute monarch.[101]

In a sense, the unusual prominence of women in *Fuente Ovejuna* also serves a diversionary, obscurantist purpose. The source accords women a far more peripheral role in the climactic act of vengeance, for which, in addition, it offers a wider range of motives—military, fiscal, and sexual.[102] The transference of class conflict from economic struggle to the

[99]López Estrada, pp. 17, 11–12.

[100]López Estrada, p. 15; Salomon, pp. 857 n. 30, 858 n. 32.

[101]Salomon, p. 863. But see Julio Matas, "El honor en *Fuente Ovejuna* y la tragedia del comendador," in *Lope de Vega y los orígenes del teatro español*, Actas del I Congreso Internacional sobre Lope de Vega, ed. Manuel Criado de Val (Madrid: EDI, 1981), pp. 385–90.

[102]Salomon, p. 856 n. 28; López Estrada, p. 14.

crime of rape enables the play to convert an irreconcilable opposition into an easy matter for moralism. Yet the focus on characters who are at once peasant and female makes possible the fusion of two of the oldest and most persistent forms of social oppression. In 1486, a decade after the events in Fuente Ovejuna actually occurred, a major rising against serfdom in Catalonia extracted the following concession from King Ferdinand: "We judge and declare that the aforementioned lords (señors, barons) . . . when the peasant takes himself a wife, shall neither sleep with her on the first night; nor shall they during the wedding night, when the wife has laid herself in her bed, step over it and the aforementioned wife as a sign of lordship."[103] More generally, a concern with sexual politics, indeed a feminist consciousness, runs through the play, manifest in an attack on the exploitation of women in extramarital intercourse, in an insistence on female rights in choosing a partner, in the formation of an effective military brigade of peasant women, and, most strikingly, in Laurencia's heroic leadership of the villagers, which begins with a challenge to the peasant men who run Fuente Ovejuna: "Dejadme entrar, que bien puedo, / en consejo de los hombres" ("Let me enter, for well I can, / in the council of men": 3.3.1712–13).

When the women organize themselves into a battalion, they consider the need for officers:

> *Pascuala.* Nombremos un capitán.
> *Laurencia.* ¡Eso no!
> *Pascuala.*　　　　　¿Por qué?
> *Laurencia.*　　　　　　　　　Que adonde
> asiste mi gran valor,
> no hay Cides ni Rodamontes.

(*Pascuala.* Let us name a captain. / *Laurencia.* No! / *Pascuala.* Why? / *Laurencia.* Because where / my great valor is present, / there are no Cids or Rodomontes. [3.4.1844–47])

This exchange echoes a similar discussion among the men shortly before:

> *Juan.* ¿Qué orden pensáis tener?
> *Mengo.* Ir a matarle sin orden.
> Juntad el pueblo a una voz,
> que todos están conformes
> en que los tiranos mueran.

(*Juan.* What order do you intend to have? / *Mengo.* To go to kill him without order. / Unite the village in one voice, / because all are agreed / that tyrants should die. [3.3.1804–8])

[103]Quoted in Frederick Engels, *The Origin of the Family, Private Property and the State*, ed. Eleanor Burke Leacock (New York: International Publishers, 1972), p. 116.

The rejection of hierarchy in both instances underscores the solidarity of Fuente Ovejuna, already a significant matter in the somewhat fanciful and legendary source. Lope's still more sympathetic treatment places even greater stress on the unity of the rebels. It excludes, for example, the villagers' removal of their local peasant leaders, appointees of the military order, after the killing of the comendador.[104]

Mengo's role here and elsewhere in the play suggests that solidarity in *Fuente Ovejuna* represents not a reactionary organicism but a genuine social leveling. Mengo is the fat, poor, ignorant, self-interested, materialistic, cowardly, buffoonish peasant so often ridiculed in the Spanish theater. He opposes the other peasants' commitment to Platonic love:

> *Pascuala.* Pues ¿de qué nos desengañas?
> *Mengo.* De que nadie tiene amor
> más que a su misma persona.

(*Pascuala.* Well, about what do you undeceive us? / *Mengo.* That anyone has love / for more than his own person. [1.4.400–402])

Later Laurencia, in this respect a typical humanist peasant, must correct his bungling classical allusion (2.7.1173–75). By failing to protect Jacinta from the comendador's men and by incurring a whipping for his inept efforts, Mengo then shows his martial inferiority to Frondoso, who earlier had preserved Laurencia from the clutches of the comendador himself. In the climactic village council meeting, Mengo, speaking for himself and for the lesser peasantry in general, initially proposes a somewhat timorous circumspection:

> Mirad, señores
> que vais en estas cosas con recelo.
> Puesto que por los simples labradores
> estoy aquí, que más injurias pasan,
> más cuerdo represento sus temores.

(Look, sirs, / that you proceed in these matters with suspicion. / Since I am here for the simple / peasants, who suffer more injuries, / more judiciously do I represent their fears. [3.2.1703–7])

Yet as his already-quoted critique of internal stratification indicates, Mengo, like Laurencia before him, assumes a position of leadership, rousing the other men with his battle cries:

---

[104]Salomon, pp. 856–57 n. 29, 858–59 n. 32. For the peasants' spiritual unity, see Leo Spitzer, "Un tema central y su equivalente estructural en 'Fuenteovejuna,'" in *El teatro de Lope de Vega: Artículos y estudios*, ed. José Francisco Gatti (Buenos Aires: Editorial Universitaria de Buenos Aires, 1962), pp. 124–47.

> *Mengo.* ¡Los reyes, nuestros señores,
> vivan!
> *Todos.* ¡Vivan muchos años!
> *Mengo.* ¡Mueran tiranos traidores!
> *Todos.* ¡Traidores tiranos mueran!

(*Mengo.* Long live the monarchs, our / lords! / *All.* May they live many years! / *Mengo.* Death to treacherous tyrants! / *All.* May tyrannical traitors die! [3.3.1811–14])

Following the death of the comendador, Mengo retains his comic qualities, reciting a rustic poem to commemorate the event. As the peasants prepare for the torture they expect to face, only Mengo is shown practicing his part. He is the first to say: "¡Fuente Ovejuna lo hizo!" Lope conforms to his source by having the investigator put a woman and a child on the rack, but, perhaps to emphasize both the brave resistance of the village and the cruelty of the government in picking on the weakest, he adds first an old man and then Mengo. Mengo is strategically chosen:

> *Juez.* Traedme aquel más rollizo . . .
> ¡ese desnudo, ese gordo!
> *Laurencia.* ¡Pobre Mengo! Él es sin duda.
> *Frondoso.* Temo que ha de confesar.

(*Judge.* Bring me that most rotund man . . . / that bare, that fat man! / *Laurencia.* Poor Mengo! It is he without doubt. / *Frondoso.* I fear that he must confess. [3.14.2236–39])

Of the three hundred villagers the judge claims to have tortured, only Mengo is presented in detail. Whipped in act 2, rehearsing his torture and then tortured in earnest in act 3, he seems about to confirm Frondoso's fears:

> *Mengo.*          Quedo, que yo
> lo diré.
> *Juez.* ¿Quién le mató?
> *Mengo.* Señor, Fuente Ovejunica.
> *Juez.* ¿Hay tan gran bellaquería?
> Del dolor se están burlando;
> en quien estaba esperando,
> niega con mayor porfía.
>          Dejaldos, que estoy cansado.

(*Mengo.* Wait, for I / will say it. / *Judge.* Who killed him? / *Mengo.* Sir, little Fuente Ovejuna. / *Judge.* Is there such great knavery? / They are making fun of pain; / he in whom I was hoping, / denies with greater obstinacy. / Cease, for I am tired. [3.14.2247–54])

It is, then, Mengo's heroic comic spirit that ultimately defeats royal authority, in an ideologically resonant reversal of generic expectations. As the triumphant peasant, amidst cries of "¡Vítor, Mengo!" ("Victor, Mengo!": 3.15.2258), attempts to recover by typically gulping down vast quantities of wine, Frondoso asks him, "¿Quién mató al Comendador?" ("Who killed the comendador?") "Fuente Ovejunica lo hizo" ("Little Fuente Ovejuna did it") is once again the reply (3.15.2280–81). Fittingly, when the peasants present themselves before the king and queen in the final scene of the play, Mengo delivers the longest speech, without deviating from his characteristic comic mode. In *Fuente Ovejuna*, a kidnapped, battered woman and a beaten, tortured man from the lowest order of the peasantry most dramatically represent the cause of the rebellion.

The royal pardon that closes the plot does not entirely succeed in neutralizing the revolutionary import of the preceding action. Well before the peasants storm his house, the comendador has had no doubt that he faces an antifeudal revolt. When the king learns of the killing, he unhesitatingly sides with the comendador against the villagers, ignoring the fact that he and the peasants have a common foe. Class solidarity conquers all, just as it did in fifteenth- and sixteenth-century Aragon, where promonarchical peasants who murdered local aristocrats were systematically punished by the crown. Similarly, King Ferdinand never ratifies the deeds of the peasants of Fuente Ovejuna, pardoning them not because he accepts their convincing arguments but because he has to.[105] The pseudoresolution, the final censorship of what was perhaps unthinkable and was certainly unrepresentable, does not conceal the antifeudal, revolutionary implications of the action. *Fuente Ovejuna* is the extreme toward which other peasant plays tend and hence the most reliable guide to the inner logic and historical significance of the form.

*King Lear* bears comparison with Lope's play in two important respects. First, it concludes with a similarly unsuccessful strategy of containment. But though here too the revolutionary moment gives way, at least ambiguously, to conservative closure, the emphasis falls not on deeds but on words. Lope's peasants rebel without fully developing a correspondingly radical ideological rationale for their conduct. Hence they never turn against the monarchy. Shakespeare's outcasts and lower-class characters articulate a thoroughgoing critique of hierarchy without discovering a political vehicle for their beliefs. Second, *King Lear* occupies as paradigmatic a position among Shakespearean tragedies as *Fuente Ovejuna* does among Spanish peasant plays. If, to adopt the terminology

[105]Salomon, p. 855 nn. 22–24, 857–61.

deployed earlier for satiric comedy, *Othello* and *Macbeth* are tragic *come-dias de figurón*, *King Lear* offers full disjunction. Although most of the tragedies, like most of the histories, focus on relations either within the propertied classes or between the upper and lower classes, *King Lear* gives full weight to both. It thus has among the tragedies the same position that *1 and 2 Henry IV* hold among the histories: it fully exploits the possibilities of the form. The play is a consequence of a brief conjuncture in the dramatist's own career as well as in the history of English theater. In no other work does the figurative language so consistently involve the juxtaposition of what may loosely be called feudal and bourgeois imagery.[106] Moreover, Shakespeare uniquely combines direct address with what Daniel Seltzer calls "'ensemble' episodes,"[107] the tragedy of an individual—the characteristic type in England since the late 1580s—with social tragedy—the form that was soon to replace it. Again, here alone Shakespeare fuses a commitment to the value of inner and personal struggle with a sense of the urgency of social and political action.

Thus *King Lear* can simultaneously address personal, moral, familial, social, economic, political, and metaphysical questions. This analogical structure, common in Renaissance literature, acquires unusual resonance here. Throughout the play, the characters are forced to adjust their attitudes to their changing situations. Although experience does not limit ideology in any narrow sense, every character who develops in the course of the plot acts first and only afterward offers a philosophical rationale for his or her conduct. Broadly speaking, in *King Lear* being determines consciousness.

Critical discussion testifies to the social range and depth of the play. *King Lear* has been thought to dramatize the decline of feudalism, the crisis of the aristocracy, the triumph of monarchism, the defeat of monarchism, the rise of capitalism, the persistence of the popular radical tradition, and, of course, some combination of these themes.[108] Since one

[106]Weimann, *Structure and Society in Literary History: Studies in the History and Theory of Historical Criticism* (Charlottesville: University Press of Virginia, 1976), pp. 226–33.

[107]Daniel Seltzer, "The Actors and Staging," in *A New Companion to Shakespeare Studies*, ed. Kenneth Muir and S. Schoenbaum (Cambridge: Cambridge University Press, 1971), p. 46.

[108]See Edwin Muir, *Essays on Literature and Society*, rev. ed. (London: Hogarth Press, 1965), pp. 33–49; C. H. Hobday, "The Social Background of 'King Lear,'" *Modern Quarterly Miscellany* 1 (1947): 37–56; Danby, *Shakespeare's Doctrine of Nature: A Study of "King Lear"* (London: Faber and Faber, 1949); Siegel, *Shakespearean Tragedy and the Elizabethan Compromise* (New York: New York University Press, 1957), pp. 161–88; Kettle, "From *Hamlet* to *Lear*," in *Shakespeare in a Changing World*, ed. Kettle, pp. 146–71; Sidney Finkelstein, *Who Needs Shakespeare?* (New York: International Publishers, 1973), pp. 176–87; Rosalie Colie, "Reason and Need: *King Lear* and the 'Crisis' of the Aristocracy," in *Some Facets of "King Lear"*, ed. Colie and F. T. Flahiff (Toronto: University of Toronto Press,

cannot simultaneously assent to all these judgments, it is tempting to assent to none of them. The present account, however, merely seeks to complicate, rather than to overturn, the allegorizing inevitable in such political readings and in so doing to specify with some precision the relationships among the social forces at work in *King Lear*.

The opening abdication scene makes sense only if Lear is not a traditional feudal king but a neofeudal absolute monarch. His autocratic conduct presupposes the consolidation of power, just as the alarm caused by his decision to divide the country necessarily rests on the prior establishment of the relatively modern category of nationhood. At the end of the play, Albany's first gesture of political renunciation emphasizes this point:

> for us, we will resign,
> During the life of this old Majesty,
> To him our absolute power.[109]

A strictly feudal society, by contrast, would exhibit far greater decentralization, a significant parcellization of sovereignty. Similarly, a genuinely feudal ideology would lead an aristocrat to respond to the assertion of royal authority after the fashion of Hotspur or of Chimène's father in *Le Cid*. *King Lear* presents no such characters. Kent's combination of class consciousness and loyal service to his king mark him as a member of the nobility who, while retaining a resolutely aristocratic outlook, has successfully adapted to absolutism. His sharp replies in the first scene accord with this social position, opposing as they do Lear's extreme indulgence in folly and imperiousness. In like manner, Cordelia's evocation of her "bond" and her "duty" draw on the contractual heritage of feudalism without challenging monarchical power (1.1.93, 97, 102). Edmund recognizes that Gloucester shares these principles, disingenuously telling the earl, "with how manifold and strong a bond / The child was bound to th' father" (2.1.47–48). Finally, although the first part of the play shows little of Edgar, subsequent events reveal that he lives by the same values.

---

1974), pp. 185–219; Paul Delany, "*King Lear* and the Decline of Feudalism," *PMLA* 92 (1977): 429–40; Michael Hays, "Reason's Rhetoric: *King Lear* and the Social Uses of Irony," *boundary 2* 7 (1979): 97–116; Timothy J. Reiss, *Tragedy and Truth: Studies in the Development of a Renaissance and Neoclassical Discourse* (New Haven: Yale University Press, 1980), pp. 183–203; Franco Moretti, "'A Huge Eclipse': Tragic Form and the Deconsecration of Sovereignty," *Genre* 15, nos. 1–2 (Spring–Summer 1982): 7–40; Jonathan Dollimore, *Radical Tragedy: Religion, Ideology and Power in the Drama of Shakespeare and His Contemporaries* (Chicago: University of Chicago Press, 1984), pp. 189–203.

[109]Shakespeare, *King Lear*, ed. Kenneth Muir (New York: Random House, 1964), 5.3.298–300. Subsequent references are noted in the text.

Given such a broad consensus, at least in theory, how can one explain the conflict within this group and the consequent destruction of the traditional order? Does the blindness of two old men have a social dimension? If excessive absolutism could lead to tyranny, insufficient absolutism might result in chaos. *King Lear* reveals the paradoxical linkage between authoritarianism and anarchy. Lear's division of the country works against historical trends by reintroducing feudalism. Indeed, if the play presents one truly feudal lord, it is Lear himself after his abdication. His hundred knights pose at least a potential threat to those in power. As Goneril ironically remarks to her husband,

> 'Tis politic and safe to let him keep
> At point a hundred knights; yes, that on every dream,
> Each buzz, each fancy, each complaint, dislike,
> He may enguard his dotage with their powers,
> And hold our lives in mercy.
>
> (1.4.333–37)

And Regan directly informs Lear:

> what! fifty followers
> Is it not well? What should you need of more?
> Yea, or so many, sith that both charge and danger
> Speak 'gainst so great a number? How, in one house,
> Should many people, under two commands,
> Hold amity? 'Tis hard; almost impossible.
>
> (2.4.239–44)

In this respect, Lear's daughters express typically absolutist concerns.

Yet their fundamental social logic perhaps lies elsewhere. Questioned by Lear, Goneril asserts that he is "Dearer than eye-sight, space and liberty; / Beyond what can be valued rich or rare" (1.1.56–57). Regan extends her sister's imagery: "I am made of that self metal as my sister, / And prize me at her worth" (69–70). This language of money, which transforms qualitative relations into quantitative ones, looks forward to a world of rational economic self-interest. It is a world Cordelia wants no part of, as her reversal of its vocabulary implies:

> Then poor Cordelia!
> And yet not so; since I am sure my love's
> More ponderous than my tongue.
>
> (76–78)

Lear, however, is infected by Goneril and Regan's speeches: "When she was dear to us we did hold her so, / But now her price is fallen" (196–

97). France's remarks, then, stand as a rebuke not only to Burgundy, to whom they are initially addressed, but to an entire outlook:

> Love's not love
> When it is mingled with regards that stand
> Aloof from th' entire point. . . .
>
> . . .
>
> Fairest Cordelia, that art most rich, being poor;
> Most choice, forsaken; and most lov'd, despised!
> Thee and thy virtues here I seize upon:
>
> . . .
>
> Not all the dukes of wat'rish Burgundy
> Can buy this unpriz'd precious maid of me.
>
> (238–59)

France's resort to paradox may testify to the psychological difficulty of reconverting quantity back into quality. Yet the commitment to married love also anticipates the very bourgeois world view whose financial considerations France clearly rejects. Although this internal contradiction never comes to consciousness, it does indicate the impurity of social and ideological distinctions in *King Lear*, an impurity definitive as well of the age of absolutism. Finally, the belief in married love, which Cordelia apparently shares, does not, in its orientation toward the future, conflict with Cordelia's allegiance to her bond, with its turn to the past. From opposite historical positions, both stand against the power of the crown and the power of money.

Subsequently, Goneril and Regan give abundant evidence of the calculating, amoral individualism only adumbrated in the first scene, before lapsing into animalism. Yet Edmund is surely the principal theorist and practitioner in the play of the instrumental reason diagnosed and deplored by the Frankfurt school. "Thou, Nature, art my goddess," he asserts at the opening of his first soliloquy (1.2.1). "What men want to learn from nature is how to use it in order wholly to dominate it and other men," write Adorno and Horkheimer, in what could almost be a gloss on the character.[110] Like Goneril and Regan, Edmund destroys traditional relationships in the family and the state in single-minded pursuit of political, economic, and social power. The early Jacobean sale of honors to "new men" had as one of its objects the elimination of the gap that Elizabethan parsimony had opened between status and title, on the one hand, and wealth and power, on the other.[111] The new men and women of *King Lear* close this gap with a vengeance, at the expense

[110]Theodor Adorno and Max Horkheimer, *Dialectic of Enlightenment*, trans. John Cummings (London: NLB, 1979), p. 4.
[111]Stone, *Crisis*, pp. 74–77, 97–102.

of fathers who initially discover that, in the absence of power, status is worthless as well. Yet Edmund also derives from the Vice figure of popular dramaturgy. Insofar as the Vice acts as the homiletic foe of humanity, he is potentially compatible with a critique of capitalism that sees in bourgeois ideology the enemy of all that makes life worth living. But to the extent that this figure of indomitable energy is in close contact with the audience, which may partly applaud his deception of more sedate and credulous characters, he serves a very different function. Such is the Edmund who can say, "Now, gods, stand up for bastards!" (1.2.22), or can coolly contemplate the rivalry of Goneril and Regan for his love: "Which of them shall I take? / Both? one? or neither?" (5.2.57–58). In this role, then, he performs the traditional task of parodically subverting the serious aristocratic concerns of the play from a popular perspective.

In summary, then, the catastrophic collapse of the old order primarily results from the combined effect of the deviation from properly absolutist rule and the depredations of capitalism. On this reading, the problem lies not in neofeudal society itself, but in the failure of some of its members to live up to its standards and, more important still, in the conscious rejection of those standards by certain representatives of the younger generation. Kent apparently never relinquishes this view, and, forced to choose between aristocratic and bourgeois perspectives, an audience would presumably side more with the traditionally minded victims than with their upstart victimizers. Certainly the first two acts do not move beyond the reassertion of neofeudal, absolutist values. The popular dimension of Edmund's character suggests, however, that a bipolar, morally weighted interpretation will fail to do justice to the play. If *King Lear* offers a devastating attack on capitalism, it also produces Shakespeare's most powerful critique of neofeudal values, and particularly of royal absolutism. As Lear and Gloucester independently realize in adversity, their defects extend far beyond the initial acts of folly that cause their predicaments. If the measure of the cruelty of the new bourgeois order is the suffering of the traditional aristocracy, the index of the old order's shortcomings is the plight of the lower classes. Although capitalism is irretrievably evil, feudalism may perhaps be redeemed if it can combine its traditional human bonds with moral content. Hence the poor and the dispossessed play a crucial, if often passive, role in the attempt to forge a new synthesis capable of breaking the historical impasse between the rival sectors of the ruling class and of justifying the exercise of power.

In the course of *King Lear*, the errant and suffering aristocrats receive the assistance of the lower classes: the fool initiates Lear's regeneration; the old man, Gloucester's tenant, briefly guides the helpless earl; and one of Cornwall's servants kills his villainous master in an attempt to save

Gloucester's eyes. Although the servant is rewarded with instant death rather than the triumphant exoneration that ultimately awaits Fuente Ovejuna's peasants, his deed receives considerable emphasis: implicit validation from his two fellow servants (3.7.99–106), detailed recounting by a messenger and explicit justification by Albany (4.2.69–81), and still a third, briefer mention (4.7.85–87). Gloucester's blindness, Regan confesses, "moves / All hearts against us" (4.5.10–11). Cordelia's army, Albany pointedly notes, is joined by

> others whom the rigour of our state
> Forc'd to cry out. . . .
>
>           .   .   .
>
>           others, whom, I fear,
> Most just and heavy causes make oppose.
>                     (5.1.22–27)

Edmund appeals to a similar social pattern of allegiance in explaining the imprisonment of Lear,

> Whose age had charms in it, whose title more,
> To pluck the common bosom on his side,
> And turn our impress'd lances in our eyes
> Which do command them.
>                     (5.3.49–52)

But the crucial popular dimension of *King Lear*, as opposed to *Fuente Ovejuna*, arises from the experience of the aristocratic characters themselves. In the opening two acts, the fool helps force upon Lear a recognition of the consequences of his conduct. On the heath Lear in a sense reciprocates, for the first time concerning himself with the fool as a human being rather than as a mere adjunct of royalty:

> Come on, my boy. How dost, my boy? Art cold?
> I am cold myself. . . .
>
>           .   .   .
>
> Poor Fool and knave, I have one part in my heart
> That's sorry yet for thee.
>                     (3.2.68–73)

Shortly thereafter he adds: "In, boy; go first. You houseless poverty,— / Nay, get thee in" (3.4.26–27). The blinded Gloucester evinces a similar concern for Poor Tom: "bring some covering for this naked soul" (4.1.44). He follows this initial expression of solicitude with an act of generosity:

[333

Here, take this purse, thou whom the heav'ns plagues
Have humbled to all strokes: that I am wretched
Makes thee the happier.

(4.1.64–66)

For both outcast aristocrats, the unaccustomed experience of suffering
leads to gestures of kindness. These gestures in turn generate a previously inconceivable capacity for social and political reflection. Lear's
prayer to "Poor naked wretches" denounces the upper class's failure,
and especially his own failure, to alleviate the distress of the lower classes
(3.4.28–36), a charge echoed soon after by Gloucester in his lines beginning "Heavens, deal so still!" (4.1.66–71). Both men emphasize the need
to share the lot of the poor (3.4.34, 4.1.68–69). Yet the different objects
of address in the two speeches—wretches and heavens—indicate a significant divergence between Lear and Gloucester. Where the helpless
earl relies on divine intervention to ensure social equity, the more defiant king reverses the relationship. The monarch must "shake the superflux to" wretches, "And [thereby] show the Heavens more just"
(3.4.35–36). In this secular, materialist inversion of religion, social justice guarantees metaphysical justice rather than the other way around.

Lear's speech, however, like Gloucester's, is ultimately a radical version of noblesse oblige, still viewing the misery of the poor, as it does,
from the perspective of the ruling class. Gloucester never advances politically beyond this point. On the other hand, Lear in his madness eventually gains an even more revolutionary understanding of his position in
society. In an attack on the legal system that ironically conjures up "The
great image of Authority: / A dog's obey'd in office" (4.6.160–61), he rejects all hierarchy, insisting instead on his common humanity. At last
fully worthy of Cordelia, Lear movingly expresses his new consciousness
at their reunion: "For, as I am a man, I think this lady / To be my child
Cordelia" (4.7.69–70).

Lear's regeneration is complete. Even if one wishes to ignore the signs
of infantile regression that the old king soon manifests, however, it is
clear that the social experience which enables him to realize the meaning
of his relationship to his youngest daughter simultaneously precludes a
return to the throne. Although he simply transcends interest in worldly
power with a sublime indifference, the final scene of the play brutally reveals the hopeless inadequacy of this attitude. Where did this combination of radical consciousness, quietist politics, and murderous victimization come from? An important historical precedent for Lear's social
insight was the "backward-looking and idealized communism" that, according to Christopher Hill, the lower classes of Tudor England op-

posed to feudalism and capitalism alike.[112] Although this brand of communism derived in part from indigenous currents of protest or heresy, such as Lollardy, it also drew on the radical Protestantism of sixteenth-century Germany. The left wing of the Reformation interacted with popular culture in the theater, just as more standard Protestantism did with the Renaissance.

Luther, of course, had no tolerance for those he considered religious radicals or political rebels. In response to the Peasants' Revolt, for which, to take the obvious examples, Marx, Engels, and Kautsky expressed such sympathy,[113] he characteristically wrote:

> also . . . auffrur . . . verstöret alles / wie das aller grössest vnglück / Drumb soll hie zü schmeissen würgen vnd stechen / heymlich oder offentlich / wer da kan vnd gedencken / das nichts gifftigers / schedlichers / teüffelischers sein kan / deñ ein auffrürischer mensch / gleich als weñ mañ einen tollen hundt todt schlahen muss / schlegst du nicht / so schlecht er dich vñ ein ganz land mit dir.

> (Thus rebellion . . . turns everything upside down, like the worst disaster. Therefore let everyone who can, smite, slay, and stab, secretly or openly, remembering that nothing can be more poisonous, hurtful, or devilish than a rebel. It is just as when one must kill a mad dog; if you do not strike him, he will strike you, and a whole land with you.)[114]

Nonetheless Luther's Catholic foes rightly charged that his teachings, by providing the peasants with a more powerful oppositional ideology than they had previously possessed, had unwittingly abetted the rebellion. The same is true of the primarily doctrinal groups in the radical Reformation. Although their movements, like the peasantry's, drew on traditions that considerably antedated Luther, the establishment of their beliefs and organizations was inspired by the profound changes emanating from Wittenberg and Zurich.[115]

---

[112]Hill, "The Many-Headed Monster," p. 204.

[113]See the letters from Marx (April 19, 1859) and Engels (May 18, 1859) to Ferdinand Lasalle, in *Marx and Engels on Literature and Art*, ed. Lee Baxandall and Stefan Morawski (Saint Louis: Telos Press, 1973), pp. 105–12, 141–43; Engels, *The Peasant War in Germany*, in *The German Revolutions: "The Peasant War in Germany" and "Germany: Revolution and Counter-Revolution"*, ed. and introd. Leonard Krieger (Chicago: University of Chicago Press, 1967); Karl Kautsky, *Communism in Central Europe in the Time of the Reformation* (New York: Russell and Russell, 1959).

[114]*Widder die Mordischen unnd Reubischen Rotten der Bauurñ* (Mainz, 1525), sig. Aiii[r]. The translation is from *Luther's Works*, ed. Robert C. Schultz, vol. 46 (Philadelphia: Fortress Press, 1967), p. 50.

[115]George Huntston Williams, *The Radical Reformation* (Philadelphia: Westminster Press, 1962), pp. 85–86, 119–20.

Overwhelmingly drawn from the lower classes, consistently perse-cuted, tortured, and murdered by Catholic and Protestant authorities alike, the Anabaptists and Spiritualists held to such heretical and radical doctrines as adult baptism, with the consequent formation of a church limited to believers and absolutely separated from the state; the eleva-tion of the spirit over the letter, of inspiration over theology, and of lay over clerical leadership, with the related emphasis on an extremely per-sonal religion that could spill over into an antinomian denial of the pos-sibility of sin; unorthodox views of Christ, including anti-Trinitarianism; the denial of predestination, with the complementary assertion of free will; and, finally, feminism, pacifism, millenarianism, and communism. Anabaptists appeared in England no later than the 1530s leaving their mark not only on various Baptist groups, but also on the Elizabethan Thirty-Nine Articles of the Anglican church, many of which are ex-pressly directed against the sect's challenge to orthodoxy, magistracy, and property. The Familists, who arrived sometime after the middle of the century, were perhaps even more important.[116]

The subversive egalitarianism, the rejection of authority, the possible advocacy of utopian communism, and even the metaphysical ques-tioning of *King Lear* look back to Anabaptism. More specifically, the mock trial of Goneril and Regan, presided over by the fool, the mad king, and the apparently mad Poor Tom O'Bedlam, seems to recall the practices of the Union Shoe, an early-sixteenth-century predecessor of the Peasants' Revolt, which used beggar kings to organize vagabonds. In the 1530s the Strassburg authorities could not decide whether the influ-ential Anabaptist leader Melchior Hoffman was a prophet or a mad-man.[117] Lear quickly follows his absolute rejection of hierarchy with the promise, "And when I have stol'n upon these son-in-laws, / Then, kill, kill, kill, kill, kill, kill!" (4.6.188–89). This wild oscillation back toward vi-olence may recall the ill-fated and, in the event, brutally repressed com-munist government of Münster. More often, the radical, pacifist sects had no alternative to a patient acceptance of mistreatment or death. Following the reunion with Cordelia, even military defeat and the pros-pect of long imprisonment cannot dampen Lear's almost religious enthusiasm:

> When thou dost ask me blessing, I'll kneel down,
> And ask of thee forgiveness: so we'll live
> And pray, . . .

[116]Williams, pp. 401–3, 778–90 passim.
[117]Engels, *Peasant War*, p. 60; Williams, p. 293.

. . .

And take upon 's the mystery of things,
As if we were God's spies.

(5.3.10–17)

Unlike the perservering radical Protestants, however, whose convictions were challenged by the martyrdom of thousands of their fellows, Lear's new faith cannot withstand the test of Cordelia's murder.

The significance of that loss may accordingly repay scrutiny. Lear, Gloucester, Edgar, and Kent quite literally share the lot of the poor. Cordelia does not, with the exception, perhaps, of her brief moment of disinheritance and consequent penury at the beginning of the play, and of her unceremonious killing at the end. Yet she is figuratively connected to the lower classes, most obviously to the fool: "Since my young Lady's going into France, Sir," a knight informs Lear, "the Fool hath much pined away" (1.4.77–78). "And my poor fool is hang'd," Lear's final speech begins (5.3.305). Cordelia's "plainness" (1.1.129), a commitment not to a verbal style but to the language of truth, also links her to Kent (1.1.148; 1.4.35; 2.2.93, 100–102, 112). Kent and Edgar condemn Oswald for his failure to live up to this standard (2.2.74–81, 4.6.254–56), Cornwall's servant speaks truth to power, and Edgar's closing injunction, at least in the First Folio (1623), to "Speak what we feel, not what we ought to say" (5.3.324), returns to the same norm.

These cross-references may help clarify Cordelia's social resonance. Shakespeare's tragedies, unlike much European tragedy, generally relegate women to a subordinate position. The unusual attention in these plays to the public world, to the drama of a nation, establishes a relationship between gender and genre that most Jacobean and Caroline playwrights rejected. In *Hamlet* and even more in *Othello* and *King Lear*, young women appear not as tragic heroines, but as tragic victims whose deaths materially signify the costs of life. Something of the subordination of even aristocratic women in early modern Europe is dramatized in their fates. But through Cordelia's covert linkages with the lower classes, *King Lear* also acknowledges the mediating role between elite and popular culture often played by such women. At least to a limited extent, then, in Cordelia's murder sexual and class oppression coalesce, a conflation found as well, though in different forms and with an opposite resolution, in *Fuente Ovejuna*.[118]

Edgar, "godson" of Lear (2.1.91) and spiritual brother of Cordelia,

---

[118]Lisa Jardine, *Still Harping on Daughters: Women and Drama in the Age of Shakespeare* (Brighton: Harvester, 1983), p. 162.

functions primarily to counteract the dismalness of this ending, to connect Lear's personal development, however tenuously, to the future of the kingdom. In addition to paralleling and thereby generalizing the main plot, then, the subplot answers or completes it. The nature of this process will emerge from a comparison of *The Malcontent* with *King Lear*. Although the possible influence of Marston's play on Shakespeare's received extended scrutiny in Germany more than sixty-five years ago, the subject has apparently elicited almost no attention in the English-speaking world.[119] Perhaps composed in 1602–3 and performed by the Children of the Queen's Revels in 1603, *The Malcontent* entered the repertory of the King's Men in revised form the following year. Three quartos appeared in the second half of 1604.[120] Shakespeare must have known the play in the theater, where he may have acted in it, in print, or in both. If he began writing *King Lear* by the end of 1604—by no means a certainty[121]—*The Malcontent* would have been fresh in his mind.

Marston's play probably served as a kind of prism through which the two principal sources of Shakespeare's tragedy—*The True Chronicle History of King Leir* and Sidney's *Arcadia*—were generically refracted. Broadly speaking, *The Malcontent* may have inflected the main plot in the direction of satire and the subplot in the direction of tragicomedy. The railing style of Malevole, Marston's protagonist, anticipates much of the language of Kent and Lear, neither of whom in this respect resembles his model in the anonymous chronicle play. Of course, the specifically sexual character of Malevole's and Lear's vituperation, far from being unique, is widely anticipated in the contemporary satiric comedy as well as in Shakespeare's immediately preceding tragedies. Yet in *The Malcontent* and *King Lear*, the plot largely justifies the apparently hysterical tone of the protagonists in the same way. Goneril has an adulterous liaison with Edmund, in which the lovers agree to kill her husband, Albany, just as Aurelia contracts with her lover Mendoza to murder her husband, Duke Pietro.[122]

More surprising, perhaps, is the relation between Shakespeare's fool and Marston's fool, Passarello. Marston added Passarello's role for performance at the Globe, partly in response, presumably, to both the acting personnel of the King's Men and the expectations of the public-

[119]Friedrich Radebrecht, *Shakespeares Abhängigkeit von John Marston*, Neue Anglistische Arbeiten, no. 3 (Cöthen: Otto Schulze, 1918), pp. 84–112. Geoffrey Bullough, ed., *Narrative and Dramatic Sources of Shakespeare*, vol. 7 (New York: Columbia University Press, 1973), does not refer to Marston in his introduction, texts, or bibliography for *King Lear*.

[120]M. L. Wine, ed., *The Malcontent*, by John Marston (Lincoln: University of Nebraska Press, 1964), pp. xi–xvi. References to the play are noted in the text.

[121]Kenneth Muir, ed., *King Lear*, p. xxiv; Gary Taylor, "A New Source and an Old Date for *King Lear*," *Review of English Studies*, n.s., 33 (1982): 396–413.

[122]Radebrecht, pp. 89–106.

theater audience. In so doing he surely was indebted to Shakespeare's clowns. Yet the influence may have run in the other direction as well. From among a wide range of popular characters, many of them comic, Shakespeare's corpus offers few fools besides the one in *King Lear*. Though a far more integral and interesting figure than Passarello, he strikingly echoes his predecessor's language. The two fools share a satiric vein, are repeatedly called fools, refer to themselves as fools, and address others as fools. "A pestilent fool!" says Bilioso, Passarello's master (3.1.121); an "all-licensed Fool," complains Goneril (1.4.209). "A bitter fowl!" adds Bilioso, perhaps in a punning vein (3.1.137); "a bitter Fool!" exclaims Lear (1.4.142). The interchangeable mode of address has a special resonance:

> *Malevole.* Fool, most happily encounter'd. Canst sing, fool?
> *Passarello.* Yes, I can sing, fool.
>
> (1.8.1–2)

Shakespeare considerably complicates matters:

> *Fool.*   But I will tarry; the Fool will stay,
>           And let the wise man fly:
>           The knave turns Fool that runs away;
>           The Fool no knave, perdy.
> *Kent.* Where learn'd you this, Fool?
> *Fool.* Not i' th' stocks, Fool.
>
> (2.4.82–87)

Malevole draws a moral from Passarello's comments: "O world most vile, when thy loose vanities, / Taught by this fool, do make the fool seem wise!" (1.8.53–54). So does Kent: "This is not altogether Fool, my Lord" (1.4.157). During the storm, Lear's fool concludes that "This cold night will turn us all to fools and / madmen" (3.4.78–79). The positive connotations of fools and folly are enforced in Shakespeare's play not only by Goneril's hostility to the fool and by her contemptuous designation of her husband as a fool because of his sympathy for Lear (4.2.28, 37, 54, 61), but also by the king's self-description at his reunion with Cordelia: "I am a very foolish fond old man," and later, "I am old and foolish" (4.7.60, 84).

Such passages point away from satire and toward tragicomedy. Much of the action of *The Malcontent* dovetails with the material Shakespeare took from the *Arcadia* for his subplot. At the prodding of Edmund, Gloucester, a weak man, rejects Edgar for Edmund. Edmund then overthrows his father, who, now penitent, is loyally cared for by Edgar. Finally Edgar defeats Edmund, returns to his rightful position, and as-

[339

sumes power. In Marston's work the political struggle apparently lacks this fundamental familial dimension. Aided by Mendoza, Pietro, also a vacillating figure, has deposed Altofront (Malevole's real name) before the play begins. He then, however, makes Mendoza his "adopted son" and "his heir" (2.5.95, 3.3.84). Mendoza usurps Pietro's position while publicly lamenting his "good father's loss" (4.3.54). Pietro, now chastened, urges Malevole, the "pitiful surgeon" of his soul (4.5.64), "be thou son to me" (4.5.73), and goes on to repent his mistreatment of Altofront. Malevole ousts Mendoza and, as Altofront, once again becomes duke of Genoa.

Many of the parallels between *The Malcontent* and the subplot of *King Lear* are not anticipated in Sidney, however. Like Edmund, Mendoza is a social-climbing villain[123] from the Vice tradition. Malevole repeatedly calls him to his face "damnable monster," "incarnate devil," "friendly damnation," "Your devilship," and the like (2.5.106, 132, 135; 4.3.107). Mendoza's soliloquies may also provide a partial model for Edmund's. A monologue will begin, for instance, with consciously ironic metaphysical references: "How fortune dotes on impudence!" (*Malcontent*, 2.5.94) or, as noted above, "Thou, Nature, art my goddess." Mendoza calls Pietro "Honest fool duke" and later concludes, "O Heaven! / I see God made honest fools to maintain crafty knaves" (1.7.73, 2.5.97–98). For Edmund, Edgar is

> a brother noble,
> . . .
> on whose foolish honesty
> My practices ride easy!
> (1.2.186–89)

Mendoza proclaims, "I must be duke. Why, if I must, I must!"(2.5.96). Edmund's lines pick up the imperative: "Legitimate Edgar, I must have your land" (1.2.16). Finally, Mendoza ends his last soliloquy with a boast:

> O, I grow proud in prosperous treachery!
> As wrestlers clip, so I'll embrace you all,
> Not to support, but to procure your fall.
> (2.5.101–3)

Edmund echoes both the language and the rhetorical effects of this passage at the close of his first speech: "I grow, I prosper; / Now, gods, stand up for bastards!" (1.2.21–22).

[123]Radebrecht, pp. 107–12.

Yet the most important similarity between *The Malcontent* and the subplot of *King Lear* involves not the villains but the antagonists who thwart them, Malevole and Edgar. Both men assume prolonged, improbable, and at times gratuitous humble disguises, a pattern that extends to Pietro and Kent as well.[124] The title page of the First Quarto of *King Lear* (1608) seems to bear witness to the prominence of this motif, calling the play the "True Chronicle Historie of the life and / death of King LEAR and his three / Daughters. *With the vnfortunate life of* Edgar, *sonne* / and heire to the Earle of Gloster, and his / sullen and assumed humor of / TOM of Bedlam." The recourse to a convention indigenous to comedy has generic implications. Each play presents a fake suicide from a high cliff at the seashore, orchestrated by Malevole or Edgar and described by a lying, disguised witness who claims to have seen the fall from below (*Malcontent*, 3.3.103–11, 4.3.1–50; *Lear*, 4.6.1–75).[125] Physically at least, these are among the most painless of the fortunate falls characteristic of tragicomedy—a matter that chapter 7 will consider in greater detail.

In *The Malcontent*, Malevole stages the narrative of the imaginary suicide partly to save Pietro from Mendoza's murderous plans. In *King Lear*, Edgar protects Gloucester from the sword of Oswald, who has been promised a reward for the killing by Regan. These brushes with death, typically tragicomic as well, are averted by the still-disguised Malevole and Edgar, who as a result begin to acquire didactic and providential functions. Under the tutelage of these two characters, Pietro and Gloucester move from despair to patience. Having learned the worst of Aurelia and Mendoza, Pietro can only pray, "let the last day fall! Drop, drop on our cursed heads! / Let heaven unclasp itself, vomit forth flames" (4.4.2–3). "All is damnation, wickedness extreme," he decides. "There is no faith in man" (4.4.16–17). Forced to live in a much grimmer world, Gloucester prefers a transcendental location for evil: "As flies to wanton boys, are we to th' Gods; / They kill us for their sport" (4.1.36–37). "Patience," counsels Malevole; "be wise" (4.5.61–62). "Bear free and patient thoughts," Edgar urges (4.6.80). The two older men comply. "O, I am chang'd," Pietro cries:

> For here, 'fore the dread power,
> In true contrition I do dedicate
> My breath to solitary holiness.
>
> (4.5.124–26)

---

[124]Radebrecht, pp. 85–89; Kenneth Muir, ed., *King Lear*, pp. xlviii–xlix.
[125]Kenneth Muir, ed., *King Lear*, p. xlii.

Similarly, Gloucester promises:

> henceforth I'll bear
> Affliction till it do cry out itself
> "Enough, enough," and die.
>
> (4.6.75–77)

Contemplating Pietro's transformation, Malevole asks, "Who doubts of Providence, / That sees this change?" (4.5.136–37). Edgar tries to revive Gloucester's spirits by telling him, "Thy life's a miracle," to which he shortly adds, "Think that the clearest Gods, who make them honours / Of men's impossibilities, have preserved thee" (4.6.55, 72–74). Finally, Malevole expresses his belief in the possibilities of regeneration: "The time grows ripe for action" (4.5.143). In a slightly different vein, Edgar reminds his father, who has once again despaired, that "Ripeness is all" (5.2.11).

*The Malcontent* ends with the completion of the tragicomic design by Altofront's restoration and by the expulsion, though not the execution, of Mendoza. One senses that Altofront returns to power with an enriched consciousness, the product of enforced disguise, of the incorporation of the satiric voice, of the chance to observe in Pietro's agony the image of his own misfortune, and of the experience of guiding his former foe back to psychic equanimity.[126] Edgar undergoes a similar development. At the beginning of the play he is a naively ineffectual, though well-intentioned, aristocrat. Social conflict within the ruling class drives him to adopt the disguise of a mad beggar. In the subsequent acts he endures the misery of the poor and vicariously participates in the ordeals and insights of his father and of his godfather the king. His new understanding enables him to serve first as his father's teacher and protector, then as the agent of personal and political retribution, and finally, though he cannot save Cordelia or Lear, as the worthiest successor to the crown. Edgar's triumph suggests that at least some small portion of what Lear has come to represent, some sense of his radicalizing experience, will survive the final catastrophe.

In this sense the play possesses two plots with two endings, one of them, if not happy, then at least tragicomic. Whereas *The Malcontent* spares even Mendoza, however, the subplot of *King Lear* kills off not only Edmund, but Gloucester as well. The main plot too, a reworking of a nontragic tale, leaves open the possibility of a tragicomic resolution until near the end of the final scene, when Lear enters carrying the body of Cordelia. From then on Edgar fails to invoke providence and divine justice. Indeed, the painfulness of the entire play, combined with the self-

---

[126]Kirsch, pp. 32–37.

conscious inadequacy of the concluding lines, renders problematic any solution to the crisis that is *King Lear*. There is an incommensurability between the processes of destruction and of re-creation that operate simultaneously throughout the tragedy. The tragicomic redemptive pattern embodied in Edgar proves a weak antidote to the dominant movement of the play.

Such, of course, are the two poles toward which response to the play tends: *King Lear* moves toward regeneration;[127] *King Lear* moves toward absurdity.[128] The glass is half full; the glass is half empty. As the references to the Quarto and Folio above imply, however, a generic account of the work may profitably conclude by considering the two most important extant versions of Shakespeare's text. Modern editions of *King Lear* are characteristically composite affairs, based primarily on F1 but drawing substantially on Q1 as well. But the argument about textual criticism and bibliography outlined in the Introduction to this book indicates the utility of a comparative analysis. The growing recent conviction that Q1 represents Shakespeare's first draft and F1 his later, revised conception has encouraged this line of inquiry.[129]

The two texts do not differ radically from one another. Within a common unity, however, if Q1 points to the bitterness of satire, F1 leads to the reconciliation of tragicomedy. The hypothesis of rewriting in 1609–10 for performance at Blackfriars, and hence a connection with the late romances, is compatible with this shift.[130] The shorter, more streamlined Folio text deflects emphasis from commentary and interpretation toward the patterning of the plot. It reduces both the amount of vituperation directed at the evil characters and the grounds for that vituperation. It omits part of Goneril's initial decision "Not to be over-rul'd" by Lear (1.3.17–21), most of Albany's diatribe against Goneril (4.2.31–68), and some of the two sisters' sexual competition over Edmund (5.1.11–13, 18–19). Gone, too, are most of a description of Lear in the storm (3.1.7–15), the trial scene in which the king arraigns his two elder daughters (3.6.17–56), and the denunciation of Regan and Cornwall by two of their servants after the blinding of Gloucester.

The Folio adds a number of passages that gesture toward forgiveness

[127]Knights, *Some Shakespearean Themes and An Approach to "Hamlet"* (Stanford, Calif.: Stanford University Press, 1966), p. 109.

[128]J. Stampfer, "The Catharsis of *King Lear*," in *King Lear: Text, Sources, Criticism*, ed. G. B. Harrison and Robert F. McDonnell (New York: Harcourt, Brace and World, 1962), pp. 176–82.

[129]Steven Urkowitz, *Shakespeare's Revision of "King Lear"* (Princeton: Princeton University Press, 1980); Taylor and Michael Warren, eds., *The Division of the Kingdoms: Shakespeare's Two Versions of "King Lear"* (Oxford: Clarendon Press, 1983), both of which are drawn on in the following discussion.

[130]Taylor, *"King Lear*: The Date and Authorship of the Folio Version," in *Division of the Kingdoms*, ed. Taylor and Warren, esp. pp. 428–29.

and harmony. Inserted are the fool's nonsensical but also utopian prophecy (3.2.79–96), Lear's second expression of solicitude for the fool, and his climactic statement of universal pardon: "None does offend, none, I say, none" (4.6.170). The concluding scenes continue this process. In both versions Edgar attempts to arrest his father's moral backsliding by his insistence, already quoted, that "Ripeness is all." Only in the Folio does Gloucester respond, "And that's true too," a final line suggesting that he may, indeed, have achieved patience before his death (5.2.11). Lear, too, gets new closing words. His last speech in the Quarto begins in bitterness and ends with his by now oft-repeated act of undressing. The Folio appends, "Do you see this? Look on her, look, her lips, / Look there, look there!" (5.3.310–11). Lear seemingly dies in the redemptive but deluded conviction that Cordelia lives. Perhaps his final moments resemble Gloucester's:

> his flaw'd heart,
> Alack, too weak the conflict to support!
> 'Twixt two extremes of passion, joy and grief,
> Burst smilingly.
>
> (5.3.196–99)

Finally, Edgar, whose relative weight in the play may increase with the diminution of Albany's and Kent's parts and with the more compromised character of Albany's, receives in the Folio some of the lines, and hence some of the authority, attributed to Albany in the Quarto. "Haste thee, for thy life," he urges the officer who belatedly attempts to save Cordelia (5.3.252). And of course he gets to deliver the last two couplets of the play, a dramaturgical sign of his own movement from adversity to good fortune.

Thus the critical debate over *King Lear*, as represented by the composite text, reproduces the generic divergence not only between main plot and subplot, but also between Quarto and Folio. What are the political implications of this split within tragedy between satire and tragicomedy? The generic tension corresponds to the contradiction in the play between demystification and retotalization. The two tendencies cannot be separated: the utter delegitimation of the upper class makes the establishment of a new system necessary and, if not possible, then at least thinkable. As in *Fuente Ovejuna*, that new system, insofar as it comes into view at the end of the play, has many of the markings of an ideological censorship, of a conservative formal closure enforced by the national imperative of a generalizing subplot. The feudal battle by which Edgar regains his birthright from Edmund reveals the ultimate social premises of the resolution, as of Shakespearean tragedy in general. So too does the qualified adherence to absolutism, however much tempered by popular beliefs and however functional in a strategy that contrasts the baseness of an emergent, bourgeois society, not yet possessed of emotionally persuasive ideological defenses, with the supposed grandeur of the dying order it supplants. In the end, Shakespeare cannot imagine English society without the crown.

Yet Edgar's concluding military and political triumph represents more than a conservative restoration, and perhaps more even than an incorporation of lower-class perspectives into a fundamentally unchanged structure. Not just another king with the common touch, Edgar undergoes experiences inconceivable in the world of the second *Henriad*. *King Lear* to this extent moves toward something genuinely new. More generally, demystification and retotalization do not possess inherently opposed ideological valences either in drama or in cultural theory. An effective radical criticism, like an effective radical politics, has to find a place for both moments. *King Lear* ends, however, not with retotalization but with the acknowledgement of its impossibility. The inherent contradiction between artisanal base and absolutist superstructure in the public theater extends, both dramaturgically and ideologically, from the social relations between play and audience to the aristocratic action, and even beyond, to an assimilation into the private and public experience of the ruling class as well. Yet as Lear's depoliticization and Cordelia's death suggest, Edgar's accession to the throne violates the logic of that experience, in its impossible effort to integrate a properly communist vision into a monarchical order. *King Lear* points to the future, only to show that the way there is barred.

Both *Fuente Ovejuna* and *King Lear*, then, exhibit a systematic relationship between radical aspiration and its partial containment or self-censorship. What evidence is there for thinking this a seventeenth-century as well as a twentieth-century interpretation, and in particular for believing that contemporary or near-contemporary audiences and readers saw the subversive implications of the two plays? In the course of the seventeenth century, one can distinguish two parallel receptions of both *Fuente Ovejuna* and *King Lear*, one conservative and theatrical, the other revolutionary and political. The perspective of metacommentary can establish the ultimate compatibility of these two opposed "readings" or at least suggest the common basis of the antagonistic responses. Yet in this instance the history of interpretation resembles less a long-term march toward the truth than an ongoing ideological battle. As a result, the emphasis in the following pages falls on the more radical reception, a stance also in line with the conviction expressed by Hans Robert Jauss: "The horizon of expectations of literature distinguishes itself before the horizon of expectations of historical lived praxis in that it not only preserves actual experiences, but also anticipates unrealized possibility, broadens the limited space of social behavior for new desires, claims, and goals, and thereby opens paths of future experience."[131] The procedure of connecting literature to a subsequent revolution in particular entered Marxist criticism with Lenin's articles on Tolstoy. "Tolstoy is great as the spokesman of the ideas and sentiments that emerged among the millions of Russian peasants at the time the bourgeois revolution [of 1905] was approaching in Russia. Tolstoy is original, because the sum total of his views, taken as a whole, happens to express the specific features of our revolution as a *peasant* bourgeois revolution. From this point of view, the contradictions in Tolstoy's views are indeed a mirror of those contradictory conditions in which the peasantry had to play their historical part in our revolution."[132]

*Fuente Ovejuna* and *King Lear* offer the opportunity of testing a similar hypothesis about Lope de Vega and Shakespeare. Cristóbal de Monroy's rewriting of *Fuente Ovejuna* (1630s?) and Nahum Tate's of *King Lear* (1681) provide helpful negative evidence in this regard. Monroy's *Fuente Ovejuna*, largely freeing itself from the chronicle source, tacitly retreats from even the ambiguously revolutionary treatment of events provided by Lope. First the focus shifts from the peasantry, which is depicted with considerably less sympathy than in the earlier play, to the aristocracy, and particularly to the ideal protagonist, Don Juan de Mendoza. The relatively more urban feel of the work brings with it a preference for Gongoresque rather than peasant language and the introduction of a *gracioso*. Although a conventional aristocratic, even courtly, love conflict usurps the plot, Monroy apparently could not dispense entirely with the historically central struggle between predatory overlord and oppressed peasantry. Yet spontaneous lower-class insurgency all but disappears from the scene. The good aristocrats plan the rebellion against the comendador, enlist the support of the peasants, and then lead their social inferiors in the climactic killing of their foe. This upper-class dominance in turn renders superfluous Lope's subplot, in which the overlord's rebellion against the crown helps justify the peasants' rebellion against the overlord. Indeed the crown, and with it a national perspective, also disappears from the play, an absence that may owe something as well to the performance of Monroy's work in Seville rather than Madrid.[133]

---

[131] Hans Robert Jauss, *Toward an Aesthetic of Reception*, trans. Timothy Bahti, Theory and History of Literature 2 (Minneapolis: University of Minnesota Press, 1982), p. 41.

[132] V. I. Lenin, "Leo Tolstoy as the Mirror of the Russian Revolution," in *A Theory of Literary Production*, by Pierre Macherey, trans. Geoffrey Wall (London: Routledge and Kegan Paul, 1978), p. 301.

[133] López Estrada, pp. 181–88, 347–48.

Second, this aristocratic version has evident difficulty in justifying re-bellion on any terms. Though fully aware of the comendador's crimes, the noble Don Juan, who serves as the villainous overlord's *privado*, re-mains steadfastly loyal to his master. He saves the comendador's life, for example, from a nocturnal ambush by two other noblemen. Soon after, when Juan discovers the comendador on the point of murdering the aris-tocratic Doña Flor, his own beloved, he contents himself with persuad-ing his master to desist. Urged to join the rebellion against his lord, he angrily refuses. In fact, Juan abandons the defense of the comendador for a position of neutrality only after the latter draws a sword on him. But Monroy attempts to conceal the disjunction between his protagonist, who is too good to rebel, and his plot, which must justify rebellion, by having Doña Flor disguise herself as Juan and, possessed, as it were, by his martial spirit, lead the fatal attack on the comendador in her lover's name. Flor's sex explains her less than ideal conduct—"mas soy mujer, bastante / disculpa de mis yerros" ("but I am a woman, enough of an / ex-cuse of my errors": 3.4.2444–45)—and with no apparent sense of the irony, Juan succeeds to the post of comendador.

Tate's *Lear* employs some of the same techniques to weaken the force of popular radicalism. An illogical love plot, in this instance between Edgar and Cordelia, competes for the audience's attention. Much as Monroy removes the peasantry from center stage, Tate completely ex-cises the fool, perhaps Shakespeare's crucial inheritance from the popu-lar theatrical tradition. Consequently, Lear's critical comments lose some of their motivation and materialist basis. When the old king says, "Come on my boy, how dost my boy? . . . My poor knave,"[134] he is speaking not to the fool, as in Shakespeare's tragedy, but to the aged and aristocratic Kent. And it is once again Kent, rather than the fool, whose suffering in-congruously generates the "Poor naked wretches" speech. As James Black, a recent editor of the play, argues, "Where Shakespeare has re-duced his aristocrats to complete desolation—to 'the thing itself'— Tate's blue-blooded protagonists become in adversity something nearer the middle- or lower-class characters of sentimental drama."[135] Most important, the happy ending, which recalls Shakespeare's source and in which the villains die, the old men—Lear, Gloucester, and Kent—re-tire, and the fortunate lovers—Edgar and Cordelia—inherit *half* the kingdom, effectively neutralizes the subversive thrust of the play: "Our drooping country now erects her head, / Peace spreads her balmy wings, and Plenty blooms. / . . . (Whatever storms of Fortune are decreed) / . . . truth and virtue shall at last succeed" (5.6.154–60).

[134]Nahum Tate, *The History of King Lear*, ed. James Black (Lincoln: University of Ne-braska Press, 1975), 3.1.41–44. The subsequent reference is noted in the text.
[135]Black, p. xxxiii.

These basic changes, which respond to the political climate of Restoration England and particularly to the conditions of a socially exclusive theater, should not be overstressed, however. Tate even adds a popular rebellion to his Shakespearean material. Further, the recourse to Shakespearean tragedy in the late 1670s and early 1680s meant both a formal and an ideological break with the immediately preceding, uncompromisingly aristocratic heroic drama. In its return to the past, Tate's Shakespeareanism, paradoxically enough, points toward the future.

By their very elisions and evasions, then, Monroy's and Tate's plays negatively suggest the presence in Lope's and Shakespeare's works of lower-class subversiveness. Does seventeenth-century reception history offer any positive support for this contention? It does, but more clearly in England than in Spain, and for reasons implicit in the two plays and explicit in the subsequent development of the two countries. In the mid-seventeenth century, Spain experienced aristocratic rebellion, but no revolution. In England, however, the contemporaneous Civil War proved the turning point in the nation's history, as well as the crucial event for seventeenth-century literature. The conflict, and particularly the role of the radical left in it, provides an appropriate framework within which to interpret *King Lear*. In a metaphorical and perhaps in a literal sense as well, the English Revolution was the most important reception of the play.

Lope's *Fuente Ovejuna* stands in a more oblique relation to subsequent Spanish history. The work presents a communal rebellion that it then conservatively integrates into a national resolution. Its national assumptions deserve scrutiny in light of political events on the periphery of the Habsburg empire; its communal premises bear comparison with social relations in the Castilian homeland. The rebellions of the 1640s, which gave the lie to the nationalist pretenses of the monarchy, fundamentally depended on the peasantry. In Catalonia a peasant army spearheaded the revolt. In Portugal, a source of dynastic conflict in *Fuente Ovejuna* (e.g., 3.8.1936–39), the lower classes were consistently more anti-Castilian than the aristocracy. When much of the upper class opted for independence in 1640, the wavering of some of the nobility, higher clergy, and merchants posed little threat, given the enthusiasm of the mass of the population. In Italy a fisherman initially led the rebellion of 1647. In Andalusia peasant unrest erupted into violence in the 1650s but had no chance of success because of the close ties between aristocracy and crown. At the end of the century the Second Germania of Valencia, the largest *jacquerie* of Habsburg Spain, passed out of the control of the local nobility, who had to rely on the royal militia to suppress the uprising. Finally, as noted in the previous chapter, when the anti-Habsburg struggles of Catalonia and Italy turned into internal class conflicts, the aristocracies once again threw in their lot with the monarchy.[136] The Spanish periphery, then, reveals not the alliance of the peasantry with the crown against the nobility, but the revolutionary opposition of the peasantry to crown and nobility alike. It reveals, in other words, not the conservative closure of *Fuente Ovejuna*, but the revolutionary action of *Fuente Ovejuna*.

In Castile, on the other hand, where internal unity was greater than on much of the periphery, the peasantry offered scant resistance to Habsburg power. The failure of rural rebellion to extend to the imperial center, one of the tragedies of Spanish history, seems to accord with the ending of Lope's play. But if the miserable and oppressed Castilian peasants did not take arms, they most certainly did take flight. By abandoning the land, on which they could no longer survive, they contributed to the devastation of Spanish agriculture. As the deposing of the leaders of Fuente Ovejuna in Lope's source suggests, those peasants who stayed behind lived not in egalitarian communes, but in hierarchical villages whose local rulers owed their allegiance to absentee aristocratic landowners. Centuries later, in the decades before the Civil War, the triumph of anarchism and socialism among the Castilian peasantry signified a rejection of village inequality, an attack by the poor on the rich, the repudiation of injustices that had persisted at least since the Habsburg era. In the long run Castile rejoined the periphery, refusing the conclusion of Lope's play while validating its insurgent plot. Similarly, the belated phenomenon of leftist performances of *Fuente Ovejuna* in Spain, during the insurgent decade of the 1930s, reenacted the close connection between the play and upsurges of revolutionary fervor in France, Germany, and Russia during the nineteenth century, and in the Soviet Union during the twentieth.[137]

With *King Lear*, on the other hand, one need not wait in quite the same

---

[136]Elliott, pp. 340–43, 349–50; John Lynch, *Spain and America, 1598–1700*, vol. 2 of *Spain under the Habsburgs*, 2d ed. (New York: New York University Press, 1981), pp. 113–14, 118, 123, 153; Antonio Domínguez Ortiz, *The Golden Age of Spain, 1516–1659*, trans. James Casey (New York: Basic Books, 1971), pp. 100–102, 106; Casey, *The Kingdom of Valencia in the Seventeenth Century* (Cambridge: Cambridge University Press, 1979), pp. 76, 101, 116, 118–20, 204, 206–7.

[137]Domínguez Ortiz, pp. 102–3; Lynch, 2:152–53; Michael R. Weisser, *The Peasants of the Montes: The Roots of Rural Rebellion in Spain* (Chicago: University of Chicago Press, 1976), pp. 17, 114, 117–20; López Estrada, pp. 9–10; Alexey Almasov, "*Fuenteovejuna* y el honor villanesco en el teatro de Lope de Vega," *Cuadernos Hispanoamericanos* 54 (1963): 717–23; Jack Weiner, "Lope de Vega's *Fuenteovejuna* under Tsars, Commissars, and the Second Spanish Republic (1931–1939)," *Annali Instituto Universitario Orientale, Napoli, Sezione Romanza* 24 (1982): 167–223. In a similar fashion, Martin Franzbach, *El teatro de Calderón en Europa* (Madrid: Fundación Universitaria Española, 1982), pp. 114–20, has demonstated the intimate and, among Calderón's plays, unique connection between *El alcalde de Zalamea* and the revolutionary moment of the late eighteenth century in France, Germany, Holland, Italy, and Austria.

fashion for the modern era. In 1640 and 1641 rebellion on the English periphery—in Scotland and Ireland—triggered revolution in the center. What did the theater mean during the revolutionary era? Owing to Parliament's suppression of the stage and Royalist attacks on that decision, a belief in a general Puritan hostility to drama has persisted for more than three centuries. But as earlier chapters have argued, if Puritanism signifies something more than the Puritan clergy, if it broadly refers to those who supported Parliament against the king, then the opposite is probably closer to the truth. The lower classes in particular remained enthusiastic playgoers, and perhaps play readers as well, at least to 1642. Although most of the actors sided with the crown, Richard Overton, who may have belonged to a professional acting company, and John Harris, who certainly did, became leading Leveller writers. Leveller and Digger tracts are often indebted to the dramatic prose of the preceding era. More generally, pamphleteers on both sides of the Civil War, mainly trying to reach a popular audience, took for granted a familiarity with the theater and many of its plays.[138]

Shakespeare was frequently referred to by Royalist and rebel writers alike. Most, though not all, of these allusions are sympathetic: the legacy of Shakespeare was a matter of ideological struggle. Yet certain patterns are discernible. As the commentators well knew, Shakespearean tragedy dramatizes the fall of princes, perhaps contributing thereby to what Franco Moretti has recently called "the Deconsecration of Sovereignty."[139] A newspaper account from 1645 evokes Archbishop Laud's fear on the scaffold of Hamlet's "undiscovered country."[140] The Players Petition to Parliament for the reopening of the stage, from 1643, mentions Henry VI before prophetically concluding: "we can tell how / To depose Kings, there we are more than you, / Although not more then what you would."[141] Similarly, a Royalist pamphlet of 1647 contrasts "The Comedy of Errors, . . . so often presented in publicke to the rabble [by Parliament] that it grew common and out of fashion," with the more ominous theatrical plans of the New Model Army, which "intended their first show should be a King and no King, personated to the life, but wholy Tragicall."[142] For monarchists, then, although parliamentary proceedings often called to mind buffoonish comedy, the Revolution

---

[138]Heinemann, pp. 237–57; Ernest Sirluck, "Shakespeare and Jonson among the Pamphleteers of the First Civil War: Some Unreported Seventeenth-Century Allusions," *Modern Philology* 53 (1955–56): 88–90.

[139]Moretti, passim.

[140]John Munro, ed. *The Shakespere Allusion Book: A Collection of Allusions to Shakespere from 1591 to 1700* (London: Chatto and Windus, 1909), 1:488.

[141]Munro, 1:481.

[142]Quoted in Leslie Hotson, *The Commonwealth and Restoration Stage* (Cambridge: Harvard University Press, 1928), p. 29. See also p. 6.

was ultimately tragedy in its combination of illegal rebellion and royal victimization.[143]

If parliamentary pamphleteers challenged the moral valence attached to this metaphor, they did not question the metaphor itself.[144] "And if the Genius of the Land should ask thee," an anonymous piece from 1643 runs, "Who hath beene so farre mis-led, to suffer the effusion of the bloud of his loving and loyall Subjects? What wou'd Conscience say, but the King? In the Tragedie of *Richard* the third, Questions being put, who had beene seduced to this and that execrable deed, Conscience or some Spirit cry'd *Richard*."[145] Milton later developed the same analogy; earlier he had compared one of his religious foes to Polonius, that "Champion from behind the Arras."[146] Equally important, because Shakespeare was associated with the public theater and popular culture, and perhaps because the people were linked to the revolutionary cause, Royalists increasingly sought to distance themselves aesthetically, if not politically, from his plays. John Berkenhead speaks of Shakespeare's "Trunk-hose-Wit," while William Cartwright, addressing himself to the memory of Fletcher, argues that

> *Shakespeare* to thee was dull, whose best jest lyes
> I' th Ladies questions, and the Fooles replyes;
> Old fashion'd wit, which walkt from town to town
> In turn'd Hose, which our fathers call'd the Clown.[147]

Finally, although *King Lear* was probably not one of Shakespeare's most quoted plays before the Restoration, it was undoubtedly far better known than some modern scholars have suggested.[148] On occasion,

[143]See the passages quoted in Hotson, pp. 19, 28, 31, 35, 36, 37, 39, 42, 46, 51.

[144]See the passages quoted in Hotson, p. 20.

[145]George Thorn-Drury, ed., *Some Seventeenth Century Allusions to Shakespeare and His Works Not Hitherto Collected* (London: Dobell, 1920), p. 5.

[146]Munro, 1:523, and, for the quotation, 474.

[147]Munro, 1:512, 511. See also Munro, vols. 1 and 2, passim; Thorn-Drury, ed., *Some Seventeenth Century Allusions*, passim; idem, *More Seventeenth Century Allusions to Shakespeare and His Works Not Hitherto Collected* (London: Dobell, 1924), passim; Heinemann, pp. 237–57; Sirluck, p. 90; P. W. Thomas, *Sir John Berkenhead, 1617–1679: A Royalist Career in Politics and Polemics* (Oxford: Clarendon Press, 1969), pp. 102, 135.

[148]Munro, 1:200, 272, 299–300, 304, 383, 492, and 2:50–53, 58, 76, 126, 520; A. Bruce Black and Robert Metcalf Smith, *Shakespeare Allusions and Parallels* (Bethlehem, Pa.: Lehigh University Publication, 1931), p. 5; Kenneth Muir, ed., *King Lear*, pp. xiii, xx; Sirluck, p. 95; David L. Frost, *The School of Shakespeare: The Influence of Shakespeare on English Drama, 1600–42* (Cambridge: Cambridge University Press, 1968), pp. 6 n. 2, 87, 149–50, 153, 164, 197–98; Cyrus Hoy, "Shakespeare and the Drama of His Time," in *Shakespeare: Aspects of Influence*, ed. G. B. Evans, Harvard English Studies 7 (Cambridge: Harvard University Press, 1976), pp. 29–30; Heinemann, pp. 253–54; E. A. J. Honigmann, *Shakespeare's Impact on His Contemporaries* (Totowa, N.J.: Barnes and Noble, 1982), pp. 37, 48. *King Lear*'s unpopularity: Bentley, *Shakespeare and Jonson: Their Reputations in the Seventeenth Century Compared* (Chicago: University of Chicago Press, 1945), pp. 19–20, 84, 109, 112, 117, 137; Hunter, ed., *King Lear* (Harmondsworth, Middlesex: Penguin, 1972), p. 46.

echoes of the play even begin to capture its radical cast. In Massinger's *Emperor of the East* (1631), Theodosius's assertion of his common humanity with his subjects is apparently indebted to Lear's growing insight in general and to his remarks to the blinded Gloucester in particular: "They flattered me like a dog. . . . they told me I was every thing; 'tis a lie, I am not ague-proof" (4.6.97–108). According to Theodosius, "The proud attributes, / By oil-tongued flattery imposed upon us, / . . . Cure not the least fit of an ague in us."[149] And in 1648 John Harris may allude to the play in his criticism of Parliament's expected supineness before Charles I and in denouncing the corruption of the legal system by wealth.[150]

Yet the Civil War is connected to *King Lear* far more pervasively than these isolated references suggest. For Lukács, "no special perceptiveness is needed to see the relation between social collision in an extreme form [within drama], on the one hand, and social transformation, i.e. revolution, on the other."[151] First, at the level of social structure, the Civil War reenacts the three-sided conflict of Shakespeare's tragedy. A split between more and less modern sectors of the ruling class produces a deadlock that can be broken only by the intervention of popular forces. In *King Lear*, the traditional sector of that class forges the alliance. The Revolution rewrites Shakespeare's script, however, by defining the modern Parliamentarians as the proponents of tradition, an emendation partly justified by the fact that the Parliamentarians of the 1640s were indeed considerably older than their adversaries.[152] Again, although in both dramas the popular contribution proves crucial, perhaps even decisive, the main benefits of the conflict accrue to the aristocracy.

Second, at the level of ideology, the radicals of the period systematically reformulate and extend Lear's revolutionary insights. Here only glancing reference is possible to this rich and largely untapped body of material. The metaphysical questioning of the play anticipates the similar concerns of the Familists, Grindletonians, Muggletonians, and Diggers.[153] Perhaps the popular dimension of Edmund, a younger son, is echoed in the denunciation by the Digger Gerrard Winstanley of "those Lords of Mannors, so called, who have, by the murdering and cheating law of the sword, stoln the Land from yonger brothers."[154] The fool's prophecy ends with the assertion, "This prophecy Merlin shall make; for I live before his time" (3.2.95–96). The prophecies of Merlin seem to

[149]Munro, 1:300.
[150]Heinemann, pp. 253–54.
[151]Lukács, *Historical Novel*, p. 97.
[152]Hill, *World*, p. 188.
[153]Hill, *World*, pp. 83, 139–50, 166, 173–74.
[154]*The Works of Gerrard Winstanley: With an Appendix of Documents Relating to the Digger Movement*, ed. George H. Sabine (Ithaca, N.Y.: Cornell University Press, 1941), p. 274.

have been linked to radicalism. Greene connected them with Marlowe's and Tamburlaine's atheism; both the Fifth Monarchists and revolutionary astrologer William Lilly cited them, the latter perhaps with self-fulfilling effect.[155] Before the Civil War, Tom O'Bedlams—madmen previously confined to Bedlam—went begging around the countryside. At least one inmate of Bedlam was sent there for antimonarchical prophecy. Especially during the revolutionary years, but even before, fools and madmen were associated with revolutionary prophecy. According to the Seeker William Erbery, "If madness be in the heart of every man, Eccles. 9.3, then this is the island of Great Bedlam . . . Come, let's all be mad together."[156]

The Ranter Abiezer Coppe's demand that men of power "Bow before those poore, nasty, lousie, ragged wretches"[157] recalls Lear's invocation to "Poor naked wretches." Lear's soliloquy continues, "How shall your houseless heads and unfed sides, / Your loop'd and window'd raggedness, defend you / From seasons such as these?" (3.4.30–32). Overton accused Cromwell's Council of State of attempting "to wound (through my sides) the too much forsaken cause of the poor oppressed people."[158] "Take physic, Pomp," Lear urges: "Expose thyself to feel what wretches feel" (3.4.33–34). The blinded Gloucester criticizes the wealthy man "that will not see / Because he does not feel" (4.1.68–69). The Leveller William Walwyn argued: "if one suffer, all ought to suffer with that one, even by having a sympathie and fellow feeling of his miserie, and helping to beare his burden."[159] The Leveller "Agreement of the People," addressed to "fellow-Commoners," specifies that elected representatives "shall be in a capacity to tast of subjection, as well as rule, & so shall be equally concerned with your selves, in all they do. For they must equally suffer with you under any common burdens."[160] In calling for divine punishment of "the superfluous and lust-dieted man" (4.1.67), Gloucester echoes Lear's concluding injunction: "That thou mayst shake the superflux to them [the poor], / And show the Heavens more just" (3.4.35–36). In "The Humble Petition," the Levellers said that they expected the House of Commons to "have raised a stock of Money or [i.e., out] of those many confiscated Estates you have had, for

---

[155]Hill, *World*, pp. 89–91; Paul H. Kocher, *Christopher Marlowe: A Study of His Thought, Learning, and Character* (1946; rpt. New York: Russell and Russell, 1962), p. 23.

[156]Hill, *World*, pp. 223–26, 277–86. The quotation is from p. 277.

[157]Abiezer Coppe, *A Fiery Flying Roll* (London, 1649), sig. B4$^{r}$.

[158]Richard Overton, "The Proceedings of the Councel of State against Richard Overton, Now Prisoner in the Tower of London," in *The Leveller Tracts, 1647–1653*, ed. William Haller and Godfrey Davies (New York: Columbia University Press with the Henry E. Huntington Library, 1944), p. 214.

[159]William Walwyn, "Englands Lamentable Slaverie," in *The Levellers in the English Revolution*, ed. G. E. Aylmer (Ithaca, N.Y.: Cornell University Press, 1975), p. 64.

[160]"Agreement of the People," in Aylmer, pp. 91, 92.

payment of those who contributed voluntoarily [*sic*] above their abilities, before you had provided for those that disbursed out of their superfluities."[161] George Foster, perhaps a cross between a Leveller and a Ranter, believed that God "will make those that have riches give them to them that have none."[162]

Although, as these juxtaposed passages suggest, Lear here most closely anticipates the Levellers, he soon moves to the more radical positions of the Ranters and Diggers, in a consideration of the legal system. Indeed, a recent study by T. Wilson Hayes refers to Winstanley's "Lear-like" argumentation.[163] To Gloucester, Lear remarks: "see how yond justice rails upon yond simple thief. . . . change places, and, handy-dandy, which is the justice, which is the thief?" (4.6.153–56). Similar perceptions were commonplace among the Levellers and Diggers. Winstanley perhaps went furthest in placing the blame on private property, which was obtained "by murther and theft," and, relatedly, on commodity exchange, which "makes great Murderers and Theeves to be imprisoners, and hangers of little ones."[164] In an attack on enclosures, the anonymous *More Light Shining in Buckinghamshire* stresses the social double standard: "you hang a man for stealing for his wants, when you your selves have stole from your fellow brethren all Lands, Creatures, &c."[165] Lear temporarily abandons this topic for his obsession with sexuality: "Thou rascal beadle, hold thy bloody hand! / Why dost thou lash that whore? Strip thine own back; / Thou hotly lusts to use her in that kind / For which thou whipp'st her" (4.6.162–65). For Coppe, the hypocritical "Pharisee in man is the mother of harlots and being the worst whore cries Whore first."[166]

Lear then switches back to the economics of justice: "The usurer hangs the cozener. / Thorough tatter'd clothes small vices do appear; / Robes and furr'd gowns hide all. Plate sin with gold, / And the strong lance of justice hurtless breaks; / Arm it in rags, a pigmy's straw does pierce it" (4.6.165–69). Winstanley asked: "hath not Parliaments . . . made Laws . . . to strengthen the rich and the strong by those Laws, and left oppression upon the backs of the oppressed still?"[167] The Quaker

---

[161]"The Humble Petition," in Aylmer, p. 136.
[162]George Foster, quoted in Hill, *World*, p. 223.
[163]T. Wilson Hayes, *Winstanley the Digger: A Literary Analysis of Radical Ideas in the English Revolution* (Cambridge: Harvard University Press, 1979), pp. 160, 186.
[164]Winstanley, *Works*, pp. 270–71.
[165]*More Light Shining in Buckinghamshire*, in Winstanley, *Works*, p. 634.
[166]Coppe, quoted in Hill, *World*, p. 333. For more on Lear and sexuality, see Coppélia Kahn, "Excavating 'Those Dim Minoan Regions': Maternal Subtexts in Patriarchal Literature," *Diacritics* 12, no. 2 (1982): 37–41.
[167]Winstanley, *Works*, p. 557.

Francis Howgill thought the law simply enabled "the envious man who hath much money to revenge himself upon his poor neighbours."[168] Lear's previously quoted, paradoxical solution, "None does offend, none, I say, none," anticipates Coppe's pronouncement that "Sin and Transgression is finished and ended." Under severe government pressure, Coppe modified his position: "All are sinners. Sinners all. What then? Are we better than they? No, in no wise."[169] "It is an hard thing," the Leveller John Wildman believed, "by the light of nature to conceive how there can be any sin committed; and therefore the magistrate cannot easily determine what sins are against the light of nature, and what not."[170] Finally, Lear's periodic undressing looks forward to the Ranter and early Quaker tendency to go "naked for a sign," to "go naked as he [Adam] did, and live above sin and shame."[171]

In both *King Lear* and the English Civil War, one set of rulers overthrows another. The anonymous author of *Tyranipocrit Discovered* spoke for Shakespeare, Erbery, and the Leveller John Lilburne in claiming that "the new tyrants which have driven out the old are in all things so bad [as] or worse than the old tyrants were."[172] In a similar vein, Overton dramatically rejects not an upstart crow, but "our new upstart Nobility." "Now the case is altered," he writes, "the Gentleman is become one of the Grandees of the Royall palace."[173] This major political crisis leads to a popular, radical ideological breakthrough, to the consequent arousal of great expectations, and to their probably inevitable disappointment. Lear's optimistic but quietist response to the prospect of imprisonment perhaps has something in common with John Webster's representation of Erbery's acceptance of defeat: "that it was the wisdom as well as the obedience of the saints to make their captivity as comfortable as they could."[174] There may be nothing more than coincidence in the similarity between Lear's cry—"Howl, howl, howl!"—when he returns carrying the body of Cordelia (5.3.257) and Coppe's demand, "Howl, howl, ye nobles, howl honourable, howl ye rich men for the miseries that are coming upon you."[175] Yet Edgar's concluding preference for feeling over platitude surely belongs in the radical Protestant tradition.[176]

---

[168]Francis Howgill, quoted in Hill, *World*, p. 270.
[169]Coppe, *A Fiery Flying Roll*, sig. A2$^r$; idem, quoted in Hill, *World*, p. 212.
[170]John Wildman, quoted in Hill, *World*, pp. 165–66.
[171]Quoted in Hill, *World*, pp. 318, 317.
[172]*Tyranipocrit Discovered*, quoted in Hill, *World*, p. 344. See also Lilburne, "The Second Part of Englands New-Chaines Discovered," in *The Leveller Tracts*, ed. Haller and Davies, p. 187; Erbery, quoted in Hill, *World*, p. 195.
[173]Overton, pp. 219, 218.
[174]John Webster, quoted in Hill, *World*, p. 196.
[175]Coppe, *A Second Fiery Flying Roule* (London, 1649), sig. C3$^r$.
[176]Hill, *World*, p. 369.

And despite adopting different temporal perspectives, his final couplet and Erbery's expression of resignation reveal related sensibilities. "The oldest hath borne most," Edgar says; "we that are young / Shall never see so much, nor live so long" (5.3.325–26). Erbery thought, "It may be other generations may see the glory talked to be in the last times, but we are cut off for our parts; our children may possess it, but for our parts we have no hopes to enjoy it."[177]

The tragedy of *King Lear* is the tragedy of English history. The latter makes the former comprehensible. Writing on Sartre, Fredric Jameson has suggested that "the implication of this revision of past by present is that it is not the mere hypothesis of the historian which fixes the meaning of the past event in definitive form, but rather simply yet *another* concrete event in time."[178] Whatever the direct influence of the play on the Revolution, *King Lear* takes its place in a tradition of popular radicalism, noted in chapter 1, that may extend without a break from the Peasants' Revolt of 1381 to the present. And just as the radical sects have increasingly proved the present age's most valued predecessors among seventeenth-century Protestants, so too the corresponding revolutionary dimensions of such works as *King Lear* and *Fuente Ovejuna* may come to seem the most precious legacy from Renaissance theater.

[177]Erbery, quoted in Hill, *World*, pp. 196–97.
[178]Fredric Jameson, *Marxism and Form: Twentieth-Century Dialectical Theories of Literature* (Princeton: Princeton University Press, 1971), p. 211.

# [7

# The Passing of the Public Theater:
# Intrigue Tragedy and Romance

The preceding chapter primarily treated plays composed for the public theaters at the start of the new century—before 1609 in England and 1622 in Spain. Only English satiric comedy belonged to the transitional period of relative balance between the public and private stages. Its consequent distance from popular dramaturgy partly allies it with intrigue tragedy and tragicomic romance, transitional forms prominent from shortly before 1610 in England and from shortly after 1620 in Spain. Although both genres tend to remove the aristocracy from politics, both also point to the future. Together they complete the structural and historical picture of the public theater while also clarifying the contemporaneous supersession of the institution by a socially more restricted stage.

## FORMS OF INTRIGUE TRAGEDY

### Secular Tragedy

Intrigue tragedy combines a loss of a national perspective[1] with a sense of the problematic nature of moral action. Compared with Shakespearean tragedy, which itself chronicled the failure of the aristocracy, the English plays reveal a narrowing range and a deeper pessimism. In Spain, less intense social and theatrical pressures encouraged a less extreme constriction but a sharper break, with the elevation of tragedy to preeminence for the first time since the early 1580s. The end of Philip III's reign and the opening of Philip IV's saw increased agitation in favor of tragedy on the part of courtiers, Aristotelian theorists, and reli-

[1]Charles Vincent Aubrun, *La comedia española* (*1600–1680*), trans. Julio Lago Alonso (Madrid: Taurus, 1968), pp. 106–9.

gious moralists.[2] In both countries, the new form dramatizes not so much the failure of the nobility to adapt to political change as the irrelevance of that class to politics altogether. As history relinquishes its dynamic significance, the passage of time seems to produce only decay, entrapment, or stasis. In the absence of alternative modes of coherence, the characters and their deeds acquire a kind of opacity that defies clear judgment[3] and that consequently has resulted in substantial interpretive controversy over a number of plays.

Intrigue tragedy falls loosely into three main subgroups—heroic, satiric, and romantic—according to the relative influence of prior drama. The satiric strain is stronger in England, the heroic and romantic in Spain. On the London stage, the rough chronological progression from heroic to satiric to romantic, coincident with a reduction of scope, suggests a defensive reaction to rising social opposition and growing isolation. In Spain, within each type the tragedies of the 1630s present a darker vision than those of the previous decade. The peninsular theater puts on stage a class, or class fraction, disoriented not, as in England, by a threat to its hegemony, but by a loss of self-confidence, by an awareness of an inability to function effectively or to prevent collapse.

Heroic intrigue, though sharing many of the assumptions of prior national drama, portrays the values that underlay traditional aristocratic power in such a way as to drain them of political significance. In the prologue to *A Challenge for Beauty* (1635), Heywood looks back on a long career in the theater only to find that, regrettably, he can no longer justify Nashe's proud distinction between the trivial concerns of foreign stages and the great national themes of Elizabethan drama.

> For where before great Patriots, Dukes and Kings
> Presented for some hie facinorious things,
> Were the Stage-Subject; now we strive to flie
> In their low pitch, who never could soare hie:
>
> . . .
>
> I only wish that they [dramatists] would sometimes bend
> To memorise the valours of such men,
> Whose very names might dignifie the Pen.[1]

---

[2]Ruth Lee Kennedy, *Studies in Tirso*, vol. 1, *The Dramatist and His Competitors, 1620–26*, North Carolina Studies in the Romance Languages and Literatures, Essays, no. 3 (Chapel Hill: University of North Carolina Department of Romance Languages, 1974), pp. 37, 44–47, 51, 53, 57.

[3]For a roughly similar description, see Jean Alexander, "Parallel Tendencies in English and Spanish Tragedy in the Renaissance," in *Studies in Comparative Literature*, ed. Waldo F. McNeir (Baton Rouge: Louisiana State University Press, 1962), pp. 84–101.

[1]Thomas Heywood, prologue to *A Challenge for Beauty*, in *The Dramatic Works of Thomas Heywood* (1874; rpt. New York: Russell and Russell, 1964), 5:3.

Among English tragedies composed for the private theaters, Chapman's *Bussy D'Ambois* (1604) and *The Revenge of Bussy D'Ambois* (1610) have obvious affinities with Jonson's *Sejanus* and Chapman's own *Caesar and Pompey*, plays that have trouble addressing broad political concerns despite their authors' apparent purposes. The *Bussy* tragedies focus from the start on the court rather than the nation. However different the two works, in each, state power at court victimizes the protagonists, both of whom display only the most casual and intermittent interest in politics: the heroic temper proves ineffective and, more often than not, irrelevant. The earlier and more complex play dramatizes the gap between Bussy's assertion of virtue, freedom, and natural law, on the one hand, and the sordid, increasingly private conduct that defines him as a feudal aristocrat out of place at an absolutist court, on the other. *The Revenge of Bussy* culminates in the main character's suicide, a conscious withdrawal by a stoic individualist that condemns the monarchy. In both plays, then, ideology serves its classic rationalizing function. More specifically, a reactionary perspective, typically indebted to bourgeois values, produces a simultaneously critical and positive vision that, while damning the present, looks to both past and future.[5]

Philip Massinger's *Unnatural Combat* (1624–25) recreates the contradictory outlook particularly of *Bussy D'Ambois*, perhaps because it is probably a late public theater play composed by a primarily private theater dramatist not entirely comfortable with the task.[6] Its hybrid nature arises from this temporal, institutional, and authorial conjuncture. Frequently criticized for structural disunity,[7] the play begins as a heroic drama but increasingly turns into an intrigue tragedy. Similarly, although Theocrine, the protagonist's daughter, combines the innocence and virtue of the young female victims of Shakespearean tragedy, she is raped and apparently "deform'd" before she dies (5.2.190). The bluff Captain Belgarde, like Davenant's sailors in *News from Plymouth*, also belongs to the public theater, where he may have appealed to patriotic enthusiasm and lower-class pride.[8] Bursting in on an aristocratic state dinner, he rebukes the governor for not granting him his back pay:

[5]For similar descriptions but, symptomatically, opposed evaluations of the plays, see Leonard Goldstein, "George Chapman and the Decadence in Early Seventeenth-Century Drama," *Science and Society* 27 (1963): 23–48; J. W. Lever, *The Tragedy of State* (London: Methuen, 1971), pp. 37–58. For an antithetical description, see Jonathan Goldberg, *James I and the Politics of Literature: Jonson, Shakespeare, Donne, and Their Contemporaries* (Baltimore: Johns Hopkins University Press, 1983), pp. 155–61, 274 n. 48.

[6]Date: Philip Edwards and Colin Gibson, introduction to *The Unnatural Combat*, in their edition of *The Plays and Poems of Philip Massinger* (Oxford: Clarendon Press, 1976), 2:181–84. References to *The Unnatural Combat* are to this edition. Attribution to the Globe: Gerald Eades Bentley, *The Jacobean and Caroline Stage*, vol. 4 (Oxford: Clarendon Press, 1956), p. 824.

[7]E.g., T. S. Eliot, *Selected Essays* (New York: Harcourt, Brace and World, 1950), p. 187.

[8]Edwards and Gibson, 2:183–84.

and yet remember
Tis we that bring you in the meanes of feasts,
Banquets, and revels, which when you possesse,
With barbarous ingratitude you deny us
To be made sharers in the harvest, which
Our sweat and industrie reap'd, and sow'd for you.
The silks you weare, we with our bloud spin for you.

(3.3.84–90)

This extraordinary passage provides the ideological key to the play, expressing popular assertiveness and in particular an insistence on the reality and fundamental significance of surplus extraction, viewed from the perspective of the exploited class. The imagery suggests that Massinger has in mind the plight of the peasant in the feudal mode of production. As the context reveals, however, Belgarde is really talking about the booty won for the ruling class by the common sailors. In the zero-sum game of feudal economics, not technological innovation but outright expropriation offers the quickest path to accumulation. Although the metaphor of the harvest in one sense mystifies the issues, in another it accurately reveals the dramatist's precapitalist premises.

For despite the attack on the court here and elsewhere from a popular point of view, The Unnatural Combat retains a resolutely aristocratic outlook. It largely lacks the critical perspective of Chapman's works or, for that matter, of many other Jacobean intrigue tragedies, public and private. In a manner reminiscent of News from Plymouth, the passing jibes at wealthy city merchants seem to be unnaturalized immigrants from Massinger's satiric comedy. Equally important, the governor and his aides generously respond to the pleas of Captain Belgarde, who discovers as a result, and to his chagrin, what the previous scene has already shown: that a poor servant has it better than a wealthy lord. Belgarde likewise learns to know his place. At the end of the play he obtains an appropriate soldier's reward—not money, but responsibility for a fort.

This ambivalence also extends to the portrayal of the protagonist Malefort, arguably his author's finest creation, a tortured and complex figure, a genuine villain-hero.[9] Yet Massinger withholds essential knowledge about him until almost the end of the play, repeatedly surprising the audience by revealing another of his former crimes—a method totally alien to earlier technique in the tragedies of the public theater. More damaging, in the first scene the governor refers to him as "Our late great Admirall," praising "his faire actions, / Loyall, and true demeanour" (1.1.203, 208–9). Only much later, however, does the same man reveal his true opinion of Malefort:

[9]T. A. Dunn, Philip Massinger: The Man and the Playwright (Edinburgh: Thomas Nelson for the University College of Ghana, 1957), pp. 126–28.

Vertues so mix'd with vices. Valiant the world speakes him,
But with that bloody; liberall in his gifts too,
But to maintain his prodigall expence,
A fierce extortioner; an impotent lover
Of women for a flash, but his fires quench'd,
Hating as deadly.

(3.2.34–39)

The audience never finds out what purpose its ignorance, and that of the other characters, serves. Does Massinger's deviation from the traditions of the public theater evoke a sense of the opacity of the human personality, its resistance to outside judgment? Alternatively, perhaps the moralizing paraphernalia of *The Unnatural Combat* merely obscures an opportunistic piece of sensationalism, or, more simply still, dramaturgical clumsiness. Whatever the answer, the play suggests the dilemma of tragedy in the public theater after 1620.

The Spanish heroic intrigue tragedy raises theoretical issues of interpretation even more clearly. The anonymous *La Estrella de Sevilla* (1623–24) and Calderón's *El médico de su honra* (1629? 1635?) consider the painful consequences of applying the traditional and rigid standards of the honor code to complex social relations.[10] In *La Estrella de Sevilla*, unless the audience accepts the code as a premise, the play becomes incomprehensible. Relatedly, the plot presupposes the inviolability of the monarch, rooted in the medieval notion of the king's two bodies. The lecherous and murderous conduct of the young ruler, abetted by his amoral *privado*, generates the tragedy. If these two characters are modeled on Philip IV and Olivares, the uncommonly harsh portrayal of the king in particular acquires an additional critical edge.[11] To the crimes of the crown, the consistently honorable Sevillians respond with exemplary intent and effect. The erring monarch learns his lesson against his will and takes public responsibility for his deeds. Insofar as he undergoes a permanent moral conversion, the honor code, though here confined to a private affair, has demonstrated its efficacy in a manner that has potential political relevance. Just as important, however, the play reveals the costs of honor when the crown fails to act according to its principles: two people are murdered, and two others have their lives ruined.[12]

Midway through act 2, Busto tells his sister Estrella of his fear that she

[10]For the date of *La Estrella* see Kennedy, p. 308 n. 20. Donald R. Larson, *The Honor Plays of Lope de Vega* (Cambridge: Harvard University Press, 1977), pp. 162–63, notes in Lope's drama after 1620 a tendency to take a dark, even tragic view of honor and to refrain from celebrating Spanish history and heroism.

[11]For the identifications, see Kennedy, pp. 53–54, 340–41.

[12]On this play see William C. McCrary, "Ritual Action and Form in *La Estrella de Sevilla*," in *Homenaje a William L. Fichter: Estudios sobre el teatro antiguo hispánico y otros ensayos*, ed. A. David Kossoff and José Amor y Vázquez (Madrid: Editorial Castalia, 1971), pp. 505–13.

engaged in dishonorable conduct the night before when the king sneaked into their house to visit her:

> *Busto.* Esta noche fué epiciclo
> del Sol; que en entrando en ella
> se trocó de Estrella el signo.
> *Estrella.* Las llanezas del honor
> no con astrólogo estilo
> se han de decir: habla claro,
> y deja en sus zonas cinco
> el Sol.

(*Busto.* This night was an epicycle / of the Sun; because in entering in it / the sign of Estrella [Star] was changed. / *Estrella.* The plainness of honor / must be uttered without an / astrological style: speak clearly, / and leave the sun in its five / zones.)[13]

Because the entire play concerns "las llanezas del honor," however, and because both before and after this scene the noble characters, Estrella included, consistently employ precisely the rhetorical elaboration that she here reproves, the stylistic side of this critique loses much of its apparent pertinence. Elevated conduct requires elevated diction. One can escape briefly from the diction, but never from the conduct itself. At the end of the play, Estrella and Sancho's culminating feat of honor—mutual rejection, despite mutual love—elicits this sequence of comments from the *privado*, the *gracioso*, and the king:

> *Don Arias.* ¡Brava constancia!
> *Clarindo.* Más me parece locura. (*Aparte.*)
> *Rey.* Toda esta gente me espanta.

(*Don Arias.* Fierce constancy! / *Clarindo.* It seems more like madness to me. [*Aside.*] / *King.* All of these people frighten me. [3.18, p. 221]

Clarindo and the king speak for at least part of the audience, evoking the absurdity and the terror of the extravagant behavior that has dominated the action. But these qualifications do not suggest a positive alternative: in the end the play allows no ethically defensible choice but the code of honor, with its attendant tragic price.

*El médico de su honra* presents a more extreme version of the same dilemma. *La Estrella de Sevilla* concerns the violation of the code at the apex

---

[13]*La Estrella de Sevilla*, in *Peribáñez y el comendador de Ocaña; La Estrella de Sevilla*, by Lope de Vega (Madrid: Espasa-Calpe, 1938), 2.9, p. 165. The subsequent reference is noted in the text.

of the feudal pyramid—a serious matter. In Calderón's play, however, the problem is the code itself, which leads a husband to murder his innocent and beloved wife, only to be rewarded for his pains by the king. The involvement of the monarch and his troublesome half-brother in this private affair implies correlations, though uncertain ones, between dynastic and marital affairs. Nineteenth-century scholars, assuming that the playwright approved of his protagonist's conduct, found the play appalling. Only in the past thirty years have critics consistently argued that Calderón was attacking the honor code, at least in this its most extreme form.[14]

The obscurity of Calderón's own basis of judgment at least partly accounts for this disagreement. In the famous peasant plays—*Peribáñez, Fuente Ovejuna,* and *El alcalde de Zalamea*— or in *La Estrella de Sevilla,* once the audience understands the principle of honor, it experiences little difficulty in allocating its sympathies to the various characters. Here the same understanding produces no such result. Whatever Calderón's intention, this very difficulty can be explained. Wife murder over a point of sexual honor characterized the Middle Ages more than the seventeenth century, when it was almost always condemned and usually severely punished.[15] Calderón complements his return to the sources of Spanish national being with a fourteenth-century setting, in the reign of Pedro I of Castile, known to history as both *el Cruel* and *el Justiciero.*

This duality defines the code of honor in *El médico de su honra.* Not the mere excess of justice, cruelty equally inheres in the code. Attacking the hegemonic ideology from within, the play reveals that Spain cannot have it both ways. One cannot simply lament, as Alonso Carranza does in 1636, "la perdicion y estrago de los antiguos buenos vsos y costumbres" ("the destruction and ruin of old good practices and customs").[16] Calderón, unlike Shakespeare, did not live in a country in which opposed modes of production provided the means for external judgment. For this reason, *El médico de su honra* simultaneously affirms and decries the essence of aristocratic culture. It is at once a moving and a horrific sign of the impasse of Spanish society.

In both countries, then, the ideological ambivalence that accompanies the potent critique of the present arises partly from the dramatists' reactionary perspective. Those intrigue tragedies indebted to satire present

[14]A relatively moderate statement of the currently dominant position is Frank P. Casa, "Crime and Responsibility in *El médico de su honra,*" in *Homenaje a William L. Fichter,* ed. Kossoff and Amor y Vázquez, pp. 127–37.

[15]Noël Solomon, *Recherches sur le thème paysan dans la "comedia" au temps de Lope de Vega* (Bordeaux: Féret, 1965), p. 389 n. 82; Melveena McKendrick, *Woman and Society in the Spanish Drama of the Golden Age: A Study of the "Mujer Varonil"* (London: Cambridge University Press, 1974), pp. 35–39.

[16]Alonso Carranza, *Discvrso contra malos trages y adornos lascivos* (Madrid, 1636), sig. Il[r].

a more complicated picture. In England, Marston, Tourneur, Webster, and Middleton composed satiric intrigue tragedies; except for Tourneur, they also wrote satiric comedies. Indeed, Middleton's *Women Beware Women* (1621) resembles *A Chaste Maid in Cheapside* rewritten with a generic surprise at the end.[17] In varying degrees, a similar movement also characterizes Marston's *Antonio's Revenge* (1600), Tourneur's or Middleton's *Revenger's Tragedy* (1606), Tourneur's *Atheist's Tragedy* (1609), and Webster's *White Devil* (1612) and *Duchess of Malfi* (1614). Yet the extremism of Middleton may indicate both his atypicality and the special properties of satiric intrigue tragedy. The detached, morally rigorous, and consistent perspective of *Women Beware Women* and *The Changeling* (1622, with the comic subplot by William Rowley) probably derives from Middleton's adherence to the parliamentary Puritan cause, a decidedly progressive, rather than reactionary, position.[18] Webster, moveover, does not seem unquestionably backward looking either. Precisely because of the predominant negativity produced by satire, playwrights of opposing outlooks could employ the same form—just as opposition to Stuart policy at least temporarily united groups and classes that had little else in common. Symptomatically, scholars cannot decide whether to attribute *The Revenger's Tragedy* to the conservative Tourneur, the radical Middleton, or someone else entirely. The generic linkage between satiric tragedy and satiric comedy had an institutional basis as well. Like satiric comedy, satiric intrigue tragedy, however much it owed to the private theater, often had some contact with the public stage, especially in the transitional era from 1609 or a little earlier to 1614. Middleton's late tragedies, composed primarily for the private theater, therefore reveal institutional change, much as *The Unnatural Combat* does in the opposite sense.

Finally, a brief recapitulative comparison to other kinds of tragedy will suggest the negative relevance of satiric comedy to satiric intrigue tragedy. The narrowly political focus of a heroic play like Jonson's *Sejanus* makes it the true tragic complement of satiric comedy. Shakespearean tragedy, by contrast, incorporates satire into a large political framework rather than merely complementing it. Intrigue tragedy does neither, instead taking over satire wholesale, to the exclusion of politics. This procedure, however, risks undermining the recipient form altogether in a play like *Women Beware Women*, where Middleton had recourse to an unsatisfying melodramatic finale in order to give the illusion of tragic doom to decidedly untragic characters and events.[19]

[17]T. B. Tomlinson, *A Study of Elizabethan and Jacobean Tragedy* (Cambridge: Cambridge University Press, 1964), p. 158.

[18]Margot Heinemann, *Puritanism and Theatre: Thomas Middleton and Opposition Drama under the Early Stuarts* (Cambridge: Cambridge University Press, 1980), esp. p. 173.

[19]Robert Ornstein, *The Moral Vision of Jacobean Tragedy* (Madison: University of Wisconsin Press, 1960), p. 179.

In Spain, the failure of Olivares's policies provoked an increasing volume of satirical writing, especially by the late 1630s.[20] Attempting to defend the count-duke, Gonçalo de Cespedes y Meneses complained in 1634 that:

> no solamente el baxo vulgo sin fundamento se atreuia a las mas intimas y ocultas, mas aun ingenios superiores regidos de su mismo espiritu y liuiandad, con sus liuelos, discursos, versos, inuectiuas, dieron escandalo a la Corte, y assaz materia a los mas infimos.

> (not only the common multitude without basis dared [to discuss] the most intimate and hidden matters, but even superior minds, ruled by their own spirit and imprudence, with their libels, discourses, verses, invectives, gave scandal to the court and enough material to the vilest people.)[21]

But even earlier, Tirso's *El burlador de Sevilla* and Lope's *El castigo sin venganza* (1631) in some ways approached a satiric vision. If *Tan largo me lo fiáis*, apparently the first version of Tirso's play, dates from as early as 1616, it followed closely upon the author's relatively satiric comedy, *Marta la piadosa*. The final title of the work conceals a double meaning: "de Sevilla" can designate the home town of Don Juan or the victim of his "burlas" ("tricks").[22] In the latter sense, it points to a function of the protagonist that links him to important characters in the English tragedies. Like Webster's malcontents, for example, "el burlador" combines witty insouciance with an at times murderous immorality in such a way as to reveal the sordid reality lurking just beneath the surface of society. More generally, Tirso treats Don Juan's activities, as well as the sexual immorality and social climbing of many of the other characters, with an ironic, but scarcely tragic, detachment that may recall Middleton's technique in *Women Beware Women*.[23] Although Don Juan in his concluding damnation functions as something of a lightning rod for the sins of society, the play does not produce a sense of moral order fully restored, despite the best efforts of a good king.[24]

---

[20]Shirley B. Whitaker, "The Quevedo Case (1639): Documents from Florentine Archives," *MLN* 97 (1982): 368–79.

[21]Gonçalo de Cespedes y Meneses, *Historia de Don Felipe IIII, Rey de las Españas* (Barcelona, 1634), sig. LL8ʳ.

[22]Henry W. Sullivan, *Tirso de Molina and the Drama of the Counter Reformation* (Amsterdam: Rodopi, 1976), pp. 152–53.

[23]Raymond R. MacCurdy, introduction to his edition of *"El burlador de Sevilla y convidado de piedra" and "La prudencia en la mujer"*, by Tirso de Molina (New York: Dell, 1965), p. 19. The reference to *El burlador de Sevilla* below is to this edition.

[24]Edward M. Wilson and Duncan Moir, *The Golden Age: Drama, 1492–1700*, vol. 3 of *A Literary History of Spain*, gen. ed. R. O. Jones (London: Ernest Benn, 1971), p. 90. But see Manuel Durán and Roberto González Echevarría, "Luz y oscuridad: La estructura simbólica de *El burlador de Sevilla*," in *Homenaje a William L. Fichter*, ed. Kossoff and Amor y Vázquez, pp. 208–9.

Darker in tone than Tirso's play, *El castigo sin venganza* parallels the English tragedies in drawing on Italian sources and in recreating an Italian milieu centered on the sexual corruption of the court.[25] Lope condemns his protagonists to a claustrophobic world of passion from which they can find no escape[26] and which they intensify by a pattern of self-deception. But though deeply ironic, the play avoids satire, developing the characters with unusual psychological depth and hence with some sympathy, and pervading the action with a tragic sense.[27] Guilty at once of incest and adultery, the doomed young lovers recognize their wrongdoing and its inevitable consequence but can do nothing about it.

In both countries, earlier efforts in the Italian Senecan revenge tradition also influenced the satiric tragedies. For the English playwrights, *The Jew of Malta*, even more than Kyd's *Spanish Tragedy* and Shakespeare's *Hamlet*, anticipates the characteristic Jacobean combination of satire and revenge.[28] Sixteenth-century Elizabethan revenge tragedy, despite its significant popular dimension, did not completely succeed in striking roots in English soil. The final nationalization of Seneca was carried out partly by Shakespeare, but also by Marston and the author of *The Revenger's Tragedy*, who accomplished this end, paradoxically enough, by setting their tales in Italy.[29] The increasing replacement of a personal by a social perspective in seventeenth-century tragedy did not usually allow for detailed scrutiny of the psychology and morality of the avenger in the manner of Kyd and Shakespeare. But revenge motifs and at times even characteristic revenge structures continued to appear in the drama of Chapman, Webster, Middleton, and others

Particularly in the satiric intrigues, the revenge tradition gave a specificity to social criticism by centering it on the well-established Renaissance opposition of court and country. A Senecan critique of tyranny soon yielded to a primarily social, rather than political, attack, to the portrayal of the treacherous surrender of the feudal aristocracy, supposed

[25]Amado Alonso, "Lope de Vega y sus fuentes," in *El teatro de Lope de Vega: Artículos y estudios*, ed. José Francisco Gatti (Buenos Aires: Editorial Universitaria de Buenos Aires, 1962), pp. 200–212, discusses Lope's reworking of his sources in this play.

[26]Diego Marín, *La intriga secundaria en el teatro de Lope de Vega* (Toronto: University of Toronto Press, 1958), p. 128, shows how the Gonzaga-Aurora subplot intensifies the main characters' feeling of imprisonment.

[27]Kossoff, introducción to his edition of *El perro del hortelano; El castigo sin venganza*, by Lope de Vega (Madrid: Editorial Castalia, 1970), p. 28, praises the psychological acuity of Lope's characterization.

[28]See Fredson Bowers, *Elizabethan Revenge Tragedy, 1587–1642*, rev. ed. (Gloucester, Mass.: Peter Smith, 1959). Una Ellis-Fermor, *The Jacobean Drama: An Interpretation*, 4th ed., rpt. with biography and bibliography by M. Cardwell (London: Methuen, 1965), pp. 1–27, treats Marlowe as a proto-Jacobean.

[29]G. K. Hunter, "English Folly and Italian Vice: The Moral Landscape of John Marston," in *Jacobean Theatre*, ed. John Russell Brown and Bernard Harris, Stratford-upon-Avon Studies, no. 1 (London: Edward Arnold, 1960), pp. 91–106.

guardian of medieval morality, to forces loosely associated with capitalism. As in Shakespeare's late tragedies, the absolutist state is betrayed from within—an important if not wholly accurate perception. Yet one can hardly speak of the state at all in these plays. As the social status of the protagonists becomes increasingly incidental to their deeds, the scene shifts to the country or the city, where gentry and merchants, respectively, take the leading roles: *The Atheist's Tragedy* and *Women Beware Women* exemplify the trend. This democratization reflects not an ideological allegiance to capitalism, but a grim recognition of its presence.[30] The metaphysical optimism of Tourneur's play thus coexists with a social pessimism. Moreover, the change in social setting entails a diminution of scope: the experience of these classes cannot yet coincide with the fate of the nation.

Usually, however, the country retains its standard connotation as the innocent antithesis of the court. *Bussy D'Ambois* opens with its main character in a green world and proceeds to assess the impact of the court on a natural man. *Antonio's Revenge* and *The Revenge of Bussy* conclude with stoical retreats from court to monastery, with dubious efficacy, however, at least in Marston's play. In *The Duchess of Malfi*, even a flight from court to country cannot protect private, family experience, based on interclass marriage. For the duchess:

> The birds that live i' th' field
> On the wild benefit of nature, live
> Happier than we; for they may choose their mates,
> And carol their sweet pleasures to the spring.[31]

In *The Revenger's Tragedy* Vendice, a country gentleman, comes to cleanse a court whose corruption he instead succumbs to. Speaking for the gentry, he complains of the court's impoverishment of the land. His morally ambiguous but ultimately successful testing of his family thus generates a fundamental contrast between the lust and greed of the court and the chastity and poverty of the country. Given the class background of Vendice and his family and the dynamic, if unequal, relationship established between the two social poles of the action, the reactionary ideological assumptions of *The Revenger's Tragedy* contribute, ironically, to the historically progressive formation of precisely the gentry-dominated country party that later overthrew the monarchy.[32]

[30]Ornstein's characterization (p. 192) of *Women Beware Women* as "realistic bourgeois tragedy" is in this respect misleading.

[31]John Webster, *The Duchess of Malfi*, ed. John Russell Brown (London: Methuen, 1964), 3.5.18—21.

[32]This conclusion may be contrasted with the conventional and by no means groundless insistence on the medieval outlook of the play. See, among many others, Irving Ribner, *Jacobean Tragedy: The Quest for Moral Order* (London: Methuen, 1962), pp. 72—86.

In Spain, with its far weaker revenge tradition, *El burlador de Sevilla* nonetheless draws on Juan de la Cueva's Senecan tragicomedy, *El infamador*,[33] and in its concluding act evokes "venganza" insistently and ominously.[34] Don Juan, for instance, tells the statue of the man he has killed:

> Larga esta venganza ha sido.
> Si es que vos la habéis de hacer,
> importa no estar dormido,
>     que si a la muerte aguardáis
> la venganza, la esperanza
> agora es bien que perdáis,
> pues vuestro enojo y venganza
> tan largo me lo fiáis.

(This vengeance has been long. / If you have to do it, / it is important not to be asleep, / because if you await death / for vengeance, it is well that now / you lose hope, / since you trust your anger and / vengeance so long to me. [3.2260–67])

But this very issue implies a symptomatic incongruity between human and divine justice. The sympathetic portrayal of the king may owe something to Tirso's admiration for Philip III.[35] Throughout most of the play, however, the monarch remains in the dark about Don Juan's true conduct, busying himself with futile efforts to marry off the powerful aristocrat and thus maintain social stability. Only after the actual execution of divine vengeance does he call for the protagonist's death. This orthodox theology inevitably raises doubts about even the best of human institutions. Reciprocally, the difficulty most critics have had in finding in Don Juan's deeds sufficient cause for his damnation raises questions about divine justice. In addition, the vitality of "el burlador," the alarmingly and attractively anarchical challenge he presents to human and metaphysical order, perhaps inadvertently transforms a superficially didactic work into a tragedy both personal and social.[36]

The title of *El castigo sin venganza* reveals a similar concern, although in this instance the morality of revenge receives a deeply ironic treatment. The duke sees his concluding murder of his wife and son as "el castigo sin venganza" ("punishment without vengeance"). But his own considerable responsibility for their sins, his near-lifelong commission of

---

[33]MacCurdy, pp. 14–15.
[34]For the rise in tension near the end of the play, see I. L. McClelland, *Tirso de Molina: Studies in Dramatic Realism*, Liverpool Studies in Spanish Literature, 3d ser. (Liverpool: Institute of Hispanic Studies, 1948), pp. 61–64, 202–7.
[35]Kennedy, pp. 58–61.
[36]MacCurdy, pp. 19–21. But see Wilson and Moir, pp. 90–91.

the very same ones—perhaps an allusion to Philip IV's possible nocturnal philandering[37]—and the covert and underhanded method by
which he executes his sentence produce the opposite result, vengeance
without punishment or justice. To preserve social appearances, to give
the illusion of "el castigo sin venganza," the duke's son "is punished," in
R. D. F. Pring-Mill's words, "for a crime he did not commit in revenge
for a crime which he did." From the perspective of divine justice, however, the resolution of the plot does produce "el castigo sin venganza,"
not only for the duke's wife and son, but also for the duke himself, who
must live on with the knowledge of having killed the two people about
whom he cared most and thus of having deprived himself in addition of
a much-desired heir to the throne.[38] In the intractable dilemma of the
belatedly reformed duke, in the slippery, often antithetical relation between human and divine justice, in the discrepancy between intention
and consequence, Lope's drama offers a critique of the state that may respond as well to the country's growing inability to control its own destiny.

Both Spanish plays, then, investigate the ironic interplay of revenge
and justice far more deeply than do the comparable English tragedies,
where the very possibility of justice dispensed at court all but disappears.
Complementarily, the contrast between country and court does not figure prominently in El burlador de Sevilla and El castigo sin venganza. In a
way, Tirso's play effaces the distinction: Don Juan sexually deceives four
women—first an aristocrat, then a peasant, then another aristocrat, and
finally another peasant—in a pattern more iterative than developmen-
tal. Although Tirso does not conflate the two classes, he emphasizes the
range both of Don Juan's subversiveness and of society's failings. To do
so, however, he has to take seriously not just the honor of the nobility,
but that of the peasantry as well. The flawed conduct of the lower class
could not acquire its full force except as a deviation from that class's own
ideals. Here Tirso's experience with peasant drama probably served him
well. His Santa Juana trilogy (1613–14), which offers the closest anticipation of a figure like Don Juan, belongs to the Golden Age theater's distinctive genre.[39] Finally, although the concentration on court intrigue
in El castigo sin venganza limits the geographical range of the representation, the country no longer offers even a fleeting alternative. The illicit
passion between Federico and Casandra begins not in the back rooms of

[37]Jonathan Brown and J. H. Elliott, A Palace for a King: The Buen Retiro and the Court of
Philip IV (New Haven: Yale University Press, 1980), p. 32.

[38]R. D. F. Pring-Mill, introduction to his edition of Lope de Vega (Five Plays), trans. Jill
Booty (New York: Hill and Wang, 1961), pp. xxxi–xxxv. The quoted passage appears on p.
xxxiii.

[39]See Salomon, pp. 864–70; Paul M. Lloyd, "Contribución al estudio de tema de Don
Juan en las comedias de Tirso de Molina," in Homenaje a William L. Fichter, ed. Kossoff and
Amor y Vázquez, pp. 449–51.

the palace, but in a pastoral *locus amoenus*. By 1631 peasantry and pastoral had lost their redemptive powers, at least for Tirso and Lope.

The distance between these two plays and the comparable English works suggests the different historical function of satiric intrigue tragedy in each country. In England the form specialized in destruction: despite a primarily anticapitalist outlook that even today retains an appeal, it helped remove the remaining ideological justifications of absolutism, to clear away the detritus of a disintegrating social system.[40] In Spain, with fundamental change out of the question, the tragedies could only have the effect of drawing attention to the crisis confronted by their nation and of clarifying its nature. They portray a more normal world, governed more firmly by traditional morality, than do the English plays. Hence, although Tirso and Lope fail to approach the cynicism or nihilism of the Jacobean satiric tragedians, they also lack the moments of not quite conscious re-creation that occur in Chapman, *The Revenger's Tragedy*, and *The Duchess of Malfi*.

Even sharper contrasts emerge from a review of romantic intrigue tragedy, in part because of the inappropriateness of the comparison. The 1620s and 1630s, the period in which most of the relevant plays fall, was in effect an earlier historical and theatrical era in Spain than in England. Accordingly, the pathetic tragedies composed for the private stage in London qualitatively differ from the love tragedies designed for the *corrales* of Madrid.

Pathetic tragedy takes English intrigue tragedy to an extreme, recapitulating and intensifying selected features of the form. In its pure state, it mainly aims to elicit a pitying response from its audience. Although out of touch with moral and political issues, it skillfully plays with them so that they will heighten the emotional effect without acquiring any significance in the process. Beaumont and Fletcher's *Maid's Tragedy* (1610) both founds and perfectly represents the form.[41] The heyday of pathetic tragedy did not come until the Caroline era, however, with plays

[40]Franco Moretti, "'A Huge Eclipse': Tragic Form and the Deconsecration of Sovereignty," *Genre* 15 (1982): 7–40; Catherine Belsey, "Tragedy, Justice and the Subject," in *1642: Literature and Power in the Seventeenth Century*, Proceedings of the Essex Conference on the Sociology of Literature, July 1980, ed. Francis Barker et al. (Essex: University of Essex, 1981), pp. 166–86; Jonathan Dollimore, *Radical Tragedy: Religion, Ideology and Power in the Drama of Shakespeare and His Contemporaries* (Chicago: University of Chicago Press, 1984). A similar assessment, though not linked as clearly to a social context, is made by J. R. Mulryne, introduction to his edition of *The White Devil*, by Webster (Lincoln: University of Nebraska Press, 1969), esp. pp. xix–xxviii.

[41]Corroborating descriptions, which inform the following discussion, may be found in John F. Danby, *Poets on Fortune's Hill: Studies in Sidney, Shakespeare, Beaumont and Fletcher* (Port Washington, N.Y.: Kennikat Press, 1952), pp. 152–83; Arthur C. Kirsch, *Jacobean Dramatic Perspectives* (Charlottesville: University Press of Virginia, 1973), pp. 38–47; William Shullenberger, "'This for the Most Wrong'd of Women': A Reappraisal of *The Maid's Tragedy*," *Renaissance Drama*, n.s., 13 (1982): 131–56.

like Ford's *Broken Heart* (1629) and Shirley's *Traitor* (1631). The dominant moods of such works include aristocratic quiescence, withdrawal, indifference to life, and attraction to death.

Slightly to one side stand two other works by Ford, *'Tis Pity She's a Whore* (1632) and *Perkin Warbeck* (1633). The former, like *Women Beware Women*, sets its scene among the merchant patriciate, a class whose sordid social life provides a contrast and impediment to the protagonists' idealistic, incestuous, and doomed love. The latter, an English history play, conscientiously investigates national issues, particularly through the character of Henry VII. Yet the protagonist of the piece is not Henry but the titular figure, a fraudulent pretender whose persistent self-delusion finally turns into a tribute to his nobility. Politically defined and damned by his lower-class following, and easily defeated by Henry, he nonetheless triumphs in the private sphere, where the pattern of devotion he engenders, centered on his loyal wife, evokes Ford's characteristic heroic pity. Shakespearean tragedy, despite its repeated depiction of aristocratic failure, almost always leaves open a path to the future, if not for the protagonist then at least for his society. In intrigue tragedy, however, the conclusion of the play signifies the end of history, the closing off of opportunities. But as *Perkin Warbeck* shows, pathetic tragedy pays an even higher temporal price: for the protagonist, for several of the supporting characters, and at least in part for the author himself, the past has disappeared as well.

Pathetic tragedy is also a form in which women came into their own. The feminization of tragedy, discernible in Shakespeare's final efforts with the genre, gained some impetus from *The Maid's Tragedy* and even more from the plays of Webster and Middleton. Behind the growing prominence of women lay a broader emerging concern with the sex's social position. To this extent, intrigue tragedy in general helped extend the range of tragedy, its frequent depiction of the oppression of women representing a humane and progressive perception. At the same time, such an orientation entailed the abandonment of politics and a consequent reduction of scope. But women became uniquely functional even in intrigue tragedy only with the full exploitation of their helpless victimization and sentimental appeal characteristic of pathetic tragedy.

These contradictory implications provide a useful context in which to evaluate the ongoing concern with the decadence of Jacobean and Caroline tragedy. The critical debate, which turns far more on the interpretation than on the nature of the evidence, has not developed along obvious ideological lines: Marxists and non-Marxists, for example, appear on both sides.[42] The charge of decadence, which of course presupposes an

[42]Within Marxist criticism, Goldstein's position (see n. 5 above) contrasts with that of Miklós Szenczi, "Decay and New Birth in post-Shakespearian Drama," *Acta Litteraria* (Bu-

earlier period of health, often extends back to Marston and sweepingly includes virtually all his successors as well. The plays of the pathetic tragedians, however, provide the obvious targets.

Although Caroline tragedy at times displays a hostility to both the court and the bourgeoisie, it lacks the aggressive destructiveness that distinguishes the generally earlier satiric intrigue tragedies. Pathetic tragedy dramatizes the feelings of a class, or section of a class, when it senses that it no longer has a social function, that history has passed it by. It is a form of self-understanding. Of course the substitution of nobility of sentiment for a now-elusive coherence expresses not universal truth but accommodation by a class that has lost its hegemony. Ironically, however, in this fashion pathetic tragedy unwittingly serves the progressive purpose of reconciling one sector of the aristocracy to its own supersession. The special prominence it accords to women likewise undermines the ostensible intention of the form. Even female characters of the highest social birth rarely can exercise the power and freedom ordinarily available to male members of their class: their sex systematically reduces their status. The women of pathetic tragedy thus mark a break with a class-based conception of tragedy. In these ways, then, the form contradictorily retains not just a historical and theoretical interest, but a human plausibility and social significance as well.

Spanish love tragedies such as Lope's *El caballero de Olmedo* (1620?) and Luis Vélez de Guevara's *Reinar después de morir* (by 1644) share with pathetic tragedy, and especially with Ford's plays, a sense of fated defeat, of doom linked to a preoccupation with private life that a superficial interest in affairs of state scarcely obscures. But these two works, especially Lope's, recall more closely *Romeo and Juliet* and *El marqués de Mantua* and thus a tradition of tragedy with deep affinities to romantic comedy: critics have even faulted *El caballero de Olmedo* for the excessively comic tone of its first two acts.[43] The relatively recent tendency to view Lope's work as a tragedy of moral failing and deserved retribution has given way to a more defensible, traditional insistence on the innocence of the protagonist in a just and divinely ordered, but nonetheless inscrutable, universe.[44] Although Inés de Castro, the heroine of *Reinar*

---

dapest) 4 (1961): 353–59. Similarly, in non-Marxist scholarship, M. C. Bradbrook, *Themes and Conventions of Elizabethan Tragedy* (Cambridge: Cambridge University Press, 1935), pp. 240–67, speaks of "the decadence," while S. Schoenbaum, "Peut-on parler d'une 'décadence' du théâtre au temps des premiers Stuart?" in *Dramaturgie et société: Rapports entre l'oeuvre théâtrale, son interprétation et son public aux xvi⁰ et xvii⁰ siècles*, ed. Jean Jacquot, with Elie Konigson and Marcel Oddon (Paris: Editions du Centre National de la Recherche Scientifique, 1968), 2:829–45, questions its existence.

[43]See Wilson and Moir, p. 67, who reject the charge.

[44]Just punishment: A. A. Parker, "Approach to the Spanish Drama of the Golden Age," *Tulane Drama Review* 4 (1959): 42–59; Wilson, *Spanish and English Literature of the 16th and*

*después de morir*, has remained free of any comparable suspicion of misconduct, the play apparently attacks *Realpolitik* as much as it celebrates love.[45] In fact, Vélez suppresses the political issue. Only the king even feels a conflict between private morality and reasons of state; his son and heir, as Inés's lover, cannot without compromising the purity of his love. More generally, since a focus on national problems would force the audience to share the king's dilemma, Vélez makes certain that it responds exclusively to the lovers' predicament.

What assumptions underlie the dramatization of a tragic destiny? Like much other Renaissance drama, both plays appropriate bourgeois values to serve aristocratic ends, here borrowing marriage for love, with all its attendant idealism. In the name of this principle, *Reinar después de morir* rejects the class-conscious condescension of Inés's more nobly born rival. Vélez returns to more traditional aristocratic terrain in his attack on the king and his *privados* and in his antithetical praise of the country. Yet he complicates the pattern not only by linking the country to domesticity and family life but also, as in *El caballero de Olmedo*, by expressing the central love relationship in courtly, Petrarchan terms.

The less ambiguous feudal dimension of Lope's play produces a greater social resonance in the tragic irony of its crisis. The chivalric valor that brings Don Alonso fame also leads him to his death. Although a supernatural warning in the form of a popular refrain frightens him, his feudal code forces him to press on.[46] A matchless swordsman like Bussy D'Ambois, he too is murdered by gunshot, military symbol of the supersession of medieval aristocratic warfare.[47] The repetition of the portentous refrain earlier in the play develops a feudal perspective in another way as well. Like some of the *romances* in *Bamba*, it produces a double vision. Most of the time the audience involves itself in a sequence of events unfolding in the present. But the refrain encourages distance from the action, an at least historically detached view of a tragedy set in the romantic, glamorous, but irrecoverably past early fifteenth century. In this way *El caballero de Olmedo* simultaneously celebrates feudalism and intuits its inevitable demise, conceiving of the latter as part of a divine plan whose meaning remains hidden from seventeenth-century

---

*17th Centuries: Studies in Discretion, Illusion and Mutability* (Cambridge: Cambridge University Press, 1980), pp. 184–200. The counterposition: Willard F. King, introduction to her edition and translation of *The Knight of Olmedo (El caballero de Olmedo)*, by Lope de Vega (Lincoln: University of Nebraska Press, 1972), pp. xi–xxvii.

[45]Aubrun, p. 151. For an emphasis on fate see Margaret Wilson, *Spanish Drama of the Golden Age* (Oxford: Pergamon Press, 1969), p. 143.

[46]Leon Livingstone, "Transposiciones literarias y temporales en *El caballero de Olmedo*," in *Homenaje a William L. Fichter*, ed. Kossoff and Amor y Vázquez, p. 444.

[47]Lawrence Stone, *The Crisis of the Aristocracy, 1558–1641* (Oxford: Clarendon Press, 1965), p. 243.

Spaniards. In common with *Reinar después de morir* it evokes a sense of loss, although the later tragedy, despite its title, does not offer even enigmatic metaphysical consolation. Despite the far more peripheral role of politics in Lope's play than in Vélez's, *El caballero de Olmedo* reveals a surer grasp of historical process, one not really equaled in pathetic tragedy, even by *Perkin Warbeck*. Perhaps with plays such as these in mind, the 1644 government attack on Lope de Vega quoted in chapter 5 also demanded that henceforth "las comedias se reduxesen á materias de buen exemplo, formándose de vidas y muertes exemplares, de hazañas valerosas, de gobiernos políticos, y que todo esto fuese *sin mezcla de amores*" ("*comedias* be confined to materials of virtuous example, modeling themselves on exemplary lives and deaths, on valiant exploits, on political government, and that all this should be *without mixing in love*").[18]

## Religious Tragedy

Although intrigue tragedy jettisoned a national perspective more completely in England than in Spain, a narrowing of range occurred in both countries. Religious tragedy constituted the major, though problematic, exception to this trend. Plays such as Argensola's *Isabela, Dr. Faustus, The Atheist's Tragedy,* and the ultimately unclassifiable *El burlador de Sevilla*—all referred to earlier—fail to develop significant political material, however. On the other hand, Middleton's *A Game at Chess* (1624) and Calderón's *El príncipe constante* (1629) effect that total fusion of national and theological commitments characteristic of an age in which religion usually meant state religion. *A Game at Chess* scarcely goes beyond ingenious patriotic allegory. Indeed, it belongs to a specifically anti-Spanish tradition on the English stage that extends back through *The Alchemist*, Beaumont and Fletcher's *Philaster* (1609), and *1 The Fair Maid of the West*, all the way to *The Spanish Tragedy*. *El príncipe constante*, on the other hand, investigates personal as well as political dimensions of Christian conduct.

Both of these plays depend on nationalist chauvinism and imperialism. But playwrights found another way of addressing larger issues of government through religious drama. The tragedy of martyrdom, typically set in late classical times, exploited the conflict between early Christianity and the secular authority of the Roman Empire. The heroic temper often associated with sainthood[19] achieves special prominence when

[18]*Consulta del Consejo de Castilla*, in Emilio Cotarelo y Mori, ed., *Bibliografía de las controversias sobre la licitud del teatro en España* (Madrid: Real Academia Española, 1904), p. 164.
[19]Parker, "Santos y bandoleros en el teatro español del Siglo de Oro," *Arbor* 13 (1949): 401, 416.

the prospective saint must face a gruesome and painful death. Given the overall direction of tragedy during the early seventeenth century, moreover, such works as Lope's *Lo fingido verdadero* (c. 1608), Dekker and Massinger's *The Virgin Martyr* (1620), and Calderón's *El mágico prodigioso* (1637) possessed a distinct advantage over *A Game at Chess* or even, to an extent, *El príncipe constante*. Free from the limitations of the national history play, they deal with royal power without necessarily endorsing it. The martyr plot, then, could fulfill the traditional political demands of tragedy in an age when dramatists were finding national destiny increasingly problematic.

How did this subgenre develop in the two countries? *The Virgin Martyr* draws on the Counter-Reformation Italian *tragedia sacra*, itself a neoclassical reworking of the late medieval *sacra rappresentazione*. Massinger's possible crypto-Catholicism may explain the work's anomalous position as the sole post-Reformation saint's play on the London stage.[50] *El mágico prodigioso*, on the other hand, grows out of Thomistic theology and the prior tradition of Spanish religious drama.[51] It also responds to the continuing reports of the martyrdom of Spanish missionaries in America and Asia.[52] Yet the two plays belong together. In each the virgin martyr defeats the machinations of the devil, thereby leading a pagan man unwittingly in danger of damnation (Theophilus, Cipriano) to religious conversion, martyrdom, and salvation. Although bystanders attribute the convert's public confession of faith to madness, he brushes aside this potential excuse, instead calling for his own death. Earlier, the heroine, though wooed by the governor's son (Antoninus, Lelio), rejects earthly love while receiving divine protection against seduction or rape. Once she also manages to convince her secular suitor (Antoninus, Cipriano) to transfer his love to heaven, the two characters come together in death. In both plays, finally, the virgin martyr is beheaded, the lower-class figures seem destined for hell,[53] and, despite clear indications of what has just occurred, the ruler remains a staunch unbeliever and persecutor of Christians. These similarities suggest that *El mágico prodigioso* may also owe something to Italian *tragedia sacra*. In general, Italy had far

[50]Louise George Clubb, "*The Virgin Martyr* and the *Tragedia Sacra*," *Renaissance Drama* 7 (1964): 103–26; Dunn, pp. 49–51, 184–91.

[51]Bruce W. Wardropper, "The Interplay of Wisdom and Saintliness in *El mágico prodigioso*," *Hispanic Review* 11 (1943): 116–24; Parker, "The Devil in the Drama of Calderón," in *Critical Essays on the Theatre of Calderón*, ed. Wardropper (New York: New York University Press, 1965), pp. 14–23.

[52]Padre Fray Pedro de Frias, *Relacion del martirio* . . . (1633), and Alonso de Benavides, *Memorial ala sancidad de Vrbano* . . . , Huntington Library MS 16690 (February 12, 1634).

[53]Parker, "The Rôle of the 'Graciosos' in *El mágico prodigioso*," in *Litterae Hispanae et Lusitanae: Festschrift zum fünfzigjährigen Bestehen des Ibero-Amerikanischen Forschungsinstituts der Universität Hamburg*, ed. Hans Flasche (Munich: Max Hueber Verlag, 1968), pp. 325–26.

closer ideological and political ties to Spain than to England in the early seventeenth century; in particular, Calderón's *oeuvre* shows a clear debt to late-sixteenth-century Italian drama.

Another play by Massinger, *The Roman Actor* (1626), closely recalls *Lo fingido verdadero*. Both works turn on the relationship between a Roman emperor and a leading actor, increasingly blur the division between art and reality through a series of plays within the play, dramatize the transformation of the ruler's initial friendship for the performer into a murderous enmity that leads to the latter's death, and, because of a concern with both politics and playing, lack a genuinely integrative structural unity. On the other hand, Lope presents in Diocletian a generally positive figure, whereas Massinger creates in Domitian a lustful tyrant. Thus, although *Lo fingido verdadero* reaches a climax in the actor's execution, *The Roman Actor* continues for a whole additional act, in which the surviving victims of the emperor's crimes successfully band together to assassinate him. Most important, the Spanish work ultimately centers on the conversion and consequent martyrdom of the actor, while the comparable figure in the English tragedy dies for having an affair with the imperial mistress. Anyone familiar with *Lo fingido verdadero* will wait, but in vain, for the religious issue to emerge in *The Roman Actor* and for the accompanying world as a stage metaphor to provide a thematic coherence for the action. But even in *Lo fingido verdadero* this metaphor cannot conceal the division in Lope's interest between the world and its renunciation.[54]

The most common means of connecting the religious drama of the two countries is to enumerate Hispanic analogues to *Dr. Faustus*. *El mágico prodigioso* and Mira de Amescua's *El esclavo del demonio* (1605–10)[55] both involve a pact with the devil in which necromancy serves the sinner's sexual desires. *El condenado por desconfiado* (1622)[56] portrays the death and damnation of an intellectual whose belief in predestination leads him to despair of divine forgiveness. The devil's unwilling proclamation of heaven's plan at the end of *El mágico prodigioso* echoes the conclusion of a play influenced by Marlowe's work, *The Atheist's Tragedy*, where the titular figure explains God's justice to the benighted operatives of the human judicial system. Yet *Dr. Faustus* obviously stands apart from all of these plays, English or Spanish. In *El esclavo del demonio* and *El mágico prodigioso* the diabolical contract is abrogated, in *El condenado*

---

[54]Alan S. Trueblood, "Rôle-Playing and the Sense of Illusion in Lope de Vega," *Hispanic Review* 32 (1964): 312, notes that the miracle play in *Lo fingido verdadero* occurs only in the third act.

[55]Date: Courtney Bruerton, "La versificación dramática española en el período 1587–1610," *Nueva Revista de Filología Hispánica* 10 (1956): 347.

[56]The date is from Kennedy, p. 87 n. 30, who also rejects, pp. 298 n. 3 and 351 n. 58, the traditional attribution of the play to Tirso.

*por desconfiado* the salvation of Enrico fully balances the damnation of Paulo, and in *The Atheist's Tragedy* the earthly reward of the virtuous Charlemont similarly answers the just death of D'Amville. But Marlowe's play is not merely more pessimistic than these other works; through its humanist and individualist assertiveness, it more fully transcends homiletic categories than does most religious tragedy, posing unanswered questions about human destiny in a world that has apparently lost its social and metaphysical cohesion.

*Dr. Faustus* achieves this distinctiveness by thematizing the relation between Renaissance and Reformation outlined in chapter 3. Luther once noted, "Multa dicebant de Fausto, welcher den Teufel seynen schwoger hies" ("Much has been said of Faustus, who called the devil his brother-in-law").[37] In the same conversation, he recounted the tale of a debtor who tore off a Jew's leg, thereby causing his creditor to flee without collecting, and of a monk who, having paid a peasant a penny for the right to eat as much as he could of the latter's hay, proceeded to consume half a wagonload. This folkloric material, here already juxtaposed with Faustus, had entered his story no later than the mid-1580s, when it appears in the Lutheran Wolfenbüttel manuscript of the Faust Book. It recurs in the printed version of 1587, the English translation of 1592, and the 1616 quarto of Marlowe's play.[38] Yet these different accounts of the legend are hardly homogeneous. The English narrative departs from the German in giving Faustus what John D. Jump calls "a genuine intellectual ardour," a process that Marlowe, of course, continues.[39] The nobility of Faustus in Marlowe's conception particularly stands out if the recent bibliographical scholarship cited in the Introduction to this book is correct in attributing most of the episodes of Faustus's pointless magic and buffoonery to a revision carried out a decade after the playwright's death and the remainder to Marlowe's collaborator on the original version.[60] Lukács does not specify which text of the play he is referring to when he claims that although Marlowe sought to remove the Lutheran excrescences from the initial, Renaissance tale of Faustus, "too often he dwelled on its external aspects (the witchery, charlatanry, the grandilo-

[37]*D. Martin Luthers Werke: Tischreden*, vol. 3 (Weimar: Hermann Böhlaus Nachfolger, 1914), p. 445. Translation: *Table Talk*, ed. and trans. Theodore G. Tappert, vol. 54 of *Luther's Works* (Philadelphia: Fortress Press, 1967), p. 241.

[38]H. G. Haile, introduction to *The History of Doctor Johann Faustus*, trans. Haile (Urbana: University of Illinois Press, 1965), pp. 1–16.

[39]Willard Farnham, introduction to *Twentieth Century Interpretations of "Doctor Faustus": A Collection of Critical Essays*, ed. Farnham (Englewood Cliffs, N.J.: Prentice-Hall, 1969), pp. 6–8; and, for the quoted phrase, John D. Jump, ed., *Doctor Faustus* (Cambridge: Harvard University Press, 1962), p. xlii.

[60]Fredson Bowers, textual introduction to *Doctor Faustus*, in *The Complete Works of Christopher Marlowe*, ed. Bowers, 2d ed. (Cambridge: Cambridge University Press, 1981), 2:123–59, esp. 155–58.

quence, the magical and mystical) so that its counter-effect could not be effective and enduring."[61]

Yet *Dr. Faustus* derives its power precisely from its dramatization of the conflict between Renaissance and Reformation. The resolution of the plot reveals that religion has more power than humanism. The ideological outcome, on the other hand, leaves something of a stalemate. Individualist aspiration, however attractive, leads to damnation. Protestant conventionality, by contrast, offers safety at the price of vitality. At once humanist tragedy and morality play, *Dr. Faustus* is in essence neither.

The unusual pessimism of *Dr. Faustus*, then, arises partly from its Protestantism. In a sense, Luther had made penitence more difficult by stressing the necessity of a genuine inner change:[62] Faustus is damned not for his deeds but for his thoughts. More generally, the tragic morality play resulted from a Reformation revision of a previously comic form, in the Dantean sense. Yet the impasse represented by *Dr. Faustus* lacks the symmetry and absolutism these remarks might suggest. If the Elizabethan soliloquy derives from a synthesis of Renaissance and Reformation, Protestanism enters the play on both sides of the conflict. On the one hand, it stands for orthodoxy; on the other, its emphasis on interiority fuses with a radical, humanist individualism in the very formation of the protagonist's character. The play accordingly turns on a conflict not only between humanism and Protestantism, but also within Protestantism itself. Furthermore, the overwhelming sense of paralysis finally produced by Faustus's restless activity is a consequence of Marlowe's relentlessly metaphysical turn of mind. When Shakespeare substituted an ethical, social, or political framework, the contradiction remained, of course, but with new, dynamic possibilities. *Dr. Faustus* is at once the last important English morality play and one of the founding works of Elizabethan tragedy.

In other words, whereas Spain had a thriving religious drama, England did not, the relatively secular *Atheist's Tragedy* and *A Game at Chess* and the relatively foreign *Virgin Martyr* notwithstanding. Religious differences between England and Spain cannot in any simple sense explain this generic divergence. Catholics opposed the public theater as much as Protestants, with Argensola particularly objecting to religious drama. Nor did he stand alone: Fray Marco Antonio de Camos, though not absolutely opposed to the stage, explained, "Ni me agradan las representa-

---

[61]Lukács, *Goethe and His Age*, trans. Robert Anchor (London: Merlin Press, 1968), p. 165. For a similar position, see George Santayana, "The Rehabilitation of Faustus," in *Twentieth Century Interpretations*, ed. Farnham, pp. 12–14.

[62]Harry Levin, "The Design of *Doctor Faustus*," in *Twentieth Century Interpretations*, ed. Farnham, p. 53.

ciones á lo divino" ("Nor do biblical plays please me").[63] Moreover, the Jesuits' didactic exploitation of the theater, which undoubtedly spurred Spanish religious plays, had a parallel in the Christian Terence, primarily a Protestant project.[64] As chapter 2 argued, the relatively secular and modern cast of English society ultimately determined the eclipse of religious drama, its influence proving decisive above all in the political arena. Unable to eliminate heterodoxy even within the Reformed church, and aware from painful experience of the subversive possibilities of stage polemic, the crown found it safer to suppress religious drama altogether. English Protestantism could unify the country only when conceptually vague and explicitly linked to national politics, but even then, as *A Game at Chess* reveals, it might well embarrass the monarchy.

In Spain, however, the powerful church combined ideological hegemony with subordination to the interests of the monarchy. Under these conditions, Catholic dogma could function as an important vehicle of national self-definition. The annual Corpus Christi *autos sacramentales*, begun early in the sixteenth century, also encouraged the explicit treatment of religious themes in the regular *comedia*. The control of the *corrales* by the religious confraternities, as well as the clerical attacks on the stage, may have had a similar effect. A number of the resultant plays, including *El esclavo del demonio* and *El condenado por desconfidado*, develop a complex parallel between rebellion against God and rebellion against society in the form of banditry. Critical interpretation of this relationship has generally taken a conservative tack, conceding that the resort to a life of crime may reveal the heroic spirit necessary to true saintliness but insisting that submission to God requires submission to social norms, and especially to the authority of the family.[65] Although the playwrights may often have had something of this sort in mind, merely following the authors' ideological footsteps does not sufficiently clarify the significance of Spanish religious drama.

Brigandage represents a primitive, unselfconscious, and prepolitical form of social rebellion.[66] Bandits overlapped with vagabonds on the Hispanic peninsula as well as in other parts of Europe. After 1600 their numbers and impact increased, particularly in Catalonia, where they produced a virtual state of anarchy between 1611 and 1615. Their activities had the protection of the poorer, mountain nobility who, along with

[63]Fray Marco Antonio de Camos, *Microcosmia, y govierno vniversal del hombre christiano, para todos los estados y qvalquiera de ellos* (1592), excerpted in Cotarelo y Mori, p. 130.

[64]On the Christian Terence, see Marvin T. Herrick, *Tragicomedy: Its Origins and Development in Italy, France, and England* (Urbana: University of Illinois Press, 1962), pp. 16–62.

[65]Parker, "Santos y bandoleros."

[66]McKendrick, pp. 130–33.

the lesser clergy, were active in the revolt of Catalonia against Castile in 1640. The same decades saw a rise of murder even among the great nobles, whose heritage of private violence fed into aristocratic rebellion. Banditry, in other words, was part of the general crisis of the seventeenth century, a symptom of social breakdown, a response to both the growing tensions between class and state and the widening gap between rich and poor.[67] Spanish religious drama, especially that section of it dealing with the life of crime, dates primarily from the seventeenth century as well.[68] It gave expression to inarticulate protest, but in such a way as to conceal the contradictions and injustices from which that protest arose and thus to make possible the reestablishment of traditional order and values.

Yet the dramatists could not always achieve this end. By about 1620, Spanish religion had taken a path that corresponded to the general direction of the country. The moral code narrowed, emphasizing sexual conduct and its elaborate taboos; the chivalric ideal, compatible with Christian piety in the sixteenth century, now formed the antithesis to religious life; and that life took on a gloomy cast, emphasizing death and damnation while rejecting the world and its pleasures. The religious drama had to situate itself in this cramped ideological space. Relatively early works like *Lo fingido verdadero* and *El esclavo del demonio* attach the highest value to renunciation, self-sacrifice, martyrdom, and the afterlife, but they also affirm the worth of earthly existence. Although in the former play Diocletian persecutes Christians, he otherwise comes off so well that Lope spends considerable time admiringly following his career. The disunity of the work thus follows from a contradictory intention, one that reproduces a widespread ideological ambivalence. Mira de Amescua largely avoids this problem by steering clear of politics. Although Leonor wins the hand of the king of Portugal by her virtuous behavior, her subplot does not differ greatly from typical *capa y espada* material and thus does not compete with the main action, which emphasizes the transcendental conduct of her sister Lisarda.

*El condenado por desconfiado* and *El príncipe constante* occupy an intermediate position. Here, though moral approbation heavily favors the next life at the expense of this one, the latter retains some significance. In *El condenado por desconfiado* secular action, especially filial obedience, wins Enrico salvation. Calderón's play apparently solves the structural di-

---

[67]Elliott, *Imperial Spain, 1469–1716* (New York: St. Martin's Press, 1964), pp. 299, 327; Antonio Domínguez Ortiz, *The Golden Age of Spain, 1516–1659*, trans. James Casey (New York: Basic Books, 1971), p. 100; Fernand Braudel, *The Mediterranean and the Mediterranean World in the Age of Philip II*, trans. Siân Reynolds (New York: Harper and Row, 1972), 2:741, 753–56; Perry Anderson, *Lineages of the Absolutist State* (London: NLB, 1974), pp. 47–48, 53–54.

[68]McKendrick, p. 109.

lemma of *Lo fingido verdadero* by conflating Christian martyrdom and national politics. But insofar as the latter requires the former, involvement in the world loses its claims. More important, within the moral hierarchy of *El príncipe constante*, the protagonist, through his self-abasement, occupies a far more exalted position than does Fénix, the symbol of earthly beauty.[69]

*El mágico prodigioso* takes this tendency to its logical conclusion. It replaces the more capacious ideology of earlier religious drama with a mutually exclusive choice between pagan, courtly love, or more accurately lust, and Christian, divine love. At the end of the play not Diocletian or even Fénix, but the debased *graciosos* represent the secular world. Paradoxically, full renunciation eliminates the political difficulty of the form. Unlike Lope, Calderón can organically portray the operation of state power, because that power has meaning for him only as the threat to his main characters, as the mechanism of their martyrdom.

Perhaps partly as a result, Shelley, all but alone among his English contemporaries, prized Calderón's plays in general and this one in particular. His affection poses the same problem as does the English Romantic claim that in *Paradise Lost* Milton unconsciously belonged to the devil's party. From *El mágico prodigioso*, Shelley translated scenes between the heroine Justina and the devil or his agents.[70] When, on at least one occasion, the English version adds emphasis to the devil's speech as it appears in the Spanish, Shelley may not be reversing Calderón's overt moral hierarchy so much as responding to something in the source. The rebelliousness with which the English poet presumably identified characterizes both the devil, who may owe something to the popular tradition, and Justina, who challenges the state to the point of assuring her own martyrdom. That martyrdom, in turn, negates political concerns in a structurally compelling but ideologically illusory solution to intrigue tragedy's problem in representing the nation. The play attempts to come to terms with the decline of Spain at a time when the course of events already seemed to deprive secular existence of its meaning. *El mágico prodigioso* constitutes a powerful critique of the state, but in the absence of a material alternative: its active spiritual rejection of worldly authority and affirmation of a higher reality translate into a political passivity that reproduces the historical impasse of Habsburg absolutism. Shelley's enthusiasm, then, points to crucial features of Cal-

[69]Leo Spitzer, "The Figure of Fénix in Calderón's *El príncipe constante*," in *Critical Essays on the Theatre of Calderón*, ed. Wardropper, pp. 137–60.

[70]Salvador de Madariaga, *"Shelley and Calderón" and Other Essays on English and Spanish Poetry* (London: Constable, 1920), pp. 3–48; Eunice Joiner Gates, "Shelley and Calderón," *Philological Quarterly* 16 (1937): 54; Durán and González Echevarría, "Historia: Calderón y la crítica," in their edition of *Calderón y la crítica: Historia y antología* (Madrid: Editorial Gredos, 1976), 1:48–54.

derón's drama and the society from which it emerged that have otherwise gone relatively unnoticed, both before and since.

## Conclusion

Critics have often denied Spanish religious drama, and indeed Golden Age theater in general, the status of tragedy,[71] although recent decades have seen something of a reversal of this attitude.[72] The present discussion may help resituate the debate. Throughout western Europe during the sixteenth and seventeenth centuries, intrigue tragedy's characteristic combination of depoliticization and moral uncertainty represented a response to a crisis in the state. The predominance of intrigue tragedy in most of sixteenth-century Italy testifies to the absence of an indigenous absolutism, to the lack of a political organization that could serve as the object of dramatic reflection. In France the movement from Corneille's heroic drama to Racine's tragedies of private experience, pessimism, and moral relativism corresponds to the changing relations between nobility and monarchy, and in particular to the latter's definitive suppression of the Fronde and with it of centuries of aristocratic political independence. The late-seventeenth-century pathetic tragedies of Dryden, Lee, Otway, and their successors, following hard upon more than a decade of heroic drama, constitute a belated, disillusioned realization that the Restoration of the monarchy in 1660, with the attendant return of the Cavaliers, did not involve a true restoration of an absolutist state or a neofeudal nobility.[73] In all three instances, the audience for intrigue tragedy was dominated culturally, if not always numerically, by the crown and aristocracy.

Unlike the tragedies of Shakespeare or the peasant plays of Lope de Vega, then, English and Spanish intrigue tragedy of the early seventeenth century belonged to a broadly international generic movement.

[71]Arnold Reichenberger, "Calderón's *El príncipe constante*, a Tragedy?" in *Critical Essays on the Theatre of Calderón*, ed. Wardropper, pp. 161–63; for the assumptions behind this position, idem, "The Uniqueness of the 'Comedia,'" *Hispanic Review* 27 (1959): 303–16.

[72]Edwin S. Morby, "Some Observations on 'Tragedia' and 'Tragicomedia' in Lope," *Hispanic Review* 11 (1943): 185–209; Parker, "Towards a Definition of Calderonian Tragedy," *Bulletin of Hispanic Studies* 39 (1962): 222–37; A. Irvine Watson, "*El pintor de su deshonra* and the Neo-Aristotelian Theory of Tragedy," in *Critical Essays on the Theatre of Calderón*, ed. Wardropper, pp. 203–23. But see MacCurdy, *The Tragic Fall: Don Alvaro de Luna and Other Favorites in Spanish Golden Age Drama*, North Carolina Studies in the Romance Languages and Literatures, no. 197 (Chapel Hill: University of North Carolina Department of Romance Languages, 1978), pp. 17–37; and the important study by José María Díez Borque, *Sociología de la comedia española del siglo xvii* (Madrid: Ediciones Cátedra, 1976), who speaks of "el fracaso de la tragedia," p. 364.

[73]Laura Brown, *English Dramatic Form, 1660–1760: An Essay in Generic History* (New Haven: Yale University Press, 1981), chap. 3.

Again unlike Shakespearean tragedy, but like ancient Greek and Roman tragedy, Renaissance European intrigue tragedy characteristically accorded women a position of prominence. As the previous chapter suggested, attempts to establish correlations between gender and genre, and in particular to discern formal imperatives in tragedy that lead to the exclusion of women, thus err in taking the exception for the rule. Yet however unpromising in the present instance, such an enterprise rests on more than etymological punning. Women do tend to fall outside the generic boundaries of the national history play in England and Spain. Still anchored in the public theater, Shakespeare drew on this national, if antifeminist, orientation, as well as, perhaps, on Marlowe's aggressively masculine drama, to produce tragedies that relegated women to relatively subordinate roles. By contrast, the triumph of intrigue tragedy in London and Madrid indicated a turn away from the unique theatrical institution that has provided the focus for this book.

For that very reason, however, the form lends itself to a reconsideration of the baroque. In "The Concept of Baroque in Literary Scholarship," René Wellek has in mind "a general European movement whose conventions and literary style can be described fairly concretely and whose chronological limits can be fixed fairly narrowly, from the last decades of the sixteenth century to the middle of the eighteenth century in a few countries." But characteristically, although Wellek believes that the "most promising way of arriving at a more closely fitting description of the baroque is to aim at analyses which would correlate stylistic and ideological criteria," he remains "unconvinced that we can define baroque either in terms of stylistic devices or a peculiar world view or even a peculiar relationship of style and belief."[74] Despite a sympathy for the formalism of the American New Critics and a keen awareness of what he himself called "The Revolt against Positivism in Recent European Literary Scholarship," Wellek was perhaps forced to his negative conclusion by the positivism of his own scholarly approach. The "correlation of stylistic and ideological criteria" may yield more satisfactory results if undertaken from a different methodological perspective.

From the point of view of the ideology of form, the baroque constitutes a legitimate periodizing concept, uniting the aesthetic not only with the ideological, but also with the social and political. The structural asymmetries, stylistic tensions, and philosophical conflicts in seventeenth-century literature and theater both responded and contributed to the crisis of absolutism. Although the baroque did not inhabit courtly or even aristocratic literary cricles alone, this crisis provided the prob-

[74]René Wellek, "The Concept of Baroque in Literary Scholarship," in *Concepts of Criticism* (New Haven: Yale University Press, 1963), pp. 93–94, 108, 113.

lematic within which it thrived most successfully and from which it most often emerged. Even when the baroque work neither supported nor challenged the monarchy, its form was ultimately defined by the tensions arising from the centralization of power. Because the opposition between crown and nobility was an intraclass rather than an interclass struggle, the underlying solidarity of the two antagonists reasserted itself whenever another class began to pose a serious threat. The dynamic but, paradoxically, closed and contained tension of baroque form aesthetically worked out a historically structured complex of rebellion and collaboration. As a result, the baroque may appropriately designate an apparently bewildering variety of writers, styles, and genres.

Obviously, much English and Spanish drama of the early seventeenth century fits neatly into this capacious category. Yet the very terms of the definition also suggest certain limits. If baroque theater thrived on the antagonism between aristocracy and monarchy, between class and state, it had correspondingly less to do with popular culture. Walter Benjamin insisted on the baroque poetics, absolutist orientation, and exclusion of popular impulses in the seventeenth-century *Trauerspiel* (mourning play). Logically enough, he found the purest form of the baroque not in Shakespeare or Lope de Vega, but in Calderón.[75] Popular traditions transform the absolutist crises with which *King Lear* and *Fuente Ovejuna* begin into qualitatively different conflicts. Intrigue tragedy, by contrast, was the true home of the baroque.

## THE FORMS OF TRAGICOMIC ROMANCE

### Influences, Form, and Ideology

Though temporally and institutionally akin to intrigue tragedy, tragicomic romance has a different generic shape and hence ideological perspective. The distinctive sense of recapitulation produced by the form, particularly in its pastoral manifestations, makes it the appropriate end point for a history of Renaissance public theater. Especially in the plays of Shakespeare and Calderón, long periods of suffering ultimately issue in the triumphant reconciliation of family and of nation. Pastoral, tragicomedy, and romance were traditional features of both English and Spanish dramaturgy. Works such as *The Winter's Tale*, *The Tempest*, and *La vida es sueño* (1634–35), however, represent amalgams that may awkwardly be designated pastoral tragicomic romance (hereafter referred to simply as romance).

---

[75]Walter Benjamin, *The Origin of German Tragic Drama*, trans. John Osborne (London: NLB, 1977), pp. 48–49 and passim.

What caused the triumph of romance? From about 1608 on in England, the works of Beaumont and Fletcher spurred the vogue for theoretically self-conscious tragicomedy first evident at the turn of the century. They primarily influenced the private theaters, but also such public-playhouse love-and-honor tragicomedies as Middleton and Rowley's *A Fair Quarrel* (1617) and Heywood's *A Challenge for Beauty* (1635). Unlike these two works, which eschew pastoral or romance or both, *Philaster* represents a genuine synthesis. Indebted to *Hamlet* and perhaps to *Cymbeline* as well, it nonetheless stands out for its successful naturalization of Italian pastoral tragicomedy.[76] Although Shakespeare almost certainly knew late-sixteenth-century Italian drama—*commedia grave*, *commedia dell'arte*, and pastoral tragicomedy—throughout his career,[77] his renewed and deepened interest particularly in the latter form beginning shortly before 1610 may have owed something to Beaumont and Fletcher. At the very least, he belonged to a general movement in the English theater.

In Spain, the *comedia* form itself almost carries the connotation of a loose kind of tragicomedy. Partly for this reason, critics have not consistently noticed Calderón's generic innovation, recognized his romances as such, or made much of their pastoral elements. But *La vida es sueño* and *Hado y divisa de Leonido y Marfisa* (1680) bear comparison with *The Tempest*, which, along with *Cymbeline*, in turn resembles *En la vida todo es verdad y todo mentira* (1659).[78] The overall similarities between these three works by Calderón and Shakespeare's four main romances—*Pericles* (1608), *Cymbeline*, *The Winter's Tale*, and *The Tempest*—constitute a virtual catalog of romance motifs. In one or more plays by each dramatist a nobleman flees the court for the country, where he secretly brings up royal children who display instinctive martial temperaments. The first meeting between these future monarchs and equally aristocratic youths of the other sex from the court produces astonishment, usually on both sides. If the encounter unites a brother and sister unaware of

[76]For Italian pastoral tragicomedy and the general course of English tragicomedy, see Herrick, pp. 125–71, 215–312.

[77]For Shakespeare and late-sixteenth-century Italian drama, see Clubb, "La mimesi della realtà invisibile nel dramma pastorale italiano e inglese del tardo rinascimento," *Misure Critiche* 4 (1974): 65–92.

[78]*La vida es sueño*: Jackson I. Cope, *The Theater and the Dream: From Metaphor to Form in Renaissance Drama* (Baltimore: Johns Hopkins University Press, 1973), pp. 236–60. *Hado y divisa*: Angel Valbuena Briones, ed., *Comedias*, vol. 2 of Calderón's *Obras completas* (Madrid: Aguilar, 1956), p. 2094. The reference to this play below is noted in the text. *En la vida*: Don William Cruickshank, introduction to his edition of the play (London: Tamesis, 1971), pp. lxix–lxxvi. Two recent accounts of Calderonian romance, both published in *Studies in Honor of Everett W. Hesse*, ed. McCrary and José A. Madrigal (Lincoln, Nebr.: Society of Spanish and Spanish-American Studies, 1981), are William R. Blue, "Romance Elements in Calderón's Last Plays," pp. 23–36; Susan L. Fischer, "Calderón's *El mayor encanto amor* and the Mode of Romance," pp. 99–112.

their kinship, an instantaneous attraction occurs as well. A magician or astrologer at odds with an Italian duke also makes his home in the country, raises both the lost children and a benign, even providential, storm, has charge of aerial spirits, and gives up his magic at the end of the play. Lower-class comic characters—sometimes drunk, usually foolish, and occasionally wise—occupy the pastoral world, either as natives or as unwilling refugees from court or city. A man-beast who often has spent his entire life in the wilds sexually threatens the heroine, who escapes unharmed, however. The plot not only teaches a major character the virtues of patience and self-discipline, but also and more important reunites and reconciles parents and children, redeeming the former by the latter and distributing the appropriate rewards to the surrogate father.

The parallels also involve the specific details of setting. The countryside is less often an Arcadian than a "hard" pastoral, frequently centered on a cave. A nearby seacoast enables the characters barely to survive nautical disaster as they wander around a Hellenistic Mediterranean at times reconceived in the terms of medieval chivalric romance: in addition to the plays already mentioned, Shakespeare and Fletcher's *Two Noble Kinsmen* (1613) employs a number of these motifs. The action may take place exclusively on an island or a group of islands, replete with music, masque, and spectacle. In *The Winter's Tale* and *Hado y divisa*, Sicily, though the setting for Theocritus's pastorals, mainly becomes the scene of court life, while the rural action occurs instead in eastern Europe. This reversal at once calls into question the standard opposition between court and country and, paradoxically, permits the entire sequence of events, regardless of locale, to be set in a pastoral world. In nearly all these works, of course, the movement between court and country retains the complex symbolic resonance traditional to pastoral.

Finally, the resemblances between Shakespeare and Calderón extend to the larger thematic shapes of their plays. In *Hado y divisa*, Marfisa mistakes her brother's discarded suit of armor for a corpse; in *Cymbeline*, Imogen weeps over the decapitated body of the villainous Cloten, wrongly thinking it her husband's. Characters return to life from figurative death, apparently tragic prophecies ultimately have comic meanings, and the Fall into Original Sin proves a *felix culpa* after all. The transcendence of Oedipal conflict in Calderón reproduces the movement described in Guarini's influential theory of tragicomedy, which depended on the generic conversion of the main model of the *Poetics*. At least by the time he composed *En la vida*, Calderón had some awareness of this tradition: in 1656 he collaborated on a play entitled *El pastor fido*.

For both playwrights, supersession of tragedy requires time. The protagonist of *Hado y divisa* asks his trusted friend how he might best escape from the maze of conflicting obligations in which he finds himself.

"Dando tiempo al tiempo" ("Giving time to time") comes the reply, "que él / sabe ciertas sendas varias / que acá ignoramos" ("because it / knows various sure paths / of which we here are ignorant": 2.2120). But Calderón came to this perception far earlier: he probably wrote *Dar tiempo al tiempo* in 1650.[79] The autonomous working of time does not in itself resolve the dramatic conflicts, however. The plays get their shape from a primarily unseen providence, the existence of which the characters intermittently intuit and with which the best of them eagerly cooperate. The controlling Neoplatonic pattern, modified by the perspective of the Counter-Reformation, reveals human beings lost in a physical and spiritual labyrinth, rescued by supernatural forces usually beyond their control, and thereby permitted both earthly felicity and at least a glimpse of eternal reality.

This lengthy catalog by no means exhausts the structural affinities between Shakespeare's and Calderón's plays. It has served its purpose, however, if it has demonstrated that the latter are romances, and if it has suggested what would require far more detailed discussion to prove: that as early as *La vida es sueño* Calderón's romances, like Shakespeare's final works, draw on the theory and practice of Italian pastoral tragicomedy. As a young man Calderón may have traveled in Italy, with which, as noted above, Spain had far closer ties than did England.[80] By the time of *La vida es sueño*, he had composed at least a dozen romantic comedies with Italian settings, as well as *Argenis y Poliarco* (1634), a play set primarily in Sicily that culminates in the union of a royal father with the grown-up son he has never before met.[81]

Institutional parallels also help explain the formal similarities between Shakespearean and Calderonian drama, as well as the possible recourse to a common tradition. Shakespearean romance roughly coincides with the initial years in which the King's Men used Blackfriars for the winter season. The spectacular effects of the plays respond to the technical capacities newly available to Shakespeare at the indoor theater, to the recent development of the court masque, and to the general impact of courtly art.[82] The growing impact of the monarchy, one critic has ar-

---

[79]Robert ter Horst, *Calderón: The Secular Plays* (Lexington: University Press of Kentucky, 1982), pp. 51–58, 214–33, emphasizes the importance of time in *La vida es sueño* but sees the play generically as a psychological epic.

[80]Kurt und Roswitha Reichenberger, *Bibliographisches Handbuch der Calderón-Forschung*, vol. 3 (Kassell: Thiele und Schwarz, 1981), p. 724.

[81]Inferred from Richard W. Tyler and Sergio D. Elizondo, *The Characters, Plots and Settings of Calderón's Comedias* (Lincoln, Nebr.: Society of Spanish and Spanish-American Studies, 1981), pp. 122–419.

[82]Stephen Orgel, *The Illusion of Power: Political Theater in the English Renaissance* (Berkeley and Los Angeles: University of California Press, 1975), esp. pp. 45–49; Gary Schmidgall, *Shakespeare and the Courtly Aesthetic* (Berkeley and Los Angeles: University of California Press, 1981).

gued, accounts for the redemptive role assigned to royal children, itself a reflection, perhaps, of the popularity of James's offspring, Prince Henry and Princess Elizabeth.[83] Post-Shakespearean playwrights often designed their romances exclusively for the private theaters. Similarly, *La vida es sueño* was probably first performed as a *particular* before the king,[84] at a time of already substantial Italian influence on the court stage. And Calderón unquestionably wrote *En la vida* and *Hado y divisa* for the theaters at Buen Retiro.

On the other hand, *La vida es sueño* is a *corral*-type play,[85] its elevated diction and intellectual subtlety notwithstanding. In England, records survive of early performances of Shakespeare's romances at the Globe, but not at Blackfriars. More important, *Pericles*, probably the earliest of the romances, was intended for and initially acted at the Globe.[86] Institutional affiliations cannot adequately account for the generic impulse. Finally, *Henry VIII*, perhaps composed for performance at court, apparently opened instead at the Globe on June 29, 1613. A discharge of the "chambers," one of the stage effects, accidentally ignited the roof thatch, caused the theater to burn down, and impelled various members of the audience to memorialize the event. The most revealing comment comes from Sir Henry Wotton, who noted that the play represented "some principal pieces of the reign of Henry VIII, which was set forth with many extraordinary circumstances of pomp and majesty, even to the matting of the stage; . . . sufficient in truth within a while to make greatness very familiar, if not ridiculous."[87] The subversive contradiction between artisanal base and absolutist superstructure characterized Shakespearean dramaturgy even in the final plays.

Many of the romances thus fall in the years of institutional transition, at the historical turning point in seventeenth-century English and Spanish absolutism. Yet what relation do they have to an era of deepening crisis, to the last, embattled age of national unity? Do they not instead reveal, especially in England, a fuller and easier reconciliation than occurs in Shakespeare's tragedies, written a decade earlier during a time of less

[83]Paul N. Siegel, "Shakespearean Comedy and the Elizabethan Compromise," in *Shakespeare in His Time and Ours* (Notre Dame, Ind.: University of Notre Dame Press, 1968), pp. 200–203.

[84]N. D. Shergold, *A History of the Spanish Stage from Medieval Times until the End of the Seventeenth Century* (Oxford: Clarendon Press, 1967), p. 554.

[85]Shergold, "*La vida es sueño*: Ses acteurs, son théâtre et son public," in *Dramaturgie et société*, ed. Jacquot, 1:93–109.

[86]James G. McManaway, introduction to his edition of *Pericles Prince of Tyre*, in *William Shakespeare: The Complete Works*, gen. ed. Alfred Harbage (Baltimore: Penguin, 1969), p. 1260, argues that the first performance of the play could not have occurred later than July 1608. Burbage did not acquire the lease to Blackfriars until August of the same year: see E. K. Chambers, *The Elizabethan Stage* (Oxford: Clarendon Press, 1923), 2:54.

[87]Sir Henry Wotton, quoted in Chambers, 2:419.

overt antagonism? Might one then deny any connection between romance and reality, or accuse Shakespeare's and Calderón's plays of escapism, of an evasion of direct tragic confrontation? Similarly, in what ways do romances and intrigue tragedies contemporaneously respond to the same social phenomena? These questions require a systematic consideration of the ideology of romance.

Here some rough generic comparisons may again clarify the argument. The transcendence of tragedy is central to the form. Symptomatically, all three of Calderón's romances and all of Shakespeare's with the exception of *The Tempest* include at least one actual death, as well as a number of near misses. However many the parallels between Shakespeare's romantic comedies and romances,[88] only in the latter does one consistently feel a somberness, urgency, and temporal depth that attest to the continuing power of the experience of the intervening tragic years. As early as *King Lear* and *Macbeth*, the conclusion of the plot hints at a process of reconciliation that anticipates the movement of the last plays. Indeed, to oversimplify, Shakespeare's entire theatrical career constitutes one vast Hegelian dialectical progression, in which the comedies engender their own antithesis in the subsequent tragedies, which the synthetic vision of the romances in turn negates and supersedes. In the structure of each of the final works, moreover, and especially in *The Winter's Tale*, Shakespeare internally recapitulates the general progression of two decades. But although that play moves from joy to adversity and from there to a concluding restoration of happiness, it really begins with the tragedy of *Othello* (acts 1–3), shifts to the romantic comedy of *As You Like It* (act 4), and only then issues in the romance conclusion (act 5). Shakespeare found no easy and immediate path from tragedy to romance.

Calderón's corpus possesses a similar shape. The opposition between father and son in *La vida es sueño*, which issues in the comic resolution of Oedipal conflict typical of Counter-Reformation tragicomedy and which also responds to more genuinely Freudian analysis, probably reworks tensions within Calderón's own family. The dramatist had treated the same relationship at least once and possibly twice before, both times providing a tragic resolution to the struggle. After *La vida es sueño*, he never again made the antagonism between father and son the center of a work, although it has some significance in *En la vida*. Segismundo's forgiveness of Basilio, then, enables Calderón, like Shakespeare before him, to incorporate tragedy into a larger, nontragic view of life.[89]

[88]Northrop Frye, *A Natural Perspective: The Development of Shakespearean Comedy and Romance* (New York: Harcourt, Brace and World, 1965).
[89]Parker, "The Father-Son Conflict in the Drama of Calderón," *Forum for Modern Language Studies* 2 (1966): 99–113.

If romantic comedy dramatizes the successful accommodation of the aristocracy to change, whereas tragedy depicts the failure of the same class to make the necessary historical adaptation, how does romance fit in? Like romantic comedy, does it merely portray the success of the nobility, despite abundant empirical evidence to the contrary? Whatever the truth of this position, an alternative perspective, drawing once again on the distinctive structure of *The Winter's Tale*, may specify more accurately the ideology of the form. Its opening three acts on the one hand constitute the dramatic past of the play, but on the other correspond to the conflict-ridden present of the tragedies. Its final two acts occur after the conclusions of the tragedies. Shakespeare and Calderón usually narrate rather than dramatize the past in most of the other romances, so that the audience apparently sees a rendition of the present. In the context of Shakespeare's entire career, however, *The Winter's Tale* reveals a different relationship. Its final two acts, like the entire plot of *The Tempest*, for example, represent not the present but an idealized future that overcomes the sufferings of that present. Far from denying tragedy's insistence on the contemporary failure of the aristocracy, romance takes that perception as its point of departure, only to continue, however, by asserting the triumphant adaptation of the class in the future.

In this context the temporal vistas offered by the form acquire their most profound meaning. Romance is genuinely utopian, considerably more so, anyway, than romantic comedy with its elaborate mechanisms of repression. In *The Tempest*, Gonzalo proposes a utopia, just as Brome does in two late English private-theater romances, *The Antipodes* and *A Jovial Crew* (1641). Although the dramatists treat these alternative visions with irony or at least some qualification, the very presence of alternatives signals fundamental thematic preoccupations as well as the inherent tendencies of the form. In *En la vida*, the protagonists live out a section of their future in the present; the hero of *Hado y divisa*, analogously, can view events occurring across the sea. Calderón's romances generally allow their characters an opportunity to try out unexpected and even unimagined existences, to obtain magical second chances in life. Though unusually painful and philosophically resonant, Segismundo's experience conforms in this respect to the norm.

Calderón's method thus has affinities with the play within the play and the blurring of the distinction between drama and reality typical of Shakespeare and Brome, in which men and women observe or, better still, act out their deepest aspirations. It also underlies the playwright's own ability to represent reality, in this instance to produce a plausible version of an increasingly elusive national unity. *The Tempest, A Jovial Crew*, and *Hado y divisa* stand at the end of their respective authors' dramatic careers: *The Tempest* may bid farewell to the public theater; Calderón composed *La vida es sueño* precisely at the moment when he first began writing extensively for the court stage; and *A Jovial Crew* was perhaps the last play performed before the closing of the theaters in 1642.[90] In each case, a dramatist at the end of an age found a way out of the persistent conflict of the present only in a utopian view of the future. Though not literally descriptive,[91] the titles of Calderón's romances— *La vida es sueño* and *En la vida todo es verdad y todo mentira*—like Prospero's famous conclusion that "We are such stuff / As dreams are made on,"[92] evoke the problem the playwrights confronted and the fragility of the solution they could propose. A similar outlook, though transferred to an explicitly transcendental plane, also shapes the Spanish religious plays of this period.

The utopian dimension of romance may help explain the relative depreciation of the form in much dramatic theory since the Renaissance. Although romance by no means constitutes an evasion, it has not moved critics or perhaps audiences as profoundly as has tragedy. Not only does its inherent logic preclude the potential fidelity to a historical moment of the more prestigious form; up to now tragedy has apparently spoken more compellingly to subsequent eras as well. Yet this difference has nothing to do with any timeless, intrinsically greater truth content of tragedy. Indeed, Marxism has always wagered that in the long run human history would have, or at least could have, the structure of romance. Precisely in its utopianism, then, romance may offer a legitimate vision not of the prehistory lived in class society, but of that authentic history that may someday succeed it.[93]

## The Quest for the Nation

The tension between civil conflict and national unity evident from a primarily formalist analysis also emerges from a more properly sociological inquiry. Northrop Frye has argued that in "every age the ruling social or intellectual class tends to project its ideals in some form of romance. . . . This is the general character of . . . aristocratic romance in the Renaissance. . . . Yet there is a genuinely 'proletarian' element in romance too which is never satisfied with its various incarnations."[94] These comments have obvious parallels to the general theory of public

[90]*Hado y divisa*: Valbuena Briones, 2:2093; *A Jovial Crew*: Bentley, vol. 3 (Oxford: Clarendon Press, 1956), p. 71.

[91]Wilson, *Spanish and English Literature*, pp. 27–47.

[92]Shakespeare, *The Tempest*, ed. Frank Kermode (London: Methuen, 1958), 4.1.156–57. Subsequent references are noted in the text.

[93]For a provocative discussion of utopia, see Fredric Jameson, *The Political Unconscious: Narrative as a Socially Symbolic Act* (Ithaca, N.Y.: Cornell University Press, 1981), pp. 281–99.

[94]Frye, *Anatomy of Criticism: Four Essays* (Princeton: Princeton University Press, 1957), p. 186.

theater drama developed in this study. The immediately foregoing discussion has tended to substantiate Frye's claim for the aristocratic function of romance. To see how the form allows for the interaction of ruling-class and popular perspectives, to understand both the possibilities and the limits of its representational capacity, requires a review of the means by which it seeks to reestablish national unity and thus the connections it posits between court and country.

For intrigue tragedy, particularly in England, the relationship between court and country usually proves irreconcilably antagonistic. Romance, of course, works toward the opposite perception, perhaps nowhere more clearly and completely than in *Philaster*. Beaumont and Fletcher portray an aristocracy hostile to the usurping king and, like the common people, sympathetic to the protagonist and rightful heir. The country woodmen ridicule Philaster's rival Pharamond, an affected and decadent Spanish prince; a "country fellow" opportunely prevents the hero from murdering the woman he loves; and later, while members of the nobility stand by as passive, albeit reluctant, spectators at the imminent execution of Philaster, the citizens stage a rebellion that wins him his rightful social and political position. Thus the urban and rural lower classes, treated with affectionate condescension by aristocratic dramatists and characters alike, not only guide the audience's judgments of Philaster, but also enable him ultimately and justly to triumph. The dramatic resolution of the play consequently incorporates all social classes. The capaciousness of this vision perhaps testifies to the effort of two private theater playwrights to construct a plot that would appeal at least in part to the audience at the Globe. But like *The Maid's Tragedy*, *Philaster* approaches the status of intrigue in the sense that the resolution of the plot has scant relation to the problems raised in the course of the action. Beaumont and Fletcher's solution to conflict combines dramaturgical exploitation with ideological evasion: it ignores all difficulty.

Failing to adopt a similar approach, Shakespeare could not easily achieve as inclusive a final synthesis. In *The Winter's Tale*, Perdita is the embodiment of that synthesis, uniting court with country and upper class with lower. The product of her own innate nobility, as well as of sixteen years of life with shepherds in a landscape ostensibly set in Bohemia but actually resembling the English countryside, she is supposedly the daughter of an old shepherd and sister of his son, the clown. Half of what she is they are, and to the extent that she sums up the movement of the play, they bear half the meaning of *The Winter's Tale*. More specifically, the father and son represent the spirit of popular comedy, both in terms of humor and, more generally, as an antidote to the aristocratic tragedy of the first three acts. They also assert or practice a series of values that link them to nature and to Perdita, in this way providing a commentary on the court. Finally, their thinking reveals a synthetic impulse that anticipates Perdita's role and that receives social ratification in their metamorphosis into courtiers at the end of the play.

Most of these themes emerge during the shepherds' first appearance, in act 3, scene 3. In contrast not only to the doomed Antigonus, who has the immediately preceding lines, but also to all that has gone before since the very first scene, the shepherd comes in speaking prose. Meditating on sexual promiscuity and looking for his lost sheep, he instead discovers Perdita. Like her irrationally jealous father, he wrongly thinks her the offspring of an illicit affair; unlike Leontes, he takes pity on her and is soon after rewarded by the discovery of gold. The shepherd summons his son in language that comically ties miraculous life to the natural processes of death and decay: "If thou'lt see a thing to talk on when thou art dead and rotten, come hither."[95] The clown, though aghast at the gruesome and disastrous scenes he has just witnessed, cannot resist a punning reference to the manner of Antigonus's death—"land-service" (3.3.90). Similarly, when the shepherd wishes he could have aided Antigonus, the boy replies, "I would you had been by the ship side, to have helped her. There your charity would have lacked footing" (3.3.103–5). The clown, too, demonstrates "charity" in his plan to bury Antigonus's remains. "Heavy matters, heavy matters!" the shepherd remarks, but in adding, "thou mettest with things dying, I with things newborn" (3.3.105–7), he laconically summarizes the movement of the scene as well as of the entire play. And he appropriately and resonantly concludes, "'Tis a lucky day" (3.3.125).

Sixteen years later in act 4, the clown, though now a comic fool and dupe, can nonetheless get at the truth. Thinking well of the court, he still somehow knows its limitations. "There's no virtue whipped out of the court. They cherish it to make it stay there, and yet it will no more but abide" (4.3.86–88). Later in the same act, when King Polixenes angrily reveals himself, both father and son show a healthy sense of self-preservation. But Shakespeare minimizes their fault by juxtaposing their plan with the stratagem of the courtier Camillo. The latter lies to fulfill a personal desire; they tell the truth to save their lives. Both actions, moreover, contribute to a providential pattern that culminates in the revelation to the proper people of Perdita's identity.

The old shepherd in particular retains close contact with natural processes. Polixenes' threats cause him to lament not being able

> to fill his grave in quiet, yea,
> To die upon the bed my father died,
> To lie close by his honest bones.
>
> (4.4.447–49)

[95]Shakespeare, *The Winter's Tale*, ed. Baldwin Maxwell, in *William Shakespeare*, gen. ed. Harbage, 3.3.77–78. Subsequent references are noted in the text.

At the recognition scene, he "stands by like a weather-bitten conduit of many kings' reigns" (5.2.53–54). Soon after, when the clown tells Autolycus that "there was the first gentleman-like tears that ever we shed," his father adds, "We may live, son, to shed many more" (5.2.136–38). *The Winter's Tale* teaches, and Leontes and his court must learn, precisely this nontragic suffering and endurance.

Perdita shares the values of the shepherds. She reciprocates their human sympathy, both toward the shepherd—"O my poor father!" (5.1.201)—and toward the mother she has never met. When Leontes narrates Hermione's death, "how attentiveness wounded his daughter, till, from one sign of dolor to another, she did, with an 'Alas,' I would fain say, bleed tears" (5.2.82–85). Perdita also insists on her rustic simplicity. When Florizel expresses his love for her in elevated rhetoric, she merely replies:

> I cannot speak
> So well, nothing so well; no, nor mean better.
> By th' pattern of mine own thoughts I cut out
> The purity of his.
>
> (4.4.373–76)

Finally, after Polixenes' abusive tirade, she remarks:

> I was not much afeard; for once or twice
> I was about to speak and tell him plainly
> The selfsame sun that shines upon his court
> Hides not his visage from our cottage but
> Looks on alike.
>
> (4.4.435–39)

Although Perdita's noble birth renders her lines unintentionally ironic, the egalitarianism of her statement does not suffer on that account. Perdita says "our cottage," not "my cottage," and thus looks ahead to the end of the play.

Earlier in the same act the clown remarks, "If I were not in love with Mopsa, thou shouldst take no money of me; but being enthralled as I am, it will also be the bondage of certain ribbons and gloves" (4.4.229–31). Like Perdita's brave words, his courtly conceit foreshadows the conclusion of *The Winter's Tale*. As the clown explains, "the king's son took me by the hand and called me brother; and then the two kings called my father brother; and then the prince my brother and the princess my sister called my father father" (5.2.132–35). The shepherd characteristically responds to his new social status: "We must be gentle now we are gentlemen" (5.2.144–45). Less logically, but with the same intention, the clown promises to perjure himself for his "friend" Autolycus. After all those years, the clown proves a "gentleman born." Although the main reconciliation of the play occurs through the unconscious agency of Perdita, the shepherds also achieve a comic, philosophical reconciliation of their own. "Gentlemen born" "these four hours" (5.2.121–31), they bring together rich and poor and court and country in the penultimate harmonious vision of *The Winter's Tale*.

To a considerable extent, then, Shakespeare's hopes of national unity depend on the rural lower classes. If the play does indeed take a utopian perspective, perhaps one should not point out that in early-seventeenth-century England shepherds did not and indeed could not play this role. Their prominence in *The Winter's Tale* instead indicates Shakespeare's popular heritage. In the intrigue tragedians, by contrast, the country and its rulers, the gentry, provide a far feebler alternative to the corruption of the court. *The Winter's Tale* thus continues the ideological argument of *King Lear*. In both works the final synthesis, insofar as it occurs at all, incorporates only the two primary and indeed antagonistic classes of feudal society. Although the conversion from agriculture to pastoralism in the late Middle Ages had great importance for the development of English capitalism, the exclusion from *The Winter's Tale* of any member of the capitalist classes, with the dubious and minor exception of Autolycus, suggests the elusiveness of full social reconciliation by 1610.

A related problem arises in *La vida es sueño*. Discussion of the play has focused far more on demonstrating the coherence of main plot and subplot than on investigating the relationship of court and country.[96] Rosaura obviously occupies a crucial position in the complex process whereby Segismundo develops his own humanity, comes to view life from the perspective of eternal reality, recognizes the vanity and pomp of worldly power, and thus emerges as an ideal prince.[97] In particular, she symbolically brings light to the dark world of his literal and spiritual imprisonment.[98] Yet *La vida es sueño* does not take the antipastoral step of favorably contrasting civilization to brutishness. Segismundo learns nothing during his stay at the seriously defective Polish court. On the other hand, he learns a good deal *from* his stay there. Although he gains wisdom only in the rural world, his moral growth turns on the interaction of court and country.

Yet unlike Shakespeare Calderón does not populate his landscape. He

---

[96]See, for example, A. E. Sloman, "The Structure of Calderón's *La vida es sueño*," in *Critical Essays on the Theatre of Calderón*, ed. Wardropper, pp. 90–100.

[97]On this last point see Everett W. Hesse, "Calderón's Concept of the Perfect Prince in *La vida es sueño*," in *Critical Essays on the Theatre of Calderón*, ed. Wardropper, pp. 114–33.

[98]William M. Whitby, "Rosaura's Role in the Structure of *La vida es sueño*," in *Critical Essays on the Theatre of Calderón*, ed. Wardropper, pp. 105–7.

accordingly cannot establish an organic relationship between his protagonist and the lower classes. Throughout the tradition of Spanish dramatic and nondramatic literature on Russo-Polish themes to which *La
vida es sueño* belongs, a national uprising inaugurates the reign of justice.[99] But once Segismundo has gained his ends, he punishes the rebel
soldier who understandably enough comes forward to request his reward. Although the protagonist's conduct here conforms to the specific
ethical assumptions of the plot, it leads to political contradiction.[100]
Good government either requires the spontaneous and independent activity of the lower classes, or it does not. Calderón, however, both needs
and fears popular rebellion. As a result, the moral basis of regeneration
in *La vida es sueño* is as strong as its social basis is weak: the distance between the monarchy and the people proves unbridgeable. Ironically, the
re-creation of national unity entails the simultaneous dissolution of that
unity.

Still greater obstacles to a similar goal trouble *A Jovial Crew*. The play
attempts a last-minute social resolution of the crisis that almost immediately thereafter resulted in civil war.[101] Brome's plot covertly works
out a providential pattern in which the otherwise perfect gentleman
Oldrents expiates and makes good both his sexual failing toward the
sister of the beggar Patrico and the economic crimes of his grandfather
against Patrico's grandfather. This resolution depends on the class reconciliation of the gentry and the beggars, a unity ideally embodied, both
physically and spiritually, in Springlove, the faithful steward of Oldrents
and, as it turns out, his natural son as well. The wandering and mirthful
beggars, whose progress through the countryside parodies a royal progress, present—they are amateur actors—and represent a utopia, in both
senses attractive but inadequate or impossible.

Given the gentry's fear of the social dislocation caused by its own enclosures, however, the partial idealization of vagabondage points to profound social conflict. A 1621 law, to which Brome alludes, in theory restricted the rural lower class's freedom of movement. In practice, by
1641 antienclosure riots were threatening the social stability of the countryside. During the revolutionary era, the radical religious sects probably
found ready converts among the many masterless men and women who
roamed England and who eagerly embraced millenarian and utopian

[99]N. I. Balachov, "Les thèmes slaves chez Calderón et la question Renaissance-Baroque
dans la littérature espagnole," in *Actes du V<sup>e</sup> Congrès de l'Association Internationale de Littérature Comparée, Belgrade 1967*, ed. Nikola Banašević (Amsterdam: Swets and Zeitlinger,
1969), p. 123.

[100]Ciriaco Morón Arroyo, "*La vida es sueño* y *El alcalde de Zalamea*: Para una sociología
del texto calderoniano," *Iberoromania* 14 (1981): 28–32.

[101]Joe Lee Davis, *The Sons of Ben: Jonsonian Comedy in Caroline England* (Detroit: Wayne
State University Press, 1967), p. 140.

hopes. Samuel Sheppard entitled his 1651 attack on the antinomian Ranters *The Joviall Crew*.[102] Whatever Brome's intentions, then, *A Jovial Crew* sympathetically anticipates the revolutionary aspirations that briefly came to the surface of English society only a few years later. As a result, however, like *The Winter's Tale* the play all too easily reconciles antithetical class interests. Yet the radicals generally did support the country party during the Civil War, at least in preference to the Stuarts. Perhaps most notable of all, the resultant harmony excludes not only the urban capitalist classes, but the crown as well. Although like many other dramatists Brome opted for royalism in the Civil War, *A Jovial Crew* reveals the difficulty of imagining a monarchical solution to the national crisis.[103]

Yet the London playwrights found a way out, a means of creating a utopian version of a genuinely encompassing national unity. Its dependence on maritime imperialism and colonization may help clarify both the relationship between Spanish and English drama and the larger significance of the public theater. Brome's *Antipodes*, though composed for the private stage, provides a convenient introduction. Like *A Jovial Crew*, it places Jonsonian satiric comedy at the service of Shakespearean romance. Indeed, Jonson himself had taken a similar tack in his last plays, evoking the past romantic age of Elizabeth and Shakespeare, both of whose names increasingly acquired oppositional connotations under the Stuarts. Something similar may even be true of Ford in *Perkin Warbeck*.[104] The central three acts of *The Antipodes* consist of a play within the play on the utopia of the Antipodes, in which "the world turn'd upside down" both geographically and socially—a recurrent theme in popular prints from the mid-sixteenth century—produces a therapeutic effect.[105] Again like *A Jovial Crew*, the play eulogizes the country and opposes both city and court. Yet the dramatic resolution involves, however ambiguously, the English navigators and the utopian speculation that the discovery of the New World inspired.[106] Both have ties, though here, too, oblique ones, to the rise of English capitalism. Perhaps despite

---

[102]Christopher Hill, *The World Turned Upside Down: Radical Ideas during the English Revolution* (Harmondsworth, Middlesex: Penguin, 1975), pp. 39–56, 87–106, 204, 358, and passim.

[103]R. J. Kaufman, *Richard Brome: Caroline Playwright* (New York: Columbia University Press, 1961), pp. 169–73.

[104]Anne Barton, "Harking Back to Elizabeth: Ben Jonson and Caroline Nostalgia," *ELH* 48 (1981): 706–31; Philip Edwards, *Threshold of a Nation: A Study in English and Irish Drama* (Cambridge: Cambridge University Press, 1979), pp. 183–87.

[105]Richard Brome, *The Antipodes*, ed. Ann Haaker (Lincoln: University of Nebraska Press, 1966), 2.2.12; Peter Burke, *Popular Culture in Early Modern Europe* (New York: Harper and Row, 1978), pp. 188–89.

[106]On the sources of the play, see Clarence Edward Andrews, *Richard Brome: A Study of His Life and Works* (1913; rpt. Hamden, Conn.: Archon Books, 1972), pp. 113–28.

the playwright's intent, a bourgeois dimension enters into the ideology of the play.

This conclusion in turn suggests the basis for contrasting *La vida es sueño* and *The Tempest*. Although romance had its geographical home in the Mediterranean, these two works suggest an opposition between eastern Europe and America. Calderón, in his lack of concern with the religious differences between Greek Orthodox Russia and Catholic Poland, perhaps advocates in *La vida es sueño* a tolerant, universalist Catholicism implicitly opposed to the more dogmatic tendencies of the Counter-Reformation.[107] The eastern European setting of the play also testifies to Spain's traditional preoccupation with the region. Although Castile discovered, colonized, and exploited the New World, very little of the literature, and even less of the drama, that has thus far made the reputation of Golden Age culture attempts to understand that experience. On the other hand, Castro, Lope, Luis Vélez de Guevara, Coello, Pérez de Montalbán, Rojas Zorrilla, Moreto, Belmonte Bermúdez, and of course Calderón himself all contributed to the body of drama on eastern Europe.[108]

That half of the continent particularly attracted the playwrights after the outbreak of the Thirty Years' War. Because the region faced Christendom's most immediate and omnipresent threat from the forces of Islam, however, it had long concerned western Europe and especially Spain, which of course had a legacy of peninsular conflict with the Moslems and, during the sixteenth and seventeenth centuries, a predominant role in the Mediterranean wars with the Turks. Spanish imperialism, in other words, remained irreducibly feudal. Although America provided Renaissance Europe with a source of primitive accumulation for capitalist development, Spain squandered the unique opportunities offered by an early, lucrative empire. The country's resulting ideological narrowness apparently precluded a penetrating grasp of the great theme raised by the discovery of the New World: the confrontation between totally alien cultures. On the other hand, the dramatic orientation toward a familiar and comprehensible eastern Europe accorded with the monarchy's feudal emphasis on continental land wars. Insofar as the Habsburg state played out its destiny in Europe rather than America, *La vida es sueño* signifies the historical dead end of Spanish absolutism.

In England, the New World proved fertile literary terrain. One might mention, among many others, the major works by More and Bacon, and the subordinate treatments by Spenser, Burton, Jonson, and Brome. *The*

[107]Balachov, pp. 119–24.

[108]Balachov, p. 120; Sister Mary Austin Cauvin, O.P., "The *Comedia de Privanza* in the Seventeenth Century," Ph.D. diss., University of Pennsylvania, 1957, pp. 184–207; ter Horst, pp. 216–20.

*Tempest* belongs both to this tradition and to the larger European reflection on the subject. As the discussion of romance should suggest, however, the play consists of more than a meditation on America, a dramatization of the Virginia pamphlets, or even a response to the whole body of travel literature available in early Jacobean England. Although Shakespeare had read some of the documents relating to Jamestown, he ignored the major justifications offered for the settlement: religious conversion of the natives, economic gain, and relief of England's overpopulation. He thus entirely sidestepped various classic expressions of imperial ideology. For instance, *A True Declaration of the Estate of the Colonie in Virginia* (1610), which Shakespeare knew, proudly argued that the English, "by way of marchandizing and trade, doe buy of them [the Indians] the pearles of earth, and sell to them the pearles of heauen."[109] Nonetheless, *The Tempest* repays consideration in light of America. From a generic point of view, Shakespeare's breakthrough in the play was to yoke the utopian thrust of romance to the source of Renaissance utopianism in the discovery of the New World.

This conjunction allows for the reestablishment of national unity on a broader social basis than in *The Winter's Tale.* The opening scene, echoing a common motif of the literature on Virginia, valorizes the labor of the master, the boatswain, and the mariners at the expense of Antonio and Sebastian. More than a mere leveler of class distinctions, the storm actually inverts customary hierarchies: unlike the crew, the courtiers find themselves utterly functionless. This obvious instance of the critical dimension of popular dramaturgy resonates in the issue of useful labor throughout the play.[110] In the final scene, the master and boatswain return to participate in a concluding reconciliation that thus transcends the limits of the aristocracy to include men who, loosely speaking, belong to the urban lower and middling classes. The manuscript of a fundraising circular issued by "The Councell and Companye of Virginia" in late 1610 refers to the "divers Lords, Knights, Gentlemen, and worthie citizens of London [who] have at this time subscrybed, . . . [and who] sollicyte . . . well affected gentlemen . . . to subscribe" and asks the latter "if there be in your countrye any honest labouring men, or artizens, that are willing to go in person."[111] Similarly inclusive appeals frequently occur in other manuscript and printed documents of the period. The historical basis of the unusual concluding unity of *The Tempest* was thus

---

[109]Council of Virginia, *A True Declaration of the Estate of the Colonie in Virginia* (London, 1610), sig. B3ʳ.

[110]Leo Lowenthal, *Literature and the Image of Man: Sociological Studies of the European Drama and Novel, 1600–1900* (1957; rpt. Freeport, N.J.: Books for Libraries Press, 1970), pp. 57–97, esp. 221–29.

[111]Council of Virginia, "To the right worshipfull our very loving friendes," 5 December 1610, Huntington Library MS HM 961, San Marino, Calif.

overseas expansion itself, in its combination of commerce and colonization, its involvement of a wide social range of the English people, and
its temporary incorporation of capitalist enterprise in a neofeudal order.[112] As Robert Gray puts it in *A Good Speed to Virginia* (1609), by
means of the colony "the territories of our kingdome [may be] inlarged,
. . . his Maiesties customes wonderfully augmented, and the honour and
renown of our *Nation* spred and propagated to the ends of the
world."[113]

This achievement had its victims, however, in *The Tempest* represented
by Caliban. To modern critics appalled by the legacy of European imperialism since the Renaissance, the play has at times seemed a disturbing
document, but one that, despite its obfuscatory and subtly didactic Neoplatonic allegory, unwittingly provides insight into an early stage in the
formation of colonialist ideology. For instance, the critique of hierarchy
in the opening scene apparently does not extend to the treatment of Caliban by Prospero, a relationship seen almost entirely from the latter's
point of view. The civilized European nobly attempts to bring language
and culture to the racially inferior native, who proves, however, both
unteachable and ungrateful. In *Nova Britannia* (1609), Robert Johnson
proposes that those natives who resisted religious conversion "shall bee
dealt with as enemies of the Commonwealth of their country."[114] The
same year Thomas Gates, governor of the colony, learned that to further the spreading of the Gospel among the Indians he "must remove
from them some convenient number of their children to be brought up
in your language and manners" and must capture and, if necessary, kill
the Indian priests, "those murtherers of soules and sacrificers of gods
images to the Divill."[115] In *The Tempest*, repeated demonstrations of
Prospero's superior power ultimately lead Caliban to recognize his own
inferiority and thus flatteringly to confirm the opinion of his master.[116]
To this extent, the play reveals that the self-defined rationality of European man—the choice of gender is deliberate—dialectically depends on
the simultaneous insistence on the irrationality of all those who are today
often called Third World peoples. For Robert Gray, native Americans
"differ very little from beasts, hauing no Art, nor science, nor trade."[117]

[112]Bruce Erlich, "Shakespeare's Colonial Metaphor: On the Social Function of Theatre
in *The Tempest*," *Science and Society* 41 (1977): 51–53.
[113]Robert Gray, *A Good Speed to Virginia* (London, 1609), sig. B2ᵛ.
[114]Robert Johnson, *Nova Britannia* (London, 1609), sig. C2ʳ.
[115]Council of Virginia, "Instruccions orders and constitucions . . . to Sir Thomas Gates,"
pp. 3–4, Huntington Library MS BR 685.
[116]See Erlich, passim; Lorie Jerrell Leininger, "Cracking the Code of *The Tempest*," in
*Shakespeare: Contemporary Critical Approaches*, ed. Harry R. Garvin (Lewisburg, Pa.: Bucknell
University Press, 1980), pp. 121–31.
[117]Gray, sig. C2ᵛ.

In other words, *The Tempest* uncovers, perhaps despite itself, the racist and imperialist bases of English nationalism.

Yet Shakespeare's attitude toward colonialism, though undeniably ethnocentric, does not adequately emerge from a catalog of demystifications. Although the audience generally sympathizes with Prospero, it also sees him undergo the difficult process of self-mastery. The problem of social hierarchy broached in the opening scene recurs in the main body of the play as the question of freedom, often at Prospero's expense. Caliban, indeed, receives far more of our sympathy than do Sebastian and Antonio or Stephano and Trinculo. Clearly mistreated by Prospero as well as by others, he in one instance even gains a moral victory over his master. At the end of the play, Prospero admits a bond to Caliban but leaves it, like Caliban's fate, unclear. The colonial experiment itself ends abortively, when the Europeans all willingly leave the island[118]—precisely the eventuality most feared by the Council of Virginia, "especially since the consequence is so pregnant, that without this or the like [settlement], the state cannot subsist without some dangerous and imminent mutation."[119] Moreover, the redemptive quality of the experience, the imperial solution to national dilemmas, proves equally problematic: the villainous Antonio and Sebastian, though temporarily pacified, remain morally unregenerate.

The utopianism of *The Tempest* also counterbalances the play's partial propagation of colonial ideology. The authors of the *True Declaration* considered their reports of Virginia so favorable that they took pains to deny that they were promulgating "Vtopian, and legendarie fables."[120] In Shakespeare's Jacobean tragedies, a neofeudal hero may oppose the forces of amoral bourgeois individualism. *The Tempest* instead more closely recalls *Hamlet*. Antonio and Sebastian's ideology, like Claudius's, lacks the specificity of the beliefs associated with the Jacobean villains. Prospero, correspondingly, shares with Hamlet his contact with the audience, his humanism, and perhaps even his bourgeois traits.[121] A basic trilateral relationship suggests the utopian dimension of this position. As a former Italian duke, an unparalleled master of "the liberal Arts" (1.2.73), and for twelve years the governor of an obscure island, Prospero literally embodies the interaction of the Old World, the Ancient

---

[118]Stephen J. Greenblatt, "Learning to Curse: Aspects of Linguistic Colonialism in the Sixteenth Century," in *First Images of America: The Impact of the New World on the Old*, ed. Fredi Chiappelli (Berkeley and Los Angeles: University of California Press, 1976), 2:568–71; Edwards, pp. 103–9.

[119]Council of Virginia, *True Declaration*, sig. I1ʳ.

[120]Council of Virginia, *True Declaration*, sig. E3ʳ.

[121]Erlich, pp. 59–60; Robert Weimann, *Shakespeare and the Popular Tradition in the Theater: Studies in the Social Dimension of Dramatic Form and Function*, ed. Robert Schwartz (Baltimore: Johns Hopkins University Press, 1978), p. 235.

World, and the New World that may have ushered in the age of capitalism. The same goes for *The Tempest* as a whole, which combines Italian characters and an observation of the classical unities with an American theme.

But the bourgeois world, in all its ambivalence, does not mark the visionary limits of what perhaps remains a prebourgeois point of view. The utopianism of the play goes even further, hinting at the antithesis of capitalism and the abolition of class society, at the formation of a postbourgeois world. Ariel's certain and Caliban's possible freedom at the close of the play more than merely suggest the end of colonial domination, a position also favored by the radicals during the revolution. Compare, for example, many of the statements quoted above from the Virginia pamphlets with the attack on "our Indian merchants" in *Tyranipocrit Discovered*:

> but consider their practices, and the profit that we have by their double dealing, first in robbing of the poor Indians of that which God hath given them, and then in bringing it home to us. . . . although their dealing concerning the Indians' goods be bad, yet they deal worser with their persons: for they either kill them, which is bad, or make them slaves, which is worse. I know not what to say concerning such impious proceedings with them poor innocent people.[122]

More striking still, in act 2, scene 1, Gonzalo posits a society without hierarchy, private property, or labor, loosely based, perhaps, on the medieval peasant village and the communal aspirations of its inhabitants. These sentiments echoed through the German revolutionary tradition, most notably at Münster in 1534, where the Anabaptists proclaimed that "all things were to be in common, there would be no private property and nobody was to do any more work, but simply trust in God."[123] Gonzalo's command that nature produce ample food for the population also looks forward, however, to Mary Cary's still more extravagant prediction in 1651 that poor believers "shall have abundance of gold and silver" on earth.[124] But as Sebastian and Antonio maliciously observe, royal edict initiates Gonzalo's utopia. The same contradiction underlies More's *Utopia*; it testifies if not to the intractable realities of sixteenth- and seventeenth-century Europe, then at least to the ideological parameters of the civilization, which prevented Renaissance intellectuals from even imagining a plausible historical inception for such a society. The harsh treatment accorded Gonzalo's vision may cap-

---

[122]*Tyranipocrit Discovered*, quoted in Hill, p. 337.
[123]Quoted in Burke, p. 175.
[124]Mary Cary, quoted in Hill, p. 322.

ture the political disillusion about the governance of the Virginia colony that had begun to set in by 1609 or 1610. Earlier discussions reveal the democratic and utopian enthusiasms that the settlement aroused. The Council of Virginia's *True and Sincere Declaration* (1610), however, blamed the food shortage at Jamestown on "the Idlenesse and bestiall slouth, of the common sort, who were active in nothing but adhering to factions and parts. . . . no man would acknowledge a superior: nor could from this headlesse and vnbrideled multitude, bee any thing expected, but disorder and ryott."[125] Other documents of the time insisted on the necessity of imposing a strict hierarchy on the colonists.

Gonzalo's scheme also cuts against the overall ideological thrust of *The Tempest*. Prospero's success depends on hard work, on the conscious mastery of nature. The geographical contrast between *La vida es sueño* and *The Tempest* thus finds a parallel in the opposing valuations of science in the two plays, of Basilio's astrology[126] and Prospero's magic. Yet to recognize that the scientific enterprise retained a certain ambivalence even in England, one need only recall the famous lines:

> But this rough magic
> I here abjure; . . .
>
> . . . I'll break my staff,
> Bury it certain fadoms in the earth,
> And deeper than did ever plummet sound
> I'll drown my book.
>
> (5.1.50–57)

After the Restoration of 1660, the mastery of nature proceeded apace, but only with the concomitant rejection of popular magic. During the revolutionary decades, however, science and magic developed together as part of an often radical program of social, economic, religious, and educational change.[127] Similarly, the recent discovery of the New World helped justify a revolutionary belief in the continuous revelation of truth. For John Goodwin, writing in 1642, "if so great and considerable a part of the world as America is . . . was yet unknown to all the world besides for so many generations together: well may it be conceived, not only that some but many truths, yea and those of main concernment and importance, may yet be unknown."[128]

---

[125]Council of Virginia, *A True and Sincere Declaration of the Purpose and Ends of the Plantation Begun in Virginia* (London, 1610), sigs. B3ᵛ–C2ʳ.
[126]Arroyo, *Calderón: Pensamiento y teatro* (Santander: Sociedad Menéndez Pelayo, 1982), pp. 76–78.
[127]Hill, pp. 288–95.
[128]John Goodwin, quoted in Hill, p. 367.

In *The Tempest*, Prospero's prototechnological magic offers precisely the mechanism by which Gonzalo's dream might someday come into being. The fusion of feudal communism and bourgeois science points beyond the two main modes of production of Shakespeare's England and indeed of postclassical European history as a whole. Although *The Tempest* does not effect this fusion, the very copresence of two such radical alternatives to Jacobean society testifies to the inherent utopian tendency of the play. As Raymond Williams has argued, "the notion of creativity, decisively extended to art and thought by Renaissance thinkers, should then, indeed, have a specific affinity with Marxism." And a little earlier: "The notion of self-creation, extended to civil society and to language by pre-Marxist thinkers, was radically extended by Marxism to the basic work processes and thence to a deeply (creatively) altered physical world and a self-created humanity."[129] *The Tempest* belongs to this tradition of thought. Probably the last work that Shakespeare composed unaided exploits the full possibilities of romance form, finding in the materials of the present the shape of the future. *La vida es sueño*, by contrast, insists on the limits characteristic of Spanish drama, particularly after 1620. Yet as the peninsula's religious plays suggest, England possessed no monopoly on utopian scenarios. In both countries intrigue tragedy and romance, however illusory their visions, made way for the future, either negatively or positively. On the verge of eclipse, the public theater intimated solutions to the very conflicts that were then determining its own historical supersession.

[129]Raymond Williams, *Marxism and Literature* (Oxford: Oxford University Press, 1977), p. 206.

# CONCLUSION

In 1780 Ulrich Bräker, a poor Swiss peasant, composed a manuscript on Shakespeare that records his enthusiastic opinion of the plays. In general he understood and liked best whatever he could connect most directly to his own experience. For instance, although he concluded that Prospero and Miranda were "perhaps the finest" figures in *The Tempest*, he found them rather "too fine." On the other hand, he appreciated the mixture of comedy and tragedy in *1 Henry IV*, loved the nurse in *Romeo and Juliet*, approved of the mechanicals in *A Midsummer Night's Dream*, had heard his fellow peasants talk like Jack Cade in *2 Henry VI*, had met both Gobbos from *The Merchant of Venice*, and was struck by the three kinds of madness—Lear's, the fool's, and Poor Tom's—dramatized in Poor Tom's hovel. His favorite work was *Hamlet*, from which he singled out the gravediggers scene. Indeed, Eric Blackall, whose findings are summarized in this paragraph, suggests that a response to Shakespeare like Bräker's had occurred at least once before. Bräker "seems to me in some ways to be a counterpart of the Elizabethan groundling. . . . What I have been describing is a confrontation similar, I believe, to that which took place in the Globe Theater." Bräker's analysis obviously had its blind spots. But it was alert and sympathetic to the popular dimensions of Shakespearean dramaturgy, disliked by many of his contemporaries. Schiller, for instance, did not care for the witches or porter of *Macbeth*.[1]

This book has attempted to combine the perspective of Bräker with the perspective of Schiller. The public theaters of Renaissance England and Spain offered possibilities for the interaction of popular and learned culture that were not available on the stage elsewhere. As the

[1] Eric A. Blackall, "Shakespeare as Viewed by a Swiss Peasant of the Eighteenth Century," *Proceedings of the American Philosophical Society* 117 (1973): 112–16. The quotations from Bräker appear on p. 114, those from Blackall on p. 116.

preceding chapters have sought to demonstrate, such an assertion has advantages over alternative models. In particular, it helps specify the conditions of possibility of the drama; the character of the plays and through them the character of their age; and, finally, the pattern of their reception, as historical record and political potential. On this view, although the genesis, structure, and impact of a Renaissance play are far from congruent, they are correlative; they are dialectically linked.[2] And the premise of such claims is, to quote Fredric Jameson, that "the human adventure is one; . . . a single great collective story; . . . for Marxism, the collective struggle to wrest a realm of Freedom from a realm of Necessity."[3]

But the English and Spanish public theaters raise a distinctive problem for the procedure adopted here. This matter may be approached by noting that Renaissance dramatic theory was generally incapable of grasping the nature or significance of Renaissance dramatic practice in these two countries. The failure was largely a consequence of an inability to theorize the social heterogeneity, and especially the popular elements, that gave the drama its unique quality and that make it an attractive subject for a radical, activist-oriented criticism. The distance between Renaissance and Marxist theory may not be as great as this formulation suggests, however. In both instances the difficulty is the gap between theory and practice. Marxist theory, whatever its intentions, will tend to reproduce the defects of Renaissance theory whenever it remains isolated, as it currently does in the United States, from a now scarcely existent larger contemporary movement for social and political transformation capable of once again uniting learned and popular culture, and thereby both justifying a project like the current one and providing much of this drama with its most resonant context at least since the seventeenth century.

[2]Robert Weimann, *Structure and Society in Literary History: Studies in the History and Theory of Historical Criticism* (Charlottesville: University Press of Virginia, 1976).
[3]Fredric Jameson, *The Political Unconscious: Narrative as a Socially Symbolic Act* (Ithaca, N.Y.: Cornell University Press, 1981), p. 19.

# INDEX

A., T.: *The Massacre of Money,* 199
Absolutism: defined, 19–20, 83, 104–5; control of theater, 107–8, 126, 151–52, 155–56, 265, 267–68, 271–72. *See also* Censorship; Closing of theaters; Patronage of theater
Acosta, Christóbal: *Tratado en loor de las mugeres,* 188
Acting companies: Spain, 19, 134, 175, 176, 178–79, 267, 274, 278; France, 73, 74, 105, 106, 107, 116; Italy, 103, 167. *See also Commedia dell'arte*
—England: 19, 27–28, 129, 153, 161, 175–79, 265–70 passim, 274, 275; Queen's Men, 153, 155, 161, 176, 266; Essex's Men, 161; Leicester's Men, 161; Lincoln's Men, 161; Sussex's Men, 161; Warwick's Men, 161; Chamberlain's Men, 161, 176, 265, 269, 302; Admiral's Men, 173, 176; boys, 266, 268–69; King's Men, 266, 269, 270, 274, 275, 338, 387; Prince Henry's Men, 266, 270; Children of Paul's, 269; Children of the Chapel, 269; Children of the King's Revels, 269; Lady Elizabeth's Men, 269, 270, 274; Children of the Queen's Revels, 269, 274, 338; Duke of York's Men, 270; Prince Charles's Men, 270, 274; Queen Anne's Men, 270, 274
*Adam,* 51, 53, 54–56, 61
Adam de la Halle, 64; *Le jeu de la feuillée,* 61–63; *Le jeu de Robin et Marion,* 61
Adorno, Theodor, 27, 331
Aguilar, Gaspar de, 170; *La fuerza del interés,* 191; *El mercader amante,* 190, 211–18, 243, 245
Alba, dukes of, 130, 153–54, 154–55
Alfonso X: *Estoria de España,* 242
Alleyn, Edward, 175, 177
Almela, Diego de: *Valerio,* 242

Althusser, Louis, 27, 62, 145, 186
America. *See* New World
Anabaptists, 336, 402. *See also* Reformation
Anderson, Perry, 20, 33, 83, 102, 119, 120, 139, 141, 147, 180
Annunciation mystery play (Byzantium), 79
*Antichrist,* 53–56 passim
*Arden of Feversham,* 315, 317
Aretino, 96; *La cortigiana,* 99, 298; *La Orazia,* 102–3, 112
Argensola, Lupercio Leonardo de, 160, 184, 378; *Isabela,* 222, 374
Ariosto, 98; *La Lena,* 99
Aristotelian theorists, 357
Armada, Spanish, 142, 144
Arras, theater of, 59–63, 68
Artisan theater, 20, 179–85, 189–90, 211, 221, 265, 279, 322
Audiences: Spain, 19, 127–28, 130, 167–70, 249, 272, 278; England, 19, 166–70, 196, 270–75 passim, 302–3; medieval, 35, 49–50, 58, 68; Italy, 98, 99, 103; France, 106, 107
Augustinianism, 147
Austrian theater: liturgical, 48; 16th–17th century, 85
*Auto de los reyes magos,* 51, 53–54
*Auto sacramental,* 17, 126, 127, 153, 166, 379

*Babio,* 52
Bacon, Francis, 398
Baker, Will, 15
Bakhtin, Mikhail, 27, 61
Bale, John: *King John,* 129
Ball, John, 71
Bances y López–Candamo, Francisco Antonio de: *El esclavo en grillos de oro,* 311, 313
Baroque, 383–84

# Index

Barthes, Roland, 113

Beaumont, Francis, and John Fletcher, 385; *A King and No King*, 350; *The Knight of the Burning Pestle*, 290; *The Maid's Tragedy*, 370, 371, 392; *Philaster*, 374, 385, 392

Belcari, Feo: *La rappresentazione de Abramo ed Isac*, 72

Bell, Thomas: *The Specvlation of Vsurie*, 197, 201

Belmonte Bermúdez, Luis de, 398

Benedict of Aniane, 42–43

Benjamin, Walter, 121, 384

Berkenhead, John, 351

Bibliography and textual criticism, 22–24, 343–44, 377

Bindoff, S. T., 137

Bisbe y Vidal, Fructuoso, 274

Blackall, Eric, 405

Bodel, Jehan, 63; *Le jeu de Saint-Nicolas*, 61–62

Botero, Giovanni, 203

Bourgeoisie and theater, 84–85, 91–96, 98–99, 157–66, 171–73, 194–95, 212–13, 235–37, 253, 267, 278–79, 284, 299–301, 307–9, 397–98. *See also* Tragedy, bourgeois

Bowers, Fredson, 23–24

Bräker, Ulrich, 405

Braudel, Fernand, 138

Brecht, Bertolt, 29, 62

Bredero, G. A.: *The Spanish Brabanter*, 96

Brome, Richard, 398; *The Antipodes*, 275–76, 390, 397; *A Jovial Crew*, 390, 391, 396–97; *The Northern Lass*, 287, 288, 291

Bruno, Giordano, 98; *Il candelaio*, 99, 298

Buckingham, duke of, 257

Burbage, James, 153, 164, 167, 269

Burbage, Richard, 175, 177, 269

Burghley, Lord, 158, 161

Burke, Peter, 18, 112

Burton, Robert, 398

Bush, Douglas, 25–26

Byzantium: history, 78, 79, 80; theater, 78–81

Calderón de la Barca, Pedro, 15, 22, 30, 98, 103, 271, 273, 278, 398; romances, 384–91 passim; *El alcalde de Zalamea*, 315, 316, 317, 321, 363; *Argenis y Poliarco*, 387; *Dar tiempo al tiempo*, 387; *En la vida todo es verdad y todo mentira*, 385–91 passim; *Hado y divisa de Leonido y Marfisa*, 385–90 passim; *El mágico prodigioso*, 375, 376, 381–82; *El médico de su honra*, 361, 362; *El príncipe constante*, 374, 380–81; *La vida es sueño*, 384–91 passim, 395–96, 398, 403, 404

Calvinism, 100, 129

Camos, Fray Marco Antonio de, 212, 378–79; *Microcosmia*, 243

Capitalism: early history of, 82; defined, 162–63

Carnival, 61, 73, 189, 193

Carolingian empire and liturgical theater, 40–43, 47, 48, 49, 81

Cartwright, William, 351

Cary, Mary, 402

Castillo, Iulian del: *Historia de los reyes Godos*, 242

Castro, Guillén de, 171, 398; *El amor constante*, 229; *Los mal casados de Valencia*, 192, 194, 285; *1 Las mocedades del Cid*, 314; *2 Las mocedades del Cid*, 311

Catalan theater: liturgical, 44, 45, 46, 49; 14th–15th century, 65, 66, 72

Censorship, 19, 126, 155–56, 302

Cervantes, 170, 171, 231; *El cerco de Numancia*, 223

Cespedes y Meneses, Gonçalo, 365

Chambers, E. K., 155

Chapman, George, 268, 285, 366, 370; *All Fools*, 291, 292; *Bussy D'Ambois*, 359, 367; *Caesar and Pompey*, 304, 305, 359; *The Revenge of Bussy D'Ambois*, 359, 367; *The Widow's Tears*, 290

Charlemagne, 42

Charles I (England), 225, 257, 258, 259, 262, 275, 352

Charles V (Spain), 122, 123

Chettle, Henry, 159, 170, 171. *See also* Munday, Anthony, Thomas Dekker, Henry Chettle, and William Shakespeare

Chicago neo-Aristotelianism, 22–23

Christian Terence, 379

*Christos paschon* (Byzantium), 79

Ciceronian prose, 210

Civil War. *See* English Revolution

Cixila, bishop of Toledo, 240

Claramonte, Andrés de, 171

Closing of theaters, 17, 37, 152, 157, 166, 264, 265, 274, 276–78

Clown, 178, 179, 210–11, 266, 292, 339, 351. *See also* Fool

Cluny, monastic reforms of, 45–46, 47

Coello y Ochoa, Antonio, 273, 398

Cofradía de la Pasión, 152, 165

*Cofradías*, 166, 268

Colet, John, 146

*Comedia* (Spain): defined, 17; *a lo divino*, 126; *de capa y espada*, 187, 284, 380; *de figurón*, 285–87; *de privanza*, 313

Comedy: popular, 18, 19, 61–63, 73–76, 90–91, 96, 99–100, 105, 106, 107, 116–20, 125, 128, 132–35, 189–95 passim, 209–11, 217–18, 253, 287, 292–93, 297–99; intrigue, 18, 19, 193–94, 209; satiric, 18, 20, 96, 99, 116–20, 282–301, 305, 339, 343, 344, 357, 364; romantic, 18, 20, 100–101, 127, 133, 187–218, 252–53, 283–84, 288,

Comedy (*continued*)
292, 311; Roman, 18, 128, 130, 182, 187,
292, 293; farce, 19, 74, 89, 99–100, 105,
106, 107, 116, 117, 119, 128, 132–33; in
Arras, 61–63; 14th–15th century, 73, 76;
neoclassical, 90–91, 96, 99–100, 116–20,
124–25, 130–35 passim, 195, 283,
292–301; Dantean, 128, 209, 378. *See also*
*Fastnachtsspiel*; *Sottie*
*Commedia* (Italy): *erudita*, 103; *dell'arte*, 103,
116, 167, 181, 385; *grave*, 385
Common law, 144, 206, 207, 209–10, 258
*Comuneros*, revolt of, 123
Coppe, Abiezer, 353, 354, 355
Corneille, 98, 103, 107; heroic drama, 108,
113, 115, 116, 382; *Le Cid*, 109–11, 112,
314, 329; *Horace*, 111–13, 116, 303
*Cornish Ordinalia, The*, 72
Cornish theater, 72
Corpus Christi plays. *See* Mystery play; *Auto*
*sacramental*
*Corrales*, defined, 159. *See also* Spain; Theaters
Counter-Reformation, 85, 90, 100, 101, 102,
121, 127, 188, 209, 313, 375, 387, 389
*Courtois d'Arras*, 61
Croatian theater, 86
Cromwell, Oliver, 260, 353
*Crónica de Alfonso III*, 241
Cueva, Juan de la, 231; *El infamador*, 229, 368;
*Los siete infantes de Lara*, 222, 227
Cultural homogeneity, 19, 90, 121, 141
Czech theater: 14th–15th century, 65, 66;
16th–17th century, 85

*Daniel* (Beauvais), 53
Danish theater, 89
Danson, Lawrence, 195, 196
Davenant, William: *News from Plymouth*,
287–88, 359, 360
Day, John, 268
Dekker, Thomas, 171, 222, 271, 274; *Old*
*Fortunatus*, 190; *The Shoemakers' Holiday*,
191. *See also* Munday, Anthony, Thomas
Dekker, Henry Chettle, and William
Shakespeare
Dekker, Thomas, John Ford, and William
Rowley: *The Witch of Edmonton*, 315, 316,
317
Dekker, Thomas, and Philip Massinger: *The*
*Virgin Martyr*, 375, 378
Della Porta, Giambattista, 98; *Gli duoi fratelli*
*rivali*, 100–101, 114, 116
Derrida, Jacques, 23
Diamante, Juan Bautista, 278
Dickens, A. G., 146
Díez Borque, José María, 26–27, 30
Diggers, 303, 350, 352, 354. *See also* English
Revolution
Digges, Leonard, 15

Dollimore, Jonathan, 26
Doran, Madeleine, 26
Doubling of parts, 128, 177
Dramatists, 19, 98, 103, 130, 131, 170–74,
271, 273, 274, 278
Dryden, John, 382; *An Essay of Dramatic Poesy*,
15, 290
Dutch. *See* Low Countries

Eastern Europe: theater, 48, 49, 65, 66,
84–88; history, 83
Eagleton, Terry, 171
Edward II, 233
Eliot, T. S., 26
Elizabeth I, 126, 129, 137–44 passim, 152,
153, 154, 161, 166, 176, 183, 233, 237, 256,
257, 388
Encina, Juan del: *Aucto del repelón*, 132;
*Eglogas*, 129–30, 131, 132
Engels, Friedrich, 335
England: theater, 17, 38, 46, 51–56 passim,
66–73 passim, 124–29, 131, 132, 150–85,
264–81; history, 120–23, 136–50, 255–60
English Revolution: 27–28, 121, 147, 162,
255, 256, 258–60, 348, 367; radicals in, 27,
76, 235, 352–56, 397; and theater, 277,
280–81; and *King Lear*, 348, 349–56
*Entremés*, 17
Erasmus, Desiderius, 145, 146
Erbery, William, 353, 355, 356
Essex, earl of, 183
Essex Rebellion, 289
*Estrella de Sevilla, La*, 361–63
Euripides, 115
*Everyman*, 70

Familists, 336, 352
*Famous Victories of Henry V, The*, 221, 223
Farce. *See* Comedy
*Fastnachtsspiel*, 73, 74, 75, 90, 91. *See also*
Comedy
Ferdinand and Isabella, 120–21, 123, 322,
323, 324
Fernández, Lucas, 130, 131; *Farsa o cuasi*
*comedia de una doncella, un pastor y un caba-*
*llero*, 132
Feudalism, defined, 33
Fifth Monarchists, 353
Fletcher, John, 351. *See also* Beaumont,
Francis, and John Fletcher; Shakespeare,
William, and John Fletcher
Folz, Hans: *Ein Fasnachtspil von einem*
*Pawrngericht*, 74; *Ein Spil von konig Salomon*
*und Markolfo*, 74
Fool, 332, 333, 336, 337, 338–39, 344, 347,
352. *See also* Clown
Ford, John: *The Broken Heart*, 371; *Perkin*
*Warbeck*, 371, 374, 397; '*Tis Pity She's a*
*Whore*, 371. *See also* Dekker, Thomas, John
Ford, and William Rowley

# Index

Foster, George, 354
Foucault, Michel, 27
France: theater, 15, 16, 43–49 passim, 51–56 passim, 59–63, 65, 69–74 passim, 104, 105–20; history, 40–46 passim, 59–60, 104–8 passim, 113–16
Frankfurt school, 331
French Revolution, 119
Frye, Northrop, 391–92

Gammer Gurton's Needle, 125, 132
Ganassa, Alberto, 153, 158, 159, 171, 179
Garnier, Robert, 103, 105
Gascoigne, George, 103; Supposes, 125
Gates, Thomas, 400
Gens nouveaux, Les, 74, 75
Germania of Valencia, Second, 348
Germany: history, 40–48 passim, 67, 86–87, 89–90
—theater: liturgical, 43–49 passim; 12th century, 51, 52, 53; 14th–15th century, 65, 67–68, 71, 73, 74; 17th century, 86–87; 16th century, 89–91
Girard, René, 26
Góngora y Argote, Luis de, 346
Goodwin, John, 403
Gorze, monastic reforms of, 45–47
Gosson, Stephen, 184
Gracioso, 135, 179, 182, 184, 267, 292, 315, 381
Gramsci, Antonio, 18, 28–29, 30, 145, 186
Granada, rebellion of 1568, 138
Gran comedia de los famosos hechos de Mudarra, La, 222, 227
Gray, Robert: A Good Speed to Virginia, 400
Greek tragedy, 383
Greenblatt, Stephen, 26–27, 145
Greene, Robert, 170, 171, 222, 353; Friar Bacon and Friar Bungay, 191; The Scottish History of James IV, 190. See also Lodge, Thomas, and Robert Greene
Greg, W. W., 23–24
Grindletonians, 352
Grotius, Hugo, 93
Gryphius, Andreas: Papinianus, 86–87
Guarini, Giambattista, 386: Il pastor fido, 100
Guerra di Carnevale e quaresima, La, 73
Gunpowder Plot, 289

Harbage, Alfred, 26, 271, 275
Hardy, Alexandre, 105–6, 107; Mariamne, 105–6; Scédase, 106
Harrington, John 158
Harris, John, 350, 352
Hayes, T. Wilson, 354
Hegelian dialectics, 196, 389
Henrietta Maria, 275
Henry V, 122
Henry VII, 120
Henry VIII, 121–22, 167

Henslowe, Philip, 164, 173
Herod (Fleury), 53–54
Heroic drama, 20, 108–13, 115, 116, 282, 310–15, 382
Hessische Weihnachtsspiel, Das, 67
Heywood, John: Four PP, 128–29; Johan Johan, 128; Play of the Weather, The, 125
Heywood, Thomas, 171, 222, 271, 274; A Challenge for Beauty, 358, 385; 1 The Fair Maid of the West, 191, 374; The Four Prentices of London, 192; A Woman Killed with Kindness, 315–18 passim
Hilarius: Lazarus, 52
Hill, Christopher, 28, 151, 334
History. See individual countries
Hoffman, Melchior, 336
Holinshed, Raphael, 233
Holland. See Low Countries
Honor, code of, 192–93, 312–13
Hooft, P. C.: Baeto, 93–96 passim
Horace, 158, 293; Beatus ille, 247
Horkheimer, Max, 331
Hosley, Richard, 167
Howgill, Francis, 355
Hrosvita, 81
Humanism, 18, 85–90 passim, 97, 124–32 passim, 141, 145–46, 158, 188, 219, 378. See also Neoclassicism; Renaissance
Hundred Years' War, 122
Hungarian theater, 48 n. 54, 85
Hunsdon, Lord, 161
Hunter, G. K., 200
Hussite rebellion, 65, 71

Iceland, theater, 89
Ildefonso, Saint: De virginitate perpetua Sanctae Mariae adversus tres infideles liber unicus, 240
Independents, 225, 289. See also English Revolution
Indies. See New World
Inquisition, 127, 139, 142, 313
Italy: history, 96–98
—theater: 16th century, 18, 96–104, 182; liturgical, 43–48 passim; 12th century, 51, 53; 14th–15th century, 66–67, 71, 72, 73

Jack Straw, The Life and Death of, 223, 227–28
James I, 256, 257, 258, 266, 274, 275, 302, 308, 388
Jameson, Fredric, 28, 186, 356, 406
Jansenism, 115, 146–47
Jardine, Lisa, 26
Jauss, Hans Robert, 345–46
Jesuits, 85, 157
Johnson, Robert: Nova Britannia, 400
Jones, Inigo, 272, 273
Jones, Marion, 155
Jonson, Ben, 98, 103, 171, 174, 273–76 passim, 283, 292–301, 397, 398; satiric comedy, 96, 99, 285, 303, 397; The Alchemist,

Jonson, Ben (*continued*)
292–300 passim, 305, 374; *Bartholomew Fair*, 271, 288, 292–95 passim, 297–99, 300; *The Case is Altered*, 355; *Epicene*, 290; *Every Man in His Humour*, 287, 291, 299; *Every Man out of His Humour*, 291, 299; *Sejanus His Fall*, 298, 303–4, 305, 314, 359, 364; *Volpone*, 291, 293, 294–95, 297, 299, 300, 305
*Joseph* (Laon), 53
Julian, Saint: *Beati Hildefonsi elogium*, 240; *Historia rebellionis Pauli adversus Wambam Gothorum regem*, 240
Jump, John D., 377
Juvenal, 293, 303

Kahn, Coppélia, 26
Kautsky, Karl, 335
*King Leir, The True Chronicle History of,* 338
Knights, L. C., 26, 198
Kochanowski, Jan: *The Dismissal of the Grecian Envoys*, 87–88
Kyd, Thomas, 135, 170, 171, 253; *The Spanish Tragedy*, 228, 229, 230, 366, 374

*Lancelot of Denmark*, 76–77
Langley, Francis, 164
Laud, Archbishop, 350
*Lauda drammatica*, 66
*Lauda in decollatione Sancti Johannis Baptiste*, 71
*Lazarillo de Tormes*, 96
Lea, K. M., 103
Leavis, F. R., 26
Lee, Nathaniel, 382
Lenin, V. I., 346
Lepanto, battle of, 138
Lerma, duke of, 262
Levellers, 27, 260, 278, 280, 281, 303, 350, 353, 354, 355. *See also* English Revolution
Lilburne, John, 355
Lilly, William, 353
Liturgical theater, 34, 35, 39–56, 65, 77–81 passim
Lodge, Thomas, 170, 171
Lodge, Thomas, and Robert Greene: *A Looking Glass for London and England*, 190
López de Castro, Diego: *Marco Antonio y Cleopatra*, 231
Lotti, Cosme, 272, 273
Louis the Pious, 42
Low Countries: theater, 48, 69, 76–77, 91–96, 99; history, 89–90, 91–92
Lucas, Bishop of Túy: *Chronicon mundi*, 242
Luján, Micaela de, 171
Lukács, Georg, 21, 29, 62–63, 186, 224, 299–300, 316, 352, 377
Luther, Martin, 146, 335, 377, 378. *See also* Reformation
Lyly, John, 125, 154, 171
Lynch, John, 137

Machiavelli, Niccolò, 25, 98; *La mandragola*, 99
Machiavellianism, 236
Madrid, City of, *Memorial*, 158–59, 162
Main and Bye Plot, 289
*Maistre Pierre Pathelin*, 74
*Mankind*, 70
Manrique, Gómez: *Representación del nacimiento de Nuestro Señor*, 66
Maravall, José Antonio, 26–27, 30
Marlowe, Christopher, 25–26, 98, 120, 126, 130, 135, 136, 170, 171, 176, 252, 275, 293, 383; *Dr. Faustus*, 23–24, 128, 229, 237, 374, 376–78; *Edward II*, 220, 223, 224, 228, 231, 232–39, 243, 245, 250, 311; *The Jew of Malta*, 206, 229, 237, 238, 366; *Tamburlaine*, 231, 237, 238, 353
Marprelate controversy, 156
Marston, John, 268, 366, 372; *Antonio and Mellida*, 289; *Antonio's Revenge*, 364, 367; *The Dutch Courtesan*, 289; *The Malcontent*, 289, 338–42
Martin, Saint, 247
Marx, Karl, 163, 165, 173, 175, 180, 203, 204, 211, 296, 299, 300, 308, 335
Marxist cultural theory: and contemporary politics, 9, 26–27, 29–30, 31, 356, 406; explanatory power of, 9, 31; heterogeneity of, 21; totalization, 21–31, 63, 68, 344–45; critique of organicism, 26, 29, 62–63, 69–70, 140; (counter) hegemony, 28–29, 35, 41, 62–63, 70, 77, 78, 84, 192, 224, 235, 294; ideological state apparatuses, 29, 35, 50; internal debates, 29, 62–63; ideology of form, 35 62, 68, 186, 206, 238; relative autonomy, 38, 68, 78; class consciousness, 62–63, 72, 186, 224; symptomatic reading, 186; commodity fetishism (reification), 186, 299–300; metacommentary, 186, 345; critique of instrumental reason, 331; and reception aesthetics, 346–47; and Renaissance theory, 404, 406
*Mary of Nijmeghen*, 69
Massinger, Philip, 274, 375; *The City Madam*, 290; *The Emperor of the East*, 352; *A New Way to Pay Old Debts*, 290; *The Roman Actor*, 376; *The Unnatural Combat*, 359–61, 364. *See also* Dekker, Thomas, and Philip Massinger
Medici, Lorenzo de': *La rappresentazione di San Giovanni e Paulo*, 67
Medieval history, 36–37, 40–44, 47, 56–58, 59, 63–65
Medieval towns: history, 56–58, 64–65
—theater, 34–39, 56–77, 78, 80; 14th–15th century, 63–77; secular, 73–77
Medwall, Henry: *Fulgens and Lucrece*, 125; *Nature*, 125
Melanchthon, Philipp, 145. *See also* Reformation
Mendicant clergy, 70–71
Mercado, Thomas de, 212

# Index

*Mestier et Marchandise,* 74, 75

Metford, J. C. J., 157

Middleton, Thomas, 274, 366, 371; *A Chaste Maid in Cheapside,* 271, 291, 292, 364; *A Game at Chess,* 275, 374, 375, 378, 379; *A Trick to Catch the Old One,* 289; *Women Beware Women,* 364, 365, 367, 371. *See also* Tourneur, Cyril, or Thomas Middleton

Middleton, Thomas, and William Rowley: *The Changeling,* 364; *A Fair Quarrel,* 385

*Mieulx que devant,* 74, 75

Milton, John, 56, 95, 351; *Paradise Lost,* 381

Mimic theater, 36–39, 78–79, 81

Miracle play, 69, 73

Mira de Amescua, Antonio: *El esclavo del demonio,* 376, 379, 380

Molière, 98, 103, 116–20; *L'avare,* 116; *La jalousie du Barbouillé,* 116; *Le mariage forcé,* 116; *Le médecin volant,* 116; *Le misanthrope,* 116; *Sganarelle, ou Le cocu imaginaire,* 116; *Le Tartuffe,* 116–20

Monroy, Cristóbal de: *Fuente Ovejuna,* 346–47, 348

*Monti de pietà,* 201

Moore, Jr., Barrington, 27

Morales, Ambrosio de: *Corónica general de España,* 242

Morality play, 70, 73, 91, 127–29, 190, 195, 218, 252, 283, 292, 378, 387

More, Thomas, 145, 398; *Utopia,* 402

*More Light Shining in Buckinghamshire,* 354

Moreto, Agustín de, 278, 398; *El desdén, con el desdén,* 286; *El lindo don Diego,* 286; *No puede ser el guardar una mujer,* 286, 292

Moretti, Franco, 350

Mosse, Miles, 198, 199

*Mucedorus,* 193

Muggletonians, 352

Mummers' Play (England), 73

Munday, Anthony, 170, 171; *The Downfall of Robert, Earl of Huntingdon,* 193

Munday, Anthony, Thomas Dekker, Henry Chettle, and William Shakespeare: *The Book of Sir Thomas More,* 223, 228

Münster, 336, 402

Mystery play, 66–73 passim, 79, 126–27, 145

Nashe, Thomas, 150, 158, 159, 171, 183, 358

National history play, 18, 20, 93–95, 108, 136–37, 150, 159, 183–84, 187, 218–52, 253, 301, 302, 306–15 passim, 358

*Nativity* play (Benediktbeuern), 51, 52

Neoclassicism: defined, 17–20 passim, 25–30 passim. *See also* Comedy; Humanism; Renaissance; Tragedy

Neoplatonism, 187–88, 209, 387

Netherlands. *See* Low Countries

New Criticism, 22–23, 383

New World, 122, 123, 138, 142, 147–49, 227, 256, 260, 261–62; in drama, 295–96, 397–404

Norfolk peasant revolt, 126

Norton, Thomas. *See* Sackville, Thomas, and Thomas Norton

Norway, theater, 89

*Novella,* 197

Ocampo, Florián de: *Cronica de España,* 242

Oedipal conflict, 386, 389

*Officium pastorum,* 45, 50

Olivares, count-duke of, 262, 263, 365

Opposition to theater, 26, 157–62

Osorio, Elena, 171

Ostrogoths, 37

Otto I, 47

Otway, Thomas, 382

Overton, Richard, 350, 353, 355

Parcellization of sovereignty, 33–35, 38–39, 40, 41, 53, 63, 77, 80, 81, 84

Parker, Alexander A., 26

*Particulares,* 153, 268, 272, 388

*Passion* (Benediktbeuern), 51, 52, 53

*Passion du Palatinus, La,* 69, 72

*Passione e resurrezione del Colosseo, La,* 67

*Passion* (Montecassino), 51

*Passion Provençale, La,* 69, 72

*Passion* scenario (Cyprus), 79, 80

*Passion* (Wales), 72

Pastoral, 61, 100, 106, 132–35, 153–55, 189–90, 193–94, 207–8, 209–10, 222, 239–52, 284, 319, 384–404. *See also* Romance; Tragicomedy

Patronage of theater, 19, 37, 106, 107, 130, 131, 153–56, 265–74 passim

Peasant play (Spain), 18, 20, 239–52, 282, 315–27, 333, 337, 344–49 passim, 356, 363, 382, 384

Peasants' Rebellion (England), 71, 76, 356

Peasants' Revolt (Germany), 335, 336

Peasant theater, medieval, 34, 35, 36–39, 73, 77, 78, 79

Peele, George, 170, 171; *The Arraignment of Paris,* 154; *The Old Wives Tale,* 193

*Peregrinus* (Beauvais), 52

Pérez de Montalbán, Juan, 398

Petrarch, 320

Philip II, 138–42 passim, 148, 149, 153, 158, 159, 165, 166, 222, 242, 256

Philip III, 256, 262, 265, 268, 279, 357, 368

Philip IV, 262, 272, 357, 369

Plautus, 182, 187, 293

Players. *See* Acting companies

Playgoers. *See* Audiences

Playhouses. *See* Theaters

*Play of the Furnace* (Russia), 79

Playwrights. *See* Dramatists

Plutarch, 106

Poland: history, 87–88; theater, 87–88
Polymetric system, 217, 245–49
Popular–learned synthesis, 170–71; England and Spain, 17–19, 22, 25, 31; medieval, 34, 56, 63, 68, 71, 75
Popular theater, early medieval, 36–39
Popular tradition: defined, 17–20 passim, 25–30 passim. *See also* Comedy; Peasant play; Peasant theater; Popular theater; Tragedy
Porter, Henry, 171; *1 The Two Angry Women of Abingdon*, 191
Poststructuralism, 23, 26–27
*Pou d'acquest*, 74, 75
Preston, Thomas: *Cambyses*, 129
Pring-Mill, R. D. F., 369
*Prophets* (Laon), 53–55, 81
Protestantism. *See* Reformation
Psychological complexity, 51–52, 95, 111, 113, 146–47, 178, 189, 194–95, 221, 238, 244, 288–89, 307, 309, 334, 360, 366, 378
Puppet theater, 79
Puritans, 142, 144, 188, 199, 258, 260, 289; hostility to theater, 145, 157–61 passim, 276, 277, 350; sympathy for theater, 161, 191, 280, 350, 364. *See also* Reformation

Quakers, 354, 355
*Quem quaeritis in praesepe*, 44–45
*Quem quaeritis in sepulchro*, 39, 43, 45, 46, 49, 50
Quevedo, Francisco de, 284

Rabelais, 27
Rabkin, Norman, 208, 209
Racine, Jean Baptiste, 98, 108, 113–16, 146, 382; *Athalie*, 113–14, 115; *Phèdre*, 94, 114, 115–16, 239
Ranters, 354, 355, 397
*Rappresentazione di Rosana, La*, 67
*Rare Triumphs of Love and Fortune*, 154
Rastell, John (?): *Gentleness and Nobility*, 125, 132
Rebellion: popular, 27–28, 39, 60, 63–66 passim, 69, 71, 75–76, 101 n. 51, 123, 126, 138, 145, 259–60, 277–81 passim, 303, 336, 348–49, 352–56; aristocratic, 64, 101 n. 51, 108, 113, 121, 126, 137–38, 148, 255–56, 258–59, 260, 263, 280–81; bourgeois, 76, 91–92, 94, 123, 258–59, 280–81. *See also* English Revolution
Rebellion of the North (England), 126, 137
Reception aesthetics, 23, 345–56
Reconquest (Spain), 164, 226, 227, 249, 251, 252
*Redentin Osterspiel, Das*, 67
Redford, John: *Wit and Science*, 125
Reformation, 121, 188; and theater, 46, 48, 86–87, 90, 121, 122, 126, 129, 146–47, 161; and Renaissance, 144–47, 307, 377–78; Lutheran, 145; radical, 335–37, 355, 356, 402
Religious theater: 12th century, 50–56; 14th–15th century, 65–73, 75–76. *See also* Liturgical theater; Tragedy
Renaissance: Carolingian, 41; 12th century, 52–53; defined, 84; Italian, 96–98. *See also* Humanism; Neoclassicism
*Respublica*, 125
Resurrection play (Catalonia), 65, 72
Revels, master of the, 155, 159
Rey de Artieda, Micer Andrés, 231; *Los amantes*, 228, 229
Ribner, Irving, 218
Richard II, 183
Richelieu, Cardinal, 107, 116
Ridolfi Plot, 137
Robin Hood, 38
Rojas Zorrilla, Francisco de, 273, 398; (?) *Del rey abajo, ninguno o El labrador más honrado*, 316, 320
Roman–Germanic synthesis, 33–36 passim, 40–44 passim, 58, 73, 80
Romance, 20, 76–77, 127, 155, 190, 218, 222, 253, 357, 384–404. *See also* Pastoral; Tragicomedy
*Romances*, 179, 242, 246, 248–49, 314, 315, 373
Rosenplüt, Hans (attrib.): *Des Turken Vasnachtspil*, 74, 75; *Vom Babst, Cardinal und von Bischoffen*, 74
Rowley, William. *See* Dekker, Thomas, John Ford, and William Rowley; Middleton, Thomas, and William Rowley
Rueda, Lope de, 134, 172; *Las aceitunas*, 134; *Comedia Armelina*, 134–35
Ruiz de Alarcón y Mendoza, Juan: *Ganar amigos*, 313; *La verdad sospechosa*, 286, 314
Russian formalism, 193
Russian theater, 79, 80, 85
Ruzante, 99–100; *Bilora*, 100; *Parlamento*, 100

Sachs, Hans, 90–91
Sackville, Thomas, and Thomas Norton: *Gorboduc*, 125, 126
*Sacra rappresentazione*, 66–67, 71, 72, 73, 375
Saint Gall, 43, 44
Saint Martial de Limoges, 43, 44
Saints' plays, 52, 67, 71
Salingar, Leo, 321
Salomon, Noël, 27, 316, 321
Sánchez, Miguel: *La guarda cuidadosa*, 193
Sánchez de Badajoz, Diego, 131, 134; *Farsa militar*, 133, 134
Sartre, Jean-Paul, 356
Scandinavia: theater, 48, 88–89; history, 88
Schiller, Freidrich von, 405
Schlegel, August Wilhelm, 16, 17, 187

# Index

*Scrutiny*, 26

*Seinte resureccion, La,* 53, 54

Seltzer, Daniel, 328

Semiotics, 23

Seneca, 93, 106, 126, 128, 135, 229–31, 304, 366, 368

Shakespeare, William, 9, 15, 30, 31, 98, 103, 126, 136, 151, 176, 196, 211, 281; and baroque, 384; blank verse, 246; classical heritage, 283, 293; court dramatist, 154; downstage monologue, 248; and Marlowe, 239, 378; member of acting company, 134, 161, 171, 175, 177, 266; national history play, 159, 220–28 passim, 252–53, 302, 308, 311, 345; plays of the 1590s, 199; preconditions of, 120, 123, 130, 135; reception of, 30, 345–56; romance, 127, 271, 384–404 passim; romantic comedy, 127, 182, 189–95 passim, 292; social background, 170; successors, 275–76; text, 22–23

—works: *All's Well That Ends Well,* 197, 285; *Antony and Cleopatra,* 302, 305, 310; *As You Like It,* 189, 194, 253, 389; *Comedy of Errors, The,* 253, 350; *Coriolanus,* 302, 303, 309, 310; *Cymbeline,* 270, 385, 386; *Hamlet,* 303–10 passim, 337, 350, 351, 366, 385, 401, 405; *1 Henry IV,* 221, 225–26, 233, 253, 302, 309, 328, 329, 405; *2 Henry IV,* 137, 221, 225–26, 253, 302, 309, 328; *Henry V,* 137, 221, 225, 226, 253, 265; *Henry VI,* 350; *2 Henry VI,* 223, 228, 405; *Henry VIII,* 270, 388; *Julius Caesar,* 265, 302–7 passim; *King John,* 136; *Love's Labour's Lost,* 154, 193; *Macbeth,* 93, 94, 95, 237, 305–10 passim, 328, 389, 405; *Measure for Measure,* 197, 285; *The Merry Wives of Windsor,* 154, 191; *A Midsummer-Night's Dream,* 154, 193, 405; *Much Ado about Nothing,* 192, 253; *Othello,* 305, 309, 310, 318, 328, 337, 389; *Pericles,* 385, 388; *Richard II,* 183, 225, 228, 237, 302; *Richard III,* 228, 237–38, 351; *Romeo and Juliet,* 220, 228, 229, 372, 405; *The Taming of the Shrew,* 191; *The Tempest,* 270, 384–91 passim, 398–405; *Timon of Athens,* 302–10 passim; *Titus Andronicus,* 220, 229; *Troilus and Cressida,* 302–10 passim; *Twelfth Night,* 192, 253; *The Two Gentlemen of Verona,* 193; *The Winter's Tale,* 270, 384–90 passim, 392–95, 397, 399. *See also* Munday, Anthony, Thomas Dekker, Henry Chettle, and William Shakespeare

—*King Lear,* 183; setting of, 302, 306; and satiric comedy, 305; as synthesis, 310; analyzed, 327–45; reception of, 345–56; popular culture in, 384, 395; and romance, 389; and madness, 405

—*The Merchant of Venice,* 214, 235, 245, 405; and law, 102; love and economics in, 188, 217; disguise in, 190; analyzed, 195–211; critique of romantic comedy in, 236, 284;

oppositional ideologies in, 243; as anticipation of problem comedies, 253

—tragedy, 20, 144, 202, 253, 311, 382; and satiric comedy, 285, 364; analyzed, 302–10; social relations in, 315, 352, 357, 367, 401; resolution of, 322, 371, 388; women in, 359, 383

Shakespeare, William, and John Fletcher: *The Two Noble Kinsmen,* 386

Shelley, Percy Bysshe, 381

Sheppard, Samuel: *The Joviall Crew,* 397

Shirley, James, 277; *The Lady of Pleasure,* 290; *The Traitor,* 371

Sidney, Philip, 158; *Arcadia,* 338, 339–40

Skelton, John: *Magnyfycence,* 128

Soliloquy, 146, 178, 211, 217–18, 246, 247, 248, 353, 378

Solís y Ribadeneyra, Antonio de, 273; *El doctor Carlino,* 286

*Son of Getron, The* (Fleury), 53

*Sottie,* 74–75. *See also* Comedy

Sources, dramatic, 115–16, 201, 234, 239, 240–43, 325, 338–42, 349, 377–78

Spain: theater, 17, 46–47, 49, 51–54 passim, 66, 124, 129–35, 150–85, 264–80; history, 120–23, 136–50, 212–13, 255–56, 260–64

Spanish Civil War, 349

Spenser, Edmund, 398

Spiritualists, 336. *See also* Reformation

Spitzer, Leo, 26

*Sponsus,* 52

Stalinism, 21

Stone, Lawrence, 259

Stubbes, Philip, 159

Sweden: theater, 48, 89

Swift, Jonathan: *Gulliver's Travels,* 298

Switzerland: theater, 43, 44, 45, 48, 49

Synthesis, dialectical. *See* Marxist cultural theory; Popular-learned synthesis; Roman-Germanic synthesis

Syria, Pedro de, 213

Tacitus, 93, 303

*Tanaweschel, Der,* 74

Tarlton, Richard, 177

Tárrega, Francisco: *El prado de Valencia,* 192

Tasso, Torquato, 98; *Aminta,* 100

Tate, Nahum: *King Lear,* 346, 347

Terence, 18, 128, 187, 293

Theater. *See individual countries*

Theaters: court, 17, 51, 85–90 passim, 98, 99, 100, 113, 124, 130–31, 153–55, 268, 272–73, 275, 278, 387–88; Spain, 17, 134, 164, 272, 278, 388; school, 85, 86, 89, 90, 92, 124; Low countries, 91, 92; France, 105, 106

—England: private, 17–18, 266, 268–69, 274, 275, 280, 289–91, 292, 301, 310, 388, 397; Theatre, 153, 164, 167; Swan, 164,

Theaters: England: private (continued)
270, 271; Rose, 164, 271; Fortune, 167,
265, 266, 270, 271, 274, 275, 278; Hope,
167, 270, 271, 274; Red Bull, 265, 266, 270,
271, 274, 275, 278; Globe, 265, 269, 270,
271, 274, 275, 281, 285, 302, 338, 392, 405;
Saint Paul's, 266; Blackfriars, 266, 269, 270,
275, 387, 388; Whitefriars, 269; Boar's
Head, 270, 271; Curtain, 270, 271; Phoenix, 274, 275, 278; Salisbury Court, 275,
278
Theatricality, 30, 35, 36, 189, 194
Theocritus, 386
Theodoric the Great, 37
Thirty Years' War, 86, 87, 262, 398
Three Children in the Furnace, The, 79
Timoneda, Juan de, 134; Aucto de la fee, 134
Tirso de Molina, 98; El burlador de Sevilla, 287,
365, 369, 370, 374; El condenado por
desconfiado, 376–77, 379, 380; Marta la
piadosa, 288–89, 365; La prudencia en la
mujer, 311, 313, 314; Santa Juana, 369; Tan
largo me lo fiáis, 365
Tolstoy, Leo, 346
Torres Naharro, Bartolomé de, 103; Ymenea,
130–34 passim
Totalization. See Marxist cultural theory
Tourneur, Cyril: The Atheist's Tragedy, 364,
367, 374–78 passim
Tourneur, Cyril, or Thomas Middleton: The
Revenger's Tragedy, 364, 366, 367, 370
Tragedia (Italy): di fin lieto, 102; sacra, 375
Tragedy, 150; bourgeois, 18, 20, 92–96, 106,
202, 315–19, 322; religious, 28, 67, 95–96,
374–82; neoclassical, 86–88, 95–96,
102–3, 105–6, 107, 108–16, 125–26,
301–5; and legitimacy, 93, 102, 108; popular, 106, 129, 239–52, 303, 309, 310,
315–19, 328, 332–39, 340, 345, 347–48,
352–56; intrigue, 218, 357–84; late
16th–century English and Spanish,
228–52, 254; early 17th–century English,
282, 301–10; classical, 383; baroque, 384.
See also Seneca; Shakespeare
Tragicomedy, 100, 102–3, 107, 108–13, 150,
218, 229, 285, 289, 338–45 passim,
384–404. See also Pastoral; Romance
Trauerspiel, 86–87, 384
Tropes, origins of, 42–43
Trotsky, Leon, 144
Twelfth–century theater, 50–56
Tyndale, William, 145, 146
Tyranipocrit Discovered, 355, 402

Udall, Nicholas: Ralph Roister Doister, 125
Union Shoe, 336
United Provinces. See Low Countries
Urban theater. See Medieval towns
Usury, 197–206
Utopia, 34, 36, 50, 61, 103, 189–95 passim,
206, 209–11, 215, 336, 344, 396–404
passim

Valencia, theater of, 134, 195
Vega Carpio, Lope de, 9, 31, 98, 103, 120,
123, 130, 135, 136, 151; and acting companies, 172; attacks on, 274, 374; and baroque, 384; and duke of Alba, 153–55; and
Eastern Europe, 398; generic innovation,
253; pastoral and peasantry, 154–55, 182,
193; peasant plays, 239–52, 315–27,
344–49 passim, 363, 370, 382; printing of
plays, 174; and stage machinery, 268, 273;
and state power, 381; subversiveness, 183
—works: Arauco domado, 137, 224, 227; La Arcadia, 284; Arte nuevo de hacer comedias en
este tiempo, 248; El asalto de Mastrique, 137,
224, 227; Belardo el furioso, 191, 193; Las
bizarrías de Belisa, 283, 292; El caballero de
Olmedo, 372, 373–74; El castigo sin
venganza, 365, 366, 368–70; Los donaires de
Matico, 193–94; Las ferias de Madrid,
192–93; Lo fingido verdadero, 375, 376, 380;
Fuente Ovejuna, 183, 315, 317, 321, 322–27,
333, 337, 344–49 passim, 356, 363, 384; La
imperial de Otón, 228, 231–32, 254; El
marqués de Mantua, 228, 229, 254, 272; El
mejor alcalde el rey, 315, 316, 320–21;
Peribáñez y el comendador de Ocaña, 315, 317,
319–20, 321, 363; El perro del hortelano,
288–89; Rimas, 15; El rufián Castrucho, 194,
285; El sufrimiento premiado, 192; El
testimonio vengado, 222; La vida y muerte del
rey Bamba, 223, 224, 228, 239–52, 254, 311,
319, 373; El villano en su rincón, 316, 319,
321
Vélez de Guevara, Juan, 278
Vélez de Guevara, Luis, 398; Reinar después de
morir, 372–73, 374; La serrana de la Vera,
315–16, 321
Vice figure, 128, 129, 178, 211, 305, 309, 332,
340
Vicente, Gil, 131; Auto da barca de Glória, 133;
Auto da sibila Casandra, 132; Don Duardos,
130, 133
Vilar, Pierre, 262
Virgil, 130; Aeneid, 94, 95
Virginia pamphlets, 398–404; A True Declara-
tion of the Estate of the Colonie in Virginia, 399,
401; A True and Sincere Declaration, 403
Virués, Cristóbal de: La cruel Casandra, 229
Visitatio sepulchri, 40, 45–50, 52
Voltaire, 15–16, 17
Vondel, J. van den: Gijsbreght van Aemstel,
94–95, 96; Lucifer, 95–96

Wager, W.: The Longer Thou Livest the More
Fool Thou Art, 128
Wakefield Master, 70, 72; Secunda pastorum, 70
Walsingham, Francis, 161

# Index

Walwyn, William, 353
Webster, John (radical), 355
Webster, John (dramatist), 365, 366, 371; *The Duchess of Malfi*, 364, 367, 370; *The White Devil*, 271, 364
Weimann, Robert, 27, 184
Wellek, René, 383
Whetstone, George, 158
Whitgift, Archbishop, 142, 158
*Wiener Passionsspiel, Das*, 67
Wildman, John, 27, 55, 355
William of Orange, 93–94
Williams, Raymond, 404
Wilson, Edward M., 26
Wilson, Robert, 171; *The Three Ladies of London*, 190
Winstanley, Gerrard, 352, 354
Women: feminist criticism, 24, 26; and popular culture, 112, 132, 311, 314, 321, 323–24, 327, 337, 372; and intrigue tragedy, 113, 114–15, 371–72, 383; actresses, 152, 160, 171; in theater audience, 168, 169, 272; and romantic comedy, 187–88, 189; and satiric comedy, 283; and bourgeois tragedy, 316; and peasant play, 316, 321, 323–24, 327, 347; and radical Reformation, 336; and Shakespearean tragedy, 337, 359, 383
Wotton, Henry, 388

Ximénez de Rada, Rodrigo: *De rebus Hispaniae*, 242

*Yorkshire Tragedy, A*, 315, 316

Zeeveld, W. Gordon, 206